PERSONS, ANIMALS,
SHIPS AND CANNON
—— IN THE ——
AUBREY-MATURIN
SEA NOVELS
—— OF ——
PATRICK O'BRIAN

Persons, Animals, Ships and Cannon

— in the —

Aubrey-Maturin Sea Novels

— of —

Patrick O'Brian

by Anthony Gary Brown

McFarland & Company, Inc., Publishers

Jefferson, North Carolina, and London

Library of Congress Cataloguing-in-Publication Data

Brown, Anthony Gary, 1953–
Persons, animals, ships, and cannon in the Aubrey–Maturin sea
novels of Patrick O'Brian / by Anthony Gary Brown.
p.   cm.
Includes bibliographical references.
ISBN 0-7864-0684-4 (sewn softcover : 50# alkaline paper) ∞
1. O'Brian, Patrick, 1914–   Dictionaries.   2. Maturin, Stephen
(Fictitious character) — Dictionaries.   3. Aubrey, Jack (Fictitious
character) — Dictionaries.   4. O'Brian, Patrick, 1914–   — Characters —
Dictionaries.   5. Naval art and science in literature — Dictionaries.
6. Historical fiction, English — Dictionaries.   7. Animals in
literature — Dictionaries.   8. Sea stories, English — Dictionaries.
9. Ships in literature — Dictionaries.   10. Ordnance — Dictionaries.
I. Title.
PR6029.B55Z459   1999
823'.914 — dc21   99-30996
                                                                               CIP

British Library Cataloguing-in-Publication data are available

Manufactured in the United States of America

*McFarland & Company, Inc., Publishers
Box 611, Jefferson, North Carolina 28640
www.mcfarlandpub.com*

For my father

Albert Joseph 'Tony' Brown
(1923–1985)

Fleet Air Arm of the Royal Navy,
1940–1968

Contents

Introduction

*O'Brian ... writes with humour, irony and an eye for
those telling details that give you a man in a moment.*
Alan Judd writing in the
London *Sunday Times*, 1992.

Over the past 25 years the Anglo-Irish writer Patrick O'Brian* has produced from his small study in the south of France a series of novels, set in the early 19th century and featuring the adventures and friendship of Captain Jack Aubrey, RN, and Doctor Stephen Maturin. These books have been variously described as 'a brilliant achievement ... of staggering erudition' (T.J. Binyon in the *Times Literary Supplement*), containing a 'far-ranging web of wit and allusion' resulting in 'the best historical novels ever written' (Richard Snow in the *New York Times Book Review*).

Why should this praise be quite so high? In good 'nautical fiction,' readers want to feel the heave of the deck underfoot and hear the cannon's roar. O'Brian gives us this a-plenty but very much more besides: the smell of the operating room, the deceptive elegance of the political *salon*, the crisp workings, often in several languages, of the natural scientist's mind, the domestic economy of the English landed — and sometimes landless — gentry, and the cultural pulse of many different lands and societies. It is not without good reason that O'Brian has been called a 'Modern Homer' (a title he modestly and insistently declines) and, rather like that great Master, he fills his world with a quite extraordinarily rich array of characters and ships, some invented, some historical, but every one of them real flesh-and-blood, even when fleetingly sketched. O'Brian is also that rare thing, a genuine polymath (and that even rarer thing, a polymath with both an angelic pen and a sense of fun) and, not very far into any of the books, even the most accomplished reader can feel in turn dazzled, bemused and ultimately intrigued by the ocean of people and ships before him. The present volume seeks to celebrate that bedazzlement by offering comfort to the bemused and modest satisfaction to the intrigued.

Here you will find an alphabetic guide to every person and ship (together with assorted

Mr O'Brian is renowned for the close guard he keeps on his privacy: he thus attracts no biographical note of his own in this volume. For those who wish to know more, he has revealed himself to a limited extent in the Cunningham volume noted in the Bibliography.

animals, cannon, etc.) referred to by name in the first 19 books of the Aubrey-Maturin series, from *Master and Commander* of 1969 through to *The Hundred Days* of 1998, some 4500 entries in all. Many of these are purely the product of O'Brian's delightful imagination: their careers in the novels are summarised in roman type, with comprehensive reference to the chapters of the various novels in which they appear. On the other hand, many are either directly historical or have their roots in the real: again their careers in the novels are first summarised in roman type, and then expanded in *italic type* from sources outside O'Brian (the sources being detailed in the Bibliography). Hence the presence of text set in italics is usually a handy visual indication that there is a direct historical inspiration for the character or ship in question. Italics are also occasionally used to discuss those entertaining and intriguing errors and contradictions in the presentation of the purely fictional that inevitably creep into such a long series (yet it should also be remembered that O'Brian often quite deliberately has his characters misunderstand or misrecall events and names). In turn, where there is no italicised annotation to an entry, this is an indication that I have been unable to find any source confirming or suggesting the 'real' existence of the character or ship in question. I will receive any and all enlightenment with gratitude!

Authors must, of course, draw their *fictional* names from somewhere, whether from the sublime (e.g., their circles of intimates and or enemies) or the mundane (e.g., the local telephone directory). In occasionally making guesses at the real characters that may have inspired O'Brian's choices, I have commented only when the underlying name both would be familiar in Jack Aubrey or Stephen Maturin's own cultural worlds and has some clear connection, usually naval or scientific, to the immediate context. Where otherwise familiar names seem to me to have been chosen purely at random, I have passed them by without comment. For example, perhaps O'Brian was simply listening to his beloved *Mozart [words preceded by an asterisk have entries in this dictionary] when he needed names for two fleeting characters in the novel, *Sarastro (a.k.a. the High Priest in *Magic Flute*) and *Schikaneder (a.k.a. the singer and impresario who wrote that opera's libretto).

The format of this dictionary is, then, intended to appeal to the hunter for a particular fact and to the browser alike and I hope that it will lead its readers to turn *to* the joys of O'Brian's books quite as often as it is used to elucidate some tricky reference *from* them.

Abbreviations and Cross-Reference Signs Used

The Novel Titles (with details of first editions)

1. M&C *Master and Commander* (first published in 1969 by Lippincott, Philadelphia)
2. PC *Post Captain* (first published in 1972 by William Collins Sons & Co., London)
3. HMS *HMS Surprise* (first published in 1973 by William Collins Sons & Co., London)
4. TMC *The Mauritius Command* (first published in 1977 by William Collins Sons & Co., London)
5. DI *Desolation Island* (first published in 1978 by William Collins Sons & Co., London)
6. FW *The Fortune of War* (first published in 1979 by William Collins Sons & Co., London)
7. SM *The Surgeon's Mate* (first published in 1980 by William Collins Sons & Co., London)
8. IM *The Ionian Mission* (first published in 1981 by William Collins Sons & Co., London)
9. TH *Treason's Harbour* (first published in 1983 by William Collins Sons & Co., London)
10. FSW *The Far Side of the World* (first

published in 1984 by William Collins Sons & Co., London)

11. RM   *The Reverse of the Medal* (first published in 1986 by William Collins Sons & Co., London)

12. LM   *The Letter of Marque* (first published in 1988 by William Collins Sons & Co., London)

13. TGS   *The Thirteen Gun Salute* (first published in 1989 by William Collins Sons & Co., London)

14. NC   *The Nutmeg of Consolation* (first published in 1991 by William Collins Sons & Co., London)

15. C/T   *Clarissa Oakes / The Truelove* (first published in 1992 by HarperCollins Publishers, London; then published later in the same year in the USA by W.W. Norton & Co., New York, as *The Truelove*)

16. WDS   *The Wine Dark Sea* (first published in 1993 by HarperCollins Publishers, London)

17. COM   *The Commodore* (first published in 1994 by HarperCollins Publishers, London)

18. YA   *The Yellow Admiral* (first published in 1996 by W.W. Norton & Co., New York)

19. HD   *The Hundred Days* (first published in 1998 by HarperCollins Publishers, London)

In General

a.k.a.	also known as		*always indicates membership of the House*
c.	*circa* (approximately)		*of Commons rather than that of the Lords)*
DNB	*Dictionary of National Biography*	OED	*Oxford English Dictionary*
fl.	*floreat* (flourished)	RN	Royal Navy
HEIC	Honourable East India Company	sic	thus, or exactly as printed
HMS(S)	His Majesty's Ship(s)	US(S)	United States (Ship)
MP	Member of Parliament (*N.B.: the term*		

Cross References

(i) Every name mentioned in the roman-type sections drawn from O'Brian's own text has, by definition, its own headline entry.

(ii) In the *italic-type* annotations, * precedes the first use of any name for which there is also a headline entry: e.g., '*In 1804 Lord *Nelson...*'

(iii) The occasional use in the italicised sections of a fully capitalised name—e.g., *LAVERY*—indicates an entry in the Bibliography.

Notes for General Guidance

Chapter References

Chapter references are thought to be handier than specific page references, for only in the last third of the 19-book series is pagination standardised across the various U.K. and U.S. hard- and paper-back editions, with the many foreign translations of O'Brian now appearing having yet different pagination again. Furthermore, O'Brian often introduces salient facts about a person or ship in dialogue spread over many pages, quite often repeating the name many times over or even not using a name at all until a much later point. Consequently, chapter references are, I hope, at once 'easy on the eye,' yet sufficiently detailed to allow for easy location of the source of the information. They follow this format:

(M&C 1,2,7), *references in* Master and Commander, *Chapters 1, 2 and 7.*
(TH 4–9), *references in* Treason's Harbour, *Chapters 4 to 9.*

(YA 2+), *multiple references in* The Yellow Admiral *from Chapter 2 onwards.*

(YA 7; *also* M&C 6; TGS 9), *indicates, as a final item in an entry, that there is a reference to a specified event in* The Yellow Admiral, *Chapter 7, and then also further passing references to the headline entry in* Master and Commander, *Chapter 6, and* The Thirteen Gun Salute, *Chapter 9.*

Names and Details of Persons

(i) O'Brian often replicates the easy-going approach to precision in spelling of his chosen period and readers are advised always to explore possible variants of the name in his text that they wish to look up. When, in the italicised annotations, 'corrections' are made to the spelling in the books themselves, this has been done purely to ease further research in the chief biographical sources, with no suggestion that the author's own choice is necessarily incorrect.

(ii) Where there are multiple characters with but a single name (e.g., **William**) they are listed within their entry in order of appearance in the series. Otherwise all entries follow the usual rules of alphabetisation.

(iii) A problem presents itself with regard to the many references to figures from classical mythology, in that these may be in several, slightly variant forms (e.g., English, French, Latin, Greek) and may also be given as the names of both ships and persons. Although I have usually placed their biographical note in the *first* of the several entries, this has not always proved practicable and readers are advised to cast their net a little more widely in these instances.

(iv) As regards the careers of the historic sea-officers in the series, I have always used the promotion dates given in SYRETT & DiNARDO, which often differ slightly from those found in CLOWES, DNB, etc.; the rationale for this preference is given in the Bibliography. In following the post-series careers of commissioned officers, I have somewhat truncated notice of the dates at which they passed through every grade of Admiral, noting only the years of advancement to the basic 'bands' of Rear-Admiral, Vice-Admiral, Admiral and Admiral of the Fleet.

(v) The long entries for Jack Aubrey and Stephen Maturin do some double-duty. In addition to outlining their own careers, they provide brief summaries of the plot of each of the novels, from the somewhat different perspective of each character. The unusual length of the entries has necessitated that some italicised interpolations be included *within* the O'Brian-derived material, in order to save readers having to jump back and forth between text and comment.

Names and Details of Ships

(i) Even where ship names are identical to personal names (e.g., Venus), the vessels are italicised and listed *after* the personal entries. Then strict alphabetisation is followed: so **Essex**; **Essex, Harry**; and ***Essex**, USS are all separate entries, appearing in that order.

(ii) 'HMS' was in common usage as the prefix for British warships during Jack Aubrey's time period but was not yet wholly standard, official practice; the characters in the series sometimes use it, sometimes not. However, I have chosen to follow modern usage in *always* attaching it to Royal Navy ship names as this usefully serves to distinguish them from those of all other navies.

(iii) Many ships changed hands between the combatants, often several times, resulting in seamen of all nationalities referring to them in a variety of spellings and languages. Readers are advised to explore several options if they cannot track down a given ship at first attempt.

(iv) For French, Italian or Spanish ship names that contain a pronoun, e.g. *El Gamo* or *l'Annibale*, this is omitted or reversed in the headline: so **Gamo, El**, or **Annibale**. For similarly named English ships, e.g., HMS *La Flèche*—I have retained and reversed the pronoun in the headline: so **Flèche, HMS La**.

(v) In the italicised annotations for British ships I have usually given the *rated* number of guns carried (e.g. *HMS* Weymouth, *60-gun*) as detailed in COLLEDGE. As LAVERY, CLOWES and others explain, this official figure almost always differed, and often substantially, from the *actual* number of guns on board, and O'Brian's characters are often referring to what they know or guess this latter number to be.

Other Entries

(i) All geographic names have been excluded unless a personal name component of them is discussed by O'Brian's characters in its own right or seems in some other way especially pertinent.

(ii) A very few place names have been included if they could either be mistaken in their context for personal names or are being used as collective terms for an organisation or household.

(iii) The names of cannon found on various British ships are included and treated, in terms of their typeface, as if they were ship names. Just as the Admiralty named ships for its national heroes and sentiments, so the crews were often permitted by captains to name cannon for their own, more local heroes, very often prizefighters.

The Chronology of the Series

O'Brian's readers will themselves know from the 'author's notes' prefacing several of the novels that strict chronological accuracy is, quite properly, put at the service of art. In many of the entries for historical characters and ships I have indicated where there are simple mismatches between O'Brian's immediate context and the 'historical record.' These notes should in no way be taken to indicate that the author is 'wrong'; rather, they are simply attempts to elucidate what the starting point or inspiration for his creativity may have been. Indeed, in researching the present volume I have been utterly delighted, yet not in the slightest surprised, to find only the merest handful of anachronisms and straightforward errors amongst many thousands of entries; and, as befits O'Brian's polymathy, these tend to reflect that splendid Italian saying, *se non è vero, è ben trovato*!

Nevertheless, an outline chronology of the books may here serve as a useful guide.

Many further date details and, occasionally, puzzles are discussed in the entries for the characters or ships most directly affected.

Master and Commander— from April 1800 to mid–1801.

Post Captain— from late 1801 or early 1802 through to October 1804.

HMS Surprise— from late 1804 to late 1805 or early 1806.

The Mauritius Command—from mid–1809 to December 1810.

Desolation Island— from 1811 to early 1812.

The Fortune of War— from early 1812 to June 1813.

The Surgeon's Mate through to *The Commodore*— all of necessity take place in the latter half of 1813, although each of these eleven books occupies about one calendar year. (See O'Brian's witty remarks on this compression of time in the Author's Note to *Fortune of War*.)

The Yellow Admiral— from late 1814 through to March 1815.

The Hundred Days— from spring (probably late April) until late June of 1815

Acknowledgements

I am exceptionally grateful to Don Seltzer for undertaking the formidable task of reviewing several drafts of this work. Not only has he saved me from innumerable careless slips, he has also suggested many lines of enquiry and made astute observations on consequent matters of emphasis and interpretation: and always in double-quick time. Naturally, I alone am responsible for the final product, errors and all.

Don is a regular contributor to two Internet discussion groups dedicated to naval fiction, 'The Gunroom' (run by Patrick O'Brian's U.S. publishers, W.W. Norton) and 'The Searoom' (run by the independent nautical book-seller John Berg). The breadth of knowledge and experience in these two groups on matters naval and historical is quite astonishing, as is the cheerful lightness with which such learning is always worn. I commend them to readers' attention as prime examples of the social world being enhanced by technology. So many hints and clues for the present work have I picked up from Gun- and Searooms over the past two years that it would be quite genuinely inappropriate here to mention single individuals by name, Don himself of course excepted. For the work of tracking down, confirming and (all too often) just browsing, the Charles E. Young Research Library in the University of California at Los Angeles is, quite simply, all such an institution should be.

Finally, an acknowledgement should be made to Antoine-François, Compte de *Andréossy, whose entertaining way with English titles had stuck in my mind for many years, with the question 'who he?' appended. That, some two years ago, I discovered not only who Andréossy was but that he was very far from being the most obscure character in O'Brian's pantheon perhaps says something about the attention I gave my lessons when small; but it was nevertheless he who made me decide to write this book.

GARY BROWN
Los Angeles, June 1999

The Dictionary

A

A., Captain
see **Aubrey, Jack** or **John**

A., Mrs
see **Aubrey, Sophie** or **Sophia**

Abbas Effendi
An Egyptian official who meets Aubrey and his expeditionary force at the port of Tina (TH 5).

Abbot, the
A protector of Maturin in either Peru or Chile (WDS 10).

Abbott
1: Mother or Mrs Abbott, the owner of a whorehouse in Dover Street (DI 1), near Button's club (LM 2). Clarissa Harvill *(later *Oakes)* had at one time been in her employ (C/T 6,9; YA 7).
2: an artist famous for his portraits of naval officers (TH 2).
Lemuel Abbot or Abbott (1760–1803) painted a number of well-known portraits of Lord *Nelson and was a favourite of many other sea-officers and society figures.

Abdallah
A predecessor referred to by Emperor Suliman of Morocco (IM 4).
The reference may be to his Muslim lineage, for Abdallah ben Abdelmottalib (545?–570?) was the father of the prophet *Mahomet.

Abd-ar-Rahman
A man whose mosque stands in Cordova (HD 7).
The Great Mosque at Cordova (or Córdoba), in southern Spain, is one of the glories of Islamic architecture and the decorative arts. Its construction was started in 784 during the reign of Sultan ʼAdb ar-Rahman I (fl. 750–788), the Syrian founder of the Umayyad Moslem dynasty in Spain, with its size and splendour being increased by his successors during the following two hundred years. Since 1236 the edifice has been a Roman Catholic Cathedral, undergoing substantial rebuilding, along liturgical plans, in the 16th century.

Abdon, St
A reference is made to his name-day (FSW 4).
Saints Abdon and Sennen were two high born Persians martyred in Rome in 250; although little is known of their lives they became widely venerated and are the patron saints of coopers. Saint Abdon has feast days celebrated on a variety of dates, including October 1st in Spain and July 30th in Italy.

Abdul
1: the Sultan of Pulo Prabang's beautiful cupbearer, suspected by Maturin of having a sexual liaison with the traitor Ledward; the Doctor compares him to Jupiter's favourite, Ganymede (TGS 6–9). Betrayed by Fox, he is discovered by the Sultana Hafsa's men in bed with both Wray and Ledward and horribly put to death (TGS 8,9).
2: a servant in the Raffles' household (NC 4).

Abdul Reis
An Algerine corsair, also known simply as 'the Reis,' who gives Maturin and Jacob passage out to William Reade's *Ringle* (HD 8).
Reis or rais is Arabic for Captain (or, in political contexts, Governor). The character of Abdul (and that of *Murad Reis) somewhat recalls Hamidou Rais, the Commander-in-Chief of the Algerian navy from 1809 until 1815, in the middle of which latter year he was killed in an action between his small fleet and a squadron led by Commodore Stephen Decatur's USS Guerrier.

Abednigo
A slave at George Herapath's house in Boston (FW 8).

Abel
1: the injured brother of the street-urchin Margaret (RM 4).
2: the boot boy at the Grapes Inn (DI 2).
3: with Mr Keyne, a Royal Navy lieutenant held prisoner on parole in Boston. They rescue Maturin from Pontet-Canet's attack (FW 7).
4: an agent of British intelligence in Paris who had been discovered and killed (COM 5).
5: see ***Cain**; *also see* ***Seth**

Abel, George
A seaman in HMS *Surprise* (FSW 10).

Abel, Sir John
A doctor referred to by Captain Nevin (M&C 6).
The name may perhaps be inspired by that of a protégé of Sir Joseph *Banks, the physician and naturalist Clarke Abel (1780—1826) who made well-regarded scientific studies on Royal Navy expeditions to China and became Chief Surgeon to the Governor-General of India.

Abercrombie, General
The officer who is rumoured to be the incoming commander of an enlarged force intended to take Mauritius. He then supersedes the furious Colonel Keating, who has done all the arduous preparatory work (TMC 10).
Sir John Abercrombie (1772–1817) was a career soldier from a large and distinguished military family. He had visited France during the Peace of Amiens and been interned from its collapse in 1803 until he was exchanged for a captured French General in 1808. He was then appointed Commander-in-Chief, Bombay and in late 1809 given the task of taking Mauritius. After the fall of

*Réunion to his subordinates, he and his staff were on their way to Mauritius in HMS *Ceylon (see *Bombay, HMS) when she was taken by *Vénus and then almost immediately re-taken by HMS *Boadicea. He eventually arrived off Mauritius in late 1810 and took command as the senior General present, almost immediately accepting the capitulation of the island.*

Abergavenny

An East Indiaman in Muffit's China Fleet, protected by HMS *Surprise* from Admiral Linois' French squadron. Her Master is the faint-hearted Captain Gloag (HMS 9).

*The Earl of Abergavenny, 1182 tons, made 7 round trips from India to England between 1789 and 1804; she was named for Henry Neville, 2nd Earl of Abergavenny (1755–1843). The action is based on the defence of a Honourable East India Company merchant fleet against *Linois' attack in February 1804. However, no Royal Navy ship was present during the fight, the squadron being organised by the senior Master, Nathaniel Dance of *Earl Camden. On this occasion John Wordsworth was Abergavenny's Master.*

Abernethy

A doctor referred to by Redfern and Maturin (NC 9,10).

*John Abernethy (1764–1831), an eminent surgeon of Irish/Scots origin, was an exceptionally talented lecturer at St *Barts Hospital, and a writer of treatises on surgical practice. He had been a pupil of the great John *Hunter.*

Abhorson

A horse owned by Mrs Morris' manservant Briggs that throws Jack Aubrey (COM 1).

Abijah

A slave belonging to Johnson in Boston (FW 7).

Aboukir, HMS

A ship on the Brest blockade that, with HMS *Bellona* and others, prevents two French 74-guns from slipping out to sea (YA 9).

*HMS Aboukir, 74-gun, was launched in 1807, sent for harbour service in 1824 and sold out of the service in 1838. She was the second ship to bear her name, taken from *Nelson's great victory in 1798 at the Battle of the Nile/Aboukir Bay.*

Abraham

The Biblical patriarch (COM 8; YA 10) referred to by Aubrey for the prolific fathering of children (TMC 6) and great age (TGS 1), and by Mould for his polygamy (COM 5). He is also used a codeword to identify Maturin on a spy mission (PC 14), referred to by Admiral Drury as having wrangled with God over Sodom and Gomorrah (FW 1,2), and claimed by the religious Shelmerstonian seamen as a descendant of Seth (LM 5).

*Abraham — Hebrew for 'father of a multitude' — was the first of the Biblical patriarchs, a remote descendant of *Adam's third son *Seth. He first came to *God's service at the age of 75 and eventually had many children by his two successive wives, Sarah and Keturah, and by Sarah's servant Hagar. He negotiated with God over the exact extent of the destruction of the corrupt city of Sodom and eventually died at the age of 175, honoured by God for his constancy.*

Abraham-men or 'Shamming Abraham'

A reference to slackers aboard ship (PC 7,12; FSW 2).

*The reference is to the *Abraham ward at the *Bedlam Hospital for the Insane in London, supposedly populated by those who only pretended to be mad to facilitate theft and idleness.*

Absalom

A reference by Billy Sutton to the long, flowing hair of the disgraced Midshipman Albert Tompkins (FSW 1).

*Absalom was one of the sons of the Biblical King *David and was famed for his physical beauty and the annual cropping of his abundant hair.*

Abse

1: a pawnbroker who had known Aubrey as a Midshipman (SM 4).

2: an unpopular seaman in HMS *Nutmeg of Consolation* who dies of the marthambles (NC 5).

Abulfeda

An Oriental author over whom Graham and Pocock had bitterly argued (TH 3).

Abulfeda, Prince of Hamah (1273–1331) was a Syrian warrior and administrator, the author of many important books on history, geography, literature and medicine.

Acapulco

A British whaler, first captured by USS *Norfolk* but soon re-taken by Aubrey's HMS *Surprise* (FSW 6).

Acasta, HMS

A 40-gun heavy frigate promised to Jack Aubrey in place of the condemned HMS *Leopard* (FW 1,8). Jack believes that she will be ordered to the North American Station now war with the USA has been declared (FW 2) but, during his own long delay in reaching England, she is given to a temporary Captain, Peter Fellowes (FW 3). However, Jack later learns that she has been given as a permanent command to Robert Kerr, partly because of his own prolonged absence (SM 1,2) and partly because of the slow vengeance of Andrew Wray, a vengeance aided by General Aubrey's embarrassingly radical election speeches (SM 4). Years later she is seen moored at Torbay (YA 4), afterwards appearing in the Mediterranean (HD 10).

*HMS Acasta, 40-gun, was launched in 1797 and broken up in 1821. From 1806 to 1809 she was commanded by Philip Beaver (see *Carrol); *Kerr commanded her from 1813 until at least 1815. In Greek myth Acasta was a minor sea deity.*

Achates, HMS

A 16-gun brig-sloop that had assisted in the taking of *Clorinde* (YA 9). Later she is part of the Brest blockade squadron sent home to be paid off on Buonaparte's abdication (YA 10).

*HMS Achates, 16-gun, was launched in 1807 as the French Milan; she was captured and renamed in 1809 and sold in 1818. The action against the 44-gun *Clorinde described in the text took place off Brest in late February 1814, with the brig under Commander Isaac Hawkins Morrison (d.1860, as a retired Vice Admiral). In Roman mythology Achates was the armour bearer of *Aeneas, renowned for his loyalty.*

Achilles

1: the Greek hero of the *Iliad* (M&C 9,12; FSW 4,7; COM 5,7,8).

*In Greek legend, the son of Peleus and *Thetis, and the greatest of the heroes of the Trojan war. He is the central figure of *Homer's Iliad, and as a warrior he is unsurpassed in every aspect of the martial arts. His mother Thetis supposedly dipped him into the river Styx as a baby to ensure his invulnerability; however, she held his heel out of the water and it was here that he received his fatal wound from Paris' arrow. The Greek dramatist Aeschylus later portrayed Achilles and his warrior-friend *Patroclus as lovers.*

2: a seaman in HMS *Diane*, the swiftest runner in the crew (NC 1).

*In *Homer, Achilles is often referred to as 'swift-footed' (see **1** above).*

Achilles, HMS

A ship into which an unpopular Third Lieutenant in HMS *Lively* had been forced to exchange by his fellow officers (HMS 2). She is later on the Brest blockade (SM 9) and in Admiral Thornton's Mediterranean fleet (IM 6). Aubrey's secretary Mr Adams had once served in her under Captain King (NC 9).

*HMS Achilles, 74-gun, was one of several ships built by the Royal Navy based on the design of the captured French *Pompée. Named for the Greek hero *Achilles, she was launched in 1798 and sold out of the service in 1865. *King took command of her in 1805, fighting her with distinction at the Battle of Trafalgar.*

Achmet

1: Maturin's servant in HMS *Surprise* (HMS 5–7).
2: Mr Wallis' servant (FW 1).
3: a servant at Fatima's boarding-house in Algiers (HD 8).

Actaeon

An attempted classical reference by Aubrey (PC 1).

Actaeon was the great huntsman of Greek myth who came upon the goddess Artemis bathing naked. Affronted, she turned him into a stag, whereupon he was torn apart by his own hounds.

Active, HMS

1: a ship, now expected at Pulo Batang (FW 1), that had been commanded in 1801 by Harry Lambert (FW 3). Mr Harding had later served in her at Hoste's victory at the Battle of Lissa (HD 5).

*HMS Active, 38-gun, was launched in 1799 and took part in *Hoste's Adriatic campaign of 1808–1814 mostly under her Captain James Alexander Gordon (1782–1869; d. as retired Admiral of the Fleet), who led her at Lissa in 1811. Sent for harbour service in 1826 and renamed HMS *Argo in 1833, she was broken up in 1860. *Lambert was not made Post until 1805 and never commanded this ship.*

2: a schooner in Aubrey's squadron (COM 8).

*The 84-ton schooner Active, commanded by acting Lieutenant Michael *Fitton, was the tender to the flagship on the West Indies station in 1800–1801.*

Adam

1: the biblical first ever man (HMS 6; DI 4; IM 1; COM 1).

*In the Old Testament tradition Adam and *Eve were the first man and woman created by *God and are the progenitors of the human race; Eve was made from Adam's rib whilst he was in a deep sleep. Given the perfect Garden of Eden in which to dwell in naked innocence, Eve was tricked by the serpent into eating from the forbidden tree of knowledge, sharing the fruit with Adam. God then cast the pair from Paradise down to Earth.*

2: the name of two brothers, formerly poachers and now convicts in HMS *Leopard* (DI 3).
3: Babbington's clerk in HMS *Oedipus* (SM 11).

Adam, Thomas

A seaman in HMS *Diane*, an ex-whaler (TGS 5).

Adams

1: a suitor of Sophie Williams with a large estate in Dorset (PC 3).
2: an Admiralty official (PC 5).
3: a Midshipman in HMS *Polychrest* (PC 11).
4: a seaman in HMS *Boadicea* (TMC 2).
5: a Bostonian officer in USS *Constitution* (FW 4).
6: the name of friends of Johnson, Villiers and Wogan in Boston (FW 5,7).
7: a Boston politician well regarded by Native Americans (FW 6).

This could be a reference to any one of a number of distinguished Boston Adams: John Adams (1735–1826), second president of the USA from 1797 to 1801; his second cousin Samuel Adams (1722–1803); or John's son, John Quincy Adams (1767–1848), sixth president from 1825 to 1829, who later became a formidable opponent of the institution of slavery.

8: the Lieutenant who brings Aubrey his recall orders to the Royal Navy following Buonaparte's escape from Elba (YA 10).

Adams, David

Jack Aubrey's clerk, secretary and acting purser in a number of his ships: HMSS *Worcester* (IM 1), *Surprise* (IM 9; TH 4+; FSW 2–9; RM 2; NC 7+; C/T 1+; WDS 1+; COM 1) and *Nutmeg of Consolation* (NC 4–7). He becomes Commodore Aubrey's private secretary in HMSS *Bellona* (COM 3–9), *Pomone* and, once again, *Surprise* (HD 2+). There are references to him having been Jack's famously efficient clerk in his early days as a Post Captain in HMSS *Lively* (NC 4) and *Surprise* (RM 2) but he does not appear by name — or suggestion — in either PC or HMS. Adams had also once served under Captain King in HMS *Achilles* (RM 2).

Adams, John

A member of the crew of USS *Norfolk*, injured in a scuffle with some of HMS *Surprise*'s crew (FSW 10).

Adams, USS

An old, 28-gun frigate referred to by Aubrey (FW 2).

> USS Adams *was launched as a 32-gun frigate in 1799 but rebuilt as a 24-gun sloop in 1807. In 1814 she was sunk by the Royal Navy in the Penobscot River and burned by her crew to avoid her being captured and refloated. The ship is named for John Adams (1735–1826), who served as second president of the USA from 1797–1801.*

Adamson

The Captain of HMS *Thetis* (COM 8).

Adanson, Michael

A French naturalist, the author of *Familles Naturelles des Plants* and many other unpublished works (RM 3; COM 8,9; YA 1).

> *Michel Adanson (1727–1806) came from a Scottish family, gone into exile for their support of the exiled King *James II of England. After study in France, he spent the years from 1748–53 in Senegal, publishing a natural history of that country in 1757. With the publication in 1763 of* Familles Naturelles des Plants *Adanson established a claim to be one of the leading taxonomic naturalists of his age, yet his proposed classification system was finally not a success, being superseded by that of *Linnaeus. He fell into obscurity and poverty and was consequently unable to find a commercial publisher for his immense* Ordre Universel de la Nature.

Addington

see **Sidmouth, Lord**

Addington

An East Indiaman in Muffit's China Fleet, protected by HMS *Surprise* from Admiral Linois' French squadron (HMS 9).

> *The* Henry Addington, *1200 tons, made 9 round trips from India to England between 1795 and 1813; she was named for Henry Addington, 1st Viscount *Sidmouth. The action is based on the defence of a Honourable East India Company merchant fleet against *Linois' attack in February 1804. However, no Royal Navy ship was present during the fight, the squadron being organised by the senior Master, Nathaniel Dance of *Earl Camden.*

Addison

A naval parson travelling out in Aubrey's HMS *Worcester* to join his new ship in the Mediterranean (IM 3).

Adeane, Captain

A neighbour of the Aubreys in Dorset and a great favourite with the local married ladies, to whom he is known as 'Captain Apollo.' Diana Villiers half-seriously suggests him as a potential lover for Sophie Aubrey (YA 8).

Adi

The Captain's cook in HMS *Surprise*, a devil-worshipper (LM 5; TGS 5).

Adonis

A model of male beauty (HMS 7; FW 6; C/T 4).

> *In Greek myth Adonis was a son of the King of Cyprus, adored by the goddess *Venus for his beauty. When he was killed hunting a boar she arranged for him to spend half of every future year with her on earth, with the other half being passed in Hades.*

Aeneas

The hero of the *Aeneid*, the epic Latin poem recited in its entirety by Stephen Maturin in his delirium (HMS 11). Later Stephen refers to the relationship between Jack Aubrey and Amanda Smith as rather similar to the tale of Aeneas and Dido (SM 2).

> *Aeneas, the Trojan son of *Anchises and *Venus, is the hero of *Virgil's Aeneid. In this epic, Aeneas escapes from the destruction of Troy — as previously described in *Homer — and eventually travels to Italy, where he marries Lavinia of Latium and lays the foundations of Rome's later dominance of the Mediterranean world. Whilst on his journey he is driven by a storm into Carthage, whose Queen *Dido falls desperately in love with him. Despite consummating the relationship, Aeneas soon abandons Dido to continue his mission to Italy, whereupon Dido, distraught, burns herself on a funeral pyre.*

Aeolus, HMS

A frigate initially blockading Boston (FW 5) that afterwards escorts the transport fleet taking the Grimsholm Catalans back to Spain (SM 8). Later, under her Captain Edward Long, she is known to have recently sunk (TH 1).

> HMS Aeolus, *32-gun, was launched in 1801 and broken up in 1817; there is no record of her ever having sunk or been commanded by an Edward Long. In Greek myth Aeolus was the god of the winds.*

Aetna, HMS

A Royal Navy bomb-ketch commanded by Evans (M&C 9), later a ship thought by Aubrey to be more suited to the attack on *Fanciulla* than his own HMS *Polychrest* (PC 10).

> HMS Aetna, *a bomb-ketch, was bought into the navy in 1803 (a little after M&C is set), serving until 1816; in 1808 she was the first Royal Navy ship to use* Congreve *rockets. For the* Fanciulla *attack, O'Brian may be thinking of this vessel or may possibly have had in mind the sloop* HMS Cormorant, *the ex-French 20-gun* Etna, *launched*

in 1794, captured by the Royal Navy in 1796, but wrecked in 1800, well before PC is set. The names are taken from Mount Etna, an active volcano on the island of Sicily.

Africa, HMS

A ship on the North American station, currently unavailable for active service (FW 5).

HMS Africa, 64-gun, was launched in 1781 and broken up in 1814. In 1805 she fought in *Nelson's great victory at Trafalgar under her Captain Henry Digby (1770–1842; full Admiral 1841). In 1812, under her Captain John Bastard, she was the somewhat decrepit flagship of Vice-Admiral Herbert *Sawyer at Halifax, Nova Scotia.

Africaine, and Africaine, HMS

An over-manned French ship that had been taken by HMS *Phoebe* (PC 4). Later as HMS *Africaine*, 36-gun, she unexpectedly arrives at Réunion under Captain Corbett, the savage former Captain of HMS *Néréide* (TMC 8), having been met at sea by Tom Pullings' HMS *Emma* and told of the poor situation at Mauritius (TMC 9). Joining in the campaign, she becomes separated from Jack Aubrey's HMS *Boadicea* and after a fierce action is taken by *Astrée* and *Iphigénie*. Very badly mauled, she is immediately abandoned by the French ships and retaken by Jack, her crew denying all knowledge of the fate of the missing Corbett (TMC 8). Many of her crew then volunteer to join *Boadicea* to have their revenge on the French (TMC 9).

Africaine, 38-gun, was launched in 1795. In February 1801, whilst she was sailing just off Gibraltar en route to Egypt, encumbered by 400 troops and their supplies as well as her own crew of 315, she was attacked by HMS *Phoebe, 36-gun, and taken after a two-hour running fight. Africaine fired high at Phoebe's rigging, whilst the British ship poured broadside after broadside into her enemy's packed hull and deck; consequently, Africaine suffered 344 dead and wounded to Phoebe's mere 13, only one of whom was killed. She was taken into the Royal Navy as HMS Africaine (N.B., CLOWES, Vol. 4:538, is mistaken in stating she was re-named HMS Amelia). On 12th September 1810, under Robert *Corbett, she was forced to surrender off the island of Réunion to the French frigates *Astrée and *Iphigénie after a furious fight, but was re-taken the following day by HMS *Boadicea (these 1810 events are not noted in COLLEDGE, but may be found in VICHOT). HMS Africaine was broken up in 1816.

Afzelius

An unpublished Swedish botanist who had lived in Sierra Leone (COM 8).

Adam Afzelius (1750–1836), a pupil of *Linnaeus, was botanist to the Sierra Leone Company from 1792 to 1794; he later became a Professor of Materia Medica (an early form of pharmacology) at Uppsala University. His publications on his botanical interests and discoveries are to be found in learned journals, rather than in entire books under his own name.

Agag

A carronade in Aubrey's HMS *Nutmeg of Consolation* (NC 5).

Agamemnon

One of the leading characters in Homer's *Iliad*, often referred to as a model of imposing military bearing (FSW 4,7; RM 4; LM 8).

In ancient Greek myth, King Agamemnon of Mycenae, the brother of Menelaus, led the Greek forces in the Trojan War.

Agamemmnon, HMS

A ship in which Jack Aubrey had once been a Midshipman (M&C 1) and Lieutenant (TMC 2,3). She had been commanded at one time by Nelson (LM 1) and later took part in his great victory at the Battle of Trafalgar (FW 2); according to Jack she is a famous sailer (HMS 4). She is also referred to several times in passing (TMC 3; IM 1; WDS 4; COM 1).

HMS Agamemmnon, 64-gun, was launched in 1781; from 1793 to 1796 she was commanded by *Nelson and in 1805 fought at Trafalgar under Captain Edward *Berry. Under Captain Jonas Rose, she was wrecked in the River Plate in 1809, and thus her later arrival at Portsmouth (LM 1) is a minor anachronism. She was named for the Greek King *Agamemnon.

Agathocles

A classical figure discussed by Maturin and Graham (IM 10).

Agathocles (361–289 BC) was an Sicilian adventurer and mercenary who became the ruler, and later King, of Syracuse. After unsuccessful campaigns against his Carthaginian rivals on his home island and in Africa itself, he invaded southern Italy but was assassinated before he could consolidate his power.

Agg, William

A quartermaster's mate in HMS *Sophie* (M&C 11).

Aggie

A passenger on an East Indiaman who, together with her sister, upsets Stephen Maturin with gossip about the affair between Diana Villiers and Richard Canning (HMS 9).

Agha

The title of the head of the Algerian janissaries (HD 6).

see also **Omar Pasha**

Agnes

1: a sheep in HMS *Diane*, eventually eaten (TGS 5).

2: the tame auk belonging to Dr Falconer, surgeon of the whaler *Daisy* (C/T 5).

Agrippa

A poet who ended in the poorhouse (RM 3).

This may be a reference to either one of two men: Henry Cornelius Agrippa (1486–1530), a physician, occult philosopher and writer who died in poverty in Grenoble; or Théodore-Agrippa d'Aubigné (1552–1630), a French soldier, poet and polemicist who published under the name 'Agrippa' and died in exile in Geneva.

Aguillières, Madame de

The aunt of Captain Christy-Pallière, residing at Laura Place, Bath (PC 4).

Ahab

A mule at Woolcombe House (YA 3).

Ahasuerus

According to Mr Woodbine, a famous mathematician (HD 6).

*Ahasuerus is a name various associated with the father of King Darius the Great, with King *Xerxes, with King Artaxerxes and with the 'Wandering Jew' of legend. I am uncertain as to why *Woodbine should think any of them appropriate to be mentioned in the same context as Sir Isaac *Newton.*

Ahmed

1: a cousin of Mr Fox's man, Ali, given a job as a servant by Stephen Maturin (TGS 4–9; NC 1–4).

2: a minor Algerian functionary (HD 7).

Aimable Louise

A French merchantman captured by HMS *Sophie*, she is Jack Aubrey's first ever prize as a Commander (M&C 5).

Ajax

1: a classical figure (PC 1) referred to for his impatience (FSW 2) and his protective shield (COM 1).

*In *Homer, Ajax was the son of King Telamon of Salamis. Enormously large and strong, he was second only to *Achilles amongst the Greek warriors, famous for carrying a huge ox-hide shield that he used as an offensive weapon more than as a defence. That Ajax relied too much on pure aggressive strength, and too little on patience and cunning, is shown in his wrestling match with his wily colleague, *Odysseus.*

2: the deceased male ape whose dried head belongs to George Rogers (PC 12).

Ajax, HMS

1: a ship in which Jack Aubrey had been a youngster (FW 3), and in which Poll Skeeping may once have served (HD 2). She was also a former command of Admiral Sir Francis Ives (TH 8).

*HMS Ajax, 74-gun, was launched in 1767 and sold in 1785. The fictional *Ives could have commanded either her or her replacement, also a 74-gun, launched in 1798 and accidentally destroyed by fire in 1807; Poll *Skeeping could perhaps have served in either ship, or in Ajax #2 below. The 1798 ship fought under Captain William Brown in*

*Calder's indecisive 1805 action, and then in *Nelson's victory at Trafalgar under her First Lieutenant John Pilford (d.1834), Brown having gone home to attend Calder's court martial (Pilford was rewarded with Post rank soon after the battle).*

2: a ship commanded by Captain Collard (TMC 1) and afterwards offered to Jack Aubrey, who declines her in favour of a somewhat independent cruise in the smaller HMS *Leopard* (DI 1). A little later, Jack reads that she has just taken *Méduse* (SM 11) and she is afterwards seen anchored at Portsmouth (IM 1). Poll Skeeping may once have served in her (HD 2).

*The third HMS Ajax, 74-gun, was launched in 1809; the action against *Méduse is fictional. In 1846 she was fitted with a steam-driven propeller and re-fitted with 60 modern guns and, in this configuration, saw a great deal of active service until her break-up in 1864.*

Akers

1: an aged Admiralty intelligence clerk (PC 14).

2: one of Governor Raffles secretaries (NC 3).

Akers, Lemuel

The one-legged First Lieutenant of HMS *Boadicea* when Jack Aubrey takes command. Jack soon forms a low opinion of his abilities and gladly sends him into Gibraltar in the *Hébé* prize (TMC 2).

Alacrity, HMS

A ship in Admiral Ives' Mediterranean fleet (FSW 1).

HMS Alacrity, 18-gun brig-sloop, was launched in 1806 and captured in the Mediterranean by the French in 1811 (some time before FSW is set); as Alacrité, she served in their navy until 1822.

Alastor

A French pirate ship, fought and taken by Aubrey's *Surprise* and Pullings' *Franklin* (WDS 5,6,9); she is then sold in Peru (WDS 10).

In Greek myth, Alastor was an avenging deity representing the curse of guilt.

Albemarle, HMS

A ship once commanded by Nelson (LM 1).

*HMS Albemarle was the ex-French merchantman Ménagère, captured by the Royal Navy in either 1779 or 1781 (the sources do not agree) and converted into a frigate; she was commanded by *Nelson from 1781 to 1783 and sold out of the service in 1784. A French naval frigate also named Ménagère, acting as a transport ship and armed only en flûte, was captured by the Royal Navy in December 1782; her fate is unknown, but VICHOT confuses her with the earlier ship in stating that she became Albemarle. Nelson's ship was named for George Monck (1608–1670), the English General and Admiral who in 1660 had negotiated the restoration of King *Charles II and who was then created 1st Duke of Albemarle for this service. Somewhat later, the *Keppel family were also Earls of Albemarle.*

Albini

A great flautist to whom Maturin favourably compares Lieutenant Howard (DI 6).

Alcmene, HMS

A ship referred to by Aubrey as one of several very desirable frigates into which he would like to be made Post (M&C 11).

HMS Alcmene, 32-gun, was launched in 1794, fought at *Nelson's victory at Copenhagen in 1801, and was wrecked off the French coast in 1809. In Greek mythology, Alcmene was the mother of *Hercules/Heracles.

Aldham

The purser of HMS *Shannon*, killed in action against USS *Chesapeake* (FW 9).

Purser George Aldham (d.1813), a Suffolk man like *Broke, was hit in the stomach by a burst of grape whilst standing near his Captain and died an hour or so later.

Aldington, Colonel Tom

An officer of the First Foot Guards with an odious reputation amongst the ladies. A distant cousin of Jack Aubrey, he warns the Captain of Amanda Smith's indifferent virtue (SM 2).

Alert, HMS

A ship in which Aubrey had served as a youngster (PC 5).

HMS Alert, 14-gun brig-sloop, was launched in 1779 and sold in 1792.

Alex

Here presumably used by Killick as short-hand for the port of Alexandria in Egypt (IM 6).

Alexander

1: the Greek warrior king (YA 5; TMC 4) who, according to Maturin, was as vain and ambitious as Buonaparte (LM 6) and a similarly odious coloniser (C/T 3).

Alexander III — 'the Great' — of Macedonia (356–323 BC) was one of the most ambitious and energetic military expansionists of all time. His father, King Philip, had sent him as a very young man to study under *Aristotle, a man who was to have an enormous impact on his vigorous intellectual development. Once turned to the military life, before Alexander was 25 years old he had pushed Persian influence out of the Mediterranean and come to control all the Greek city-states of Asia Minor. He later invaded and conquered much of north India but was soon compelled to withdraw because of the final unwillingness of his troops to fight seemingly interminable wars in conditions of great hardship; his contemporaries supposed that his early death at Babylon was due to poison. The English poet Alexander *Pope summed up Alexander's remarkable career and personality thus, that he 'all things but himself subdued.'

2: an elderly, reliable quartermaster in HMS *Sophie* (M&C 7).

3: a seaman in *Surprise*, the cousin of the rock-climber McLeod (HD 10).

Alexander, John

The murdered Superintendent of HMS *Leopard*'s convicts (DI 3).

Alexandria, HMS

A small frigate on the Brest blockade (YA 4), Captain Nasmyth (YA 6).

HMS Alexandria, 32-gun fir-built, was launched in 1806 and broken up in 1818.

Alfred

An East Indiaman in Muffit's China Fleet, protected by HMS *Surprise* from Admiral Linois' French squadron. (HMS 9).

The Alfred, 1198 tons, made 8 round trips from India to England between 1790 and 1809. She was probably named for Alfred, King of Wessex (849–899), he who supposedly burnt a lowly, if well-intentioned, housewife's cakes whilst disguised as a wandering peasant. The action is based on the defence of a Honourable East India Company merchant fleet against *Linois' attack in February 1804. However, no Royal Navy ship was present during the fight, the squadron being organised by the senior Master, Nathaniel Dance of *Earl Camden.

Algaroth

Maturin refers to 'powder of Algaroth' (PC 14).

The powder is antimony oxychloride, an expectorant and emetic, named for the 16th century Italian physician, Vittorio Algarotto.

Algiers, Dey of

The ruler of Algiers and its hinterland (PC 8; HD 1,5,6), strangled in a coup and replaced successively by Omar Pasha (HD 6), Ali Bey (HD 8) and Hassan (HD 10).

'Dey' (Turkish for 'maternal uncle') was the traditional title of the rulers of Algiers from 1689 until the French conquest of 1830.

Algren

A helmsman in HMS *Sophie* (M&C 7).

Ali

A Malay servant of Mr Fox (TGS 4–7).

Ali, Mehemet or **Mohammed**

The Pasha of Egypt (IM 4), thought to be a French ally (TH 3–8).

Muhammad Ali (1769–1849) was Viceroy and Pasha of Egypt from 1805 until his death. He was of Greek or Albanian origins, and made his reputation as one of the Sultan of *Turkey's military commanders opposing *Buonaparte in Egypt. After being appointed Pasha he threw his energies partly into the modernization of the county and rather more into establishing a powerful family dynasty — partly by trying to play British and French interests against each other — that ruled until the middle of the following century. His son *Ibrahim was one of his leading military commanders.

Ali, Pasha of Iannina or **Ali Arslan**

An Albanian Muslim Bey in the Ionian region

thought by his good friend Professor Graham to be on the point of open revolt against the Sultan of Turkey, having already defeated his rival, the Bey of Scutari (IM 9–11). Secretly, he really sees Capitan-Bey Mustapha as the main threat to his plans and, after forming an alliance with him, provokes him into a first rebellion against Constantinople. Mustapha is then defeated by Jack Aubrey — Turkey's ally for the occasion — and a clear path is left for Ali Pasha's plans (IM 11).

> *Ali Weli Zade (1750–1822), called 'Arslan' ('Lion'), was a notorious brigand and adventurer who in 1798, after service as Lieutenant— and eventually successor— to the Derbend-Pasha of *Rumelia, was appointed Pasha of Yannina. He spent his subsequent years plotting independence from the Sultan of *Turkey, whose most powerful Prince he had soon become. Eventually an outright rebel, Ali was shot whilst resisting arrest by the Sultan's forces.*

Ali Bey

The new, somewhat pro-British Dey of Algiers who has replaced Omar Pasha in a coup (HD 8). Later, he stakes a vigorous claim to the Moslem gold captured by Jack Aubrey but is soon deposed and killed by Hassan (HD 10).

> *Although *Omar Pasha remained Bey throughout the period covered by HD, the name and general context perhaps recalls Ali Bey el Abbassi, a *Buonapartist spy born in Catalonia as Badia Castillo y Leblich (1766–1818), who was active in Morocco and the Mahgreb from 1802 to 1805 and then in the Moslem eastern Mediterranean lands until about 1808. SPILLMANN describes him as one of Napoleon's many 'James Bonds'!*

Alice

A relative of Peter Willis and Art Compton (COM 1).

Alice B. Sawyer

An American merchant brig allegedly fired on by Aubrey's HMS *Leopard* (FW 4,6).

al-Jabal, Sheikh

The leader of the Muslim sect of Assassins, a.k.a. 'The Old Man of the Mountains' (HD 1).

> shaykh al-jabal *is Arabic for 'mountain chief' (mis-translated by the Crusaders as 'the old man of the mountain'), the title given to the Assassin war-lord Rashid ad-Din as-Sinan (d.1192), the ruler of the Syrian mountain fortress of Alamut, and his immediate successors. Rashid operated almost entirely independently of Assassin headquarters in Iran, sending his devoted and determined followers on missions to murder his enemies, largely moderate opponents of his extreme shi'ite sect.*

Alkmaar

A Dutch merchantman, encountered by Aubrey and HMS *Nutmeg of Consolation*, whose Master had once been pressed into HMS 'Billy Ruffian'/ Bellerophon (NC 5,6).

> *The ship is probably named for the poet Henrik van Alk-*

maar (fl. late 15th century), supposedly the author of a version of the fable Reynard the Fox, *a work famously adapted into English in 1481 by the printer William Caxton.*

Allah

The name of God in the Muslim faith (TGS 6).

> *Before the coming of the prophet *Mahomet, Allah was the Arabic name for 'the god,' merely the most important amongst many tribal deities. The new religion of Islam proclaimed Allah as the one true *God, the same supreme being worshipped in Christianity and Judaism.*

Allen

1: an American Loyalist Royal Navy officer, promoted from Commander of HMS *Sophie* to Post Captain of HMS *Pallas*, thus creating a vacancy for Jack Aubrey (M&C 1+).

2: a Master's Mate in HMS *Polychrest* (PC 7,8,11).

3: a former suitor of Sophie Williams (PC 8).

4: the acting bosun in HMS *Leopard* once Lane and all his mates have abandoned ship (DI 9). He has a brother who had deserted to the USA from HMS *Hermione* (DI 10).

5: the former Captain of HMS *Skate*, thought by her crew to be a bolder man than Aubrey (IM 7; *N.B., Skate's commander had earlier (IM 2) been named as Captain *Hall*).

6: Admiral Sir John Thornton's confidential secretary and intelligence advisor (IM 4,8,9). It is strongly suggested that, in order to prevent disclosures during a trial, he has poisoned a traitorous Maltese naval clerk (a cousin of the French spy Giuseppe) held prisoner in HMS *Ocean* (IM 4; TH 1).

7: the Master of a transport, expected by Jack Aubrey at Kutali, but which has in fact been taken by Capitan-Bey Mustapha (IM 11).

8: the Master of the *Dromedary* transport (TH 4,5,7).

Allen, George

A seaman in HMS *Lively* (PC 14).

Allen, Michael

An ex-whaler who had been Master of HMS *Tiger* until falling ill. He joins HMS *Surprise* as replacement for the promoted Mr Gill (FSW 2–6; RM 2).

Allen, Tom

Barret Bonden is said to resemble Nelson's coxswain, Tom Allen (COM 9).

> *Tom Allen (1760–1834) lived in *Nelson's Norfolk village of Burnham Thorpe and volunteered for HMS *Agamemnon in 1793 when, after five years on shore, Nelson was appointed to her command. In 1798 he became the great man's principal retainer, remaining with him for almost the entirety of his career, yet missing the Battle of Trafalgar itself by being been sent with Captain *Louis to Gibraltar on various errands. After the*

*Admiral's death Allen fell on hard times but, after 1830, managed to secure a berth as a pensioner at Greenwich Naval Hospital; on his death, Admiral Sir Thomas Hardy (HMS *Victory's Captain at Trafalgar) arranged for a headstone in the hospital cemetery. Allen's job—he is usually described as servant, not coxswain—and personality were far more like those of *Aubrey's *Killick than *Bonden. A contemporary portrait of him can be found in O'BRIAN's own* Men of War: Life in Nelson's Navy.

Almack's

A gambling club in London (PC 10; DI 2; SM 2; YA 7).

Almack's Club in Pall Mall, founded by William Almack (d.1781), was famed for its high-stakes play and élite society members. Almack and his family also owned many other popular clubs and assembly-rooms in the capital.

Almathea

HMS *Surprise*'s goat (WDS 4)

*In classical legend Almathea was the goat that gave suck to *Zeus when he was hidden by his mother, Rhea, to save him from his father Cronos' indiscriminate appetite.*

Almaviva

see **'Marriage of Figaro'**

Almighty, the

1: a reference to Jack Aubrey as a Captain (YA 5).
2: *see* **God**

Alphonso

The name of an army barracks in Port Mahon (HMS 3).

The barracks is named for one of the many Alfonsos who had been Kings of Castile, Leon and, later, the united Spain.

Alton, Lord

A gentleman who unsuccessfully writes to Jack Aubrey in the hope of getting him to take his son to sea in HMS *Worcester* (IM 2).

Amanda

1: a name scratched on the wall of the nunnery/ prison in Brest where HMS *Ariel*'s officers are held (SM 10).
2: *see* **Smith, Amanda**

Amasis

A king whose reign Goodridge had studied in Tacitus (PC 10).

*Amasis, Pharaoh of Egypt (ruled 570?–525? BC), enjoyed a notably prosperous and peaceful reign; he left many monuments and temples, amongst which is the grand temple of *Isis at Memphis.*

Amati

Stephen Maturin owns a cello made by Geronimo Amati (PC 3; WDS 1) and Jack Aubrey a violin from the Amati family (SM 4).

*The Amati family were leading instrument makers in the Italian city of Cremona. There were two men named Girolamo—or Geronimus—Amati, the first living from 1561–1630, and his grandson from 1649–1740. The intervening son, Nicola (1596–1684), was the greatest genius of the family and had both *Stradivari and *Guarnieri as his pupils.*

Amazon, HMS

A frigate referred to by Captain Griffiths as having taken the 74-gun *Droits de l'Homme* in company with HMS *Indefatigable* (PC 1; FSW 2; YA 5).

*HMS Amazon, 36-gun, was launched in 1795. In the early morning of 14th January 1797, under Captain Robert Reynolds, she and HMS *Indefatigable, Captain Sir Edward *Pellew, pursued *Droits de l'Homme onto rocks off the French coast. The French ship and almost her entire crew were lost; shortly afterwards Amazon too was wrecked nearby but then enjoyed more fortune, having all but 6 of her crew saved by local inhabitants. Her similar replacement (see *Riou) was launched in 1799 and broken up in 1817. In Greek myth the Amazons were a race of warrior women.*

Ambrogio

Jack Aubrey's first Italian teacher in Malta, soon warned off by French agents (TH 1).

Ambrosian

A plainchant mode (TH 2).

This ancient mode, now lost, is named for Saint Ambrose of Milan (374–397), who restructured the vocal music of the early Christian church.

Amelia

A whaler, Master Mr Shields (FSW 3), taken by USS *Norfolk* (FSW 7).

Amelia, HMS

A British frigate operating in the Western Mediterranean (M&C 7+), referred to by Jack Aubrey as one of several very desirable ships into which he would like to be made Post (M&C 11). She later gives the victorious Jack and his HMS *Sophie* a full naval cheer at Port Mahon (M&C 11), with Mr Trollope a Midshipman in her at the time (TMC 2). Years afterwards she is reported by Captain Billy Holroyd to be overdue at Sydney (NC 8).

*HMS Amelia was a 28-gun frigate, the ex-French Prosperine, launched in 1785, captured by HMS *Dryad in 1796, and broken up in 1816. She was named for Princess Amelia (1783–1810), the youngest child of King *George III.*

Amélie

Diana Villiers' maid in Bombay (HMS 7).

Amethyst, HMS

A frigate commanded by Captain Seymour, an exshipmate of Jack Aubrey (PC 3+). She is encountered by HMS *Polychrest* at sea (PC 7) and later takes a merchantman that had escaped Jack's ship (PC 9). Sailing in company with Jack's HMS *Lively*,

she is out-paced in order to impress the visiting Sophie Williams (PC 14), even though she is known
as an especially fine sailer (FSW 2). Mr Davidge
had served in her in an action against *Thetis* (C/T
2) and, years later, she is briefly seen by Jack's HMS
Bellona tender, *Ringle* (COM 5).

> HMS Amethyst, 38-gun, was launched in 1799 but was
> not commanded by *Seymour until well after PC is set.
> In November 1808, under Seymour, she engaged the
> significantly heavier *Thétis and forced her to strike after
> a particularly bloody night-action. She was wrecked off
> Plymouth in 1811— some years before COM is set— and
> not replaced until 1844.

Amiable Catherine or Catherine

A merchant ship met by HMS *Surprise* off the coast
of Brazil (FSW 4).

Amos

1: a coachman (HMS 4).
2: *see* **Jacob, Dr Amos**

Amphion, HMS

Under her Captain Sutton, a member of the
squadron that takes Bustamente's Spanish treasure
ships (PC 14). However, as the action took place before war was formally declared, the ships are not
prizes but *droits* of the Crown, leaving the Captains
very much less rich than they had hoped (HMS 1).
Later, perhaps commanded by Captain Brenton,
she is encountered by Jack Aubrey at Funchal,
Madeira (HMS 11).

> HMS Amphion, 32-gun, was launched in 1798, sunk as
> a breakwater at Woolwich in 1820, and sold in 1823. The
> action described in PC took place in October 1805, pro-
> ducing treasure worth one million pounds sterling at the
> time, which did indeed go straight to the Crown. In Greek
> myth, Amphion was that son of *Zeus and *Antiope who
> rebuilt Thebes.

Amphitrite

A character in the ship-board ceremony of 'crossing the line' (TMC 2).

> In Greek myth Amphitrite was a *Nereid, the wife of
> *Neptune and mother of *Triton.

Ananda

A Buddhist monk met by Maturin at the temple of
Kumai (TGS 7,8).

Ananias

A dishonest Gosport wine-merchant (IM 1).

Anchises

A man guessed at by Jack Aubrey as being responsible for the poor treatment of Dido (TH 9), and
as a man of very great age (TGS 1).

> In Greek mythology Anchises, a Prince of Troy, was the fa-
> ther of *Aeneas by the goddess *Venus. After the destruc-
> tion of their city by the Greeks, Anchises fled across the
> Mediterranean with his son, and it was this young man
> who, on the journey, met and then abandoned Queen

> *Dido of Carthage. The ancient Anchises is supposed to
> have later died in Sicily.

Andersen

A Swedish medical authority on the treatment of
fractures, especially by the Basra plaster method
(LM 9).

Anderson

1: a seaman in HMS *Polychrest* believed by Aubrey
to be about to mutiny (PC 11).
2: a Danish seaman in HMS *Ariel* (SM 8).
3: an HMS *Surprise* seaman on Aubrey's Mubara
expedition (TH 7).

Anderssen

A Danish seaman in HMS *Sophie* (M&C 5).

Andréossy

A former French envoy to Britain (LM 7).

> Antoine-François, Compte de Andréossy (1761–1828), the
> French General and diplomat, was Ambassador to Lon-
> don in 1802, negotiating the terms of the Treaty of Amiens.
> A military engineer by training, he was promoted Gen-
> eral in 1797, and served as *Buonaparte's Chief of Staff
> in 1799, before becoming Ambassador to London, Vienna
> and Constantinople successively. He was part of the team
> that negotiated the armistice following the Emperor's de-
> feat at Waterloo in 1815, thereafter following a minor po-
> litical career under the *Bourbon restoration.

Andreotti

A man referred to by members of Lesueur's organisation in Malta (TH 10).

Andrew

Mr Norton's coachman (LM 8).

Andrew, John

A seaman in HMS *Lively* killed in action when the
Spanish *Mercedes* blows up (PC 14).

Andrew, Merry

see **Merry-Andrew**

Andrew, Saint

A reference is made to the style of his crucifixion,
imitated by Captain-Bey Mustapha in his treatment
of captured Greek pirates (IM 9).

> Andrew was one of the biblical Twelve Apostles of *Jesus,
> a brother of Saint *Peter. He is supposed to have preached
> the gospel both in Greece and northwards across the
> Danube before suffering martyrdom on an X-shaped cross
> in about 60 or 70 AD.

Andrews

1: the ship's corporal in HMS *Sophie* (M&C 6).
2: a seaman in HMS *Sophie* (M&C 7,9), possibly
later serving in HMS *Surprise* (FSW 3).
3: a Royal Navy officer referred to by Captain
Fowler (PC 3).

4: a British official in Boston who deals with issues relating to prisoners-of-war (FW 5,7).

The British consul/agent in Boston at the outbreak of war in 1812 was a Mr Allen. He resigned in mid-1813 in protest at being required by U.S. officials to move his office some 40 miles inland from the port, a demand designed to limit his ability to pursue his responsibilities for prisoners promptly and effectively. The senior Royal Naval officers at Halifax then recommended similar, retaliatory measures against American officials to the Admiralty in London.

5: the landlord of an inn in Woolcombe (YA 3).

Andrews, Joe

The servant of a Marine officer in HMS *Bellona* (COM 9).

Andrews, Tom

A former Captain of HMS *Leopard* (DI 1), perhaps the unnamed relative of Admiral Bertie earlier given the ship (TMC 6).

Andromache

A classical figure referred to by Aubrey (M&C 12) whose child had been dashed from the battlements of Troy (FSW 4).

In Greek myth Andromache was the wife of the Trojan hero *Hector. Her famous lament over his death in *Homer's Iliad *leads her to represent all women who suffer loss in war. In other versions of the myth, Andromache's daughter, Astyanax, is thrown from the city walls as Troy is sacked by the Greeks.*

Andromache, HMS

A ship on service in the Mediterranean (IM 1,2), later referred to in passing (LM 9). She is the ship from which Sir Williams Hastings had obtained the newspaper bearing the announcement of the birth of Stephen Maturin and Diana Villiers' daughter (NC 10).

HMS Andromache, *38-gun, was launched as the French *Junon in 1782; she was captured by the Royal Navy in 1799 and taken into service as HMS* Princess Charlotte. *Renamed* Andromache *in January 1812, she was broken up in 1828. For the name derivation see *Andromache above; see also *Masher, Andrew, the common Royal Navy nickname for the ship.*

Andromeda, HMS

A ship, once commanded by the Duke of Clarence, in which Lieutenant Parker of HMS *Polychrest* had served (PC 9,10,11) and in which Mr Thomas of HMS *Nymphe* had once been surgeon's mate (TH 9). Jack Aubrey had also served in her as a boy (FW 7).

HMS Andromeda, *32-gun, was launched in 1784 and broken up in 1811; *Clarence commanded her in 1788–1789. In classical myth, Andromeda was that daughter of Cephus and *Calliope with whom the hero Perseus fell in love, he turning potential rivals to stone by showing them the severed head of *Medusa.*

Andronicus, Titus

A reference by Maturin to the gory scene following his slaying of Pontet-Canet and Dubreuil (FW7).

The reference is to *Shakespeare's tragedy Titus Andronicus, *written in about 1590. Andronicus, a Roman general, is both victim and perpetrator of numerous plots and feuds that give rise to extraordinarily gory murders, mutilations and rapes: the final scene is especially gruesome.*

Andros, Father

The leader of Kutali's Orthodox Christians and political advisor to Sciahan Bey (IM 10,11), later once again visited by Aubrey and Maturin (TH 9).

Angelica

see **Orlando and Angelica**

Angelo

A fencing-master who had employed Davidge after his dismissal from the Royal Navy (LM 6).

The Angelo family were famous equestrians and fencing-masters in England from about 1755 onwards: the dynasty was founded by the Italian immigrant Domenico Angelo Malevolti Tremamondo (1716–1802) and continued by his son, Henry Angelo (1760–1839), and grandson, also Henry (1780–1852).

Anglars, d'

A gentleman known to Stephen Maturin, associated with Talleyrand-Périgord's intelligence network; he is also in La Mothe's closet, homosexual circle. Having accompanied Stephen and Jack Aubrey to England in order to visit his cousin Blacas, a member of the Bourbon exile court in England (SM 11), he rather later restores Diana Villiers' 'Blue Peter' diamond to Stephen (RM 10; LM 9).

The reference may perhaps be to François Antoine Boissy-d'Anglas (1756–1826), a powerful French politician who had voted against the execution of *Louis XVI and who went on to serve under both *Buonaparte and the *Bourbon restoration.

Aniceto, Saint

A saint referred to in passing (TH 4).

Saint Anicetus reigned as Pope from about 155–166 AD, working to prevent the splitting of the infant Church by heresies and variant practices; little is known of his life.

Anigoni

A dishonest apothecary in Malta (TH 3).

Anna, Saint

The saint for whom a church in Port Mahon is named (HMS 3).

In the Christian New Testament, Saint Anne is the mother of the Virgin *Mary.

Anne, Queen

A Queen of England (SM 10) who had given a silver teapot to Mr Lowndes' grandmother (PC 8).

Queen Anne (1665–1714) was the second daughter of the exiled *James II; in 1702 she succeeded her childless brother-in-law King *William III (who had married and outlived Anne's elder sister, Queen Mary II) to the three separate thrones of England, Scotland and Ireland. All of Anne's children died very young, leading her in 1701 to agree to an Act of Settlement that provided for the Elector of Hanover to become King George I after her death. In order further to secure the exclusion of the deposed, male line of the (originally Scottish) Stuarts, in 1707 the thrones of England and Scotland were amalgamated into the single Kingdom of Great Britain.

Annibale

A French 74-gun in Toulon Harbour that had been captured, as HMS *Hannibal*, from the Royal Navy (PC 4).

HMS *Hannibal *had been launched in 1786 and was captured in 1801 by the French *Formidable at Algeçiras after having run aground in the action between *Saumarez' and *Linois' squadrons; Annibale (the French spelling of the Latin name) remained in French service until 1823.

Annie

A lady of Kutali to whom Tom Pullings has become attached (IM 11).

Anon., Dr S.

The name by which Maturin ironically refers to himself when hoping not to have been discovered by Johnson as an intelligence agent (FW 7).

Anselmo

The keeper of an inn on Gibraltar (FSW 2).

Anson, Commodore

A famous and wealthy seaman of a former age (PC 14; DI 1; FSW 5; NC 1; WDS 10), an account of whose voyages is owned by Captain Yorke (FW 2).

Lord George Anson (1697–1762) was the leading English seaman of his age and is regarded as the father of the modern British naval profession. Made Post in 1724, he was promoted Rear Admiral in 1744, Vice Admiral in 1746, Admiral in 1748 and rose to Admiral of the Fleet in 1761. He served as a Commissioner of the Admiralty from 1744 to 1751, as an MP from 1744 onwards, and as First Lord from 1751 to 1756 and from 1757 until his death. From 1740 to 1744 Anson embarked with a small squadron on both actions against the Spanish and a circumnavigation of the globe; the remarkable adventures and hardships of this voyage form the basis of O'Brian's early sea novels, The Golden Ocean and The Unknown Shore. During this time Anson's HMS *Centurion took a Spanish treasure galleon, his share of the prize money making him rich for life. Following these adventures, Anson's career as a fighting seaman and naval administrator was a story of uninterrupted success, enabling him to introduce many reforms — especially in the areas of training and professional discipline — and act as mentor to many of the leading Captains and Admirals of the next generation. In 1748 Centurion's chaplain, Richard Walter, published A Voyage Round the World, an account of the great circumnavigation, based closely on log books and diaries.

Antaeus

A figure referred to by Martin in connection with his confession that he is at heart a landsman (NC 8).

In Greek myth, Antaeus was the son of Poseidon ('Sea') and Ge ('Earth'), whose strength was drawn primarily from contact with his earth-mother.

Anthony, Saint

An extreme ascetic referred to by Maturin (PC 2).

Two Anthonies are possible, Saint Anthony Abbas (251?–305?) a religious hermit and monk in Egypt, or Saint Anthony of Padua (1195–1231), a Portuguese Franciscan Friar and Patron Saint of the Poor.

Antiope, HMS

A ship, Captain Harvey, that had passed up the chance of capturing a prize in the southern Mediterranean in order to avoid any suggestion of a breach of the complex neutrality laws in place in the various Turkish outposts (IM 6).

The ship is fictional; in Greek myth Antiope was a daughter of King Nycteus of Thebes and the mother, by *Zeus, of *Amphion.

Antonine

A passing reference is made to the 'Antonine Age' (TH 2).

The Antonine Age covers the reigns of the Roman Emperors Antonius Pius (ruled 138–161 AD) and his immediate successors, including his adopted son Marcus *Aurelius Antoninus (ruled 161–180 AD). The age was marked by peace, prosperity and good government; Antonius Pius was especially admired by Edward *Gibbon.

Aphrodite

A reference to female beauty (SM 1).

Aphrodite is the Greek name of the goddess *Venus.

Apicius

A writer on food referred to by Dr Jacob (HD 3).

Marcus Gavius Apicius (fl. early 1st century AD) is reported by the historian and critic Seneca (his contemporary) to have been a wealthy gourmand and writer on food topics, legendary for his devotion to excess. The On Matters Culinary often seen under his name is, however, a work dating from about three hundred years after his death. The name Apicius is also given to several other minor Latin authors, all concerned with aspects of luxury.

Apollo

1: a Greek fisherman, a.k.a. 'Sponge,' now a seaman in HMS *Sophie* (M&C 3,6).
2: a reference to Aubrey's protégé Mr Richardson, the beautiful Flag Lieutenant of HMS *Irresistible* (RM 1).
3: a reference to the handsome Jagiello by Maturin (SM 8) and d'Anglars (SM 11).

The Greek god Apollo, son of *Zeus, is a symbol of light, reason and youthful, manly beauty.

Apollo, Captain
see **Adeane, Captain**

Apollon
A ship that had been fought by HMS *Ajax* (FW 3).
> *Apollon was the name of many French warships, the best known of which was a 74-gun launched in 1788, renamed* Gasparin *in 1794 and* Marceau *in 1797; her fate is unrecorded. I have not found a record of an action between* Apollon *and HMS *Ajax.*

Appleby
A Midshipman in HMS *Worcester* (IM 1,5).

Aquinas
A philosopher referred to by Professor Graham (TH 1).
> *Saint Thomas Aquinas (1225?–74) was the pre-eminent scholar of the middle ages, whose many works remain profoundly influential in the Roman Catholic church to this day. Despite all the advantages of an aristocratic birth and, later, fame as a scholar throughout Europe, Aquinas spent his working life as a Dominican monk, refusing all offers of important and influential posts. He produced an enormous number of philosophical and religious works, chief amongst them the vast, though unfinished,* Summa Theologica, *in which he attempts to reconcile Christian faith with *Aristotelian reason.*

Arab, the
A thug in Malta employed by the French agent Lesueur (TH 10).

Archbold
1: Major Beck's second-in-command in Halifax (SM 1,2).
2: a medical manual referred to by Maturin (COM 6).

Archer
A seaman in *Surprise* (C/T 7).

Archimède
A French 74-gun that slips out from Toulon, avoiding the British blockade (IM 4).
> *The ship is fictitious; Archimedes (287?–212 BC), a Sicilian of Greek origins, was an exceptionally talented practical scientist and also the greatest geometer of his age.*

Arcturus
A merchant vessel belonging to George Herapath (FW 5) in which Maturin, Aubrey and Villiers briefly hide during their escape from Boston (FW 8).

Arden, Matthew
The political advisor to Admiral Lord Barmouth (HD 9,10).

Ardent
A French ship in the Adriatic that, after declaring for Buonaparte, is engaged and sunk by Jack Aubrey's small squadron (HD 5).

Ardent, HMS
A 64-gun ship, with Midshipman Aubrey aboard, that had been badly mauled by the Dutch *Vrijheid* at the Battle of Camperdown (DI 6). Many years later she is in sight of HMS *Ajax* when she takes *Méduse* (SM 11).
> *HMS* Ardent, *64-gun, was the former East Indiaman* Princess Royal, *bought into the Royal Navy in 1797. In October 1797 she fought in Admiral *Duncan's great victory over the Dutch at the Battle of Camperdown; however, Jack *Aubrey had already been promoted Lieutenant in 1792 and he nowhere else mentions his presence at this battle.* Ardent *was sent for harbour service in 1812 (a little before SM is set) and was broken up in 1824.*

Arethusa, HMS
A ship under the command of Captain Billy Harvey (IM 1) of which Robin Clerk, once a Midshipman in HMS *Surprise*, is later Master (C/T 2). Jack Aubrey had served in her as a Lieutenant (COM 1) and she had been John Daniel's first ever ship (HD 3).
> *HMS* Arethusa, *38-gun, was launched in 1781 and broken up in 1814. In Greek myth, Arethusa, a *Nereid, was an attendant of Diana, the goddess of the moon, childbirth and hunting.*

Argand
The inventor of a patent lamp (IM 2; HD 2,4).
> *Aimé Argand (1745?–1803) was a Swiss chemist and inventor who developed his very bright oil-lamp, equipped with a hollow glass wick, in England during 1784.*

Argenson
A great man who attends Maturin's lecture in Paris (SM 5).
> *The reference is probably to Marc René de Voyer d'Argenson (1771–1842), an elected Prefect from a distinguished political family. After *Buonaparte's abdication he was strongly opposed to a *Bourbon restoration, spending his later life in parliamentary opposition to the King.*

Argo, HMS
A ship referred to as being famous for the golden dress of her bargemen (RM 2).
> *HMS* Argo, *44-gun, was launched in 1781 and sold out of the service in 1816; from 1798 until 1802 Samuel *Walters was a Midshipman in her under Captain James *Bowen. The* Argo *of classical myth carried *Jason and his Greek heroes — the 'argonauts' — in search of the Golden Fleece.*

Argonauta
A Spanish ship engaged in Admiral Saumarez' great fleet actions (M&C 12).
> Argonauta *was an 80-gun ship, Captain Don Jose Herrera, that avoided capture by the English fleet in *Saumarez' second action — of July 13th 1801 — and escaped to Cadiz. Later, under Captain Don Alphonso Parejo, she fought at Trafalgar, surrendering to Captain*

King's HMS *Achilles. Being badly damaged, she was scuttled by her prize-crew in the storm that followed the battle. For the derivation of her name see HMS *Argo, above.*

Argus, HMS

A sloop once commanded by Captain Griffiths (YA 2).

*HMS Argus, 10-gun sloop, was the ex-French privateer Argus, launched in 1798 and captured by HMS *Pomone in 1799; she was broken up in 1811. Her name is the Latin form of the more usual Greek *Argo.*

Ariadne

A classical figure to whom Jack Aubrey's sometime lover Amanda Smith compares herself (SM 5).

*In Greek myth, Ariadne fell in love with the hero *Theseus. After helping him escape from the beast *Minotaur, she was cruelly abandoned on the island of Naxos.*

Ariadne

An HM Hired Vessel referred to by Aubrey (NC 10).

*An HMS Ariadne, 20-gun, was in full service from 1776 to 1814, being rebuilt as a 24-gun in 1792; for the derivation of her name see *Ariadne, above.*

Ariel, HMS

A sloop, an 18-gun ex-French corvette, initially under Commander Draper but then given as a temporary command to Aubrey for the Grimsholm mission (SM 6+). After success in the Baltic she heads south to Spain but, mistaking her position in foul weather, and after a dreadful mistake by her First Lieutenant Mr Hyde, she runs onto rocks near Brest and slowly sinks (SM 9+; RM 10). At one time the ship had possessed a Sumatran rhinoceros (IM 6).

*An HMS Ariel, 18-gun, was launched in England in 1806 and sold in 1816. In Greek fable, Ariel was a spirit of the air, later appearing as a sprite in *Shakespeare's Tempest.*

Aristides

An attempted classical reference by Aubrey (PC 1).

There were at least four Aristides of note, variously politicians, writers and philosophers from the 5th century BC to the 3rd century AD.

Aristotle

The ancient Greek scientist and philosopher (M&C 2; TGS 5) whose *Poetica* is being translated by Mr Martin for Lieutenant Mowett to versify (LM 6).

*Aristotle (384–322 BC), one of the very greatest of all thinkers, studied under *Plato in Athens, and later became the tutor of *Alexander, son of Philip of Macedon. On Alexander's succession to the throne, Aristotle founded his Lyceum, a research and scholarship community; however, on his royal patron's death he was forced into exile. Of the 400 books Aristotle is thought to have written, only the contents of 100 have come down to us; even these are thought to be teaching materials rather than works intended for publication. Aristotle's philosophy is distinguished by an exquisitely logical method of enquiry, applied with great thoroughness to those phenomena of the natural world that excite wonder—and, often, a consequent misunderstanding—in the human mind.*

Arklow

The senior bosun's mate in HMS *Leopard* who replaces his drunken superior, Mr Lane (DI 7).

Arklow, James

A seaman in HMS *Boadicea* wounded in the *Hébé* action (TMC 2).

Arliss

The chief British intelligence agent in Paris (SM 11).

Arminianism or Arminians

A heretical doctrine refuted by Mr White (HMS 8), later said to be one of the religious sects in Shelmerston (WDS 1).

*The doctrine is named for Jacob Arminius (1560–1609; a.k.a. Jacob Harminsen), a Dutch theologian who became Professor of Divinity at Leiden University in 1603. Opponents of *Calvin's strict doctrine of predestination, Arminius' supporters were later relentlessly persecuted for heterodoxy and heresy but elements of their religious views were very influential on John Wesley (1708–1791) and his development of Methodism.*

Armstrong, Mrs

The wife of HMS *Lively's* gunner, serving with him aboard, who had once nursed Lieutenant Simmons back from a near-fatal fever (PC 12,14).

LAVERY notes that despite restrictive Admiralty regulations, the wives of officers and warrant officers were quite often to be found at sea, although always at the Captain's discretion.

Arne

A composer (RM 1).

Thomas Augustine Arne (1710–1788) was famous for the sheer tunefulness of his many vocal compositions, amongst them God Save the King and Rule Britannia.

Arnold

A maker of fine naval chronometers, a pair of which are owned by Aubrey (SM 9; FSW 5; COM 5).

John Arnold (1736–1799) made many important improvements in the design of precision time-pieces for use at sea. His great contribution was to make his instruments extremely reliable in a variety of temperatures and other conditions, thus enabling mariners to have one clock permanently set to Greenwich mean time whilst the other of the pair was adjusted to a local time determined by celestial observation. The difference between the two times thus shown allowed accurate computation of longitude, the distance east or west of the Greenwich meridian.

Arrowsmith, John and Lizzie

A somewhat elderly, ship-less Royal Navy Lieutenant resident, with his daughter and family, at Gibraltar (HD 1).

Arslan, Ali
see **Ali, Pasha of Iannina**

Art

1: a nephew of Captain Goffin, sailing with him in the privateer *Triton* (NC 7).
2: *see* **Grimble, Arthur**

Artemisia

1: the wife of Mausolus (SM 8).
Artemisia (d. 350? BC) was both wife and sister of Mausolus of Caria, and reigned as Queen after his death; the magnificent tomb she built for him gives rise to the term 'mausoleum.' She was also a noted botanist and practical doctor.
2: the Queen of Cos, Lygdamus' daughter (SM 8).
*This Artemisia lived in the first half of the 5th century BC, a vassal of the Persian King *Xerxes; Maturin's account of her battle technique is drawn from *Herodotus. However, Lygdamus is usually supposed to have been her son or nephew, rather than her father.*

Artemisia, HMS

A frigate in the West Indies (SM 8).
*This is probably intended as a joking riposte by Jack *Aubrey to Stephen *Maturin's classical acumen (see *Artemisia, above) for there was no such English frigate. There were, however, two French frigate Artémises, the first launched in 1794 and destroyed at the Battle of the Nile in 1798 (at which Jack was of course present), the second (not listed in VICHOT) driven on to rocks off Brest by HMS *Minerva in 1808.*

Arthur

A waiter at Black's club (LM 7).

Arthur, King

The name of a game played by HMS *Surprise*'s crew in hot weather (FSW 3).
King Arthur is supposed to have united the British people against Saxon invaders in the fifth or sixth centuries. However, there is scarcely any contemporary evidence of even his existence and none at all of his deeds. In medieval romance literature he became a model for the brave, somewhat mystical ruler of a courtly and wholly imaginary England of past times.

Asa Foulkes

An American barque at Recife (DI 5).

Asclepia

The name of Mr Choate's hospital in Boston (FW 4+).
*In Greek myth Asclepius was a hero and god of healing, with a widespread cult centred on the island of Cos—where *Hippocrates supposedly later continued the healing tradition—and on the popular religious shrine of Epidaurus. Many ancient hospitals and healing centres called themselves Asclepiea.*

Ashgrove

*'Ashgrove' is sometimes encountered in the books as a reference to 'the *Aubrey household at Ashgrove Cottage, Hampshire,' the family's first home.*

Ashton, Captain

The one-time commander of HMS *Defender* (FSW 2).

Aspasia

HMS *Surprise*'s goat (FSW 3,5,7,9; RM 3).
Aspasia, equally famous for her beauty, intellect and political skills, was the mistress of the Athenian statesman Pericles in the middle of the 5th century BC.

Aspen, John

A Philadelphian member of Mr Jay's London delegation, and a member of Louisa Wogan's circle in London (DI 6).

Assei and Assou

Two Bengali (or 'lascar') seaman in HMS *Sophie* (M&C 3).

Astley's

A London pleasure-garden (PC 6; HMS 6).
Philip Astley (1742–1814) was a famous horseman, soldier and theatrical manager who founded circus shows in London and Paris. From 1798 onwards 'Astley's Royal Amphitheatre' on the south side of Westminster Bridge was a popular attraction and it is here that the 'Polish Giant' referred to in the text could be seen.

Aston

A medical colleague of Maturin (TGS 4).

Astrea, HMS

A ship at Gibraltar (M&C 12), later said to have recently been wrecked (TMC 1).
*HMS Astraea (sic), 32-gun, was launched in 1781 and wrecked off Antigua in 1808. In classical myth, Astrea was a daughter of *Jupiter and Themis and a goddess of justice; she is regarded as the last of the immortals to have left the earth at the end of the Golden Age, taking her place amongst the stars as 'Virgo.'*

Astrée

1: a French frigate, said by Aubrey to be famous for her speed (M&C 9).
*Astrée, 36-gun, was launched in 1780 and served until 1795; her replacement—see #2 below—was not launched until 1803, some two years after M&C. For the name derivation see HMS *Astrea above.*
2: a 38-gun frigate that joins Commodore Hamelin's Indian Ocean squadron at Réunion (TMC 5–9), said by Jack Aubrey to be so new that he has no reports of her sailing qualities, which he soon discovers to be only average (TMC 8). She plays a crucial role in the French victory at the Battle of Port South East on Mauritius (TMC 7) and, in company with *Iphigenie*, soon takes HMS *Africaine*, abandoning her on the immediate approach of Jack's HMS *Boadicea* (TMC 8).
*Astrée, 38-gun, was launched in 1803 and taken by Admiral *Bertie's squadron when Mauritius fell in December 1810; in early 1811 she was renamed HMS *Pomone and finally broken up in 1816. For the name derivation see HMS *Astrea above.*

Astronomer Royal

Aubrey favourably compares Marshall's powers of navigation to those of the Astronomer Royal (M&C 7).

This title, which is still extant, was created in 1675 for John Flamsteed (1646–1719). At the time of M&C the post had been held since 1765 by the fifth Astronomer Royal, Nevil Maskelyne (1732–1811). In 1763 he had published his British Mariner's Guide, *containing a new method of calculating longitude by lunar observation, and in 1766 he published the first volume of the navigation serial* Nautical Almanac.

Astruc

The author of a medical text (C/T 3; WDS 4).

Jean Astruc (1684–1766), the leading French physician and author of his age, published his Treatise on Venereal Disease *in 1736.*

Atahualpa

The Inca defeated and duped by the Spanish conqueror Pizarro (WDS 9).

Atahualpa (d.1533), the son of *Huayna Capac and brother of *Huascar, was the ruler of the northern half of Peru. Following his defeat of his brother in a civil war, Atahualpa met the invader *Pizarro on terms of friendship; however, he was almost immediately seized and imprisoned. Having offered the Spaniards a colossal quantity of gold for his release, this too was seized on delivery and Atahualpa was put on trial for his life. Sentenced to be burned alive at the stake, he was offered — and accepted — the mercy of prior strangulation in return for conversion to Christianity.

Atalante, HMS

The ship into which Aubrey's colleague Edward Calamy had first been made Post (IM 2).

No HMS Atalante *was a Post ship in the Royal Navy of the period, all of her name — in the English form of Atalanta — being small sloops or brigs. *Aubrey may have been thinking of the French 38-gun frigate* Atalante, *launched in 1768 and taken by HMS *Swiftsure in 1794; renamed HMS Espion, she was wrecked in 1799. In Greek myth Atalanta was the swiftest runner of all the mortals; challenged to a race by Milanion, she lost by stopping to pick up golden apples, a gift from *Venus, that her wily opponent dropped in her path. Milanion's prize from the gods was Atalanta's hand in marriage; his consolation prize for losing would have been death.*

Athena

The goddess, famous for her owl (HD 7).

In Greek legend Athena, a daughter of Zeus, is a goddess famed equally for her wisdom, her domestic craft-skills and her ferocity as a warrior, being often portrayed as the special helper of mortal, male heroes. Athens, taking her owl as its symbol, claimed her as its own protecting deity (though it is not certain which of the two was named first), yet in early legend she is also a guardian of several other cities, such as Sparta and even Troy. Sometimes called Pallas Athene ('Athena, City-Guardian') in Greek, she was identified by the Romans with their own *Minerva. See also **Renault, Mary**

Atkins

1: Mr Stanhope's unpopular secretary on HMS *Surprise*'s voyage to India (HMS 5+). On a shore outing he makes an unwelcome pass at Diana Villiers, who later recalls him as 'Perkins' (HMS 7). Following Stanhope's death, he transfers to an East Indiaman for the voyage to Calcutta (HMS 9) and there Maturin obtains him a post with Canning, who soon comes to believe he is the Doctor's spy (HMS 10).

2: a bosun's mate in HMS *Leopard* (DI 3).

Atlas

A French 74-gun in Toulon Harbour (PC 4).

The ship, paid for by France's ally Spain, was launched in 1800 as Atlante; *in 1803 — a little after PC 4 is set — she was re-named* Atlas *and in 1808 was handed back to Spain. In Greek mythology, Atlas supported the pillars that kept heaven and earth separate.*

Attila

A name often invoked for its ferocious connotations (DI 6; FSW 1; LM 9; NC 9).

Attila (c.406–53), King of the Huns, was famous for his ferocity both in and after battle: he is reputed to have said, 'the grass cannot grow where my horse has passed.' The Huns were a nomadic tribe from north of the River Danube, who invaded Germany, Gaul, Italy and Byzantium under Attila's leadership. In 447 he soundly defeated the armies of the Eastern Roman Empire, but in 451 those of the Western Empire, with their Visigoth allies, inflicted a heavy defeat on him in northern Gaul. Attila now ravaged northern Italy but was eventually persuaded to withdraw back across the Danube by Pope Leo I.

Attlay

A lawyer who wrote a long analysis of Lord Cochrane's fraud trial, used as a source by O'Brian for Aubrey's predicament (RM author's note).

James Beresford Atlay (sic; 1860–1912) published The Trial of Lord *Cochrane before Lord *Ellenborough *in 1897.*

Aubin

The author of a nautical French-English dictionary referred to by Mr Scriven (PC 6).

Pierre François Aubin (1655?–1737) was a prolific author on a wide variety of topics, and is especially remembered as the author of The Devils of Loudon, *of which town he was a native. His* Dictionnaire de la Marine *was published from 1702 onwards.*

Aubrey, Caroline
see **Aubrey, Charlotte**

Aubrey, Charlotte

Jack and Sophie Aubrey's joint-eldest child with her twin sister, Fanny; she is first met as a very young baby (TMC 1), Jack having great difficulty in telling the girls apart (DI 1; LM 4; COM 2). Now somewhat grown up, she visits HMS *Worcester* with the family to see her father off to the Mediterranean

(IM 1); curiously, she is perhaps twice referred to as 'Caroline' in letters to Jack from home (IM 5). Some years afterwards the twins are pupils at their widowed Aunt Frances' school in Ulster (YA 1), later visiting their parents at Woolcombe House (YA 6,8) and travelling with them to Madeira on *Surprise* (YA 10). Often alluded to at other times by the central characters in the series, Charlotte is only occasionally spoken of by name (SM 4, C/T 7 and COM 3).

Aubrey, Fanny, Fan or Frances

Jack and Sophie Aubrey's joint-eldest child with her twin sister, Charlotte; she is first met as a very young baby (TMC 1), Jack having great difficulty in telling the girls apart (DI 1; COM 2). Now somewhat grown up, she visits HMS *Worcester* with the family to see her father off to the Mediterranean (IM 1). Some years afterwards the twins are pupils at their widowed Aunt Frances' school in Ulster (YA 1), later visiting their parents at Woolcombe House (YA 6,8) and travelling with them to Madeira on *Surprise* (YA 10). Often alluded to at various times by the central characters in the series, Fanny is only occasionally spoken of by name (LM 4; C/T 7; COM 3) and only once is she called by her full name of Frances (SM 4).

Aubrey, General

The General is Jack Aubrey's father (M&C 1), portrayed throughout the books as an uneducated, often boorish throwback to a coarser age (e.g. HMS 7; RM 3). A widower of about 64, he tells Jack that he intends to marry a twenty-year-old woman from a humble background, with the intention of fathering more children (M&C 9). His new wife turns out to be his former dairy-maid (PC 1), by whom he soon has a son (PC 3; HMS 7). The General also becomes the Tory MP for the Cornish constituency of St Muryan through the influence of its effective owner, Mr Polwhele (PC 13,14; TMC 10); though this seat is later referred to as 'Great Clanger' (HMS 1; *N.B., 'clanger' is English slang for an embarrassing mistake)* and Gripe (SM 4). In this new role he begins a habit of making intemperate speeches on naval affairs (PC 13,14). Some years later, having been both a Tory and a form of Whig, he stands in an General Election as a fiery Radical, now making speeches so critical of government policy they help to deprive Jack of the promised command of a fine frigate (SM 4,5). He is nevertheless elected to two seats at once — by implication one of them being Milford (LM 8; TGS 1) — and continues to hinder Jack's career by foolish and opportunistic Parliamentary interventions (IM 1,9; TH 1; FSW 9; RM 1; YA 1). Out of a straightforward filial loyalty, Jack later passes on the stock-market tip he has received from 'Ellis Palmer,' letting slip that he has recently been on the cartel ship plying between France and England (RM 4). The General puts these two — in fact, wholly unrelated — pieces of information together, buys stock with dubious cronies, and starts false rumours that peace is about to be declared; Jack too has bought stock and is soon arrested, tried and convicted for a conspiracy to defraud the market (RM 4,7+). The General flees and goes into hiding (RM 7; LM 7) and is later found dead — of natural causes — in a ditch near an ale-house where has been hiding under the name of 'Captain Woolcombe' (after the name of the family home); the estate is left impoverished and much encumbered (LM 8; YA 2). In somewhat curious later passages, Philip Aubrey, the fruit of the General's perfectly legal marriage to the second Mrs Aubrey (LM 8), is referred to as only recently legitimised (YA 2) and refers to himself as the *grand*son of the General via his second marriage to a Miss Stanhope (YA 8).

Aubrey, George

The youngest of Sophie and Jack Aubrey's children, conceived on the night of his departure for Mauritius (TMC 10). The news of his birth reaches Jack via a newspaper announcement spotted by Tom Pullings (TMC 10) although the moment of his birth may be alluded to in a sudden, intensely real image of Sophie that a little earlier had flashed into Jack's mind (TMC 9). Stephen Maturin jokingly refers to the baby as *stupor mundi* ('the wonder of the world'); Jack and Sophie name him George (DI 1,4; FW 1; SM 1,2,4; FSW 2; RM 2,3; LM 4; TGS 4; COM 2,3; IM 10; YA 1+). With the family, he later visits HMS *Worcester* to see his father off to the Mediterranean (IM 1) and, later still, goes on a short cruise to Madeira on *Surprise* (YA 10), returning to England when Jack is summoned back to duty (HD 2). Jack intends a sea career for the boy (e.g. TH 6).

Aubrey, Jack or John

This entry traces Jack Aubrey's professional and domestic career in each of the 19 books of the series. A final section lists all the ships in which he served or saw action before the series opens. In order to keep the length of this entry somewhat manageable, many further details of Jack's career are to be found under the main entry for the ships in or against which he fought.

Master and Commander opens in the Governor's House at Port Mahon, Minorca, late in the evening of 18th April 1800 (*see* ***Baldick, Richard William**). Jack Aubrey, a Royal Navy Lieutenant in his 20s, is sitting next to Dr Stephen Maturin during a Locatelli concert; the pair quarrel and appear to be intent on fighting a duel the following day (M&C 1). However, Jack soon receives the joyous and long awaited news that he is to be promoted Master and Commander into the brig-sloop HMS *Sophie*, a reward for his service in HMS *Leander* both at the Battle of the Nile and in her subsequent action with

Généreux; he reconciles himself to Stephen and invites him to a celebratory dinner (M&C 1,2). Jack's superior, Captain Harte (with whose wife, Molly, he is having a scarcely concealed affair: M&C 1+), has delayed news of the promotion, leaving Jack no time to replace *Sophie*'s departing officers before he assumes command (M&C 1); he therefore invites the impoverished Stephen to sail as the ship's surgeon (M&C 2). Their first task is to escort and protect a small merchant convoy, giving Jack a chance to work on *Sophie*'s indifferent sailing and gunnery techniques (M&C 2–4). So absorbed is he that he fails to notice an attack on the convoy by an Algerine galley until Stephen draws attention to the ship (M&C 4). The galley is beaten off but is not taken or sunk, leading the newly appointed First Lieutenant — the wealthy Irishman James Dillon — to doubt Jack's fighting spirit (M&C 4). Jack is nevertheless rewarded for this action with a series of independent cruises, soon becoming famous as 'Lucky Jack Aubrey' for the number of merchant prizes that he seizes; yet these successes only serve to frustrate Dillon's desire for glorious action directly against enemy warships (M&C 4–10). Jack, by his loud and lewd behaviour ashore, manages to lose even more friends, leaving himself open to Harte's enmity (M&C 6). The effectiveness of *Sophie* as a commerce-raider leads to the Spanish *Cacafuego* being engaged by Spanish merchants hunt her down (M&C 7–10); to Dillon's fury Jack initially manages by a ruse to avoid conflict with the much larger enemy ship (M&C 8). However, they soon meet again and in a short, bloody fight Jack boards and takes the frigate: Dillon is killed at the very height of the action (M&C 10). Although this victory leads to fame and admiration for both Jack and *Sophie*, Captain Harte contrives to deny him proper reward by querying *Cacafuego*'s status as a national warship and by delaying the sending of the victory dispatch to England; Jack's troubles are compounded by a venereal disease, probably contracted from Molly Harte (M&C 11). Now again reduced to escort duty, *Sophie* runs into a powerful French squadron led by Admiral Linois; despite a spirited attempt to run clear, Jack is forced to surrender to *Desaix*, a 74-gun commanded by Captain Christy-Pallière (M&C 11). A captive in *Desaix*, Jack sees the defeat of Sir James Saumarez' squadron in Algeçiras Bay but, exchanged a few days later on parole to Gibraltar, he then sees the subsequent British victory on the distant horizon (M&C 12: *these actions took place in July 1801*). As a matter of form, Jack is now court-martialed on board HMS *Pompée* for the loss of his *Sophie* and, of course, most honourably acquitted (M&C 12).

Post Captain opens in late 1802 with Jack enroute home to England, hoping to be promoted Post Captain; however, he hears that a peace treaty between France and England has just been signed *(the Peace of Amiens, agreed in October 1801, signed March 1802: O'Brian conflates these dates and delays the signing until October 1802)*, dashing his hopes for the time being (PC 1). He and Stephen Maturin take a house in Hampshire and soon meet their neighbours, the beautiful and wealthy Sophie Williams and her equally beautiful but poor cousin, Diana Villiers (PC 1,2). Jack admires them both but takes especially to Sophie; and she to him (PC 2+). However, Mrs Williams, Sophie's mother, is turned against the match both by Jack's uncertain career prospects and his sudden reduction to poverty and debt by the failure of his prize agent; Jack's own confidence is seriously undermined (PC 3+). Desperate for a ship, he has a most unhappy and unsuccessful interview with the formidable First Lord, Earl St Vincent; on the point of arrest for debt, he then flees to France with Stephen (PC 3). On the collapse of the Peace *(in May 1803)*, the pair flee to Spain — with Jack disguised as a dancing bear — and take passage home to England (PC 4,5). Still heavily in debt and thus frustrated in his desire for Sophie, Jack accepts command of the experimental sloop HMS *Polychrest* (PC 6), narrowly escaping arrest by bailiffs before getting safely to sea (PC 7–9). Jack has now grown increasingly attached to Diana Villiers, occasioning growing unease between himself and Stephen, who has also fallen for her (PC 8–10). On Jack's return from the Baltic, the pair quarrel furiously over Diana and arrange, once again, to duel; the affair is postponed by Jack's being given by his old enemy Harte (now an Admiral) the very difficult task of cutting out the French corvette *Fanciulla* from her harbour (PC 10). After a near-mutiny on the unhappy *Polychrest*, Jack attacks and takes the Frenchman but loses his own ship to cannon fire from shore in the process; yet both the glory of the action and Jack's wounds in the fight enable a reconciliation with Stephen (PC 11). Jack now has the joy of being made Post — as of May 23rd *(1804)* — by a new and friendly First Lord, Melville, from whom he accepts temporary command HMS *Lively* (PC 12+). Although still debt-ridden, this improvement in his prospects allows Jack to come to an informal arrangement with Sophie Williams for marriage, with Stephen Maturin largely responsible for negating in Sophie's mind Mrs Williams' continuing disapproval (PC 13,14). In his (newly revealed) role as an influential intelligence agent, Stephen also arranges for Jack to participate in the capture of Admiral Bustamente's enormously rich, Spanish treasure squadron *(October 1804)*; *Lively* takes *Clara* and *Fama*, and Jack looks forward to wealth and happiness (PC 14).

(N.B., 1804 happened to be a thin year for the appointment of new Post Captains, yet O'Brian has over fifty being appointed just after Jack (PC 14). This early 'acceleration of time' has some significance much later in the

series when Jack frets about his prospects of promotion to Rear Admiral: if time ran 'normally,' he would not in fact have been eligible for flag rank until early 1837, when the survivors of the small 'class of 1804' were advanced.)

As **HMS Surprise** opens, the action against Bustamente's squadron should have put both Jack and Stephen Maturin in the way of being wealthy men, but events turn out otherwise. As the battle occurred before war with Spain was formally declared, the pair are denied their prize money. Moreover, Jack's prize agent has absconded with what little money he possessed and a court has reversed payment for some disputed neutral merchant prizes, leaving him very heavily in debt (HMS 1). Although the engagement to Sophie Williams has now been announced (HMS 2), his uncertain financial and career prospects make Jack dither over the marriage (HMS 4+). In the meantime he remains in temporary command of HMS *Lively* (now engaged in Lord Nelson's blockade of Toulon), breaking off from his immediate duties to rescue Stephen Maturin, discovered to be held captive, under torture, on Minorca (HMS 3; *the island had been handed to the French during the recent Peace*). On *Lively*'s arrival back in England, Captain Hamond returns from parliamentary duties to her command and Jack is left ship-less; furthermore, he is then is arrested and briefly imprisoned for debt (HMS 4,6). Fortunately, Stephen's intelligence colleague, Sir Joseph Blaine, secures Jack command of HMS *Surprise* for a diplomatic mission to Bombay and the South China Seas (HMS 4+: *N.B., the Battle of Trafalgar of October 21st 1805 takes place—unmentioned—at about this time*). During the outward voyage, Jack teaches Stephen to swim (HMS 5) and infamously gets the Doctor's captive Brazilian sloth drunk on rum-soaked bread (HMS 6). On active duty, *Surprise* has several encounters with Jack's old foe Admiral Linois, eventually beating off his attack on the China merchant fleet and badly mauling his *Marengo* (HMS 9; *based on events that had taken place in February 1804: see* **Linois, Admiral**). Soon after arriving in Calcutta (to which he has diverted following the death by illness of his passenger, the envoy Mr Stanhope: HMS 8), Jack witnesses Stephen, in an illegal duel over Diana Villiers' affections, kill the wealthy merchant Richard Canning and then whisks his badly injured friend away to the safety of his ship (HMS 10,11); on his recovery, Stephen soon names a captured, hitherto non-descript turtle as the *testudo aubreii* in his saviour's honour (HMS 11; TMC 4). Moderately wealthy from his successful cruise, the homeward-bound Jack now arranges to collect Sophie Williams at Madeira, well away from her mother's influence (HMS 10). In fact the lovers' ships meet just off the island, Jack and Sophie immediately confirming their pledge to marry as soon as they are home (HMS 11).

The Mauritius Command opens some years later *(probably in mid-1809)* with Jack in much changed circumstances. Ship-less, on half-pay, and pining for a command, he is now married to Sophie Williams, the couple living at Ashgrove Cottage, Hampshire, with their new-born, twin daughters as well as their now-impoverished mother-in-law (TMC 1). Jack does have some scientific consolations, having addressed the Royal Society on astronomy and having built his own observatory; the family are also still tolerably affluent from his Indian Ocean cruise in HMS *Surprise* (TMC 1). Through Stephen Maturin's influence at the Admiralty, Jack soon obtains command, as a junior Commodore, of HMS *Boadicea* and the expedition to take French Mauritius (TMC 1, 3+; *N.B., the ensuing campaign is closely based on real events that took place in the second half of 1810:* TMC author's note*). For the first ever time, Jack has now to deal with subordinate commanders. He had long ago served with Lord Clonfert in HMS *Agamemnon* and found reason at that time to doubt the latter's courage (TMC 2), a fact that clouds their uneasy relationship throughout the campaign (TMC 3–10). He also reacts with fury to the news that the harsh Captain Corbett has had his own regular coxswain, Barrett Bonden—temporarily under Corbett's command—flogged for a trifling offence (TMC 3). Whilst at the Cape, Jack raises his broad pennant in HMS *Raisonable* (TMC 3) and then goes on to enjoy initial success by raiding, with his army colleague Colonel Keating, the French island of Réunion, capturing the frigate *Caroline,* and re-taking the valuable East Indiamen *Europe* and *Streatham* (TMC 4). At this point the British do not have the forces available to hold the island, but they later return to make it a permanent acquisition (TMC 6). Yet the first assault on Mauritius itself is very much less successful, for, on detached duty, Captains Pym of HMS *Sirius* and Clonfert of HMS *Néréide*—into which he has been promoted by Jack, an honour accepted with very mixed feelings (TMC 4)—make a poor fist of the Battle of Port South East, even when somewhat fortuitously reinforced by HMSS *Magicienne* and *Iphigenia*. In a heavy reverse, all four British ships are taken or sunk (TMC 7). Nevertheless, Jack and *Boadicea* (to which he has returned) re-organise and augment his forces, gradually isolating Mauritius by inflicting defeats on individual French ships and exploiting, with Stephen Maturin's aid, political and religious dissatisfaction with French rule (TMC 8, 9). At long last ready to assault the island, Jack is thereupon superseded by the arrival of Admiral Bertie from the Cape with a powerful squadron and a large army: Mauritius immediately capitulates (TMC 10). Feeling that Jack may have been rather hard done by in this last-minute intervention, the usually grasping Bertie gives him the great honour of taking the news of the victory home to England (TMC 10). During the course of the campaign Jack has learned, from a newspaper obtained by Tom Pullings, that Sophie has given birth to a son, whom he calculates to have been conceived on the night of his departure (TMC 10). He may earlier have had a curious premonition of the birth when his wife springs suddenly and vividly to mind as he prepares for action against *Vénus* and *Victor* (TMC 9).

Desolation Island opens with Jack at home in England *(sometime in 1811)*, prosperous from his earlier re-taking of valuable East Indiamen at Réunion and Mauritius (DI 1). He has a new baby son, George (DI 1), owns a fine Beechey portrait of himself as a senior Post Captain wearing the sash of Order of the Bath (DI 1; *N.B., nowhere else in the series is this award of a senior knighthood mentioned and indeed Jack elsewhere states that he does not care for honours: TMC 7; SM 5*), and has been given the sinecure of command of the local Sea Fencibles (DI 1; *curiously, he also states that he is due to be promoted to Flag rank in the next five years or so: see note at end of **The Post Captain** section above*). However, certain aspects of life ashore lie somewhat beyond his expertise: he is involved in mining speculations with the con-man Kimber (DI 1) and is cheated at cards by the influential Andrew Wray, this latter leading to a public row and the possibility of a duel (DI 1,2; *see also* TH 1). With relief, Jack soon learns that he is to have HMS *Leopard* for a voyage to Australia, there to assist the troubled Governor Bligh (DI 1+); yet he is furious to learn that the ship is also to transport common criminals to the penal colony (DI 2). On the outbound voyage fever breaks out amongst these passengers and rapidly spreads to the crew, depleting *Leopard*'s fighting strength (DI 4,5); many seamen die and many, including First Lieutenant Tom Pullings, have to be put ashore in Brazil to recover (DI 5). Carrying on with the mission, *Leopard* then falls in with the much larger, Dutch 74-gun *Waakzaamheid*, an opponent Jack had very much hoped to avoid (DI 6,7). After a long, running chase, *Leopard* dismasts her enemy with a single shot, Jack and his crew watching with horror as she immediately founders in a monstrous sea (DI 7,8). During the short exchange of fire, Jack has received bad leg and head wounds that leave him temporarily disabled and at the mercy of First Lieutenant Grant, an elderly, opinionated, often incompetent man, jealous of Jack's fighting reputation (DI 7,8). Driven far south, *Leopard* approaches an iceberg to take on fresh water but strikes on it and is badly holed (DI 8). After prodigious efforts to save and repair the ship, Grant and Jack differ as to whether she can remain afloat; Grant and many of the crew abandon her in the boats, albeit with Jack's somewhat reluctant permission (DI 8). Jack just

manages to get *Leopard* and her remaining men — together with the convict and spy Louisa Wogan, under the care and attention of Stephen Maturin — to the deserted and inhospitable Desolation Island (DI 9). The island is visited by the American whaler *La Fayette*, a ship with a forge badly needed by the *Leopard*s for repairs; however, as tensions are running high between the two countries, the necessary assistance is secured only with some difficulty and duplicity (DI 10). The book closes *(in early 1812)* with Jack preparing to remain on the island for some time in order to render his battered ship seaworthy (DI 10).

The Fortune of War opens *(a little later in 1812)* with Jack and HMS *Leopard* safely at Pulo Batang on Java. Here he tells Admiral Drury that he sailed his ship from Desolation Island to New South Wales — discovering there that Governor Bligh's difficulties had already been resolved — and thence to Pulo Batang for such refits and repairs as are possible (FW 1). Jack is greeted with the welcome news that he has been appointed to the command of a crack frigate — HMS *Acasta* — in England, news all the more welcome as he had fully expected to be promoted into a ship-of-the-line engaged on tedious blockade duty (FW 1). After a game of his beloved cricket against HMS *Cumberland*, Jack takes passage to England in HMS *La Flèche*, accompanied both by Stephen Maturin and his immediate followers such as Bonden, Killick and Babbington; at Cape Town they hear of the state of war with the USA (FW 2; *war was declared by the USA in June 1812*). As the journey continues *La Flèche* is destroyed by an accidental fire: Jack and all his men escape in small cutter, drifting off the coast of South America, desperately short of food and water, until being rescued by the passing HMS *Java* (FW 3). Knowing of the several defeats the U.S. Navy has inflicted on the Royal Navy, *Java* encounters USS *Constitution* and is herself rapidly taken, burned and sunk by the American; Jack fights the forecastle gun batteries in the battle and is severely wounded in the head and arm (FW 3). Too ill to be off-loaded in Brazil with the rest of the prisoners, Jack — accompanied by Stephen — is taken to Boston, where he is sent to Choate's hospital to recover (FW 4). Whilst there, he is interrogated by U.S. Navy Department officials, who at first suspect him of having carried out an earlier intelligence coup against the spy Louisa Wogan (FW 4). Once it is discovered that it is Stephen who is in fact the intelligence agent, the almost-recovered Jack escapes with his friend — together with Diana Villiers, now living unhappily in the USA — in a small boat, meeting his cousin Philip Broke's HMS *Shannon* off Boston Harbour (FW 8). Jack then plays an active role in Broke's swift victory over USS *Chesapeake* (FW 9; *an action that took place in June 1813*).

*(N.B., all books from this point in the series until **The Yellow Admiral** remain notionally set in the second half of 1813, even though each in fact occupies about one calendar year.)*

At the opening of **The Surgeon's Mate** Jack is in Halifax, Nova Scotia, waiting for passage home to England and enjoying his part in HMS *Shannon's* recent triumph (SM 1). Wrongly conceiving that his wife, Sophie, has neglected to write to him in Canada, Jack becomes indignant at her imagined heartlessness and, at Admiral Colpoys' Ball, engages and takes the far-from-unwilling Amanda Smith (SM 2). Jack here suggests that Sophie has little interest in physical love-making (SM 1,4) and reveals that he has had a number of passing affairs in recent years (SM 6). Miss Smith afterwards bombards her new, and now-departed, lover with dramatic letters — including a claim of pregnancy — until he learns with great relief that she has married a Captain Lushington of the Royal Marines (SM 5,6,11). Shortly after the affair, Jack, Stephen Maturin and Diana Villiers travel home to England — narrowly avoiding capture by privateers en route (SM 3) — and here Jack finds both his domestic affairs horribly complicated by the doings of the fraudster Kimber and his cronies (SM 4+), and his career held back by the political idiocy of his father, the General, and the slow revenge of Andrew Wray (SM 4,5). Denied both the promised HMS *Acasta* and a knighthood (in any case unwanted), he is offered the shore-post of command of the receiving ship HMS *Orion*, an easy sinecure that he nevertheless declines (SM 4,5). After learning of a further complication — that Lieutenant Grant, of HMS *Leopard* days, is now alleging that *Waakzaamheid* was in fact an unarmed transport ship (SM 6) — he is offered temporary command of the sloop HMS *Ariel* for a political mission that Stephen is to undertake at the fortified Baltic island of Grimsholm (SM 6+). Once this is successfully accomplished, Jack takes the Doctor and his new Catalan colleagues southwards towards Spain (SM 8,9). However, *Ariel* runs onto rocks on the French coast and slowly sinks, with Jack, Stephen and her entire crew being taken prisoner (SM 9). The consequences of the intelligence activities and confusions in America now catch up with Jack, and he and Stephen (together with their new associate, Jagiello) are taken to Paris for interrogation (SM 10+). Jack tries various clever methods of effecting an escape from the Temple prison with ropes and pulleys but in fact all three obtain release as a result of Stephen's subtle political machinations (SM 11). The trio — together with Diana Villiers, now living in Paris — travel home to England in the cartel HMS *Oedipus*, aboard which Jack has the honour of giving Diana away in marriage to Stephen, a ceremony performed by their long-time friend, Commander William Babbington (SM 11).

The Ionian Mission opens with Jack fitting out, for the North American station, the brand-new frigate HMS *Blackwater*, a reward for his recent successes (IM 1). Yet his financial mire with the con-man Kimber has deepened and he has even been involved in a physically violent dispute with his various creditors' lawyers; urgently needing to get away to sea, Jack accepts temporary command of the decrepit 74-gun HMS *Worcester*, due for blockade duty in the Mediterranean (IM 1+). Moreover, both the continuing malign influence of Andrew Wray and General Aubrey's political indiscretions soon result in *Blackwater* being awarded to a different commander (IM 1+). After a spell in Sir John Thornton's fleet off Toulon, Jack is ordered by Harte, the Admiral's second-in-command and Jack's old enemy, on a mission to the supposedly neutral ports of Barka and Medina, in company with William Babbington's HMS *Dryad* (IM 6,7). Following Harte's curiously written orders to the letter, Jack sends *Dryad* unaccompanied into Medina, only then to learn that French ships were waiting and that his young colleague very narrowly escaped capture (IM 6). Jack immediately attempts to provoke the enemy into an open fight but finds that they too appear to be under strict orders under no circumstances to violate Medina's neutrality; *Worcester* and *Dryad* return somewhat crestfallen to Thornton's fleet, with some of their people feeling that Jack should have tried bolder strokes to bring about an action (IM 6,7). To his anger and dismay, Jack now learns that the intention was in fact to have *allowed* Babbington to be captured at Medina, then using this breach of neutrality as an excuse to attack the French. However, when Admiral Thornton comes to see that Harte had incompetently drafted the orders, he absolves Jack of blame (IM 7). After another spell of blockade duty — including a secret landing of Stephen Maturin on the French coast and some involvement in an abortive attempt to bring the French fleet to battle — the storm-battered *Worcester* is sent to Malta to refit and Jack is once again given command of his beloved HMS *Surprise* for a mission to the Ionian sea (IM 9). The French must be turned out of the Greek mainland port of Marga, a task for which Jack needs the aid of the fortifications of Kutali, a neighbouring town disputed by three rival Beys: Ismail of Mesenteron, Mustapha of Karia, and Sciahan (the latter temporarily in possession of Kutali itself). Jack's orders are therefore to support for the rule of Kutali whichever of these rulers seems to him to be most willing to assist in an attack on Marga itself (IM 9). After a series of interviews Jack chooses Sciahan as the British ally but, before his fort can be fully rearmed with cannon, they learn that the rejected

Mustapha is at sea with his frigates *Torgud* and *Kitabi*, heading for the town. Immediately setting sail in *Surprise*, Jack inflicts a brisk defeat on the rebellious Turks (IM 10,11).

Treason's Harbour opens with Jack, having since turned the French out of Marga, now at the British base on the Mediterranean island of Malta, with both HMSS *Worcester* and *Surprise* undergoing major repairs (TH 1). Here he proudly displays the diamond *chelengk* decoration given him by the Sultan of Turkey for defeating the rebel Mustapha Bey (TH 1; *a valuable possession later both lost and found*: TH 6). Whilst in Malta Jack strikes up a friendship with Laura Fielding, the pretty Sicilian wife of a fellow-officer held prisoner-of-war in France (TH 1+). After the rescue of her guard-dog, Ponto, from a fall into a well (TH 1), the mastiff's public devotion results in all Malta assuming Jack and Laura are lovers (TH 2+). Jack indeed soon tries to put truth into the rumour, but the virtuous Laura politely rebuffs his advances, and the two remain on good terms (TH 3). Whilst at leisure, Jack also visits his former commander Admiral Hartley, now living in sadly reduced circumstances on the nearby island of Gozo (TH 2). On the service front, Admiral Thornton having died, the new Commander-in-Chief, Sir Francis Ives, soon gives Jack charge of an expedition to the troublesome island of Mubara in the Red Sea. He is to sail to Egypt in the *Dromedary* transport, cross overland to Suez with many of his *Surprise* crew, and there take command of an 18-gun East India company sloop, *Niobe*. He is then to capture a galley, supposedly carrying an enormous French bribe, before replacing the present ruler of Mubara with a man more amenable to British interests (TH 4–7). From the very outset this plan has been betrayed to the Mubara forces and their French allies (TH 6): unknown to Jack, the traitor is his old foe Andrew Wray (TH 2+). In due course, suspecting that the galley is trying to lure him into the range of French guns on Mubara island, Jack sinks her and then, using Stephen Maturin's diving bell, recovers one of her 'treasure' chests, finding that it contains just lead ingots and an abusive note (TH 6). Seeing no prospect whatever of success in an attack on the heavily fortified island, Jack returns to Malta to report his failure to the Admiral (TH 6,7). Although he here learns that his beloved *Surprise* is to be laid up, or even sold, as too small for modern duties, they are in the meantime given some last duties together (TH 8+). They first accompany a convoy from Malta to Trieste, a voyage during which Jack learns both that HMS *Blackwater* has been permanently given to a Captain Irby and that Laura Fielding's jealous husband, Charles, has escaped from France, via Italy, to the nearby HMS *Nymphe* (TH 8,9). Jack and his ship are then given a further mission to Zambra at the western end of

the Mediterranean, there to deal with the independent-minded Dey of Mascara (TH 10). Once again the mission has been betrayed by Wray and is consequently something of a failure: *Surprise*'s consort, HMS *Pollux*, is destroyed by a powerful French squadron — Admiral Harte, a passenger, is killed — and, under Stephen's official, political advice, Jack retreats to Gibraltar to consult and obtain reinforcements (TH 10). The only saving grace of the affair has been that the French 74-gun ship *Mars* was badly damaged in its action with *Pollux* and that *Surprise* has managed to leave a heavy French frigate onto a reef in Zambra Bay (TH 10; FSW 1).

The Far Side of the World opens with Jack at Gibraltar to explain the Zambra incident to Admiral Ives who, fortunately, is not at all critical of Jack's conduct in the bizarre circumstances (FSW 1). In view of the mixture of intelligence triumphs and fiascos in the Mediterranean, Sir Joseph Blaine has arranged for Stephen Maturin to go on a relatively minor mission to South America: in the temporarily reprieved HMS *Surprise*, Jack is to both support his friend and to hunt down the marauding USS *Norfolk* (FSW 1+). The intelligence component of the voyage is soon accomplished but *Surprise* is damaged in a storm and has then to undergo substantial repairs in Brazil (FSW 4,5). As these are almost complete, *Norfolk* is spotted heading south and Jack sets off in immediate pursuit. Unfortunately, a drunken pilot promptly grounds *Surprise* on a sandbank and it takes over two weeks to haul her off (FSW 5) before Jack can eventually pursue the American round Cape Horn and into the Pacific (FSW 5+). During the ensuing long chase, Stephen falls into the sea whilst leaning far out of the stern windows to catch sea organisms by night: Jack immediately follows and saves his friend from drowning but *Surprise* stands on, unaware that the two are overboard (FSW 7). After some considerable time and close to death, Jack and Stephen are picked up by a South Seas *pahi*, crewed entirely by women. On board, they narrowly escape emasculation and death (FSW 7) before being abandoned on a desert island, from which they are then rescued by *Surprise*'s searching launch (FSW 7,8). During another storm, the unlucky Stephen falls and receives a severe concussion, leading Jack to sail *Surprise* to the remote Old Sodbury's Island in order to aid his friend's recovery; here they discover the crew of *Norfolk*, their ship wrecked on a reef (FSW 9). Jack goes ashore with just a few men, whereupon *Surprise*, under Lieutenant Mowett, is driven far away from the island by the tail of the storm. A very uneasy relationship is established with the numerically far superior Americans, who are also found to have a number of Royal Navy mutineers from HMS *Hermione* hidden amongst them (FSW 9,10). Just as open warfare breaks out, *Surprise* re-appears off the island in hot pursuit of an American whaler, which she then easily takes before dropping anchor in the bay (FSW 10).

The Reverse of the Medal opens with HMS *Surprise* now at Barbados on her way home to England with Jack back in command (RM 1). Rumours abound that, following his speculative land schemes at home, the Captain is in deep financial trouble but, during a dinner, he learns that hints of peace with France will certainly cause the currently depressed London stock market to shoot up, giving great returns to anyone 'in the know' (RM 1; *also see Sir Joseph *Blaine's remarks on this phenomenon in* SM 4). Whilst still in port, Jack receives a startling visit from Sam Panda, his hitherto-unknown, black son from a youthful liaison with Sally M'puta, causing him extreme apprehension as to the likely reaction of his wife, Sophie (RM 1–3). Before leaving for home Jack sits on the court-martial of the captured HMS *Hermione* mutineers, enduring the distasteful task of sentencing them all to death (RM 1,2). When finally he gets away, he and *Surprise* chase the heavy American privateer *Spartan* across the Atlantic all the way to the French coast (RM 2,3) before eventually arriving in England (RM 4). On the coach journey from Dover up to London, Jack meets 'Ellis Palmer,' supposedly a confidential agent returning from France, who persuades him that peace is indeed soon to be declared and that a quick investment in stocks and shares will make him rich. Once in London, Jack buys shares and passes the tip onto his father, the General, and his somewhat disreputable associates (RM 4). He also learns both that *Surprise* is finally to be sold and that, for the present, he is not to be offered another command (RM 5); these disappointments are offset by the steady rise of the market as rumours of peace spread (RM 6). Home at Ashgrove, Jack announces his intention to buy *Surprise* as a private vessel and also discovers that Sophie has reacted much less intolerantly to the existence of Sam Panda than he had feared (RM 6). But calamity soon strikes: Jack is suddenly arrested for conspiracy to defraud the stock exchange (RM 6) and confined in the Marchalsea prison (RM 7–9). In a vicious, political trial — the Government wishing to destroy General Aubrey and his Radical allies by first destroying his son — Jack is convicted (RM 8) and sentenced to both a huge fine and a spell in the public pillory (RM 9). At the ordeal itself, a large crowd of officers and seamen prevent any harm coming to Jack, giving him the rousing support of a full naval cheer (RM 9); the humiliating sentence, passed on such a distinguished fighting officer, also turns out to be deeply unpopular in the country at large (RM 10). Yet a far worse punishment awaits Jack, his dismissal, as a convicted criminal, from his beloved Royal Navy (RM 9). In the meantime. Stephen Ma-

turin, seeing early that the case against his friend is driven by unstoppable political revenge, has conceived with Sir Joseph Blaine a scheme to buy *Surprise* himself and to sail, with Jack as her private Captain, to Chile, there to offer support to the independence movement in Peru (RM 8+); Jack accepts the command (RM 9+). Whilst Jack begins to fit the ship out at the West Country smuggling port of Shelmerston (RM 10), Stephen finally learns that Andrew Wray is a French spy and has also been at the bottom of the plot to ruin Jack, his old enemy (RM 10).

The Letter of Marque opens with Jack still in a state of emotional disarray at having been struck off the Royal Navy list, with his new job of private Captain of the letter-of-marque *Surprise* offering scant consolation (LM 1). Nevertheless he busies himself fitting out the ship for her next voyages to the Baltic (for supplies) and South America (for intelligence purposes), crewing her with a mixture of old shipmates and local, Shelmerston smugglers (LM 1). She soon sets out on sea-trials in the English channel with Jack working up the new crew into a fighting unit (LM 2,3) but also enduring an unpleasant encounter with the insolent Lieutenant Dixon, the son of his old foe Admiral Harte (LM 2). Whilst at sea he hears from Stephen Maturin both of Andrew Wray's treachery and of the full extent of the plot by which Wray had brought him down; to his joy, he also learns that evidence of his innocence has at last been unearthed (LM 2). Filled with new verve, Jack conducts offensive operations in the Azores against the privateer *Spartan*, soon taking her and re-capturing several of her very valuable prizes (LM 3), victories that make him both popular and wealthy (LM 4). Sir Joseph Blaine now suggests to Stephen that Jack can greatly enhance his claims to be re-instated in the Navy by cutting out the French frigate *Diane*, currently being fitted out in her home port for a subversive expedition to South America, very similar to the one planned for *Surprise* (LM 4). Back in his ship from a spell at home, Jack encounters the very great difficulties of dealing with the curious religious sects amongst his Shelmerstonian seamen and also begins to plan his attack on *Diane*, currently blockaded in her harbour by a very small Royal Navy squadron headed by his own young *protégé*, Commander William Babbington (LM 5). As anticipated, William is happy to play only a minor role in the attack, allowing all credit to go to his former Captain: in a short but fierce action Jack and his men capture *Diane* and take her back to England, Jack being rather severely injured in the fight (LM 6). Although the victory gives his friends a very strong argument for his restitution, Jack still has powerful enemies in the appropriate Ministries and the matter is far from a foregone conclusion. Moreover, he then refuses to accept the conditions on which an offer of pardon is made — he has no notion of being forgiven for what he asserts he did not do — and his hopes appear thereby to be dashed (LM 7,8). Yet matters quickly change on the sudden death of his father, for Jack is offered by his wealthy cousin, Edward Norton, the General's old Parliamentary seat of Milport. His ensuing ownership of a vote prompts Viscount Melville to promise full (though not quite immediate) restoration to the Navy in exchange for his support of the Government in the House (LM 8). In the meantime, Jack still intends to travel to South America after first taking *Surprise* to the Baltic, where he intends to collect Stephen, currently in Sweden searching for the missing Diana Villiers (LM 8). Jack meets the reconciled pair in Stockholm and, joyously, they all head back to England (LM 9).

The Thirteen Gun Salute opens with Jack in England finishing off the preparation of *Surprise* for his and Stephen Maturin's naval/political mission to South America (TGS 1+). Although he had been promised reinstatement in the Navy for the cutting out of *Diane*— a promised reinforced on his election as MP for Milford — the Tory government's uncertain future gives him and his friends continuing unease and Jack finally sets sail before matters are fully settled (TGS 1). However, when Britain's Spanish allies hear rumours of *Surprise*'s plans, it becomes expedient to postpone the political elements of the voyage (TGS 3+). This in fact works to Jack's advantage for he is instead offered temporary command of the newly bought-in HMS *Diane* for a mission to Pulo Prabang (in the South China Sea), after which he will make a rendezvous at sea with *Surprise*, given in the meantime to Tom Pullings (TGS 3+). To Jack's intense joy, Lord Melville now restores him to the Navy (as of May 15th 1813) with all his former seniority (TGS 3,4). As events turn out, Jack and his new ship play a relatively minor role in the Pulo Prabang affair (TGS 5–8) and, once the envoy, Mr Fox, has concluded a successful treaty, Jack immediately sets sail with him back to Java, intending *en route* to keep his appointment with *Surprise* (TGS 9). However, *Diane* soon runs onto an uncharted reef off a small, uninhabited island (TGS 9) and is totally destroyed in an ensuing typhoon. Jack gets most of his crew safely ashore and announces plans to escape in a schooner, to be built from the wreckage of his former ship (TGS 10).

The Nutmeg of Consolation commences with Jack and the crew of HMS *Diane* still on their shipwreck island, slowly building a schooner for the voyage back to Java when a large party of Dyak pirates appear, attacking the seamen in a ferocious battle (NC 1,2). Although the Dyaks are beaten off, they first burn the makeshift schooner: fortunately a Chinese merchant junk then appears and takes

the stranded *Diane*s back to Batavia (NC 2). Here Jack learns that the French frigate *Cornélie* is about to put to sea and, given the 20-gun HMS *Nutmeg of Consolation* by Governor Raffles, he sets out to destroy or capture her before making the long-delayed rendezvous with *Surprise* (NC 3,4); the ships soon meet and commence a series of actions and chases (NC 5,6). Just as Jack is about to bring the Frenchman to a decisive action, Tom Pullings' *Surprise* appears: although *Cornélie* makes her escape, she soon founders in the heavy seas (NC 6). Jack now transfers back into his old frigate, sending *Nutmeg* back into Java and then heading on to Australia for stores before finally setting out for South America (NC 6,7). However, the impromptu duel that Stephen Maturin fights with an important army officer on arrival in New South Wales causes Jack severe problems in his plans to refit and resupply *Surprise*, as do the many attempts by his seamen to smuggle escaped convicts aboard (NC 8–10). To make matters worse, after Stephen has already conceived a plan to smuggle his imprisoned servant Padeen Colman from the colony in the ship, Jack makes a specific promise to Governor Macquarie that he will allow no absconders aboard (NC 10). The great tension that this situation causes between the two friends is resolved by Stephen's near death ashore from a platypus sting. Padeen helps bring him aboard the departing *Surprise*, with Jack having little option but to accept the *fait accompli* (NC 10).

Clarissa Oakes (*published in the USA as* **The Truelove**) opens with Jack heading east from New South Wales in His Majesty's Hired Vessel *Surprise* to resume the South American mission given to them some time previously. *Surprise* herself has been bought from Stephen Maturin by Jack, in plentiful funds owing to a large inheritance from his late cousin, Edward Norton (C/T 1,3). Jack soon discovers a runaway convict, Clarissa Harvill, hiding in the ship (C/T 1): she agrees to marry her rescuer, Midshipman Billy Oakes, and is given away by Jack, being presented by him with a scarlet dress — silk really intended for his own wife, Sophie (C/T 2; COM 6). *Surprise* soon receives new orders to divert to the Pacific island of Moahu where a British whaler, *Truelove*, has been detained in a dispute between two warring chiefs (C/T 2+). Here Jack assists Queen Puolani to defeat her French-assisted rival Kalahua, sleeps with the Queen after the celebration feast, and easily recaptures the whaler (C/T 9). The French/American privateer *Franklin* had been assisting Kalahua and, after his defeat, is pursued by *Surprise* (C/T 9).

The Wine Dark Sea opens with Jack still sailing *Surprise* towards the coast of South America in pursuit of the privateer *Franklin*, an easy prize that he soon takes though not before encountering a great and strange volcanic eruption from the sea-bed (WDS 1,2). On arrival off Peru, Jack intends to remain at sea in *Franklin* with a prize-crew, whilst sending Stephen Maturin into Lima in *Surprise*, under Tom Pullings' command (WDS 3). However, *Franklin*'s captured owner, the social revolutionary Jean Dutourd, begins to exert an influence on some of the more religious of his English captors (WDS 3–7) and eventually escapes with their connivance (WDS 7). Jack immediately sets sail for Lima in the ship's launch in order to warn Stephen that Dutourd may be about to disrupt his plans, but he and the small crew are much delayed and battered by a storm, arriving far too late to do any good (WDS 7,9). Ashore, Jack again meets his black, illegitimate son, Sam Panda (now a Catholic priest) who tells him that Stephen has indeed been denounced by Dutourd and forced to flee over the Andes to Chile (WDS 9). Taking command of *Surprise*, Jack heads along the coast and picks Stephen up off Valparaiso, intending now to abandon the mission and return to England. However, they soon encounter a heavy U.S. frigate and are forced to flee far south into the ice-fields, losing the ship's rudder during the chase (WDS 10). Fortunately they meet Heneage Dundas' HMS *Berenice*, *en route* to England from New South Wales, and, having made emergency repairs, sail homeward in her company (WDS 10).

The Commodore opens with *Surprise* nearly home in England, Jack having won from Heneage Dundas *enroute* his tender, *Ringle*, in a game of backgammon (COM 1). To his joy, Jack soon learns that he is to be appointed a first-class Commodore for a mission against the slave trade in West Africa (COM 1), hoisting his broad pennant in the 74-gun HMS *Bellona* with his *protégé* Tom Pullings made Post under him (COM 2+). At home for a spell, Sophie and Jack are gradually moving from Ashgrove Cottage to the inherited family seat of Woolcombe House in Dorset (COM 3; *although earlier guessed at by Maturin as being in Somerset:* TGS 9). Jack becomes very jealous of Sophie's old suitor Mr Hinksey, and she in turn suspects her husband of a ship-board affair with Clarissa Oakes, both ladies having been presented by him with the same scarlet Batavian silk. Although these concerns are somewhat lessened by the news of Hinksey's betrothal to a Miss Lucy Smith, they have already led to many domestic arguments on a wide variety of topics (COM 6). During the anti slave-trade mission Jack receives further orders to intercept, in due course, a French invasion of Ireland (COM 7). After capturing and destroying many illegal slavers in and around Sierra Leone (COM 8,9), Jack and all his larger ships leave the African coast, soon locating and defeating the invasion squadron (COM 10).

The Yellow Admiral does not, however, see all these successes work out quite as Jack would have liked, for the legality of his many seizures of slave-ships is being disputed in court and consequently the family is once again in reduced financial circumstances (YA 1+). Furthermore he is taking frequent absences from HMS *Bellona*— now on the Brest blockade — to attend Parliament and make speeches critical of the Government (YA 1). All these events combine to make him fret that, although still some years from a flag promotion by seniority (YA 1,9; *also see note at the end of* **The Post Captain** *section above*), he may in due course be 'yellowed' onto the superannuated flag-list rather than given an active command (YA 1+), and all this despite his status as MP, Justice of the Peace (NC 10; YA 2), Lord of the Manor (YA 2) and Fellow of the Royal Society (e.g. RM 5; NC 10; C/T 2). Change for the worse is afoot at home too for, during a long walk on a common near Woolcombe House, Jack explains to Stephen Maturin that he sees land enclosure as the ruin of the traditional rural economy and declares his opposition to the schemes of his naval neighbour, Captain Griffiths (YA 2+; *N.B., the contrary view on enclosures is later set out by Lord* Stranraer: YA 4). Successful in his opposition to the proposed changes (YA 2,3), he nevertheless earns the enmity of Griffith's influential uncle, Admiral Lord Stranraer, unfortunately his current, immediate superior in the Channel fleet (YA 3+). Purely domestic relationships also go awry, with Jack now being furiously accused of past adultery with Amanda Smith by his wife Sophie, who threatens to divorce him (YA 6): but the worldly intervention of both Diana Villiers and Clarissa Oakes soon brings about a reconciliation (YA 8). At sea, Jack runs further foul of Stranraer when two French frigates slip the blockade, getting past *Bellona* in the fog (YA 6), but later somewhat redeems himself when he helps prevent a larger squadron from making its escape (YA 9). The war is now drawing to its close and, on Buonaparte's abdication, *Bellona* is sent home to be paid off, leaving Jack and his naval colleagues with very uncertain prospects (YA 10). Fortunately, Stephen Maturin too has been worried about Jack's career outlook and has suggested that he consider leaving the Royal Navy and taking service in the new Chilean navy as that country seeks its independence from Spain (YA 4+). Through his political contacts Stephen obtains for Jack an offer of a role in advising and training this force, nominally on attachment to the Admiralty Hydrographic Survey and with a promise of full reinstatement to the Royal Navy in due course (YA 8,10). Jack now enjoys a rare period of domestic bliss in England whilst *Surprise* (*rather mysteriously once more belonging to Stephen:* YA 10) is refitted for the coming voyage. Eventually he sets sail, carrying his family as far as Madeira for a short holiday (YA 10). Here, however, dramatic news awaits: Buonaparte has escaped from Elba and Jack is immediately recalled to the Royal Navy by his old patron, Admiral Lord Keith, who has appointed him into HMS *Pomone* as a Commodore (YA 10).

The Hundred Days opens in early spring of 1815 with Commodore Jack Aubrey, his pennant raised in HMS *Pomone*, arriving at Gibraltar after a delayed departure and passage from Madeira (HD 1). At the Rock he learns from Lord Keith that new, Buonapartist warships are nearing completion in the Adriatic and that Moslem plots are afoot both to finance these ships and to prevent the union of the Russian and Austrian armies against the newly-restored Emperor (HD 1). Jack and his small squadron are ordered to protect Mediterranean trade against increasingly active corsairs and to investigate conditions in the Adriatic, a mission for which the Commodore transfers his pennant to HMS *Surprise*, his old ship now being restored to the Royal Navy (HD 1,2). After rescuing some East Indiamen from the corsairs (HD 2) and a call at Port Mahon (HD 3), Jack encounters his old friend Christy-Pallière — now a Bourbon Captain — and learns further details of the complex situation in the Adriatic (HD 4). On arrival in those waters, Jack engages and sinks the Imperial frigate *Ardent* and then supports Stephen Maturin's political successes in both subverting the loyalty of other potential Buonapartist converts and in arranging for the destruction of a number of 'rebel' ship-yards and vessels (HD 5). He then conveys Stephen and his colleague Dr Jacob to Algiers, where they are to try to prevent passage of Moslem gold from Morocco back to the Adriatic (HD 6–8). As this mission is only partly successful, Jack now intends to intercept the delayed treasure-galley at sea, but must first obtain fresh orders from the newly arrived, and somewhat unfriendly, Commander-in-Chief, Lord Barmouth (HD 9). Although the Admiral orders Jack, now largely bereft of his former squadron, to strike his Commodore's pennant and return *Surprise* to the status of a private vessel, he does agree to the plan to take the galley (HD 9) and Jack soon intercepts her as she passes through the Straits of Gibraltar (HD 10). After a long chase, he then forces the enemy ship to take shelter in a small bay at the deserted Cranc/Fortnight Island and here, after hauling cannon up to the top of the cliffs, forces her to surrender (HD 10). On his triumphant return to Gibraltar, Jack learns that Buonaparte has just been defeated at Waterloo and is immediately ordered by Lord Barmouth to resume his, and Stephen's, mission to South American waters (HD 10).

Jack Aubrey's Royal Naval Service Prior to April 1800.

Curiously, Jack Aubrey says he *first* went to sea as

a boy at the time of the 'Spanish Armament' (FW 2): this must be a slip on his part, for the first 'Spanish Armament' *(i.e., the re-arming of the Royal Navy against what was seen as Spanish aggression)* was in 1770, around the time of his birth (*see e.g.,* HD 1, *where he is said to be 7 years junior to Lady *Keith), and the second in 1790–1791, which he elsewhere says was the occasion for his 1792 promotion to commissioned Lieutenant (FSW 3; WDS 3). Nevertheless, his first Royal Navy service was under a nephew of Admiral Boscawen, though in an unnamed ship (C/T 7) possibly in the West Indies (COM 3).

He went on to serve as a boy or youngster (which could include the rank of junior Midshipman) in HMSS *Alert* (PC 5), *Ajax* (FW 3), *Andromeda* (FW 7), *Goliath* (FW 7), *Minerva* (WDS 1), *Queen* (IM 10), *Ramillies* (TMC 6), *Sylph* (NC 8), and *Tonnant* (DI 1). He served as a Midshipman in HMSS *Agamemnon* (M&C 1), *Bellerophon* (COM 1,5), *Britannia* (PC 7), *Circe* (TMC 2), *Fortitude* (TH 2), *Namur* (FSW 10), *Resol/Resolution* (multiple references; *the ship in which Jack was temporarily turned before the mast as topman and sailmaker's crew*), *Success* (M&C 7), and *Surprise* (HMS 4,5,8; SM 7; LM 1; C/T 2). Jack also says he served as a Midshipman in HMS *Ardent* at the Battle of Camperdown (DI 6): however by the date of this battle, October 1797, he had already been a Lieutenant for 5 years. Jack served as a senior Midshipman — i.e., Master's Mate — in HMSS *Formidable* (FSW 4), *Surprise* (HMS 4,5,8) and *Sybille* (HD 9).

In 1792 he was promoted from unemployed Master's Mate to Fifth Lieutenant of HMS *Queen* (FSW 3; WDS 3). His subsequent ships as Lieutenant were HMSS *Agamemnon* (TMC 2,3); perhaps *Ardent* (DI 6; *he may have intended to say 'Lieutenant' not the impossible — given the date of service — 'Midshipman'*); *Arethusa* (COM 1); *Bellerophon* once again (LM 4); *Colossus* (TGS 4; *but he also says he was in* Orion *at the same battle, Cape St Vincent*); *Eurotas* (TH 10); possibly *Fortitude* again (TH 2; *the context is uncertain*); possibly *Foudroyant* (PC 8; *as mentioned by Sophie Williams, although Jack himself never claims such service*); *Fox* (DI 1); *Hannibal* (M&C 4); *Queen* (WDS 3); *Leander* (M&C 2,3,11,12; PC 12; TMC 3); *Orion* (PC 2; HMS 8; *but he also says he was in* Colossus *at the same battle, Cape St Vincent*); *Theseus* (M&C 3; DI 7; IM 2); and *Thunderer* (M&C 1,3).

Jack also served in unspecified ranks on HMSS *Euryalus* (RM 2), *Euterpe* (FW 9), *Isis* (TGS 4), *Marlborough* (PC 3), and *Minerva* (WDS 1).

No Aubrey — Jack or otherwise — served in the Royal Navy of the period. However, it is of interest that in O'Brian's 1952 novel Testimonies *(not a sea-tale) the narrator is named Joseph Aubrey Pugh, and once makes a reference to one Maturin, a former university colleague.*

Aubrey, Jacques

A reference to Jack Aubrey by Jeannot, one of Captain Christy-Pallière's orderlies (PC 4).

Aubrey, Mrs

1: Jack Aubrey's long-deceased mother, the first wife of General Aubrey (SM 5).

2: the second wife, and subsequently widow, of General Aubrey: when still a dairy maid, she had also been Jack Aubrey's occasional lover (HMS 7; SM 5; LM 8). Although usually referred to as the mother of Jack's half-brother, Philip Aubrey (e.g. HMS 7; LM 8; WDS 10), there are two curious later passages in which Philip is first said to have been born illegitimate (YA 2) and then declares himself to be the *grand*-son of the General and his second wife, a Miss Stanhope (YA 8).

3: *see* **Aubrey, Sophie**

Aubrey, Philip

Jack Aubrey's much younger half-brother, the son of General Aubrey and his second wife (HMS 7; LM 8). Jack intends to send Philip to sea in HMS *Orion* under the patronage of Heneage Dundas (TGS 4); he is later met as a Midshipman on Dundas' HMS *Berenice* (WDS 10; YA 2,3) and in the aviso HMS *Swallow* (YA 8). In *The Yellow Admiral* there are two curious passages in which Philip is first said to have been only recently legitimised (YA 2) and then declares himself to be the *grand*son of General Aubrey and his second wife, a Miss Stanhope (YA 8).

Aubrey, Sophie *or* Sophia

We meet Sophie as the beautiful, 27-year-old, unmarried daughter of the widow Mrs Williams and the elder sister of Cecilia and Frances (PC 1). Jack Aubrey and Stephen Maturin become their Hampshire neighbours and Sophie rapidly comes to prefer Jack over all her suitors (PC 2+), whilst also forming a good friendship with Stephen (PC 3+). Jack wavers between her charms and those of her cousin Diana Villiers, occasioning a violent disagreement between the two women (PC 8). Eventually Sophie and Jack come to an informal agreement to marry when she and Cecilia take a short cruise in the English Channel on Jack's HMS *Lively*. However, the grasping and snobbish Mrs Williams' blessing is not immediately forthcoming, as her daughter is moderately rich and Jack very poor (PC 14; HMS 1,4). Jack's triumph against the Spanish treasure fleet (PC 14) allows an official engagement to Sophie (HMS 2,4) but the ensuing uncertainties over the extent of any prize money raise doubts in both their minds, especially whilst he is

away in India (HMS 4–10). After much hesitation Jack asks his old friend Heneage Dundas to deliver Sophie in his HMS *Ethalion* from England to Madeira where he will meet her, on his return in HMS *Surprise* to Europe, away from the influence of her mother (HMS 10). The couple in fact meet at sea just off the island and confirm their pledge to marry once home (HMS 11).

Five years later Sophie is Mrs Aubrey of Ashgrove Cottage, Hampshire, and the mother of twin baby daughters, born after a long and difficult confinement: it is also implied that her mother has somehow contrived to lose the Williams' family fortune (TMC 1). Sophie is aware of Jack's ill-concealed impatience for a new sea-command, and encourages Maturin in obtaining one for him (TMC 1+). At sea, Jack receives a letter from his wife containing a hint—which he seems not to pick up—that she is again pregnant (TMC 6) and later receives the news that Sophie has given birth to a boy, whom he calculates must have been conceived on the night prior to his departure from home (TMC 10). When Jack comes home to meet his new son, George, he not only starts to commit his hard-won prize money to improbable land-improvement schemes but contrives to quarrel dangerously with the influential Andrew Wray over cards. Sophie is consequently happy to see her husband, who is in any case fretting for an active command, go back to sea as soon as possible (DI 1+).

Although Jack is now away for a very long time, with reports reaching England via Lieutenant Grant that he may not have survived a calamity in the far southern ocean, Sophie never doubts his well-being (FW 1+) and eventually hears news of his survival from Diana Villiers in America (FW 2). She continues to run the Ashgrove household during Jack's many long absences and fleeting presences, with financial worries constantly present (SM 1+; IM 1+; TH 2–8; FSW 1–9). However, she does at last receive from her husband a remittance of prize money equivalent to about ten years' pay (TH 3). A little later she also receives another surprise: a visit from Sam Panda, Jack's illegitimate, black son from a youthful liaison in South Africa (RM 1) and, although she later admits to having liked this fine young man, she stops short of ever specifically acknowledging any relationship between him and her husband (RM 6). After a visit to Ireland to see her sister Frances' new baby (RM 6) Sophie then has to contend with Jack's arrest for fraud: after his conviction she lives with him in the Marchalsea prison until he is fined, pilloried and released (RM 7,9). Following his temporary disgrace and dismissal from the Royal Navy she spends time at Shelmerston helping him in the clerical side of fitting out his new command, Maturin's *Surprise*, as a private letter-of-marque. Throughout the ordeal, she remains utterly convinced of her husband's innocence and certain of his eventual re-instatement (LM 8; TGS 1–5). This of course does happen (TGS 3,4), but leads to Sophie having to endure her husband's many more long absences at sea (TGS 5+; NC 1+; C/T 2,3,4,7; WDS 10; COM 1,2).

When Jack eventually returns to England Sophie has been gradually moving the Aubrey family from Ashgrove Cottage to the inherited, and ancient, Woolcombe House (COM 3+; YA 1). But what should be a happy homecoming is very tense, for Sophie has become jealous of Jack's supposed relationship at sea with Clarissa Oakes, and he jealous of her supposed new relationship with her former admirer Mr Hinksey: many tensions and arguments ensue (COM 6; YA 1–3). Furthermore the family finances suffer another reverse, putting pressure on Sophie to sell Ashgrove Cottage, long ago put into her sole name by marriage settlement (YA 1,2). She remains jealous of Clarissa Oakes until assured by Jack (choosing his words most carefully, for he is a fairly frequent adulterer: SM 6; TH 4; C/T 9) that this and similar suspicions are groundless (YA 1,3). However, she soon discovers the love letters sent to her husband by Amanda Smith some years earlier (see SM 5,6), accuses him of adultery and states her intention to leave Woolcombe with the children (YA 6). The more worldly Diana Villiers and Clarissa Oakes persuade Sophie (whom Jack regards as having no great interest in their own physical love-making: SM 1,4; IM 1) to view the matter less seriously and she soon asks Jack for a reconciliation (YA 8). Following Buonaparte's abdication, they enjoy a period of rare domestic bliss (YA 10). When Jack undertakes his semi-private mission to Chile, Sophie and the children accompany him in *Surprise* as far as Madeira, learning there of his swift recall to the Royal Navy (YA 10). Sophie and the family return to England where, almost immediately, her mother, Diana and several others are killed in a coaching accident (HD 1–3).

Audacious, HMS

A ship in Admiral Lord Keith's Mediterranean fleet (M&C 3,4) that later takes part in Admiral Saumarez' action off Gibraltar (M&C 12).

HMS Audacious, 74-gun, was launched in 1785 and broken up in 1815. She was used by *Keith as his flagship for a very short period after the accidental loss of his HMS *Queen Charlotte in 1800. However, it must be to *Louis' HMS *Minotaur that Jack is headed when he pauses by Audacious (M&C 4), as she was by then Keith's preference as temporary flagship. In 1801, under her Captain Shuldham Peard, Audacious fought in both of *Saumarez' actions and, between the two fights, this Admiral briefly transferred his flag into her whilst his more usual ship, *Brenton's HMS *Caesar, underwent emergency repairs.

Auden

A seaman in *Surprise*, a Sethian lay preacher ((LM 5; TGS 2; NC 7).

Audubon

An well-known ornithologist (WDS 6), by implication the bird-artist whose paintings Johnson had once offered to Maturin as a thinly described bribe (FW 6).

John James Audubon (1785–1851; originally, Jean-Jacques Fougère Audubon) was the author and illustrator of The Birds of America *(first published in London from 1827–1838), as well as a number of other illustrated wildlife books. Although a considerable ornithologist, he is chiefly famed for the high artistic qualities of his works. Haitian-born, at an early age he was taken by his father home to France, where he began to develop his interests and expertise. In 1803 he then moved to the USA, building there a wide reputation as a talented amateur illustrator. Persistent business failures in other ventures eventually drove him to publish by subscription his many drawings, a commercial course he had long resisted: indeed, Audubon had to travel to London to find engravers and publishers who could meet his exacting standards. His several books met with both considerable financial success and great artistic and scientific acclaim.*

Auger, Colonel

A French dragoon officer and security chief on Minorca (HMS 3,4), responsible for Stephen Maturin's imprisonment and torture. He is killed when Stephen is rescued by Jack Aubrey and a party of seamen from HMS *Lively* (HMS 3).

Augusta, Princess

A lady referred to by Lord Panmure (LM 7).

Princess Augusta Sophia (1768–1840) was the sixth child of King *George III.

Augustine, Saint

The African churchman (RM 2) who had begged God for the gift of inclination towards chastity, preferably somewhat delayed (SM 6; C/T 3).

Saint Augustine of Hippo (354–430) was one of the most influential Fathers of the early Christian Church. He was born in Tagaste (located in modern Tunisia), North Africa, and went on to study and teach philosophy in Carthage, Rome and Milan. In 386, under the influence of Saint Ambrose, he converted to Christianity and soon returned to Africa, becoming Bishop of Hippo in 396. He died there whilst the city was under siege by the Vandals. Augustine wrote an autobiography, Confessions, *in which he describes, with great psychological penetration, his early immorality, his struggles with his conscience and his eventual conversion.*

Aunt Sally

A fairground game (YA 2).

'Aunt Sally' is a cut-out woman's figure, often with a clay pipe in her mouth: the object of the game is to break the pipe—or knock over the figure—with thrown wooden balls. Hence, figuratively, an 'Aunt Sally' is an argument or person set up in order to be knocked down.

Aurangzeb

The Indian potentate in whose time Diana Villiers' 'Blue Peter' diamond had supposedly been appropriated by a sailor (SM 3).

Aurangzeb (1618–1707; Emperor from c.1657) was one of the greatest Moslem rulers of northern India, consolidating the power of his father, Shah Jehan (whom he deposed and imprisoned, along with his own brothers) and extending his dominion to the extremely wealthy city-states of Golconda and Bijapoor. However, his reign was later marked by intolerance of the Hindu faith and consequent widespread insurrection amongst its adherents.

Aurelius, Marcus

An Emperor of Rome (TH 2).

*Marcus Aurelius Antoninus (121–180 AD), a Roman Emperor famed for his benign rule and intellectual acumen, was an adherent and eloquent advocate of *Zeno's school of Stoicism. In 161, at the Senate's urging, he succeeded his adopted father Antoninus Pius as Emperor, ruling jointly with Lucius Commodus until the latter's death in 169 and alone thereafter. Aurelius continued the *Antonine Age of his predecessor, ruling effectively and justly, yet (somewhat curiously, given his otherwise attractive personality) he admitted to a great dislike of the rising Christian religion, persecution of which rose under his regime. Engaged in wars and disturbances on the fringes of his Empire throughout his reign, he died on campaign near modern Vienna, Austria. He wrote, in Greek, a book of* Meditations, *an influential treatise on moral discipline admired by Admiral William *Bligh, amongst many others.*

Aurora, HMS

A 28-gun frigate of Jack Aubrey's squadron, Captain Francis Howard (COM 3+).

HMS Aurora, *28-gun, was launched in 1777 and sold in 1814, being replaced in that year by the recently captured *Clorinde. In Greek myth Aurora was the goddess of the dawn.*

Aurore

A French merchant vessel in the Mediterranean (IM 6).

Aurore, HMS

An Royal Navy vessel commanded by Captain Bennet, moored at Port Mahon (M&C 6).

The French-built 32-gun ship was laid down in 1766 as Envieuse, *but launched in 1768 as* Aurore. *She was captured from the French in 1793, but then used only as a prison ship until about 1803, after which her fate is unknown.*

Autun, Bishop de
see **Talleyrand-Périgord**

Auvergne, Prince d'

A French Royalist Post Captain in the Royal Navy with whom Marine Captain Moore had once served (DI 10).

Philippe de la Tour d'Auvergne (1745–1816), Prince de Bouillon, was born on the island of Jersey into a cadet branch of a noble French family, receiving most of his ed-

ucation in France. *He then spent the better part of his adult life in the service of the British Crown, being commissioned as a Royal Navy Lieutenant in 1777, promoted Commander in 1781, made Post in 1784, and advanced to Rear Admiral in 1805 and Vice Admiral in 1810; from 1803 until the end of the war he served as Naval Commandant of Jersey. After being promoted Commander he had travelled to France and become the heir of an elderly, distant relative, the Prince de Bouillon; however, the Revolution then prevented him ever taking possession of the estates following the Prince's death. At the first *Bourbon restoration of 1814 d'Auvergne assumed the Prince's title and commenced litigation against other claimants, but his claim of inheritance was rejected by the French courts in 1816, the year of his death. His younger brother, Corbet James d'Auvergne (d.1825), also served in the Royal Navy, rising to Post Captain in 1811.*

Avaray, d'

A courtier of King Louis XVIII whilst in exile in England (SM 5).

*A reference to either Claude Antoine de Bésiade d'Avaray (1740–1829) or his son Antoine Louis, Duc d'Avaray (1759–1811), both fervent royalists. The younger d'Avaray had helped the future King *Louis XVIII escape from France in 1791; the elder d'Avaray in 1814 delivered the loyal address of the French Senate to the restored king.*

Avicenna

A famous doctor of former times (TMC 2; TGS 6).

Ibn-Sina (980–1037; a name often Latinized to Avicenna) had an unrivalled reputation as the leading scholar and polymath of his age. Born in central Asia, before the age of 20 he had become famous as a philosopher, mathematician, natural scientist and physician. A prolific author, his System of Medicine *remained influential for many centuries.*

Avon, HMS

A ship that arrives at Gibraltar carrying dispatches (FSW 1).

HMS Avon, *18-gun brig-sloop, was launched in 1805 and sunk in 1814 by USS* Wasp *in the English Channel; she is named for a river in southern England.*

Axel

A servant of Countess Tessin (LM 9).

Ayliffe

A seaman in HMS *Leopard* put ashore in Brazil to recover his health (DI 5).

Ayrton, Ezekiel

A seaman in HMS *Surprise* (WDS 4).

Azéma

The 'second captain' of the French privateer *Bellone*, a former Royal officer, who takes command of the *Lord Nelson* as a prize but soon strikes to HMS *Seagull* and a large British squadron (PC 5).

The name is perhaps inspired by that of the famous French General François Bazile Azémar (1776–1813), killed in action at the Battle of Gross Drebnitz.

Azgar, Sheikh of
see **Ibn Hazm**

Azul
A Spanish privateer chartered by Guzman's brother

to convey a valuable cargo of quicksilver to the New World (LM 3); she is taken by the American *Spartan* privateer, immediately re-taken by Aubrey's HMS *Surprise*, and promptly sinks (LM 3).

B

Babbington, Mr and Mrs
The parents of William Babbington, Mr Babbington being a Tory MP (PC 3,12).

Babbington, William (*on one occasion, Charles*)
A well-connected Royal Navy officer, a follower and protégé of Jack Aubrey from an early age. They first meet in HMS *Sophie*, where the very young William Babbington already serves as a Midshipman of enthusiastic yet indifferent seamanship (M&C 1+) with an early devotion to lechery (M&C 6); in her, William takes part in the glorious capture of *Cacafuego* (M&C 10). Ashore during the Peace of Amiens (PC 2,3), he enthusiastically escorts Diana Villiers on a coach journey to Jack and Stephen Maturin's Ball (PC 2).

On the resumption of war he follows Jack — who now holds him in high regard — into HMS *Polychrest* and is badly wounded in the *Fanciulla* action (PC 11; LM 7), with Stephen Maturin saving his shattered arm from amputation (PC 12). He next serves as a Master's Mate in Jack's HMS *Surprise* (HMS 5+). Still three months short of his mandatory six years sea-service before he can sit the promotion exam, he is soon made an acting Lieutenant by his Captain; overcome with both gratitude and guilt, he then confesses to having eaten Stephen's experimental rats (HMS 6). He is later sent across to the East Indiaman *Royal George* for the battle with Linois' French squadron (HMS 9).

Some years now pass before William is again encountered: after service on the West Indies station, he returns to England to become Third Lieutenant in Jack's HMS *Leopard* (DI 1+). By now he is a prime sea-officer, although severely reprimanded by his Captain for lecherous approaches to the prisoner / passenger Louisa Wogan (DI 4). When *Leopard* nears the icebergs of the far southern ocean, William's far-northern experiences in HMS *Erebus* are ignored by the dogged First Lieutenant and cannot be brought to the attention of the ailing Jack Aubrey: *Leopard* is sucked into the berg and badly holed (DI 8). William remains with Jack in the near-foundering ship, later reaching Desolation Island with those crew who had also chosen to remain

aboard (DI 9). As *Leopard*'s First Lieutenant since Grant's departure, he eventually arrives safely in Pulo Batang with Jack, who intends to take him back to England for a post in his new command, HMS *Acasta* (FW 1). Although a considerable cricketer by reputation, William fails first ball in the match against HMS *Cumberland* shortly before accompanying Jack home as a passenger in HMS *La Flèche* (FW 1,2). With his colleagues, he then escapes from the accidental destruction of this ship by fire, is picked up by HMS *Java*, and fights in her disastrous encounter with USS *Constitution* (FW 3,4): the victorious Americans then put William and most of their other prisoners ashore in Brazil (FW 4,5).

Having arrived back in England (SM 5+), he is quickly promoted Commander into HMS *Sylphide* (SM 11). Shortly afterwards, he is encountered as Commander of the sloop HMS *Oedipus*, running between France and England as the cartel ship, and in her, under Jack's watchful eye, he marries Stephen Maturin and Diana Villiers (SM 11). Now Commander of the sloop HMS *Dryad* of Admiral Harte's Mediterranean squadron (IM 5), William accompanies Jack on the mission to the neutral ports of Barka and Medina: sent ahead to Medina he narrowly escapes capture by the powerful French ships unexpectedly present there (IM 6). Jack soon discovers that it was intended that *Dryad* be captured in order to provide an excuse to attack the French (IM 7); in turn, William suspects that Harte had chosen him for this fate in order to separate him from his daughter, Fanny, leaving open the prospects of her marriage to the influential civilian, Andrew Wray (IM 5). William later accompanies Jack and HMS *Surprise* to the Ionian sea but returns to Malta before seeing any significant action (IM 9–11). Although Fanny Harte has now been compelled by her father to marry Wray, she and William remain very much in love (TH 1): William, swearing off general lechery for the first time ever, remains on active service in command of *Dryad* (TH 3,9,10).

Some years later, this affair is still in progress (RM 6,9) although, somewhat curiously, Fanny now refers to William as 'Charles' (RM 9), afterwards giving an elaborate explanation for her slip (LM 2). Still a Commander, he is now given the sloop HMS *Tartarus* (RM 6). At some risk to his career, he loyally attends the now-disgraced Jack Aubrey's ordeal in the pillory (RM 9). In *Tartarus*, he later finds himself senior officer of the tiny squadron blockading the French frigate *Diane* in harbour (LM 5) and, secure in the knowledge that he himself is soon to be made Post, happily agrees to let Jack — now commanding a privateer — take full credit for her capture (LM 6). He also remains much attached to Fanny, now separated from her traitorous husband (LM 2,6). Perhaps a little surprisingly, William is only once again mentioned in the series, purely in passing (C/T 7).

> There are 3 naval Babingtons (sic) who may have provided O'Brian with inspiration for the name: James Babington, a Lieutenant of 1801 who died in 1808; William Maitland Babington, Lieutenant of 1796, died 1798; and James Boyle Babington, Lieutenant of 1810, Commander of 1816, died 1826.

Babylon, Whore of

A reference by 'Broad-Brim' to the supposed iniquities of Franchon's Hotel in Boston (FW 5).

> The ancient city of Babylon (whose ruins lie just south of modern Baghdad, Iraq) was fabled for its power, opulence and dissipation. The Whore of Babylon appears in the biblical Book of Revelations as a figure for the moral and economic corruption of unbelieving empires: *God's judgement on her was death.

Bacchante, HMS

A frigate forming part of the small inshore squadron blockading St Martin's (LM 4).

> HMS Bacchante, 38-gun, was launched in 1811 and broken up in 1869. Named for the god *Bacchus, at the approximate time of LM she was commanded by the dashing young William *Hoste.

Bacchus or Baccho

The god of wine (FW 8; TH 3; FSW 2,3).

> In classical myth Bacchus (a.k.a. Dionysus) was a son of *Zeus and the god of wine, intoxication and transcendent experience.

Bach

'London Bach,' a composer who had written some works for Jack Aubrey's uncle Fisher and who Jack himself had met (IM 2,5). Jack also refers to his father, 'Old Bach,' as being a somewhat obscure composer working in an old-fashioned style, but he nevertheless explores the profundity of some of his scores (IM 2,3; COM 6).

> 'Old Bach' is the great Johann Sebastian (1685–1750); 'London Bach,' perhaps more usually known as the 'English Bach,' was his youngest son, Johann Christian (1735–1782). Johann Sebastian Bach is today regarded as one of the greatest of all polyphonic composers but, during his own lifetime, his fame was primarily as a virtuoso organist, with his prodigious creative output neither widely known nor highly regarded, being thought old-fashioned

even by his contemporaries. His reputation improved a little after his death and in 1801 received a considerable boost with the publication of his Well-Tempered Clavier studies. However, it was not until a 1829 performance of the great St Matthew Passion in Berlin that interest started to flourish, and even then systematic publication of his works did not begin until 1850. Johann Christian Bach went to Italy in about 1755 but, after several of his early operas received poor receptions in Milan, moved on to London in 1762. Appointed Music Master to the Queen in the following year, he continued to write operas and instrumental works, but now with considerable success. Towards the end of his life his popularity declined and he died in London in considerable debt and some obscurity, being buried in a mass-grave. However, his early reputation for charming melody, agreeably scored, remained high, especially in the eyes of other great musicians such as *Mozart, *Haydn and, a little later, Beethoven.

Bacon

1: a Friar referred to by Captain Billy Sutton (FSW 1).

> Roger Bacon (1214?–1292?) was an English Franciscan monk and polymath of immense reputation in his own lifetime and for many centuries thereafter. As well as being a theologian of very wide influence, he was also famous as a linguist, mathematician and scientist, especially in the field of optics: he invented reading spectacles (at least in the Western world: they were separately and earlier known in the East) and described a basic form of telescope. In about 1265 he composed his Opus Maius, a rigorous treatise on all known sciences. However, in 1278 he was condemned by his order for heretical propositions and imprisoned for over ten years until his death. The saying quoted by Sutton is more usually associated with Sir Francis Bacon: see **2** below.

2: Maturin makes a passing reference to the theory that Bacon wrote the plays of Shakespeare (FSW 5).

> Sir Francis Bacon (1561–1626), Baron Verulam and Viscount St Albans, rose to prominence as a brilliant lawyer, parliamentarian, intellectual and Royal favourite in the reigns of Queen Elizabeth I and King James I, rising to Lord Chancellor in 1618 and being made a Viscount in 1621. In that same year he was convicted of accepting bribes in his capacity as a judge and driven out of public life: he devoted himself thereafter to study and writing. His many books and pamphlets — on scientific method, the law, mythology, systems of thought, education and natural philosophy — were as popular as they were influential and display a brilliantly erudite and supple mind. It is, in part, the contrast in learning and cultural finesse between the elegant Bacon and what little is known of *Shakespeare's humble origins that led some authors to suppose that the plays must have been from Bacon's pen, a theory supposedly supported by encoded claims of authorship in the text. However, these theories — not today given much regard — were not propounded in writing until the middle of the 19th century, well after Maturin's remarks.

Badger, HMS

A sloop at Funchal in Madeira (HMS 11).

> A brig HMS Badger was in service from 1777 to 1784, and a 10-gun brig-sloop Badger from 1808 until her final

break-up in 1864; however, no Badger *was in service at the time of* HMS.

Badger-Bag

A character in the ceremony of 'crossing the line' (HMS 6; TMS 2; FSW 4) to whom Maturin's eccentric appearance is compared (PC 12).

*'Badger-bag' is the traditional name for the gaily dressed members of Father *Neptune's Court in the lower-deck naval ceremony of 'crossing the line' (i.e., the equator).*

Bailey

The owner of an hotel in Halifax, Nova Scotia (SM 1).

Bainbridge, Commodore

The commander of USS *Constitution*, injured in the action against HMS *Java* (FW 4,7; TGS 8).

William Bainbridge (1774–1833) was promoted Captain into the frigate USS Philadelphia *in 1800. In late 1804, she ran aground near Tripoli in an action against the pirates of the Mediterranean Barbary coast, with Bainbridge and his officers then spending a year and a half in captivity. Appointed in mid-1812 Commodore of a small squadron led by USS *Constitution, he took HMS *Java in December of that same year. On the ending of the Anglo-American war in early 1815, Bainbridge then commanded the U.S. fleet in the Mediterranean, largely acting against commerce-disrupting pirates and privateers.*

Baines

A Royal Navy officer whose career had been wrecked by an arrest for debt (PC 6).

Bainton

A secretary at the Admiralty (PC 12).

Baker

1: Captain Fellowes' steward in HMS *Thunderer* (IM 6).
2: the Captain of HMS *Iris,* who likes his bargemen to have surnames taken from colours of the rainbow (FSW 2).
3: a seaman in HMS *Diane* (TGS 10).
4: a naturalist and student of bees referred to by Maturin (NC 7).

The reference may be to Henry Baker (1698–1774), a naturalist, educator and minor poet. A Fellow of the Royal Society, he was distinguished for his advances in the use of microscopic techniques, and his very popular Microscope Made Easy *(1742) contains observations on both pollen and fleas as well as on his more usual crystallography.*

5: the author of a *Chronicle* in the Woolcombe House library (YA 2).

Sir Richard Baker (1568–1645) wrote a very popular Chronicle of the Kings of England, *long a standard reference work in schools and private homes.*

Baker, Tom

The Captain of HMS *Phoenix*, 36-gun, who had taken the 44-gun *Didon* (FW 2).

Thomas Baker (1771–1845) entered the Royal Navy in

*1781 and was made Post in 1797. In August 1805 he intercepted the heavy frigate *Didon, Captain Milius, in his much lighter HMS *Phoenix; Didon, carrying dispatches from Admiral *Villeneuve, should properly have declined the engagement but instead chose to fight. Despite the French ship's much superior broadside weight, Baker's superior gunnery—firing three broadsides for every two received—eventually told and after a 16 hour running fight* Didon *struck. A little later in the same year it was Baker spotted the small French squadron that had escaped from *Nelson's victory at Trafalgar, being then able to inform Sir Richard *Strachan's squadron of their whereabouts. Baker was promoted Rear Admiral in 1821 and Vice Admiral in 1837.*

Baldick, Richard William

The Lieutenant of HMS *Sophie* under Captain Allen, whom he follows into HMS *Pallas*. Baldick, temporarily ill ashore in Port Mahon, is visited by Jack Aubrey (M&C 1,2)

Mr Baldick provides the solution to an often posed puzzle: exactly when do Jack Aubrey and Stephen Maturin first meet? HMS Sophie's *log records that Baldick had left her on April 18th 1800 (M&C 2) and he is said to have then immediately hospitalised himself, this occurring on the day before the newly promoted Jack Aubrey pays him a courtesy call (M&C 1). From this snippet we can deduce the time of the opening scene of* Master and Commander *as being in the evening of April 18th, with Jack receiving in the early hours of the following morning the delayed news that he had been promoted Commander as of April 1st.*

Baldwin

A boyhood neighbour of Jack Aubrey in Dorset (YA 2).

Balfour, Captain

A Post Captain who, in 1787, had been passed over for expected promotion by seniority to Rear Admiral, thus becoming the first victim of the new notion of 'yellowing,' i.e., promotion to retired, squadron-less, Rear Admiral (YA 4).

George Balfour (1725?–1794) had been commissioned Lieutenant in 1745 and made Post in 1758; he saw no active service after about 1781. In 1787 he was passed over for automatic promotion by seniority to Rear Admiral of the Blue, causing a great fuss amongst other senior Post Captains who feared the same eventual fate. There was already in existence a 'retired list' for Admirals who had once held active flag commands, however briefly or nominally, and within a few months the Admiralty relented, promoting Balfour to Rear Admiral but placing him straight onto this list as a 'yellow' admiral without benefit of squadron. The entry for Balfour in John Charnock's contemporary Biographia Navalis *strongly implies that he was not the only Captain so passed over in 1787, although I have been unable to identify the others.*

Ball

A Post Captain met by Aubrey and Pullings on the island of Gozo (TH 2).

The reference could possibly be to Henry Lidgbird Ball (d.1818) who was made Post in 1795 and promoted Rear-

Admiral in 1814: however, he had been placed on the half-pay list—i.e., without a ship to command—in 1813, about the time TH is set. From 1786 to 1792 Ball had commanded the brig HMS *Supply, part of the 'First Fleet' sent out to colonise Australia, and in 1799 had commanded HMS *Daedalus in her bombardment of Kosseir. See also **Hildebrand, Sir.**

Ballocks, Mr

An officer commanding a signal post on Réunion, as referred to by Jenkins and Trecothic (TMC 9).
The name is perhaps generic disrespect, 'ballocks' or 'bollocks' being British slang for testicles.

Banks, Sir Joseph

The wealthy naturalist and politician, on whose temporary commission as a Post-Captain in the Royal Navy that given to Stephen Maturin is to be modelled (PC 14; HMS 1). He is often referred to by Stephen and others, almost always with great admiration (DI 1; FSW 7; RM 6+; TGS 2–6; NC author's note, 8,10; C/T 9; YA 4,10).
Sir Joseph Banks (1743–1820) was at the centre of English scientific life for many years, becoming president of the Royal Society in 1778. Enormously wealthy, Banks had financed *Cook's voyages of exploration in HMS *Endeavour, and accompanied him on his first circumnavigation; he is the subject of a biography by O'Brian, Joseph Banks: a Life *(London: Collins, 1987). However, Banks was never commissioned in the Royal Navy, the reference being perhaps inspired by the position given to Sir Edmund *Halley, the great astronomer.*

Banterer, HMS

A 22-gun ship recently wrecked (TMC 1).
HMS Banterer, *22-gun, was launched as HMS* Banter *in 1805 and re-named in 1807; she was wrecked on shoals in the St Lawrence River in December 1808.*

Bantock

A seaman in HMS *Polychrest* picked out by Aubrey as being perfectly reliable during a the near-mutiny (PC 11).

Baptist, John

An Italian seaman in HMS *Sophie* (M&C 10).

Barabbas

The biblical figure referred to by Martin in connection with what he sees as the grasping business practices of Mowett's publisher (RM 2).
Barabbas was the biblical thief released by Pontius *Pilate, at the mob's behest, in place of *Jesus Christ.

Barber

A seaman in *Surprise* (C/T 5).

Barclay de Tolly

A Russian general marching to join Wellington in the Low Countries (HD 1).
Mikhail, Prince Barclay de Tolly (1755–1818), a Russian of Scottish ancestry, made a name for himself as a soldier (at first, in the ranks) in the wars with Turkey, Sweden

and Poland of 1788–1794 and later fought in the Polish forces themselves in their wars with the French. He first rose to real distinction in the Franco-Russian campaign of 1806–1807, being badly wounded at Eylau early in the latter year. Promoted to field rank, Barclay de Tolly became a confidant of the *Czar himself and in 1810 was made Minister of War, soon enjoying success as a reformer and moderniser. In 1812 he was also appointed Army Commander in the West but, under the weight of dual responsibilities, did not flourish in the field. He was soon replaced in his active command by Marshall Kutusov, under whom he then served with some distinction at Borodino. In 1813–1814 he commanded army divisions under the Czar in the invasion of *Buonaparte's empire, fighting in each of the major battles of that campaign. In 1814, following the Emperor's first abdication, he led for a short time the Russian army of occupation in France, being made both Prince and Field Marshal. When Buonaparte escaped from Elba in 1815 for his final 'hundred days,' Barclay de Tolly, back in St Petersburg, led a fresh advance from the east but *Wellington and *Blücher had defeated their old rival at Waterloo before the Russian army had even set foot in France.

Barka, Pasha of
see either **Esmin, Pasha of Barka** *or* **Mohammed, Pasha of Barka**

Barker
1: a seaman in HMS *Polychrest* (PC 11).
2: a seaman in HMS *Bellona* who contracts and recovers from yellow fever (COM 9).

Barlow
1: Mrs Barlow, Sir Joseph Blaine's house-keeper (RM 5+; LM 4,7).
2: a Master's Mate in HMS *Bellona* (COM 6).
3: the owner of a gentlemen's outfitters at Gibraltar (HD 9).

Barmecide
A reference by Aubrey to the meagreness of his available rations (HMS 2; NC 8).
In the Tales of the Arabian Nights, *a member of the wealthy Barmecide family plays a cruel joke on a beggar by serving him with an wholly imaginary feast.*

Barmouth, Admiral Lord
The newly appointed Commander-in-Chief, Mediterranean, replacing Lord Keith (HD 8); he has recently married Admiral Horton's widow, a lady who, as Miss Isobel Carrington, had been a close friend of the young Jack Aubrey (HD 9,10). Barmouth, no especial admirer of Jack—whose Captain in HMS *Sybille* he had once been and under whom his own son, Arklow, had unsuccessfully served—orders him to strike his Commodore's pennant and return HMS *Surprise* to its former status as a private ship (HD 9). However, he does give Jack permission to intercept an Algerine galley carrying a huge sum of gold from Morocco to the Adriatic, a prize in which he is then most happy to share

(HD 10). Under his commoner's name of Captain Richardson, Lord Barmouth had a built a most brilliant reputation as a frigate Captain but, in Jack's view, has become a far less impressive man since rising to flag rank (HD 9,10). After Jack's success at sea, Barmouth grows somewhat piqued at his new wife's attentions to her old friend and rapidly orders *Surprise* away to South America (HD 10).

> *Lord Barmouth is to some degree modelled on Admiral Lord Exmouth, the former Sir Edward *Pellew, who in HD 1 was indeed said to be due to supersede Lord *Keith in the Mediterranean command.*

Barmouth, Lady

The former Miss Isobel Carrington, a friend of the young Jack Aubrey, who had first married Admiral Horton and, after his demise, has now just wed Admiral Lord Barmouth (HD 9,10). Whilst in Gibraltar, she seems most attached to Jack, causing her new husband some irritation (HD 10).

Barnes, Peggy

A convicted child-killer, acting as Louisa Wogan's servant in HMS *Leopard*, who spreads a venereal disease to the ship's crew (DI 6–10). Later, she is reported to have arrived safely in the penal colony at Botany Bay (FW 5).

Barney

A character in a verse sung by Maturin to a snake he has brought aboard HMS *Sophie* (M&C 6).

Barr

The Third Lieutenant of HMS *Charwell* (PC 1).

Barrington

A famous pick-pocket who had been transported to New South Wales (DI 3).

> *George Barrington (1755 — after 1806) was an Irish pick-pocket, specialising in robbing London's social elite in the guise of a parson, who was arrested in 1790, after a long and notorious career, and sentenced to transportation to New South Wales. On the voyage out he gave information to the ship's Master of an impending convicts' mutiny and was rewarded shortly after his arrival (in 1792) with the first ever 'warrant of emancipation' issued in the colony. Barrington rose to the position of Superintendent of Convicts at Botany Bay and also became a minor playwright as well as the author of a number of popular books on the geography, customs and inhabitants of the colony.*

Barrow

The author of sermons used by Mr Martin (FSW 7).

> *Isaac Barrow (1630–1677) was a famous mathematician, theologian and church orator who, already holding Professorships of Greek and Geometry, was in 1663 appointed to the Lucasian Chair of Mathematics at Cambridge University. He resigned this post in favour of his pupil and friend Isaac *Newton in 1669 and in 1672 became Master of Trinity College. His famous Sermons appeared in 1685 in an edition by Dr *Tillotson.*

Barrow, Isaac

A seaman in HMS *Polychrest* who has been illegally punished by Parker (PC 7).

Barrow, Sir John

The Second Secretary at the Admiralty, responsible for intelligence matters. Taken severely ill, he is temporarily replaced by Andrew Wray (SM 4; IM 1,5; RM 2,5).

> *Sir John Barrow (1764–1848) rose from humble origins to become a statesman and scientific explorer of great renown. After long travels in China and South Africa he returned to England in about 1802 and in 1804 was appointed by Lord *Melville Second Secretary to the Admiralty, a post in which he was responsible for the entire civil administration of the Royal Navy for the next forty years. A Fellow of the Royal Society of 1805, Barrow was the author of several biographies of leading naval characters as well as works on geography and exploration. In the realm of intelligence matters his expertise on all matters to do with China and Southern Africa was often consulted by governments throughout his long career. Although occasionally referred to in the series as 'Sir John,' Barrow did not in fact receive his baronetcy until 1835.*

Bart, Jean

The subject of a toast by Maturin (NC 7).

> *Jean Bart, or Barth, (1650–1701) was a famous French privateer and Admiral. Having gone to sea at age 15, he became the equivalents of Commander in 1686, Post Captain in 1689 and Rear Admiral in 1697. As an independent commander Bart took or sank several hundred fishing and merchant vessels belonging to his King's enemies; he also played a distinguished role in warfare waged directly on enemy forces. For many French sea-farers of subsequent generations Bart was revered as the very model of a bold, attacking officer; his son, grandson and nephew all became Captains in the French Navy.*

Bartholomew Fair

A fair often referred to as a symbol of lively chaos (PC 7; FW 3; IM 5; FSW 10; LM 5; C/T 7).

> *A fair that took place in London on St Bartholomew's Day — August 24th — was the subject of a rollicking farce by Ben Jonson (1573–1637), first performed in 1614. Saint Bartholomew himself was one of the 12 New Testament Apostles of *Jesus, although almost nothing is known of his own life or work.*

Bartlet, N.

A woman searching for Ellis Palmer/Paul Ogle (RM 7).

Bartolo

see '*Marriage of Figaro*'

Bartolomeu

A Catalan agent referred to by Maturin (PC 3).

Barton

1: a Scottish pirate, the subject of a ballad sung by Mr Orrage (FSW 3).

> *Sir Andrew Barton (d.1511) was a Scottish sea-captain*

and commerce raider whose exploits and demise were a popular subject for ballads. Under the protection of King James III of Scotland Barton attacked English shipping in his Lion before being hunted down, and then killed in a fierce sea-action, by Sir Edward and Sir Thomas Howard, sons of the Earl of Surrey.

2: an authority on birds referred to by Fabien (WDS 6).

This may be a reference to either of two Bartons, both distinguished American physicians and botanists, although neither especially noted for their ornithology. Benjamin Smith Barton (1766–1815) was Professor of Natural History and Botany at the University of Pennsylvania from 1789; his nephew, William Barton (1786–1856), succeeded him to the Professorship but did not publish extensively on botany until about 1820.

Bartram

The name of two authorities on birds referred to by Fabien (WDS 6).

John Bartram (1699–1777) and his son William (1739–1823) were American naturalists of great reputation. John Bartram held the position of American botanist to King *George III and was greatly admired by *Linneaus and other leading European scientists. William Bartram came to enjoy a scientific reputation almost as strong as that of his father, being especially known for his ornithological studies.

Bart's

A hospital in London (TGS 2; IM 1).

St *Bartolomew's Hospital, or 'Bart's,' was founded in Smithfield, London in 1137 next to a recently built priory. It was re-built in 1730 on the same site and remains today as London's oldest medical facility.

Basilio

A colleague of the French intelligence agent Lesueur (TH 8).

Bates

1: a secretary to Lord St Vincent (PC 3).
2: an officer in the *Lord Nelson* Indiaman (PC 5).
3: HMS *Surprise's* armourer (HMS 11).
4: a Midshipman in HMS *Boadicea* (TMC 9).
5: an ex-Flitch killed in action on HMS *Java* (FW 3).
6: a name scratched in the wall of the Brest nunnery/prison where HMS *Ariel's* officers are held (SM 10).
7: a Captain admonished by Admiral Ives in a letter (FSW 1).
8: Lady Bates, a ferocious lady of Aubrey's acquaintance (RM 3).
9: a Master's Mate in HMS *Pomone* (HD 4).

Bates, Abraham

A seaman in HMS *Polychrest* (PC 8).

Bates, John

A seaman in HMS *Africaine* who has his foot am-

putated following the action with *Astrée* and *Iphigenie* (TMC 9).

Bates, Joseph

A seaman referred to in a court-martial on board HMS *Ocean* (IM 4).

Bates, William

A marine in HMS *Boadicea* wounded in the *Hébé* action (TMC 2).

Bates, Zeke 'Butcher'

A notorious murderer confined as a madman in Choate's Boston hospital, where he is befriended by Jack Aubrey (FW 4).

Baudelocque

A French doctor said by his old friend Stephen Maturin to be the best attendant for pregnancies in Europe. He cares for Diana Villiers, agreeing with Stephen that she is likely to miscarry (SM 5,10,11).

Jean Louis Baudelocque (1746–1810) became the chief surgeon and accoucheur at the Hôpital de la Maternité in Paris and the principal attendant to *Buonaparte's second wife, Marie Louise of Austria. Although certainly the leading expert of his day on issues of pregnancy and childbirth, by the time of SM he had been dead for several years.

Bayard

A reference by Farquar to dashing military behaviour (TMC 9).

Pierre de Terrail (1475–1524), Chevalier Bayard, was known as 'the knight free from fear or reproach.' As a soldier and general under successive French kings, Bayard enjoyed a reputation for immense personal valour, great generosity and sound tactical sense; he was killed in battle against the forces of the Duke of *Bourbon.

Bazajet

A man referred to by Mr Martin in connection with Tom Pullings' ferocious driving of *Surprise* to her rendezvous with Jack Aubrey (NC 8).

Bayazid, or Bazajet, I, King of the Ottomans (1347–1403) was a famous warrior, given the surname 'Ilderim' ('Lightning') for the rapidity of his military movements across Asia Minor, Bulgaria and Greece. Finally defeated by *Tamerlane's armies in 1401, he died in captivity.

Beach

A neighbour of the Aubreys in Hampshire (TMC 6).

Beale

An apothecary in Portsmouth (COM 4).

Beales, Reverend

George Aubrey's Latin tutor (C/T 2).

Beatson

A naval historian referred to by O'Brian (M&C author's note).

Robert Beatson (1742–1818) was a Scottish writer and

compiler who in 1790 published his Naval and Military Memoirs of Great Britain from 1727 to the Present Time; *he also wrote an analysis of Admiral *Keppel's controversial 1778 action off Ushant.*

Beatty
The carpenter of *Surprise* (LM 6).

Beaumont
A Lieutenant in HMS *Briseis,* formerly of HMS *Worcester* (COM 5).

Beauprin
A colleague of Maturin who had sired 16 children when past the age of 80 (SM 6).

Beauvilliers
The hotel in Paris used by Maturin when he addresses the *Institut* (SM 5,11).

Beaver
An 'HM Hired Vessel' referred to by Aubrey (NC 10).
At the time of NC there was, in full Royal Navy service, an HMS Beaver, *10-gun brig-sloop, launched in 1809 and sold in 1829. For a few months in 1801— very much earlier than NC— a Beaver gunboat had been hired into the navy.*

Bechell, Fra.
A seaman referred to in Captain Allen's HMS *Sophie* log as having been lashed (M&C 2).

Beck, Major
The well-regarded Royal Marine officer in charge of intelligence activities on the North American Station (SM 1,3,4).

Beckett
A seaman in HMS *Surprise* (FSW 7).

Beckford
The author of *Vathek,* who had designed a house near Lisbon visited by Blaine and Maturin (TGS 3).
William Beckford (1759–1844) was an immensely wealthy Member of Parliament, Lord Mayor of London, traveller, collector and exotic novelist; his oriental tale Vathek, *highly regarded by Lord *Byron, was published in French in 1784 and in English two years later. In 1794 Beckford built a vast mansion on the outskirts of Lisbon, and in 1796 started to built Fonthill Abbey, Wiltshire, on a scale that eventually even he could not afford to sustain. After a life of combined seclusion and scandal in this art- and curio-stuffed palace, he was in 1822 forced to sell up and retire to Bath, far more moderately affluent than before.*

Bede
An ancient historian (NC 3,8).
The Venerable Bede (673–735) was a Northumbrian monk, historian and scholar, the author in about 731 of Historia Ecclesiastica Gentis Anglorum *('An Ecclesiastical History of the English People'). He also wrote many other works of biblical commentary, rudimentary science and natural philosophy.*

Bedlam
A reference to chaos (PC 7; HMS 9; HD 3).
Short-hand for the Hospital of St Mary of Bethlehem, a lunatic asylum in London from the early 15th century onwards. The hospital was named for Saint *Mary, who gave birth to *Jesus in Bethlehem.

Beechey
An artist who has executed a portrait of Jack Aubrey (DI 1) and many other naval officers (TH 2).
Sir William Beechey (1753–1839) was one of the most fashionable portrait painters of his age, executing commissions for King *George III and Queen Charlotte as well as for military figures such as *Nelson and the *Cornwallis brothers.

Beelzebub
A slang expression for anyone tyrannical (M&C 8; DI 4; IM 5,8; TGS 2; YA 2; HD 3).
Beelzebub is an adaptation of the Hebrew for 'Lord of the Flies,' used in the Bible as a name for a Philistine god. Although also used by John *Milton in Paradise Lost *for that fallen angel who was *Satan's 'second-in-command,' the name has come to be a reference to the *Devil himself.* See also **Evans, Black**

Beelzebub
Jack Aubrey's brass, long-9 chaser in HMS *Nutmeg of Consolation* and in *Surprise* (NC 5+).

Begum
see **Blue Peter**

Begum Lala
A reference to Diana Villiers by Dil (HMS 7).
'Begum Lala' is the Muslim term for a high-ranking lady, used especially for widows.

Behemoth
A reference to the villainous Master Cooper of Gibraltar dock-yard (FSW 2) and later the name first contemplated for Emily Sweeting (NC 8).
'Behemoth' is Hebrew for a monstrous beast.

Behemoth, HMS
A ship in which John Daniel had served (HD 3).

Behn, Aphra
A playwright and spy mentioned by Blaine to Maturin (DI 2).
Aphra Behn (1640–1689) was, according to the novelist Virginia Woolf, the first English woman to earn her living solely by writing. In 1664 she had married Behn, a London city merchant probably of Dutch origins and, after his death in 1666, she went on an intelligence mission for King *Charles II to Holland, where she extracted, supposedly from several lovers, information on Admiral De *Ruyter's plans to attack British shipping in the Rivers Thames and Medway. She received no

financial reward for this work and on her return was soon imprisoned for debt; once released, she turned, most successfully, to her pen in order to raise cash. Her many plays, written from 1670 onwards, were hugely popular in her day and are often revived; her several novels are also still held in high regard. Mrs Behn was frequently accused of both lewdness and plagiarism in her works, criticisms that she justly regarded as motivated entirely by the fact of her sex.

Belcher, Jem

A famous prize-fighter (FSW 9; YA 3) after whom a neckerchief is named (RM 4)..

*Jem, or Jim, Belcher (1781–1811) was a famous pugilist (one-eyed after a racquets accident in 1803) after whom multi-coloured, spotted neckerchiefs, very popular amongst the sporting set of all ranks of society, were named. In the year of his accident he had succeeded 'Gentleman' John *Jackson as Champion of England, although the two never themselves met in the ring. Jem's younger brother, Tom (1783–1854), was also a notable prize-fighter.*

Belcher, Tobias

A Sethian seaman in *Surprise* (HD 10).

Belcher

A cannon on Jack Aubrey's *Surprise* (LM 2; NC 7) and HMS *Diane* (TGS 5).

*Undoubtedly named by the crew for Jem *Belcher.*

Belette, HMS

The former ship of Mr Horner, the new gunner of HMS *Surprise* (FSW 2).

HMS Belette, 18-gun brig-sloop, was launched in 1806 and wrecked off Denmark in November 1812 with the loss of all but five hands. 'Belette' is French for 'weasel.'

Bell, John

A bosun's mate in HMS *Sophie* (M&C 6).

Belle-Poule

A French ship referred to by Admiral Parr that had been taken in 1778 (HMS 1). Later she appears as a 40-gun frigate in Admiral Linois' squadron (HMS 6,9) and, many years later still, she is compared by Jack Aubrey to HMS *Pyramus* (COM 3).

*Admiral Parr's 36-gun Belle-Poule was launched in 1765, taken by the Royal Navy in 1780 and sold in 1801. Her 38-gun French successor—which served with *Linois in 1804 under her Captain Bruilhac—was launched in 1802 and, in 1806, was captured by the Royal Navy in the South Atlantic; she became a troopship in 1814, a prison ship in 1815 and was sold in 1818. 'Belle poule'—literally 'pretty hen'—is French slang for a 'racy girl.'*

Bellerophon

A member of a criminal gang connected to the Duke of Habachtsthal (COM 4).

Bellerophon, HMS

A ship at Port Mahon (M&C 1), Captain Bennet (M&C 11), often subsequently referred to in the se-

ries (HMS 11; IM 1; NC 7; WDS 7). Cumby had served in her at the Battle of Trafalgar (FSW 1) and Jack Aubrey had served in her both as a Midshipman (COM 1,5) and, in 1797, as a Lieutenant (LM 4). Amongst mariners, she is sometimes referred to as the '*Billy Ruffian*' (NC 5).

*HMS Bellerophon, 74-gun, was launched in 1786 and in 1794 fought in *Howe's great victory at the Battle of the Glorious First of June. In 1798 she fought in *Nelson's victory at the Nile under Henry d'Esterre Darby, who was still her Captain at the time of M&C, 1800–1801. Mr *Cumby was her First Lieutenant at Trafalgar in 1805, assuming command when his then Captain John Cook was killed, and in 1815 she was the ship to whose Captain Frederick Maitland *Buonaparte surrendered at La Rochelle after his flight from Waterloo. Bellerophon was reduced to a prison ship in 1815, renamed HMS Captivity in 1824 and sold in 1836. She was named for the Greek mythical hero who, riding his winged horse *Pegasus, slew the monster Chimera.*

Belling

A Post Captain or Commander, a protégé of Admiral Drury (FW 1).

Bellingham, Mrs

A friend of Edward, Clarissa Oakes' childhood 'guardian' (C/T 6).

Bellona, HMS

A 74-gun that Commodore Jack Aubrey is to have as his pennant-ship for the expeditions to Africa and Ireland, with Tom Pullings made Post as her Captain (COM 2+). She later continues as Jack's ship on the Brest blockade (YA 1+; HD 1,2), for a time under the temporary command of Captain Jenkins whilst Jack attends Parliament (YA 1–4). Following Buonaparte's abdication, she is sent home to be paid off (YA 10).

*HMS Bellona, 74-gun, was launched in 1760, and in 1801 took part in *Nelson's victory at the Battle of Copenhagen under her Captain Thomas Boulden Thompson (1766?–1828; died in the rank of Vice Admiral). Named for the Roman goddess of war, Bellona was broken up at Woolwich in September 1814 (N.B., see also Bellone # 1 below).*

Bellone

1: a 34-gun Bordeaux privateer, Captain Dumanoir, that takes the *Lord Nelson* Indiaman with Aubrey, Maturin and Pullings aboard (PC 5+). Pursued a little later by Aubrey in his HMS *Polychrest*, she runs aground and capsizes (PC 9).

*Bellone was launched in 1797 and soon became famous for both her commerce raiding and fighting abilities; she took Lord Nelson off Brest in August 1803. In July 1806 (giving weight to *Harte's doubting that Jack *Aubrey had in fact destroyed her!) she was intercepted off the coast of Ceylon by the 74-gun HMS Powerful. The British ship's dismal standard of gunnery allowed Bellone to fight her for two hours, inflicting significant damage, before being* *forced to strike. Taken into the Royal Navy as HMS Bellona (the same name as the co-existing 74-gun noticed above), she was re-named HMS *Blanche in 1809 and broken up in 1814.*

2: a new French 40-gun frigate said by Maturin to be intended for service in the Indian Ocean (TMC 1+), where she soon arrives under her Captain Duperré, capturing HMS *Victor* and the Portuguese heavy frigate *Minerva* (TMC 3,5). During the Battle of Port South East she is one of the many ships to run aground, emerging victorious none the less (TMC 7). Later in the campaign she is rumoured to have been disabled at Mauritius by disaffected Papists or Royalists (TMC 10).

Bellone, 38-gun, was launched in 1803 and taken by the Royal Navy at the fall of Mauritius in December 1810; re-named HMS Juno in the following year, she was broken up in 1817. Bellona was the Roman goddess of war.

Belvidera, HMS

A frigate blockading Boston (FW 5) into which Jack Aubrey later hopes to be appointed (SM 4).

HMS Belvidera was launched in 1809, sent for harbour service in 1846 and finally broken up as late as 1906. She was named for the tragic Venetian heroine of Thomas Otway's (1652–1685) popular, often revived play Venice Preserv'd.

Ben

1: a porter at Black's club (LM 4).
2: an aboriginal servant lent by Blaxland to Martin and Maturin (NC 10).

Benbow, HMS

A ship in which John Bullock had served, losing his leg in an action (SM 1).

HMS Benbow, 74-gun, was not launched until early 1813, only a very little before SM is set; she was sent for harbour service in 1848, made a coal-hulk in 1859, sold in 1892 and broken up in 1895. She was named for Vice-Admiral John Benbow (1653–1702), a brave, enterprising but very fiery-tempered commander of a former age. In a four day fight off Jamaica with a French squadron he was first deserted by several of his discontented Captains (two of whom were later shot and two of whom were dismissed the service) and then mortally wounded in the leg, dying on shore a few months later.

Benckendorf

A European scientist at Maturin's lecture in Paris (SM 5).

Benda

A composer played by Aubrey and Maturin (WDS 3; YA 5), a member of a larger family of musicians (COM 6).

The Bohemian Benda family produced at least five composers and performers of considerable reputation. Aubrey and Maturin are most likely to have played the violin and cello works for which two of the family were especially

known, Georg, or Jiři, Benda (1722–95) and his son, Friedrich Ludwig (1752–92).

Bénévent, Prince de
see **Talleyrand-Périgord**

Beni Khoda

A Bedouin tribesman met by Aubrey in northern Egypt (TH 5).

Bennelong

A drunken aboriginal, asked to demonstrate the boomerang to Maturin and Martin (NC 10).

This is possibly a reference to Bennelong (1773?–1814), an Iora tribesman who, according to *Hughes, was the first Australian black to learn English and associate with the white men. He visited England from 1792 to 1795, the first aboriginal to do so. Eventually driven to the margins of both his own and the settlers' societies, he was later given a small, solitary hut on what is now Bennelong Point (the site of the Sydney Opera House). His sad story is used by Hughes to show the pernicious effects of white culture and dark rum on the native Australian population.

Bennet

The Captain of HMS *Aurore*, met by Maturin and Aubrey at Molly Harte's party (M&C 6). He later commands HMS *Bellerophon* (M&C 11).

Bennet or Bennett, Harry

The Captain of HMS *Berwick*, formerly of HMS *Theseus*, who had dallied with his lover Miss Serracapriola in Sicily (IM 5). He later gives the parson Mr Martin leave of absence, finding that having him aboard cramps his amorous propensities (TH 4). Later still his attentions have been transferred to a Miss Perkins (FSW 1,2).

Bennett

A Master's Mate in HMS *Diane* (TGS 5), very severely injured in the island battle (NC 1,2). He nevertheless makes a recovery and later serves in HMS *Nutmeg of Consolation* (NC 4,6).

Bentham

1: a Captain whose 'foolish' court-martial is referred to by Jack Aubrey (M&C 2).
2: the social philosopher (HMS 2; FW 4), whose acquaintance Ellis claims (M&C 8) and to whose theories on punishment Paulton refers (NC 9).

Jeremy Bentham (1748–1832) was the great jurist and political scientist who wrote, amongst many other works, the Defence of Usury *of 1787, the strongly utilitarian* Introduction to Principles of Morals and Legislation *of 1789, and the* Panopticon Letters *of 1791 on the improvement of prison discipline. In accordance with his principles, Bentham left his body to science and his fully dressed skeleton still sits in a glass case in the lobby of University College, London. His brother, Sir Samuel Bentham (1757–1831), was a distinguished naval architect and en-*

gineer who served both King *George III and the Tsar (or *Czar) of Russia.

Bentinck

1: a naval Captain famous for innovations in sail and rigging arrangements (TMC 1; IM 3; COM 4).

John Albert Bentinck (1728–1775) was made Post in 1758. An energetic and innovative sailor, he introduced: a) 'Bentinck triangular storm-courses' for square-rigged ships (these fell out of favour in the Royal Navy, being replaced by storm staysails, but remained popular in the U.S. forces); b) the 'Bentinck boom,' used both to spread and quickly raise the foot of the main foresail in brigs and, especially, whalers, greatly enhancing visibility forward; and c) 'Bentinck shrouds' that reinforced the usual mast supports in heavy weather. His son, William (d.1813), also served with great distinction in the Royal Navy, being made Post in 1783, promoted Rear Admiral in 1808 and Vice Admiral in 1810: there is a fine portrait of the pair in O'BRIAN's Men of War.

2: a cavalry Major in Batavia (NC 3).

Bentinck, Sophie

A neighbour of the Williams family engaged to George Simpson (PC 3).

Bentley

1: Maturin's bookseller (HMS 4).

2: a man referred to, with Porson, as a model of prodigious learning (RM 3).

Richard Bentley (1662–1742) was a famous polymath, scholar and critic who became Master of Trinity College, Cambridge.

3: *Surprise's* carpenter, who, injured during the attack on *Diane* (LM 3, 6), recovers and resumes his duties (TGS 2; C/T 1–6; WDS 3,10).

4: the coachman in the Aubrey household (COM 3).

Benton

The Purser of HMS *Leopard* (DI 3+), one of those who follow Mr Grant in abandoning ship after the collision with an iceberg (DI 9; FW 1).

Beppo

A thug employed in Malta by the French agent Lesueur (TH 10).

Berceau

A French 22-gun corvette in Linois' squadron that engages HMS *Surprise* and is heavily damaged. She makes sufficient repairs to engage in the attack on the China Fleet shortly afterwards (HMS 9).

*Berceau, 22-gun, was launched in 1794 and served until 1804 in *Linois' Indian Ocean squadron under her Commander Halgon; her fate thereafter is unknown. 'Berceau' is French for a cradle or cot.*

Berenice, HMS

A decrepit 64-gun ship commanded by Heneage Dundas (WDS 10; COM 1; YA 2,3).

The only HMS Berenice ever in the Royal Navy was a paddle sloop that served from 1836 to 1866, when she was accidentally burned in the Persian Gulf. Berenice was the Greek/Egyptian goddess representing benefaction.

Beresford, Lieutenant

The promotion-seeking, well-connected subject of a letter from Lord St Vincent to Sir Charles Grey (PC 3).

*The Lieutenant is probably intended as a member of the great Irish family of the same name (see *Beresfords, the), although only Sir John Poo Beresford (1766–1844) served in the Royal Navy of the time and he had been made Post in 1795. In 1828 Sir John rose to full Admiral.*

Beresfords, the

An Irish family referred to by Maturin (M&C 5).

The Beresford family were variously Earls of Tyrone and Marquesses of Waterford, supplying over the centuries many admirals and generals to the Crown.

Berkeley

An attaché to Mr Stanhope (HMS 6,8).

Berkely or Berkeley

The 'Honourable Berkely' is a former Captain of Tom Pullings (PC 5) and, as Admiral Berkeley, is a friend and admirer of Jack Aubrey (IM 1).

*The reference is probably to be Sir George Cranfield Berkeley (1753–1818), a younger son of the 4th Earl of Berkeley and hence an 'Honourable'; he was also a cousin of Admiral Augustus *Keppel. Made Post in 1780, he commanded HMS *Marlborough at *Howe's Battle of the Glorious First of June, receiving an incapacitating head-wound during the action. Unfounded, though persistent, rumours accused him of 'skulking in the cockpit' during the rest of the fight and, in 1794, Berkeley won substantial libel damages against a newspaper for repeating the old tale. Promoted Rear Admiral in 1799 and Vice Admiral in command of the North American station from 1805 to 1807, Berkeley's orders in that latter year resulted in the controversial attack on USS *Chesapeake by *Humphreys' HMS *Leopard. In his final sea-command, the Portuguese station from 1808 to 1812, his reputation as an energetic innovator from time to time exasperated the very conservative General *Wellington, who complained that the Admiral often seemed unable to support the Peninsula campaign by simple, well-tried methods alone; he did, however, commend Berkeley's zeal and declined an offer to have him replaced. After his retirement, Berkeley rose by seniority to Admiral of the White in 1814.*

Bernadotte

A man unfavourably compared to Judas by Sir Joseph Blaine and said to be hardly an ally of Britain at all (SM 6). His position is also thought to be at risk from the legitimate Swedish Royal family, the Vasas (LM 4).

*Jean-Baptiste Bernadotte (1763–1844) was one of the French army's most distinguished commanders, rising in 1794 from humble origins as a private in the Royal Marines to the rank of General. Although his personal relationship with *Buonaparte was always uneasy, his bril-*

liant roles in the victories of Piave (1797), Austerlitz (1805) and Halle (1806) brought him political office, important commands and high honours. Briefly Minister of War in 1799, he was promoted a Marshall of France in 1804 and created Duke of Ponte Corvo in 1806. In 1807–1808 Bernadotte commanded the Northern Armies against Sweden, a campaign for which his unusually humane conduct both in the field and in manoeuvre through civilian areas won him admiration in Stockholm. In 1810, on the death of the *Vasa family heir to King Charles XIII, the Swedish Diet offered Bernadotte the succession. This he accepted, gaining Buonaparte's consent even though the Emperor had recently been publicly critical of his conduct at the Battle of Wagram (1809). However, as Swedish Crown Prince, Bernadotte pursued policies opposed to Buonaparte, going to war against France in 1813 and leading armies in the victories at Gross-Beeren, Dennewicz and Leipzig. In 1814 he led the conquest of Norway, which then became a possession of the Swedish Crown, and in 1818 succeeded to the throne as King Carl XIV. The current Swedish Royal Family are Bernadotte's indirect descendants.

Bernard, Inigo

A Barcelona merchant who has become chief assistant to the Spanish naval intelligence agency and who now accompanies Stephen Maturin on a mission to France (YA 5,7).

Bernardino

A relative of Father O'Higgins living in Chile (WDS 8).

Berry

1: a Midshipman in HMS Charwell (PC 1).
Two young Midshipman Berrys are possible: John (d.1809), who was made Lieutenant shortly before Trafalgar in 1805, being wounded on HMS *Revenge in the battle; and William, made Lieutenant in 1803, but executed in 1807 for reasons tantalisingly not recorded in SYRETT & DiNARDO.
2: the Captain of HMS Jason, one of the judges at the trial of the HMS Hermione mutineers (RM 2).
The name may be inspired by Sir Edward Berry (1768–1831), known as one of *Nelson's 'Band of Brothers' having served in 1797 as the First Lieutenant of his HMS *Captain at the Battle of Cape *St Vincent. Made Post shortly after that great victory, Berry was knighted in 1798 after being Nelson's *Flag Captain at the Battle of the Nile in HMS *Vanguard. In 1805 he commanded HMS *Agamemnon at Trafalgar and in 1821 rose to Rear Admiral. However, Berry never commanded an HMS *Jason and by the time of RM (c.1813) he was commanding ships-of-the-line, which did not serve on the West Indies station where the trial takes place. See also *Foudroyant, HMS, *Généreux and *Leander, HMS.
3: a seaman in Ringle (HD 8).

Bertie, Admiral and Mrs

The Commander-in-Chief of the Cape Station (TMC 1+), a man whose wife is most anxious for him to get a baronetcy (TMC 1,3); on account of his somewhat grasping nature, Jack Aubrey calls him 'Sir Giles Overreach' (TMC 3). Having given Jack an independent command to take Réunion and Mauritius (TMC 3), Bertie then arrives, at the very last, to supersede him and accept the glory for himself (TMC 10). From a residual sense of guilt, he sends Jack — rather than one of his own relatives or protégés — home to England with the great news of the victory (TMC 10).
Sir Albemarle Bertie (1755–1824) was made Post in 1782, promoted Rear Admiral in 1804, Vice Admiral in 1808 and Admiral in 1814. In 1792, as Captain of the 74-gun HMS Edgar, he had helped take a French privateer laden with an enormous treasure, his share of the prize money making him rich for life. For his accomplishments at Mauritius in December 1810, he was in 1812 given a baronetcy; however, DNB does not record whether he ever married.

Bertolucci's

A Buonapartist ship-yard in the Adriatic, destroyed by fire as a result of Maturin's activities (HD 5).

Bertrand

A French politician, nominally out of office, yet still very influential through a private organisation (SM 10).
This may be a reference to Antoine-François, Marquis de Bertrand de Molleville (1744–1818), a politician who had served as the head of *Louis XVI's secret police and who continued similar activities whilst in exile in England from 1791 to 1814, in which latter year he returned with *Louis XVIII to France, living out his days in retirement.

Berwick or Berwick, HMS

1: a French 74-gun, captured from the Royal Navy some years previously (PC 4; HMS 2; FW 9).
HMS Berwick, 74-gun, was launched in 1775. In 1795, whilst jury-rigged and hardly capable of making sail, she was captured by three French frigates, her newly appointed Captain Adam *Littlejohn being the only man killed in the brief fight. As le Berwick she was re-taken from the French at the Battle of Trafalgar in 1805 but wrecked in the storm that followed the great victory.
2: HMS Berwick, the ship that Mr Martin is to join as Parson under Captain Harry Bennet (IM 5). She is known as a swift sailer (IM 8; FSW 1,2).
HMS Berwick, 74-gun, was launched in 1809 and broken up in 1821. The Berwicks (pronounced 'Berrick') were all named for a town on the English/Scottish border.

Bess

1: A horse owned by George Herapath (FW 8).
2: A spaniel at Woolcombe House (YA 2).

Bessie

The Aubreys' Welsh cook/housekeeper who resigns in protest at her treatment by Mrs Williams (TMC 1).

Betterton

Admiral Lord Barmouth's Flag Lieutenant (HD 10).

Bettesworth, Captain
The Captain of HMS *Curieux* (YA 3).
> *Captain George Edmund Bryon Bettesworth was made Post in 1805 but killed in action on his frigate HMS Tartar in 1808, some years before* YA *is set.*

Betty
A serving girl at a low pot-house in Dover whose advances Aubrey rejects (PC 10).

Beveridge
The senior Captain in Admiral Lord Stranraer's offshore squadron (YA 9).

Bevis of Hampton
A romantic hero referred to by Maturin (TH 9).
> Bevis of Hampton *was a popular medieval romance based on a 12th century French chanson entitled* Beuves de Hanstone. *The Countess of Southampton arranges for the murder of her husband the Earl by her secret lover, the future Emperor of Germany. Once the deed is done she sells her son Bevis into slavery and marries the Emperor. After many adventures in the East—where, amongst other things, he weds the daughter of the King of Arabia after converting her to Christianity—Bevis returns to England and takes his deadly revenge on his father's murderer.*

Bhonsli raja
A Mahratta chief (HMS 7).

Biela
A comet studied by Goodridge (PC 10).
> *The comet was discovered by the German astronomer Wilhelm, Baron von Biela (1782–1856), but not until 1826 (see also* *Encke*).*

'Big Buck'
An insulting reference to Jack Aubrey by Dr McAdam (TMC 10).

Bill
1: a quartermaster in HMS *Leopard* (DI 3).
2: a seaman in HMS *Surprise* (FSW 9; WDS 9).
3: *see* **Grimshaw, William or Bill**

Billings
One of Mr Stone's clerks (RM 1).

Billy, King
see **William III, King**

Billy, Prince
see **Clarence, Duke of**

Billy Ruffian, HMS
A ship into which the Master of *Alkmaar* had been pressed (NC 5).
> *'Billy Ruffian' was a common nick-name for HMS* *Bellerophon.

Bimbashi, the
see **Midat Bimbashi**

Bingham
A whaler who had once sailed with Mr Allen (FSW 3).

Birmingham, Father
An Irish priest who, together with Father Power, had accompanied Sam Panda to England in order to find Jack Aubrey, his father (RM 1).

Birnbaum
A medical authority cited to Maturin by Geary (WDS 6).

Bishop, the
A Roman Catholic bishop whose authentication of Pius VII's excommunication of Buonaparte is used by Maturin to suborn the strongly Catholic inhabitants of Mauritius, as well as the Irish emigré troops stationed there (TMC 9).

Blacas, Compte de
The chief advisor to Louis XVIII's exile court in England (SM 5), a cousin of d'Anglars (SM 11).
> *Pierre Louis Jean Casimir (1770–1839), Duc de Blacas d'Aulps, was a constant supporter of the* *Bourbon line, *serving in England as Minister of War to the exiled* *Louis XVIII *from 1800 onwards. During the frequent illnesses of the younger d'**Avaray, *Blacas assumed the role of Chief Minister.*

Black
A member of the barge-crew of Captain Baker's HMS *Iris*, chosen for his colour-related surname (FSW 2).

Black, Abel
A seaman in HMS *Bellona* injured in an accident (COM 8).

Blackburne, Dr
The Archbishop of York in Blaine's father's time, and said by him to have perhaps been a privateer on the Spanish main (LM 4).
> *Lancelot Blackburne (1658–1743) was ordained in 1681 and then spent an number of years in the West Indies, possibly on secret government service. In 1695, back in England, he became sub-Dean of Exeter Cathedral but in 1701 was forced to resign for a brief period when his enemies circulated rumours that, in his youth, he had become Chaplain on board a buccaneer. Although these stories dogged him all his life—and were given some credence by his infamously lusty life-style in England—Blackburne rose to Bishop of Exeter in 1717 and Archbishop of York in 1724.*

'Black Coat'
1: an elderly intelligence official at the British Admiralty (PC 3).
2: *see* **Palmer, Ellis**

'Black Dick'
see ***Howe, Admiral Lord**

'Black Frank'

An imaginary figure supposedly preferred by
Queeney Keith to her Catholic step-father (M&C
4).

Black Lopez

A servant, or possibly monk, at a Capuchin
monastery high in the Andes (WDS 9).

Black's

The fashionable London club of which Aubrey, Maturin and Blaine are members (RM 5+; LM 2,8;
TGS 4; C/T 6,9; COM 2,5,6; YA 1+).

Blackstone

1: a legal authority (FSW 2) and the author of the
    Commentaries (YA 2).
    *Sir William Blackstone (1723–1780) was Professor of Eng-
    lish Law at Oxford University from 1758 to 1766; his*
    Commentaries on the Laws of England *(1765–1769)
    were for many years the standard text on the historical de-
    velopment of the English legal system. However, the work
    was criticised by *Bentham, amongst many others, both for
    its lack of intellectual depth and for its avoidance of ques-
    tions of necessary future reform.*
2: the Dorsetshire hunt, referred to by Lieutenant
    Thomas Edwards (HD 1).

***Blackwater*, HMS**

A new frigate, still on the stocks, that Melville offers
to Jack Aubrey as a possible command. Jack, however, begs for an immediate sea-posting and is given
temporary command of HMS *Lively* (PC 12). Many
years later, *Blackwater* has eventually been launched
and is now being fitted out by Jack for the North
American station. However, both the machinations
of Andrew Wray and the political indiscretions of
General Aubrey work to deny him formal appointment to her (IM 1). Although Jack retains hopes for
the command (TH 4), having been freshly promised
the ship by Croker, the Admiralty First Secretary,
himself (TH 8), Stephen Maturin soon hears that
she has been given instead to a Captain Irby (TH
8), a final disappointment of which Jack later receives confirmation (TH 9; FSW 1).
    No HMS Blackwater *served in the Royal Navy until 1903.*

'Black Whiskers'
see **Griffiths, Captain**

Blagden, Colonel

An aide-de-camp to the Duke of Habachtsthal
(COM 2).

Blagrove, Jemmy

An acquaintance of Cecilia Williams (PC 1,3).

Blaine, Sir Joseph

Blaine, initially met simply as 'Sir Joseph,' is Dr
Stephen Maturin's principal contact in British naval
intelligence (PC 3). Also an entomologist — an enthusiasm he shares with the Doctor — and a bachelor of comfortable wealth (PC 14), he has risen
from very humble, working-class origins (RM 5).
Learning from Stephen that Spain is soon to enter
the war as an ally of France, the two plan the in-
terception of Bustamente's treasure squadron, Sir
Joseph arranging both for Jack Aubrey to participate
in the mission and Stephen, as a temporary Post
Captain, to take a share in any prize money (PC 14).
We next learn that Sir Joseph — initially surnamed
'Blain' before his usual 'Blaine' — is in fact the long-
serving Head of Naval Intelligence (HMS 1), intending soon to retire (HMS 4): as part of this
process he uses his influence to secure command of
HMS *Surprise* for Jack (HMS 4,6,7). Although he
carries through his resignation plan (TMC 3; DI 2),
he remains an important intelligence co-ordinator,
using Stephen — now a close friend — as one of his
most trusted agents (DI 2–10).
    Yet soon Sir Joseph resumes his old formal role,
with even greater powers than before (FW 1,4; SM
1–6). He tells Stephen of a mission to Grimsholm
in the Baltic (SM 4) and later entrusts the job to his
friend and Jack Aubrey (SM 6). He also lets slip
that he is contemplating marriage to a Miss Blenkinsop and is somewhat concerned for his fading
virility, although only about 50 (SM 4; *see note at
end of entry*): a minor medical problem is in fact
successfully treated by Stephen but he eventually
decides not to pursue the match (RM 5). Sir Joseph
remains as Stephen's main contact and confidant
during his and Jack's troubled, betrayed missions in
the Mediterranean (IM 4,5; TH 2,8). Later, concerned that Stephen's secret role may have been
compromised, he arranges for his friend and Jack to
go on a relatively minor mission to the South Seas
(FSW 1,5).
    On their return, Sir Joseph is still Head of Intel-
ligence (RM 1) but with his power much reduced
owing to curious political machinations in London
and France (RM 5). Later, he helps in the unsuccessful attempts to discovery exculpatory evidence
in Jack's prosecution for fraud, gradually discovering that the Captain's enemies may be closely linked
to his own and Stephen's (RM 7+). Blaine now
arranges political support for Stephen's plan to send
the disgraced Jack on an intelligence mission to Peru
(RM 8,9). Still trying to discover the source of high
level treason in the government, he is given the startling news by Stephen that his intelligence associate Andrew Wray, and his even more powerful
colleague Ledward, are in fact the suspects (RM 10).
After Wray and Ledward's exposure Sir Joseph is
restored to full power in his office and begins to
plan with Stephen how they might bring about
Jack's restoration to the Royal Navy: an attack on
the French frigate *Diane* is suggested as the best
course of action, especially as she is intended for a

competing mission to South America (LM 4+). Sir Joseph nevertheless remains puzzled and concerned at the enmity Stephen and Jack both still face in certain political quarters (LM 7).

Continuing as the Head of Naval Intelligence, Sir Joseph confirms his support for Stephen's mission to South America (TGS 1; NC 3,9; C/T 3+). However, when the Spanish — now allies again — learn of the scheme, it must be postponed (TGS 3). Intercepting Stephen in Lisbon, he offers the temporary, alternative task of intelligence advisor to Mr Fox's mission to Pulo Prabang (TGS 3+); an added bonus of this arrangement is that Sir Joseph is finally able to use his influence to help secure Jack's restoration to the Navy List (TGS 1–4). On the scientific front, Sir Joseph — almost certainly a Fellow of the Royal Society from before the beginning of the series — has at some point become President of the Entomological Society of London (C/T 6). Stephen eventually carries out the delayed Peruvian mission, yet it ends in fiasco and all agree that it would next time be better aimed at independence supporters in neighbouring Chile (WDS 8; COM 1).

Sir Joseph next asks Stephen to accompany Jack on a mission against the slave trade in West Africa and then to help thwart a French invasion of Ireland (COM 2+). In the continuing saga of betrayals in London, he tells Stephen that the patron of the now-dead traitors Wray and Ledward has been identified as the powerful Duke of Habachtsthal (COM 2), a man now pursuing revenge against his enemies, the Doctor included (COM 4+). After the Duke's exposure and suicide (COM 10), Sir Joseph obtains a long-overdue pardon for Stephen for his 1798 activities in Ireland (YA 1), his energies in this being enhanced by enthusiastic use of Stephen's coca leaves (YA 1+). With Stephen, he now stages an intelligence coup at home, catching the Spanish secret agent Diego Diaz in the act of burgling his house (YA 7). As peace with France finally arrives, Sir Joseph shares Stephen's fears for Jack Aubrey's career prospects and is influential in arranging his temporary attachment to the new Chilean navy, with Stephen as his political advisor (YA 7+; also HD 1,4,9,10).

> In SM 4 — notionally set in 1813 — Sir Joseph refers to a bottle of wine as being nata mecum consule Buteo, Latin for 'born with me, under Bute's consulate.' He has in mind here a line from *Horace, Odes III, where the poet dates both himself and a bottle of wine in the accustomed Roman manner of reference to a one-year term of political office: nata mecum consule Manlio. Blaine's little joke only works because John Stewart, 3rd Earl of Bute (see *Buteo), was Prime Minister of the United Kingdom for just twelve months in 1762–1763.

Blaine, Sir

Sir Joseph Blaine, as referred to by a number of Frenchmen (HMS 4; RM 10).

Blair

An author of sermons (COM 2).
> Hugh Blair (1718–1800) was a Scottish minister who, in 1762, became Professor of Rhetoric in the University of Edinburgh. His immensely popular sermons were published in five volumes from 1777 to 1801.

Blake

1: Miss Blake, Sophie Aubrey's tutor and governess when young (HMS 1).
2: a Lieutenant in HMS Caledonia, once a Midshipman under Jack Aubrey, who has invented a new carronade slide (FSW 1).

Blakeney, William

A young Midshipman in HMS Surprise, the son of Jack Aubrey's old shipmate Lord Garron (FSW 3+; RM 3).

Blanche, HMS

1: a ship that Jack Aubrey says was out-sailed by the French Bellone privateer (PC 6).
> HMS Blanche, 36-gun, was launched in 1800 and captured and burned by the French off Jamaica in 1805 whilst carrying dispatches to *Nelson's fleet.
2: a ship in which Admiral Mitchell had once been a Lieutenant (IM 4), whose Captain Sawyer had been broken for sodomy in 1796, and which had then been given to Captains Preston and Hotham (COM 9).
> For Mitchell either: a) HMS Blanche, 36-gun, launched as the French Blanche in 1766, captured by the Royal Navy in 1779 but lost in a hurricane in 1780; or b) her 32-gun replacement, launched in 1786 and rendered unserviceable in 1799 after repeatedly grounding on shoals in the Texel. *Sawyer, *Preston and *Hotham obviously commanded the latter ship.
3: a ship, Captain Robert Morley, newly arrived in England from the West Indies (COM 5).
> This HMS Blanche should be well known to Jack Aubrey, for she was the captured French privateer *Bellone that he had fought many years before.

Blanckley

1: the author of the Naval Expositor, referred to by Mr Scriven (PC 6).
> Thomas Riley Blankley (sic; dates unknown) published his Naval Expositor, an illustrated dictionary of sea-terms and techniques, in 1750; nothing is known of his life.
2: an elderly, deceased Master's Mate, late of the bomb-ketch HMS Carcass, whom Maturin has recently dissected (PC 12).

Blane

The author of Diseases of Seamen (M&C 2; HMS 5).
> Sir Gilbert Blane (1749–1834) was a distinguished Scottish doctor who became personal physician to Admiral Lord *Rodney. In 1780 he first went to sea with his client — a martyr to gout — and was soon appointed Physician to

the Fleet, a post in which he produced a remarkable improvement in the health of the men under the Admiral's command. In 1785 Blane first published his Observations on the Diseases of Seamen, *a very influential text that went into several expanded editions. Although after 1785 he had little direct contact with seamen, becoming instead a leading figure in London medical circles, Blane did serve on the Sick and Hurt Board from 1795 to 1802, during which time he pushed through the long-overdue issue to all ships of lemon-juice as an anti-scorbutic — a procedure long advocated by James *Lind — and a number of other practical health reforms. He was also consulted over the reforms of 1805 by which naval surgeons received very substantial improvements in their pay and conditions (indeed, up until that date they had not even enjoyed quarterdeck status). In 1812 Blane was knighted for services to the Royal Navy — the first doctor ever so honoured — and throughout his long career continued to advocate good health at sea as a vital military consideration: he often asserted that, had his reforms not been put into place, Britain would have run out of seamen long before *Buonaparte could finally have been defeated.*

'Blank,' Mr

A device used to indicate any one of several, unnamed, mutual acquaintances (C/T 4).

Blaxland

A member of the Royal Society met by Maturin and Martin in New South Wales (NC 10).

Gregory Blaxland (1771–1853), a friend of Sir Joseph *Banks, was a prosperous Kent farmer who emigrated to New South Wales in 1805–1806, being, according to Robert *Hughes, 'the first settler of unimpeachable respectability.' Even so, the brothers John (1769–1845; in NSW from 1807) and Gregory Blaxland were both signatories to the petition of 1808 calling for Governor *Bligh's arrest. Later, Gregory, accompanied by William Wentworth and William Lawson, made in 1813 the first crossing by a colonist of the Blue Mountains into the Australian interior.

Blenkinsop

1: Miss Blenkinsop, Sir Joseph Blaine's intended wife (SM 6), later rejected (RM 5).
2: a Foreign Office official, an acquaintance of Aubrey (RM 4).
3: an English political agent in Algiers (HD 10).

Blew, John

A seaman in HMS *Edinburgh* whom Captain Baker of HMS *Iris* would like for his barge-crew on account of his colourful surname (FSW 2).

Bligh, William

An Admiral, the head of the British administration in Australia, who has been deposed in a mutiny, a situation Jack Aubrey is sent in HMS *Leopard* to resolve (DI 1+; NC 2,3,8,10). Bligh is known to Jack as an officer commended by Nelson for his role in the Battle of Camperdown (DI 1) and as a fine practical seaman and navigator, legendary in the service for his open boat journey after the HMS *Bounty*

mutiny (DI 8; TGS 10; WDS 10). Jack's friend Captain Peter Heywood, who had served as a Midshipman in *Bounty* and played a role in the mutiny, seems to regard Bligh as a fool rather than villain, but clearly is somewhat uneasy in discussing the matter at all (DI 1; *but also see* TGS 2 *where Bligh is described as an odious man*). By the time the long-delayed Jack arrives in Australia, the rebellion has already been in some way resolved (FW 1).

William Bligh (1754–1817) earned his reputation as a prime seaman and navigator whilst sailing Master of *Cook's HMS *Resolution during its final circumnavigation of 1775–1779. He was commissioned Lieutenant in 1781, made Post in 1790, promoted Rear Admiral in July 1810 (though this was not officially gazetted until his return to England in August 1811), and rose to Vice Admiral in 1814. In 1801, sponsored by Sir Joseph *Banks, he was elected a Fellow of the Royal Society. In 1787, whilst still a Lieutenant, Bligh had been given command of the small armed transport HMS *Bounty, with a mission of taking live breadfruit seedlings from Tahiti to the West Indies (where it was hoped they would provide cheap food for the slave population). However, his harsh tongue and capricious command techniques, in combination with the many temptations of life in the Pacific Islands, led many of his officers (led by acting Lieutenant Fletcher *Christian) and crew to mutiny. Bligh was seized whilst Bounty was sailing off the Friendly Islands and set adrift in an open boat with 18 other men and only a very few provisions. In one of the most famous feats of navigation in the annals of the Royal Navy, Bligh took the boat and its crew 3,500 miles to Timor without the loss of a life: in doing so he won his promotion to Post rank. He now dedicated the next few years to justifying his role in the Bounty affair and to supporting the hunting down, prosecution, and imprisonment or execution of those mutineers who could be found. Yet a number of influential sea-officers clearly took a very much less favourable view of Bligh's conduct and, under their patronage, several mutineers won pardons and thereafter enjoyed successful careers in the Royal Navy (see *Heywood, Peter). Bligh, too, continued a sea-career, playing distinguished parts in the battles of Camperdown (1797; see *Duncan) and Copenhagen (1801), where he won *Nelson's praise for his conduct. At the Nore mutinies of 1797, Bligh was among the last of the commanders to be ejected from their ships and was not amongst those whose conduct was complained of by the mutineers: indeed he was employed by Nepean (see *Evan, Sir) as a member of the group of officers who visited such ships as would receive them, attempting to recall the men to their duty. Yet, in 1804, Bligh was court-martialed on charges of foul language and tyranny brought by Second Lieutenant Frazier of his HMS Warrior, and, although acquitted, was admonished by Admiral Sir Charles Cotton to pay attention to the correctness of his language to fellow officers, whether junior or not. In 1805 he was appointed Governor and Captain-General of New South Wales, at that time traditionally a Royal Navy post. His vigorous opposition — as ordered by London — to the local rum trade and his clumsy attempts to impose his personal authority both led to another mutiny against his command and, in 1808, the local army officers deposed him (with considerable civilian support), even confining him for a year (see *Macarthur, Captain). In early 1810, *having already left for England, he was formally super-seded by the soldier *Macquarie (N.B., O'Brian delays these events by two years or so for plot purposes). Bligh saw no further service, but spent his time and energy attempt-ing to vindicate his administration in Australia.*

Blodge
An ex-shipmate of Aubrey in HMS *Orion* (HMS 8).
The name may not be intended as real, 'Blodge' being a common British usage for 'some typical, though unnamed, person.'

Bloggs, Joe
An imaginary prize-fighter referred to by Bonden (YA 3).

Blücher
An Allied general now in the Low Countries, marching to join up with Wellington's forces against those of the newly restored Buonaparte (HD 1).
Gebhard Leberect von Blücher (1742–1819), Prince of Wahlstadt, was a native of Mecklenburg who first served in the Swedish cavalry in campaigns against Prussia. He swopped sides in 1760 and served as a Prussian hussar until 1773, when he retired to life as a farmer. Recalled to Prussian service in 1786, on the outbreak of war with France in 1793 he immediately established a dashing rep-utation, rising to Major-General in the following year. During the peace of 1795–1806 Blücher remained vio-lently opposed to *Buonaparte, welcoming the resumption of hostilities in that latter year. However, the rapid crush-ing of the Prussian armies by the French (with Blücher himself being forced to surrender to *Bernadotte) again sent him into a long retirement until hostilities re-opened in early 1813. Taking command of the Prussian armies, and soon promoted Field Marshall, Blücher inflicted a se-ries of defeats on some of Napoleon's better generals and led the invasion of France at the very end of 1813, even-tually reaching Paris (with other Allied forces) and forc-ing the Emperor's first abdication. Blücher, his health long suspect, now prepared a final retirement from the army, but recalled himself once more when Napoleon escaped from Elba for his final 'Hundred Days.' The old warrior suffered a defeat at Buonaparte's hands at Ligny, and was himself injured in the battle, but rallied his forces to join *Wellington on the field of Waterloo two days later, ar-riving in the late afternoon and forcing the French re-serves to commit in defence of their flank and rear. When Wellington thereupon broke the Emperor's unsupported centre, Blücher's Prussians led the pursuit of the shattered French army southwards. The Marshall, long known and loved as 'Old Forwards' by his men, was created Prince of Wahlstadt when Buonaparte abdicated a few days later and now, at long last, retired from a life of campaign. See also **Prussia, King of**

'Blue Breeches'
An author met in the English countryside by Ma-turin (LM 1).

Blue Edward
A Malay seaman in HMS *Lively* (PC 14).

'Blue Peter'
The name recalled for Diana Villiers' great diamond by Maturin, who first hazards it may have been called either Nabob or Mogul and relates that it had supposedly been appropriated by a sailor in the time of Aurangzeb (SM 3,5; *N.B., the original name of the stone was in fact the *Begum:* FW 6). Stephen later learns that Diana has used the gem as a bribe to se-cure his safety and freedom from French captivity: yet, in the political deal that eventually does secure his release, the future restitution of the stone is promised by Duhamel (SM 11). When this promise is kept (RM 10 LM 4), Stephen is able to return the gem to Diana, by now his wife (LM 9; TGS 1). Later still, Diana puts it into pawn to alleviate tem-porary family poverty (YA 6,8). Somehow recov-ered, the great stone is buried with her following her death in a coaching accident (HD 7).

Blyth
The Purser of HMS *Diane* (TGS 4+) who dies of a sudden heart attack as the shipwreck island is at-tacked by Dyak pirates (NC 2,3,4).

Boadicea, HMS
A 38-gun frigate, initially commanded by the ail-ing Charles Loveless, of which Commodore Jack Aubrey is given command for the campaign in the Indian Ocean (TMC 1+). When Jack temporarily moves to the elderly HMS *Raisonable* as his pennant ship, Captain Eliot assumes command (TMC 3) but Jack is soon back on board taking very valuable prizes (TMC 5,9; DI 3). Later *Boadicea* is on the Brest blockade under a Captain Mitchell (SM 9; *also* LM 8).
HMS Boadicea, *38-gun, was launched in 1797 and bro-ken up in 1858. The 1809–1810 campaign for Rodriguez, Réunion and Mauritius was led by Commodore (eventu-ally Admiral Sir) Josias Rowley (1765–1842) in both HMS* Boadicea *and *Raisonable.* Boadicea *(or Bonduca, Boudicca), the Queen of the Iceni in Eastern Britain and a leader of campaigns against the Roman occupation, committed suicide following a heavy defeat in 61 AD.*

Boanerges
A reference to the power of Canning's singing (PC 8).
'Boanerges' is Greek for 'a vociferous orator' and is used in the New Testament as a name for the Apostles *James and *John, both fiery zealots for their faith.

Bob
1: a carpenter's mate *in* HMS *Leopard* (DI 5).
2: an assistant in a silversmith's shop (RM 6).
3: a seaman in *Surprise* (C/T 9).

Boccanegra
A ship-builder of Sicilian origin with a yard on the Adriatic coast (HD 5).

Boccherini

An Italian composer, a perpetual favourite of Aubrey and Maturin (M&C 1,11; PC 7; HMS 6,9,10,11; C/T 3; WDS 2,3,4,10).

Ridolfo Luigi Boccherini (1743–1805) was famed as a virtuoso cellist and instrumental composer in a style similar to that of *Haydn. Having held important musical positions in Vienna and Madrid, from about 1789 he lacked a major patron and, after 1798, lived in poverty and obscurity.

Body, William

A coroner's assistant in London (RM 7).

Boethius

The author of *De Consolatione Philosophae* (PC 4; FSW 7).

Anicius Manlius Severinus Boethius (475?–525) was a Roman author, statesman and neoplatonic philosopher. He held office under the Emperor Theodoric the Goth, but was eventually tried and executed for involvement in a political conspiracy. His famous On the Consolation of Philosophy *was written in prison, shortly before his death.*

Boguslavsky

A member of the barge crew in HMS *Surprise* (HMS 6).

Bolt

An injured seaman *in HMS Lively* (PC 14).

Bolter

The owner of a debtors' gaol in Portsmouth (HMS 4).

Bolton

1: a seaman in HMS *Polychrest* whom Jack Aubrey saves from drowning — the 22nd or 23rd such man he says he has rescued — (PC 8), but who later conceives a great jealousy for other similarly rescued men (DI 4). He serves in Corbett's HMS *Néréide* before rejoining Jack in HMSS *Raisonable* and *Boadicea* (TMC 3,6). Mrs Bolton, in England, is said to be in a state of delicate health (TMC 6).

2: a Captain who has invented a new type of jury-mast (IM 3).

3: an elderly member of the Royal Society (HD 3).
Matthew Boulton (sic; 1728–1809) was an engineering member of the Royal Society, a colleague of the great James *Watt in his development of steam-power. Boulton also designed machinery for the manufacture of coins, supplying his presses to the Royal Mints of several European powers.

Bombay

A transport ship at Réunion (TMC 7).
A Bombay did serve as part of Commodore Josiah Rowley's squadron in the taking of the Indian Ocean islands but nothing is otherwise known of her.

Bombay, Governor of

The administrator at whose residence Envoy Stanhope tries to recover his shattered health (HMS 7).

Bombay, HMS

According to Barret Bonden, a 40-gun, Indian-built frigate in which his cousin George had once sailed (TMC 9). Witnessed from a small boat by Bonden and Stephen Maturin, she is engaged and taken by *Vénus* and *Victor* but later re-taken by her crew when *Vénus* is captured by HMS *Boadicea* (TMC 9).

The ship was launched in 1793 in India and purchased by the Royal Navy in 1805 as HMS Bombay, *38-gun. Renamed HMS* Ceylon *in 1808, it was under this name she fought in the Mauritius campaign of 1810 (as accurately described in TMC). In the first encounter, her Captain Charles Gordon was killed along with his Master, William Oliver. Her crew were then led in re-taking their ship by Lieutenant Philip Gibbon, accompanied by General Sir John *Abercrombie and his staff. Later in the campaign, she was briefly commanded by James *Tomkinson. Ceylon was sold in 1857. The HMS* Bombay *of the time was a 74-gun launched in 1808, re-named HMS* Blake *in 1819, sent for harbour service in 1828 and broken up in 1857; she played no part in the Indian Ocean campaign described.*

Bombay Castle

An East Indiaman in Muffit's China Fleet, protected by HMS *Surprise* from Admiral Linois' French squadron (HMS 9), that later calls at Madeira on her way to England (HMS 11).

The Bombay Castle, *1200 tons, made 6 round trips from India to England between 1792 and 1804, her final year of service. The action is based on the defence of an Honourable East India Company merchant fleet against *Linois' attack in February 1804; however, no Royal Navy ship was present during the fight, the squadron being organised by the senior Master, Nathaniel Dance of *Earl Camden. On this occasion Archibald Hamilton was* Bombay Castle's *Master.*

Bonaparte

see **Buonaparte or Bonaparte, Napoleon,** *or*
see **Buonapartes, the**

Bonden, Barret

Barret Bonden is Jack Aubrey's coxswain in almost all his commands. First met in HMS *Sophie*, he is a member of the boat crew (M&C 6,7), captain of the maintop and Captain's coxswain, said to be unusually young for this latter role (M&C 8). Jack soon offers to rate him Midshipman but he declines in favour of his better-educated young cousin, George Lucock (M&C 8; *Bonden's first name is here given as Barret, but, for some curious reason, he is called 'George' by the ship's crew a little later:* M&C 9). As coxswain, Bonden is alongside Jack when he takes *Cacafuego* (M&C 10). He then follows his Captain ashore as a servant (PC 1+) until joining his HMS *Polychrest*, again as coxswain (PC 7–11): at one point Jack refers to having saved him from drowning some time previously (PC 9). Bonden later follows Jack into HMSS *Lively* (PC 12; HMS

2,3) and *Surprise* (HMS 4+). Here, Stephen Maturin finds Bonden can read but not write and starts to give him lessons (HMS 4,6; *N.B. Stephen later recalls teaching Bonden to read on HMS* Sophie*: YA 4*). Some years later, when he is given HMS *Boadicea* after a spell ashore, Jack is without his usual coxswain (*see* ***Moon**) as Bonden is serving, with Preserved Killick, under Captain Heneage Dundas in the West Indies (TMC 3+). During this intervening period he has also served in HMS *Druid* under Philip Broke (SM 4; **Broke commanded her from mid-1805 to mid-1806*) and perhaps also on HMSS *Ajax* (FW 3) and *Isis* (IM 10). Hearing of Jack's being back at sea, Bonden transfers to the harsh Captain Corbett's east-bound HMS *Néréide* and, aboard this ship, is flogged for a trifling offense, his first ever such punishment (TMC 3). Afraid that Corbett will not allow him to transfer to Jack's ship at the Cape, he seeks Stephen Maturin's assistance in letting his Captain know of his predicament: Jack then arranges his transfer, as coxswain, to his new pennant-ship HMS *Raisonable* (TMC 3,4) and in due course back to HMS *Boadicea* (TMC 6). After this campaign Bonden follows Jack ashore as a servant at Ashgrove Cottage (DI 1) and then into HMS *Leopard* (DI 3+; FW 1). He accompanies his Captain as a passenger on HMS *La Flèche* (FW 1,2) and with him escapes in a small boat from the accidental burning of the ship before being picked up by HMS *Java* (FW 3). On this ship Bonden is the first man to identify the approaching USS *Constitution*, a ship that he had visited in the Mediterranean to see his friend Joe Warren (FW 3). When *Java* is defeated, it is this 'Boston Joe' that shackles his captured English friend (FW 4). Bonden is later put ashore in Brazil with all the prisoners, except Jack Aubrey and Stephen Maturin (FW 4). When he arrives home in England, he now joins Jack's new HMS *Acasta* to await the Captain's arrival from Canada. However, when Robert Kerr is appointed to the ship in Jack's place, as a courtesy he sends Bonden (and Killick) ashore to Sophie Aubrey (SM 4).

Bonden eventually follows Jack into HMS *Worcester* (IM 1–9) and than back into *Surprise* (IM 9–11; TH 1+; FSW 1+; RM 1,2) before again becoming a servant ashore in England (RM 6+). When Jack is tried and disgraced for fraud Bonden attends his Captain's public pillorying as part of his 'protection squad' (RM 9). He now joins his dismissed Captain on Stephen Maturin's private letter of marque, the old *Surprise* (LM 1+; TGS 1–3) and follows him into HMS *Diane* on his restoration to the Royal Navy (TGS 4+; NC 1–3). After *Diane* is wrecked he next serves with Jack in HMS *Nutmeg of Consolation* (NC 3–7) before they both rejoin *Surprise* (NC 8+; C/T 2–9; WDS 1+; COM 1). He

then moves upwards with Jack to HMS *Bellona*, a pennant-ship (COM 2+; YA 1+).

Ashore with the Captain at Woolcombe House, Bonden gets into a row with 'Black Evans,' Captain Griffith's game-keeper, and is challenged to a boxing match (YA 2). Although once champion of both the Mediterranean Fleet (YA 1) and the Portsmouth squadron (FSW 9), he is beaten in the brutal fight and badly injured (YA 3), only slowly making a full recovery (YA 3–5). When *Bellona* is paid off on Buonaparte's abdication Bonden returns with Jack to Woolcombe House as a servant (YA 10). After (presumably) travelling to Madeira with his Captain in *Surprise*, Bonden next follows Jack to his Commodore's appointment in HMS *Pomone* (HD 1) and then once again back into *Surprise* (HD 2–9). When she first engages Murad Reis' treasure-galley, Bonden is killed by a cannon-ball that strikes his own long-gun (HD 10).

Although born on HMS *Indefatigable* (DI 1), Barret Bonden was brought up in a tough part of central London (YA 4). At some point in his sea career he had served under Lord Nelson (DI 5), perhaps at the Battle of Cape St Vincent (TGS 7): indeed he is said to resemble Tom Allen, Nelson's coxswain (COM 9). In addition to his cousin George Lucock, Bonden's other, much older, cousin Joe Plaice is a frequent shipmate (*see* ***Plaice Joe or Joseph**), as is on one occasion another cousin, Miller (DI 4). Bonden's brother, Bob, serves in the flagship HMS *Irresistible* (RM 1,2).

Bonden, Robert or Bob
Barrett Bonden's brother, a sail-maker in HMS *Irresistible* (RM 1).

Bonelli
A tavern keeper in Malta (TH 10).

Boney
see **Buonaparte** or **Bonaparte, Napoleon**

Bonhomme Richard
A richly laden, French merchant-brig, taken in the Mediterranean by Jack Aubrey's HMS *Surprise* and then given to Lieutenant Rowan to take into Malta (IM 9–11). Later condemned as a lawful prize, she brings Jack a very useful sum of money, equivalent to at least ten year's pay (TH 3).

Booby
A reference by Aubrey to a clumsy seaman, possibly Fazackerley (TGS 9).

Booby, Captain J., RN
The name by which Aubrey refers to himself for having signed his marriage contract unread (SM 2).

Boodle's
A London club referred to by Aubrey (YA 2).

Booerhaave

The author of a medical text consulted by Maturin and Martin (WDS 4).

Herman Booerhaave (1668–1738), the Dutch physician and anatomist, was the most famous medical teacher and author of his time. At the University of Leyden he simultaneously held the Chairs of Medicine, Botany and Chemistry, as well as twice serving as Rector. In 1730 he was elected Fellow of the Royal Society, a British recognition of his immense international reputation.

Boreas, HMS

A ship in which Macdonald had once served (PC 9), later encountered in Admiral Thornton's Mediterranean fleet (IM 6).

Macdonald's HMS Boreas, 28-gun, was launched in 1774, turned into a slop-ship in 1797 and sold in 1802; her 20-gun replacement was launched in 1806 but wrecked in 1807. The 36-gun frigate Hanfrue was taken by the Royal Navy when the Danish fleet surrendered at Copenhagen in late 1807. At first to have been re-named Boreas, she was in fact taken into service as HMS Harfruen (sic), serving until being sold in 1814. In ancient Greece, Boreas was the north or north-east wind, very often portrayed as a horse.

Borée

A dull-sailing ship in Emeriau's Toulon fleet (IM 8).

Borée was launched in 1805 and served until 1825. For name derivation see Boreas, HMS above.

Borell

see **Borrell**

Borgia

A Pope despised by Maturin for his contribution to the colonisation of the New World (C/T 3).

Roderigo Lenzuoli Borgia y Doms (1431–1503) was a Spanish lawyer and soldier, a member of a wealthy and influential family. In 1455 his uncle became Pope Calixtus III, leading Roderigo to pursue a career—a very worldly one—in the Church: made Cardinal in 1456, he was in 1492 elected Pope Alexander VI. It was the ruthless attitude towards the acquisition and deployment of power by both Roderigo and his son, Cesare (1475?–1507), that provided the impetus for the writings of *Macchiavelli. Although before and during his reign Roderigo was infamous for cruelty, duplicity and high corruption, yet, in keeping with his times, he was also a patron of the arts on a lavish scale. Stephen Maturin's hatred of the Borgia Pope stems from his approval, in 1494, of the Treaty of Tordesillas between *Columbus's Spanish patrons and the King of Portugal, a pact that divided the New World into exclusive spheres of influence and put each monarch in control of the missionary churches in their colonies.

Borgia, Lucrèce

In a note to Captain Christy-Pallière, Jack Aubrey jokingly claims Borgia as his mother (PC 4).

Lucretia Borgia (1480–1519) was the daughter Roderigo *Borgia—later Pope Alexander VI—and sister of the notorious Cesare. Several times married, she is often supposed—with little certain evidence—to have been involved in dynastic murders and poisonings. Like her father, she was a noted patron of the arts.

Borgo, Pozzo di

An authority on the bird-life of Malta (TH 1).

The name may be inspired by that of Carlo Andrea Pozzo di Borgo (1764–1842), a Corsican lawyer and diplomat who supported General Paoli's plans for the independence of his home island from France, if necessary under British protection, a scheme despised by a local young activist, Napoleon *Buonaparte. Pozzo di Borgo, regarding Napoleon as his personal enemy, entered the service of the *Czar of Russia in 1803 and, after the Emperor's defeat, acted as Russian ambassador to Paris from 1815 to 1835, in which final year he was moved to England, as having become too closely associated with purely French interests.

Borrell or Borell, Mr and Mrs

HMS *Worcester's* gunner and his wife, who sail together as tradition allows (IM 2). Mr Borrell later follows Jack Aubrey to HMS *Surprise* (IM 9,10; TH 5,6,8,10) and is eventually promoted into HMS *Burford*, 74-gun (FSW 1,2).

Borwick

Jack Aubrey's attempt at a Shakespearian reference (M&C 4).

The reference is to Yorick, the deceased court-jester recalled by the Prince in *Shakespeare's *Hamlet, Act V.

Boscawen

A famous British Admiral whose exploits inspired O'Brian (M&C author's note) and who is greatly admired by Aubrey (C/T 7).

Edward Boscawen (1711–1761) was a commander famous both for his fighting spirit and his care for seamen's health and welfare. Having served as a Midshipman in *Hosier's fleet, he was commissioned Lieutenant in 1732; made Post in 1742, he was promoted Rear Admiral in 1747 and Vice Admiral in 1755. He rose to full Admiral in 1758, having served as an Admiralty Commissioner from 1751 onwards; he was also an MP from 1742 until his death. Boscawen fought in many engagements against the Spanish as a young Captain, and later against the French as one of the leading British Admirals of the Seven Years War. In 1756, he was one of those many officers outraged at the conduct of Admiral *Byng off Minorca, having regarded the latter's courage as suspect from the time they were young Lieutenants together. In his capacity as a Commissioner, Boscawen signed the subsequent order for Byng's trial and as Commander-in-Chief, Portsmouth, signed his execution warrant.

Bosset, Major de

The Commander of the British garrison at Cephalonia (IM 9).

Bossuet

A reference by Maturin to a great orator (TH 5).

Jacques-Bénigne Bossuet (1627–1704) was a renowned theologian, priest and pulpit orator whose great performances in Metz and Paris were said to have converted many Protestants to the Catholic faith. In his lifetime

Bossuet was France's leading Roman Catholic rhetorician and author, becoming a close advisor to King *Louis XIV. To this day, he is regarded as one of the great stylists of French literature.

'Boston Bean'
A reference by Bonden to the Master of the American brig, *Asa Foulkes* (DI 5).

Boston Joe
A seaman in USS *Constitution* who manacles the captured Barret Bonden. He is presumably the same Joe Warren mentioned, shortly before the battle, as Bonden's old friend (FW 4).

Bosville
A supporter of slavery with whom Maturin once had a heated altercation in Barbados (WDS 4).

Boswell
A writer referred to in passing (NC 3).
James Boswell (1740–1795) was a Scottish lawyer and writer, famed for his biography of Dr Samuel *Johnson.

Boswell, Salubrity and Leopardina
A pregnant, convict gypsy *in HMS Leopard* (DI 3+) who, having convinced the crew that the ship is haunted (DI 6), is regarded by many of them as a witch (DI 7). She goes into labour during a terrible storm (DI 7) and is delivered of her baby by caesarian section (DI 8): the child is named 'Leopardina' (DI 9). Somewhat later, Salubrity is reported to have found her already-transported husband in Botany Bay (FW 5).

Bougainville
The author of a nautical volume owned by Captain Yorke of HMS *La Flèche* (FW 2), later said to have enjoyed a safe-passage for scientific travel between England and France in time of war (SM 11).
Comte Louis-Antoine de Bougainville (1729–1811) was a French explorer and circumnavigator (during 1766–1769) whose Voyage Autour du Monde *of 1771 brought him international acclaim and, amongst many other honours, a Fellowship of the Royal Society. His exploration voyages were similar in extent to those of *Cook and *Wallis. Bougainville had served as an army officer from 1756 to 1763 but, having turned to the sea, rose to Admiral in 1782. In this capacity he was made to bear a large measure of the blame for the heavy defeat by Admiral *Rodney at the Battle of the Saints in 1782, losing his command. Having later narrowly escaped execution in the French Revolution, he managed in 1793 to retire to his estates in Normandy and was able thereafter to travel widely in his capacity as a scientist.*

Boughton
An officer in HMS *Hannibal* (M&C 12).

Boulay
A British Channel Islander, working in Sir Hildebrand's Maltese administration, who is revealed as a French spy in the pay of Lesueur (TH 10). On the collapse of Lesueur's network, he takes his own life, or is perhaps murdered (FSW 1).

Boulter
The owner of a wharf in Shelmerston (LM 8).

Bounty, HMS
The ship that had mutinied under Captain Bligh, with Peter Heywood a Midshipman in her at the time (DI 1).
HMS Bounty *was a small, armed transport, launched as* Bethia *and bought into the Royal Navy in 1787 for Lieutenant William *Bligh's breadfruit-collecting voyage to the South Seas. Her crew mutinied off Tofua on April 28th, 1789, discontented with Bligh's capricious manner and harsh tongue, and drawn by the many temptations of Tahiti, which they had just left. The mutineers, led by Master's Mate (and now acting Lieutenant) Fletcher *Christian, sailed* Bounty *to the remote Pitcairn Island, where she was run ashore and burned in 1791.*

Bourbon
A code word used by Maturin (PC 8), the name of the French Royal family (TMC 4; SM 5; HD 1+).
The French Royal House of Bourbon had its origins in the Compte de Clermont's acquisition of the Duchy of Bourbon l'Archanboult in 1327. The Bourbons went on to rule France from 1589 to 1848, the Revolution and *Buonaparte's regimes excepted. After the execution of King *Louis XVI and the death in prison of his young son Louis XVII, French Royalists remained dedicated to the 'Bourbon Restoration,' eventually accomplished in the person of *Louis XVIII in 1814. Buonaparte's brief return to power for the 'hundred days' of early 1815 forced Louis to flee, but he was soon restored following *Wellington and *Blücher's victory at Waterloo.

Bourbonnaise, HMS
The name Jack Aubrey gives to the captured French *Caroline*, there already being an HMS *Caroline* in the Royal Navy. She is given to Corbett to take the good news of the capitulation of Réunion to Admiral Bertie at the Cape (TMC 4, 5).
Caroline was launched in 1806 and captured by HMS *Sirius in September 1809. Re-named HMS Bourbonnaise—*after the French Royal House of *Bourbon—she was eventually broken up in 1817.*

Bourgeois, Père
A famous French scholar with whom Herapath had studied (DI 6).
N.B., the name partly recalls that of the Sinologist, Père du *Halde.

Boursicot
The French author of *South Seas*, a work which was to have been translated by Mr Scriven (PC 6).
The name is perhaps suggested by a combination of Edme Bourscault (1638–1701), a leading French playwright and Pierre-Louis Boursault (1781–1833), a purser, Admiral's secretary and, later, leading Marine Ministry administrator.

Bourville

A writer and critic referred to by Martin (NC 9).

Bowden

1: a seaman in the exploration ship *Rattler*, killed in an accident (FSW 3).

2: a seaman in HMS *Bellona* operated on by Stephen Maturin, who uses spirits of wine as a mild local anaesthetic and hints at, though is scientifically unaware of, some possible antiseptic effect (YA 9).

Bowen

A Post Captain who had risen from the ranks (DI 3), having been Lord Howe's sailing Master at the Battle of the Glorious First of June (C/T 4).

James Bowen (1751–1835) served in the merchant marine until entering the Royal Navy as a Master some time before 1781. In 1789 he returned to commercial activities as Inspecting Agent in the Port of London but on the outbreak of war was asked by *Howe to serve as Master in his HMS *Queen Charlotte. In 1794, shortly after the battle, Bowen was promoted Lieutenant as a reward for his services and rapidly rose to be Queen Charlotte's *premier. In the following year he was promoted both Commander and Post Captain; in his HMS *Argo, 44-gun, he was later a patron of Samuel *Walters, like him a Devonian from Ilfracombe. In 1806 Bowen, always regarded as a prime navigator and disciplinarian, served as Lord *St Vincent's *Captain of the Fleet in the Channel command. From 1816 to 1825 he was a Commissioner of the Navy; in that latter year DNB notes that he was promoted retired Rear Admiral, an advancement not however recorded in SYRETT & DiNARDO or CLOWES. Despite his early naval service as a Master, Bowen did not come from humble stock: his two brothers, Richard and George, and both of his sons, James and John, all served as Post Captains, entering the officer class by the more usual means.*

Bowers

A Royal Marine officer at a dinner aboard HMS *Caledonia* (FSW 2).

Bowes

1: either the Gunner or a Lieutenant in HMS *Charwell* (PC 1).

2: the club-footed purser of HMS *Surprise* whose brother was a Royal Navy Captain, a career he himself would dearly love to have followed (HMS 5+). Despite his disability, Mr Bowes loves a cutting-out expedition and is a very able gunner (HMS 5+), having pointed a piece at the Battle of the Glorious First of June (HMS 6) and now being the man who brings down *Berceau*'s topmast (HMS 9). For the battle with Linois' squadron, he goes to the *Earl Camden* as a gunner (HMS 9) but receives a head-wound in the action and soon dies (HMS 10).

3: an Admiral referred to in passing (SM 1).

Bowles

1: a senior official in the East India Company who gives Tom Pullings a position in the Indiaman *Lord Nelson* (PC 5).

2: a parson, an admirer of Sophie Williams (PC 8,10).

Bowyer, Admiral

An Admiral — possibly the Port Admiral — at Plymouth (IM 2).

Boyle

1: a Midshipman in HMS *Leopard* (DI 3).

2: a Midshipman in HMS *Surprise* (FSW 3–9), injured during a storm (FSW 6).

3: an HMS *Surprise* youngster, the son of an old shipmate of Jack Aubrey (RM 2,3).

4: a priest in Ireland who assists Maturin in preventing a rebellion against the Crown (COM 10).

Boyne, HMS

1: a ship that caught fire and exploded, witnessed by Aubrey (M&C 3,11).

HMS Boyne, *98-gun, launched in 1780, took accidental fire at Spithead in 1795 and soon blew up. Although her crew were mostly saved, several men in other ships nearby were killed by* Boyne's *cannon firing as the flames reached them. The ship was named for King *William III's victory in Ireland over King *James II at the Battle of the* Boyne *(a river) in 1690.*

2: a ship in Admiral Thornton's Mediterranean Fleet, Captain Lord Garron (IM 5,6).

HMS Boyne, *98-gun, the replacement for # 1 above, was launched in 1810, renamed HMS* Excellent *and appointed as a gunnery training ship in 1834, finally renamed HMS* Queen Charlotte *in 1859 and broken up in 1861.*

Bradby, James

The deceased Royal Navy Captain of HMS *Pallas* (M&C 1).

No Captain Bradby quite fits either HMS *Pallas or a death in early 1800. However, the reference may echo Captain James Bradby of HMS *Ariadne, who had been made Post in 1797 and who died in June 1801.

Brahminical

A reference to cleanliness and superstition (PC 6; HMS 7).

Taking their name from Brahma, the impersonal Supreme Being, the Brahmins are the highest, priestly sect in the Hindu caste system, practising rigorous religious purity and cleanliness.

Braithwaite

A senior Midshipman in HMS *Surprise*, Babbington's rival for promotion to acting Lieutenant after Mr Nicholls' death (HMS 6,8,9).

Brampton

A cousin of Jack Aubrey, in favour of the land enclosures near Woolcombe House (YA 2).

Brampton, John

A Polynesian-speaking, Sethian seaman in *Surprise*, a nephew of Nehemiah Slade (LM 5; NC 7; C/T 4,5).

Brand

An officer — possibly the Captain — of HMS *Implacable*, glimpsed by Jack Aubrey in London (PC 6).

Brawley

The Captain of HMS *Rainbow* (HD 2).

Bray

A servant of the Aubreys at Ashgrove cottage (RM 6).

> *N.B., there is also an Amos *Dray in the same role (RM 6; LM 4).*

Bray, the Vicar of

A song given by Dillon and Babbington after dinner (M&C 10).

> *The song was extremely popular in the 18th century: the Vicar of Bray declares himself ready to accommodate himself to whatever religious beliefs his Sovereign holds, so long as he can retain his living. The character in question is often identified with Symon Symonds, vicar of Bray in Berkshire during the late 16th and early 17th centuries, who switched from Catholicism to Protestantism with ease and frequency.*

Breadalbane, Lord

A wealthy member of Louisa Wogan's circle in London, her sometime lover (DI 4,6).

> *John Campbell (1762–1834), 4th Earl and 1st Marquis Breadalbane, was the largest land-owner in Britain, having vast Scottish estates as well as extensive possessions in England and Ireland. He had served as a soldier in his youth and was later made a Lieutenant General in recognition of his having raised several regiments from his lands during the various French wars.*

Breen

see **Maturin, Brigid**

Bréguet or Breguet

The maker of a pocket-watch often carried by Maturin (M&C 12; PC 6, 9; SM 9; RM 3; COM 4; HD 6,7).

> *Adam Louis Bréguet (1747–1823), the famous Swiss-French watchmaker, was the leading master of the craft in his age. Bréguet also produced nautical and astronomical instruments, all of exquisite workmanship and ingenuity, and became a member of the French Academy of Sciences.*

Brendan, Saint

The Irish saint and sea-voyager (PC 7; NC 7; YA 1).

> *Saint Brendan (484?–577), Abbott of Clonfert in County Galway, is first revealed in the* Navigation of St Brendan *(dating from 1050) as supposedly having been a solo sea-traveller to the outlying British Isles*

Brenton

1: an officer referred to by Jack Aubrey, presumably the Captain of either HMSS *Amphion* or *Badger* (HMS 11).

> *N.B. This could perhaps be a reference to either Edward or Jahleel *Brenton (see separate entries below) although neither commanded HMSS *Amphion or *Badger.*

2: a Polynesian-speaking seaman in *Surprise* (C/T 1).

Brenton, Edward or Ned

An officer known to Jack Aubrey (FW 4).

> *Edward Pelham Brenton (1774–1839) was made Commander in 1802 and Post Captain in 1808 but saw no active service after 1809. Mainly recalled for two books,* The Naval History of Great Britain from 1783 to 1822 *(1823) and* The Life and Correspondence of John, Earl *St Vincent (1838), Edward was the younger brother of the much more famous Sir Jahleel *Brenton. The* Naval History *was a most controversial book in its own day, including as it did many direct criticisms of the actions and character of Brenton's fellow officers (as well as many inaccuracies of fact).*

Brenton, Jahleel

1: the Captain of Saumarez' flagship HMS *Caesar*, one of the officers who court-martials Jack Aubrey for the loss of HMS *Sophie* (M&C 12). He is well known to Jack as a religious, American-born officer, recently made a baronet, a protégé of the equally religious Admiral Saumarez (FW 4).

> *The brothers Jahleel (1770–1844) and Edward Brenton (see *Brenton, Edward or Ned) were the Rhode Island-born sons of an American Loyalist Admiral, also Jahleel (made Post 1781 and Rear Admiral in 1801; d.1802). Jahleel Brenton the younger was commissioned Lieutenant in 1790, having served as a Midshipman in both the Royal and the Swedish Navies. He served at the Battle of Cape *St Vincent in 1797 and in 1799 was promoted Commander into HMS *Speedy, being in April 1800 made Post and replaced in her by Thomas *Cochrane (N.B., O'Brian has the fictional, American-born Commander *Allen being promoted out of HMS *Sophie and replaced by Jack *Aubrey). Brenton's first command in his new rank was as *Flag Captain of *Saumarez' HMS *Caesar, a ship in which he quickly established a great reputation for zeal and efficiency. In 1803 Brenton was appointed to the frigate HMS *Minerve, but was soon wrecked on the French coast, being then held prisoner-of-war in Verdun until 1806. On his return he went on to make a further brilliant reputation in the frigate HMS* Spartan *— gaining a baronetcy in 1812 — before being appointed in 1814 to the plum jobs of, firstly, Commissioner of the Naval Arsenal at Port Mahon and then, until 1822, Resident Com-*

missioner at the Cape of Good Hope. Brenton was pro-moted Rear Admiral in 1830 and Vice Admiral in 1840.
2: an official of the U.S. Navy Department who interrogates Jack Aubrey in Boston. Jack initially suspects him to be a mad inmate of Choate's hospital, masquerading as Captain Sir Jahleel Brenton of the Royal Navy (FW 4,6).

Bretonnière

The Lieutenant in command of *Hébé*, whose Captain had recently been killed in action. He himself is wounded when his ship is taken by Jack Aubrey's HMS *Boadicea* (TMC 2) and then left at the Cape as a prisoner-of-war (TMC 3).

Brett, Lucy
see **Turnbull, Harry** and **Lucy**

Breughel

The painter (HD 7).
Pieter Breughel/Brueghel the Elder (1525?–1569), a Dutch artist who spent most of his working life in Brussels, was often later known as the 'Peasant Brueghel' from the scenes of everyday, rural life that were his most frequent topic. A simple cheerfulness of both subject and style is Brueghel's most obvious gift, yet his quirky imagination and satirical edge (as well as considerable technical abilities) have raised him very high in the pantheon of great Flemish artists. His two sons, Pieter the Younger (1564–1638) and Jan (1568–1625), also enjoy considerable reputations, the former as an artist very much in his father's mould and the latter as an expert producer of still lives and landscapes. The painting of the elder Brueghel referred to in the text is The Misanthrope *of 1568, currently housed in Naples.*

Brian of the Tributes

A High King of Ireland referred to by Maturin (YA 5).
Brian Boru (941–1014) succeeded his father as King of Munster in 978 and set about extending his power by defeating both rival clans and Danish invaders. By 1002 he had established dominance as High King and frequently progressed through the island taking hostages and taxes ('boru' or 'boroihme' being Gaelic for 'tributes') to support his war efforts. Brian was killed by Danish marauders shortly after he and his son Murchad had defeated their main force at the Battle of Clontarf, and was succeeded by *Maelsechlinn II.*

Brideen
see **Maturin, Brigid**

Bridey
see **Donohue, Bridey**

Bridges, Admiral Sir John
A guest at the Keiths' Ball (PC 6).

Bridie
see **Maturin, Brigid**

Briggs
A Midshipman in HMS *Néréide* (TMC 7).

Briggs, Frederick

The Roman Catholic manservant of the Honourable Mrs Selina Morris, the friend of Mrs Williams (COM 1–3). He becomes very unpopular in the Aubrey household, being beaten by his sailor enemies before accompanying his mistress back to Bath (COM 3). To Mrs Williams' later horror, Briggs runs off with and marries Mrs Morris (YA 6) but is soon arrested and prosecuted for bigamy (YA 8).

Brighton, the Rev. Dr, M.D.

The author of the *Memoir of Admiral Sir P.B.V. Broke, Bart., KCB, etc.* (FW author's note).
J. G. Brighton's Memoir *was published in 1866, but no details of the author's own life are recorded beyond that he was a country parson with a medical degree. He was still active in 1892, when he published his* Memoir of Admiral of the Fleet Sir Provo W. P. *Wallis.

Brigid
see **Maturin, Brigid**

Brigid, Saint

A saint referred to by Maturin (COM 8).
Saint Bridget or Brigid, the Patroness of Ireland, was active in the middle of the 5th century and became famed as a religious teacher and scholar.

Brillat-Saverin, Anthelme

The French author of *Physiologie du Goût*, whose eccentric English words are given to one of O'Brian's characters (FW author's note).
Jean-Anthelme Brillat-Saverin (1755–1826) was a lawyer and local politician in Belley, France—an area well known for gastronomy—who fled from the Revolution in early 1793 and then led a life as an itinerant violinist and language teacher, visiting America in this capacity for about three years. He returned home in 1796 and soon became both an appellate judge and celebrated bon vivant. His Physiology of Taste *was published in 1825: the passage in question is from Chapter 14 of the* Miscellanea *section of the book and, in FW 4, is delivered by O'Brian's* *Pontet-Canet.

Brindley

The name of the ship-yard where HMS *Shannon* was built (FW 7).
Brindley's Yard lay on the Medway River in Kent at Frindsbury, near Chatham.

Briseis, HMS

A 74-gun, Captain Lampson, met at sea by Jack Aubrey's *Surprise* (TGS 3) and later met by *Ringle* (COM 5). Now a frigate, she is encountered as a member of Jack's squadron at Madeira (YA 10) and, under her Captain Harris, follows Jack to the

Mediterranean (HD 1,2), until being detached for service in the eastern part of that sea (HD 4).

*The HMS Briseis of the time was a 10-gun brig-sloop, launched in 1808 and wrecked off Cuba in 1816. In *Homer, Briseis was the slave and concubine of *Achilles, taken from him to his intense fury by King *Agamemmon but later restored.*

Brissac, Charles and Latrobe
Two brothers in Peru, Swiss missionaries and possibly French spies (WDS 7).

Brisson
An author whose books are owned by Sir Joseph Blaine (SM 4).

Mathurin Jacques Brisson (1723–1806), a Professor of Physics at the University of Navarre, in 1756 published The Animal Kingdom *and in 1787 his 6-volume* Ornithology.

Britannia, HMS
A ship, known in the Royal Navy as *Old Ironsides* (HMS 6; COM 8), in which Jack Aubrey and Heneage Dundas had served together when young (PC 7) and in which Lieutenants Arrowsmith and Edwards had once served together (HD 1).

HMS Britannia, *100-gun, was launched in 1762 after being on the stocks for 11 years. She fought at the Battle of *St Vincent in 1797 and then at Trafalgar in 1805, where she was the flagship of *Nelson's third-in-command, Rear-Admiral William, Earl of Northesk (1756–1831). In January 1812 she was re-named HMS* Princess Royal *for just two weeks before becoming HMS* St George; *under her 1819 name of HMS* Barfleur, *she was broken up in 1825. I have not located a reference to her as* Old Ironsides, *a name more usually associated in naval history with USS *Constitution.*

Broad
1: Mrs Broad, the owner of the Bunch of Grapes in the Savoy district of London (PC 12,14; HMS 4; TMC 1; DI 2; IM 1; RM 5; LM 4,8,9; TGS 4; NC 10; C/T 6,9; COM 2,5; YA 1,8,10). On one occasion Stephen Maturin — who has long kept bachelor rooms in the establishment — returns to London to find the Grapes burned down, and Mrs Broad removed to her sister whilst the insurance claim is resolved (RM 5). The inn is, however, soon rebuilt (LM 4).
2: a hatter in Gibraltar (HD 1).

'Broad-Brim'
An American Puritan met by Maturin in Boston (FW 5).

Brocas
The Royal Navy pay-agent in Malta (TH 2).

Broke
The father of Jack Aubrey's cousin, Captain Philip Broke of HMS *Shannon*. He is thought by Jack to be a mean man, though his friendship with the politician Pitt had secured early promotion for his son (FW 7,9).

Philip Bowes Broke (d.1801) was a substantial, though far from wealthy, landowner from a very old Suffolk family.

Broke, Sir Philip and Louisa
Sir P.B.V. Broke, on whose famous action the final part of *The Fortune of War* is closely based (FW author's note). The somewhat dour Broke went to sea late, having attended a naval academy ashore rather than serving as a youngster in ships; Jack Aubrey, a distant cousin, has known him well for over 20 years (FW 7; RM 3; TGS 9; IM 10). Broke had served under Captain Hope in HMSS *Bulldog*, *Eclair* and *Romulus*; he was then the Third Lieutenant of HMS *Southampton* at the Battle of Cape St Vincent. Promoted Commander into HMS *Shark*, he was soon made Post — ahead of Jack — through his father's influence with the politician Pitt (FW 7; FSW 2). Before being given HMS *Shannon* five years previously, Broke had commanded HMS *Druid* (FW 7,8; FSW 2). Eager to avenge the defeats suffered by the Royal Navy at the hands of the U.S. Navy, he now issues a challenge of single-ship combat to Captain Lawrence of USS *Chesapeake* (FW 9). Lawrence in any case stands out to do battle shortly before the message is received and is rapidly and heavily defeated by Broke's well-trained and well-motivated crew, assisted by the passenger Jack Aubrey. Yet, just at the moment of triumph, Broke is clubbed down by an American seaman and severely wounded, scarcely understanding Jack's congratulations (FW 9): he is reported as critically ill following his great victory (SM 1,2,4,5). Something of a scientific officer, Broke had invented a gun-sight and, during the Peace of Amiens, seen a steamer operating on a Scottish loch (FW 8); whilst ashore unemployed for a spell, he had demonstrated his zeal by forming his own militia (FSW 2). Both Barret Bonden (SM 4) and Mr Nuttall of HMS *Ariel* had served under him (SM 7). According to Jack, Philip Broke is somewhat unhappily married to a rich hypochondriac (FW 7–9) named Louisa (SM 4).

Sir Philip Bowes Vere Broke (1776–1841) was commissioned Lieutenant in 1797, promoted Commander in 1799 and made Post in 1801 (although he was not given a sea-command until HMS Druid *in 1805). Appointed to the new HMS *Shannon in 1806, in 1813 he fought and took USS *Chesapeake *in a famously brisk, 15-minute fight. Broke received a severe head injury in the action and never again served at sea once* Shannon *returned to England; he was immediately knighted for this victory and in 1830 rose by seniority to Rear Admiral. In 1802 Broke had married the wealthy heiress Sarah Louisa Middleton (1778–1843) and, after 1855, the family added the Middleton surname: many Broke-Middletons pursued naval careers, with one of Philip's grand-daughters marrying a grandson of Sir James de *Saumarez. Although Mrs Broke does appear to have been a delicate and somewhat timid soul (like Sophie *Aubrey, she was afraid of horses), Philip's many letters to her are most affectionate, usually being* *addressed to 'my beloved Loo/Looloo.' The steamer seen by Broke may well have been the first ever commercial steam driven craft, the* Charlotte Dundas *(named for the daughter of a non-naval member of the *Dundas family) that first operated on a Scottish canal in 1802.*

'Broken-nose'

A bailiff who tries to arrest Jack Aubrey (PC 7).

Bromley

An official to whom Jack Aubrey has written requesting command of HMS *Diane*, but who has rejected his entreaties (TMC 1).

Brönte

'Brönte XXX' is inscribed on a cask of lemon juice presented by the Duke of Clarence to Maturin (NC 7).

*The inscription indicates that the juice comes from Lord *Nelson's own estates in Sicily, he having been made Duke of Brönte in 1799 by the King of Naples.*

Brook's

A gaming-club in London's St James Street, whose members Jack Aubrey regards as having wild, radical sympathies (WDS 4; YA 2,7), even though he himself had once been a member (TGS 1).

*Brook's Club was founded in the middle of the 18th century by William *Almack and rapidly became famous for both high-gambling and fast-living.*

Broughton

A Lieutenant in HMS *Java*, killed in action (FW 3).

Brown

1: the head of the Port Mahon dockyard, with an unnamed wife and a daughter, Fanny. Mr Brown is also an amateur composer (M&C 2+).

2: a seaman on Mr Parker's punishment list in HMS *Polychrest* (PC 7).

3: a member of the barge crew in HMS *Surprise* (HMS 6).

4: a man referred to by Harry Johnson, presumably a British intelligence agent in the USA (FW 7).

5: the owner of a hotel in Halifax, Nova Scotia (SM 1).

6: a flashy, radical friend of General Aubrey (SM 5).

7: a member of the barge-crew of Captain Baker's HMS *Iris*, chosen for his colourful surname FSW 2).

8: the founder of one of the Shelmerstonian religious sects (WDS 1).

Robert Brown or Browne (1550?–1630) was an English theologian who believed that ministers should be elected by their congregations alone; his followers were known as 'Brownists' or 'Independents.'

Brown, Admiral

1: the crew's slang expression for HMS *Boadicea's* effluent (TMC 2).

2: an officer who had been good to the young Jack Aubrey, in consequence of which Jack now takes his nephew, Elphinstone, into HMS *Worcester* as a Midshipman (IM 2,4).

*The only one of many Browns who have served in the Royal Navy who could be the reference here is John Brown (d.1808), made Post in 1779 (and hence a Captain during *Aubrey's first years at sea), promoted Rear Admiral in 1795, Vice Admiral in 1801 and Admiral in 1808, only a few days before his death.*

Brown, Joe

The master-at-arms of HMS *Lively* (PC 12).

Brown, William

Captain Dockray's coxswain, temporarily in HMS *Dart* with Lieutenant Dillon (M&C 3).

Browne

An elderly, sick Irishman whom Stephen Maturin had accompanied as doctor on a sea voyage to Port Mahon. Having died on arrival, he has left Stephen stranded, with neither money nor prospects (M&C 2).

Brueys

Nelson's opponent at the Battle of the Nile (COM 10).

*François-Paul Brueys d'Aigalliers (1753–1798) had been expelled from the French navy in 1793 as a Royalist, but then re-instated and promoted Rear Admiral in 1795 by *Buonaparte's influence. As Vice Admiral, Brueys commanded the fleet that brought General Buonaparte's forces to Egypt in 1798 but, at his 'safe' anchorage in Aboukir Bay, he was attacked by *Nelson's forces and comprehensively defeated in a famous British victory that cut the French army off from its chain of supplies. Brueys was killed early in the action and later his flagship, *Orient, blew up with a very heavy loss of life.*

Bruno, St

The saint after whom a variety of mushrooms are named (TMC 1).

The reference could be to any one of several Saints Bruno — the best known lived from about 1040 to 1101 and founded the Cathusian order of monks — and the mushrooms are perhaps (like St George's mushroom) thought to be at their peak on his feast day. (N.B., 'collops' usually means 'meat, cut up small,' but I take it in the context to be a reference to an especially meaty fungus).

Brunswick, Duke of

The Emperor of Morocco refers to 'Duke of Brunswick' as one of the titles of King George III (IM 4).

*King *George III came from the Hanoverian family of Brunswick-Lüneberg but the Dukedom in fact remained in a different branch of the clan. Karl Wilhelm Ferdinand (1735–1806), Duke of Brunswick, was a leading Prussian General, mortally wounded at the Battle of Auerstädt. His son, Wilhelm Frederick (1771–1815), was prevented by the Franco Russian Treat of Tilsit of 1807 from taking possession of the family Dukedom until 1813: in 1815, he* *was killed at the Battle of Quatre Bras leading his Brunswick Corps against the French.*

Brunswick, HMS

A ship on which three HMS *Bounty* mutineers had been hung, witnessed by young Jack Aubrey from HMS *Tonnant* (DI 1). Years later, she is seen at Gibraltar (IM 3).

HMS Brunswick, *74-gun, was launched in 1790, taking part four years later in *Howe's victory at the Glorious First of June. After service from 1807 to 1808 in the Baltic fleet, he was sent for harbour service in 1812 and broken up in 1826. She is named for the Hanoverian holders of the Duchy of *Brunswick in Germany.*

Brutus

A reference is made to Brutus' being the model for the modern short haircut (TGS 3; WDS 3).

Marcus Junius Brutus (80–36 BC) was a leading Roman republican and, eventually, the enemy of the imperial schemes of his erstwhile friend, Julius *Caesar. After participating in Caesar's assassination, Brutus fought his heirs Octavius (later the Emperor Augustus) and Marcus Antonius but was defeated by them at Philippi, committing suicide on the battlefield. In 1789 the great French Neoclassical painter Jacques-Louis David (1748–1825) showed in Paris his The Lictors Bringing to Brutus the Bodies of His Sons. *In a reaction against the then-prevailing Rococo style, Brutus was portrayed with a close-cropped, bare head (as in ancient busts of him and his contemporaries), starting a fashion against both wig-wearing and flowing locks that gradually spread across Europe.*

Bryant, Timothy

A seaman in HMS *Sophie* (M&C 6).

Brydges

see Miller, Mrs

Bryman, William

A seaman in *Surprise* badly wounded in the action on Moahu Island (C/T 9).

Bucentaure

A French ship seen at the Battle of Trafalgar by Captain Yorke (FW 2).

Bucentaure, *80-gun, was launched in 1803 and in 1805 was the flag-ship of Vice Admiral *Villeneuve at Trafalgar, where she lay in the centre of the Franco-Spanish line (see *Yorke, Charles). After the great defeat by *Nelson, she was briefly re-taken by her own crew before being wrecked on rocks off Cadiz.*

Buchan

1: the Master of HMS *Boadicea*, a man not greatly admired by Jack Aubrey (TMC 2, 6), later killed in action against *Astrée* (TMC 8).
2: the author of *Domestic Medicine* (FSW 2; RM 4).

William Buchan (1729–1805) was an Edinburgh physician and medical author whose very successful book was first published in 1769.

3: the Flag Captain of Admiral Lord Keith's HMS *Royal Sovereign* (HD 1).

Buckmaster

A naval tailor in London (TGS 4).

Buddha

The Asiatic spiritual leader (TGS 8).

'Buddha' is derived from a Sanscrit word indicating knowledge, understanding or wisdom, and is widely used as a title for spiritual leaders in various eastern religions. By far the most influential Buddha was Gautama Sidhartha, who lived in India and Ceylon in the 6th century BC. He founded a non-theistic, non-dogmatic religion whose aim is eventual annihilation of the individual into a state of nirvana, *but only after many years, and even lifetimes, of contemplation of the transitory and illusory nature of material phenomenon.*

Buffon, de

A French naturalist referred to by Maturin (M&C 6; PC 12; RM 5; LM 2).

Georges Louis Leclerc (1707–1788), Comte de Buffon, was a scientist and naturalist of great distinction in both France and England, where he was elected a Fellow of the Royal Society. He produced a prodigious body of work in the realm of natural history and ornithology, as distinguished for its literary style as for its content. Buffon's son became a French army officer but was executed in the Revolution for his aristocratic rank.

Bugge, Ole

The Captain of the Danish merchant brig, *Clomer* (M&C 5).

Bulbuljibashi

Ismail Bey's Keeper of the Nightingales (IM 10).

Bulkeley

1: Mr Stanhope's classics master in his school-days (HMS 8).
2: *Surprise*'s bosun (LM 1+; TGS 2; NC 7,9; C/T 1+; WDS 1+), a fluent Polynesian speaker nicknamed 'Old Chucks' (C/T 1,5). He is later dismissed the ship for gross embezzlement (WDS 10).

Bull, Captain

The subject of a letter from Lord St Vincent to the Marquis Cornwallis (PC 3).

Bulldog

A cannon in HMS *Surprise* (RM 3).

Bulldog, HMS

A Royal Navy vessel, possibly commanded by Darley, mentioned in HMS *Sophie*'s log (M&C 2). Philip Broke had once served in her as a Midshipman (FW 7).

HMS Bulldog, *16-gun sloop, was launched in 1782, turned into a bomb-vessel in 1798 and captured by the French for much of 1801. Re-taken by the Royal Navy at the end of that year, she was converted to a powder hulk, being finally broken up in 1829. In November 1799 — the date referred to in the text — she was under Commander Barrington Dacres (Post Captain 1802; d.1806).*

Buller, Mrs

A Calcutta lady who tries to call on Diana Villiers following the death of Canning (HMS 11).

Bullock, John

A former seaman of HMS *Surprise*, now a servant of Admiral Colpoys in Halifax. Stephen Maturin had once saved his leg but he had later lost it in action on HMS *Benbow* (SM 1,2).

Bulwer

1: the owner of a hay-yard in Dorset (SM 5).
2: a Lieutenant of HMS *Belvidera*, taken captive by the U.S. navy whilst in command of a prize and now held prisoner in Boston (FW 4).

Bunce

The owner of a tavern in Port Mahon (IM 7).

Bungs, Jemmy

A ship-board name for the master cooper (RM 2; TGS 10).

Buonaparte or Bonaparte, Napoleon

The ruler of France, a man especially loathed by Stephen Maturin (referred to by name many times in PC, HMS, TMC, DI, FW, SM, IM, TH, FSW, RM, LM, TGS, NC, C/T, WDS, COM, YA, HD). *(N.B., O'Brian almost always uses the Italian/Corsican spelling 'Buonaparte,' although the French form of 'Bonaparte' is occasionally encountered and is used exclusively in HD.)*

Napoleon Buonaparte (1769–1821), the brilliant Corsican-French soldier and statesman, was the effective autocrat of France from 1799 to 1814 and again for three months in 1815; he reigned as Emperor from 1804 to 1814 and in 1815. Buonaparte (the French spelling of the name — Bonaparte — was adopted by Napoleon in mid-1796) was born into a family (see **Buonapartes, the** *below) of strong supporters of General Paoli's movement for Corsican autonomy and it was to his mother that he later always attributed his astonishing energy and powers of decision. At the age of 10 Napoleon was sent to military schools in Brienne and Paris and in 1785 became a Lieutenant of Artillery. By 1789 he had become an enthusiast for revolutionary ideas, and in 1792 moved his entire family from Corsica to France rather than follow Paoli's acceptance of English protection for the island. In 1793 Napoleon made his military reputation, and earned promotion to General, by capturing the port of Toulon from Spanish and English occupation, and in 1794 led the Convention's defeat of the rebellion by the National Guard, as a result of which he was made effective Commander-in-Chief of the army of the interior.*

In 1796, shortly after his marriage to Josephine

*Beauharnais (the fashionable widow of a General and the daughter of a naval Captain), Napoleon took command of the French army in Italy and began a series of campaigns whose brilliant success has seldom been rivalled in history. In 1798 he was then entrusted by the Directory with planning the invasion of England but the political powers of the time soon decided to concentrate their attack on Britain's overseas Empire by sending the young General to Egypt and thence, by intention, to India. He enjoyed considerable military success in Egypt itself but *Nelson's great victory at the Battle of the Nile in August 1798 and Sir Sidney *Smith's defence of Acre in 1799 so limited the French army's supply routes that the campaign had to be abandoned. Whilst in Cairo Buonaparte had, for political purposes, courted Islam, encouraging by both proclamation and action a belief that he had even embraced the faith (see COM 10; HD 1+). Although the General had a genuine and intelligent interest in matters of belief and religious observation, and some considerable sympathy for the combined holy and organisational tenets of Islam in particular, he later stressed that he had merely given Arabic Moslems the respect due to all great faiths, especially by invaders in search of local allies.*

*In 1799 Napoleon returned to France — narrowly escaping capture by British cruisers en route — where he found the whole country grossly dissatisfied with the Directory's war effort. He immediately used his own great popularity to secure the post of First Consul, taking near-absolute power for himself. Resuming command in the field, he won decisive victories against the Austrian armies in Italy and compelled them to sue for peace. Britain's consequent isolation led to the Treaty of Amiens of March 1802. Amongst other things, this period of peace enabled Napoleon greatly to increase his system of domestic control, particularly by the use of *Fouché's talents as Chief of Police.*

*The peace with England broke down in early 1803 and plans to invade her were again raised. In May 1804 Buonaparte crowned himself Emperor Napoleon of the French in a ceremony conducted by Pope *Pius VII and then immediately began campaigns against the Austrians and Russians, inflicting on them a series of heavy defeats. However, even the great victory at Austerlitz in December of 1805 was partially offset by Nelson's triumph over the combined French and Spanish fleets a few months earlier at Trafalgar, after which French strategic sea-power never seriously rivalled that of Britain. Although by 1810 Napoleon was the undoubted master of continental Europe, he had failed to reduce Britain by either invasion or trade blockade and he was still embroiled in a long, costly campaign in Spain and Portugal (lasting from 1808 to 1814). Furthermore in 1808 he had fallen out with his former ally the Pope and in 1809 had invaded Rome, annexing the Papal States: in June 1810 Pius excommunicated all involved in this affair (and was imprisoned for his pains from 1811 to 1814), an act which tended to unite staunch Catholic opposition to Napoleon's rule, especially in northern Europe and in France's out-lying, colonial possessions.*

In December 1809 Napoleon had divorced the Empress Josephine, she having failed to bear him an heir, and in 1810 he married Princess Marie-Louise of Austria, who in 1811 bore him a son (see **Buonapartes, the***). In 1812 Napoleon then invaded Russia with an army of 500,000 men, initially winning brilliant victories but soon over-stretching his supply lines and being forced to withdraw:*

by December the exceptionally hard Russian winter had reduced the French force to less than 100,000. Following this first real sign of French strategic mis-judgement, in 1813 much of Europe rose up against the Emperor's rule. Whilst his military talent remained largely intact, his enemies were growing stronger and France herself was tiring of the costs of 20 years of near-continual war. Following a heavy defeat at Leipzig in 1813 itself, the Emperor was unable to raise sufficient new forces to defend Paris effectively and in March 1814 he was forced by his discontented Generals to abdicate. He was banished to the small Mediterranean island of Elba (of which he was made Head of State) and the *Bourbon monarchy was restored to France (see YA 9,10).

However, the new King *Louis XVIII failed to obtain popular support, whilst Napoleon himself kept in close contact with his own former supporters. In February 1815 he left Elba (see YA 10) and marched in triumph to Paris, being joined by his former armies along the way amidst legendary scenes of the old imperial charisma (HD 1+). Once in his capital, he resumed the position of Emperor for the famous 'Hundred Days,' and struck northwards against his enemies: however, he was soon finally defeated at Waterloo in Belgium by *Wellington and the Prussian General *Blücher (see HD 10). Napoleon now hoped to flee to the USA, but at the Atlantic port of La Rochelle soon realised that he had no means of getting through the British naval blockade. On July 15th 1815 he surrendered to Captain Frederick Maitland of HMS *Bellerophon and was taken to England. On August 7th he was conveyed to his final exile on the Atlantic Island of St Helena aboard HMS *Northumberland, the flag-ship of Admiral Sir George *Cockburn, under the command of Captain Charles *Ross.

On May 5th 1821, Napoleon died of stomach cancer: the Empress Marie Louise had left him on his first abdication in 1814 and the ex-Empress Josephine — with whom he remained passionately in love — had died of diphtheria during his exile on Elba.

Buonapartes, the

The large family of Napoleon Buonaparte (SM 5).
*The reference here is specifically to those of his brothers and sisters who held significant political power, but it is useful also to note other members of the remarkable clan. Napoleon's father **Carlo** (1746–1785) was a Corsican lawyer and politician who, whilst an ardent nationalist, believed strongly in the link with France and eventually rejected General Paoli's campaign for total independence. His wife, **Letizia Ramolino** (1750–1836), bore him 13 children of whom 8 survived to adulthood. Under her son Napoleon's rule of France, Letizia became known as 'Madame Mère,' regarded by all as a formidable, canny and yet unpretentious lady. Always financially very prudent, she regarded her family's astonishing elevation to wealth and glory as inevitably subject to the vagaries of fate. From 1815 she lived in retirement in Rome, wealthy yet preferring a simple life-style. Napoleon's four brothers and three sisters were all elevated by him, in varying degrees, to positions of glamour or power. **Joseph** (1768–1844), the eldest of the family, was an effective politician and diplomat who became King of Naples in 1806. Forced to abdicate in favour of his brother-in-law General Murat in 1808, in that same year he became King of Spain, ruling until being compelled by military reverses*

*again to abdicate in 1813. He lived in Philadelphia, USA, from 1815 to 1832 and from 1837 to 1839, before finally retiring to Italy. **Lucien** (1775–1840) was the least ambitious of the brothers: active as a politician until 1804, he then retired to Rome, refusing all further honours offered by his brother. **Louis** (1778–1846) served as a soldier before becoming King of Holland in 1806: in 1810 he quarrelled with Napoleon, abdicated and retired. His son, **Charles Louis Napoleon** (1808–1873), ruled France as Emperor Napoleon III from 1853 to 1870: in that year he was deposed and moved to England, where three years later he died. **Jérôme** (1784–1860) entered the French Navy in 1800 and rose to Rear Admiral in 1806, in which year he moved to senior army commands. He was made King of Westphalia in 1807 but lost his crown in the military reverses of 1813. He fought very effectively for his brother at Waterloo in 1815 and thereafter lived a wandering life until allowed to return to Paris in 1847. Promoted a Maréchal de France in 1850, in 1852 he was made President of the Senate and given the title 'First Prince of the Blood.' In 1803 he had married the American Elizabeth Patterson but, under great pressure from his brother, had divorced her in 1807 and made a more suitable political match. Napoleon's eldest sister, **Elisa** (1777–1820), was made Grand Duchess of Tuscany in 1809. She lost this position on the Emperor's 1814 abdication and thereafter lived in Triest with her very wealthy husband, the Prince of Piombino. **Pauline** (1780–1825) married the Italian Prince Borghese in 1803 but lived apart from him as a lively society hostess in Paris until her brother's final fall in 1815, when she retired to Italy. **Caroline** (1782–1839) married General Murat in 1800 and became Queen of Naples on his elevation to that throne in 1808: her husband died in 1815 and she then retired to private life. Napoleon's son by his second Empress, Marie-Louise of Austria, **Napoleon François Charles Joseph** (1811–1832), was made King of Rome immediately after his birth and held that post until his father's first abdication in 1814. On his father's final abdication in 1815, he was recognized by Bonapartists as Emperor Napoleon II, but never held any power. Under the guardianship of his grandfather, the Emperor of Austria, he was later made Prince of Parma and Duke of Reichstadt: never in strong health, he died of consumption after a brief military career.*

Burdett, Mrs

A neighbour of Aubrey and Maturin in Sussex (PC 1).
Possibly a reference to Sophia *Coutts, the wealthy wife of Sir Francis *Burdett.

Burdett, Sir Francis

A wealthy member of Louisa Wogan's circle in London, and her sometime lover (DI 6). He is possibly the same Sir Francis Burdett who later accompanies General Aubrey on a visit to his daughter-in-law, Sophie (SM 4).
Sir Francis Burdett (1770–1844) was elected to Parliament in 1795 as a liberal Whig, soon after his marriage to Sophia, the daughter of a wealthy banker Thomas *Coutts. An opponent of the wars against France, Sir Francis was a strong supporter of electoral reform in Britain. After 1807, he sat as MP for Westminster for the next 30 years:

in 1810 he was briefly imprisoned, after a political show-trial, for supposedly libelling the dignity of the House of Commons.

Buren, Cornelius and Mevrouw van

A distinguished Dutch East Indies anatomist (TGS 4). No admirer of Buonaparte, he assists Stephen Maturin with his intelligence activities as well as his scientific investigations (TGS 6–8; NC3,4; *N.B., earlier in the series van Buren is referred to in passing as an intelligence source:* FW 1). The pair even dissect the bodies of the traitors Ledward and Wray following their assassination (TGS 8). Van Buren is married to a Malay lady, Mevrouw (TGS 6,7).

Buren, Kitty van

A Baltimore friend of Louisa Wogan and Diana Villiers (DI 5).

Burford, HMS

The ship in which Lieutenant Dillon arrives at Port Mahon (M&C 2), later the 74-gun into which Gill and Borrell of HMS *Surprise* are promoted Master and Gunner respectively (FSW 2).

The last HMS Burford, *70-gun, had been launched in 1757 and sold in 1785, well before the series opens; she was named for a town in Oxfordshire.*

Burgess, Tom

Killick's mate in HMS *Surprise* (RM 1).

Burgoyne, General

The British commander under whom the American George Herapath, then a Tory loyalist, had served in the Revolutionary War (FW 7).

Sir John Burgoyne (1722–1792) was both an English General and a playwright. In the former career, 'Gentleman Johnny' took command of a British army in Canada in 1777 and marched south into New York state. He was soon forced to surrender at Saratoga, a victory that gave great encouragement to the revolutionary party in America. In his writing and social career he was famous as a wit and charmer, writing a very successful satire, The Heiress, *in 1786, having earlier (1774) written a comedy of country life,* The Maid of the Oaks.

Buridan

A medieval philosopher referred to by Maturin (M&C 10).

*Jean Buridan (1295?–1358) was a Frenchman who spent his life teaching the works of *Aristotle at the University of Paris. He was supposedly killed by being tossed into the Seine in a sack, although just for what offence remains uncertain.*

Burke

A Colonel in the East India Company service, Canning's second in the duel with Maturin (HMS 10).

Burke, Aloysius and Sheridan

Two Irish seamen *in HMS Sophie* (M&C 3).

Burke, Dumb

A famous prize-fighter (YA 3).

*The name may be inspired by that of the well-known pugilist, 'Deaf' James Burke (1810–1845), who, in a bout in 1833, killed Simon Byrne, the '*Myrtle Bough.'*

Burnet

1: a Midshipman in HMS *Isis*, met by Jack Aubrey at Molly Harte's salon (M&C 1).
2: a seaman on Mr Parker's punishment list in HMS *Polychrest* (PC 7).

Burney, Admiral

A Captain under whom Jack Aubrey had once served, and who had himself sailed with Captain Cook. His sister was a novelist (FW 2).

*James Burney (1745?–1821), a son of the composer Charles Burney (1726–1814), sailed under *Cook as Midshipman and, from 1773, Lieutenant. Made Post in 1782, he was placed on the retired list in 1804 and not promoted Rear Admiral—still on the retired list—until 1821. His sister, Fanny Burney (1752–1840), spent her youth in the glittering literary society cultivated by her father and published her own first novel* Evelina *in 1778, then going on to enjoy success with* Cecilia *(1782) and* Camilla *(1796), all about the entry of beautiful young women into the world of social experience. Fanny, also a prodigious essayist and letter-writer, in 1793 had married an exiled French Royalist General, d'Arblay: during the Peace of Amiens of 1802, they visited France but were arrested and interned until 1812.*

Burney, Ned

An officer of Heneage Dundas' HMS *Excellent* (IM 4).

Burrel, Captain

The officer appointed to HMS *Leopard* in place of Jack Aubrey. However, he has already died of dysentery before the ship arrives at Pulo Batang (FW 1).

Burrowes, William

A seaman in *Surprise* (COM 1).

Burton

1: a member of Mr Savile's hunt (PC 1).
2: an author referred to by Maturin (LM 2; YA 2).
Robert Burton (1577–1640) was an extremely well-educated Oxford vicar who in 1621 published The Anatomy of Melancholy. *Ostensibly a medical treatise on his own mild mental illness, it is rather more a wide-ranging satire on the human condition.*
3: HMS *Leopard's* gunner, a man admired by Jack Aubrey (DI 6).

Busbequius

A scientific authority referred to by Dr Ramis (M&C 12).
Augier Ghislaine de Busbecq (1522–1592), a Flemish scholar, traveller and diplomat, was twice ambassador to

*Constantinople on behalf of the Holy Roman Emperor Fer-
dinand II and also travelled widely in the whole of western Europe. In 1589 he published, in Latin, his
observations on life, culture and natural philosophic matters in the many countries he had visited.*

Bushel

1: the Captain immediately below Jack Aubrey on
the Navy List (TGS 4).
2: an army officer serving Governor Raffles in
Batavia (NC 3).

Bussell, Joseph

A seaman in HMS *Sophie* (M&C 2+).

Bustamente, Admiral don José

The commander of the Spanish treasure
squadron—*Medea* (his flagship), *Fama*, *Clara* and
Mercedes—that surrenders to the British squadron
led by Captain Graham, and including Jack
Aubrey's HMS *Lively* (PC 14).

*Don José Bustamente y Guerra (1759–1825) did indeed
command the Spanish squadron that forms the basis of
O'Brian's tale. Having intercepted the four 'enemy' ships,
on October 5th 1804 Captain *Graham Moore sent a
Lieutenant Ascott from HMS *Indefatigable to *Medea
to demand their surrender without the necessity of blood-
shed: Bustamente of course refused, and commenced a
short, hopeless action for the sake of his country's honour.
Captured, he was soon paroled home to Spain where he
was honourably acquitted for the defeat. The seized ships
held treasure worth about one million pounds sterling at
the time but, as war had not actually been declared when
the action took place, the spoils largely went direct to the
British Crown as droits, rather than being part-shared out
as—colossal—prize money.*

Butcher

1: the cry in a ship when someone takes a tumble
(HMS 9; FSW 4; NC 8).
*Not in fact a name at all: in an abattoir, once a slaugh-
terman has downed an animal he calls for the butcher to
commence the dismemberment. In NC 8 the cry is in fact
given as the non-capitalized 'butcher.'*
2: the surgeon of USS *Norfolk*, formerly the assistant to Mr Evans in USS *Constitution*, who is
amongst the crew marooned on Old Sodbury
Island after *Norfolk* is wrecked (FSW 9,10); he
refers in passing to Mrs Butcher (FSW 9).
Later, he is a prisoner-of-war at Barbados (RM
1,2).
3: the First Lieutenant of Dundas' HMS *Eurydice*
(RM 10).
4: the assistant loblolly-boy in HMS *Bellona* (YA 9).

Butcher, Elijah

Jack Aubrey's clerk in HMS *Diane* (TGS 5,10),
killed in the Dyak attack on the shipwreck island
(NC 2,3).

'Butcher Jeffrey'

A highwayman, possibly imaginary (HMS 4).

Buteo

Sir Joseph Blaine refers to himself and a bottle of
wine as *nata mecum consule Buteo* (SM 4).

*The line is Latin for 'born with me, during Bute's con-
sulate.' Blaine has in mind here a line from *Horace, Odes
III, where the poet also dates both himself and a bottle of
wine in the accustomed Roman manner of reference to the
date of a one-year Consulship: nata mecum consule Man-
lio.' Blaine's little joke only works because John Stewart
(1713–1792), 3rd Earl of Bute, was a close confidant of
King *George III and served as his—immensely unpopular—Prime Minister for just twelve months in 1762–1763.
Bute, a considerable patron of the arts, was also a published botanist of some renown.*

Butler

1: the Captain of HMS *Naiad* (M&C 11).
2: a Midshipman in HMS *Lively* (PC 12; HMS 2).
3: a noble family referred to by Maturin as genuinely Irish, rather than being English implants
(TMC 2).
*The Anglo-Norman soldier Theobald Walter (d.1205)
served on campaigns in Ireland under King Henry II's son
Prince (later King) John from about 1182, receiving large
grants of land as a reward and becoming Chief Butler (in
effect, 'treasurer') of Ireland, a title that he adopted as the
family surname towards the end of his life. By the mid-
16th century the Butler family had become Earls of Or-
monde and were amongst the largest land-owners in
Ireland. Amongst their various cadet branches were the
Montgarret family: see *Butler, Simon*
4: a former Captain of HMS *Druid* (FW 9).
5: Lady Butler, a friend of the Aubreys in Dorset
(YA 10).

Butler, Jane and Mr

The wife of Mr Butler of HMS *Calliope*, said by Sophie Aubrey to have been left penniless by his death
from wounds received in a duel (DI 2).

Butler, Sir John

A doctor who, in company with the President of the
College of Physicians, attends Mrs Williams (HMS
6).

Butler, Molly

A friend of Lizzie Arrowsmith (HD 1).

Butler, Simon

A Protestant United Irishman. In the vain hope of
diffusing a growing tension between the Irish Lieutenant, James Dillon, and his English Captain, Jack
Aubrey, Stephen Maturin tells Jack that many
United Irishmen were well-educated Protestants
and not merely 'Catholic rebels,' as Jack might have
supposed (M&C 3).

*Simon Butler (1757–1797), a son of Viscount Montgar-
ret, was a leading Dublin lawyer who became first President of the United Irishmen. He died of natural causes
shortly before the 1798 rising. See also **Butler #3**, above.*

Butoo

A person who had helped Stephen Maturin to learn Eastern languages (HMS 7).

Butterbox, Old

A reference to *Waakzaamheid*'s Dutch Captain (DI 6).

Butterworth and Kyle

The firm that owns the whaler *Acapulco* (FSW 6).

Button

An able-seaman in HMS *Lively* (PC 12).

Button, Joseph

A marine sentry in HMS *Sophie* (M&C 11).

Button's

A London club of which both Jack Aubrey and his father are members (RM 4; LM 2, 4; C/T 6).

Byng

A British Admiral who had been shot, on his own quarterdeck (TMC 6), following a court-martial for what Ferris refers to as 'an error of judgement and being unpopular with the mob' (M&C 12). Admiral Russell later refers to his 'judicial murder' (LM 1).

*Admiral John Byng (1704–1757) was the forth son of Viscount Torrington, Admiral of the Fleet, and rose to flag rank in 1745 through influence rather than ability or experience: the charge later levelled against him was that he had failed to do his utmost to prevent the loss of Minorca to the French in 1756. Whatever Byng's actual failings in the campaign, there is no doubt that the government of the day badly needed a scapegoat to divert attention for their own neglect of the rise of French power in the Mediterranean, and his subsequent execution by firing-squad on the quarterdeck of HMS Monarch (which was not his flag-ship) inspired *Voltaire's famous line that the English shoot an Admiral from time to time simply pour encourager les autres ('to motivate all the others'), a view rather endorsed in CLOWES' lengthy treatment of the whole affair. Views on Byng's character, conduct and fate varied in the Royal Navy from those expressed by O'Brian's characters to the outright hostility of, e.g., Admiral *Boscawen. However, the court that tried him was at pains to note that he was accused of negligence, not cowardice or disaffection, and in consequence made a recommendation—ignored—for mercy. Byng had been made Post in 1727, only four years after being commissioned Lieutenant; he served as Governor-General of Newfoundland from 1741 to 1744 and was promoted Rear Admiral in 1745, Vice Admiral in 1747 and full Admiral in 1756. He was also MP for Rochester from 1751 until his death.*

Byrne

A seaman from HMS *Surprise* on Jack Aubrey's Mubara expedition who owns a lucky snuff-box (TH 6).

Byron

A Midshipman in HMS *Leopard* (DI 3,4) promoted acting Lieutenant (DI 5+), a rank later confirmed (SM 6). He is a relative of both Lord Byron the poet and Admiral 'Foulweather Jack' Byron (DI 3). Having accompanied Jack Aubrey homewards to England from the Cape (FW 1), he escapes with Jack from the accidental burning of HMS *La Flèche* and is picked up by HMS *Java*. Badly wounded in her action with USS *Constitution,* he is later put ashore in Brazil with most of the prisoners (FW 3,4,5).

*A number of relatives of Admiral *Byron and Lord *Byron served in the Royal Navy, although none quite fits the dates of *Aubrey's young protégé.*

Byron, Admiral 'Foulweather' Jack

A famous British Admiral whose exploits inspired O'Brian (M&C author's note). Byron had served as a Midshipman in HMS *Wager* with Tom Pullings' grandfather amongst her crew and the old man had later become bosun of the now Admiral Byron's flagship, HMS *Indefatigable* (DI 3). The Admiral, the grandfather of the poet Lord Byron and hence doubly admired by Mr Mowett, was also the circumnavigator under whom Jack Aubrey's cousin, Admiral Carteret, had once served (RM 2,8; FSW 7; NC 8). His final service was as an Admiral on the American Station in 1779 (FW 2).

*John Byron (1723–1786) had served in *Anson's fleet as a Midshipman on HMS *Wager, enduring great adventures and hardships for four long years following her wreck on the coast of Chile in 1741. He is the leading character in O'Brian's early novel about these events,* The Unknown Shore, *a work in which he somewhat prefigures Jack *Aubrey. On his return to England, Byron's fortitude was rewarded by promotions to Lieutenant, Commander and Post Captain, all in 1746. From 1764 to 1766, as Captain of HMS *Dolphin, he made a brisk circumnavigation but few significant discoveries. After service as Governor General of Newfoundland (1769–1772), he was promoted Rear Admiral in 1774 and Vice-Admiral in 1778. Sent in 1779 to relieve British forces in North America during the Revolutionary War, en route he met—by no means for the first time in his career as the famous 'Foulweather Jack'—a fearsome gale that much reduced the fighting power of his force. This, combined with his own tactical disarray, led to a subsequent engagement with a French fleet being a most inconclusive affair, as a result of which he was soon recalled to England. Byron was then prevented by ill-health from ever again seeing service at sea. 'Foulweather Jack' was the grandfather of the poet Lord *Byron, their family being for many years highly distinguished in Britain's military and naval services.*

Byron, the Honourable

The sometime Captain of HMS *George* (COM 1).

*Various members of the Byron family served in the Royal Navy, two of whom were 'Honourable' in rank: Jack *Byron and his great nephew George Anson—later Lord—Byron (d.1868). However, neither man commanded an HMS *George.*

Byron, Lord

The famously dashing, romantic poet (FW 6; IM 9; TH 4; HD 4), a relative of whom serves as a Midshipman in Jack Aubrey's HMS *Leopard* (DI 3). Byron is greatly admired by his fellow-poet Lieutenant Mowett, especially as he is the grandson of an Admiral (RM 2,8).

> *George Gordon Noel, Lord Byron (1788–1824), the romantic poet frequently criticised in his time for immorality in both his work and life, published his verse from 1807 onwards, enjoying public success after 1812, the year in which the first part of his* *Childe Harold *was issued.*

From 1809 to 1811 Byron had travelled widely in Europe, including visits to Greece and Turkey. Having left England permanently in 1815, by 1822 had become greatly attached to the cause of Greek independence from Turkish rule. He soon became a dashing and idealistic military adventurer, leading a private brigade to Missolonghi and attaining there a surprising (to his many critics) reputation for organisational ability and personal toughness. However, he soon died in Greece of fever contracted on the ill-fated expedition. Lord Byron was a grandson of Admiral Jack *Byron, both members of a large and distinguished military and naval family.

C

C., Mrs

The wife of Cooper the druggist (LM 4).

Cacafuego

A Spanish 32-gun xebec frigate, Captain Don Martin de Langara (M&C 11), hired by the merchant Mateu to hunt down Jack Aubrey's marauding 14-gun sloop HMS *Sophie* (M&C 7+). She is soon famously engaged and captured by Jack, although Lieutenant James Dillon and Midshipman Ellis die at the height of the action, as does Captain Langara (M&C 10; PC 1+). As *Cacafuego* was not under the command of her regular Captain and her status was not technically that of a national ship (M&C 10), she is not bought into the Royal Navy and Jack is not made Post for the victory (M&C 11; PC 1). This action, Jack's first great triumph as an independent commander, is frequently mentioned in the series (HMS 9; TMC 1,2,3,7; FW 5,7; IM 4; FSW 2; RM 1; LM 6,7; TGS 4; WDS 5; YA 9).

> *The battle is closely based on Commander Thomas* *Cochrane's *taking on May 6th 1801 of the Spanish* El *Gamo *with his HMS* *Speedy. CUNNINGHAM *gives* Cacafuego *as a frequent Spanish ship nick-name meaning 'shits fire'; GOSSETT even has an HMS* Caca Fuego, *gunboat, wrecked off Gibraltar in early 1809, but this vessel is not recorded in COLLEDGE or NORIE.*

Cadafalch, Ramon Mateu

A Catalan acquaintance of Maturin in Tarragona (M&C 8).

Cadmus

A reference by Admiral Hughes to miraculous ways of producing fresh manpower (FSW 2).

> *In Greek myth Cadmus, the founder of Thebes, killed a dragon and sowed its teeth in the ground: fully armed men then sprang up from these 'seeds.'*

Cadogan, Edward

A member of Black's club (COM 2).

Caesar, Julius

Caesar, several times referred to as a figure of power (PC 10; TGS 6; COM 1; YA 4), is disliked by Stephen Maturin as an early coloniser (C/T 3). The captured Midshipmen of HMS *Ariel* facetiously claim 'Sir Julius Caesar' for a parent (SM 10).

> *Gaius Iulius Caesar (100–44 BC) was an ambitious, high-born politician, administrator and general who had served in the Roman army from an early age. Having already held the consulate in 59 BC, Caesar set out in the following year with an army for Gaul and its German borders, here conducting a long series of tough campaigns that, by 51, resulted in the complete pacification of Gaul; he had also conducted invasions of southern Britain in 55 and 54. By 50 Caesar's personal power and popularity had become so awesome that he was ordered by the Senate, encouraged by his political rival Pompey (see* ***Pompee, HMS**), *to disband his army and return to Italy. Caesar instead chose civil war, crossing the Rubicon River with a relatively small contingent of his force and occupying the towns in the north of his homeland, usually welcomed by the citizenry. Soon appointed dictator of Rome itself, Caesar quickly subdued opposition in Spain and, after some reverses, defeated Pompey's forces and allies first in Greece, and then in Egypt and North Africa. Spain briefly rose again under Pompey's sons, but by 46 Caesar had all but eliminated military opposition and been declared sole dictator of the Empire. Yet political opposition to imperial rule being in the hands of just one man continued in a faction led by Caesar's bitter enemy, Cassius, and by the republican idealist* *Brutus. *On March 15th of 44 BC they and their associates stabbed Caesar to death in the Senate, starting yet another series of civil wars, eventually won by Caesar's adopted son, Octavius (who, as first Emperor of Rome, took the name 'Augustus Caesar'). In addition to his military and civic feats, Caesar also wrote two famous multi-part books,* The Gallic War *on his early campaigns and* The Civil War *on his path to near-imperial power. 'Caesar' soon became the title by which Emperors were known, although by the time of* *Diocletian, *they now took the title 'Augustus,' with 'Caesar' being reserved for their chief aide and heir.*

Caesar, HMS
One of Admiral Saumarez' flagships, Captain Brenton (M&C 12). In the initial reverse against the French off Gibraltar she is so badly damaged that Saumarez transfers his flag to another ship: *Caesar*'s crew then petition Brenton to be allowed to work round the clock to get her ready for the next encounter (M&C 12; HMS 7)

> HMS Caesar, 80-gun, was launched in 1793 and in the following year took part in *Howe's great victory at the Glorious First of June. From 1800, as the principal Mediterranean flag-ship of Sir James de *Saumarez, she was commanded by his protégé, Jahleel *Brenton. After the first action of 1801 Saumarez shifted his flag to HMS *Audacious, stating that he did not believe that the battered Caesar could be made ready for him in time to tackle *Linois again. The feats of Brenton and his crew in having her fit for the Admiral within five days became the benchmark for energy, determination and innovation in emergency refits for many years to come. In 1805 Caesar was commanded by Sir Richard *Strachan in his taking of the small French squadron that had escaped from *Nelson's triumph at Trafalgar. The ship, named for Julius *Caesar, saw a great deal more action before being reduced to an army depot/transport in 1814 (see La *Flèche, HMS) and broken up in 1821.

Cain
A reference is made to the 'mark of Cain' and to a heretical 'Cainite' sect (YA 5; HD 4,7).

> In the Book of Genesis, Cain, a son of *Adam and Eve, killed his brother Abel and was then visibly marked by *God so that people on Earth should know to preserve him for his intended punishment: a long, wandering life of extreme toil and misery. The Cainites were an extreme Gnostic sect (see *Valentinius) who revered many of the rejected figures of the Old Testament, believing them to have been unjustly persecuted by Hystera, a jealous associate of the otherwise perfect God, later becoming the guardians of the supreme deity's hidden knowledge. See also *Seth.

Cain, Tubal
The person that Admiral Ives believes discovered the art of writing (FSW 1).

Calamy, Edward and Mrs
A deceased, former shipmate of Jack Aubrey in HMS *Theseus* and his widow. Edward had been made Post into HMS *Atalante* and later been given the decrepit HMS *Rochester*, soon lost with all hands in a storm. Jack takes the Calamys' son, Peter, into his HMS *Worcester* as a Midshipman (IM 2).

Calamy, Peter
The young son of Jack Aubrey's deceased shipmate, Captain Edward Calamy, taken by Jack as a Midshipman into HMS *Worcester* at Mrs Calamy's request (IM 2–9). He later follows Jack to HMS *Surprise* (IM 9+; TH 2+; FSW 2+; RM 3).

Calder, Admiral Sir Robert
An officer who had been court-martialed for an insufficiently good performance against a superior enemy squadron (FW 3; COM 10).

> Sir Robert Calder (1745–1818), a Scotsman, was commissioned Lieutenant in 1762 and almost immediately became wealthy for life by participating in the capture of an enormously valuable Spanish treasure ship. Made Post in 1780, in 1797 he served as *Captain of the Fleet at the Battle of Cape *St Vincent, resulting in a immediate knighthood, with a baronetcy in the following year; he was promoted Rear Admiral in 1799 and Vice Admiral in 1804. In 1804–1805 Calder served as a squadron commander under Admirals *Cornwallis and *Nelson, attempting to keep *Villeneuve's Franco-Spanish fleet from joining up with ships blockaded in Brest and Ferrol. On July 22nd 1805, in very heavy fog, he intercepted Villeneuve's force — about a third larger again than his own — and fought a confused, partial action in which he nevertheless took two Spanish ships-of-the-line. During the following two days Calder had the opportunity to bring Villeneuve to battle again but declined to do so, conceiving his orders to mean that he should at all costs preserve his own squadron intact and prevent, by manoeuvre rather than by battle, the enemy fleets from uniting. Calder's decisions caused outrage in London — although Nelson himself was sympathetic to the dilemma that his old comrade had faced — and he was recalled to face a court-martial. The trial took place in December 1805 (a few weeks after Nelson crushed Villeneuve at Trafalgar), with Calder receiving a severe reprimand for failure to use his utmost endeavours to defeat the enemy. Although he never again served at sea, Calder continued to rise in the Royal Navy by seniority, becoming a full Admiral in 1810.

Caledonia or *Caledonian*, HMS
Admiral Sir Francis Ives' flag-ship in the Mediterranean (TH 4,8), also briefly seen at other times and places (TMC 1; FSW 2; LM 1).

> HMS Caledonia was launched in 1808 as a 100-gun three-decker, becoming the model for heavy warship design. Renamed the hospital ship HMS Dreadnought in 1856, she was broken up in 1875. Caledonia is the Latin name for Scotland.

Caley
1: an Admiral who had told Mrs Martin that her husband Nathaniel's intemperate pamphlet on Royal Navy reform meant that he could never be re-employed in the service (LM 1).
2: a Commander known to Tom Pullings and his wife (TGS 1).
3: the man who had been shot dead by Clarissa Oakes, leading to her transportation to New South Wales (C/T 7).
4: a seaman in HMS *Bellona* (COM 6).

Caligula
The Roman Emperor referred to by Brendan Lawrence, Jack Aubrey's lawyer (RM 8).

> Gaius Julius Caesar Germanicus (12–41 AD), 3rd Emperor of Rome, was often known by his childhood nickname of Caligula ('Little Boot') from the army uniform he wore when he was a small child in the camp of his soldier-father, Germanicus). Gaius, a cultured and intelligent man,

succeeded *Tiberius as Emperor in 37 and, although initially popular, soon developed a deserved reputation for hedonism, caprice and cruelty. Assassinated, along with his wife and daughter, after a reign of four years, he was succeeded by Claudius, his uncle. 'Caligula' was regarded by many contemporaries and subsequent historians as having become clinically insane, a medical diagnosis that there is in fact very little direct evidence to support.

Callaghan, James or Paddy
A Master's Mate in HMS *Bellona*, sometimes in command of *Ringle*, her tender (YA 3,4,5).

Calliope, HMS
The ship that had brought to Malta both Andrew Wray and the confirmation of Tom Pullings' promotion to Commander (TH 1). She is later referred to in passing (YA 5).
HMS Calliope, 10-gun brig-sloop, was launched in 1808 and broken up in 1829. In Greek myth Calliope, the Muse of Poetry, was supposedly the mother of *Orpheus.

Callow
1: a volunteer in HMS *Surprise* (HMS 5+), one of the members of the larboard Midshipman's mess guilty of the theft and consumption of Maturin's experimental rats (HMS 6). Wounded in the head in the action against *Berceau*, he soon recovers (HMS 9).
2: a Midshipman in HMS *Bellona* (YA 6).

Calpe, HMS
A sloop of Saumarez' squadron, Captain Dundas, whose boats attempt to come to the aid of the stranded HMS *Hannibal* (M&C 12).
HMS Calpe, 14-gun, was the ex-Spanish San Joseph taken in 1800. At Algeçiras in 1801, under her Commander George Heneage Lawrence *Dundas, she played almost exactly the role O'Brian describes. Calpe, sold out of the service in 1802, was named for one of the pillars of Hercules, the term later being also used for the Rock of Gibraltar.

Calvert, Captain
Admiral Lord Stranraer's Captain of the Fleet in HMS *Queen Charlotte* (YA 6,7,9).

Calvin
Stephen Maturin fears that Lieutenant Macdonald may hold some Calvinist (HD 7) doctrines peculiar to the Royal Marines alone (PC 10).
John Calvin (1509–1564) was the French Protestant theologian and reformer who strongly supported Church control of the State, being himself virtual dictator of Geneva from 1541. Central to his thought was the belief that all but a chosen few humans, these possessed of God's grace, were predestined to a life of wretched depravity.

Cambrensis, Giraldus
A historian referred to by Maturin (HMS 11).
Giraldus de Barri (1146?–1220?) was a Welsh (Cambrensis being Latin for 'of Wales') priest who, after a turbulent political career in the Church, lived from 1196

onwards in retirement, a scholar in a Lincoln monastery. There he wrote a number of histories of Wales and Ireland, as well as lives of British saints.

Cambridge, HMS
A ship in Admiral Ives' Mediterranean fleet, Captain Scott (FSW 1).
The 80-gun HMS Cambridge, launched in 1755, had been broken up in 1808, some years before FSW is set; her replacement was not launched until 1815, well after FSW. The ships were probably named for King *George III's seventh son, Frederick, Duke of Cambridge (1774–1850).

Camden
The 'Camden faction' in New South Wales have become enemies of Stephen Maturin following his duel with Colonel Lowe (NC 9).
John Jeffries Pratt, 2nd Earl and 1st Marquis Camden (1759–1840) was Lord Lieutenant of Ireland from 1795 to 1804 (and thus a suppressor of the 1798 United Irishman uprising), Secretary of State for War from 1804–1805, and, with one brief interruption in 1807, President of the Council from 1806–1812. He was a patron in England of John *Macarthur, who consequently named his New South Wales estates 'Camden Park' (now the town of Camden), and the reference is therefore to 'the adherents of the Macarthur family.'

Camden
see **Earl Camden**

Camel, HMS
A store ship forming part of the small inshore squadron blockading St Martin's (LM 4).
HMS Camel was bought in 1798 and eventually sold in 1831.

Camilla, HMS
A 20-gun brig-sloop, Commander Smith, in Jack Aubrey's squadron (COM 3+).
HMS Camilla, a 20-gun 6th rate (and therefore a Postship, not a sloop), was launched in 1776, sent for harbour service in 1814 and sold in 1831. In Greek myth, Camilla, the daughter of King Metabus of the Volscians, was a fleetfooted attendant of the goddess *Diana.

Campbell
1: one of Colonel Fraser's officers (TMC 6).
2: Admiral Lord Keith's confidential secretary (HD 1).

Canaletto
A famous Italian painter to whose works O'Brian compares the view of Port Mahon from HMS *Sophie*'s stern windows (M&C 1).
Antonio Canal (1697–1768), a.k.a. 'Canaletto,' the Venetian painter renowned for his architectural views of his watery home city, made his initial reputation as a designer of sets for opera and theatre, his father's profession before him. Both he and his city were especially popular with English travellers and collectors, leading to Canaletto's long stay in London from 1746–1755.

Candish

The new purser of HMS *Surprise* who, reluctant to return to England to face a disagreeable domestic situation, joins the Royal Navy at sea from a rescued East Indiaman (HD 3,6).

Canning

1: Mrs Canning, the wife of Richard Canning, is a member of two families of powerful Jewish financiers, the Goldsmids and Mocattas. Incensed at her husband's relationship with Diana Villiers (HMS 1), she prepares to travel to India to confront him (HMS 7) and is due to arrive in Calcutta at about the same time that Canning is killed in the duel with Maturin (HMS 10).
2: a gentleman who had duelled with his fellow-politician, Castlereagh (TGS 4).

George Canning (1770–1827) was a Tory politician and writer who in 1807 became Foreign Secretary in the administration of the Duke of Portland. In 1809 Britain suffered a military fiasco at the island of Walcheren off the coast of Holland (see *Chatham and *Strachan). In the aftermath of the affair Canning quarrelled bitterly and publicly with Lord *Castlereagh, the Secretary for War, and the pair soon fought a pistol-duel in which Canning was slightly injured. He then resigned and held no formal position in government until returning as Foreign Secretary in 1821; in 1827, the year of his death, he served very briefly as Prime Minister.

3: a mate in the whaler *Daisy* (C/T 5).

Canning, Richard

An enormously wealthy, Jewish merchant of Bristol who offers the shipless Jack Aubrey command of a heavy privateer (PC 6+). Although Jack turns him down in favour of HMS *Polychrest*, Canning cheerfully celebrates this career step at a dinner on the ship (PC 8). Canning, a member of the Prince of Wales' set (PC 10), soon becomes an intimate admirer of Diana Villiers (PC 10), later reported by Cecilia Williams to have 'gone into keeping' with him (PC 14). In order to escape his wife's fury at this open affair, the couple move from England to Bombay (HMS 1,6+), where he becomes 'Mr Commissioner Canning' of the East India Company (HMS 6). Increasingly jealous of Diana's fondness for the visiting Stephen Maturin, he strikes the Doctor in the face when he finds them kissing (HMS 10). In their subsequent pistol-duel, Canning first fires and wounds Stephen, who in turn — yet not by intent — drops his opponent dead (HMS 10; SM 10).

Canning is a distinguished political name in England: see *Canning above. The Cannings were part-descended from the medieval Bristol merchant family, the Canynges. However, all appear to have been Christians.

Cannonière

A French ship that had recently taken HMS *Laurel*. She is said by Jack Aubrey to be ancient, dating from around 1710, but still very fast (TMC 1,3).

Known to be at Mauritius (TMC 1), she is later said to have been de-gunned, owing to her decrepit state (TMC 4,5).

Cannonière had a most eventful career but was not a very old frigate. She was launched as *Minerve in 1794 and captured the following year by the Royal Navy, being renamed HMS *Minerva. Under her Captain Jahleel *Brenton, she ran aground off Cherbourg in 1803, was taken by French gunboats, and then renamed Cannonière ('gunboat'). In late 1808 she took the 22-gun HMS *Laurel off Mauritius, but was herself so badly damaged in the hull that she was soon disarmed, and renamed Confiance, transport ship. In early 1810, en route to France with treasure, she was taken by the 74-gun HMS Valiant; she was sold later that year.

Canopus, HMS

A ship in Admiral Thornton's Mediterranean fleet (IM 8). James Fielding had served in her as a Lieutenant, narrowly missing participation in the Battle of Trafalgar (TGS 4).

HMS Canopus, 80-gun, was launched in 1797 as the French *Franklin. Taken by *Nelson at the Battle of the Nile in 1798, in 1805 she was the flag-ship of his subordinate commander, Admiral Thomas *Louis, but shortly before the Battle of Trafalgar was sent with a small squadron to Gibraltar for water and other supplies. Her Captain at this time was Francis William Austen (1774–1865; the brother of the novelist Jane Austen, 1775–1817), who in 1863 rose to become Admiral of the Fleet Sir Francis Austen (see also *Smith, Tom). His younger brother, Charles John Austen (1779–1852; see also *Phoenix, HMS), was also a Royal Navy officer, rising to Rear Admiral in 1846. The ship, eventually sent for harbour service in 1863 and sold for break-up in 1887, was named by Nelson for the ancient Egyptian city of Canopus.

Canterbury, Archbishop of

A prelate referred to by Jack Aubrey as a model of religious rectitude (FSW 9).

The See of Canterbury is the most senior Archbishopric in the Church of England, its occupant being the effective head of the Church, albeit under the Monarch in his or her capacity of 'Defender of the Faith.'

Capel

A senior Royal Navy officer in Halifax who, together with the Commissioner of the Dockyard, writes the injured Philip Broke's victory dispatch (SM 2).

The Honourable Thomas Bladen Capel (1776–1853) was a younger son of the Earl of Essex. At the Battle of the Nile in 1798, he was *Nelson's Flag Lieutenant in HMS *Vanguard. Quickly promoted Commander into HMS *Mutine, he carried the victory dispatch first to Naples and, having left Mutine to *Hoste, then on to London, where he was promptly made Post Captain. At the Battle of Trafalgar in 1805, Capel was one of Nelson's 'eyes of the fleet,' commanding the frigate HMS *Phoebe. From 1811 to 1814 he commanded HMS *Hogue on the North American station, being Senior Naval Officer in Halifax at the time of *Broke's great victory. Capel was promoted Rear Admiral in 1825, Vice Admiral in 1837 and Admiral in 1847.

Capell, Mrs

The owner of a school once attended by Molly Harte and Laetitia Ellis (M&C 8).

Capitan-Bey

see **Mustapha, Capitan-Bey of Karia**

***Captain*, HMS**

A 74-gun ship from which Nelson boarded the Spanish *San Josef* and *San Nicolas* (M&C author's note).

> *HMS* Captain, *74-gun, was launched in 1787, sent for harbour service in 1809, and in 1813 part-destroyed by fire and broken up. In 1797, under her Captain Ralph Miller (see* *Theseus, HMS*), *she was Commodore* *Nelson's pennant-ship at the Battle of Cape* *St Vincent.*

Captain of the Fleet

A type of flag officer (IM 3–5; FSW 1; HD 2,9).

> *The Captain of the Fleet was the Chief-of-Staff to the commanding Admiral and was either a very senior Post Captain or even a Rear Admiral. If not of flag rank in his own right he was paid as a Rear Admiral (e.g., FWS 1), dressed as one, and could issue orders under his own name to officers more senior than himself. Sometimes known as the 'First Captain,' he was almost always stationed in the same ship as his Admiral, with one vessel therefore containing a senior Admiral, a Captain of the Fleet and a* *Flag Captain (sometimes known as 'Second Captain'), the latter being the actual day-to-day commander of the ship itself.*

Caraciolo

Marine Lieutenant McDonald believes that Lord Nelson behaved badly in the 'Caraciolo affair' (PC 14).

> *Francesco Caracciolo (sic; 1752?–1799), Duca di Brienza, was a distinguished Neapolitan Commodore—fairly well known to* *Nelson—who had briefly joined a French-inspired rebellion against Britain's ally, King Ferdinand of Naples (see* *King of the Two Sicilies). The city soon fell to British and Royalist forces, accepting terms of surrender that explicitly excluded reprisals. However, neither Nelson nor Ferdinand had been party to the negotiations and, on arrival from Sicily, refused to be bound by them: Caracciolo and thousands of others were immediately arrested. The Commodore was summarily tried for treason on board HMS* *Foudroyant, albeit by a court composed of Neapolitan officers and nobles rather than British officers, and sentenced to be hung from the yard-arm of his own pennant-ship, Minerva, without further ado. Despite pleas for clemency, or at least the dignity of a firing-squad, Nelson confirmed the sentence and within two hours the Duke was dead. His manacled body was then tossed into the harbour, where, a few days later, it gruesomely bobbed to the surface in the full sight of the horrified King, Nelson having to order it retrieved and taken ashore for disposal. Whilst Nelson and* Foudroyant *lay offshore, scores—perhaps hundreds—of the other prisoners were executed by Ferdinand's supporters in the piazze of Naples with hundreds more being sentenced to life imprisonment.*

***Carcass*, HMS**

A bomb-ketch in which both a deceased Master's Mate, Blanckley, (PC 12) and the young Nelson had once served (NC 7).

> *HMS* Carcass, *8-gun bomb vessel, was launched in 1759 and sold in 1784, some 20 years before* *Blanckley's death. In 1773, the young* *Nelson served as Captain Skeffington Lutwidge's coxswain on HMS* Carcass' *Arctic exploration voyage.*

Cardan

A famous doctor and mathematician (M&C 2; HD 5).

> *Girolamo Cardeno (1501–1576) was an Italian physician, mathematician and astronomer who, although the first clinician to describe the course of typhus fever, is better remembered today for his works on probabilities and games of chance.*

Cardinal, the

A Prelate, related to Buonaparte family, who attends Maturin's lecture in Paris (SM 5).

Carew, Mr

The Chaplain of HMS *Lively* (HMS 2).

Carey

A manufacturer of quack medical remedies (WDS 7).

Carling

An Admiralty official (HMS 4), later secretary to Sir Joseph Blaine (YA 1).

Carlos

A French spy in Malta (TH 1).

Carlotta

1: a singer referred to by Jack Aubrey (TMC 1).
2: the owner of an hotel in Valetta, Malta (TH 8).

Carlow

1: a seaman in HMS *Polychrest* punished for theft (PC 8).
2: the Captain of HMS *Immortalité* who wishes to attend Parliament in his capacity as an MP. Lord Melville contemplates offering Jack Aubrey the frigate as his first, temporary, Post command (PC 12).
3: a man—or perhaps place—in Bath, visited by Maturin (HMS 4).
4: a seaman in HMS *Surprise* killed in action against Linois' *Marengo* (HMS 9).
5: the Commander of HMS *Orestes* (COM 4).

Carnegia, Fortunato

A seaman referred to in Captain Allen's HMS *Sophie* log (M&C 2).

Carol

1: a Midshipman in HMS *Otter* (TMC 4).
2: the surgeon's mate in Jack Aubrey's HMS *Boadicea* (TMC 5,9). We later learn that his share of the ship's prize money was so great that he was able to retire in considerable style (DI 3).

Caroline

1: a relative or friend of the Aubrey family who attends General Aubrey's funeral feast (LM 8), perhaps the same girl that the young Jack Aubrey had once clumsily insulted (NC 4).

2: the niece of Philip Aubrey (TGS 4).

N.B., in the context this looks like a slip for either Philip's half-niece Charlotte *Aubrey—whom O'Brian once elsewhere calls Caroline—or his more distant niece, little *Cecilia, daughter of Cecilia *Williams.

3: *see* **Aubrey, Charlotte**

Caroline

1: a new French 40-gun frigate (TMC 1) that takes the East Indiamen, *Europe* and *Streatham* (TMC 3). She is soon taken by Jack Aubrey at Réunion, and, as there is already an HMS *Caroline* in the Royal Navy, re-named HMS *Bourbonnaise* and given to Corbett (TMC 4,5). *Caroline was launched in 1806 and captured by HMS *Sirius in September 1809, having taken *Europe and *Streatham earlier that year. Re-named HMS *Bourbonnaise, for the French Royal House of *Bourbon, she was eventually broken up in 1817.*

2: a Bourbon frigate commanded by Captain Christy-Pallière (HD 4).

Caroline, **HMS**

When Jack Aubrey takes the French *Caroline*, he renames her HMS *Bourbonnaise*, there already being an HMS *Caroline* in the Royal Navy (TMC 4).

HMS Caroline, *36-gun, was launched in 1795 and, after long service in the Indian Ocean, broken up in 1815. She was named for Caroline of Brunswick (1768–1821), the wife from 1795 of the Prince of *Wales (see also *Fitzherbert, Mrs).*

Carpenter's Mistake

A nickname for Jack Aubrey's ill-conceived, and worse-built, HMS *Polychrest* (PC 6,7).

Carrick

A junior colleague of Sir Joseph Blaine (TGS 3).

Carrier, Joe

The name used by the landlord of the Marquess of Granby inn for the local haulier (LM 1).

Carrington

1: an agent who had been tortured and killed by Dubreuil (FW 7).

2: an Admiralty official who has fallen into the power of the spy Diego Diaz (YA 7).

Carrington, Isobel

The maiden name of the new Lady Barmouth, the widow of Admiral Horton (HD 9,10).

Carrington, Lucy

A lady who has given a ball attended by Diana Villiers (IM 1).

Carrol

1: the First Lieutenant of HMS *Hannibal*, whom Lieutenant Jack Aubrey once challenged to a duel (M&C 4).

The reference echoes a dispute between Philip Beaver (1766–1813), the First Lieutenant of Lord *Keith's flag-ship HMS *Foudroyant, and his junior officer Thomas *Cochrane, the model for many of Jack *Aubrey's early exploits. Both men were protégés of the Scotsman Keith, but Beaver, himself both an Englishman and a famously taut Premier, felt that his many Scottish subordinates had been appointed more on interest than merit, the fiery Cochrane first amongst them. In 1798 Beaver insisted—against Keith's advice—on having Cochrane court-martialled for passing a sarcastic comment on what he considered excessive attention to the perfection of the ship's appearance. The young Lieutenant was acquitted of the charge, although he was admonished by Lord Keith for displaying 'flippancy' on the quarterdeck. Beaver, a fine seaman, was promoted Commander in 1799 and made Post in 1801, serving from 1806 to 1809 in HMS *Acasta. Somewhat ironically, in 1810 he was one of the Captains who arrived at Mauritius with Admiral *Bertie's fleet after all of the hard work in preparation for the assault had been done by Commodore Josias Rowley, who in TMC is the partial model for Jack Aubrey. Having in 1811 played a distinguished role in the taking of Java, in 1813 Beaver died at the Cape of an illness contracted on his way home to England from New South Wales.

2: an officer in HMS *Indefatigable* (PC 14).

Carteret, Admiral

A cousin of Jack Aubrey, who had discovered Sweeting's Island. A circumnavigator with both Byron and Wallis, he commanded HMS *Swallow* in the latter's squadron (NC 8).

Philip Carteret (1738–1796) was commissioned Lieutenant in 1757, promoted Commander in 1766, and made Post in 1771; DNB records that he was promoted retired Rear Admiral in 1794 but SYRETT & DiNARDO do not confirm this. Carteret, having been a Lieutenant on Jack *Byron's HMS *Dolphin voyage of 1764–1766, was promoted on his return to England into HMS *Swallow and immediately accompanied *Wallis, now Dolphin's Captain, on another voyage of discovery. The ships became separated off Cape Horn and Carteret continued the circumnavigation alone. In 1767 he discovered a large number of South Sea islands (including Pitcairn Island, later of HMS *Bounty fame), naming them for himself, his colleagues and the great and good of Britain: however, a *Sweeting was not among them.

Cartwright

The Captain of HMS *Ganymede* (HD 2).

Cary, Mother

Grimble refers to the giant petrel as 'Mother Cary's Goose' (TGS 5).

The storm petrel, a blue-water ship-follower, is known to sailors as either 'Mother Carey's Chicken' (origins obscure) or, from its loud, challenging whistle, the 'bosun's mate.'

Casademon, En Ramon d'Ullastret

The senior Catalan officer on the French-held Baltic island of Grimsholm. He is both a descendent of Wilfred the Shaggy and the godfather of Stephen Maturin, who undertakes a mission to subvert his allegiance (SM 6–9). Casademon soon agrees to switch sides (SM 8), taking passage with his men back to Spain in a transport fleet led by Jack Aubrey's HMS *Ariel* (SM 8,9). When the ship is wrecked on the French coast, he disguises himself as the Royal Marine private 'Ludwig Himmelfahrt,' and soon escapes (SM 9). *See also* ***Ramon # 2**.

> *Casademon is, to some degree, based on a distinguished Spanish soldier, General Pedro Caro y Suredra, Marquis de La Romana (1761–1811). In 1807 he was appointed to command of a Spanish corps incorporated into *Buonaparte's army following a treaty arrangement with *Godoy. This body of about 9,000 troops was promptly sent to the far north of Europe, there to serve under General *Bernadotte. When, in 1808, Buonaparte put into action a coup in Madrid that effectively deposed King *Charles IV, *Wellington arranged for Romana's loyalty to be suborned in a style somewhat reminiscent of Maturin's adventure. The Foreign Secretary, *Canning, soon sent the Scottish Benedictine monk and secret government agent, James Robertson (1758–1820; his religious name was 'Father Gallus'), to Romana's base on Fünen, the second largest island in Denmark. Disguised as a cigar and chocolate merchant, Robertson crossed the enemy lines and appraised Ramona of the treachery at home in Spain: the Marquis agreed to change sides and was given a Royal Navy transport fleet—initially lead by Rear Admiral *Keats in his HMS *Superb—to take himself and his men southwards. The entire force arrived in Spain without incident, but was soon defeated and dismembered by the French and their local allies. In 1810 Romana was appointed Commander-in-Chief of a new, independent Spanish army, operating alongside Wellington's forces in Portugal, but the Marquis died of illness in the following year. James Robertson lived in Dublin from 1809 to 1813, but in that latter year returned to diplomatic and intelligence service with Wellington in Spain. In 1815 he was given a large pension by the British government and then retired to his home monastery—which lay in Bavaria—to take up a final career as a successful educator of the deaf and dumb. In 1863 his nephew, Alexander Clinton Fraser, published Robertson's* Narrative of a Secret Mission to the Danish Islands in 1808.

Caspar

One of the Three Magi, referred to by Maturin for his blackness (RM 2).

> *The* Magi *(Latin for 'wise ones') and their role in *Jesus's birth are recorded in, e.g., Matthew 2. However, the name Caspar (or Gaspar/Gathaspa) does not appear as one of their number before the 8th century.*

Cassandra

The last-remaining of HMS *Lively*'s gibbon apes, according to Maturin a declining alcoholic (PC 12, 14).

Castlereagh

A politician referred to disparagingly by Maturin (M&C 3), later said by Blaine to be responsible for British relations with Sweden (LM 4). He is famous for having duelled with Canning, a fellow politician (TGS 4).

> *Robert Stewart (1769–1822), Viscount Castlereagh, was British Chief Secretary for Ireland from 1798 to 1801. Though strongly in favour of the British/Irish Union (which *Maturin of course opposes) that finally occurred through his efforts in 1801, he nevertheless resigned in protest in that same year when King *George III rejected concomitant Catholic emancipation (which Maturin of course supports). Castlereagh next served as Secretary of State for War from 1805 to 1809 and then as Foreign Secretary from 1812 to 1822. In 1809 he had fought a non-fatal duel with George *Canning, the then Foreign Secretary, over a public dispute the two had over the fiasco of the attempt to seize Walcheren Island (see *Chatham and *Strachan). Only a year before his own death, Lord Castlereagh inherited the Marquisate of Londonderry from his father.*

Castro, Garcia de

A Spanish government agent in Peru, of uncertain loyalty (WDS 7+).

Catherine

*see **Amiable Catherine***

Catiline

A Roman referred to by Maturin (RM 7).

> *Lucius Sergius Catilina (110?–62 BC) was a Roman politician and general famous for his reckless ambition. He was an enemy of *Cicero, who, in one of his most famous orations, denounced him in the Senate and soon brought about his downfall and eventual death in battle.*

Cato

Aubrey refers to a mild dispute with Maturin over the pronunciation of Cato (RM 6).

> *Ancient Rome had a number of distinguished Catos, members of the Porcius family. Cato the Censor (234–149 BC) became a byword for austerity and rectitude; his great-grandson Cato the Younger (95–46 BC) was a famous Stoic and a staunch enemy of Julius *Caesar's political ambition. *Aubrey would have pronounced Cato in the 'old English' style, 'kay-toe,' whilst *Maturin would probably have favoured the 'continental' Italian/Roman style 'chaa-toh.'*

Catullus

A Latin poet quoted by Maturin (FW 4).

> *Caius Valerius Catullus (84?–54? BC) was a wealthy and fashionable young poet, born in Verona. His passionate and ultimately unsuccessful affair with a married woman, Clodia, led him to write many love-poems (in which Clodia is disguised as 'Lesbia'), using the models of classical Greece rather than the recent Roman styles. Catullus is regarded as one of the very finest Latin poets, fresh and 'modern' to this day.*

Cavaignac

A Frenchman shot as a result of Maturin's intelligence coup in *Desolation Island* (FW 1).

Ceasoir

According to Maturin, a daughter of Noah who had visited Ireland (TGS 4).

*Queen Ceasoir/Ceasair, usually said to have been a grand-daughter of Noah, was the leader of a tribe supposed to have invaded Ireland before the great flood. In this calamity she perished with all her people, the sole escapee being Finntam, who escaped by changing himself into the Salmon of Knowledge (see *MacCool, Finn). In Gaelic poetry, Ceasair is often seen as a synonym for Ireland herself.*

Cecilia

1: Sophie Aubrey's very young niece, living with her at Ashgrove Cottage. She is the daughter of Cecilia Williams, who is away following her — unnamed — husband's regiment (TMC 1).

2: Saint Cecilia, the subject of a piece of music either owned or written by Maturin (TGS 10).

Saint Cecilia was a Roman virgin supposed to have suffered martyrdom for her Christian faith in the late second century. The patroness of musicians, she is as such a frequent subject of musical compositions and historical paintings.

3: *see* **Williams, Cecilia**

Centaur, the

A classical reference by Aubrey (YA 9).

The Centaurs were a mythical tribe of wild and dangerous beasts, half-human and half-horse.

Centaur, HMS

A ship whose surgeon, Mr Edwardes, is visited by Stephen Maturin in order to witness his first ever naval amputation (M&C 2). Later, under her then Captain Hood, she had taken and fortified the Diamond Rock (HD 10).

*HMS Centaur, 74-gun, was launched in 1797 and broken up in 1819. She became famous, under her Captain *Markham, for the adoption in the late 1790s of a new and healthier design of sick-berth. In 1804, now as the pennant-ship of Commodore Samuel *Hood, she took the small, precipitous Diamond Rock, off Martinique, and by prodigious efforts of rigging and endurance, hoisted cannon to her summit. The little island was even commissioned as the 'sloop-of-war' HMS Diamond Rock, but was taken by a French assault in the following year.*

Centurion, HMS

A large ship (LM 1) in which Grainger's grandfather had served under Commodore Anson (WDS 10).

*HMS Centurion, launched in 1732, was *Anson's 60-gun flag-ship for his 1740s circumnavigation; she was broken up in 1769. Centurions were the principal professional officers of the Roman army, commanding around one hundred men.*

Cerbère

A new French ship about to be launched in the Adriatic (HD 4). Under some forceful encouragement from Aubrey and Maturin, her Captain Delalande declares for Louis XVIII (HD 5)

For her name definition, see **Cerberus**.

Cerberus

A classical reference by Sir Joseph Blaine (RM 9).

In Greek myth Cerberus was the monstrous, three-headed dog that guarded the entrance to the underworld.

Cerberus, HMS

A ship at Trieste whose surgeon visits HMS *Nymphe* in order to watch Maturin perform an operation (TH 9).

*HMS Cerberus, 32-gun, was launched in 1794 and sold out of the service in 1814. In 1811, under Captain Henry *Whitby, she took part in *Hoste's dashing victory at Lissa.*

Cerutti

A European scientist at Maturin's lecture in Paris (SM 5).

César

A French ship due to join the squadron bound for Ireland (COM 9).

*César, 74-gun, served in the French navy from 1807 to 1817. Her name is derived from the line of Roman rulers established by Julius *Caesar.*

Cestos, HMS

A brig in Jack Aubrey's inshore squadron commanded by Mr Whewell (COM 9).

Ceylon

An East Indiaman taken by the French (TMC 7) that later, as part of the enemy squadron, strikes to HMSS *Iphigenia* and *Magicienne* but runs before she can be secured. With many other of the ships involved in the battle, she then runs aground (TMC 7).

*Ceylon, 818-tons, made four round trips to England for the British East India Company between 1802 and 1809. In July 1810, under her Master Henry Meriton, she and several consorts were taken by a French squadron after a brisk fight. Taken into the French service under the same name, she was then used as a prison ship at Mauritius. When that island fell to the British at the end of the same year, she was repossessed; her fate thereafter is unknown, but she was not taken back into Company service. See also *Bombay, HMS.*

Chads

The wealthy First Lieutenant of HMS *Java*, a scientific officer who loves gunnery and has invented new cannon-sights (FW 3). Although himself wounded in the action against USS *Constitution*, after his Captain Lambert is disabled he struggles up to take command, yet soon has to surrender his battered, sinking ship (FW 3). Acquitted at the necessary court martial (FW 8), he later visits Sophie Aubrey in England, bearing news of her badly injured husband (SM 2).

*Sir Henry Ducie Chads (1788?–1868) was commissioned Lieutenant in 1806 and in 1810 served on Henry *Lambert's HMS *Iphigenia in the Mauritius campaign. After* *the HMS* Java *fiasco of 1812, Chads was nevertheless promoted Commander in 1813 for his personally valiant defence of the ship. Made Post in 1815, he was promoted Rear Admiral in 1854, Vice Admiral in 1858 and Admiral in 1863. Throughout his long career — except as noted below — he held active, fighting commands, especially in campaigns in Burma, China and the Crimea. As a well-known enthusiast, he was in 1845 appointed to command of the Royal Navy School of Gunnery in HMS* Excellent, *a post that he held with distinction for several years.*

Challoner, Bishop

A prelate who was a source of information about the number of closet Catholics serving King George (M&C 6).

Richard Challoner (1691–1781) was Roman Catholic Bishop of Debra from 1738, de facto *leader of the English Roman Catholic community from 1741, and the Rome-appointed Apostolic Vicar of London from 1758 onwards.*

Cham

1: the 'Cham of Tartary,' a joking reference by Maturin to an imagined Eastern potentate (HMS 1).
2: the 'Great Cham,' a reference to Sir Joseph Banks (RM 6).

Cham is an obsolete form of 'Khan,' or 'Ruler/King,' and hence *Banks *is the 'pre-eminent figure' in his field: Dr Samuel* *Johnson *was known in his own lifetime as 'the Great Cham of Literature.'*

Chambers

A seaman on HMS *Sophie* (M&C 6+).

Chameleon, HMS

A ship at Bombay to which HMS *Java* is carrying some fresh crew (FW 3).

HMS Chameleon *or* Cameleon, *16-gun brig-sloop, was launched in 1795 but broken up in 1811, rather before HMS* *Java *must have set sail. Her 10-gun replacement, built in Bombay, was not launched until 1816, being broken up in 1849.*

Champflower

A physician to whom Blaine favourably compares Maturin (PC 3).

Chapel, Mrs

The wife of the Master-Attendant of Gibraltar naval yard (FSW 2).

Chapman

An author who had translated Homer (FSW 4).

George Chapman (1559?–1634) had a career as a soldier and playwright before making his reputation as a translator of *Homer *from 1598 until 1616. His overall output was prodigious, yet very little is known of his life and it is thought that he may have died in poverty and obscurity. Although his translations of both the* Iliad *and* Odyssey *were long well known and well regarded, their reputation was given an enormous boost by the publication in 1816 of a sonnet by John Keats (1795–1821) in praise of the work, 'On First Looking into Chapman's Homer.'*

Charles

1: a relative or friend of the Colpoys family (PC 6).
2: a doorman at Black's club (RM 5+; YA 8).
3: a waiter at Black's club (LM 7).
4: a street-crossing sweeper in London (YA 1).
5: *see* **Babbington, William**

Charles II, King

The King of England whose restoration to the throne is commemorated by gunfire in the Royal Navy (FSW 2); his favourite dish is said to have been eggs and ambergris (FSW 3). Jack Aubrey later refers to King Charles when describing his own lack of desire to lose his position and travel around waiting for restoration (NC 10).

King Charles II of England, Scotland and Ireland (1630–1685) was the eldest son of that Charles I who was dethroned by Parliament and, in 1649, executed. The younger Charles fought in his father's army and was even crowned King by the Scots shortly after the elder's execution. However, his remaining forces were soon defeated by those of *Cromwell *and, in 1651, he fled to Europe. In 1659, after Cromwell's death, the republican regime in England began to collapse, allowing General George Monck (later 1st Duke of* *Albemarle) *to negotiate the restoration of Charles as King, an event that took place in May of 1660. The subsequent reign was marked by many religious controversies, in particular by Parliament's attempts to exclude from the succession the childless King's brother, the Roman Catholic James, Duke of York. Charles, something of a religious liberal and himself eventually a closet Romanist, annulled the penal laws against Catholics and Dissenters; Parliament responded in 1673 with the a Test Act that specifically excluded non-Protestants from service under the Crown (the very law often referred to in relation to* *Maturin's Catholicism). *After further struggles, Charles ruled without a Parliament from 1681 until his death. His brother thereupon did succeed to the throne as King* *James II, *in due course occasioning yet another revolution in England.*

Charles IV, King

A King of Spain referred to in passing (WDS 8).

King Charles IV (1748–1819) succeeded his father to the Spanish throne in 1788, falling rapidly under the influence of *Godoy, *the favourite of his Queen Maria. In 1808, under pressure from both Godoy and his French allies, Charles abdicated in favour of his own son, Ferdinand, but both were soon forced by* *Buonaparte *to resign their family claim to the throne (also see* ***Buonapartes, the***). After a period of confinement, Charles was given a large pension by Paris and, in about 1811, retired permanently to Rome.*

Charles V

A monarch in past times (M&C 12; TGS 1).

Charles (1500–1558) inherited, in three tranches, one of the greatest Empires of all time: on the death of his father in 1506 he became Duke of Burgundy and the Netherlands; in 1516 he succeeded one of his grandparents as King Charles I of Spain and Naples; and in 1519 he was elected Holy Roman Emperor (i.e. Emperor of Germany) in succession to another grandparent. His various reigns were oc-

cupied by wars with France and her Italian allies and by the upheavals of the rise of Protestantism under the Reformation. Exhausted by his labours (and eventually forced to compromise with both France and Protestantism), in 1558 he handed his Spanish possessions to his son, Philip II, and his German possessions to his brother, Ferdinand I. He then retired to a Spanish monastery, where he soon died.

Charlie

1: a half-witted seaman in HMS *Diane* (TGS 10).
2: *see* **Ricketts, Charles**

Charlotte

see **Aubrey, Charlotte** *or* **Colpoys, Mrs**

Charlotte, HMS

see ***Queen Charlotte*, HMS**

Charlton

1: the Captain of the unhappy HMS *Superb* in Thornton's Mediterranean fleet (IM 4).
2: a man whom Admiral Schank says went too high in a balloon and consequently froze (LM 1).

Charlton

A merchantman taken by *Vénus* and *Manche* (TMC 5).

Charlton, 818-tons, made 6 round trips for the British East India Company between 1798 and 1808. In November 1809 she was taken by the French off Mauritius and then re-taken by the Royal Navy when that island fell in December 1810. Her subsequent fate is unrecorded.

Charnock

HMS *Lively*'s carpenter (PC 14).

Charnock, Harry

A cousin of Jack Aubrey (LM 8).

Charon

A gem-dealer in Paris (SM 5).

Chartres, Colonel

A famous lecher referred to by Reverend White (HMS 11) and Jack Aubrey (YA 3).

*'Colonel' Francis Charteris (1675–1732; the name is pronounced and sometime spelled 'Charters/Chartres') was a notorious Scottish gambler, usurer and rake, earning for himself the awful title 'Rape-Master General of Great Britain.' He served in both the British and Dutch armies (never rising above Captain), being dismissed from both for dishonesty. So great was his reputation that both the satirist Alexander *Pope and the painter William Hogarth (1697–1764) used him as an archetype for the wild debauchery of their age.*

Charwell, HMS

A 32-gun frigate, Captain Griffiths, in which Aubrey and Maturin travel as passengers (PC 1).

HMS Charwell was in fact an 18-gun sloop, the ex-French Aurore, launched in 1799, captured by the Royal Navy in 1801 and eventually sold in 1813. The Charwell, or Cherwell, is a river flowing through Oxford.

Chastity

A British merchant vessel seized by the French on the re-declaration of war (PC 4).

Chatham

A former First Lord of the Admiralty, once served by Blaine (HMS 1).

*John Pitt (1756–1835), 2nd Earl of Chatham, was the eldest son of the great William Pitt, the 1st Earl, and brother to the younger William *Pitt. Although by background an army officer, he served in his brother's Ministry as *First Lord of the Admiralty from 1788 to 1794, as Lord Privy Seal from 1794 to 1796 and as Lord President of the Council from 1796 to 1801. In 1801 he rejoined the army and in 1808 vied with *Wellington for high command in Spain. Disappointed of this, in 1809 he was given charge (with Rear Admiral *Strachan) of the expedition to capture the island of Walcheren, lying just off the Dutch coast. He was quite rightly held responsible by the Prime Minister, Spencer *Perceval, for the ensuing fiasco (the island taken but the victory not exploited; the loss of over 4000 men by malaria and the subsequent embarrassing withdrawal) and soon fired. Nevertheless appointed full General in 1812 (although, after Walcheren, he never again commanded troops in the field), from 1820 to 1835 he served as Governor of Gibraltar.*

Chators

A supplier of venison (PC 12).

Chatterton

An author referred to by Martin (RM 3).

*Thomas Chatterton (1752–1770) was a Bristol writer and poet who produced a large number of clever pastiches of ancient forms — including those of *Ossian — that enjoyed some popularity and admiration for their near-authenticity and precocious brilliance. For the purpose of his initial deceit, he had invented a 15th century monk named 'Rowley': once revealed as the true author, Chatterton then moved from the west-country to London in high hopes of literary success. Within a few months of arrival he had committed suicide, apparently reduced to despair by immediate poverty, unrelieved by his anticipated patrons.*

Chaucer

The great author, whose free borrowing of plot from other writers is noted by O'Brian (FSW author's note), also referred to by Maturin and others (FW 7; YA 4).

Geoffrey Chaucer (1343?–1400) served as a soldier under King Edward III and was a protégé of John of Gaunt, who paid him a pension from 1367 onwards. Having seen both diplomatic and military service in France and Italy, he then held a number of administrative positions in England. In the late 1360s Chaucer achieved considerable renown as a poet, his work being greatly influenced by earlier exposure to contemporary, continental European literature. The famous Canterbury Tales, written from 1387 onwards, consist of 22 lively, often scurrilous stories, told to each other by pilgrims in order to ease the rigours of the journey from London to Canterbury and back (with

*Chaucer himself contributing 2 more tales in his author-ial voice). Many of the tales draw for their basic plots on French romances and the Italian works of Boccaccio and *Plutarch.*

Chauncy, William B.

The American sailing master of the *Franklin*, killed by HMS *Surprise*'s gunfire (WDS 2).

Cheal, Maggie

A female sailor who comes aboard HMS *Surprise* (perhaps from HMS *Leviathan*), where she acts as a nurse alongside Mrs Poll Skeeping. She is the sister-in-law of *Surprise*'s bosun (HD 2–10). *See also* **Defiance, HMS**

Cherubini

A composer whose works are played by Aubrey and Maturin (IM 5).

*Luigi Cherubini (1760–1842) wrote nearly 30 operas, several Masses and Requiems and six string quartets. Having enjoyed great success in Italy and London, he settled in Paris in 1788 and he soon became the city's leading composer. However, he gradually fell out of favour with *Buonaparte and, in 1805, was forced to leave for Vienna (where he was to be a strong influence on Beethoven). Following the *Bourbon restoration, Cherubini in 1815 returned to France, immediately becoming a Professor at the Paris Conservatoire, and serving as its director from 1821 to 1841.*

Cherubino

*see '**Marriage of Figaro**'*

Chesapeake, USS

An American frigate that had been fired on, most controversially, by Salusbury Humphreys' HMS *Leopard* (FSW 9). Several years later she arrives at Boston, having eluded the British blockade (FW 2,4,5,8). Under her newly appointed Captain Lawrence, she soon sails out to meet HMS *Shannon* in single-ship combat but is rapidly defeated and captured (FW 9; SM 1,3,4; FSW 3; RM 6).

*USS Chesapeake was authorised in 1794 as one of the new 44-gun ships of the new U.S. Navy. Her construction was then delayed by several changes in official policy and she was not launched until 1799, and then as a 38-gun. In 1807 Vice-Admiral the Honourable George *Berkeley, the British commander at Halifax, Nova Scotia, ordered his ships to seize any Royal Navy deserters that it suspected were in U.S. warships, even though no state of war existed between the two countries. *Humphreys, in his 50-gun HMS *Leopard, intercepted Chesapeake, under her Captain James Barron (1768–1851), off Norfolk, Virginia and demanded the right to search his ship. Barron was dumbfounded at the order and of course determined to resist such an outrage but, at the disadvantage of his ship being wholly unprepared for any hostile encounter, before he could run his own guns free he received three full broadsides from the British ship, compelling him to strike. As alluded to several times in the series, this incident caused great resentment in the U.S. and was a contributing factor to war breaking out in*

*1812. (Captain Barron himself was largely excused blame for his performance, although he was reprimanded and suspended for his failure to prepare the ship quickly enough once he realised he was about to be attacked. Yet the affair lingered on, and in 1820 Barron fought a duel with the dashing Commodore Stephen Decatur (1779–1820), who had continued to voice public criticism of his earlier conduct: Decatur was killed and Barron badly injured.) In May 1812 the very successful Captain James *Lawrence was promoted into Chesapeake from the smaller USS *Hornet, his first task being to complete the major refit his new ship was undergoing in Boston. With an over-confidence hitherto the preserve of British Captains in the area, Lawrence almost immediately stood out with his under-manned ship and under-trained crew to do battle with Philip *Broke's highly efficient HMS *Shannon, a ship of about the same weight of broadside. Chesapeake was forced to strike within 15 minutes, Lawrence having been fatally shot by one of Shannon's Royal Marine officers as the two ships closed. The battered Chesapeake was taken into Halifax by Shannon and bought into the Royal Navy as HMS Chesapeake (never seeing any active service). Later sent to England, in 1819 she was sold out of the service and gradually broken up. Some of her timbers went to make Chesapeake Mill, in Wickham, Hampshire, a business that survived until at least 1864 (when it was visited by the Reverend *Brighton) and probably for many years afterwards.*

Cheseldon

Maturin refers to the operation known as 'Cheseldon's lithotomy' (PC 10).

William Cheselden (sic; 1688–1752) was a renowned English surgeon and a pioneer of high-speed lithotomy (i.e., stone-removal, especially from the bladder), for which operations he received enormous fees from his predominantly wealthy, agony-ridden patients. The author of a number of standard textbooks on human anatomy, Cheselden also held important posts in several of the leading London hospitals.

Cheslin

A sick seaman aboard HMS *Sophie*, formerly a 'sin-eater,' who becomes Maturin's loblolly-boy (M&C 6+).

Chevènement

A seaman in HMS *Surprise* who hails from the island of Jersey and consequently speaks some French (LM 5).

Cheyne, Dr

A physician referred to by Maturin for his theory that the mind and body influence each other's well-being (IM 4).

George Cheyne (1671–1743) was a mathematician and physician who wrote many popular treatises on health and medicine, including The Natural Method of Cureing *(sic) the Diseases of the Body and the Disorders of the Mind Depending on the Body, etc. (1742, and many subsequent editions).*

Cheyney, Aunt
The elderly sister of Clarissa Oakes' childhood 'guardian,' Edward (C/T 6).

'Childe Harold'
A poem by Lord Byron (SM2; IM 9).

Lord *Byron published the four Cantos of Childe Harold's Pilgrimage from 1812 to 1818 ('Childe' is an Old-English title meaning, roughly, 'young gentleman'). In the first two Cantos, published in 1812, Harold has become jaded with his life of dissolution and, in need of distraction, sets out on a pilgrimage through Europe, the sensations of which journey he narrates in an enthusiastic, even histrionic style: the work immediately made Byron wildly famous. Canto III was written in 1816 and contains Harold's further travels, together with reflections on the Peninsular War and the Battle of Waterloo (see *Wellington). In Canto IV, Byron uses his own authorial voice to muse on time and history, especially as symbolised by the 'eternal sea.'

Childers
see **Flying Childers**

Child's
The name of a London banking house (C/T 4).

The bank was founded by the goldsmith and bullion dealer Sir Francis Child (1642–1713). He was several times an MP and served a term as *Lord Mayor of London, a career pattern followed by several later generations of his family.

Chilon
An ancient figure referred to by Aubrey, who entertainingly believes him to have been an ironmonger (WDS 9).

Chilon of Sparta (active c.556 BC) was one of the Seven Wise Men of Greece, said to have had 'saws' (or sayings) such as 'Know Thyself' and 'Nothing in Excess' inscribed on the Temple of Apollo at Delphi.

'Chips'
The traditional nick-name, encountered frequently in the series, for all ships' carpenters.

Choate, Dr Otis P.
The brother-in-law of Surgeon Evans of the USS *Constitution*, who runs a hospital in Boston — the Asclepia — predominantly for the insane. However, the standard of general medical care is also high and it is here that Jack Aubrey is sent to recover from his serious wounds (FW 4–7).

Choles
The loblolly-boy in HMS *Surprise*, a former butcher (HMS 9,11).

Choles, Henry
A member of the carpenter's crew in HMS *Surprise* (FSW 10).

Cholmondeley
A wealthy cousin of Diana Villiers (YA 1,2,3,8), killed alongside her in a coaching accident (HD 1).

N.B., in Britain the name is usually pronounced 'Chumley.'

Chorley, Reverend
An acquaintance of George Herapath in Boston (FW 8).

Chose, Madame
A French dress-maker and fabric smuggler in Halifax, Nova Scotia (SM 1).

Christ
see **Jesus**

Christian
The Master's Mate in HMS *Bounty* who had to endure Captain Bligh's mood swings (D1 1).

Fletcher Christian (1764–1793?) had already served for a few years in the Royal Navy as a Midshipman when, in late 1787, he was appointed Master's Mate to Lieutenant William *Bligh, a family acquaintance who was now the commander of the little exploration ship, HMS *Bounty. Once in the South Seas, Bounty remained at Tahiti, a virtual paradise for European sailors, for five months, with Bligh allowing discipline to slacken ashore. When the ship eventually sailed for the West Indies, Christian — a man of limited sea-faring talent, long led a sad dance of it by his foul-mouthed commander, a most unpredictable friend — seized the ship with the aid of some similarly discontented petty officers, setting Bligh and some loyal followers adrift in an open boat (in which they eventually reached the distant Timor). Christian, instantly aware of the enormity of what he had done, decided that he must leave Tahiti and eventually, with only eight followers, sailed the ship (now joined by his local wife, Mauatua, and some other island natives) to the remote, uninhabited Pitcairn Island. In 1808 a sole survivor of the mutinous band, John Adams, was found on this somewhat inhospitable rock with some of the descendants of the natives. He reported that the island had soon become a hotbed of discontent and murder, and that Christian and all the English sailors were long dead (Adams was allowed to remain, unmolested by the Navy, and Pitcairn is inhabited by his family and others to this day). Nevertheless, there is an enduring tale — unverifiable one way or the other — that Christian had in fact escaped from Pitcairn in 1808 and returned to England in the following year.

Christie-Pallière
see **Christy-Pallière, Guillaume**

Christie's
The London auction house (RM 8).

The firm was founded in London in about 1766 by James Christie (1730–1803). DNB states that he was a former commissioned naval officer but he is not recorded as such in SYRETT & DiNARDO. However, one of his sons, Edward, did enter the Royal Navy as a Midshipman, dying of fever at Jamaica in 1821.

Christine, cousin
see **Wood, Christine**

Christy
The family name of Captain Christy-Pallière's English cousins (M&C 12). The family, residing at Laura Place in Bath, consists of Mrs Christy, Miss Christy (the eldest daughter, who may perhaps be named 'Polly'), Miss Susan, Tom, and Madame de Aguillières (PC 4,7).

Christy-Pallière, Guillaume
The Captain of *Desaix* to whom Jack Aubrey surrenders HMS *Sophie*, being allowed to keep and wear his sword. The Frenchman then plays a leading role in the initial defeat of Saumarez' squadron off Algeçiras (M&C 11+). A man with English cousins (M&C 12; *also* HMS 2,7; FW 4; IM 6), he immediately becomes a personal admirer of Jack, later giving his visiting friend a discrete warning to leave France before war is re-declared following the collapse of the Peace of Amiens (PC 4). Many years later, Jack, knowing that his old friend he has been promoted Admiral, first meets and then captures his young nephew, Pierre Dumesnil, a Lieutenant in *Cornélie* (TGS 8; NC 5–7). Later still, during Buonaparte's 'hundred day' return to power, Christy-Pallière, now a Bourbon loyalist, is in command of the frigate *Caroline* (and once again a mere Captain) and is able to give Jack many valuable details concerning the complex political and military situation following the Emperor's restoration (HD 4,5).

> *It was to Jean-Anne Christi-Pallière (sic; sometimes seen as 'Pallière-Christi') of *Desaix that Commander Thomas *Cochrane surrendered HMS *Speedy in 1801, the basis for the events of M&C 11.*

Chubb, Miss
Tom Pullings' fiancée (PC 7).
see also **Pullings, Tom** and **Mrs**

Chuck
The Master's Mate of a captured American whaler (WDS 5).

Church, William
A Midshipman in HMS *Surprise*, one of the members of the larboard Midshipman's mess who stole and ate Maturin's experimental rats (HMS 6–9).

Churchill
The author of a book of voyages (FW 2; HD 6).

> *Awnsham Churchill (d.1728) and his brother John (dates unknown) were well-known publishers and printers who, in 1704, produced the very successful, multi-volume A Collection of Voyages and Travels, a work that went on to appear in many later, expanded editions.*

Cicero
The great Roman orator (TMC 9; RM 7).

> *Marcus Tullius Cicero (106–43 B.C.) was a great Roman orator, lawyer, philosopher, writer and politician; although now usually known as 'Cicero,' until quite recently he was often referred to by English-speakers as 'Tully.' The power and elegance of Cicero's oratory — in court, in the Senate and in voluminous correspondence — has had a profound effect down through the centuries on the development of many languages beyond his native Latin, and his works remain as models of classical acumen. A political opponent of the imperial ambitions of Julius *Caesar, Cicero was a witness to his assassination, a deed of which he approved. He then continued as a vocal opponent of Caesar's competing heirs, Octavius, Lepidus and, especially, Marcus Antonius, by whose soldiers he was eventually murdered.*

Cimarosa
The composer of *Le Astuzie Femminile*, a work enjoyed by Blaine and — somewhat later — heard by Maturin (PC 14).

> *Domenico Cimarosa (1749–1801) was the composer of some 65 operas as well as symphonies and keyboard sonatas. A supporter of the French Revolution, he had been sentenced to death in 1799 for political activities in his native Naples (see *Caraciolo), although this was soon commuted to permanent exile in Venice.*

Circe, HMS
A ship in which Midshipman Jack Aubrey (TMC 2) and Phelps of HMS *Worcester* (IM 2) had once served.

> *HMS Circe, 28-gun, was launched in 1785. Having served in *Duncan's victory at Camperdown in 1797, she was wrecked off Yarmouth in 1803. Her 32-gun replacement, which could also be Phelps' ship, was launched in 1804 and sold in 1814. In Greek myth Circe was the sorceress on the island of Aeaea who tempted passing sailors with a drink that turned those who consumed it into swine.*

Cissy
see **Williams, Cecilia**

Citoyen Durand
A French merchant ship, fully laden with gunpowder, taken by HMS *Sophie*. Aboard is her Master's pregnant wife who, under Maturin's care, gives birth to a son shortly after the capture (M&C 5).

Clapham, Nelly and Sue
Young lady friends of William Dolby and Harry Lovage (YA 3).

Clapier
A French army major who interrogates Maturin (SM 11).

Clapton
Sophie Aubrey's maid (COM 6).

Clara

A Spanish frigate, part of Admiral Bustamente's treasure squadron, that strikes to Jack Aubrey's HMS *Lively* (PC 14; *also* HMS 6; TMC 2).

After her capture in October 1804, the 38-gun Clara was briefly re-named HMS Leocadia, but soon reverted to HMS Clara; sent for harbour service in 1811, she was sold in 1815.

Clare

The author of a medical book consulted by Maturin on the subject of venereal diseases (C/T 4).

The physician Peter Clare (1738–1786) published in 1780 two books detailing new methods for administering mercury as a cure for venereal diseases.

Clarence, Duke of *(often referred to as Prince William)*

A former shipmate of Jack Aubrey (M&C 8), referred to by St Vincent in his letter to Sir Charles Grey on the subject of Lieutenant Beresford (PC 3); he is also a former shipmate of Lieutenant Parker, whose claim to promotion he presses (PC 7,12). At one time Captain of HMS *Pegasus* (WDS 10), he was never a popular commander (TMC 5). The Duke remains as a friend and supporter of Jack, especially when the latter is dismissed from the Royal Navy, but unfortunately has little influence with his elder brother, the Prince Regent (TGS 1; YA 7). He is also an admirer, and sometime patient, of Stephen Maturin (TMC 1; DI 4; SM 1; LM 2,7; NC 7; COM 1; YA 1,4; HD 1). Clarence is also mentioned many times in passing (e.g. RM 1,5,9; LM 2,4; TGS 5; NC 6,7; COM 4,10).

Prince William Henry (1765–1837), King *George III's third son, was created Duke of Clarence in 1789. Clarence was for a time a career naval officer, albeit one with the ultimate patron: a Midshipman of 1779, he was commissioned Lieutenant in 1785 and made Post in the following year, soon commanding HMS *Pegasus on the West Indies station with a rigorous discipline, much admired by *Nelson and *St Vincent. However, amongst his junior officers, his reputation was that of a man under whom it was almost impossible to serve without being eventually dismissed the service. By a rushed seniority, the Duke rose to Rear Admiral 1790 (although he was never given a sea-command), Vice Admiral in 1794 and Admiral in 1799. He became Admiral of the Fleet in 1811 (overreaching the man who should have had the position, Earl *St Vincent) and *Lord High Admiral in 1827. In this specially revived post he made a final, disastrous foray into assuming command of the fleet during manoeuvres, being forced to resign in 1828 by an outraged King and Prime Minister. In 1830 the Duke succeeded his elder brother George IV (formerly the Prince *Regent) as King William IV, 'the Sailor King.'

Clarges

1: Sir Joseph Blaine's sister (HMS 4).
2: Clonfert's steward in HMS *Néréide* (TMC 7).

Clarissa

1: *see* **Harlowe, Clarissa**
2: *see* **Oakes, Clarissa**

Claude

see **Lorraine, Claude**

Clavering

A Midshipman in HMS *Shannon* (FW 9).

Douglas Charles Clavering (d.1827) served as a youngster on *Broke's HMS *Shannon and was eventually commissioned Lieutenant in 1814. Promoted Commander in 1821, he was presumed drowned when his HMS Redwing, 18-gun, vanished off the coast of West Africa.

Clegg

An officer in HMS *Pomone* (HD 1).

Cleghorn

A former Surgeon-Major to the British army garrison at Port Mahon (M&C 6).

George Cleghorn (1716–1789) was an Edinburgh physician and author of studies of diseases amongst discrete populations, e.g., of soldiers. Surgeon-Major at Mahon from 1736 to 1749, he was from 1751 onwards Professor of Anatomy at Trinity College, Dublin.

Clement XIV, Pope

The Pope who had suppressed the Jesuit order in the 1770s (RM 2).

Giovanni Vincenzo Antonio Ganganelli (1700?–1774) became Pope Clement XIV in 1769 and suppressed the very powerful Jesuit order (see *Loyola) in 1773. For many years after his death it was rumoured that he had been soon poisoned for his pains, but no evidence of such a crime has ever been produced. The order was re-instated by Pope *Pius VII in 1814.

Clementi

A piano manufacturer (PC 2; COM 5,6) and popular composer (FW 5; SM 2; NC 4; C/T 3; COM 5,6).

Muzio Clementi (1752–832) was born in Rome and soon made a reputation as a keyboard prodigy. In 1766 he moved to England to study and in 1775 made his London début to great acclaim. Touring Europe from 1781 to 1783, he performed at concerts where the prodigies of the age, including *Mozart, vied with each other in playing, improvising and sight-reading. Once again living again in England for extended periods, Clementi composed an enormous number of piano sonatas and studies, his influence on his instrument's subsequent repertoire being profound. In about 1800 he founded in London the manufacturing firm of Clementi & Co, remaining as a partner in the firm until his death.

Clements

A seaman in HMS *Polyphemus* (IM 6).

Cleopatra

The subject of a side-show at an entertainment park visited by the young Jack Aubrey and Philip Broke (FW 7).

*Cleopatra VII of Egypt (69–30 BC) succeeded her father to the throne in 51 BC, ruling jointly with a succession of younger brothers. The final monarch of the Greek Ptolemaic dynasty, Cleopatra was supposedly the first of them ever to learn to speak Egyptian. As an astute, if beleaguered ruler, she sought to preserve Egyptian independence and power from the jealous attentions of Rome by a series of alliances and romances, firstly with Julius *Caesar and, later, with General Marcus Antonius (a.k.a., Mark Anthony). However, *Plutarch observes that it was supposedly her brilliant conversation, rather than purely physical charms, that so enticed her potential enemies. In the wars that followed Caesar's assassination, Cleopatra allied herself with Marcus Antonius against Octavius, Caesar's heir (who later became the Emperor Augustus), but soon found herself reviled by Rome as a 'foreign temptress.' On Octavius' occupation of her capital of Alexandria, she committed suicide by the bite of her royal asp.*

Clerk
A seaman in HMS *Surprise* (HMS 9).

Clerk, Robin
A Midshipman in HMS *Surprise* when she cut out *Hermione*, Clerk much later became Master of HMS *Arethusa* (C/T 2).

Clerk of Eldin
The author of a book sent by Stephen Maturin to Sophie Williams (HMS 4).

*John Clerk (1728–1812) was a merchant from Eldin, Scotland, who achieved considerable fame as an authority on naval tactics even though he had no experience of warfare and only small estuary-boat experience of the sea. From reading accounts of sea-battles, he came to the view that British Admirals understood only hard, line-to-line fighting in battle and had no notion of manoeuvres that could concentrate their force against key points in the enemy's formation by 'breaking his line.' In 1782, the year in which *Rodney won the Battle of the Saintes by unexpectedly cutting through the French line, Clerk had distributed an early version of his* Essay on Naval Tactics, *which was then fully published in 1790 with a further three parts following in 1797. Clerk claimed that his works had a profound influence on contemporary British successes, and it was stated by him, and widely believed, that Rodney had studied the early pamphlet before his victory (although this would in fact have been materially impossible). Certainly many officers—including *St Vincent, Sir Alexander *Cochrane and *Nelson—read and admired his books but it is far from certain that they were either the only source of tactical thinking available (several similar French works had been published in England before Clerk set to work) or that the most senior officers thought them uniquely insightful.*

Clerk of the Cheque
A harbour official in Malta (TH 3).

Clerk of the Hanaper
A minor official present at the King's Birthday Levée (RM 5).

The 'Hanaper' is a hamper, a wicker basket for collecting documents.

Clerke
A Midshipman in HMS *Diane* (TGS 5,8) who has either died or been killed in action (NC 4).

Clermont
The family name of friends of La Mothe in Paris (SM 5).

Clifford, Lady Isabel
The wife of the British Minister in Algiers, both formerly residents of Sierra Leone (HD 6). Although friendly to Stephen Maturin, she refuses his request to take care of the young FitzPatrick twins, a rebuff that puzzles Stephen (HD 8).

Clifford, Sir Peter
The British Minister in Algiers, formerly on the staff of Governor Wood in Sierra Leone (HD 6,8).

Clio, HMS
A frigate in Admiral Thornton's Mediterranean fleet (IM 6), later the ship from which Miller and Oakes have carelessly 'deserted' by overstaying their shore-leave in Batavia (NC 4)..

HMS Clio, *18-gun brig-sloop, was launched in 1807 and broken up in 1845. In classical myth Clio was the Muse of History.*

Clive
The General to whom Charles Villiers is compared in potential (PC 1).

*Sir Robert Clive, Baron Clive of Plassy (1725–1775), was a British colonial soldier and administrator, a leading member of the East India Company from 1743 and Governor of Bengal from 1765 to 1767. He was chiefly responsible for establishing British political and commercial supremacy in India, in part by military and diplomatic campaigns and in part by administrative genius and the pursuit of robust anti-corruption measures (although he had been by no means above such practices himself in the early years of his rise to power). His health broken, Clive returned to England in 1766, only to be himself attacked and hounded on corruption charges by a group of vengeful politicians, whose narrow, selfish interests he had effectively curtailed during the course of his administration. Although his service in India was publicly vindicated in 1773, Clive—always a moody man—had by then succumbed to gross opium addiction, and soon took his own life. In 1753 Clive had married Margaret Maskelyne, the sister of the *Astronomer Royal.*

Clive
see **Lord Clive**

Clomer
A Danish brig, Captain Ole Bugge, stopped by HMS *Sophie*. By co-incidence, she is a near copy of *Sophie*'s design (M&C 5).

*In 1800, as a rûse de guerre, Commander Thomas *Cochrane painted his brig HMS *Speedy to resemble the Danish brig* Clomer, *which was well known along the western Mediterranean coast. Cochrane then placed a*

Danish quartermaster, in the uniform of an officer of that nation, at Speedy's *helm to complete the deception.*

Clonfert, Lady

The elegant wife of Lord Clonfert who asks Jack Aubrey for a passage to the Cape in order to join her husband and then visits Ashgrove Cottage to pursue her request (TMC 1). Jack however, somewhat fearful of the reaction of his own wife, Sophie, to his granting the favour, contrives to abandon Lady Clonfert in Plymouth before she can board HMS *Boadicea* (TMC 2), leaving her to arrange passage in an Indiaman (TMC 3,10).

Clonfert, Lord

The Commander of the sloop HMS *Otter*, at one time ship-mates with Jack Aubrey, in whose squadron he now serves (TMC 1+). Clonfert's title is in the Irish peerage, although the family is English, surnamed Scroggs (TMC 2). In earlier days, when they were both Lieutenants in HMS *Agamemnon*, Clonfert had in fact been the senior man but, in a cutting out expedition, he had given Jack—and perhaps others—reason to doubt his courage, and very shortly afterwards had transferred into HMS *Mars* (TMC 2). At one point in his subsequent career, he has conducted a very public affair with a Mrs Jennings, ending in a court-case (TMC 2,5). Later, in HMS *Ramillies*, Clonfert was court-martialed for striking a fellow officer and dismissed the service. After a short spell in the Turkish forces, he was reinstated to the Royal Navy but with loss of seniority (TMC 2). Subsequently he had served under Admiral Sir Sidney Smith at Acre and has now, at long last, been promoted Commander (TMC 2).

Clonfert's personality, at once showy and insecure, leads him into very uneasy relationships with Corbett (TMC 3), Pym (TMC 5) and Jack Aubrey himself (TMC 3+), the latter exacerbated by the Commodore's failure to transport Lady Clonfert from England to the Cape (TMC 3). He is nevertheless a dashing and active officer, soon playing a leading role in the successful raid on Réunion, an effort for which Jack makes him Post and promotes him into HMS *Néréide* (TMC 3, 4). Throughout the campaign Clonfert is driven by conflicting feelings of envy, resentment and admiration of Jack, as well as by his own need for reassurance, and even worship. The resulting medical symptoms, both physical and mental, are analysed at length by Doctors Maturin and McAdam (TMC 4+), who also observe his tendency to surround himself with sycophants—albeit able ones—on his own quarterdeck (TMC 7).

Clonfert's curious traits, in combination with the more senior Pym's indecision, now produce a disaster at the Battle of Port South East on Mauritius. At the outset, Clonfert attempts to seize glory for himself rather than to summon reinforcements and he then draws Pym, with a misleading signal of 'enemy of inferior force,' into an unequal fight (TMC 7). In the ensuing action Clonfert is severely wounded in the face and neck and is eventually forced to surrender his devastated HMS *Néréide* to *Bellone* (TMC 7). Held as a prisoner in the French hospital on Mauritius, he hears of the eventual great victory of the British fleet. Pulling the bandage off his neck wound, he immediately bleeds to death, preferring to avoid either the commiserations or the judgement of his nemesis, Jack Aubrey (TMC 10; *also* TGS 5).

Lord Clonfert is a fictional character but several incidents in the book are based to some degree on the exploits, both during and before the campaign, of the very different—but equally fascinating—Sir Josiah Nesbit Willoughby (1777–1849). Willoughby had entered the Royal Navy in 1790 and by 1798 was a Lieutenant in the 74-gun HMS Victorious. *In 1799 he was court-martialed for showing disrespect to his Captain Clark and sentenced to be dismissed his ship. His reputation for zeal and bravery soon obtained him another post, on HMS* Russell, *but here the argumentative and even brutal side of his nature once more showed itself, leading to an ugly dispute with his Captain Wood. Both officers were brought to court-martial in 1800, Wood being acquitted but Willoughby being broken and dismissed the service. Zeal again won through and in 1803 Willoughby obtained a volunteer's berth on HMS* Hercule, *the flag-ship of Sir John Duckworth, soon getting his previous dismissal remitted for showing the outstanding personal courage and dash that characterised his entire career. Promoted Commander into HMS* *Otter *in 1808, by the following year had so fallen out with his officers that he was again hauled before a court, this time being merely admonished for his high-handed, driving ways. A member of Sir Josias Rowley's squadron in the Mauritius campaign, he was soon made Post (in circumstances very similar to those of Clonfert) into HMS* *Néréide *but lost her in August 1810 in the disaster of Port South East. Having in June of that same year being horribly injured in the face and neck by the accidental explosion of a musket, in this final battle Willoughby now lost an eye as well as receiving other severe wounds during the desperate fight. At his subsequent, routine court-martial the question of the mis-leading 'enemy of inferior force' signal was raised, but the conduct of both Willoughby and his crew had been so outstanding that he was fully acquitted, with only a note that his signal had been 'injudicious' for being evidently wrong. After a period of recuperation Willoughby, unable to get a command, joined the Baltic fleet as a volunteer but, immediately chafing at the lack of action in* *Saumarez' *largely political campaign, in 1812 then took the extraordinary step of accepting a commission in the Russian army. Soon taken prisoner, he had the most unusual distinction of marching as a captive on the retreat from Moscow, surviving the ordeal to end up in a French prison. Never lacking enterprise, Willoughby then escaped back to England in 1814 but his active military career was now finally over. Yet curious incidents still attended the man: knighted by George IV (see* *Regent) *in 1827, he was given exactly the same honour by William IV (see* *Clarence, Duke of) *in 1832,* *the previous award having been forgotten. Willoughby rose by seniority to Rear Admiral in 1847, just two years before his death.*

Clorinde
A French frigate taken by HMSS *Eurotas*, *Dryad* and *Achates* after a very long and valorous fight (YA 9).

Clorinde was launched in 1808 and taken by the Royal Navy— as described by Jack *Aubrey— in February 1814; renamed HMS *Aurora she was eventually broken up in 1851. In the Jerusalem Delivered *of Torquado Tasso (1544–1595), Clorinde is the pagan, warrior daughter of the King of Ethiopia who had been suckled as a baby by a tigress. Later unwittingly wounded by her enemy and admirer, the crusader Tancred, she receives baptism into his faith before expiring in his arms.*

Clotworthy, Mr
Frances Williams' Irish husband, by whom she has just had a baby (RM 6): many years later, she is a somewhat impoverished widow (YA 1).

N.B., Frances *Williams is initially said to have married one Sir Oliver *Floode (HMS 7).

Clousaz
The author of *Examen de Pyrrhonisme* (COM 1).

Jean Pierre de Crousaz (sic; 1663–1748) was a Swiss mathematician and philosopher who, like many of his contemporaries, wrote prolifically on a wide variety of topics; his Examen de Pyrronism, ancien et moderne *was published in 1733. Originally developed by the Greek philosopher Pyrrho of Elis (360?–272 BC), 'Pyrrhonism,' or Scepticism, calls for a suspension of judgement in the face of necessarily incomplete knowledge of the world.*

Clowes
1: Envoy Stanhope's doctor in Bombay (HMS 7).
2: a Royal Navy Captain, an old friend of Aubrey and Dundas (HMS 10).

The name may perhaps be a passing tribute to Sir William Laird Clowes (1856–1905), the British naval journalist and historian who from 1897 to 1903 produced his great, 7-volume work, The Royal Navy *(see* **Bibliography***).*

Cluentius
A Roman defended in court by Cicero (RM 7).

Aulus Habitus Cluentius (dates unknown) was successfully defended by *Cicero in 66 BC against a charge of murder, the great orator later boasting that his trial technique had been one of 'throwing dust in the eyes of the jury.'

Clusius
An authority on the flora of Malta (TH 1).

Charles L'Ecluse (1526–1609; in Latin, Carolus Clusius) was a French physician and botanist who spent many years travelling in Spain, France, Italy and Austria. In 1593 he became Professor of Botany at Leiden University in Holland and in 1601 he collected his many botanical publications into a History of the Rarer Plants.

Clutton
A silversmith to whom the impoverished Aubreys try to sell a dinner service (YA 1).

Clytie
A ship that had made a record crossing of the North Atlantic in 1794 (SM 3).

Cobbald, Robert or Bob
A member of the barge-crew in HMS *Bellona* (YA 4).

Cobbold
The Captain of HMS *Hyperion*, who has offered to take Philip Aubrey to sea as a protégé (WDS 10).

Cochet
The First Lieutenant of Earl Howe's HMS *Queen Charlotte* at the Battle of the Glorious First of June (C/T 4).

John Cochet (1760–1851) was commissioned Lieutenant in 1789 and promoted Commander in 1795 for his services under *Howe in the previous year. Made Post in 1796, Cochet was promoted Rear Admiral in 1819, Vice Admiral in 1830, and full Admiral in 1850.

Cochrane
1: Lord Cochrane, O'Brian's avowed inspiration for many of Jack Aubrey's early exploits (M&C author's note; FSW author's note). Cochrane is often later referred to as showy and eccentric, although undoubtedly very able (PC 12; HMS 5; TMC 3,4,7; IM 8). His prosecution and conviction for fraud in 1814 provide the basis for the events in *The Reverse of the Medal* (RM author's endnote).

Thomas Cochrane (1775–1860), 10th Earl of Dundonald, was a notoriously fiery navy Captain, Member of Parliament, mercenary foreign adventurer and, finally, British Admiral. Cochrane went to sea rather late in life, at age 17, a fellow-Scots protégé of both his uncle Captain Alexander Cochrane (see below) and George Elphinstone, Lord *Keith (also see *Carrol). Many of the events of M&C are based on Cochrane's cruise in the 14-gun HMS *Speedy, into which he was promoted Commander in March 1800: for example, on May 6th 1801 Cochrane famously captured the Spanish 32-gun xebec frigate El *Gamo, the model for O'Brian's *Cacafuego. Made Post later in 1801, he then enjoyed a brilliant— if exceptionally independent and controversial — career both at sea and in Parliament (as MP for Honiton from 1806 to 1807 and Westminster from 1807 to 1814 and 1816–1818); he was knighted in 1809. In 1814 Cochrane became involved— perhaps innocently, perhaps not— in a stock market fraud. Tried and convicted by an extremely biased court, he was sentenced to fines, imprisonment and the pillory, this last being commuted for fear of riots. Dismissed the Royal Navy, he was also forced to resign his seat in the House of Commons (although, by virtue of his overwhelming popularity with the voters, he soon regained it). Cochrane's fighting reputation, coupled with always vigorous self-promotion, soon led to offers of high service abroad: from 1817 to 1822 he led the Chilean Navy, from 1823 to 1825, the Brazilian Navy, and from 1827 to 1828 the Greek Navy (where he became an enthusiastic proponent of steam-power for fighting ships). Having in 1831 succeeded to the family Earldom of Dundonald, in May 1832 Cochrane was restored to the Royal Navy list as a Rear Admiral by former seniority; he rose to Vice Admiral in 1841 and full Admiral in 1851. Cochrane wrote extensively about his career and adventures, publishing in the year of his death a brilliantly engaging Autobiography of a Seaman (usually found indexed under his Dundonald title).

2: Admiral Cochrane, an officer referred to in passing (PC 14).

Sir Alexander Forrester Inglis Cochrane (1758–1832), the uncle of Thomas Cochrane, was made Post in 1782 and served as a senior Captain in the Mediterranean fleet from 1799 to 1804, in April of which year he was promoted Rear Admiral. Knighted in 1806, he was promoted Vice Admiral in 1809, served as Commander-in-Chief, North America, from 1814 to 1815, and rose to full Admiral in 1819.

Cockburn, Miss

A young lady who has recently married Captain Ross of HMS *Désirée* (SM 11).

Charles *Ross married Miss Cockburn, a sister-in-law and cousin of George *Cockburn, in Jamaica in 1803. Their only son died as a Commander in the Royal Navy.

Cockburn, George

The Captain of HMS *Meleager*, well known to Aubrey and Maturin. He had once denounced Captain Sawyer of HMS *Blanche* as a sodomite (COM 9).

The Honourable Sir George Cockburn (1772–1853) was an extremely well-connected officer who in 1793 was both commissioned Lieutenant and promoted Commander, being made Post in 1794 (fighting in HMS *Minerva at the Battle of Cape *St Vincent in 1797), promoted Rear Admiral in 1812, Vice Admiral in 1819, Admiral in 1837, and Admiral of the Fleet in 1852. Cockburn served as a Commissioner of the Admiralty from 1818 to 1827 and 1828–1830 and was four times an MP; knighted in 1815, he inherited a baronetcy in 1852. In addition to the advantages of his connections, he also had a reputation as a sound seaman and an energetic, lucky officer, being especially recalled as the Admiral who in 1814 attacked Washington and burned The White House and as the commander of the squadron that in 1815 took *Buonaparte to his final exile on St Helena (where Cockburn remained as Governor until 1816). The *Sawyer affair took place in *Nelson's Mediterranean squadron during 1795–1796.

Codlin, Joseph

A seaman in HMS *Sophie* (M&C 3).

Codpiece, Abram

An Italian seaman in HMS *Sophie* (M&C 10).

Codrington

A Lieutenant in Earl Howe's HMS *Queen Charlotte* at the Battle of the Glorious First of June (C/T 4)

and later Charles Yorke's Captain aboard HMS *Orion* at the Battle of Trafalgar (FW 2).

Sir Edward Codrington (1770–1851) was a protégé of *Howe and his immediate aide-de-camp in the great 1794 battle. Having the honour of taking the victory dispatch home to England, he was immediately promoted Commander and then made Post in the following year, aged just 25. In early 1805 he was given command of the newly re-fitted HMS *Orion, 74-gun, fighting her in *Nelson's great victory later that year at Trafalgar. Promoted Rear Admiral in 1814 and Vice Admiral in 1825, he rose to full Admiral in 1841. In 1827 Codrington was Commander-in-Chief of the Mediterranean fleet and led a combined British, French and Russian fleet against the Sultan of *Turkey at the Battle of Navarino, the last fleet action fought wholly under sail. For the crushing victory he inflicted on the enemy he was given knighthoods by France, Russia and Greece to add to the British honour he had received in 1815.

Coffin

The First Lieutenant of HMS *Burford* (M&C 2).

Many members of the distinguished Coffin family became Captains, Admirals and Generals in the British forces, several of them originally American Tory loyalists at the time of the Revolutionary War: none, however, were Lieutenants in 1800, when M&C 2 is set.

Coke

1: the civilian Judge-Advocate at Aubrey's court-martial for the loss of HMS *Sophie* (M&C 12).

The Judge-Advocate was secretary and legal advisor to the panel of Captain-judges.

2: a famous English judge referred to by Maturin (RM 7).

Sir Edward Coke (1552–1634; always pronounced 'Cook') was the Chief Justice of the King's Bench from 1613 to 1616, when he was dismissed for his continual lack of sufficient obedience to the Crown. Coke is renowned as the leading author both of his time and for several centuries thereafter on the rules of Common Law: his Reports were published from 1600 to 1615 and his Institutes of the Laws of England from 1628 until ten years after his death.

Cole

The Purser of HMS *Goliath*, a published poet (IM 3).

Colebrook

A family of Blaine's acquaintance (RM 7).

The Colebrooke (sic) family of the time were variously distinguished for both commerce, banking and learning, Henry Thomas Colebrooke (1765–1837) being the leading British Oriental scholar of his day as well as an important officer of the East India Company.

Coleman, Captain

Harry Tennant's uncle, sometime Captain of the scrapped HMS *Phoebe* (RM 4).

Colin

A Francophone seaman pressed from Franklin to HMS *Surprise* (WDS 4).

Collard

The Captain of HMS *Ajax*, a ship in which Killick had once served (TMC 1).

The reference may be to Valentine Collard (1770–1846) who was the first Lieutenant of HMS *Britannia, 100-gun, at the Battle of Cape *St Vincent in 1797, being promoted Commander after the action as reward (although he then wrecked his first command, the 16-gun HMS Fortune, off Oporto just a few months later). Collard was made Post in 1807 and rose to Rear Admiral in 1841.

Colley, Tom and Mrs

A seaman in HMS *Boadicea* injured in action against *Astrée* and *Iphigenie* (TMC 8). His depressed cranial fracture is trepanned by Maturin and Cotton, to the imagined concern of his wife in England (TMC 9). Having become regarded by Aubrey as an omen for the success or failure of the coming assault on Mauritius, Colley then recovers his health (TMC 9).

Collingwood

A member of a Northumberland family (TH 9), he was Nelson's second in command at the Battle of Trafalgar (FW 2) and is renowned as an efficient and effective officer (IM 2; FSW 2; RM 3).

Cuthbert Collingwood (1748–1810) was one of the foremost naval commanders of his age. From a north country family with no influential connections, he went to sea at the age of 11 and rose by merit alone to Lieutenant in 1775, Commander in 1779 and Post Captain in 1780. In this rank he played outstanding roles in the battles of the Glorious First of June (fought by *Howe in 1794) and Cape *St Vincent (1797). Promoted Rear Admiral in 1799 and Vice Admiral in 1804, in 1805 he served as second-in-command at the Battle of Trafalgar, assuming sole control of the fleet when *Nelson fell. Raised to the peerage for his role in this great victory, Lord Collingwood became Commander-in-Chief of the Mediterranean fleet thereafter. However, during this period he was plagued by ill-health and developed what was probably stomach cancer: having resigned his command in 1810, he died at sea off Minorca on his way home to England. In his early career as a Post Captain Collingwood spent long periods ashore, taking regular country walks on which he always carried a pocketful of acorns, tossing them about to ensure future supplies of ship-oak.

Collins

1: a Captain who had taken Bustamente's Spanish treasure squadron in company with Aubrey, Graham and Sutton (IIMS 1).

By implication, Collins must be the commander of HMS *Medusa, the only Royal Navy ship in the PC 14 action not to have her Captain named. However, in the 1804 action on which the incident is based, a Captain John Gore had HMS Medusa (and was in fact senior to HMS *Amphion's *Sutton). Gore was made Post in 1794, knighted in 1805, and promoted Rear Admiral in 1813; he rose to Vice Admiral in 1825 and died in 1836 (see also *Revenge, HMS). In 1799 his then HMS *Triton had assisted in the taking of the *Santa Brigida and El *Thetis, an action which made him a very wealthy man. None of

the several Collins who held Royal Navy commands was a Post Captain in 1804.

2: a quarter gunner in HMS *Surprise* sent to *Lushington* for the battle with Linois (HMS 9).

3: a senior Master's Mate in HMS *Boadicea* (TMC 6,8).

4: a Lieutenant in Aubrey's HMS *Worcester* (IM 2–8).

5: the Governor of Van Diemen's Land (NC 8).

David Collins (1756–1810) had been a Captain in the Royal Marines before serving from 1787 as an administrator in New South Wales and being appointed in 1804 to the charge of Van *Diemen's Land (renamed Tasmania in 1856).

Colman, Bridie

'Bridie Colman's Washing Day,' a phrase used by Maturin to compliment to the appearance of HMS *Surprise* under full sail (WDS 10).

Colman, Padeen or Patrick

A giant Irishman from County Clare, confined as a lunatic on Gibraltar. Stephen Maturin, realising that Padeen is simply suffering from a cleft palate and a lack of command of English, takes him onto HMS *Surprise* as his servant (FSW 2+) and back to England in the same capacity (RM 6+). Padeen later follows Stephen into the private letter-of-marque *Surprise*, where a painfully burnt hand and a severe toothache are treated with laudanum, leading to addiction and eventual theft of the drug (LM 2–5). Whilst Stephen is absent, Padeen is caught red-handed by Tom Pullings and put in irons (LM 9). However, he soon manages to desert from *Surprise* at Leith in Scotland where, having broken into an apothecary's shop, he is apprehended and condemned to death. Saved only by the intervention of his naval friends, he is then sentenced to transportation to New South Wales (TGS 1,3; NC 8,9). On a subsequent voyage, Stephen locates Padeen in Sydney and finds he has been most cruelly treated (NC 9). The Doctor arranges for his former servant's escape in *Surprise*, although initially only with Jack Aubrey's most unwilling cooperation (NC 10). Padeen returns to his sick-bay duties for Stephen (C/T 1+; WDS 1+) and eventually returns with him to England (COM 1). Left at Barham House to guard both Clarissa Oakes and Stephen's strange, young daughter Brigid (COM 2), he forms a special bond with the infant, teaching her to speak Irish (COM 3+). Political machinations delay his promised pardon (COM 2) and soon necessitate his fleeing to Spain with Stephen (COM 4,5,9,10), who promises him a small farm in Ireland as reward for his continued protection of Clarissa and Brigid (COM 5). Eventually Padeen receives his pardon and arrives back in England as a retainer of the Maturins (YA 1+), remaining there after the death of Mrs Maturin in a coaching accident (HD 1,2). However, he seems reluctant to take up the offer of the farm, possibly out of fear of a consequent marriage (YA 4) and possibly because of a deep, silent devotion to Clarissa Oakes (YA 10).

Colnett

A Royal Navy officer who had commanded the exploration sloop *Rattler* on a voyage in 1792–1793. On his return to England, he had written a book on the South Seas whaling trade (FSW 2,3,5,6).

*James Colnett (1755?–1806) was one of the leading explorers of his age, with a reputation not only for expert cartography but also for astute investment in the commercial aspects of his voyages. Colnett had served as a Midshipman on *Cook's second voyage to the Pacific of 1771–1775 and later went on to command the exploration sloop* Argonaut *in the northeastern Pacific. Here, in Nootka Sound at *Vancouver Island, Colnett was one of the explorers and traders arrested by the Spanish in 1789. British reaction to this 'outrage', a powerful fleet assembled under Lord *Howe, became known as the 'Spanish Armament' of 1790–1791, a development to which Jack *Aubrey attributes his initial appointment to commissioned rank (FSW 3, WDS 3).*

*In 1792 Colnett was invited to command a joint Navy-commercial voyage to the Pacific in *Rattler *in order to locate alternate whaling and naval bases to those now denied to Britain by Spain. The voyage lasted from early 1793 to late 1794 and explored the full length of the eastern Pacific, though it found only two small islands entirely suitable for British purposes. On his return to England, Colnett was soon made Post (1796) and given command of a 28-gun frigate, HMS* Hussar; *he almost immediately lost her to a storm on the French coast and then spent some six months in captivity. Colnett's final command seems to have been HMS* Glatton, *56-gun, on an 1802–1803 voyage to Australia transporting convicts to the penal colony. In 1798 Colnett had published an account of the* Rattler *voyage, a splendidly illustrated work that later drew the favourable attention of both Charles Darwin (for its observations on the Galapagos Islands) and the novelist Herman Melville (for whaling insights useful for* Moby Dick*). Oddly, Colnett is almost entirely unmentioned in the standard British and Royal Navy biographical reference works, a curious omission perhaps hinted at in Jack *Aubrey's claimed ignorance of the man.*

Colonel, the

see **Casademon, Ramon d'Ullastret**

Colossus, HMS

1: the ship in which Jack Aubrey served at the Battle of Cape St Vincent, standing alongside her Lieutenant John Fitton when he was killed (TGS 4).
   Aubrey's 74-gun HMS Colossus *was launched in 1787, fought at Cape *St Vincent under Captain George Murray in 1797 but was wrecked of the Scilly Isles in December of the following year (N.B., in PC 2 Aubrey says he was in HMS *Orion at the same battle). She (and her replacement, below) were named for the Colossus, a giant, bronze statue of Helios the Sun-God that in ancient times supposedly stood at the entrance to Rhodes harbour.*
2: a ship whose appearance, in company with HMS *Tonnant*, forces the French-captured *Lord Nelson* Indiaman to re-strike to HMS *Seagull* (PC 5). Years later she serves in Sir John Thornton's

Mediterranean fleet (IM 2) and is joined by HMS *Worcester*'s recently disgraced Lieutenant Somers (IM 5).

This HMS Colossus *was launched in 1803, fought at Trafalgar in 1805 under Captain James Morris (d.1830 as a Vice Admiral), and was eventually broken up in 1826. The *Lord Nelson incident occurred in August 1803, Colossus being commanded at the time by a Captain Thomas Alexander (d.1843 as a full Admiral).*

Colpoys

The Admiral commanding the Brest blockade in 1796 (YA 5).

*Sir John Colpoys (1742?–1821) was made Post in 1773 and promoted Rear Admiral in 1794; promoted Vice Admiral in 1795 (commanding off Brest under Lord *St Vincent from 1796 to 1797), he became full Admiral in 1801. From 1803 onwards he occupied a variety of shore-commands in England. In the great Spithead mutinies of 1797, Colpoys came close to being hanged by the rebellious seamen of his flag-ship, HMS* London, *when he rescued the ship's First Lieutenant from them, saying that this officer had only been obeying his, the Admiral's, orders in shooting at them as they emerged from the hatchways against his specific command. Fortunately Admiral Colpoys was later put safely ashore, but not until a very tense 24 hours of confinement had passed during which time he was certain he was to die. Sir John was the uncle of Admiral Sir Edward Griffith, who took the Colpoys name on inheriting his uncle's estate in 1821 (see *Colpoys, Lady Harriet *and* Admiral*).*

Colpoys, Mrs Charlotte and Colonel

Admiral Haddock's sister and her husband, guests at the Keith's Ball, with whom Diana Villiers is staying in London (PC 6).

Colpoys, Lady Harriet and Admiral

The Port-Admiral of Halifax, Nova Scotia, and his wife (SM 1,2) who give a great ball to celebrate the victory of HMS *Shannon* over USS *Chesapeake* (SM 2).

*The reference is to Sir Edward Griffith (1767–1832), who in 1821 took the name Colpoys on receiving an inheritance from his deceased uncle, Admiral Sir John *Colpoys. He had been made Post in 1794 and then commanded his uncle's HMS* London *until the mutinies at Spithead in 1797. In 1805 Griffiths, now in HMS* Dragon, *took part in Sir Robert *Calder's indecisive pre-Trafalgar action. Promoted Rear Admiral and sent to North America in 1812, he commanded the North American Station from 1815 to 1817 (superseding Sir Alexander *Cochrane) and again from 1819 to 1821, in which year he was promoted Vice Admiral.*

Columbus

The famous explorer who, having been a colonist, is not admired by Maturin (C/T 3).

Cristoforo Colombo (1451–1506; often Latinised to Chrispherus Columbus) was born in Italy but spent the crucial years of his career of exploration and discovery in the service of King Ferdinand and Queen Isabella of Spain, the Queen being his chief supporter. By his own account he went to sea at the age of 14, seeing both commercial and *military service. With an early reputation as a talented navigator, he then moved to Portugal and there developed his conviction that there existed a western passage to Japan, China and the riches of the East. Thwarted in Lisbon of his plans, in about 1484 he moved to Spain in search of fresh patronage. From 1492 to 1504 Columbus made four round-trips westward, becoming the first European to both reach the New World and then disseminate systematic knowledge of its geography: his landfalls and observations being of the Caribbean islands and parts of the north-eastern coast of South America (although he himself always maintained that he had in fact discovered a hitherto unknown region of far-eastern Asia). Yet Columbus' position, as an Italian, was never wholly secure in the complex world of Spanish court politics, and he was eventually recalled to Spain. Here, whilst following Ferdinand's retinue around the country in the hope of what he felt were his due rewards, he soon died of several combined illnesses. For many years Columbus' reputation was that of the discoverer of the potential of the New World and especially as the enricher of Spain, which country, along with their Portuguese rivals (see *Borgia), had rapidly colonised the new lands. Stephen Maturin touches on a more modern theme — though one which had currency almost from the very time of Columbus' discoveries — of the pernicious nature of colonisation and exploitation. Despite these legitimate concerns, Columbus' reputation as a prime navigator and an exceptionally determined explorer remains substantially intact.*

Columptons, the
Friends of Diana Villiers in London (TH 2).

Coluthon, Anna
A reference by Stephen Maturin to the upset and flustered Sophie Williams (PC 3).
'Anacoluthon'— Greek for 'not in proper sequence'— is the technical, linguistic term for a sudden break or change of direction in the flow of speech, e.g. 'I hear that Jack Aubrey—his surgeon's Irish, you know—has been made Post.'

Colville, Lord
A gentleman whose wine-cellar had been bought by Andrew Wray (TH 10).
The reference is probably to John, 8th Baron Colville of Culross (1725–1811), but may perhaps be to his son the 9th Baron, also John (1768–1849), a Royal Navy officer who was made Post in 1796, promoted Rear Admiral in 1819, Vice Admiral in 1820 and Admiral in 1841.

Colvin
1: a Master of Foxhounds near Woolcombe House (YA 10).
2: an Admiralty intelligence agent at Port Mahon, a Roman Catholic (HD 3).

Comfort, Mrs
The inn-keeper of the Jericho (RM 6).

Comfrey
A naval parson travelling out to the Mediterranean in Aubrey's HMS *Worcester* to join his new ship (IM 3).

Comic, Mr Farcical
An angry retort made by Maturin to Marshall, whom he imagines to be making jest of him (M&C 10).

Commendatore, the
An elderly friend of Laura Fielding in Malta (TH 3,10).

Commissioner, the
The Commissioner of Portsmouth Dockyard (PC 7).
*At the time of PC this post was held by Captain Sir Charles Saxton (d.1808), who had been made Post in 1762 and appointed to the Dockyard in 1791. Before 1806 the Commissioner of a naval base was merely a liaison officer with the Navy Board in London, lacking any real power even though he was usually a retired, senior Royal Navy Captain, for dockyard departmental heads dealt direct with London and all navy officers and ships were under the command of the *Port Admiral. The 1806 re-organization of all dockyard administration gave substantial executive powers to the Commissioners: in Portsmouth the new post went to Captain the Honorable George Grey (d.1828).*

Commisioner of Halifax Dockyard, the
One of the senior Naval officers on the North American Station who, together with Captain Capel, writes the injured Philip Broke's victory dispatch (SM 1,2).
*From 1811 to 1819 the Commissioner at Halifax was Captain the Honourable Philip *Wodehouse.*

Commodore, the
In the context of The Hundred Days, *see* **Aubrey, Jack**

Compton
1: a seaman in HMS *Boadicea* (TMC 3).
2: HMS *Defender*'s barber, a ventriloquist and a troublemaker, who is transferred into HMS *Surprise* (FSW 2,3,6).
3: a helmsman in HMS *Bellona* (YA 6).

Compton, Art
A boy at Shelmerston harbour, the nephew of Peter Willis (COM 1).

Condorcet
An adherent of Rousseau referred to by Maturin (WDS 8).
*Marie-Jean-Antoine-Nicholas Caritat, Marquis de Condorcet (1749–1794) was a leading figure in the French Enlightenment, immensely distinguished as a mathematician, scientist, intellectual historian and radical politician. He was a member, along with *Rousseau and *Buffon, of the group of philosophes who were all greatly active in propagating scientific and cultural knowledge far more widely that had ever been previously attempted. Through the brilliant salons of his beautiful wife, Sophie (1764–1822), daughter of the famous General Grouchy, Condorcet was also a well-known society figure. In his political life a member of the Girondin faction bested by the *Jacobins, he became a revolutionary victim, rumoured to*

have killed himself shortly after being arrested. Condorcet's most lastingly influential work, a lengthy outline of an intended magnum opus on human perfectibility in the 'age of reason,' was written whilst he was in hiding, shortly before his downfall.

Confucius

The Chinese philosopher whose *Analects* had been quoted to Maturin by Michael Herapath (SM 6).

K'ung fu-tsu (551–479 BC; often Latinised to Confucius) is regarded the greatest philosopher of the Chinese culture and language. Relatively little is known of his career, and very little of his work or authentic wisdom has survived, the Analects being thought to contain the most direct material from his working life. His philosophy — entirely secular and practical — confronted what he saw as the moral disarray of his age by advocating a return to the simpler virtues of the founders of the Chou dynasty (which lasted from 1030 to 256 BC). Although he seems never to have secured official acceptance of his views, Confucius became widely influential as a tutor to young men destined for high office, preaching to them concepts of justice, filial obedience, loyalty, humility and social propriety.

Congress, USS

A 38-gun frigate mentioned by Jack Aubrey (FW 2,5).

USS Congress, 38-gun, had been authorised in both 1794 and 1798 but was not finally launched until 1799, after being on the stocks for at least three years; she was broken up in 1836.

Congreve

A man who had disapproved of HMS *Polychrest*'s experimental design (PC 7), later referred to as a rocket inventor (TMC 1; HD 9).

*The first reference may be either to Sir William Congreve the elder (d.1814), the Colonel Commandant of the Royal Artillery and Comptroller of the Royal Laboratory at Woolwich Arsenal, or to his son and colleague, also Sir William (1772–1828), the well-known engineer and inventor. Both Congreves were influential in the design and refinement of conventional Royal Navy guns and, by at least 1805, the younger William had developed his eponymous incendiary rocket, based on devices deployed against British forces in India in the 1790s. In 1808 Congreve's now-refined rocket was first used (under his personal supervision) in a naval action conducted from the bomb-vessel HMS *Aetna, part of a small squadron under the command of Captain Thomas *Cochrane.*

Conn Céad Cathach

A song given by Padeen Colman to a group of Aboriginals in New South Wales (NC 10).

Conn 'of the Hundred Fights' was an ancient Irish King after whom the county of Connaught is named. The song in question refers to a legendary, past time when Ireland was strong and united, and begins, 'Conn of the hundred fights, rest in thy grass-grown sepulchre, and reproach not our defeats with thy victories.'

Conroy

A seaman in HMS *Surprise*, a relative of a man who had served under Aubrey in HMS *Sophie* (HMS 5).

Constance, Miss

The daughter of the young John Daniel's local parson (HD 6).

Constellation, USS

A 38-gun frigate that had taken the French *Insurgent* before being herself badly damaged by *Vengeance* (FW 2).

*USS Constellation was launched as a 38-gun in 1797 and went into commission in the following year. In mid-1798 French depredation of US commercial shipping led to a quasi-war between the two countries lasting until early 1801. In February of 1799 Constellation, under Thomas Truxtrun (1755–1822), took the 40-gun *Insurgente (sic) in the Caribbean but in the following year had a lengthy, damaging and inconclusive encounter with the 50-gun *Vengeance off Guadaloupe. Both ships were severely damaged, with the American losing her mainmast in the early hours of the morning just as she was about to board the Frenchman, which was thereby able to escape in the darkness. Both sides claimed this action as a victory, with Truxtrun even receiving a medal for the affair as Vengeance was thought by the Americans to have struck her colours at least twice during the fight. Constellation was re-built in 1812 as a heavy 44-gun but in 1853–1854 was cut back down, this time to a 24-gun corvette. As late as 1955 she was removed from the Navy List and sent to Baltimore, where she had been laid up since 1871, as a floating museum. The many plans thoroughly to restore her have, as yet, not come to fruition.*

Constitution, USS

A 44-gun American frigate, heavier than anything possessed by the Royal Navy (FW 2+). Under Captain Hull she has taken the 38-gun HMS *Guerrière* — earning the name *Old Ironsides* in the process — and later, under Commodore Bainbridge, she encounters and destroys HMS *Java* (FW 3,4; LM 3,4; also TGS 8; SM 1.2.11; FSW 4,9; COM 6,10).

*A 44-gun frigate launched in 1797, USS Constitution is still afloat, newly restored and in commission to this day at Boston, where she can be admired and visited. Constitution can claim be one of the doughtiest-ever opponents of the Royal Navy. In 1812, under Isaac *Hull, she fought and destroyed HMS *Guerrière, 38-gun, earning her nickname from the seeming imperviousness of her stout wooden sides to British cannon-fire. Soon afterwards, now under *Bainbridge, she captured and destroyed HMS *Java. In 1815 she took both HMS Cyane, 32-gun, and her 20-gun consort HMS Levant. Although Constitution was a heavier ship in both construction and weight of broadside than her enemies, in most conditions she was considerably slower through the water. In the action described by O'Brian, Java failed to take any advantage of this fact and, by preferring to fight broadside to broadside with the extremely efficient Constitution, not only suffered from the physical disparity but also exposed her own deficient gunnery technique.*

Contarini

A composer whose cello sonata is played by Laura Fielding and Maturin (TH 3).

The name may be inspired by that of Mario Contarini

(1632–1689), a wealthy Venetian patron of the arts and music who maintained a large library of music scores and a collection of rare instruments.

Conte and Contessa
*see '**Marriage of Figaro**'*

Conway
A foretopman from HMS *Diane* whom Aubrey promotes to Midshipman in HMS *Nutmeg of Consolation* (NC 4+).

Cook, Captain James
A Post Captain and explorer often referred to with considerable admiration by Aubrey, Maturin and others (PC 10; FW 2; SM 11; IM 10; FWS 5,7; LM 8; TGS 5; NC 4,10; C/T 2,5,6,8; WDS 1).

James Cook (1728–1779), a man of humble origins, went to sea in the merchant service at the age of 18 and rapidly made a reputation as a prime seaman and navigator. By 1755 he had been offered command of a coastal trading vessel but, wishing to expand his horizons, chose instead to enlist in the Royal Navy as a able seaman. His manifest talents soon led to rapid advancement and in 1759 he became Sailing Master of HMS Solebay. Although he saw considerable active service in North American waters, Cook was making his primary reputation as a scientific navigator and explorer and, from 1763 to 1768, commanded the survey ship HMS Grenville, coming to the attention of the Royal Society with his observations. In 1768 he was chosen to command HMS *Endeavour in Sir Joseph *Banks' expedition to the South Seas (after the civilian Alexander *Dalrymple had been vetoed by the Admiralty) and commissioned Lieutenant. In this first great voyage of discovery, Cook made important surveys of Tahiti, Australia, New Zealand and New Guinea, before returning to England in 1771. Promoted Master and Commander in that year, he soon set off again to explore and chart the far Southern Ocean, establishing that no habitable continent lay south of either Australia or Cape Horn. On his return to England in 1775, he was made both a Post Captain and a Fellow of the Royal Society. Almost immediately setting off on what was to be his final epic of exploration, he sailed back to the South Seas and then northward in search of the Pacific end of the fabled North-West Passage. In 1778 Cook discovered the Hawaii Island group, returning there in 1779 to refit his under-supplied, badly battered ships. To his bemusement, he was treated by the Polynesian inhabitants as a returning God, with the tribal leaders straining the limited resources of the island peoples to produce lavishly appropriate greeting ceremonies. Unfortunately, only two days after once more setting sail, Cook was forced back to the islands for further repairs, and now received only a sullen, strained welcome. Following a series of squabbles, in which the local population realised that the Europeans were neither Gods nor otherwise invulnerable, a large ship's boat was stolen. As was his habit from past similar instances of relatively petty theft, Cook went ashore to take a Chief hostage for the return of the missing goods. On the shore he was met by an armed crowd, determined to protect their Chief and, in a short melée, Cook and several other seamen were stabbed and clubbed to death before the Marine guards could come to their aid. Cook's reputation rests not only on the extent of his discoveries and surveys but on his precise and straightforward Journals of his adventures, first published in 1777.

Coolan, Bridie
A childhood acquaintance of Maturin (M&C 10).

Cooper
A London druggist used by Maturin and Martin (LM 4).

'Cooper, John'
A reference by Maturin to HMS *Surprise*'s master cooper, temporarily in the East Indiaman *Niobe* (TH 6).

Corbett, Robert
The Captain during the Mauritius campaign of HMSS *Néréide*, *Bourbonnaise*, and *Africaine* successively (TMC 1–9). He had also at one time commanded HMS *Seahorse*, in which Golovnin served as a volunteer (TMC 3). Although not known personally to Commodore Jack Aubrey, Corbett has a service reputation as a taut, fighting commander (TMC 1,3), although, in Admiral Bertie's eyes, somewhat 'irascible' (TMC 3). On the lower decks his reputation is that of a dangerously hard-driving flogger: he has had Bonden, who with Killick and others had transferred to him in order to re-join Jack at the Cape, lashed for a trivial offence, much to the Commodore's later fury (TMC 3; COM 5). After the successful assault on Réunion, Corbett is given HMS *Bourbonnaise* to take the good news to Admiral Bertie and thence on to England (TMC 4). Much later, he arrives unexpectedly back at Réunion in another new command, HMS *Africaine*, but his ship is rapidly taken by *Vénus* and *Victor* (TMC 8). When she is almost immediately recaptured by Jack's HMS *Boadicea*, Corbett is missing, with his crew denying all knowledge of what has become of him (TMC 8). Stephen Maturin later learns from HMS *Africaine*'s surgeon, Cotton, that Corbett, having first received a bad foot wound in the action, was later hit again and tossed overboard, although by whom remains uncertain (TMC 9). Cotton speculates that he may have been murdered by his own crew, who had earlier mutinied when he was appointed to command: during the awful voyage from England, HMS *Africaine*'s officers had even asked the surgeon whether Corbett could be relieved of his command on the grounds of insanity (TMC 9).

Robert Corbett/Corbet (d.1810) was promoted Commander in 1802 and made Post in 1806; he was killed in action on September 13th 1810, much as described by O'Brian's characters (although HMS *Africaine was en route from England, not the West Indies, to Madras). His reputation for severity on his ships is well-founded (he had been court-martialed and admonished for failure to keep good discipline on HMS *Néréide) and is certainly thought to have adversely affected the fighting spirit of Africaine. In his Naval History, Edward *Brenton suggested, without any evidence, that Corbett killed himself rather than be taken prisoner by the French.

Corby

A Royal Navy officer, an escapee with Lieutenants Fielding and Wilson from imprisonment in France, who was later killed by an enemy cavalry patrol in northern Italy (TH 9).

Corelli

An Italian composer often played by Aubrey and Maturin (PC 7; HMS 11; TMC 5; IM 11; FSW 2,4; TGS 4; C/T 3; WDS 1; COM 8).

Arcangelo Corelli (1653–1713) was a famous and successful violinist and composer in whose stylistic footsteps *Handel and *Bach followed. From 1690 onwards he lived under the patronage of Cardinal *Ottoboni, dying a wealthy man with a notable collection of great art.

Cornélie

A French frigate sent on the mission to Pulo Prabang (TGS 4), soon stranded there on a sand-bank (TGS 8). Later, pursued by Jack Aubrey in HMS *Nutmeg of Consolation* (NC 3+), she founders in a squall (NC 6).

A Cornélie 40-gun frigate was launched in 1794 and wrecked in 1808, some years before NC is set. Another frigate of the same name served in the French navy from 1813 to 1814 but her fate is unknown. Cornelia was the wife of *Pompey the Great. Her lamentation for his death was the subject of a well-known play by the Roman author Seneca and became a popular theme in later European art.

Cornwallis

1: an officer on HMS *Tartarus* (LM 2).
2: the Admiral commanding the Brest blockade in 1803 (YA 4).

Sir William Cornwallis (1744–1819), the younger brother of General the Marquis *Cornwallis, was made Post in 1765 and promoted Rear Admiral in 1793, Vice Admiral in 1794 and Admiral in 1799. Commander-in-Chief of the Channel fleet from 1801 to 1806, he had a reputation for superb seamanship — especially on the tedious blockade duty — and rigorous discipline. He was nevertheless a popular commander with his men, who regarded him as fair as he was taut. Cornwallis was largely responsible for preventing, by manoeuvre rather than action, a French invasion of England in 1805, thus enabling his very close friend *Nelson to bring the enemy to a decisive battle at Trafalgar towards the end of the same year (see also *Calder). Cornwallis also served as an MP for over 30 years.

Cornwallis, the Marquis

An aristocrat to whom Lord St Vincent addresses a letter about a Captain Bull (PC 3).

Charles, 2nd Earl and 1st Marquis Cornwallis (1738–1805), was the defeated second-in-command in the American Revolutionary War, with a reputation as the ablest of the British generals in the campaign. He later served as Commander-in-Chief (1786–1793) and Governor General of India (1797), before becoming Viceroy and Commander-in-Chief of Ireland from 1798 to 1801. In 1802 Cornwallis, the elder brother of Admiral Sir William *Cornwallis, was one of the chief negotiators of the short-lived Peace of Amiens.

Cornwallis, HMS

A ship at Bombay to which HMS *Java* is carrying fresh crew (FW 3).

HMS Cornwallis, 74-gun, was launched in Bombay in 1813. Having been converted into a screw-driven ship in 1855, she was taken out of service in 1865 and turned into a jetty at Sheerness. Re-named HMS Wildfire, shore-base ship, in 1916, she was not finally broken up until 1957. The ship was originally named for General the Marquis *Cornwallis, although a 20th century successor was named for his brother, Admiral *Cornwallis.

Corrigan

A 'crooked' United Irishman referred to by Maturin (M&C 5).

Corvisart

A French naturalist (SM 3–5) and physician, an advocate of 'auscultation' (SM 4; YA 8).

Jean Nicolas Corvisart-Desmarets (1755–1821) was one of the leading practical physicians of his day, with an especial reputation for diagnosis of heart complaints by the careful listening to — 'auscultation' — of body-sounds. In 1800 he became the chief physician to *Buonaparte, who regarded him as a highly able doctor, if somewhat blunt in his bed-side manner.

Cosmao-Kerjulien, Admiral

The newly appointed French second-in-command to Admiral Emeriau at Toulon (IM 4).

Julien-Marie, Baron Cosmao-Kerjulien (1761–1825), was promoted Commander in the French navy in 1792 and made Post in 1793. Made Commodore in 1797, in that rank he commanded Pluton, 74-gun, at the Battle of Trafalgar in 1805. Having escaped capture by *Nelson's fleet, two days after the great action he led a small squadron in re-taking two Spanish ships from their British prize-crews. In 1806 Cosmao-Kerjulien was promoted Rear Admiral, leading various squadrons of the Mediterranean fleet until, in 1814, being given the senior command. A Baron of the Empire of 1810, on the second *Bourbon restoration of 1815 he was made a Peer of France and in 1816 retired with full honours.

Cosnahan

A Master's Mate in HMS *Shannon* (FW 9,8).

Michael Finch Cosnahan (d.1885) was promoted Lieutenant in early 1815 but then waited for no less than 57 years until his advancement to retired Commander in 1872, a most belated recognition of his part in HMS *Shannon's great victory of 1813.

Costello, Father

The name of Irish priests in both Boston and Halifax, wished by Stephen Maturin to wed him and Diana Villiers (FW 7; SM 2).

Cotton

The elderly, ailing surgeon of HMS *Africaine* who speculates to Maturin that Captain Corbett may have been killed by his own crew (TMC 9).

Cotton, Henry or Harry

The Captain of HMS *Nymphe*, once a fellow Midshipman of Jack Aubrey in HMS *Resolution* (TH 9).

Courageux, HMS

A ship, Captain Wilkinson, in which Mr Rowan had been Third Lieutenant when she ran onto a reef, the incident being the subject of Rowan's entry to the HMS *Surprise* poetry competition (IM 9).

*HMS Courageux., 74-gun, was launched in 1800 and in 1805 took part in Sir Richard *Strachan's post-Trafalgar squadron victory. Later, under Philip *Wilkinson, she twice grounded on rocks, off Torbay in early 1811 and on the Anholt Reef in late 1812. This last accident (the subject of a poem written by her Third Lieutenant, Samuel *Walters) effectively ended her service career, and she was sent for harbour service in 1814, being broken up in 1832.*

Courser, James

A seaman in HMS *Sophie* (M&C 3).

Courteney, Hardwicke

A mathematician known to Maturin (YA 4).

Coutts

A bank referred to by a civil servant in Java (TGS 6).

*The London bank, still in business today, was first established in 1692 by an Edinburgh goldsmith, John Campbell (d.1712), for the purposes of serving the Scottish aristocracy's needs in England. By the 1760s it was managed in London by another Edinburgh merchant Thomas Coutts (1733?–1822) and his brother James (d.1778), who had married into the Campbell family. Thomas, though not himself of high birth, rapidly became the principle 'society' banker (all of Britain's monarchs since *George III have banked with Coutts) and his three daughters established very high connections for the family: Sarah married the 3rd Earl of Guildford; Frances married the eldest son of the Earl of *Bute; and Sophia married the wealthy Sir Francis *Burdett.*

Coutts

An East Indiaman in Muffit's China Fleet, protected by HMS *Surprise* from Admiral Linois' French squadron. (HMS 9).

*Coutts, 1200-tons, completed eight round trips for the East India Company between 1796 and 1813; she was named for the banker Thomas *Coutts. The action is based on the defence of a Honourable East India Company merchant fleet against *Linois' attack in February 1804. However, no Royal Navy ship was present during the fight, the squadron being organised by the senior Master, Nathaniel Dance of *Earl Camden.*

Coventry, Lady

A lady who, together with the Duchess of Hamilton, is said by Sir Joseph Blaine to have been one of the society beauties of his youth (HMS 4).

Maria Gunning, Countess of Coventry (1733–1760), came from a family of impoverished Irish gentry and, on their arrival on the London scene in 1751, she and her sister Elisabeth immediately became celebrated for their great beauty. In 1752 Maria married George, 6th Earl of Coventry (just a few weeks after Elisabeth had married the Duke of

*Hamilton) but died of consumption after bearing the Earl five children in rapid succession. As famous for her silliness as for her looks, on one occasion she told King George II that she absolutely longed to see a coronation in London. N.B., *Blaine elsewhere implies that he was in fact born shortly after Lady Coventry's death: see *Buteo.*

Cowslip

A British whaler, Master Michael McPhee (C/T 5).

Cox, Tom

The phrase 'to come it the Tom Cox's traverse' is used to mean 'to outwit.' (HMS 9).

In ship's parlance the phrase means 'to come up on deck through one hatchway and go down by another' or some similar variant on artful dodging; 'Tom Cox' himself is obscure.

Cozens

A naval friend of Tom Pullings (PC 5).

Cozens, William

A seaman in HMS *Sophie* (M&C 3).

Crabbe

A civil servant from Java attached, with his colleagues Loder and Johnstone, to Fox's Pulo Prabang mission. From their loud pomposity the three become known to HMS *Diane*'s crew as the 'Old Buggers' (TGS 6–9) and Jack Aubrey refers facetiously to Crabbe by one of the Sultan of Pulo Prabang's titles, Nutmeg of Consolation, Rose of Delight or Flower of Courtesy (TGS 9). When *Diane* is later stranded on a reef Crabbe leaves for Java with the rest of Fox's party in a small boat and Jack soon believes them all to have been lost in the typhoon that then sweeps the area (TGS 10).

Craddock

1: the navigator of the launch that escapes from the British defeat at Port South East, taking Stephen Maturin with the bad news to Jack Aubrey on nearby Réunion (TMC 7).
2: a seaman in HMS *Shannon*, injured boarding USS *Chesapeake* (FW 9).
3: a friend or colleague of Blaine and Maturin (SM 4).
4: a Polynesian-speaking seaman in *Surprise* (C/T 5).
5: a Captain recently promoted retired Rear Admiral (YA 1).
6: Admiral Lord Stranraer's secretary (YA 4,7).

Craig

The Master of an East Indiaman — possibly *Dorsetshire* — in the China Fleet protected by HMS *Surprise* (HMS 9).

Dorsetshire was commanded by Robert Hunter Brown in the action on which this incident is based.

Cramer

A great violinist referred to by Maturin (C/T 7).

Wilhelm Cramer (1746–1799) was a German orchestral

*leader and virtuoso violinist who lived in London from 1772 onwards, enjoying the encouragement of J. C. *Bach. He was chamber musician to King *George III as well as the leader of many popular festival orchestras, including those of the *Handel memorial concerts of 1784 and 1787. His son, Franz (1772–1848), was also a noted violinist.*

Craven, Lord

A gambling partner of Smithers (PC 10).

The reference is perhaps to William, 2nd Earl Craven (1770–1825), a Major-General and well-known sporting yachtsman.

Crawley, Abel

An elderly servant at Ashgrove Cottage, formerly a seaman in HMS *Arethusa* with the then Lieutenant Jack Aubrey (COM 1).

Crawshay, Frank

The MP for Westport and a friend of Jack Aubrey (YA 3).

'Creeping Jenny'

A figure whom the captured Midshipmen of HMS *Ariel* facetiously claim for a parent (SM 10).

Créole

A French corvette at Mauritius (TMC 5).

Créole was launched in 1809 and served in the French navy until 1812.

Crescent, HMS

A 36-gun ship, recently wrecked (TMC 1).

HMS Crescent 36-gun, was launched in 1784 and wrecked, with very heavy loss of life, off Jutland in late 1808.

Criana

A character mentioned in a sea-shanty (TGS 3).

Cribb, Tom

A famous prize-fighter (FSW 9; TGS 1; YA 3).

*Tom Cribb (1781–1848), the 'Black Diamond' (in his early years he fought still-begrimed from his job as a coal-miner), was one of the leading professional pugilists of his day, fighting his way to the Championship of All England. *Maturin, in FSW, has mis-recalled Cribb as Henry *Pearce's intended opponent, for Cribb's career did not start until 1805 and he never met the 'Game Chicken' in the ring.*

Crichton, Admiral

The 'Admirable Crichton,' thought by Jack Aubrey to have been an admiral (HMS 2; FW 6).

James Crichton (1560–1582) was a Scottish prodigy, often referred to as the 'Admirable' for his command, from a very early age, of many languages and philosophical tenets. He became well known as a participant in contests of knowledge and wit in France and Italy, where he also served as a dashing mercenary soldier and freelance tutor. Whilst in Italy, Crichton was killed by his pupil Vincenzo, the son of the Duke of Mantua, in a tavern brawl.

'Crimson Breeches'

The commander of the Turkish galley pursued and sunk off Mubara by Jack Aubrey's *Niobe* (TH 6).

Criseyde

O'Brian remarks that Criseyde's reading of lives of the saints is an anachronism (SM author's note).

*Chaucer's longest complete poem, Troilus and Criseyde, was written in the late 1380s and is inspired by a tale found in Boccaccio. The setting of the love story is the Trojan War, long before the Christian era and its saints.

Crockford's

A gambling club in London (YA 7).

*The club was founded in St James' Street (next door to *White's) in about 1790 by the fishmonger William Crockford (1775–1844), who had made a fortune at the gaming tables of London. It was famous for its lavish decor, for its well-bred manners and members, and for the extraordinarily high stakes that passed across its tables. The establishment closed for good shortly after William's death.*

Crocus

A reference by Aubrey to his present ample wealth (COM 1).

see **Croesus**

Croesus

A reference to legendary wealth (PC 8; FW 6; TH 8), with Blaine referring to Maturin as 'Dr Croesus' (RM 7).

*In Greek legend, King Croesus of Lydia (560?–546 BC) amassed colossal wealth by subjugating the Greek cities of Asia Minor. Eventually overthrown by his Persian rivals, he was supposedly thrown alive onto a funeral pyre but immediately rescued by the god *Apollo.*

Croft

The elderly lawyer of the Aubrey family (COM 6).

Croker

1: a neighbour of Aubrey and Maturin in Hampshire (PC 3).

2: the First Secretary at the Admiralty, the successor to Roger Hoarehound (TH 8,9). Maturin, who knew him at Trinity College, Dublin (RM 5), regards him as a villain (LM 4).

*John Wilson Croker (1780–1857) was an Irish-born politician, critic and essayist on literary topics, who attended Trinity from 1796 to 1800 as a distinguished classicist. As a reward for political service, in 1810 he became First Secretary to the Admiralty, where, despite Maturin's observation, he seems to have been well regarded as an assiduous official. He resigned his post in 1830, the year in which he achieved additional fame by being the first man to call the Tory Party 'Conservative.' In 1831 Croker produced a new edition of James *Boswell's Life of *Johnson.*

Crompton

The maker of a scientific instrument for measuring specific gravity (TGS 9).

Cromwell

The ruler of England (C/T 5) in whose time the Williams family had been Puritans (SM 4).

Oliver Cromwell (1599–1658), a strong *Calvinist, was a landowner, Member of Parliament and soldier who became Lord Protector Of England after the deposition and execution of King Charles I. For several centuries after his death, his regicide and his ruthless efficiency as military commander and dictator dominated his reputation. Yet he was also responsible to a great degree for both establishing English religious institutions as tolerant of a wide liberty of conscience (and this despite his own religious extremism as a young man) and for arresting the steady decline in his country's economic and political fortunes that had set in after the reign of Queen Elizabeth I. On Oliver's death his son, Richard (1626–1712), briefly took the title of Lord Protector but was soon forced to abdicate, allowing King *Charles II to reclaim his father's throne.

Crook

A seaman in HMS *Surprise* (NC 8).

Crosland

The Second Mate of *Diligence* (SM 3).

Cross, Thomas

A gunner's mate in HMS *Sophie* (M&C 6).

Crosse, Commodore La

The commander of *Droits de l'Homme* when she was driven onto rocks off Brest by HMSS *Indefatigable* and *Amazon* (YA 5).

Jean-Baptiste-Raymond, Baron La Crosse (1760–1829) was promoted Commander in 1786, Captain in 1793, Commodore in 1796 and Rear Admiral later in the same year. As Commodore, he led the abortive expedition to Bantry Bay in Ireland, soon being forced to retreat in his *Droits de l'Homme and being wrecked on his return journey, as described in the text. From 1801 to 1803 he served as a very troubled Préfect and Governor of Guadeloupe before returning home ill: on the voyage back to France his ship was captured by a Royal Navy frigate but La Crosse was soon released and allowed to continue on his way. From 1804 to 1811 he then commanded the French fleet at Boulogne, eventually retiring from the service in 1816 on health grounds.

Crowle

A man killed following the collapse of his hot air balloon (LM 1).

Crown

1: a reference to the owner of the Crown Inn at Port Mahon, who had married his pretty bar-maid Mercedes (IM 7).
2: the bosun of HMS *Diane* and later HMS *Nutmeg of Consolation* (TGS 5,8; NC 1–7). Badly crippled in the shipwreck island battle (NC 1), he later seems fully recovered (NC 4).

Crozet

A French explorer after whom a small group of South Seas islands are named (FW 1).

Julien-Marie Crozet (1728–1780) saw exploration service for the French East Indian company and military service for his nation from 1739 onwards, making a reputation as a prime seaman and navigator. From 1771 to 1773 he explored the South Pacific, discovering in 1772 the islands named for him. He died at sea in 1780, as commander of the warship Elisabeth.

Cucufat, Saint

A saint referred to in passing (TH 4).

Saint Cucufas (sic; d.304) was an aristocratic Carthaginian martyred near Barcelona, Spain; his feast-day is July 25th.

Cullen

A writer on mental illnesses (TGS 9).

William Cullen (1710–1790) was a Scottish physician and educator who, whilst specialising in materia medica *(i.e. pharmacology), also became known for his theories on ways in which the nervous system acts on the course and manifestation of bodily disease.*

Cullis

The Serjeant-Dentist to the Prince Regent, who operates on Padeen at Guy's (LM 4).

Culloden, HMS

A ship in which Simmons had served at the Battle of the Nile, but which had run aground and missed the main action (PC 12). She later serves in Admiral Thornton's Mediterranean fleet (IM 6).

HMS Culloden, *74-gun, was launched in 1783 and broken up in 1813. In 1798, under her Captain Thomas *Troubridge, she ran aground on a sandbar about a mile north of where the main engagement at the Nile took place and was unable to haul off until the next morning, despite the attempts to assist by Commander Thomas Hardy's brig HMS *Mutine. Her name commemorates the 1746 Hanoverian victory over the *Young Pretender at Culloden Field, near Inverness.*

Cumberland, Duke of

An aristocrat referred to by Lord St Vincent in his letter to Sir Charles Grey on the subject of Lieutenant Beresford (PC 3). His birthday is later celebrated in HMS *Surprise* (HMS 6).

Ernest Augustus, Duke of Cumberland, Earl of Armagh and King of Hanover (1771–1851), was the fifth son of King *George III and a professional soldier who saw much active service in the Hanoverian army. Appointed to both his Earldom and Dukedom in 1799, he became Chancellor of Trinity College, Dublin in 1805, a post in which he was a relentless opponent of Catholic emancipation and all political reform. In 1837 Victoria, the daughter of one of his elder — now deceased — brothers, succeeded to the Crown of the United Kingdom. However, under the prevailing Salic succession laws, she was debarred from the throne of Hanover, which therefore passed from her uncle and predecessor, William IV (see ***Clarence, Duke of***), to Ernest.*

Cumberland

An East Indiaman in Muffit's China Fleet, protected

by HMS *Surprise* from Admiral Linois' French squadron. (HMS 9).

> Cumberland, *1200-tons, made seven round trips for the East India Company between 1802 and 1815; the origins of her name may either be purely geographical or taken from the Duke of *Cumberland. The action is based on the defence of a Honourable East India Company merchant fleet against *Linois' attack in February 1804. However, no Royal Navy ship was present during the fight, the squadron being organised by the senior Master, Nathaniel Dance of *Earl Camden.*

Cumberland, HMS

A 74-gun ship, the flag-ship of Admiral Harte in the Mediterranean (PC 7) and later of Admiral Drury at Pulo Batang (FW 1).

> Harte's HMS Cumberland, *74-gun, was launched in 1774 and broken up in 1804, perhaps a little before he has her for his flag-ship. Her replacement was launched in 1807; renamed HMS* Fortitude *in 1833, she was sold sometime after 1870. The name of both of these ships appears to have been geographical in origin rather than a reference to any of the various Dukes of *Cumberland.*

Cumby

A cousin of Billy Sutton who had served in HMS *Bellerophon* at the Battle of Trafalgar, being soon made Post. He had once written a lengthy skit against the formidable Admiral Sir Francis Ives (FSW 1).

> William Pryce Cumby *(1770?–1837) had been promoted Lieutenant in 1793 and by 1805 was First Lieutenant of HMS *Bellerophon. At Trafalgar, he assumed command when his Captain John Cooke was killed, shot at much the same time as *Nelson and, like the Vice-Admiral, also by a sharpshooter. In January 1806 Cumby was made Post as a reward for this service, later briefly serving (in 1808) as Commodore of a small squadron in the West Indies. His ordeal over the skit occurred at the hands of that most formidable of Admirals, Earl *St Vincent, in about 1798.*

Cummings

1: one of Aubrey's co-defendants at his fraud trial (RM 7, 8).
2: an intelligence agent known to Sir Joseph Blaine (YA 7).

Cundall

A seaman in HMS *Sophie* (M&C 4).

Cunningham

1: a Captain who has an interview with his old ship-mate, Lord St Vincent (PC 3).
2: a British agent sent to South America in the mail packet *Danaë*, carrying enormous sums of money intended for bribes (FSW 2; RM 5). He is captured when the ship is taken by USS *Norfolk* (FSW 5).
3: a nephew of Admiral Schank who had served under Nelson in HMS *Agamemnon* (LM 1).

Curieux, HMS

A ship commanded by Captain Bettesworth (YA 3).

> HMS Curieux, *16-gun brig-sloop, was launched as the French* Bearnais *in 1808 and captured by the Royal Navy in 1809; she was sold out of the service in May 1814.*

Curtis

1: a marine in HMS *Burford* (M&C 2).
2: a Shelmerstonian seaman in HMS *Surprise* (NC 7).

Curtis, Lucius

The Captain of HMS *Magicienne* (TMC 5, 6) whose battered and grounded ship is blown up at the end of the Battle of Port South East by her own crew. They then escape to HMS *Iphigenia* and, by implication, all become prisoners on her surrender to the French (TMC 7).

> Sir Roger Lucius Curtis *(1780?–1869) was made Post in 1806 and inherited a baronetcy on the death of his father, Admiral Sir Roger Curtis (1746–1816; see also *Queen Charlotte, HMS). Promoted Rear Admiral in 1838, Vice Admiral in 1849 and Admiral in 1855, in 1864 he rose to Admiral of the Fleet. His HMS* Magicienne *was lost, exactly in the manner described, on August 25th 1810. Lucius' elder brother, also Roger (d.1802), was also a Royal Navy officer, made Post just a few months before his death.*

Cuvier, Georges and Frédérick

Georges Cuvier is a French doctor and scientist of whom Maturin and Blaine are great admirers (SM 1,4,5; RM 5,7,8,10; LM 9; TGS 6,7,8; WDS 4; COM 8,9). He is the senior of a family of *savants* that also includes Frédérick Cuvier (SM 1,4).

> Georges Chrétien Léopold, Baron Cuvier *(1769–1832), was one of the leading natural scientists of his age and is regarded as the founder of modern comparative anatomy, whose systematic work laid the foundations for Darwin's evolutionary biology. From 1802 Cuvier served as Perpetual Secretary to the French Academy of Sciences and in that capacity travelled widely in Europe consulting on the setting up of other such academies and great university departments. A prolific writer throughout his life, his great* Fossil Bones *was published in 1812 and his monumental* Animal Kingdom *in 1817. Cuvier became a Baron in 1820 and a Peer of France in 1831. His younger brother, Frédérick (1773–1838), became director of the zoo in the Jardin des Plants and also a Professor of Comparative Anatomy in the same institution.*

Czar, the

The Russian monarch who Maturin says had been strangled (HMS 1). His successor (FW 6) sends caviare to Admiral James Saumarez in the Baltic (SM 8).

> Paul I *(1754–1801), an unstable and incompetent man, succeeded his mother Catherine II—'the Great'—in 1796, plunging the country into chaos. In early 1801 he was strangled or smothered in his bedchamber by discontented nobles, a plot of which his son and heir, Alexander (1777–1825), was informed in advance (see *Vandamme). This young man, now Alexander I, was a pious, high-minded reformer by inclination but was also somewhat capricious, lacking both the skill and energy to see through his grand ideals. In foreign policy he saw himself initially as a moderator between the competing desires of France and England. However, he was*

unable to maintain a 'benevolent neutrality' and instead merely switched sides between the two great rivals and their respective allies several times, usually with calamitous results for his own armies and national borders. After an uneasy peace with *Buonaparte in the years following the crushing defeats of 1807, war again broke out with the French invasion of 1812. The harsh winter and the brilliant tactics of Marshall Kutuzov forced a French retreat but Alexander

finally decided that he must now throw in his lot with England and Prussia to defeat Napoleon once and for all. After peace finally arrived in 1815, Alexander gradually became more of a reactionary in his domestic policy and more of a religious mystic in his private life. Having several times declared that he wished to abdicate, he died in the Crimea of a fever: it was long rumoured that this 'death' was staged, to enable him to retire to a monastery.

D

D., Mr.
see **Dutourd, Jean**

'D of C'
A reference to a protector and sometime lover of Louisa Wogan (DI 2).
see, perhaps, **Clarence, Duke of** or **Cumberland, Duke of**

Dabeoc
A saint referred to in passing by Maturin (C/T 7).
Saint Beoc or Dabheog (active 5th or 6th century) was a Welsh-born monk who travelled to Ireland and founded a monastery on an island in Lough Derg; his feast day is December 16th.

Dacier, Madam
An authoress who had translated Homer (FSW 4).
Anne Lefèvre Dacier (1651?–1720) was the leading Hellenist of her age and a classical philologist of international renown. The daughter and pupil of the famous classicist Tanneguy Lefèvre (1615–1672), she married her fellow student and scholar André Dacier (1651–1722) in 1682. Madam Dacier published many editions of Greek and Latin classics, and made translations of *Homer's Iliad (1699) and Odyssey (1708) as well as numerous other ancient works.

Dacres, Tom
The Captain of HMS *Guerrière*, 38-gun, taken by the 44-gun USS *Constitution* (FW 3), later perhaps the same Captain Dacres who has just become an MP (TGS 4).
James Richard Dacres (d.1853) commanded HMS *Guerrière during this action on August 19th 1812, being wounded by musket fire during the intense, 25-minute fight. Dacres was extremely complimentary about his subsequent treatment by his American captors and became a life-long friend of USS Constitution's *Captain Isaac *Hull: he had no doubt helped himself in this matter by thoughtfully allowing 10 of his crew who were themselves Americans to stay below during the encounter. Dacres, the son and nephew of Admirals, had been made Post in 1806 and eventually rose to Rear Admiral in 1838 and Vice Admiral in 1848. N.B., none of the several members of the family who joined the Royal Navy was named Tom or served as an MP.*

Daedalus, HMS
A ship that, with HMS *Fox*, had bombarded the French-held fort of Kosseir on the Red Sea coast (TH 7).
HMS Daedalus, 32-gun, was launched in 1780. COLLEDGE records that she served as a hulk in England from 1803 to 1806 before being broken up in 1811; CLOWES, however, has her on active service in the West Indies in late 1808. The rather unsuccessful bombardment of Kosseir in the Red Sea took place in August 1799, with Daedalus being commanded by Henry Lidgbird *Ball. In Greek myth Daedalus was the artful inventor and craftsman who, amongst other things, made wings for himself and his son *Icarus. Unlike the incautious boy, he survived their subsequent flight and went on to confirm his uncanny skill in many other projects.

Daendels, Van
The Dutch commander in the Spice Islands (DI 6).
Hermann Willem van Daendels (1762–1818) was a Dutch soldier who served in the French army from about 1792 until being, in 1796, appointed General in his own national army. In 1807 he was promoted Marshall of Holland by King Louis (see *Buonapartes, the) and from 1808 to 1811 was Governor-General of the Dutch East Indies. In 1812 he returned to military service in Europe, commanding a French division in the invasion of Russia.

Daisy
A British whaler (WDS 1), Master Mr. Wainwright (C/T 5–8).

Dale
The Master of the East Indiaman *Streatham* (TMC 4).
John Dale (dates unknown) was Master of *Streatham, 30-gun transport, taken by the French *Caroline, 40-gun, in May 1809.

Dalgleish, Jamie, Mrs., and Tom
Jamie Dalgleish is the owner and Master of the British Government mail packet *Diligence* (SM 3,4), with his son Tom aboard as a seaman (SM 3). When *Diligence* is vigorously pursued by Johnson's privateers, Jamie very much has his wife's opinions on his safety and business prospects in mind (SM 3).

Dalhousie

The Hydrographer of the Navy (YA 10).

*A somewhat puzzling reference, for in 1808 Alexander *Dalrymple was succeeded as Hydrographer to the Navy by Captain Thomas Hurd (1753–1823), who then served in the post until his death. However, Dalhousie was a well-known military name of the time, with General Sir George Ramsay (1770–1838), 9th Earl of Dalhousie, being one of *Wellington's subordinate commanders in Spain and the South of France.*

Dalrymple

A hydrographer (TGS 6,9) who had made observations in the Salibabu Passage (NC 6).

*Alexander Dalrymple (1737–1808) joined the East India Company in 1752 and, ten years later, charted for them new trading routes from Madras to Canton. He made a great reputation as a scientific surveyor and in 1766 was proposed as Commander of the Royal Society expedition to the South Seas: however, the Admiralty insisted on having a serving officer lead the naval side of the mission and Lieutenant James *Cook was instead appointed to the task. In 1779 Dalrymple was appointed Hydrographer to the East India Company and in 1795 he became the first holder of the office of Hydrographer to the Admiralty, holding both of these posts until his death, from gangrene, in 1808.*

Dalton

The Captain of HMS *Theseus* (IM 5).

Dalziel, Alexander

The new First Lieutenant of HMS *Sophie*, succeeding the deceased James Dillon. He is a nephew of Lord Keith, and is accompanied to sea by his dog (M&C 11+).

Damer, Mrs.

A Mayfair neighbour of the Keith's (PC 6).

*Possibly a reference to Anne Seymour Damer (1749–1828) an artist and society hostess who produced busts of, amongst others, King *George III and Lord *Nelson.*

Damon and Pythagoras

A reference by Jack Aubrey to forbearance for the sake of friendship (PC 12).

*In legend, Damon of Syracuse (a follower of *Pythagoras's ethical system) was the close friend of Pythias, each pledging their lives for the sake of the other. Their names are consequently associated as exemplars of mutual loyalty under threat of death.*

Danae

A reference by Jack Aubrey to greed (TMC 5).

*Danaë, daughter of Acrisius and *Eurydice, was visited and seduced by *Zeus disguised as a shower of gold, wealth that she greatly desired. The myth provided a popular subject for tales and visual art though the ages.*

Danaë

A mail packet sent by the British government to South America carrying an intelligence agent, Cunningham, and very large sums of money intended to suborn local governments into rebellion. Becoming very concerned that she may be taken by USS *Norfolk*, Blaine sends Aubrey and Maturin in HMS *Surprise* to intercept her (FSW 2,5,6,8). She has indeed been taken by the American ship but is soon recaptured by HMS *Surprise* (FSW 5). Most of the money concealed in her was not found by the Americans, and is now transferred to Maturin's safekeeping, with the ship herself given to Tom Pullings to take back to England (FSW 5; RM 1,5,8).

*For her name derivation see *Danae above.*

Dandin, George

The subject of a French catch-phrase, 'vous l'avez voulu, George Dandin' (TGS 6).

George Dandin, ou le Mari Confondu, a comedy of manners by the great French playwright Molière (1622–1673), was first performed in 1668. Dandin, a wealthy peasant, marries above his station and is repeatedly cuckolded by his pretty wife, Angélique. Whenever he tries to confront her with her deception, he is tricked into having to retreat, making a constant, bitter refrain of 'you brought this on yourself, George Dandin.'

Dangeau, Madame

An agent of the French intelligence services who tries to entrap Maturin in illegal activities in Paris (SM 5).

Daniel, John

A newly joined Master's Mate in HMS *Surprise* with a bent for mathematics and navigation. The son of an impoverished book-seller, he had been forced to go to sea to save the family from ruin, and had served in Jack Aubrey's HMS *Worcester* along with several other ships (HD 3+). Daniel is rather unluckily injured in the symbolic 'action' against *Cerbère* (HD 5) and again injured in an accidental fall (HD 6).

Daphne, HMS

The sloop with Ponsich aboard that, under a recently promoted young Commander, has been sunk by fire from the island of Grimsholm (SM 6).

*An HMS Daphne, 22-gun frigate, was launched in 1806 and sold in 1816; she served extensively in the Baltic and North Sea but does not seem to have engaged in an action similar to the one mentioned in the text. In Greek myth Daphne was a mountain-nymph who was changed by Mother Earth into a laurel tree in order that she might escape the attentions of *Apollo. As a consolation prize Apollo then made for himself a wreath of laurel-leaves, this later becoming famous as the victory symbol in games held in his honour.*

'Dark Lantern'
see **Diaz, Diego**

Darkie

1: a Capetown black man who assists Maturin in

wheeling the drunken Dr. McAdam back to his ship (TMC 3).

2: a powerful black seaman in HMS *Nutmeg of Consolation* (NC 6).

*Perhaps a reference to Darkie *Johnstone.*

Darley, Captain

Possibly the commander of HMS *Bulldog*, a ship mentioned in HMS *Sophie*'s log (M&C 2).

*In November 1799 — the date referred to in the M&C text— HMS *Bulldog was under Commander Barrington Dacres (made Post in 1802; died in 1806); no Darley was serving as a Royal Navy officer at the time.*

Darley Arabian, the

A famous racehorse of a past age (DI 1).

*In 1704 (in some accounts, 1706) Mr. Thomas Darley of Yorkshire (dates unknown) imported to England a Syrian stallion that had been born in about 1700. Along with two similar horses, the Godolphin Barb and the Byerley Turk, the 'Darley Arabian' is the origin of the English thoroughbred blood-line, the sire of *Flying Childers amongst many other champions.*

Dart, HMS

The Royal Navy hired cutter previously commanded by James Dillon (M&C 2+).

Two small HMS Darts are possible sources for this incident, an 8-gun cutter hired in 1782, of which no more is known, and an 8-gun lugger, a British privateer brig of unknown launch date, captured by the French in 1802 and recaptured by HMS Apollo in 1803, being sold in 1808. However, the Royal Navy also had an HMS Dart, 28-gun brig-sloop (and, as such, not a Lieutenant's command), that was very active in the Channel waters at the time of M&C; she was launched in 1796 and broken up in 1809. The ship names are probably taken from the River Dart in Kent.

Darwin, Dr.

A scientist referred to in very favourable terms by Maturin and Martin (FSW 10).

Erasmus Darwin (1731–1802) was a physician, botanist and author of great originality. His prose meditation Zoonomia, or the Laws of Organic Life (1794–1796) and several of his other works offer interesting, if rather mystical, embryonic versions of the evolutionary theories of his more famous grandson, Charles Darwin (1809–1882). Darwin's poem The Temple of Nature or the Origin of Society was published posthumously in 1803.

Dashwood, John

A Lieutenant in HMS *Lively* (PC 12,13; HMS 2) who takes command of the captured Spanish *Fama* (PC 14).

Dato Selim

A potentate in Batavia (NC 3).

Datuk/Dato is the Malay term for a war-chief or head of a village community.

d'Auvergne, Prince
see **Auvergne, Prince d'**

Davey
see **Davy**

David

The biblical King referred to by Maturin for his religious dancing (COM 8).

*David (1090?–1015? BC) was a poet and musician who in about 1055 BC, some years after he had slain the giant *Goliath, became King of Judah and later, in about 1048, King of all Israel; he was succeeded by his son, *Solomon. David's ecstatic dance before the Lord is referred to in the Old Testament at II Samuel VI.*

Davidge

1: a helmsman in HMS *Surprise* (HMS 5).

2: the Third Mate/Lieutenant of Jack Aubrey's letter-of-marque *Surprise*, recently dismissed the Royal Navy for signing a dishonest purser's accounts without first checking them (LM 1+; TGS 1,2,4; NC 7+; CT 1–9). Later in the voyage he gradually comes to be on very bad terms with Lieutenant West over their competing desire for the stow-away, Clarissa Oakes (C/T 3+). Hoping to regain Jack's favour, Davidge is killed in action on Moahu Island, furiously leading a shore party against a group of French mercenaries (C/T 9; WDS 1). Although he had served in HMS *Amethyst* in her famously bloody fight with the French frigate *Thetis (C/T 2), he is later said to have seen little action in his career (C/T 4).

Davidson

A naval surgeon hanged at Bombay for mutiny (PC 11).

Davies

A black seaman in HMSS *Sophie* (M&C 7,9,10), *Boadicea* (TMC 9; *as 'Davis'*) and *Pomone* (HD 1; *but see Awkward *Davies, below*).

Davies or Davis, Awkward

A huge, violent, brutal seaman who enthusiastically transfers from HMS *Niobe* into his old Captain Jack Aubrey's HMS *Worcester*, Jack having once rescued him from drowning (IM 6+). He remains with Jack in many later commands, usually somewhat unwelcome (TH 4+; FSW 4–9; RM 3,9; TGS 1–3; NC 7+; C/T 3–8; WDS 1+; COM 3,7; *perhaps* HD 1). According to the Captain, he is without doubt a cannibal (TH 6) and is referred to as Jack's 'Old Man of the Sea' (TH 4).

*Awkward Davies makes a rather sudden first appearance in IM as an 'old hand.' He could perhaps be the black *Davies of HMSS *Sophie and *Boadicea (who later seems to turn up in HMS Pomone: HD 1), the mutinous *Davis of HMS *Polychrest, or Tom *Davis of HMS *Leopard (who, if he had accompanied Jack to HMS La*

Flèche, could later have eaten *Raikes). He may even be the unhandy brute *Bolton—renamed—of Polychrest, *whom Jack had certainly saved from drowning.*

Davis

1: a 'crooked' United Irishman referred to by Maturin (M&C 5).

2: a seaman in HMS *Polychrest* believed by Aubrey to be about to mutiny (PC 11).

3: the owner of a horse-yard in Plymouth (SM 4).

4: Dr. Davis, a naval parson travelling out to his new ship at Port Mahon in Aubrey's HMS *Worcester*. So disagreeable does he find sea-travel that he returns to England by as much land as he can manage (IM 3).

5: a seaman — perhaps Awkward Davies — in HMS *Surprise* who carries no immunity to smallpox (NC 8).

6: *see* **Davies**

Davis, Awkward

see **Davies** or **Davis, Awkward**

Davis, Tom

A seaman in HMS *Leopard* (DI 3).

Davy

Seamen are occasionally 'as drunk as Davy's sow' (TMC 10; SM 4; TGS 9).

According to BREWER, *David Lloyd, a Welsh farmer, had a sow with six legs that on one occasion was confused with his drunken wife, collapsed in its sty: the lady became known thereafter as 'Davy's sow.'*

Davy, Sir Humphrey or Humphry

A Fellow of the Royal Society much admired by Maturin (DI 2; SM 1,5,10; IM 2; RM 4).

Sir Humphry Davy (1778–1829) was a highly distinguished chemist and experimentalist, elected Fellow of the Royal Society in 1803. Having made an early reputation by his discovery of the effectiveness of nitrous oxide as an anaesthetic gas, he later he went on to discover many new metallic elements, as well as to invent his famous safety lamp for use in mines. Davy was knighted in 1812 and made a baronet in 1818; he served as President of the Royal Society from 1820 to *1827.

Dawkins, Mr.

An unwelcome suitor of Diana Villiers (PC 6).

Dawson

1: a neighbour of George Herapath in Boston (FW 8).

2: the Captain of HMS *Pollux*, in which Admiral Harte takes passage back to England. The ship accompanies Aubrey's HMS *Surprise* to Zambra, and is there engaged and destroyed, with the loss of all hands, by a powerful French squadron, led by the 74-gun *Mars* (TH 10; FSW 1).

3: a recently executed horse-nobbler (YA 3).

Daniel Dawson (d.1812) was a well-known betting tout around the various stables at Newmarket. After his colleague, Cecil Dawson (apparently no relation), turned King's evidence against him, he was convicted and executed at Cambridge for poisoning racehorses—two of which died—in 1809 and 1811. The case made considerable news at the time because of Daniel Dawson's close connections to well-known sporting gentlemen, some with aristocratic titles, and consequent suspicions that he was involved in a large-scale, race-fixing operation.

Dawson, Nancy

The subject of the tune that summons seamen to their grog (PC 12; FW 9; FSW 6).

In 1759 the dancer Nancy Dawson (1730?–1767) became instantly famous when she replaced the regular, male performer of the hornpipe sequence in a revival of John Gay's Beggar's Opera. *The song, with new words relating how Nancy became the star of the show and the toast of London, became immensely popular, although it is not known exactly how it achieved its status as the Royal Navy 'grog's up' call. The tune itself is also well known in the form of 'Here We Go Round the Mulberry Bush.' (see also* ***Nancy Dawson**).

Day, Amos

The captain of the foretop in HMS *Surprise*, promoted bosun into the gun-brig HMS *Fly* (FSW 2).

Day, George 'Lazarus'

HMS *Sophie's* gunner (M&C 1+), who receives a depressed cranial fracture in the ship's first battle (M&C 4). Successfully operated on by Stephen Maturin, the first of a number of famous 'trepannings' accomplished by the Doctor, he is thereafter nicknamed 'Lazarus' Day (M&C 5; HMS 9,11; TMC 9; DI 3; FSW 5). So complete is his recovery that he is later promoted into HMS *Elephant*, 74-gun (PC 8).

Dayrolle

Referred to in a note from Maturin to Aubrey, perhaps the name of the owner of a farm or inn (HMS 4).

Dayton

A neighbour of Diana Villiers (C/T 3).

Dear, the

see **God**

Deb or Deborah

A girl working at Mrs. Broad's Inn, possibly her daughter (SM 6; LM 4).

Deborah

The lady referred to by Martin as his wife (LM 5). N.B. that, earlier in the series (RM 6), Martin's betrothed is one Polly *(a diminutive of 'Mary')*, and they are later certainly married (RM 10).

Decaen, General

The French commander of the island of Mauritius (TMC 1+; TH 4).

> *Charles-Mathieu-Isidore Decaen (1769–1832), first appointed General in 1796, was in 1802 made Captain-General of all the French possessions in and around India. Forced to surrender the last of them, Mauritius, to General *Abercrombie in December 1810, he then returned to Europe, joining the Spanish campaign with some success, and in 1813 being made a Count. In 1814 he maintained his military rank under the first *Bourbon restoration but then re-joined *Buonaparte on his return from Elba in 1815, being in consequence forced to resign and go into exile on the Emperor's final defeat.*

Dédaigneuse

A French frigate that briefly pursues HMS *Sophie* (M&C 9).

> *Dédaigneuse, a 36-gun launched in 1797, was captured by the Royal Navy off the Portuguese coast in January 1801, taken in as HMS Dedaigneuse and then sold in 1823.*

Dee

An elderly Admiralty intelligence official at Gibraltar, the author of a 1764 work on Persian literature (HD 1).

Dee, HMS

A 38-gun frigate sailing in company with HMS *Charwell* (PC 1).

Deering

A former Captain of HMS *Phoebe* who had died of a fever in the West Indies (DI 4).

Deering, John

A naturalist and friend of Stephen Maturin who has recently died whilst undergoing surgery at Stephen's hands (DI 1).

Defender, HMS

An unhappy ship, Captain Marriot, in Sir John Thornton's Mediterranean Fleet (IM 4,5); long ago she had been commanded by Admiral Lord Stranraer (HD 1). Mr. Martin acts as her temporary Chaplain, giving comfort to two of her men who are to be executed (IM 4). Later the crew come close to mutiny against her incompetent set of officers, and at Gibraltar her more troublesome seamen are transferred to Jack Aubrey's HMS *Surprise*, taking some considerable time to become integrated (FSW 2–6). At some point *Defender* had been commanded by a Captain Ashton (FSW 2) and, some years later, Tom Pullings tells Stephen Maturin of a discussion he had once had with her Master on the subject of sodomy (RM 8).

> *By implication HMS Defender is a sizeable ship, a frigate at the least: however, all the Defenders of the general period were brigs, luggers or gun-boats.*

Defiance, HMS

A ship commanded by Captain Dungannon (RM 1).

> *HMS Defiance, 74-gun, was launched in 1783 but not commissioned until 1794. Until 1798 she bore the reputation of an unusually mutinous ship, no less than 15 of her crew being hanged and 20 severely punished in other ways. In 1801, under Captain Richard Retallick, she took part in *Nelson's victory at Copenhagen and in 1805, now under Philip Durham (d.1845 as a full Admiral) she fought both in *Calder's indecisive action and at Trafalgar itself a few months later. Amongst her crew was one Jane Townsend, at first recommended for the commemorative medal for her valuable service in the battle, but later denied it on the grounds that it would surely open the doors to claims from the many other female participants in great battles of the past. After seeing a great deal more active service, Defiance was converted to a prison ship in 1813 and broken up in 1817.*

Delalande

The Captain of the frigate *Cerbère* who, after some encouragement from Jack Aubrey and Stephen Maturin, declares for King Louis XVIII (HD 5).

Delaney

A missing intelligence agent in some way connected to Sir Joseph Blaine (YA 1).

Delaris

A secret policeman belonging to Laurie's Parisian organisation (SM 11).

Delarue

A gentleman who had attempted to persuade Maturin to carry a secret message from Paris to London (SM 11).

Delaunay, Madame

A fashionable dress-maker in Paris (SM 5).

Demosthenes

A classical orator (SM 5; FSW 2) referred to as having addressed the waves (LM 1).

> *Demosthenes (384–322 BC), the Athenian statesman, was generally considered to be the greatest Greek orator of all. By legend, he overcame an early speech impediment by declaiming over the noise of the sea with his mouth full of pebbles.*

Denghy

A serpent-god of the Fijians (C/T 3).

> *In the Fijian belief system, the serpent Ndengei holds up the world and therefore has the power to produce earthquakes and eruptions.*

Dent

The Commander of HMS *Grappler* (TMC 5).

Desaix

A French 74-gun ship in Linois' squadron that takes Jack Aubrey's HMS *Sophie*. She is commanded by Captain Christy-Pallière (M&C 11+; PC 4; TGS 8).

Desaix *was launched in 1793 as* Tyrannicide, *re-named* Desaix *in 1800 and wrecked in February 1802. It was aboard her in June 1801 that Thomas *Cochrane surrendered HMS *Speedy to Captain *Christi-Pallière, who insisted the Scotsman keep his sword for his gallantry. The ship is named for General Louis-Charles-Antoine Desaix de Veygoux (1768–1800), the French military hero killed at the Battle of Marengo.*

Desbrusleys, General

The French commander of the island of Réunion (TMC 3), in dispute with Captain Saint-Michiel as well as most of his other officers (TMC 4). Following Jack Aubrey's successful raid on Réunion he kills himself, partly on account of the military reverse and partly because of his marital problems (TMC 4).

Nicholas-Arnault de Rignac Desbrulys (sic; 1757–1809) had served in the French army from 1776, being appointed Brigadier General in 1794. In 1802, after a period without a command, he accepted a position under General *Decaen in the French East Indies and in 1808 was promoted General and given command of Réunion. However, when the island proved incapable of being defended against the British with the few troops he had been allocated, Desbrulys killed himself by cutting his throat and setting off two explosive charges he had wrapped round his neck. His suicide note referred only to his sense of disgrace at the military calamity that had befallen him.

Désirée, HMS

A ship whose Captain Ross has recently married a Miss Cockburn (SM 11).

HMS Désirée, *36-gun, was an ex–French ship of the same name, launched in 1796 and captured by the Royal Navy in 1800. Under her Captain Henry Inman (d.1809), she fought at *Nelson's victory at Copenhagen in 1801, but then saw relatively little service until being sold out of the service in 1832.*

Desmond

An Irish family that had forfeited land to the Scroggs/Conferts (TMC 2).

The *Fitzgeralds, Earls of Desmond from the 14th to the late 16th century, were an Anglo-Norman family that had held extensive lands and titles in Ireland from the 12th century onwards; another branch were Earls of Kildare and Leinster. In 1583 Gerald, 14th Earl of Desmond, was executed for treason and in 1586 his lands were declared forfeit to the Crown.

Desmoulins

A French politician with responsibility for foreign affairs (FW 1).

The name echoes that of Camille Desmoulins (1762–1794), the lawyer, political writer and moderate *Jacobin who, with his close friend George Danton, played a leading role in the French revolution: he was executed, with Danton, after falling out with their erstwhile colleague Robespierre. Desmoulins' wife, Lucile, was executed shortly afterwards, on the same day as their good friend General Arthur *Dillon.

Despard, Colonel

An acquaintance of Maturin who has told him of the number of closet Catholics in King George's service (M&C 6).

Edward Marcus Despard (1751–1803) was an Irish-born soldier, colonial administrator and, eventually, conspirator against the British Crown. After a successful career as a British officer, Despard became disaffected with colonial policy whilst Chief Administrator of Belize. Returning home unemployed, he may have become involved in the United Irishmen uprising of 1798 as he was imprisoned, without formal charges or trial, until 1801. On his release, he then hatched a plot in London with Irish soldiers and labourers to assassinate King *George III and start an armed uprising. His scheme was riddled with informers from the start and Despard was quickly arrested, tried and convicted of high treason. Despite testaments to his earlier character from Lord *Nelson (who had known him very well in the West Indies), he was hung and beheaded, with six others, in 1803. As was the case with Lord Edward *Fitzgerald, Hamilton *Rowan and Wolfe *Tone (and many other Irish families too), the Despard family's loyalties were complex and mixed, for, throughout this period of rebellion, Edward's elder brother, John (1745–1829), was a successful and well-regarded British general.

Despatch, HMS

A cartel ship, Captain Harry Tennant (RM 4).

HMS Dispatch *(sic), 18-gun brig-sloop, was launched in 1812 and sold in 1836.*

Despencer, Mr.

A Midshipman of HMS *Bellona*, temporarily in *Ringle*, her tender (YA 4).

Deucalion

A reference to a classical figure who had escaped a flood (HMS 6).

Deucalion is an approximate equivalent in Greek myth to the biblical *Noah. A son of the 'rebel god' Prometheus, he built a small boat for himself and his wife to escape *Zeus' flooding of the world. Once the waters subsided, they threw, as per Prometheus' instructions, stones over their shoulders, these then changing into human beings who repopulated the earth. Deucalion's son, Hellen, gave his name to Hellas, the word by which classical Greeks referred to their country.

Deux Frères

A French privateer, Master M. Dumanoir, pursued and taken by HMS *Bellona* off Brest (YA 6,8).

Devil

The Evil One (or Lucifer, Satan), very often referred to in oaths (e.g. HMS 2,7,11; TMC 5; SM 11; TH 10; FSW 2,4,7,9; LM 5; NC 1,7; C/T 1,4,6; COM 5,9; COM 9; HD 1,3,4).

In the biblical tradition, the leader of those angels who rebelled against *God was Lucifer (in Latin, the 'light-bringer'): after his expulsion from Heaven—for excessive pride—he became known as Satan or the Devil, the chief of all the souls in torment in his fiery realm. The word 'Devil' seems to be derived from the ancient Greek diabo-

los, 'slanderer,' with 'Satan' being derived from a Hebrew
and Greek word for 'adversary.'

Devlin
A quartermaster in HMS *Surprise* (TH 10).

Devonshire, Duke and Duchess of
Two aristocrats who had revealed a clumsy attempt
at bribery by members of the French delegation to
London during the Peace of Amiens (LM 7).

> *William Cavendish, 5th Duke of Devonshire (1748–1811)
> and his wife Georgina (1757–1806) were leading society
> figures, with the Duchess, a sister of Earl *Spencer, being
> the most famous hostess of the period.*

Dgezza Pasha
see **Djezzar Pasha**

Di or Diana
see **Villiers, Diana**

Diana
A Russian sloop at Capetown, commanded by
Golovnin (TMC 3,5).
see **Golovnin**

Diane, HMS
1: a ship currently being fitted out in England and
   wanted as a command by the ship-less Jack
   Aubrey (TMC 1).
   *HMS Diana (sic) was launched in 1794 and sold to the
   Dutch navy in 1815. In Greek myth Diana was the goddess of the moon, of childbirth and of hunting.*
2: initially a new French frigate, *Diane*, blockaded
   in St. Martin's and commanded by the brother
   of that Jean-Jacques Lucas who had *Redoubtable* at Trafalgar (LM 4+; TGS 7). She is
   soon cut out from her harbour by Jack Aubrey,
   hoping that his *coup* will bring about his
   restoration to the Royal Navy (LM 6; TGS 1).
   Later we learn that *Diane* had been intended to
   carry out a French mission to Chile and Peru,
   similar to that eventually undertaken by Jack
   and Stephen Maturin (TGS 1). Bought into the
   service as HMS *Diane*, 32-gun, she is initially
   given to a Captain Bushel (TGS 3,4), but,
   when Jack is finally restored, he assumes command and takes the ship on the mission to Pulo
   Prabang (TGS 3+). Just after that task is concluded, *Diane* strikes fast on an uncharted reef
   lying off a small, uninhabited island (TGS 9)
   and is totally wrecked in an ensuing typhoon
   (TGS 10; N-C 1–3; *also* C/T 1,4,8; WDS 1+;
   YA 1).
   *The French navy had a corvette named Diane from 1808
   to 1831, whilst the Royal Navy had from 1794 to 1815 that
   HMS Diana noticed in the first part of this entry. The
   wrecking of Diane and the subsequent events on the island
   are closely based on the loss of HMS Alceste in February
   1817 (see M'Leod, John Voyage of His Majesty's Ship*

Alceste etc.; London: John Murray, 2nd ed. 1818). Also see
La *Flèche, HMS.**

Diaz, Don Diego
A wealthy Spaniard acting as a private intelligence
agent in London (YA 7). Diaz is in fact an opera-
tive for the Spanish, and perhaps French, governments, to whom he had volunteered his services
after his brother was killed at the Battle of Trafalgar. In the guise of 'Black Lantern,' he attempts to
burgle Sir Joseph Blaine's home but is caught in the
act by Stephen Maturin and others (YA 7).

Dibdin
An author whose works are copied out by Bonden
as part of his learning to write (HMS 6).

> *Charles Dibdin (1745–1814) was an actor and dramatist
> who also wrote many popular songs, a great number of sea-
> songs amongst them. Reduced to poverty in his old age,
> Lord *St. Vincent gave him a small pension in thanks for
> his songs having helped pass many a tedious ship-board
> evening. Charles' son, Thomas John Dibdin (1771–1841),
> was also a prolific songwriter.*

Dick
1: a servant at a coaching inn in Devon (YA 3).
2: *see* **Richardson, Dick**

Dido
A reference by Amanda Smith to her own imagined
abandonment by Jack Aubrey (SM 2). In a different
context, Jack later ventures that Dido was poorly
treated by either Ulysses or Anchises (TH 9).

> *In *Virgil, Dido, Queen of Carthage, entered a passion-
> ate relationship with the Trojan hero *Aeneas whilst he
> was en route to Italy, with his father *Anchises, after the
> destruction of their home city by the Greeks. The heartless
> Aeneas soon abandoned Dido to continue his journey, and
> she, distraught, threw herself on a funeral pyre. *Ulysses'
> long wanderings home to Greece from victory at Troy did
> not include a visit to Carthage.*

Didon
A French 44-gun taken in 1805 by Tom Baker's 36-
gun HMS *Phoenix* (FW 2).

> *Didon— named for Queen *Dido — was launched in 1799
> and, under her Captain Milius, was captured by *Baker's
> much lighter HMS *Phoenix in August 1805. Taken in
> to the Royal Navy as HMS Didon (there already being an
> HMS Dido in service), she was broken up in 1811.*

Diego, Don
see **Diaz, Don Diego**

Diemen, Van
The man for whom Van Diemen's Land is named
(DI 4; FSW 3).

> *Anthony van Diemen (1593–1645) was a Dutch naval
> officer who rose to Admiral some time before 1631 and in
> 1636 became Governor of the Dutch East Indies, a post he
> held until his death. He was the patron and colleague of
> the explorer Abel Tasman, who in 1642 discovered a large*

island off the southern coast of Australia and named it for Van Diemen. In 1856 this island was re-named Tasmania.

Dil

A street orphan in Bombay taken up by Stephen Maturin, who then becomes greatly attached to her as a cultural and geographical guide: however, his gift of much-desired silver bracelets immediately results in her being robbed and murdered. Numb with grief and guilt, Stephen arranges for her funeral immolation (HMS 7).

Diligence

A mail packet, operating between Nova Scotia and England on behalf of the British government, owned and commanded by Jamie Dalgleish (SM 2–4). Jack Aubrey, Stephen Maturin and Diana Villiers take passage in her, being then hotly pursued across the North Atlantic by Johnson's privateers (SM 3) before arriving safely at Portsmouth (SM 4).

Diligence, HMS

A small vessel under Admiral Pellew's command at Barbados (RM 2).

> *The reference may perhaps be to either HMS Diligence, a 14-gun sloop purchased as Union in 1801 and sold in 1812, or a lugger, launched as Thistle, purchased and re-named by the Royal Navy in 1812 and sold in 1814.*

Diligent, HMS

A ship in which Jackson had once served (WDS 10).

> *Any one of some half dozen HMS Diligents — from schooners to a third-rate — may fit this passing reference.*

Dilke

1 the wardroom steward in HMS *La Flèche* (FW 2).

2: a deceased London money-man who has left a fortune to Admiral Harte (IM 5).

Dillon

The commander of the Irish Brigades in the French Royalist Army, later disbanded during the Revolution for refusing to fight against the King (SM 5).

> *Dillon is a distinguished Irish name in both politics and military affairs (e.g., Admiral Sir William Dillon, 1779–1857), with a whole emigré line of French generals — strongly Royalist and Catholic — being notable from the mid-17th century onwards. The reference here is almost certainly to Arthur Richard Dillon (1750–1794), an English-born member of the clan who entered the French service in the family Regiment at a very young age, becoming its hereditary Colonel in 1767, at age 17. An able soldier, in 1784 Dillon was appointed Brigadier General and in 1792 rose to become commander of the army of Northern France. However, in this position he soon fell out with his *Jacobin political masters, who thought him over-sympathetic to his Royalist opponents: briefly imprisoned in 1792 and again between 1793 and 1794, in April of that year he was condemned as a plotter and, on the same*

day and scaffold as his close friend Lucile *Desmoulins, guillotined. A little earlier, Arthur's distant cousin, Theobald Dillon (1745–1792), having risen to be a Brigadier General in the same family regiment, was retreating under orders through Flanders when he was murdered by his own troops, who mistakenly though he had betrayed them to the Royalists. The various 'Irish' regiments of the French army, in any case largely manned by Frenchmen, did not long survive these controversies.

Dillon, James

Having recently made a dashing reputation for himself in the hired cutter *Dart*, Lieutenant James Dillon, a wealthy and aristocratic Irishman, is transferred into Jack Aubrey's first command, the brig-sloop HMS *Sophie* (M&C 2,3). On board he soon encounters Dr. Stephen Maturin, the ship's surgeon, with whom he had once been active in the United Irishmen, a political society dedicated to Catholic emancipation and self-rule that in 1798 had staged an unsuccessful armed rebellion against British dominance (M&C 3,5). Although Dillon had been away on active service in the Royal Navy at the time of the revolt (M&C 5), his continuing confusion and unhappiness over the events spill over into his relationship with the assertively English Jack (M&C 4–10). During a number of actions Dillon forms, and scarcely troubles to conceal, the view that his Captain prefers easy prize-money from merchant ships to actually engaging enemy forces head-on (M&C 4,7,8). Retaining his commitment to both Catholic emancipation and home-rule (yet still under the Crown: M&C 5), Dillon is placed in a dreadful quandary when HMS *Sophie* is ordered to intercept an American ship thought to be carrying Irish rebels, and is driven to help them avoid detection and capture (M&C 7). Tortured by distaste for the stratagem he had adopted (blackmailing *Sophie*'s homosexual Master), thereafter James seems to loath himself quite as much as he has come to loathe Jack. Later, when HMS *Sophie* engages the far more powerful frigate *Cacafuego*, James Dillon meets his death leading a wild charge against the Spaniards (M&C 10) and is buried at sea (M&C 11,12; also PC 10; TGS 4).

> *N.B., Mr. Parker, the First Lieutenant of HMS *Speedy (Thomas *Cochrane's brig, on whose adventures M&C is part-based) was very badly wounded at the moment of the taking of El *Gamo, in circumstance similar to Dillon's demise.*

Diocletian

A Roman who could not bear to cut a cabbage (TMC 1).

> *Gaius Aurelius Valerius Diocletianus (284–305) rose from rather obscure origins to high rank in the Roman army, becoming commander of the Emperor Numerianus' bodyguard whilst on campaign. When the Emperor was assassinated in late 284, the army chose Diocletian as his successor and by 285 he had defeated and eliminated all*

rival claimants. In 286 he appointed Maximian to be Emperor of the West, whilst he himself ruled as Eastern Emperor, spending almost his entire reign on campaign along the Danube and in Asia. Diocletian also chose a *'Caesar' as aid and heir to each Emperor (himself known by the title 'Augustus') and was responsible for many of the administrative reforms that enabled the Empire to survive very troubled times. However, he is chiefly recalled for vigorous persecution of the Christian sect in the latter years of his rule. In 305, suffering from a total breakdown in his health, he retired to his country estates (in modern Bosnia), where, according to *Gibbon, he spent his remaining years dedicated to tending his beloved vegetable garden.

Diogenes

A man referred to for his eccentricity (PC 12).

Diogenes the Cynic (412?–324 BC) was a Greek philosopher and eccentric who evangelised a life of extreme simplicity and self-sufficiency. Referred to by *Plato as the 'mad Socrates,' in popular legend Diogenes was reputed to have lived in a discarded barrel.

Diomed or Diomede, HMS

A ship being broken up or refitted, from whose hull Jack Aubrey has obtained the copper for the dome of his observatory (TMC 1). Years later, now laid-up, she is the source of some new oars for Surprise (TGS 2).

HMS Diomede, 50-gun, was launched in 1798 and sold out of the service in 1815. In Greek myth Diomedes, King of Argos, was one of the great sea-captains and generals of the Trojan war.

Diomede

A 40-gun, French frigate mentioned by Jack Aubrey (HMS 2).

Diomède, in fact a 74-gun ship-of-the-line, was launched as Union in 1799 and re-named in 1803. In early 1806 she was driven onto rocks in the West Indies and then taken and burned by the Royal Navy.

Dionysius of Halicarnassus

An author whose treatment of Pyrrhus is discussed by Professor Graham (IM 10).

Dionysius of Halicarnassus (70?–10? BC) was a Greek-born historian who wrote a monumental History of Ancient Rome, stressing in it the Greek influence on Latin culture and institutions.

Dioscorides

An author referred to by Maturin for his view that the flesh of certain birds may be poisonous because of their diet (IM 5).

Dioscorides Pedanius (fl. 1st century AD) was a Greek botanist, and perhaps physician, who wrote a multi-volume work—Materials of Medicine—on the drugs of his age, travelling widely to collect his materials and knowledge. The sections of the books dealing with poisons and venomous animals are today thought not to have been part of Dioscorides' original work.

Director, HMS

A 64-gun ship commanded by Bligh at the Battle of Camperdown (DI 1).

HMS Director, 64-gun, was launched in 1784 and broken up in 1801. *Bligh commanded her in *Duncan's victory over the Dutch at Camperdown in October 1797, playing a distinguished role in the action.

'Dirty Dick's'

A supply yard at Gibraltar (FSW 2).

Dismas

see Zelenka, Dismas

Dittersdorf

A composer whose music is played by Aubrey, Maturin and Admiral Pellew (RM 2), and is elsewhere also favoured (NC 9).

Karl Ditters von Dittersdorf (1739–1799) was a prolific Austrian composer and violinist, producing many popular operas, symphonies and chamber pieces.

Dixon

(N.B., these three characters are discussed collectively, below.)

1: the ill-mannered commander of the brig HMS Viper, said to be the son of the 'scrub' Dixon of Port Mahon (LM 2).

2: the Third Lieutenant of HMS Diane, the son of Admiral Harte (the Admiral having changed his name on receiving an inheritance). Owing to the very bad relations that had existed between Jack Aubrey and Harte, Jack has Dixon replaced by Dick Richardson before assuming command (TGS 4).

3: a 'scrub' of Port Mahon, the father of the insolent Lieutenant Dixon of HMS Viper (LM 2).

Dixons 1 and 2 are probably intended to be the same man, with Dixon 3 being his father, the re-named Admiral *Harte (although it was from a Mr. *Dilke, not Dixon, that Harte was thought to have inherited). The pair are perhaps based on two real Dixons, father and son: a) Sir Manley Dixon (d.1837), made Post 1790, promoted Rear Admiral in 1808, Vice Admiral in 1813 and Admiral in 1825. From 1800 to 1801 Dixon had served as Captain of HMS *Généreux in the Mediterranean and, as the senior Captain at the Port Mahon base, was thought by Thomas *Cochrane to have delayed, out of personal enmity, his dispatch on the taking of El *Gamo reaching Lord *Keith, and thence England. To this extent Dixon may be a model for Harte, Jack *Aubrey's long time foe, who does something very similar with the *Cacafuego dispatch (M&C 11). b) Sir Manley's son, Manley Hall Dixon (1786–1864), served under his father in Généreux as a junior lieutenant (and would therefore also have known Cochrane), before being promoted Commander in 1809 and Post Captain in 1811 (i.e., both somewhat before LM is set). A Rear Admiral of 1847, he was promoted Vice Admiral in 1855 and Admiral in 1860. (See also the note under *Manby.)

Djezzar Pasha

The Turkish commander at the siege of Acre (TH 5), who had once given an impressive lamp to Clonfert (TMC 3). He was the uncle of Omar Pasha, Dey of Algiers (HD 7).

*Ahmed Djezzar Pasha (1735?–1804) was originally a Bosnian Christian who, after involvement in a murder, escaped to Cairo and converted to Islam. At first a faithful—and exceptionally murderous—retainer of Mohammed *Ali Bey, he later fled his old master, and was soon, in about 1775, appointed Pasha of Acre and Sidon by the Sultan of *Turkey. In 1799, in co-operation with Sir Sidney *Smith, he defended Acre successfully against *Buonaparte, eventually forcing the great French general to retreat in some disarray back to Egypt.*

Dockray, Captain and Mrs.

A Royal Navy officer whose wife, together with her sister Miss Jones, had travelled as passengers in James Dillon's HMS *Dart*. The two ladies had then acted as 'powder-boys' in an action with French privateers (M&C 3). Jack Aubrey had once known Captain Dockray as the First Lieutenant of HMS *Thunderer* (M&C 3).

Doctor, the

see **Maturin, Stephen**, *for whom this is a very frequent appellation throughout the series.*

Dodd, Parson

A man who had been hung for fraud (RM 5).

*Parson William Dodd (1729–1777) was a fashionable pulpit orator, well connected in literary circles and a good friend of Dr. *Johnson. He was convicted of forging on a bond the signature of his patron, Philip Stanhope, Earl of Chesterfield, and hanged at Tyburn.*

Doe, John

The literary pseudonym of Louisa Wogan (DI 4).

'John/Jane Doe' is common American usage for 'an anonymous person.'

Doggett

A reference to heroic oarsmanship (TMC 9; LM 3).

To celebrate the coronation of King George I, Thomas Doggett (1670?–1721), a very successful Irish-born comic actor, instituted in 1715 an annual sculling race on the river Thames, to be run from London Bridge up to Chelsea. The winner's prize was 'an orange coat with a badge representing Liberty' and, although the prize-coat is now red, the race is still run to this day.

Dolby, William

A friend of Jack Aubrey, met by him in Devon (YA 3).

Dolland

A London maker of superior telescopes (PC 4; FSW 7; LM 3; WDS 10; HD 5).

The Dolland, or Dollond, Instrument Company was founded by John Dolland (1706–1761) and expanded by his exceptionally talented sons, Peter (1730–1820) and

John (d.1804), together with their nephew George (1774–1852).

Dolphin, HMS

A ship to which many of Jack Aubrey's crew had been suddenly transferred just before his HMS *Leopard* left England (DI 3). Some years afterwards, she is a now-decrepit ship, forming part of the small inshore squadron blockading St. Martin's (LM 4,6). John Daniel refers to her as having been an active prize-taker at one stage in her career (HD 6).

*HMS Dolphin, 44-gun, was launched in 1781, converted into a hospital ship in 1797 (when she was briefly commanded by Josiah Nisbit, the son of Lady *Nelson by her first marriage), re-converted to a troopship in 1800, and broken up in 1817. An earlier 24-gun Dolphin, launched in 1751, was the survey ship commanded between 1764 and 1770 by *Byron and *Wallis successively; she was broken up in 1777.*

Domanova

Stephen Maturin asserts that he has a cousin Domanova, with whom Jean Dutourd has confused him (WDS 4,7).

*Domanova is part of *Maturin's full Catalan name, occasionally used by him as an alias in his intelligence activities.*

Domanova, don Esteban Maturin y

see **Maturin, Stephen**

Dommet, Admiral

The officer who gives Jack Aubrey temporary command of the sloop HMS *Ariel* for the Grimsholm mission (SM 6).

*Sir William Domett (sic, although several variant spellings are seen; 1754–1828) was made Post in 1782, promoted Rear Admiral in 1804, Vice Admiral in 1809 and Admiral in 1819; he was knighted in 1815. As Post Captain he served in many famous fights, especially when acting as *Flag Captain to his patrons, Lord *Rodney and Sir Alexander *Hood (later Lord Bridport). In 1801 Domett was Admiral Sir Hyde Parker's *Captain of the Fleet (a post he also held under *St. Vincent and *Cornwallis) in the manoeuvres leading up to *Nelson's victory at the Battle of Copenhagen. Domett, a man highly regarded in the service for his organisational abilities, served as an Admiralty Lord from 1808 to 1813 and Commander-in-Chief, Plymouth, (his final service) from 1813 to 1815.*

Donaldson, Mr.

The Master of HMS *Bellerophon*, with whom Aubrey had served in 1797.

Donne, Dean

One of the authors of the sermons typically preached by Mr. Martin (TH 5; FSW 4,9,10).

John Donne (1573–1631), a seaman, clergyman and metaphysical poet, was from 1621 onwards, Dean of St. Paul's Cathedral in London. In addition to the three very highly regarded volumes of sermons published by his son, John, after his death (in 1640, 1649 and 1660), he wrote many satires and elegies, renowned for their wit and eloquence.

In 1596 and 1597 Donne had sailed on military expeditions with the Earl of Essex and Sir Walter *Raleigh, adventures that he commemorated in his poems The Storm *and* The Calm.

Donohue, Bridey
An Irish nurse at Choate's hospital (FW 4–6).

Donovan
An acquaintance of Sir Joseph Blaine (RM 8).

Donzelot, General
The commander of the French troops on the Ionian island of Corfu (IM 9; TH 9), on very good terms with Capitan-Bey Mustapha (IM 10).

François Xavier Donzelot (1764–1843) rose from the ranks to become a staff officer of distinction, being promoted General in March 1801. Just a few months later he was the unwilling signatory of the surrender of Egypt to the British forces. Once back in France, Donzelot continued to hold important staff positions before being appointed to command the forces in Corfu and the Ionian, a post he held from 1807 to 1814. He joined *Buonaparte during his 'Hundred Day' return in 1815 and was a divisional commander at the Battle of Waterloo in the same year. After the Emperor's final defeat, Donzelot was unemployed until 1817 when he was made Governor of Martinique, remaining there until 1828.

Doodle, Faster
see **Doudle** or **Doodle, Faster**

Doris, HMS
A ship in Admiral Thornton's Mediterranean fleet (IM 8), later a heavy frigate on the Brest blockade (YA 4,6).

HMS Doris, *36-gun, was launched in 1807 as the East Indiaman* Salsette, *being renamed* Pitt *later the same year. Bought and re-named by the Royal Navy in 1808,* Doris *was present at the fall of Mauritius in 1810 and Java in 1811; she was sold in Chile in 1827. In Greek myth,* Doris *was the wife of Nereus, the sea-god.*

Dorkin, Abraham
A light and nimble seaman in HMS *Surprise* (WDS 3).

Dormer
A Midshipman in HMS *Bellona* (COM 10; YA 5).

Dorset, Marquis of
A gambling friend of Mr. Smithers (PC 10).

The Marquisate of Dorset had died out in 1554, but Charles Sackville Germain (1767–1843), 5th Duke of Dorset, was a very well-known gambler and sportsman of Smithers' time.

Dorset or *Dorsetshire*
An East Indiaman — possibly commanded by Craig — in Muffit's China Fleet, protected by HMS *Surprise* from Admiral Linois' French squadron. (HMS 9).

Dorsetshire, 1260-tons, completed nine round trips for

the East India Company between 1799 and 1821; her name is geographical. The action is based on the defence of a Honourable East India Company merchant fleet against *Linois' attack in February 1804. However, no Royal Navy ship was present during the fight, the squadron being organised by the senior Master, Nathaniel Dance of *Earl Camden. Dorsetshire *was commanded on the occasion by Robert Hunter Brown.*

Dorte Engebrechtsdotter
A Norwegian merchantman escorted by HMS *Sophie* and attacked by an Algerine galley, thus providing Jack Aubrey with the occasion for his first battle as a Commander (M&C 4).

Doudle or Doodle, Faster
A prime seaman in Jack Aubrey's HMSS *Surprise* and *Leopard* (HMS 8; TH 10; FSW 1,5; RM 3) who prefers tobacco to grog (DI 9). He is a nimble wicket-keeper in the ship's cricket team (FW 1), even though a very tall man (DI 9).

Douglas
1: the Captain of HMS *Resolution*, a friend of General Aubrey, who had temporarily disrated the young Midshipman Jack Aubrey for concealing Sally M'Puta aboard for immoral purposes (M&C 4; FW 7; TH 2; RM 1). Douglas was famous for his attention to good gunnery practice (IM 2).

Admiral Sir Charles Douglas (1725–1789) was renowned for his devotion to improving gunnery aboard his ships, a dedication Jack *Aubrey entirely follows in his later career. Douglas was made Post in 1761, knighted in 1777, and promoted Rear Admiral in 1787. In 1782, at the Battle of the Saintes, he served as *Rodney's *Captain of the Fleet in HMS *Formidable.

2: an officer made Post into HMS *Phoebe* (M&C 11).

Dover
The bosun of HMS *Bellona* (COM 5).

Dover, Dr. Thomas
A physician said by Maturin to have turned corsair (RM 8).

Thomas Dover (1660–1742), an English physician, served as Second Captain of the privateer Duke *in 1708–1711, cruising off South America. During this time he devised a popular mixture of opium and ipecacuanha to promote 'laudable sweating' in the treatment of tropical fevers.*

Dover, HMS
A former 32-gun frigate, now at Madeira as a troopship (YA 10). Under her Captain Ward, she joins Jack Aubrey's Mediterranean squadron (HD 1) but is soon detached as an escort to homeward-bound East Indiamen (HD 2,4).

HMS Dover, *38-gun, was the ex–French* Bellona, *launched in 1806 and, in 1811, captured, re-named and turned into a troopship by the Royal Navy. Sent for harbour service in 1825, she was sold in 1836.*

Draper

The Commander of the sloop HMS *Ariel*, superseded by Jack Aubrey (SM 6,7).

Dray, Amos

A one-legged, former bosun's mate of HMS *Surprise*, now in service ashore with the Aubrey family (DI 1; RM 6; LM 4; TGS 4; COM 3). Later he, or a namesake, is seen serving in Jack's HMS *Bellona* (YA 9). *See also* *Bray, *who occupies the same role.*

Dreadnought, HMS

A ship briefly seen by *Ringle* (COM 5).

> HMS Dreadnought, *98-gun, was launched in 1801 after 13 years on the stocks. Having served as the flag-ship of *Cornwallis *and* *Collingwood, *at Trafalgar in 1805 she was commanded by the Irishman John Conn (a cousin by marriage of Lord *Nelson), drowned in 1810 whilst in command of HMS* *Swiftsure *off Bermuda. Dreadnought saw little further significant service before being turned into a hospital ship in 1827 and finally broken up in 1857.*

Dredge

A Marine officer in HMS *Lively* who pays attentions to Cecilia Williams during her visit to the ship (PC 14).

Driver, Captain

The newly appointed Marine officer in Jack Aubrey's HMS *Surprise* who, in the gunroom poetry competition, recites a verse from Pomfret (IM 9–11).

Droits de l'Homme

A French 74-gun, destroyed in 1797 by HMSS *Amazon* and *Indefatigable* (PC 1; YA 5).

> Droits de l'Homme *was launched in 1794, her name being taken from* The Rights of Man *by the American-English radical author, Tom *Paine. In 1797, under her Captain La Crosse, she took part in General Humbert's abortive invasion of Ireland and, on her retreat back to France, fell in with two Royal Navy ships engaged in blockading Brest, HMSS *Indefatigable, *44-gun, under Captain Edward *Pellew and* *Amazon, *36-gun, under Captain Robert Reynolds. In the early morning of January 14th, during a long running fight in appalling weather, Droits struck on rocks south of Ushant and slowly foundered with the loss of some one thousand sailors and troops. Amazon too was wrecked soon afterwards on the nearby shore, though with few losses.*

Droll, Dr. Humorous

A facetious reference to Maturin by Aubrey (TGS 9).

Dromadaire

A French store-ship captured and burned by Jack Aubrey's HMS *Lively* (HMS 2).

> Dromadaire — *named for the type of camel — was a quite common name for French storeships, with several of them being taken by the Royal Navy, although none at the time of HMS.*

Dromedary

A British transport ship, Master Mr. Allen (TH 3–8), that brings Stephen Maturin's diving bell to Malta and takes it on to Egypt (TH 3). She also carries Jack Aubrey's expeditionary force to the Nile delta and back (TH 4–8).

Druid, HMS

Philip Broke's first command as a Post Captain (FSW 2), in which Mr. Dunn (FW 7,9) and Barret Bonden (SM 4) had once served.

> HMS Druid, *32-gun, was launched in 1783 and broken up in 1813. *Broke, made Post in 1801, was ship-less until being given* Druid *in 1805, but then held her for only a year until being appointed to the newly launched HMS *Shannon.*

Drummond's

A London banking house (SM 5,11; TGS 6).

> *The Drummonds were, and are, one of Scotland's leading families, with branches in the landed aristocracy as well as in finance, public service and the arts. The family bank was founded in Edinburgh in 1712 and, by Jack *Aubrey's day, had the chief London Branch of their bank at 49 Charing Cross; the firm was later incorporated into the Royal Bank of Scotland. A daughter of Henry Dundas, Lord *Melville (another scion of Edinburgh society), married into the banking branch of the family.*

Drury, Admiral and Mrs.

The well-connected, married Commander-in-Chief of the East Indies station (DI 1; FW 1,2,4,6; SM 2,5), a keen cricketer (FW 1).

> *William O'Bryen Drury (d.1811) was an Irish officer made Post in 1783, promoted Rear Admiral in 1804 and Vice Admiral in 1810. As a Captain he had played a leading role in *Duncan's victory at Camperdown in 1797. As Rear- and Vice-Admiral he commanded the East Indies station from his headquarters at Madras from about 1807 until his death in 1811 (which had in fact taken place on March 6th, a little before he is first met in the series: see *Stopford) and was largely responsible for the successful plan that later prised Java from the Dutch and French. His wife was a daughter of the famous engineer and Celtic scholar, General Charles Vallancey (1721–1812).*

Dryad, HMS

1: a brig met at sea by HMS *Ariel* (SM 7).

2: a sloop, Commander William Babbington, in Admiral Thornton's Mediterranean Fleet (IM 5+). She separates from Jack Aubrey's HMS *Worcester* and sails alone to Medina as per Admiral Harte's orders, narrowly avoiding capture by the French (IM 6). Having later accompanied Jack's HMS *Surprise* to the Ionian sea (IM 9+), she returns to Malta before the final, decisive action of the book (IM 11; *also* TH 9; RM 6; LM 7).

3: a 36-gun frigate that had assisted in the taking of *Clorinde* (YA 9). Later she is a member of the Brest blockade squadron, sent home to be paid off following Buonaparte's abdication (YA 10). Mr. Candish had once served in her (HD 2).

*HMS Dryad, 36-gun, was launched in 1795 and broken up in 1860; she and her companions took *Clorinde in February 1814, as described in the text. The Dryads were the wood-nymphs of classical myth.*

Dryden

A writer referred to by Maturin as the 'Prince of Poets' (RM 3) and later quoted by Aubrey in an insult directed at Lady Hertford, the mistress of the Regent (TGS 1).

John Dryden (1631–1700) was a poet, playwright, translator and critic, of prodigious output and widely admired literary style. He was Poet Laureate of England from 1668 to 1688.

Dubreuil

A French intelligence agent in Boston (FW 5), whom Stephen Maturin recognises from earlier years in Portugal and France (FW 6). Shot dead by Stephen at Franchon's Hotel (FW 7; SM 4,11; TH 2), he is later referred to by Major Beck as 'Durand,' a slip not remarked on by Stephen (SM 1).

Duchamp

A seaman in HMS *Surprise* who, hailing from the island of Jersey, has some command of the French language (LM 5).

Ducks, Jemmy and Mrs.

The generic name for a ship-board poultry-keeper (TMC 5; FW 2; FSW 3). In Jack Aubrey's HMS *Diane* and *Surprise* he is one John Thurlow and has charge of the little Sweeting girls (TGS 9,10; NC 8+; C/T 1–9; WDS 4+; COM 1), 'Mrs. Jemmy' being his wife, of sorts, back in England (COM 1).

Duclerc

A French Admiral who had attacked a British convoy, inflicting heavy losses (COM 5).

Dudley, 'Sextant'

A scientific Royal Navy Captain known to Aubrey (TH 9).

Duff, William or Billy

The Captain of HMS *Stately* in Aubrey's squadron, a fine seaman but a predatory paederast (COM 3+) whose ship-board behaviour leads to his being on appallingly bad terms with his officers (COM 9). In the action with Maistral's squadron, he loses a leg (COM 10).

Duguay-Trouin

A French naval officer compared by Dumesnil to Nelson (NC 7).

*René Duguay-Trouin (1673–1736) started his remarkable career as a privateer but in 1697 joined the Royal service as a frigate Captain; he was promoted Commodore in 1709 and Rear Admiral in 1715. With *Suffren, he is consid-*

ered by many to be the greatest naval commander ever produced by France, the very type of an enterprising, imaginative and brave officer, and is especially celebrated for his taking of Rio de Janiero in 1711. Amongst many other adventures, Dugay-Trouin was captured by the Royal Navy in 1694 and then imprisoned in England; from where he soon escaped after seducing a young woman who sold meals to the prisoners, a tale that finds an echo in *Aubrey, *Maturin and *Jagiello's attempted escape from a French prison (in SM).*

Duhamel

1: the author of a nautical book sent by Stephen Maturin to Sophie Williams (HMS 4), later said by Stephen to have made experiments on dye diffusion in bones (HMS 6).

Henri Louis Duhamel de Monceau (1700–1782) was a French scientist of very wide interests, establishing a strong reputation in every subject he studied. He published treatises on economics, botany, physiology and agriculture as well as producing, in 1758, a famous work on marine engineering and design, Elements de l'Architecture Navale.

2: a French intelligence or security agent who escorts the captured Stephen Maturin — plus Jack Aubrey and the Lithuanian hussar, Jagiello — to prison in Paris (SM 10). Duhamel, a member of Talleyrand-Périgord's organisation, wants to use Stephen to make contact with Bourbon exiles in England (SM 11) and offers the trio freedom just as they are about to attempt an escape (SM 11). On behalf of his master, he promises the return in due course of the 'Blue Peter' diamond, earlier used by Diana Villiers to buy Stephen's safety (SM 11). Some years later, Duhamel, disillusioned and wanting to retire, appears in London and fulfills the promise to restore the great gem (RM 10). In exchange for identification of the spies Wray and Ledward, Stephen then arranges passage for him to Canada in Heneage Dundas' HMS *Eurydice* (RM 10), later learning that he had been drowned whilst trying to board the ship, weighed down by his money-belt (LM 2,4,6; *also* COM 5).

Duke, the
see **Clarence, Duke of**

Dukes

A seaman in HMS *Leopard*, the first man to spot *Waakzaamheid* (DI 6).

Dumanoir

1: the confidential secretary to Captain Christy-Pallière (PC 4).
2: the Master of the French privateer *Deux Frères* (YA 6).
3: the French intelligence official who has hatched the plot to use Moslem money and troops to prevent the Austrian and Russian armies from joining forces against Buonaparte (HD 1).

Dumanoir de Plessy

The French commander of the *Bellone* privateer (PC 5–9), wounded when she takes the *Lord Nelson* Indiaman and later operated on by the captured Stephen Maturin. By implication, he is later killed when *Bellone*, pursued by Jack Aubrey's HMS *Polychrest*, runs aground and founders (PC 9).

The name may be inspired by that of two French naval brothers, sons of the Minister of Marine Dumanoir de Pelley (sic): Pierre-Etienne-René-Marie (1770–1829), who became a Rear Admiral in 1800, and in 1805 fought both at Trafalgar and against *Strachan's squadron shortly after the great battle; and Charles Jean Marie Armande (1776–1824), who became a Captain in 1812.

Dumesnil

A French General with internal security duties in Paris (SM 10).

Dumesnil, Jean-Pierre or Pierrot

The nephew of Jack Aubrey's friend Captain Christy-Pallière, who had once met the captured Jack in his uncle's *Desaix*. Later, as a Lieutenant in *Cornélie*, he encounters Jack ashore at Pulo Prabang (TGS 8) and is afterwards rescued by Jack when *Cornélie*, pursued by HMS *Nutmeg of Consolation*, founders (NC 5,6,7).

Dunbar

Stephen Maturin's junior assistant in HMS *Worcester* (IM 8).

Duncan, Admiral

An Admiral whom Stephen Maturin regards as one of the few of his rank, along with Nelson, not to have had his humanity driven out of him by the long exercise of authority (HMS 5). Jack Aubrey and others refer to his formidable reputation and bearing (IM 7; TH 9). A sailors' inn in Portsmouth is also named for the great man (RM 4).

Admiral Adam Duncan (1731–1804), a Scotsman, was the victor in 1797 of the Battle of Camperdown, an action in which he inflicted a decisive defeat on de Winter's somewhat smaller Dutch fleet. Amongst other features of a very active fighting career, Duncan was well known for his concerns for seamen's welfare and service conditions. He dealt with a severe mutiny in his fleet only a few months before his great action with notably merciful measures, and was well known for his view that the worst of lower-deck conditions could drive otherwise loyal men to desperate measures. Duncan was made Post in 1761, Rear Admiral in 1787, Vice Admiral in 1793 and Admiral in 1795; in 1797 he was created Viscount Duncan of Camperdown in recognition of his great victory. Duncan was a huge man, formidably strong and assertive, and widely regarded by his officers and crews as the very ideal of what a Commander-in-Chief should be. He was also devoutly religious, spending several minutes kneeling in prayer on his own quarterdeck before giving the order to attack at Camperdown. Like his boyhood hero and Captain, Augustus *Keppel, he was honoured by many plain seamen in the names of their retirement public houses.

Dundas, Heneage or Hen

The close friend and colleague of Jack Aubrey from boyhood (YA 2) and throughout their careers, having been Midshipmen together in their first years at sea in HMS *Bellerophon*, when they had fought a silly, childish duel (COM 10). We first meet Heneage Dundas as a prodigious mathematician, the Commander of the sloop HMS *Calpe* in the Mediterranean fleet (M&C 12). A well-connected officer (his father Henry Dundas, Lord Melville, being First Lord of the Admiralty), after only just over a year as Commander he is made Post into HMS *Franchise* (PC 6+), well ahead of the influence-deprived Jack, to whom he had been five years junior as a Lieutenant (PC 7). Heneage, concerned that Jack's amorous conduct ashore is unwise, asks Stephen Maturin to have a word with their mutual friend. The wholly unintended consequence is that Jack and Stephen quarrel almost to the point of a duel, an encounter for which Heneage agrees to be Stephen's second (PC 10). The row made up, Heneage now becomes Stephen's very firm friend, with the Doctor coming to regard him as the ideal of a good sea-officer (HMS 5).

As Captain of HMS *Ethalion*, Dundas is asked by Jack to arrange passage for his beloved Sophie Williams to Madeira (HMS 10), but, in the event, meets Jack's HMS *Surprise* at sea just off the island and transfers Sophie and her maid across (HMS 11). Some years later he is serving in the West Indies, with the ship-less Jack's usual retainers, Bonden and Killick, under his command (TMC 3). The tables are soon somewhat turned when Heneage is himself ashore in England, without a ship and somewhat impoverished. Here, at Craddock's gaming house, he comes to Jack's assistance when his friend accuses Andrew Wray of cheating at cards (DI 1,2). A few years later — with his elder brother Robert, Viscount Melville, now First Lord — Heneage is Captain of the 74-gun HMS *Excellent* in Admiral Thornton's Mediterranean fleet (IM 1,4,5,10; TH 1+; FSW 1,2) and, at Malta, makes a descent in Stephen Maturin's new diving bell (TH 3).

Heneage's reputation for siring bastards soon sours his relationships with his brother (RM 1,2,8) but he nevertheless gets command of HMS *Eurydice*, a new, heavy frigate destined for North America (RM 5,10). Whilst still in England, he loyally attends the disgraced Jack Aubrey's public ordeal in the pillory after a conviction for fraud (RM 9; LM 1). A little later he has the joy of passing onto Jack the news of Melville's offer of eventual re-instatement in the Royal Navy (LM 8).

After a spell in command of HMS *Orion* (TGS 4; *perhaps also referred to at WDS 5*), Heneage is homeward bound from New South Wales in his HMS *Berenice* when he meets Jack and the crippled *Surprise* off Cape Horn. He is able to assist with emergency repairs and then sails in company with his friend to England (WDS 10). On the voyage he loses to Jack his tender, *Ringle* (earlier found abandoned at sea: WDS 10), in a game of backgammon (COM 1,2). On arrival home, Heneage then spends a great deal of time ashore with the Aubreys whilst his own, rather decrepit ship is under repair (YA 2–4; 10): after Buonaparte escapes from Elba, he then arrives in the Mediterranean as the Captain of the frigate HMS *Hamadryad* (HD 9). In the light of the attractive, outgoing personality that Heneage presents, Jack at one point rather curiously says his friend is a small, pale, shrewish man, known throughout the service as 'Vinegar Joe' (IM 10).

> *Dundas is a lowland Scots family name of great political and military renown. In addition to the two *Melville/ Dundas' holding of the top Admiralty position, many of the family served in the Royal Navy, no less than four rising to Admiral: a) George Dundas (Post Captain 1795, Rear Admiral 1814, d. same year); b) Sir Thomas Dundas, who commanded HMS *Naiad at Trafalgar (Post-Captain 1798, Rear Admiral 1825, Vice Admiral 1837, d.1841); c) the Hon. George Heneage Lawrence Dundas, he who commanded HMS *Calpe in 1800–1801 (Post Captain 1801, Rear Admiral 1830, Comptroller of the Navy 1831–1832, d. 1834); and c) Admiral Sir Richard Sanders Dundas (1802–1861), the second son of Robert Dundas, Viscount *Melville. Although O'Brian's original inspiration for his Dundas must have been c), this officer's later career in fact bears very little resemblance to that of the fictional character (although see *Edinburgh, *Euryalus, and *Queen Charlotte, HMSS), and neither was he so closely related to the two Melvilles.*

Dundas, Henry
see **Melville, Lord**

Dundas, Robert
see **Melville, Viscount**

Dundas, William
An MP who is related to Robert Dundas, Viscount Melville (TGS 4).

> *William Dundas (1762–1845), a nephew of Henry Dundas and thus cousin to Robert, was an MP from 1794 onwards, serving as Secretary of War from 1804 to 1806 and as a Lord of the Admiralty from 1812 to 1814.*

Dungannon
The Captain of HMS *Defiance* (RM 1).

Dunn
Philip Broke's clerk in HMSS *Druid* and *Shannon*, killed in action in the fight with USS *Chesapeake* (FW 9).

> *Clerk John Dunn (d.1813) was hit in the stomach by a burst of grape whilst standing near his Captain and died an hour or so later.*

Duperré
The French Captain of *Bellone* (TMC 5).
> *Victor Guy, Baron Duperré (1775–1846), served as a com-*

mercial sailing-master before entering the Navy service in 1793. Always a highly regarded and successful officer, he was promoted Commander in 1802, Frigate Captain in 1806 and Captain of *Bellone in 1808. In her he enjoyed great success in the Indian Ocean before being taken prisoner in 1810 on the fall of Mauritius to Admiral *Bertie. On his return to France in 1811, Duperré was promoted Rear Admiral and made a Baron of the Empire, then serving in various Mediterranean commands until the end of the war, when he was dismissed at the *Bourbon restoration. Recalled to the Navy in 1818, he was promoted Vice Admiral in 1823, held several important, active commands, and was made a Peer of France in 1830. Duperré then served three terms as Minister of Marine between 1834–1843. Both his son and grandson became Admirals in the French service.

Dupin
The author of an Ionian chrestomathy referred to by Mr. Allen (IM 8: 225).

> *A chrestomathy is a collection of literary passages drawn from another language, often from a single, well-known author in that tongue. The reference here may perhaps be to* The New Library of Ecclesiastical Writers, *published in a monumental 58 volumes from 1686 to 1704 by the French theologian and historian Louis Ellies Dupin (1657–1719), although I have been unable to find why this would have been of any use in a specifically Turkish-Ionian context. Curiously, at the approximate time of* IM, *one François-Pierre-Charles Dupin (1784–1873), a distinguished engineer and scientist, was Chief Naval Engineer at the French base at Corfu, a post he held from 1807 to 1812. Having founded the Ionian Naval Academy, he became a leading supporter of the notion of Greek independence from Turkey.*

Duplessis, Jean
The nominal head of the French mission to Pulo Prabang (TGS 3–9). An ineffective man, with inadequate funds and associates, he is soon thwarted in his plans by Maturin and Fox (TGS 8).

Dupont
The American captain of the schooner *Merlin* (LM 3).

Dupont, Lewis
A seaman in HMS *Sophie* (M&C 3).

Duport
A composer played by Maturin (LM 6).
> *The reference could be to either one of two French cellist brothers. Jean-Louis Duport (1749–1819) was both a composer and the author of a still-important work on instrumental technique. His elder brother, Jean-Pierre (1741–1818), was primarily distinguished as a performer but also wrote for his instrument..*

Dupuyten or Dupuytren
A doctor friend of Stephen Maturin, with whom he has dissected (TMC 1,5; SM 4,5,10; HD 1,7). He recommends Paul Martin to Stephen as an assistant surgeon (DI 3).

Guillaume, Baron Dupuytren (1777–1835), was one of the greatest French surgeons and anatomists of his age. Having studied medicine in Paris from 1789 to 1794, he became an influential member of the Paris medical establishment from 1796 onwards. From 1803 he was firmly established as one of its leading lights, amassing great wealth through his talents. In 1823, after the *Bourbon restoration, Dupuytren became Royal Surgeon to *Louis XVIII.

Duran, William

An intelligence agent killed in past times by a booby-trapped rifle (HD 7).

Durand

A reference by Beck to Pontet-Canet's colleague (SM 1).

Presumably a slip for *Dubreuil, though Maturin makes no correcting remark.

Durand, Louis

A man recalled as Jack Aubrey's talented French cook in HMS *Sophie* (PC 8).

Durand-Rual

A French intelligence agent (FW 1).

Duranton

A French doctor who had taught the young Stephen Maturin, showing him, amongst other things, the virtues of spirits of wine as a mild, local anaesthetic (YA 9).

Duroc, Madame

The virtuous wife of a rich banker in Paris and the object of the homosexual La Mothe's pretended passion (SM 5).

Duroures, the

Royalists with whom Maturin intends to hold a clandestine meeting in France (IM 7).

The large Grimoard de Beauvoir family of soldiers and statesmen contained many Royalists as well as others who made accommodations with *Buonaparte's Empire. Nicholas-Louis-Auguste Scipion de Grimoard de Beauvoir (1753–1838), Viscomte du Roure and Comte de Brison, fled Paris with his family at the start of the Revolution in 1789, yet returned in 1802. He was appointed General in 1809 but retired from service in about 1811. His son, Auguste-François-Louis, Marquis du Roure (1783–1858), was also in Paris from 1802 but nothing is known of his activities there before he accepted a military command under the *Bourbon restoration of 1814.

Durrant

The owner of an hotel in London (RM 8,10).

Durrants, or Durants, was an hotel long popular with naval officers. In 1799 Sir John Orde (d.1824 in the rank of full Admiral) was arrested there in order to prevent him duelling later in the day with Lord *St. Vincent over a vicious disagreement the two had regarding the choice of the relatively junior *Nelson to lead the fleet at the Battle of the Nile the previous year. Both Orde and St. Vincent, the

latter arrested at the duellling-ground itself, were fined and bound over to keep the peace.

Dutch Duke, the
see **Habachtsthal, Duke of**

'Dutch Sam'

A famous pugilist (FSW 9; YA 3).

'Dutch Sam' was the nickname of Samuel Elias (1775–1816), a small and wiry English Jew, famed for his tremendous hitting power in the ring. His best-recalled bout took place against Tom *Belcher, brother of the more famous Jem, in 1807.

Dutch William
see **William III, King**

Dutourd

A French Captain and intelligence agent, a military engineer by original profession (HMS 4), killed in the raid that Jack Aubrey conducts on Port Mahon in order to free Stephen Maturin (HMS 3).

Dutourd, Jean

The commander of the privateer *Franklin*, known to Stephen Maturin as a wealthy, wild romantic whose theories on colonisation had influenced Captain Palmer of USS *Norfolk* (C/T 6,9). Dutourd intends to found an egalitarian Paradise in the South Seas, first subduing any natives present (WDS 1+). After his capture by Jack Aubrey, his enthusiasms and persuasive language begin to appeal to the leveller sympathies of *Surprise*'s Knipperdollings (WDS 3,4) and he also slowly begins to recognise Stephen (WDS 1,4), who in turn becomes concerned that the Frenchman could disrupt his plans for a rebellion in Peru (WDS 6). In due course Dutourd's new admirers are persuaded to allow him to escape to Lima (WDS 7), where he denounces Stephen (WDS 8) before himself being taken up by the local Inquisition for heresy (WDS 9; COM 2). He later turns up in Spain where he again denounces Stephen for his Peruvian activities (YA 1).

Duval

An acquaintance of Jack Aubrey who had carried the news of the Battle of the Nile from Egypt to India (TGS 6).

After the great Battle of August 1–2 1797, *Nelson sent Lieutenant Thomas Duval (or Duvall; dates unknown) overland to Bombay with the news that the threat of a French invasion from the north had been eliminated: he arrived there in late October. Duval, who had been commissioned Lieutenant in 1795 and was then promoted Commander in 1799, was drowned in January 1802 when his brig HMS Fly sank off Newfoundland with the loss of all hands.

Duvallier

1: the French commandant of Ile de la Passe, off

Mauritius, who surrenders his fort to Pym (TMC 7).

2: the New Orleans apothecary to whom Fabien had been apprenticed (WDS 6).

DV

An abbreviation often used by Maturin in his diary for Diana Villiers.

Dyce

On one occasion Aubrey says to his helmsman, 'Very well Dyce' (IM 9).

A typo for 'very well, dyce' as found elsewhere in the series meaning 'very well, just so.'

E

Eames

A seaman in HMS *Boadicea* injured in a brawl with some volunteers from HMS *Africaine* (TMC 9).

Earl Camden

An East Indiaman in Muffit's China Fleet, protected by HMS *Surprise* from Admiral Linois' French squadron. In the ensuing battle she flies a Royal Navy flag as a *ruse de guerre.* (HMS 9).

Earl Camden, 1200-tons, completed four round trips for the East India Company between 1802 and 1809; she was named for John Jeffries Pratt, 2nd Earl and 1st Marquis *Camden. The action is based on the defence of a Honourable East India Company merchant fleet—16 HEIC ships and 12 'independents'—against *Linois' attack in February 1804. However, no Royal Navy ship was present during the fight, the squadron being organised by the senior Master, Earl Camden's Nathaniel Dance (1748–1827). Dance had served in the East India Company fleet since 1759, and been appointed a Master in 1787. In this action—for which he was knighted and handsomely rewarded on arrival in England in 1805—Dance had no ship that was any match for even one of Linois' smaller frigates. He nevertheless succeeded in tricking Linois into believing that his extremely valuable convoy was protected by at least three Royal Navy ships and, after a brief action, Linois retired. The sole Royal Navy officer present in the incident was Lieutenant Robert Merrick Fowler (d.1860), serving as a volunteer in *Ganges in order to get home to England. In 1803 Fowler had been in command of a small store-ship, HMS Porpoise, when she was wrecked on a reef in the Pacific and had then spent several months marooned with his surviving crew on a small coral atoll. For his part in Dance's action Fowler was given a cash reward and a Patriotic Fund sword. A Lieutenant since 1800, he was promoted Commander in 1806, made Post in 1811 but was retired from the Captains' list in 1847.

Eclair, HMS

1: a ship in which Philip Broke had served under Captain Hope (FW 7).

HMS Eclair, 22-gun, had been launched as a French corvette of the same name in 1770. In 1793 she was captured by HMS Leda and given to *Hope later in the same year; Midshipman *Broke followed him into her for a short

period. *Eclair was turned into a powder hulk in 1797 and sold out of the service in 1806.*

2: a French-built, 14-gun dispatch cutter, commanded by Lieutenant M'Mullen, that intercepts *Surprise* at sea to deliver a change of orders for Jack Aubrey (C/T 2,3).

This may be a reference to HMS Eclair, 12-gun schooner, launched by the French in 1799 and captured by HMS Garland in 1801. In 1809—some time before C/T—she was renamed HMS Pickle (the new HMS Eclair being a 18-gun sloop launched in late 1807) and served until being sold in 1818.

Edinburgh, HMS

A 74-gun ship, Captain Heneage Dundas, in the Mediterranean fleet (TH 3,10; FSW 1,2).

HMS Edinburgh, 74-gun, was launched in 1811, turned into a screw-driven ship in 1846 and sold out of the service in 1865. She was commanded by George Heneage Lawrence *Dundas in the Mediterranean from 1812 to 1814.

Edmonton, the Witch of

A prophetess (TGS 1).

Elizabeth Sawyer (d.1621) was hanged as a witch in April 1621. Her fate of persecution and death merely for being 'poor, deform'd and ignorant' is the subject of the popular tragi-comedy by Thomas Dekker and colleagues, The Witch of Edmonton, *first performed in 1658.*

Edmunds

An Admiralty official who has fallen into the power of the spy Diego Diaz (YA 7).

Eduardo

A Spanish/Inca nephew of Father Gomez who acts as Maturin's guide on his trek across the high Andes (WDS 8,9). He is later referred to by Maturin as 'Roberto,' possibly to protect his identity (WDS 10).

Edward, Cousin

1: the sexually abusive 'guardian' of the young Clarissa Oakes and her friend, Frances (C/T 6).

2: *see* **Fitzgerald, Lord Edward**

3: *see* **Norton, Mr. Edward**

Edward, Lord
see **Fitzgerald, Lord Edward**

Edwardes
1: the surgeon of HMS *Centaur*, whose work Maturin observes to familiarise himself with naval procedures (M&C 2).
2: the Head Physician of the British hospital at Gibraltar (FSW 2).
3: an HMS *Surprise* seaman injured in action against *Ardent* (HD 5).

Edwards
1: the Captain of HMS *Pandora*, who had tracked down some of the HMS *Bounty* mutineers. He is utterly despised by one of them, Peter Heywood, whom he had captured and imprisoned (DI 1).
Edward Edwards (1742–1815) was made Post in 1781 and hunted down the Bounty *mutineers in his HMS *Pandora *from 1790 until she was wrecked in March 1791, just as described in the text. His treatment of the captured seamen was certainly every bit as awful as *Heywood recounts, and was clearly later regarded as repellent by a number of influential senior officers. Although he never held a command, Edwards was promoted to seniority Rear Admiral in 1799, Vice Admiral in 1805 and Admiral in 1810.*
2: a seaman in HMS *Surprise*, formerly of the whaler *Intrepid Fox* (FSW 10).
3: Aubrey's clerk in HMS *Bellona* (YA 5).

Edwards, David
Envoy Fox's secretary, who becomes popular with HMS *Diane*'s officers and crew (TGS 5+). Perhaps on account of this, the very unpopular Fox maligns him in his official report of the Pulo Prabang treaty negotiations (TGS 10). When, after the stranding of *Diane*, the envoy and his retinue head off to Java in a small boat, Edwards remains with the ship's company, having with him a copy of the dispatches (TGS 10; NC 1,2). Although wounded in the island battle with the Malay and Dyak pirates, he eventually gets safely with his shipmates to Batavia, where it is hinted that Stephen Maturin and Governor Raffles intend to suppress the most damaging passages of the document (NC 2).

Edwards, Dirty
A quartermaster in *Surprise* (C/T 2).

Edwards, Ezekiel or **Zeke**
A gunner's mate in the Turkish frigate *Torgud* who had once served with Barret Bonden in HMS *Isis* (IM 10).

Edwards, Peter
A seaman in HMS *Sophie* who had once served in HMS *King's Fisher* (M&C 6+).

Edwards, Thomas
1: a seaman in HMS *Surprise* who suffers a broken leg (LM 5).
2: a somewhat elderly, ship-less Royal Navy Lieutenant living at Gibraltar (HD 1).
Although there is no reason to suppose that O'Brian had any particular officer in mind for this scene, a real Thomas Edwards (d.1827) illustrates the darker side of the promotion stakes so often referred to in the series: commissioned in 1778, Edwards was not promoted to retired Commander's rank until 1820, over 40 years later (the award of, in effect, a higher pension after many years lobbying).

Edwards, William
A seaman whose cruel punishment by Lieutenant Parker results in a quarrel with Maturin (PC 7).

Egmont
A Royalist with whom Maturin intends to hold a clandestine meeting in France (IM 7).

Egyptienne, HMS
A heavy frigate that Jack Aubrey thinks should accompany his HMS *Acasta* to the North American Station (FW 1,2). When Jack is soon after denied command of *Acasta*, he hopes for a while to be appointed to *Egyptienne* herself (SM 4).
*HMS Egyptienne, 48-gun, was launched as a French ship of the same name in 1799; having initially been laid down as a 74-gun, she had been altered during construction to become a very heavy frigate. She was captured at Alexandria by Lord *Keith's squadron in late 1801. In 1805, under Captain the Hon. Charles Elphinstone Fleeming (d.1840 in the rank of full Admiral), she took part in *Calder's indecisive, pre-Trafalgar action, her Captain later giving evidence at the Admiral's court-martial. Egyptienne was sold for break-up in 1815.*

Eldon
1: the designer of HMS *Polychrest* (PC 6).
2: an especially reliable member of HMS *Worcester*'s crew (IM 7).

Elephant, HMS
A 74-gun of which Maturin's former patient Mr. Day is now gunner (PC 8).
*HMS Elephant, 74-gun, was launched in 1786, reduced to a 58-gun in 1818 and broken up in 1830. *Nelson's flagship, under Captain Thomas Foley, at the Battle of Copenhagen in 1801, by the time of PC she was commanded by Captain George *Dundas.*

Eliot
1: the Captain of Admiral Bertie's flagship HMS *Raisonable*, who in 1798, had been shipmates with Jack Aubrey in HMS *Leander* (TMC 3). When Jack temporarily raises his own Commodore's pennant in *Raisonable*, Eliot assumes command of HMS *Boadicea* (TMC 3). Although said by Bertie to want to invalid home

to England as soon as he can, he is later found back in command of *Raisonable* (TMC 3,5,6).

2: the British Consul in the rebellious Dey of Mascara's main port of Zambra (TH 10). We later learn that he and Mr. Pocock have arranged for the Dey to be murdered and replaced by one of his sons (FSW 1).

Eliseus
see **Elisha**

Elisha or Eliseus
A biblical prophet (COM 10), once referred to regarding the unluckiness of baiting bears (PC 4).

> *In the* Second Book of Kings *of the Old Testament, the Prophet Elisha ('Eliseus' in Latin) is tormented for his baldness by some children from Bethel. He thereupon summons up two she-bears, who devour 42 of his little assailants.*

Elkins
An eminent, recently deceased London cheesemonger dissected by Maturin (PC 3).

Elkins
A slave ship referred to by Mr. Whewell (COM 7).

Ellenborough, Lord
The judge at Cochrane's trial for fraud and the model for O'Brian's Lord Quinborough (RM author's note).

> *Edward Law (1750–1818), 1st Baron Ellenborough, was Lord Chief Justice of England from 1802 onwards. In June 1814 he presided over *Cochrane's trial, having previously been a Parliamentary opponent of Lord *Melville (of whom both Cochrane and Jack *Aubrey were protégés) during his impeachment proceedings in 1806. In 1816 Cochrane in turn pressed charges against Ellenborough for bias and oppression, but these were quickly dismissed. In that same year Ellenborough proved a vigorous, if unsuccessful, opponent of the legislation abolishing the pillory for all offences but perjury. See also *Law.*

Elliott, Bampfylde
The Second Lieutenant of HMS *Diane*, formerly of either *Sylph* or *Flèche*, a popular officer although an indifferent seaman (TGS 4+). Given charge by Jack Aubrey of the boat taking Fox's party to Java from the island where HMS *Diane* has been wrecked, he is almost certainly lost in the typhoon that then sweeps the area (TGS 10).

> *Ships named *Sylph *and *Flèche *served at various times in both the British and French navies. Having been unable to find a record of an action between the two, I am uncertain in which the fictional Mr. Elliott had served.*

Ellis
1: a cousin of James Dillon referred to by Mrs. Dockray (M&C 3).

2: a London money-man, met by Jack Aubrey at Molly Harte's house, who has a wife Letitia and a son Henry (M&C 8+).

3: the Captain of the privateer *Prudence*, who had once been Commander of the 18-gun HMS *Hind*. Jack Aubrey knows him, recalling that he had been dismissed the Royal Navy for some form of fraud or embezzlement (RM 3).

4: an injured seaman in *Surprise*, formerly of HMS *Agamemnon* (COM 1).

Ellis, Henry
The son of the money-man Ellis who joins HMS *Sophie* as an acting Midshipman (M&C 8+). Here he comes close to death by drowning before being revived by Stephen Maturin with the aid of tobacco smoke blown into his lungs (M&C 9). Ellis is later killed in action, alongside James Dillon, in the taking of *Cacafuego* (M&C 10).

Ellis, Laetitia
A friend of Molly Harte, the wife of the money-man Ellis and the mother of Midshipman Henry Ellis (M&C 8+).

Elmo, St.
A reference to 'St. Elmo's fire' (FSW 4; HD 2).

> *Saint Erasmus, or Elmo, (d.303?), an early Christian bishop, is reputed to have been martyred during the persecution of *Diocletian. A patron saint of seamen, his 'fire'—static electricity seen dancing at the tips of any substantial metal objects—is said to be a sign of his protecting presence.*

Elpenor
A Greek seaman in HMS *Surprise* (HD 2).

Elphinstone
1: a protégé of Admiral Brown, taken by Jack Aubrey into HMS *Worcester* as a Midshipman even though he is now 20 years old and still a very poor seaman (IM 2,4). Although, by implication, he is not one of the skilled Midshipmen later taken by Jack into HMS *Surprise* (IM 9), he nevertheless appears later to serve in that ship, now portrayed in a more flattering light (IM 9).

2: *see* **Keith, Lord**

Els Set Dolors
A merchant ship that carries Maturin from Spain to Minorca (IM 7).

Elzevier
The printer or publisher of an edition of Pomponius Mela (COM 9).

> *The Elzevier (or Elzevir) family of high-quality printers and publishers established their reputation from bases in Leyden and Amsterdam from the late 16th century onwards, with their editions being especially noted for the beauty of their typography.*

Emerald, HMS
A British ship in the western Mediterranean (M&C

8), one of several very desirable frigates into which Jack Aubrey would like to be made Post (M&C 11), later famous for the green outfits of her bargemen (RM 2).

> HMS Emerald, 36-gun, was launched in 1795 and enjoyed a long career as an active frigate in the Mediterranean and Channel commands. Only ever once in a major engagement, *Gambier's controversial 1808 action in the Basque Road, in that battle she was commanded by Frederick Maitland (later the Captain of HMS *Bellerophon to whom *Buonaparte surrendered in 1815). Maitland, with *Cochrane one of those officers most openly critical of Gambier's conduct, was never called to give evidence at the Admiral's carefully controlled court-martial. Emerald herself was finally broken up in 1836.

Emeriau

The French Admiral in Toulon (IM 4–10).

> Maxime-Julien, Comte Emeriau de Beauverger (1762–1845) had been a Commodore at the Battle of the Nile in 1798, with his pennant hoisted in Spartiate. Wounded in the action, both he and his ship were captured by *Nelson's fleet, although he was then released just a few months after the battle. Promoted Rear Admiral in 1802, he was from 1803 to 1811 Maritime Prefect of Toulon. He was made Compte in 1810 and promoted Vice Admiral in 1811, being given command of the Mediterranean fleet until the end of the war. After the second *Bourbon restoration, Emeriau was in 1815 made a Peer of France, retiring from the Navy the following year.

Emily

see Sweeting, Emily and Sarah

Emma, HMS

An armed transport ship of which Lieutenant Tom Pullings takes command on his own initiative (TMC 8, 10). She then meets Captain Corbett and his HMS *Africaine* at sea, telling him of the poor situation at Mauritius (TMC 9).

> The armed transport Emma was commanded in the taking of Mauritius by one Lieutenant Benjamin Street (dates unknown), who previously had command of the brig HMS *Staunch. Street had been commissioned in 1800 and was promoted Commander in March 1811, with CLOWES implying that this latter was a confirmation of an acting rank awarded in the Indian Ocean campaign. When Lieutenant *Tomkinson had declined command of *Windham, it was another enterprising Lieutenant from Emma, Henry Lynne (a Commander of April 1811, d.1835) who filled the breach.

Emmet or Emmett

An Irish Protestant family who were leading members of the 'United Irishmen,' a movement that Jack Aubrey wrongly supposes to have been composed wholly of 'Catholic rebels' (M&C 3). One of the family, a Doctor Emmet, had been an acquaintance of James Dillon and Stephen Maturin in Ireland and a member of the Society (M&C 5).

> Thomas Addis Emmet (1764–1827), a member of the distinguished Irish Protestant Emmett family of doctors, lawyers and politicians, had himself trained as a physician

in Dublin and Paris before switching to the law. In the early 1790s he defended various, indicted members of *Fitzgerald and *Tone's United Irish Society, becoming in the process a leading public figure. Although not militarily active in the rebellion of 1798, he was imprisoned from that year until 1802 for having been a member of the Society. He then lived briefly in France, agitating unsuccessfully for support for Irish independence, before moving to the USA and rising to a position of wealth and eminence at the New York bar. His younger brother, Robert (1778–1803), was also an active United Irishman, who in 1803 led an abortive rising against British rule, resulting in his trial and execution.

Emperor, the

1: see Buonaparte or Bonaparte, Napoleon
2: see Thomas, Captain

Emperor of France, the

see Buonaparte or Bonaparte, Napoleon

Encke

The name of a comet studied by Goodridge (PC 10).

> Johann Franz Encke (1791–1865) was a German mathematician and astronomer. However, the use of the name for the comet is a rare, straightforward anachronism on O'Brian's part for, although the comet was first observed in 1786 by Pierre Méchain, it was not given its name until Encke had confirmed its orbit in 1819, some 15 years after PC is set.

Endeavour

The exploration vessel financed by Sir Joseph Banks (FSW 7). On its visit to Java, Banks had become very ill (TGS 6).

> HMS Endeavour had been launched as the Whitby merchant collier Earl of Pembroke. Of especially strong construction, she was bought into the Royal Navy in 1768, on *Cook's advice, for *Banks' expedition to the South Seas. Now rated as a 10-gun barque, she carried out her voyage of exploration from 1768 to 1771, visiting Java in late 1770 on her way home to England. Here, Banks, *Solander and many others suffered from a severe tertian fever (possibly malaria), followed by acute dysentery almost as soon as they again set sail. Endeavour was sold out of the service in 1775.

Enderby

The owner of the whaler Amelia, who had petitioned the British government for Captain Colnett's voyage of exploration (FSW 3).

Endor, Witch of

Stephen Maturin alarms the superstitious crew of HMS Surprise by his reference to the existence of the Witch (TH 6).

> In the Old Testament First Book of Samuel, King Saul consulted the 'Witch of Endor' to obtain a prophesy regarding his forthcoming battle with the Philistines. After obtaining a promise of immunity for practising her dark arts, she — correctly — told Saul that he and his sons would be defeated and killed.

Endymion, HMS

A ship referred to by Jack Aubrey as one of several very desirable frigates into which he would like to be made Post (M&C 11). Jack later believes she will be ordered to the North American Station now that war has broken out with the USA (FW 1,2).

HMS Endymion, *built in 1797, was a famously swift sailer. She was rated 40-gun but usually carried 48 guns or more and was thus more suitable for meeting the heavy frigates of the U.S. Navy than many other British frigates. In January 1815, under Captain Henry Hope (d.1863 as Admiral Sir Henry), she took part—with HMSS* *Pomone *and* *Tenedos— *in the capture of Stephen Decatur's USS* *President, *using her speed, agility and good gunnery to great effect against her powerful opponent (who nevertheless eventually turned and dismasted her before being forced to surrender by virtue of the odds). Endymion was relegated to harbour service in 1860 and finally broken up in 1868. In Greek legend Endymion was an exquisite young man whom the Moon sent into a permanent sleep so that she could forever gaze on his beauty.*

Enghien, Duc d'

A man who had been shot in Paris on the evidence of forged documents (SM 10).

Louis-Antoine-Henri de Bourbon-Condé (1772–1804), Duc d'Enghien, was a leading exile Royalist soldier who, in 1801, retired to the neutral German principality of Baden. Constant plots by *Bourbon *adherents led* *Buonaparte *and* *Talleyrand *to order the arrest of d'Enghien, even though he was outside French jurisdiction. This was accomplished in March 1804, with the Duc being promptly tried by a rigged military tribunal, before which he was not even allowed a defence lawyer. He was shot immediately after his conviction, an act that caused outrage in Europe: indeed, of this judicial murder,* *Fouché *is reputed to have said, 'it was more than a crime, it was a mistake.'*

England, King of
see George III, King

Ennius

A classical author referred to by Lady Queenie Keith (HD 1).

Quintus Ennius (239–169 BC) started his career in a Calabrian regiment of the Roman army but soon made an impact amongst the Latin elite for his poetry and dramatic works, earning some of his living as a language tutor to aristocratic youth. Ennius produced a wide variety of influential works (including free translations of Greeks such as Euripides) and his Annales, *a narrative poem on the early history of Rome, was both popular for many centuries and very influential on later artists such as* *Ovid *and* *Virgil.

Entreprenant

A corvette in the French squadron at Réunion (TMC 6).

Entreprenant, *14-gun brig, was launched in 1808 and taken by the Royal Navy on the fall of Mauritius in December 1810; her fate thereafter is unrecorded.*

Erastianism

A doctrine referred to by Maturin (HMS 11).

Thomas Erastus (1524–1581), a Swiss physician and theologian, argued that, where all citizens shared a single religion, all offenses whether civil or ecclesiastical should be tried by the State. The theologian Richard Hooker, and others, later gave this doctrine its modern, much wider meaning of the State's authority in ecclesiastical matters being always and everywhere superior to that of the Church.

Erc

According to Maturin, the father of the Irish ruler Maelsechlinn the Wise (TGS 9).

In old legend, Erc was a pre-Christian king of Ireland and the enemy of the hero Cuchalain. He is not usually said to be the father of either of the two *Maelsechlinns.

Erebus, HMS

A ship in which William Babbington had sailed to the northern ice-fields (DI 8) and from which McLeod is later drafted into *Surprise* (HD 10).

HMS Erebus *was an experimental rocket vessel launched in 1807. She was turned into a somewhat more conventional 18-gun sloop in 1808 and, after service as a fireship, was in 1810 re-rated as 24-gun post-ship, still equipped with rockets of some sort. Erebus was sold in 1819. Curiously, in the light of Babbington's remark, her successor, a 14-gun bomb-vessel launched in 1826, was a famous explorer of ice regions; she was under Captain Sir James Ross when, in 1841, he discovered and named Mount Erebus in Antarctica. In 1844 she was then converted into a screw vessel and dispatched on an Arctic exploration voyage under Captain Sir John Franklin (1789–1847; in 1805 he had been a Midshipman in HMS* *Bellerophon *at Trafalgar). The ship and her consort vanished in the ice and were lost without a trace; the crews all perished trying to find a route back to safety. In classical myth Erebus was a dark cave at the entrance to Hades, the abode of the dead.*

Erskine

1: a Admiral serving on the Board of Admiralty (HMS 1).

2: a friend or colleague of Blaine and Maturin (SM 4).

Esau

According to a heretical Jewish sect, a descendant of Cain (HD 4).

In the Book of Genesis, *Esau (or Edom) is the son of Isaac and Rebecca and the grandson of the patriarch* *Abraham. *Hungry after an extended hunting expedition, Esau sold his rights of inheritance to Jacob, his domineering, younger twin brother, for a 'mess of pottage' (i.e., a bowl of soup). Jacob then also cheated Esau out of Isaac's death-bed blessing, but then fled to avoid a deadly confrontation with his furious twin. However, Esau later forgave Jacob in a tearful reconciliation after many years of separation.*

Esmin Pasha

Jack Aubrey reports to Admiral Thornton that he found that Esmin Pasha was being besieged by his son Muley in a dispute over the rule of Barka. However, when the Sultan of Turkey then intervened and appointed a completely new Pasha, Esmin had re-united with his son against this interloper. Jack had greeted the incoming Pasha and then sailed on to Medina, leaving the various disputes unresolved (IM 7).

> N.B. that slightly earlier Admiral *Thornton had said that the Pasha of Barka was *Mohammed, an English ally, who had been deposed by his brother *Jaffar. It was this situation that Thornton had sent Jack to reverse (IM 4).

Espiègle, HMS

A sloop once commanded by Captain Griffiths (YA 2).

> HMS Espiègle, 16-gun brig sloop, was launched in France in 1789, captured by the Royal Navy in 1793 and sold out of the service in 1802. Her name is the French for 'a mischievous child.'

Essex

1: the sheriff in charge of Aubrey's pillorying (RM 9).

2: a foreman at Seppings' ship-yard in Poole (YA 10).

Essex, Harry

The friend or client of Clarissa Oakes, who had obtained the commutation of her death sentence to that of transportation to New South Wales (C/T 7).

Essex, USS

A light frigate in the U.S. Navy (TH 8) whose pursuit by HMS Phoebe is echoed in FSW (FSW author's note).

> USS Essex, 32-gun, was launched in 1799 as an exceptionally fast sailer; in 1810 she was re-armed with 40 short-range, heavy carronades, reduced to 36 in the following year. In late 1812, Essex, under Captain David Porter (1780–1843), became the first ever U.S. warship to venture into the South Pacific, intending there to disrupt the lucrative — and hitherto mostly undisturbed — British whaling trade. Having cruised successfully at this business for over a year, in early 1814 HMSS *Phoebe, 36-gun, and Cherub, 18-gun, arrived off Chile with orders to hunt down and destroy her. After a series of long chases and bloody actions — the American ship faster and with more broadside metal from her short-range carronades, the British ships slower but armed with well-served, longer-range canon — Essex was forced to strike on March 28th. Although very badly damaged, she was taken into the Royal Navy as HMS Essex; in 1823 she became a convict ship and in 1837 was sold out of the service.

Esteban, don

see Maturin, Stephen

Esteve

see Maturin, Stephen

Estrella Polar

A Spanish merchantman met at sea by HMS Surprise (FSW 6).

Ethalion, HMS

A ship referred to by Jack Aubrey as one of several very desirable frigates into which he would like to be made Post (M&C 11). We hear later that her Captain is ill, with Lord Melville having her in mind as a first, temporary Post-command for Jack, before he finally settles on HMS Lively (PC 12). Some time afterwards she is said to be due at Bombay (HMS 7), but later still she is yet in England, under the command of Heneage Dundas, and thus able to convey Sophie Williams to Madeira (HMS 10,11).

> HMS Ethalion, 36-gun, was launched in 1802 as a replacement for her 38-gun namesake wrecked in 1799. She went into harbour service in 1823, remaining on the Admiralty lists until 1877. In classical myth, Ethalion, a sailor, was turned into a dolphin as a punishment for abducting the God *Bacchus.

Etherege

The Marine Lieutenant in HMS Surprise (HMS 5+). He acts as Maturin's second in the duel with Canning even though he has advised the Doctor that, in his own strong opinion, a gentleman need not fight a Jew (HMS 10).

Etough

The acting Master of Philip Broke's HMS Shannon (FW 8; SM 2).

> Henry Gladwell Etough (d.1854) entered *Broke's HMS *Druid as a volunteer in May 1805 and in the following year followed his Captain into HMS *Shannon as a Midshipman. He was acting Master in the action with USS *Chesapeake, being highly commended by Broke in his victory dispatch for his handling of the ship. In consequence Etough was commissioned Lieutenant in July 1813, continuing to serve in the American campaign. Although he apparently he saw no active service after 1820, Etough was promoted Commander in 1851.

Eudoxia, Saint

A Saint referred to in passing (TGS 3).

> The Roman Catholic church has several Saints Eudoxia/Eudocia, of whom the best known is the wife (lived 394?–461) of the Roman Emperor Theodosius II. Known by her original Greek name of Athenaïs before her conversion to Christianity, under her new name she became a well-known poetess, producing a verse paraphrase of the first eight books of the Old Testament.

Eulália, Cosí

A Spanish relative of Maturin (NC 5).

Europa

A classical figure who had loved a bull (SM 11).

> The great beauty of Europa, a sister of *Cadmus, drew down the attentions of *Zeus. Disguised as a fine, mild-tempered bull, the god induced Europa to climb onto his

back, whereupon he dashed into the sea, swam with her to Crete and, in his human-like form, seduced her.

Europe

An East Indiaman captured by the French *Caroline* and then retaken by Aubrey at Réunion (TMC 3,4).

Europe, 820 tons and armed with 30 light guns, completed 6 round trips for the British East India Company between 1802–1816. Under her Master William Gelston, she was taken by Caroline on May 31st 1809 and re-captured at Réunion by Commodore Josias Rowley's squadron on September 21st of the same year.

Eurotas, HMS

A ship in which Jack Aubrey had long ago been Third Lieutenant (TH 10), now on the Brest blockade (YA 9). Under Captain John Phillimore, she had recently taken *Clorinde* in a very long engagement, assisted at the last by HMSS *Dryad* and *Achates* (YA 9).

*HMS Eurotas, 46-gun, was launched in March 1813 and broken up in late 1817. The action described by Jack *Aubrey in the text took place in February 1814. As Stephen *Maturin notes, the classical Eurotas was the stream on which stood the city of Sparta.*

Euryalus, HMS

A ship in which Dillon (M&C 3), Nicholls (HMS 5) and Whewell (COM 7) had once served, and in which Jack Aubrey had once been shipmates with Foster (RM 2); Mr. Oakhurst had once been her Master (HD 3). Under her irascible Captain Miller, she and Heneage Dundas' HMS *Ethalion* are met at sea by Jack's HMS *Surprise* (HMS 11). She is later referred to in passing (LM 6) and later again referred to by Shelton as a former command of Dundas himself (WDS 5).

*The first-ever HMS Euryalus, 36-gun, was not launched until 1803, ruling out service by *Dillon and *Aubrey. In 1805 she was present, under the Honourable Sir Henry Blackwood (1770–1832), at Trafalgar, having earned herself the nick-name of *Nelson's 'Watch Dog' for her careful tracking of the enemy fleet's position in the days leading up to the action itself. In 1809 she took part in the fiasco at Walcheren (see *Chatham and *Strachan) under Captain George Heneage Lawrence *Dundas. After further distinguished service, Euryalus became a prison ship in 1826 and, under her 1859 name of HMS Africa, was sold in 1860. The early, pre-1803 references may be to HMS Eurus, 32-gun, the ex-Dutch Zefir captured in 1796. She became a store-ship in 1803, and was broken up in 1834. In *Homer, Euryalus was the companion of Diomedes, King of Argos, during the siege of Troy; in classical myth, Eurus was the south-east wind.*

Eurydice, HMS

A ship referred to as cruising off Bordeaux (SM 9), later commanded by Heneage Dundas (RM 5,8; LM 8). In a play on the name of the frigate, Stephen Maturin compares his abandonment by Diana Villiers to the death of Eurydice, Orpheus' wife (RM 5).

*HMS Eurydice, 24-gun, was launched in 1781 and, after a rather uneventful career, broken up in 1834. In one telling of the legend, *Orpheus followed the deceased Eurydice to the underworld in order to rescue her. However, by disobeying a command not to look on her face until they reached the surface world, he then lost her forever.*

Eusebio, HMS

A 32-gun frigate, a former command of Captain Thomas of HMS *Thames*, that had been lost in a storm in 1809 (COM 4).

Eusebius

An early Church father whose tomes are used as seat cushions for Sarah and Emily Sweeting (WDS 7).

There were a considerable number of men named Eusebius who were influential in the early Church. For sheer size of output, the prolific Eusebius of Caesarea (260?–339), whose 10-volume Ecclesiastical History appeared from 290 to 325, is likely to be the author in question.

Euterpe, HMS

A ship in which Jack Aubrey, the senior Littlejohn and Mr. Whewell had once served (FW 9; COM 7), now on the Brest blockade (SM 9).

Evan, Sir

An Admiralty official (PC 6).

*This is almost certainly a reference to Sir Evan Nepean (1751–1822), a naval administrator of great acumen. Nepean entered the Royal Navy as a very young man, first serving as a Captain's clerk and immediately showing an aptitude for organisation and paper-work. From 1780 to 1782 he acted as Sir John Jervis'— later Earl *St. Vincent— clerk in HMS *Foudroyant, coming to enjoy that great man's life-long patronage; he was later to win both the friendship and respect of *Nelson and other leading Royal Navy figures. In 1782 Jervis secured for his protégé a civil-service post ashore and by 1784 he had rose to the important position of Under Secretary for War. Appointed First Secretary to the Admiralty in 1795, in 1802 he was rewarded for his talents with a baronetcy. For just a few months in 1804, Nepean was appointed Chief Secretary for Ireland before being recalled to London as a Lord Commissioner of the Admiralty. Out of office from 1806 to 1812, he was then appointed Governor of Bombay, a post he held until his retirement in 1819.*

Evans

1: the Commander of the bomb-ketch HMS *Aetna*, jealous of Aubrey's success and luck (M&C 9).
2: a Commander on the West Indies station, made Post ahead of Aubrey (M&C 11).
3: the surgeon of USS *Constitution*, greatly admired by Maturin (FW 4; FSW 9). He often visits the recuperating Aubrey at the hospital of his brother-in-law, Otis P. Choate (FW 6,8).
4: Admiral Russell's servant (LM 1).
5: the lob-lolly boy in HMS *Bellona* (COM 8).

Evans, Black

Captain Griffiths' head game-keeper and Barret

Bonden's opponent and victor in a brutal boxing match. He is also referred to as 'Beelzebub' for his habitual violent behaviour (YA 3).

Evans, Evan

A seaman in HMS *Lively* who accuses George Rogers of the theft of a dried ape's head (PC 12).

Evans, Ned

A seaman in HMS *Sophie* injured in her first battle (M&C 4).

Evans, Tom

A gunner's mate in HMS *Diane* (NC 1).

Eve

The biblical companion of Adam (TMC 2; DI 4,7; IM 9)

> In the Bible *Adam and Eve, the progenitors of the human race, were the first man and woman created by *God, Eve being produced from Adam's rib whilst he was in a deep sleep. Given the perfect Garden of Eden in which to dwell in naked innocence, Eve was soon tricked by the Serpent into eating from the forbidden tree of knowledge. As punishment, God then cast the pair down from Paradise to Earth.

Eves, Francis Walwin

A deceased Midshipman of HMS *Theseus* whose obituary is read by Maturin (DI 6).

Evil One

see **Devil, the**

Excellency, His

1: *see* **Stanhope**

2: *see* **Macquarie**

Excellent, HMS

A ship in Admiral Thornton's Mediterranean fleet, Captain Heneage Dundas (IM 3–5).

> HMS Excellent *was launched as a 74-gun in 1787 and in 1797, under her Captain Cuthbert *Collingwood, fought at the Battle of Cape *St Vincent. Cut down to a 58-gun in 1820, in 1830 she became the Royal Navy's main gunnery training ship, before being broken up in 1835. Her replacement became the official School of Gunnery at Portsmouth, commanded for a while by Henry Ducie *Chads.*

Exeter

An East Indiaman in Muffit's China Fleet, protected by HMS Surprise from Admiral Linois' French squadron. (HMS 9).

> Exeter, *1200-tons, completed eight round trips for the East India Company between 1792 and 1809; she was named for a city and port in southwest England. The action is based on the defence of a Honourable East India Company merchant fleet against *Linois' attack in February 1804, during which* Exeter *was commanded by Master Henry Meriton. However, no Royal Navy ship was present during the fight, the squadron being organised by the senior Master, *Earl Camden's Nathaniel Dance (1748–1827).*

F

F., Lady

The mother of Frances Williams' new husband, Sir Oliver Floode (HMS 7).

Fabian or Fabien

A French-American apothecary's assistant, taken from *Franklin* by *Surprise,* who becomes for a time Maturin's assistant surgeon. He is also a talented ornithological artist (WDS 6+; COM 1).

Fabre

A doctor local to the Temple prison in Paris who, before being conscripted into the French Army, treats the ailing Jack Aubrey (SM 10).

Fabrice

A fictional character who was present at the Battle of Waterloo (FW author's note).

> The reference is to Fabrice del Dongo, the central character in Stendhal's Charterhouse of Parma *(1839). Fab-*

rice's anti-heroic description of the great battle inspired Tolstoy to write War and Peace.

Fahrenheit

The inventor of a type of thermometer (PC 9; TH 6; COM 9).

> Gabriel Daniel Fahrenheit (1686–1736), a German physicist and inventor, mostly resident in Holland, was the first man to use mercury in the thermometer's glass tube and also devised a new temperature scale, taking as its 'zero' the coldest moment of the winter of 1709.

Faithorne

1: an Admiral who dines at Diana Villiers' London home (IM 1).

2: the Captain of HMS *Grampus* (YA 9).

3: the surgeon of the whaler *Daisy*, a natural historian (C/T 5–9; WDS 2).

Falconer

A figure who greatly inspired O'Brian (M&C author's note). He was the author of *Dictionary of the*

Marine (PC 2), probably the book sent by Stephen Maturin to Sophie Williams (HMS 4).

> *William Falconer (1732–1769) was a Scottish poet and lexicographer who, driven perhaps by poverty, went to sea in the merchant service. Some time before 1750 he joined, as boatswain, the merchantman* Britannia, *a ship that was later wrecked in the Mediterranean, with Falconer being one of only three men saved. In 1762 he made his poetic reputation with* The Shipwreck, *a thundering work inspired by his disagreeable experience. After a further career as a Royal Navy Midshipman and Purser, under the patronage of Admiral the Duke of York, Falconer joined* HMS Aurora *but was then lost when she foundered with all hands off Cape Town. In addition to his many poems, his* Universal Dictionary of the Marine *appeared from 1768 onwards. Much of the verse written and declaimed in the series by Lieutenant *Mowett is borrowed from* The Shipwreck *and from Falconer's later* The Midshipman. *N.B., as O'Brian does not say specifically that it was the entertaining verse of Falconer — thick with sea-terms and classical allusions — that inspired him, it is possible that he may have had in mind a genuine Royal Navy fighting hero, very similarly named: Robert Faulknor (sic; 1760–1795), Captain of the light frigate HMS *Blanche that in January 1795 took on the heavy Frenchman La *Pique. In an action which caught the British public's admiration, Captain Faulknor was shot dead whilst lashing the bowsprit of* La Pique *to* Blanche's *capstan. After several more hours of point-blank gunnery exchanges,* La Pique *surrendered. Faulknor had been commissioned Lieutenant in 1780, promoted Commander in 1790 and made Post in 1794.*

Falkiner

A Lieutenant in HMS *Shannon* (FW 8,9). He later brings USS *Chesapeake* into Halifax as a prize (SM 1), travelling on to England in HMS *Nova Scotia* with Captain Broke's victory dispatch (SM 2,3).

> *Sir Charles Leslie Falkiner (1790–1858) had been commissioned Lieutenant in 1810 and was appointed to HMS *Shannon in the same year. Rewarded for his role in the great victory with promotion to Commander in July 1813, he was then immediately placed on half pay, never seeing further active service. Falkiner was promoted retired Post Captain in 1848 and in 1858 succeeded to his deceased, elder brother's baronetcy very shortly before his own death.*

Falstaff

A reference is made by George Herapath to Falstaff's basket plot (FW 8).

> *Sir John Falstaff is a character in *Shakespeare's* Henry IV Parts 1 and 2 and in* The Merry Wives of Windsor; *his decline and death is then referred to in* Henry V. *In* Merry Wives *Falstaff is smuggled out of the house of his intended lover, Mistress Ford, in a laundry basket. The name of the character was inspired by that of the soldier Sir John Fastolf (1377?–1459), who in 1415 had fought under King Henry V at Agincourt, becoming Governor of Anjou and Maine after the King's death.*

Fama

A 34-gun Spanish frigate, part of Admiral Bustamente's treasure squadron and the ship actually carrying the bullion itself. Having struck to HMS *Medusa*, she then runs, before finally striking again to Jack Aubrey's HMS *Lively* (PC 14; HMS 6; TMC 2).

> Fama *was captured on October 5th 1804 by HMSS *Lively and *Medusa off Cadiz, her companions having already been engaged by Sir *Graham Moore's squadron. Bought in as HMS* Fama, *38-gun, she was sold out of the service in 1812.*

Fanciulla

A 20-gun Ligurian corvette with French officers that Admiral Harte orders Jack Aubrey to attack in Chaulieu harbour (PC 10+). Jack takes her, losing his own HMS *Polychrest* to a sand-bank and heavy gunfire in the process (PC 11; IM 4), and she is then bought into the Royal Navy, rated a sloop and given, in compliment to Jack, to Lieutenant Parker as Commander (PC 12).

Fanning

A Midshipman in HMS *Lively* (PC 13).

Fanny

see **Harte, Fanny** or **Aubrey, Fanny**

Fanny

A merchantman due to be escorted by HMS *Sophie* (M&C 2).

Fanshaw

1: Jack Aubrey's prize-agent (HMS 4), who has received an ex-gratia payment of £10,000 on his behalf for his role in the capture of Bustamente's treasure fleet (HMS 6).
2: a British intelligence agent (SM 4).

Fanshaw, Harriet

A young lady who had been badly treated by Andrew Wray in an affair of the heart (IM 1).

Fanshawe

1: the Commissioner of Plymouth Dockyard and his wife (IM 2; COM 3). Captain Fanshawe is also once referred to as a Port Admiral (LM 7).

> *Robert Fanshawe (d.1823) was made Post in 1768 and served as MP for Plymouth from 1783 to 1790, after having commanded HMS *Namur in *Rodney's victory at the Battle of the Saintes in 1782. He became the *Commissioner (not *Port Admiral) of Plymouth Naval Dockyard in 1789, serving in the post until 1815; Captain Fanshawe's acceptance of this position took him out of the seniority list, and hence he never raised his flag.*

2: an army Captain who is a member of the British legation in Stockholm (LM 9).
3: a flag officer at Port Mahon, presumably the Port Admiral for the British naval base, who is the brother of Captain William Fanshawe (HD 3,4,8,9).

Fanshawe, William or Billy

1: the Captain of HMS *Ramillies* (YA 5–9), an old

friend of Jack Aubrey (YA 6). He conveys to Jack Admiral Lord Stranraer's fury that two French frigates appear to have slipped past HMS *Bellona* in the fog (YA 6).

2: an officer successfully treated for serious wounds by Stephen Maturin after the Battle of Algeçiras (*see* M&C). His brother, Admiral Fanshawe, implies that William has since retired from the sea (HD 3).

Farley, Tom

A seaman in HMS *Berenice*, a long-time follower of her Captain Heneage Dundas and once a ship-mate of Barret Bonden (YA 3).

Farquhar, R.T.

A colonial administrator, intended to be Governor of Mauritius, taken by Jack Aubrey to the Indian Ocean (TMC 1+). The nearby island of Réunion being captured first, Farquhar is initially installed there (TMC 6).

> *Sir Robert Townshend Farquhar (1776–1830) spent his entire active career in India and the Indian Ocean, serving as a young man as Lieutenant Governor of Pulo Prabang and then in Madras. After his spell on Réunion (from late 1809), he moved to Mauritius, being formally appointed Governor and Commander-in-Chief in 1812. He held this post until his retirement in 1823, also becoming during this time a Director of the British East India Company. In 1821 he was made a baronet, principally for his successes in suppressing the local slave trade.*

Farrell

A seaman in HMS *Surprise* under particular obligation to Maturin for medical treatment received in the past (LM 5).

Fatima

A boarding-house keeper in Algiers (HD 8).

'Fatty'

A name used by Mr Whewell for a Krooman tribesman in Sierra Leone (COM 8).

Faulkner

An author from whom Maturin had learned of the powers of coca leaves (FSW 5).

> *The reference may perhaps be to Sir Arthur Brooke Faulkner (1779–1845), an Irish doctor who served from 1808 to 1815 as Chief Physician to the British Army in Europe, making a name for himself as a strong advocate of proper military hospitals and the author of a guide to soldiers' health in adverse climates. Faulkner was also a well-known raconteur and miscellany writer.*

Fauvet

A fashionable literary man in the pay of French intelligence, whose secret messages to England Stephen Maturin refuses to carry (SM 5,11). He nevertheless later testifies against Stephen at his interrogation (SM 11).

Fawkes, Guy

A famous conspirator, closely associated in the English mind with fireworks (PC 1; HMS 9; IM 4; TGS 5; NC 6; C/T 2,3,4; COM 8)

> *Guy Fawkes (1570–1606), a fervent Catholic convert, was part of a plot to blow up the Protestant King *James I and the Westminster Parliament. The plot was betrayed and Fawkes was arrested on November 5th, 1605 whilst preparing his charges in the vaults; he was then tried and executed. In Great Britain, November 5th (Bonfire or Guy Fawkes Night) is still celebrated with firework displays and the ritual burning of stuffed mannikin 'guys.' It is a matter of continuing controversy as to whether it is the failure or the near-success of his plot that is so enthusiastically recalled.*

Faye, La

A medical authority consulted by Martin when Maturin receives a severe concussion (FSW 9).

Fazackerly

A seaman in HMS *Diane*, possibly later referred to by Aubrey as 'Booby' for his clumsiness (TGS 9).

Fearney

A Master of Foxhounds with whom Mowett had once ridden (FSW 3).

Fearney, William

One of Nelson's bargemen (M&C author's note).

> *William Fearney (dates unknown) served *Nelson in HMS *Captain at the Battle of Cape *St Vincent (1797).*

Feathers, the

The landlord of the Feathers Inn at Torbay, a former seaman who had lost a leg at the battle of Cape St Vincent (YA 4).

Featherstonehaugh

A seaman, probably a Midshipman, in HMS *Thunderer* (COM 1).

> *In Britain the name is usually pronounced 'Fanshawe.'*

Felip V

A 7-gun Spanish privateer taken by HMS *Sophie* (M&C 10).

> *Felip, or Philip, V (1683–1746), a grandson of King *Louis XIV of France, became the first *Bourbon King of Spain, ruling from 1700 to 1746 (with an interlude in 1724 when he briefly abdicated in favour of his short-lived son, Luis). However, no privateer by this name was taken by the Royal Navy in the period.*

Fell, Harry, George, Mordecai and William

Sethians — and hence known to HMS *Surprise*'s Sethians — who have been transported to New South Wales. Harry Fell is believed to have absconded from the colony in a passing whaler (NC 9).

Fellowes

1: the Flag Captain of Admiral Harte's HMS *Thunderer* (IM 4), perhaps the Senior Naval Officer at Valletta (TH 10). He still has *Thunderer* some years later (COM 1).

The reference may be to Richard Edward Fellowes (1771–1841) who, at the time of the books mentioned, was active in the Mediterranean in his HMS Conqueror, 74-gun. He had been made Post in 1795 and was promoted Rear Admiral in 1814 and Vice Admiral in 1830.

2: a passing reference is made to the mother of a Colonel Fellowes who had supposed the ill-dressed Stephen Maturin to be a street-beggar (TH 8).

Fellowes, John

The very skillful bosun of HMS *Boadicea*, thought to be young for his post (TMC 2+). Under the bad influence of his counterpart in HMS *Sirius*, he mis-appropriates a quite unacceptable quantity of HMS *Boadicea*'s stores, leading to a furious reprimand by Jack Aubrey (TMC 6).

Fellowes, Peter

The temporary Captain of HMS *Acasta* (FW 3).

Fellows

The vicar of the parish in which the Williams' family home of Mapes Court lies (HMS 7).

Fenn

A Midshipman in HMS *Shannon* (FW 9).

Tommy Fenn served on HMS *Shannon as one of *Broke's Midshipmen but his fate after the great victory of 1813 is unknown.

Fenton

1: Dr McAdam's mate in HMS *Néréide* (TMC 5,7).

2: the Second Lieutenant of HMS *Ariel* (SM 6–9).

Feretier

The Captain of the French frigate *Caroline*, badly wounded in action (TMC 4,5).

Lieutenant J. B. H. Feretier was *Caroline's acting Captain at the time of this action.

Ferris, Captain

The Captain of HMS *Hannibal*, captured by Linois' squadron off Gibraltar, a former shipmate of Jack Aubrey (M&C 12).

Solomon Ferris (d.1803), made Post in 1793, was captured with his HMS *Hannibal in July 1801. Exchanged on parole (together with *Cochrane) shortly after the action, he was acquitted of any blame for the loss of his ship at a court-martial held on September 1st of the same year.

Fidge

A Lieutenant, under whom Jack Aubrey had been a Midshipman in HMS *Surprise*, who had later died of yellow fever (HMS 8).

Fielding

1: a Lieutenant in HMS *Lively* (HMS 2,3).

2: the Captain of HMS *Nymphe* (DI 5; SM 6).

Fielding, Charles

A Royal Navy Lieutenant, held as a prisoner-of-war in the Bitche prison in France. His virtuous and beautiful Sicilian wife, Laura, is living in Malta, where she becomes a close friend of both Jack Aubrey and Stephen Maturin (TH 1+). Charles' predicament has put Laura into the hands of the French intelligence agent, Lesueur, who forces her to spy — unsuccessfully — on Stephen (TH 1,3+). Through Lesueur's organisation, Charles is able to send letters to his wife but Stephen later comes to believe that these are forged and that Charles is probably dead (TH 8). Some letters are indeed forged, but this is because the Lieutenant has managed to escape from prison with his fellow officers, Wilson and Corby. The sole survivor of the ensuing journey to freedom, Charles Fielding makes his way to Italy and is rescued from a small boat by HMS *Nymphe*, a ship in which he had once been Third Lieutenant (TH 9). Stephen, who in Malta is popularly and wrongly thought to be one of Laura's lovers, operates on the slightly wounded Charles off Trieste. Jack, widely and wrongly thought in the Royal Navy to be another of Laura's lovers, attempts to offer Charles passage to Malta, but is icily rebuffed (TH 9). Charles' escape and re-appearance in the Mediterranean immediately puts Laura in the greatest peril, she no longer being of use to Lesueur but still able to identify him and his colleagues (TH 10). Later Charles, having arrived in Gibraltar in the bomb vessel HMS *Hecla*, is soon convinced by Laura that her virtue is unsullied (FSW 1). Fielding had once been Second Lieutenant of HMS *Volage* (TH 9) and later acting First Lieutenant of HMS *Phoenix* (TH 3); he had also served under Admiral Harte (TH 10).

Fielding, James

The First Lieutenant of Jack Aubrey's HMS *Diane*. He had once served in HMS *Canopus*, and thus had narrowly missed the Battle of Trafalgar (TGS 4+). In a ship-board accident he suffers a broken leg that, set in plaster by Maturin, makes a complete recovery (TGS 5,6); in the battle on the ship-wreck island he is badly wounded, again in the leg (NC 1–3). Once safely in Batavia, Fielding follows Jack into HMS *Nutmeg of Consolation* (NC 3–7), accepting command of her to return to Java when his Captain transfers into *Surprise* (NC 7).

Fielding, Laura

The beautiful and virtuous Sicilian wife of Lieutenant Charles Fielding, a prisoner-of-war in France (TH 1+). Laura is living at the British naval base of Malta, where her husband's predicament gives the

French secret agent, Lesueur, power over her, forcing her to attempt to spy on her new friend, Stephen Maturin (TH 1). Stephen, from the very outset suspicious of her motivations in befriending and in later trying to seduce him (TH 1,3), persuades her to reveal the secret and starts to use her to feed false intelligence back to Lesueur himself (TH 3+). The Doctor does, however, retain a very strong friendship for Laura, and is solicitous of her continued well-being, leading to rumours of an affair (TH 3+). She has a devoted guard-dog, Ponto, whom Jack Aubrey rescues from drowning in a well: the dog's subsequent enthusiastic public greetings of the Captain convince many people that he too has become her lover (TH 1+). Jack himself, wanting very much to give substance to these rumours, is elegantly yet firmly rebuffed (TH 3). Later, the re-appearance in the Mediterranean of the escaped Charles Fielding puts Laura in great peril of assassination by Lesueur, for he has now lost his power over her yet can still be identified by her to the British authorities (TH 9,10). Stephen snatches her away from an attempt on her life to the safety of HMS *Surprise* and she then sails in Jack's ship to the safety of Gibraltar (TH 10). Although the jealous Charles, convinced that Laura and Jack were lovers, has now issued a veiled challenge to a duel (TH 9), she, on his later arrival in Gibraltar, easily persuades her husband that her virtue has remained unsullied. Laura is soon also granted a full pardon for her previous spying activities (FSW 1; *also* RM 5).

Figaro

see '*Marriage of Figaro*'

Findlay

A senior doctor at Guy's Hospital, for whom Alexander Macaulay had been a dresser (COM 3).

Firkins

The Penal Secretary in New South Wales, known to Maturin as 'Mealy-Mouth,' a cousin of Captain Lowe (NC 8+).

> *A name possibly inspired by that of Richard Atkins (1745–1820), the Deputy Judge Advocate in New South Wales and a man widely regarded by contemporaries and later historians as a vicious, incompetent drunk.*

First Consul

see **Buonaparte** or **Bonaparte, Napoleon**

First Lord

> *The First Lord of the Admiralty (see also* ***Lord High Admiral***) was the political head of the Royal Navy, sometimes but not always a serving Admiral. The text often attaches a particular name to the title, but it may be convenient here to list all those who served in the years 1800–1815.*

1: *Earl Spencer* (December 1794–February 1801)
see ***Spencer**

2: *Admiral Earl St Vincent* (February 1801–May 1804)
see ***St Vincent, Lord**

3: *Henry Dundas, 1st Viscount Melville* (May 1804–May 1805)
see ***Melville, Lord**

4: *Admiral Lord Barham* (May 1805–February 1806)

> *Sir Charles Middleton (1726–1813; Lord Barham from 1805) was made Post in 1750 but then only ever saw very limited service at sea, his talents lying primarily in administration. He served as Controller of the Navy — in charge of ship-building, amongst other things — from 1778 to 1790 and as a Lord Commissioner of the Admiralty from 1794 to 1795. He had been promoted Rear Admiral in 1787, Vice Admiral in 1793 and Admiral in 1795, although he never held an active command in any of the flag ranks. On Lord *Melville's impeachment in 1805, Middleton was appointed First Lord and given his peerage. His administration came at a crucial time in Britain's naval fortunes and, after initial unease, he soon gave full support to *Nelson's plans to bring *Villeneuve to a decisive battle as soon as possible. Once the great victory at Trafalgar (in late October 1805) had eliminated the threat of invasion, Barham soon retired.*

5: *Charles Grey, M.P.* (a.k.a. **Lord Howick**; February 1806–September 1806)
see ***Grey, Sir Charles**

6: *Thomas Grenville, M.P.* (September 1806–April 1807)

> *Thomas Grenville (1755–1846) was a diplomat and statesman from a leading political family. When *Grey became Foreign Secretary he accepted office as First Lord, but resigned on the change of Government of 1807, as the new administration was hostile to one of his most favoured causes, Roman Catholic emancipation.*

7: **Lord Mulgrave** (April 1807–May 1810)
see ***Mulgrave**, # 1

8: *Charles Yorke, M.P.* (May 1810–March 1812)
see ***Yorke, Charles** # 1

9: *Robert Dundas, 2nd Viscount Melville* (March 1812–September 1828)
see ***Melville, Viscount**

First Sea Lord

A very senior officer whom Jack Aubrey had always thought of as a friend (YA 2). Jack later refers to the change that comes over officers when they are elevated to such grandeur (HD 9).

> *The first reference may be a slip for Viscount *Melville, the First Lord (although he was never a sea officer) or may be intended to refer to the longest-serving Royal Navy member on the Board of Admiralty, at the time of YA one Sir Joseph Yorke, the brother of Charles *Yorke, sometime civilian *First Lord. In Jack *Aubrey's time, the Board of Admiralty always consisted of a mixture of Civil and Naval Lords (with the latter sometimes being known informally as 'Sea Lords'), all of nominally equal rank and power. Following the reforms of 1832 the Navy was put permanently under the control of a government minister, with a 'First Naval Lord' as his senior advisor (and*

Fisher • Fitzgerald   124

therefore effective professional head of the service); in 1904 this title was changed to 'First Sea Lord.'

First Secretary to the Admiralty
see **Evan, Sir** or **Croker**

Fisher
1: the Chaplain of HMS *Leopard* who, having become a close friend of Lieutenant Grant, abandons ship with him after the iceberg collision (DI 3–9; FW 1).
2: Jack Aubrey's uncle, for whom the 'London' Bach had written some works (IM 2).
3: an ex-smuggler seaman in *Surprise* (LM 1; TGS 2; NC 7).

Fisher, Harry
Either a Post Captain or a Commander, a protégé of Admiral Drury (FW 1).

Fitton, Michael and John
Michael Fitton, a Lieutenant in command of the cutter HMS *Nimble*, is the son of Jack Aubrey's old colleague, John Fitton of HMS *Colossus*. The elder Fitton had been killed, standing alongside Jack, at the Battle of Cape St Vincent (TGS 4, COM 3,4).
Michael Fitton (1766–1752) entered the Royal Navy in 1780 but was not commissioned Lieutenant until 1804. He had nevertheless enjoyed a brilliant career as an enterprising young Midshipman, although apparently one totally devoid of the family influence so often necessary to secure advancement. Given command in the year of his promotion of the 10-gun cutter HMS Gipsy, *in 1805 he fought a spirited and successful action against five small privateers, capturing one of them. In 1806, now in the 12-gun schooner HMS* Pitt, *he took the notorious 14-gun pirate brig,* Superbe. *All the naval biographies note that his career-long gallantry and energy — he captured over 40 ships in his active sea-life — were mysteriously over-looked and that he was never promoted beyond Lieutenant. From 1835 onwards, he lived as a pensioner of Greenwich Naval Hospital. The name of Michael's father is unrecorded, and no 'John Fitton' served as an officer in Aubrey's time.*

Fitzgerald
1: a friend of Jack Aubrey (M&C 2).
2: an Irish aristocratic family referred to by Maturin as genuinely Irish, rather than being English implants (TMC 2).
The Fitzgeralds, Earls and Dukes of Kildare and Leinster (see ***Fitzgerald, Lord Edward**, *below), were an Anglo-Norman family that had held extensive lands and titles in Ireland from the 12th century onwards; another branch were Earls of* *Desmond. *The family's Irish connections originate with Maurice Fitzgerald (d.1176), one of King Henry II's chief conquerors of the island. So long and deep was the connection that it is often said that the Fitzgeralds are more Irish than the Irish themselves.*
3: the father of Maturin's dead cousin Kevin, now resident in Normandy. He had once served as a Colonel in Dillon's Irish Brigade of the French Army (SM 5).

4: the family name of Mr Geoghegan's grandmother (YA 5).

Fitzgerald, Lord Edward and Lady Pamela
Lord Edward Fitzgerald was a leading Protestant United Irishman whom Stephen Maturin had tried to persuade of the folly of an armed uprising against the Crown. In the vain hope of diffusing a growing tension between the Irish James Dillon and his very English commander, Jack Aubrey, Stephen tells Jack that many United Irishmen were well-connected Protestants and not merely 'Catholic rebels' as he might have supposed (M&C 3+; YA 1). Fitzgerald is referred to by Maturin as 'Cousin Edward' (NC 10), Sir Joseph Blaine having remarked that Stephen is an illegitimate connection of the family (HMS 4). His wife, Lady Pamela Fitzgerald, is referred to fondly by both James Dillon and Stephen (M&C 5; RM 5).
Lord Edward Fitzgerald (1763–1798), 12th son of the Duke of Leinster, served with distinction as a young Ensign in the British Army during the American War of Independence. However, in 1792 he was cashiered for joining in a toast, in Paris, to the abolition of all hereditary titles. Returning to Ireland, he became active in the United Irishmen Society (see ***Tone, Wolfe**) *and by 1798 was convinced that a violent insurrection against the Crown was not only necessary but likely to succeed. During the rebellion — a ramshackle, premature and strife-ridden affair — Fitzgerald's whereabouts were betrayed to Major Henry* *Sirr, *head of the Dublin police, and he was soon captured, receiving a severe wound in the arm and dying in prison a few weeks later. The Fitzgerald family was a large one, of diverse views and loyalties: one of Lord Edward's elder brothers, Charles Lord Lacale (d.1810), rose to flag rank in the Royal Navy and in 1800 was a leading supporter of proposals for union between the British and Irish crowns. He had been made Post in 1780 and was promoted Rear Admiral in 1799 and Vice Admiral in 1804. Lady Pamela (1773–1831) married Lord Edward in Paris in 1792; she is often supposed to have been the natural daughter of her guardian Madame de Genlis and the Duc d'Orleans. After Lord Edward's death, she led a wandering and rather desperate life in Europe.*

Fitzgerald, James
A priest and cousin of Stephen Maturin, encountered by him in New South Wales (NC 10).

Fitzgerald, Kevin
A cousin of Stephen Maturin who had died in the Austrian service whilst fighting against the French. Because of this circumstance, his lands in Ireland, forfeit after his involvement in the 1798 rebellion, are to be restored to the family (FW 3; SM 5). He may also be the gentleman who had once debated the Irish problem with Dr Johnson (NC 3).

Fitzgerald, Thaddeus
A cousin of Stephen Maturin (RM 5).

Fitzgerald y Saavedra, Colonel don Patricio

A Spanish officer and friend of Stephen Maturin (COM 5).

Fitzgibbon

An opponent of the United Irishmen referred to by Maturin (M&C 3).

John, 1st Baron Fitzgibbon and 1st Earl of Clare (1749–1802), was Lord Chancellor of Ireland from 1789 onwards. A vigorous opponent of all political and religious reform in his native country, he was a leading proponent of the Act of Union between the Irish and British Crowns, finally passed in 1802.

Fitzherbert, Mrs

A lady said by Sophie Williams to be a Catholic, later referred to by Maturin as the wife of the Prince Regent (PC 10; RM 9).

Maria Anne Fitzherbert (1756–1837), a Roman Catholic who had already been twice married and widowed, went through a ceremony of marriage in 1785 with her lover, George, Prince of Wales (later the *Regent). From then until the end of her life she was treated and received in Society as his legal wife, even by the Royal family (with the almost sole exception of King *George III himself, who had no time for his son or any of his circle). However, there are aspects of the marriage that were obscure and controversial at the time and remain so to this day. Firstly, there are doubts — later encouraged to some degree by Mrs Fitzherbert herself — as to whether the marriage ceremony itself was ever properly performed. Secondly, the marriage was in any case declared invalid in 1794 on two separate grounds, a) that the legal requirement of the King's specific consent to marriage in the case of the direct Heir to the throne had never been obtained; and b) that Mrs Fitzherbert's professed Catholicism was in itself a legal barrier to marriage to the Heir. The immediate occasion of this legally correct, though widely disputed and condemned 1794 declaration was the impending marriage of the Prince to the impeccably Protestant Princess Caroline of Brunswick, a union arranged for reasons of State and in an attempt to produce a Protestant, male heir. The ceremonies (wedding and bedding) over, the Prince promptly separated from the Princess, to whom a single daughter was later born amidst public accusations that the Prince may not have been the father (Sir Sidney *Smith, amongst others, was thought a likely culprit). Mrs Fitzherbert was now advised by her Church that she could regard her 1785 marriage as canonically legal and therefore again live openly with the Prince without religious condemnation, which she did from 1796 to 1803. However, from this latter date on, the Prince's affections turned elsewhere and by 1808 he and Mrs Fitzherbert had broken, with some mutual acrimony. Nevertheless, when the Prince — by now King George IV — died in 1830, he was wearing a miniature portrait of Mrs Fitzherbert around his neck.

FitzMaurice

A man referred to by Sir Joseph Blaine as being connected to the Cabinet Office, through which he had secured the large sums of money necessary to subvert the government of Peru (RM 5).

The reference is probably to Henry Petty-Fitzmaurice (1780–1863; 3rd Marquis of Landsdown from 1809), the Chancellor of the Exchequer from 1806 to 1807. He is chiefly remembered as a vigorous proponent of money as a vital tool of war, having introduced in 1806 quite large scale taxation measures to support the campaigns against *Buonaparte. Although out of formal office from 1807 until 1827, he remained influential throughout the campaigns against *Buonaparte and in economic policy thereafter.

FitzPatrick, Kevin and Mona

Two young, twin children from Munster in Ireland, captured from a fishing boat by corsairs and later redeemed from slavery in Algiers by Stephen Maturin (HD 8). They are placed in the temporary care of Lady Keith at Gibraltar, Stephen's intention being to restore them to their family (HD 9,10).

Fladong's

An eating-house in London, much frequented by Royal Navy officers (RM 5+; LM 3).

Flag Captain

Various Flag Captains are mentioned, by title or name, throughout the series. The post itself is that of the 'day-to-day' Captain of the headquarters-ship used by an Admiral or Commodore (Commodores were not entitled to a Flag Captain unless the squadron was particularly large; Admirals were always entitled to one). Quite often Admirals appointed a relatively junior protégé as their Flag Captain and indeed it was not uncommonly a first ever appointment on being made Post, especially for men with experience as First Lieutenants of large ships. Successful Flag Captains often hoped next to be given command of a plum, independent frigate, rather than remaining forever on the often tedious fleet duties in a ship-of-the-line. The post (sometimes known as that of 'Second Captain') is not the same as that of the *Captain of the Fleet (or 'First Captain'), the Chief of Staff to a senior Admiral.

Flag Lieutenant

Various Flag Lieutenants are mentioned, by title or name, throughout the series. The post is that of chief signals officer to an Admiral, responsible both for fleet battle instructions and the handling of more routine signals and communications. Some Admirals liked to take a favoured Flag Lieutenant from command to command whilst others, such as *Nelson, preferred simply to appoint the most senior Lieutenant on any given ship as Flag Lieutenant, with the next most senior being made First Lieutenant, i.e. the second-in-command to the *Flag Captain. Although Flag Lieutenants tended to have very good promotion prospects because of the Admiral's patronage, some ambitious young officers objected to the 'Nelsonian' variant of the system, believing that 'Premiers' had far more opportunity for glory than 'Admiral's assistants.'

Flaherty

An Irish seaman in HMS *Sophie* (M&C 3).

Flèche

A ship that had fought *Sylph*. Mr Elliott of HMS

Diane had been an officer in one or the other and been wounded in the action (TGS 4).

> *Ships named *Sylph and *Flèche served at various times in both the British and French navies. Having been unable to find a record of an action between the two, I remain uncertain in which Mr Elliott had served.*

La Flèche, HMS

A ship, Captain Yorke, due in from Bombay on her way home to England with dispatches (FW 1); she was originally a French flush-deck corvette (FW 2). Jack Aubrey, Stephen Maturin and some of HMS *Leopard*'s crew take passage in her (FW 1,2) but she soon accidentally takes fire and blows up, perhaps as a result of her naturalist-surgeon McLean's carelessness in smoking near the alcohol used to preserve his specimens (FW 2). Jack's immediate companions, and large numbers — perhaps all — of the 'Flitches' (as her crew are known), escape in the boats, though it appears that only the men in Jack's cutter are ever rescued (FW 2,6).

> *None of the three La Flèches that served in the Royal Navy was a Post Captain's command and none were lost by fire. However, the description of the incident is somewhat similar to the near-loss of HMS *Caesar in 1817. She was en route from Java to England, carrying amongst others the surviving crew of Captain Murray Maxwell's HMS Alceste, which had recently been wrecked in the South China Sea (see *Diane, HMS). She took fire in mid-ocean when 'some booby' spilled onto a naked flame spirits being used to preserve a dead parrot; fortunately, the ship was spared (see: M'Leod, John Voyage of His Majesty's Ship Alceste etc.; London: John Murray, 2nd ed. 1818). In terms of La Flèche's total loss, there are also similarities to the fate that befell Governor *Raffles on his final journey back to England aboard the merchantman Fame in 1824.*

Fleischhacker

The Dutch author of *Elegant Diversions*, a work translated by Mr Scriven {PC 6).

> *Although Fleischhacker is a perfectly respectable Dutch name, the reference is possibly to Jan Michael Fleischman (1701–1768), a popular essayist and miscellany writer. However, no Elegant Diversions survives under his name.*

Fleming

A Midshipman in HMS *Diane* whose father is a well-known naturalist and Fellow of the Royal Society (TGS 5,6). He follows Aubrey into HMS *Nutmeg of Consolation* (NC 4+).

> *Mr Fleming senior is perhaps John Fleming (d.1815), a Scottish physician, botanist and FRS who in 1810 published an important* Catalogue of Indian Medicinal Plants.

Flitch

The nick-name for a member of the crew of HMS *La Flèche* (FW 2).

Flogging Parson
see **Marsden**

Flood

HMS *Surprise*'s cook, whose brother had been eaten in the Solomon Islands some years before (NC 8).

Floode, Sir Oliver

An Ulster landowner, MP for Antrim, who marries Frances Williams. His younger, penniless cousin — un-named — marries her sister, Cecilia (HMS 7).

> *N.B., some years later, Lady Frances (as she would be called) is said to be married to another Irishman, Mr Clotworthy, by whom she bears a child (RM 6). Later still, she is a somewhat impoverished widow (YA 1).*

Flora

The name given by Stephen Maturin to Jack Aubrey when the latter is disguised as a bear in order to escape from France (PC 4).

Flora, HMS

A 32-gun ship recently wrecked off the Dutch coast (TMC 1)

> *HMS Flora, 36-gun, was launched in 1780 and, under her Captain Loftus Otway Bland (d.1810), wrecked off the Dutch coast in early 1808. In Roman myth Flora (Chloris in Greek) was the goddess of the spring season and of flowers.*

Florey

A Port Mahon surgeon of Maturin's acquaintance (M&C 2+).

Florio's

A skittle alley in Port Mahon (IM 7).

Floris, Mr

The surgeon of HMS *Lively* (PC 12+).

Flower, Mrs

Sophie Aubrey's new housekeeper (YA 10).

Flower of Courtesy

A title of the Sultan of Pulo Prabang (TGS 6), later used by Jack Aubrey as a facetious reference to one of the 'Old Buggers' (TGS 9).

Fly

An 'HM Hired Vessel' referred to by Aubrey (NC 10).

> *Fly was the name of many small hired or full-service cutters and sloops during the period. However, no hired Fly is recorded after 1805.*

Flying Childers

A famously swift racehorse (M&C 11; DI 1; YA 3).

> *Flying Childers (1715–1741), an Arabian stallion and one of the origins of the English thoroughbred blood-line, was bred by a Mr Leonard Childers of Yorkshire and was a son of the *Darley Arabian (by the mare Betty Leedes). Often referred to as the first truly great racehorse, 'Childers' was also known as 'Old Careless' for his ease in out-pacing rivals.*

Flying Childers or Childers

1: a very fast ship (HMS 9).

> *At the time of Aubrey's reference, an HMS* Childers, *14-gun brig-sloop, was in service, having been launched in 1778; she was broken up in 1811. She—and no doubt the smuggling craft at 2 below—was named for the racehorse mentioned in the preceding entry.*

2: a Shelmerston smuggling craft used by Mould and Vaggers when they are not serving under Aubrey (COM 5).

Foley, John

The ship's fiddler in *Surprise* (TGS 3).

Forbes, Lady

Diana Villiers' companion and 'chaperone' in Bombay and Calcutta. They ladies were known to each other during Diana's previous time in India (HMS 7,10).

Forder

The Second Lieutenant of HMS *Africaine*, wounded in action. With Tullidge and Parker he had earlier asked Surgeon Cotton whether Captain Corbett might be relieved of command on the grounds of insanity (TMC 9).

> *Robert Forder (d.1864) had been commissioned Lieutenant in 1804. After the severe battering his HMS* Africaine *received, he was given command of the hired cutter* Egremont *and took part in the eventual fall of Mauritius. Forder was promoted Commander in 1821.*

Formidable

An 80-gun French ship fought by the tiny HMS *Sophie*. The flag-ship of Rear Admiral Linois, her Captain Lalonde is later killed in action (M&C 11,12; PC 4).

> Formidable, *80-gun, was launched in 1795, having been known as* Figuières *whilst on the stocks. She was* *Linois' *flagship in the squadron that took* *Cochrane's *HMS* *Speedy *in June 1801 and later fought in the both fleet actions against* *Saumarez, **Lalonde being killed in the first. In 1805* Formidable *fought at Trafalgar as the flagship of Admiral* *Dumanoir le Pelley, *being captured soon after the battle by Sir Richard* *Strachan's *squadron. Taken into the Royal Navy as HMS* Brave *(sometimes seen as* Braave*), she became a prison ship in 1808 and a powder hulk in 1814, before being sold in 1816 for break-up.*

Formidable, HMS

A ship in which Jack Aubrey had once been a Master's Mate (FSW 4).

> *HMS* Formidable, *90-gun, was launched in 1777 and in 1782 was* *Rodney's *flag-ship at the Battle of the Saintes. Reduced to a 74-gun in 1813, she was then broken up in the same year.*

Forshaw

A Midshipman in HMS *Leopard* (DI 5+; FW 1) who takes passage with Jack Aubrey in HMS *La Flèche* (FW 2). To his great embarrassment, his mother has written to Jack with instructions for his personal hygiene (FW 2). When the ship is accidentally destroyed by fire, Forshaw escapes with Jack in a cutter and is picked up by HMS *Java*: however, he is then killed in her action against USS *Constitution* (FW 3).

Forster

Admiral Bertie's Flag Lieutenant (TMC 3).

Forte, La

A 44-gun frigate taken by HMS *Sybille* when Charles Yorke was her Third Lieutenant (FW 4).

> La Forte, *a 44-gun, was launched in 1794 and captured by the 40-gun HMS* *Sybille *in early 1799 after a fierce fight in the Bay of Bengal. Her Captain Beaulieu was killed in the action, whilst* *Sybille's *Captain Edward Cook died a few months later of wounds received in the exchange.* La Forte *was bought into the Royal Navy under her French name but in early 1801 was wrecked entering Jeddah harbour.*

Fortesque

1: the Master of *Wasp*, an armed schooner of the East India Company attached to Aubrey's squadron (TMC 4).

> Wasp, *under her Master Mr Watkins, had been attached to Commodore Josias Rowley's squadron by the HEIC for this mission.*

2: a Royal Navy Captain and his wife, with whom Diana Villiers stays on her return from America (SM 4,5).

Fortitude, HMS

A former command of the retired Admiral Hartley, in which Jack Aubrey had served as a Midshipman (TH 2). She was once ordered by Lord Hood to make an attack on the heavily fortified Mortella tower on Corsica (SM 6).

> *HMS* Fortitude, *74-gun, was launched in 1780, turned into a prison ship in 1795 and reduced to a powder hulk in 1802 before being broken up in 1820. The attack on the Corsican fortress occurred in early 1794, with* Fortitude *under Captain William Young (d.1821 in the rank of full Admiral). She and several consorts were beaten off by fire from the high tower,* Fortitude *being set ablaze and suffering over 60 casualties. The fort itself was soon taken by a land assault, but only after a fierce battle.*

Foster

A naturalist referred to by Maturin (DI 10).

> *The reference may be to Johann Reinhold Forster (sic; 1729–1798) a German naturalist who made explorations in Asiatic Russia before moving to England and, in 1772, joining* *Cook's *second voyage to the South Seas. Having returned to Germany in 1780, he became Professor of Natural History at the University of Halle. In 1778 his son, who had accompanied his father on Cook's voyage, published their* Observations Made on a Voyage Round the World on Physical Geography, Natural History and Ethic Philosophy.

Foster, William

A Lieutenant, now in command of a privateer, who

had once been shipmates with Jack Aubrey in HMS *Euryalus* (RM 2).

Fouché

As the Peace of Amiens collapses, Fouché's men are said to be everywhere in France searching for foreign nationals (PC 4). Years later he is still very influential, although nominally out of office (SM 10).

Joseph Fouché (1759–1820), Duc d'Otrante, was a French politician, statesman and organiser of internal security under both the Revolutionary, Imperial and restored *Bourbon governments. Very early in his career he developed a reputation for both intrigue in pursuit of his own interests and for great efficiency; as a Jacobin deputy he voted for the execution of King *Louis XVI. In 1799 he attached himself to General *Buonaparte's rising star, becoming his Chief of Police and in this office he ruthlessly eliminated both revolutionary and royalist opposition to Napoleon's regime, being rewarded in 1806 with the Dukedom of Otranto in Italy. From 1807 onwards, Fouché began to engage in intrigues with Britain and the Bourbon exiles and in 1810, when these plots became known, he was replaced by the Emperor. Yet his comprehensive, personal intelligence network throughout France made him far too powerful a man to attack directly and he was now sent on various overseas missions, all the while keeping his links with both the Emperor and King *Louis XVIII. Reappointed Minister of Police by Buonaparte during the 'Hundred Days' of 1815, he then managed the trick of being confirmed in this post by the returning King. This was too much for many of the returning exiles to bear, and in 1816 he was dismissed as having been a regicide. Fouché then lived in lavish retirement in Italy until his death.

Foudroyant, HMS

Admiral Lord Keith's flagship (M&C 1+), in which Jack Aubrey had once been Second Lieutenant (PC 8).

HMS Foudroyant, 80-gun, was launched in 1798 and was one of several ships (including HMS *Audacious) of the Mediterranean fleet in which *Keith hoisted his flag from time to time after the accidental loss of HMS *Queen Charlotte in 1800. From 1799 to early 1800 she had been *Nelson's flagship, under her then Captain Edward *Berry, and had participated in the capture of *Généreux in February 1800; it is often supposed that Horatia, the daughter of Nelson and Emma *Hamilton, was conceived aboard her a little later. In 1820 Foudroyant became a guard ship and in 1862 a training ship before being was sold in 1892 and wrecked off Blackpool in 1897. The name is taken from that of the 88-gun Foudroyant (French for 'Devastator') captured by the Royal Navy in 1758 and broken up in 1787.

'Foulweather Jack'
see **Byron, John**

Fowler, Captain

An officer met at Thacker's Coffee House by Aubrey and Maturin (PC 3).

Fox

1: an English politician, known for both his wit and his ugliness (HMS 7; LM 7; WDS 4).

Charles James Fox (1749–1806), the famous radical politician, served as a Tory Lord of the Admiralty from 1772 to 1774 (in a very brief dalliance with that party), and as Whig Foreign Secretary from 1782 to 1783 and again in 1806. Fox was a towering intellectual figure in English politics of his time, a quite brilliant orator, debater and writer. His radical sympathies and constant opposition to the long wars—*Buonaparte was a great admirer, and the two met in Paris in 1802—put him at odds with both *Pitt and King *George III. Indeed, shortly before his death in 1806, he had been involved in unsuccessful negotiations for a peace treaty with France. Fox was equally famous as a gambler, a duellist and as an uncouth, dirty, raucous social companion.

2: an American diplomat and intelligence official (FW 1).

3: the surgeon of HMS *Java* (FW 3; SM 11). He is once incorrectly referred to as HMS *Shannon*'s surgeon (SM 1).

Fox, Edward

The head of the British mission to Pulo Prabang, at first greatly admired by Sir Joseph Blaine and Stephen Maturin for his many abilities as a lawyer and scholar (TGS 3+). However, Jack Aubrey, Stephen and the whole ship's company of HMS *Diane* soon come to dislike his forceful personality and sense of his own superiority (TGS 4,5+). With the aid of Stephen's intelligence information, he successfully concludes a treaty with the Sultan, having the traitors Wray and Ledward disgraced and assassinated in the process (TGS 6–8). Following his triumph he becomes both impossibly self-important and excessively eager to return to England to reap his rewards (TGS 8–10). When *Diane* is wrecked on a reef, he and his party set off to Java in a small boat and are presumed lost in the typhoon that then sweeps the area (TGS 10; *also* NC 1–3; C/T 1; COM 2).

Fox
see **Intrepid Fox**

Fox, HMS

1: a ship in which Jack Aubrey and Peter Heywood had once served together (DI 1) and which, with HMS *Daedalus*, had once unsuccessfully bombarded the French-held fort of Kosseir on the Red Sea coast (TH 7).

HMS Fox, 32-gun, was launched in 1780 and broken up in 1816. The rather unsuccessful bombardment of Kosseir took place in August 1799, with Fox under Commander, and acting Captain, Henry Stuart (d.1840 in the rank of Rear Admiral). Peter *Heywood served as a Lieutenant on her under Captain Sir Pulteney Malcolm (d.1838 in the rank of full Admiral) from January 1796 to June 1798.

2: a cutter on the Brest blockade (YA 5).

Frances

1: the childhood friend of Clarissa Oakes, and the niece of Edward, their sexually abusive 'guardian' (C/T 6).

2: *see* **Williams, Frances**

Francesc, Cosí

A Spanish relative of Stephen Maturin (NC 5).

Franchise, HMS

A 36-gun frigate into which Heneage Dundas has recently been made Post (PC 6,7,10).

> HMS Franchise, *36-gun, was an ex-French frigate of the same name, launched in 1798 and captured in 1803; she was broken up in 1815. 'Franchise' means 'Charter of Freedom.'*

Franchon, Madam

The owner of the hotel in Boston where Diana Villiers and Harry Johnson keep an apartment (FW 5–7).

Francis

1: a popular seaman in HMS *Boadicea*, injured in a fall (TMC 3).

2: a Master's Mate in HMS *Leopard* (LM 8).

Francis, Sir

see **Ives, Admiral Sir Francis**

François

The Master of the privateer *Marie-Paule* (COM 5).

Frankie

see **Williams, Frances**

Franklin

1: a seaman in HMS *Surprise* (HMS 5).

2: a flag officer mentioned by Jack Aubrey as a possible replacement for the very ill Admiral Sir John Thornton (IM 4).

3: Jack Aubrey's cook in HMS *Surprise* (HD 4,5).

Franklin, Benjamin

The American diplomat (FW 4) and scientist, who had once advocated a form of jet propulsion for ships (FW 8).

> Benjamin Franklin (1706–1790) was one of the most distinguished American statesmen and thinkers of his age, playing a leading role in the foundation of his country both by his keen intellect and great persuasiveness as practical negotiator. A leading citizen of Pennsylvania—though born in Massachusetts—he represented the colony's Assembly to Britain from 1757 to 1762 and again from 1764 to 1775, using every effort to prevent a breach between the old and new. However, when he came to see separation as inevitable, he returned home to devote his energies to forming not only a new nation but a new idea of nation, enshrined in his contributions to the Declaration of Independence. From 1776 to 1785 he was the brilliantly successful American representative to Paris, where he became—somewhat to his own amusement—the very height of 'New World' fashion. In 1778 Franklin made a treaty with France that secured both financial and military aid for the Revolutionary War and, victorious, in 1782–1783 negotiated the settlement with Britain that established the USA as a sovereign nation. If all this was not enough, Franklin was also a very successful businessman (in the printing trade), an experimental scientist of international reputation and a practical social reformer of note. From about 1746 onwards Franklin and friends had taken an interest in electricity and in 1752 his earlier proof that lightning was a form of electrical charge led to his election as a Fellow of the Royal Society; his experimental design and clarity of presentation of results and proofs were greatly admired by the likes of *Buffon and *Davy. On his way back to America in 1785, Franklin sketched out a means of propelling a ship by a steam-piston driven jet of seawater, publishing the idea in the following year. His plans and thoughts were influential on the experimental steam-driven boats of his protégé, the engineer James Rumsey (1743–1792), although the eccentric inventor John Fitch (1743–1798) later claimed that Franklin had stolen crucial elements of the idea from him.

Franklin

1: a French ship at the Battle of the Nile that had been engaged by Lieutenant Jack Aubrey's HMS *Leander* (M&C 12).

Franklin *was launched in 1797 and captured by *Nelson at the Nile in the following year. Re-named HMS *Canopus she was sent for harbour service in 1863 and sold to be broken up in 1887.*

2: a 22-gun privateer commanded, and probably owned by Jean Dutourd, and crewed by prospective settlers and a few seamen. Sailing under American colours, but as a private and somewhat anomalous ship of war, she is pursued and taken by Jack Aubrey's *Surprise* (C/T 5–9; WDS 1,2), with Tom Pullings then being made her commander (WDS 2–5). Later, whilst Tom runs Stephen Maturin into Peru in *Surprise*, Jack briefly takes command of the ship (WDS 6,7), before later selling her as a valuable prize (WDS 10; also COM 2).

Both 1 *and* 2 *are named for Benjamin *Franklin.*

Fraser, Colonel

One of Colonel Keating's subordinate officers (TMC 6–8).

> CLOWES *gives a Lieutenant-Colonel Frazier (sic) as one of Keating's officers, but I have been unable to locate any details of his career. Keating's aide-de-camp on the expedition was* Captain James Stewart Fraser (1783–1869), *a Scottish soldier and, later, colonial administrator from a distinguished military family. He served his whole career from 1800 onwards in and around India, becoming a Lieutenant Colonel in 1824, a Major General in 1838 and a full General in 1862.*

Fred

A dog resident at Mr Lowndes' house in Dover (PC 10).

Frederick

A siamang gibbon resident in Raffles' gardens (TGS 6).

Frédérick

see **Cuvier, Georges** and **Frédérick**

French Emperor

see **Buonaparte** or **Bonaparte, Napoleon**

Frere, Sir James

The Captain of the Fleet in Lord Barmouth's HMS *Implacable* (HD 9).

Frescobaldi

A composer referred to by Maturin (RM 6).

> *Girolamo Frescobaldi (1583–1643) was an Italian composer and famous virtuoso keyboard player who, from 1608 to 1628 and again after 1633, held the post of organist of St Peter's in Rome. He wrote many highly influential studies for both organ and harpsichord.*

Friend

A form of address used by Quakers to fellow members (RM 4).

> *The Quaker Society was founded in England by George Fox (1624–1691) as the 'Religious Society of Friends.'*

Frig

An Old English deity referred to in the works of Leland (WDS 4).

Frig (also Frigga, Freyia), the wife of Odin, was the 'Mother of the Gods' in old Norse legends.

Frolic, HMS

A ship commanded by Captain Hallows (PC 3), later said to have been taken by USS *Wasp*, 18-gun (FW 3).

> *The first HMS* Frolic, *18-gun brig-sloop, was not launched until 1806, some years after PC 3. In October 1812, under her Commander Thomas Whinyates (d.1857 in the rank of retired Rear Admiral), she was taken in a very bloody action by the USS *Wasp of Captain Jacob Jones (1770–1850). In the fight every British officer was wounded or killed but, despite their valour in defence of the already storm-damaged ship, it was superior American gunnery in an awkward sea that won the battle. However, just a few hours later Captain John Poo *Beresford's 74-gun HMS* Poitiers *arrived on the scene and immediately took the two battered ships.* Frolic *was not fit for further service and was broken up in 1813.*

Fugger

A great banking family referred to by Maturin as active in the time of Charles V (TGS 1,3).

> *The German Fugger family dominated European commerce and banking in the 15th and 16th centuries, establishing branches and dynasties all over the continent. Jakob Fugger — 'Jakob the Rich' (1459–1525) — financed the election in 1519 of *Charles V as Holy Roman Emperor. The family gradually gave up its commercial interests from about 1540 onwards, but remained immensely rich aristocrats for some centuries thereafter.*

--- G ---

G., Mr

1: a bookseller who had let down Mr Scriven (PC 6).
2: *see* **Grant, Mr**

G., Mrs

The wife of Mr Goodridge (PC 10).

Gabriel, the Archangel

The angel referred to as an archetype of power (PC 7; TMC 3; SM 1).

> *An 'Archangel' is a member of the most senior group of *God's attendants. In religious traditions based on the Old Testament, Gabriel is often encountered as the principle divine messenger to mortals.*

Galen

An ancient medical authority (HMS 5; FW 5).

> *Galen (in Greek, Klaudios Galenos; 129–216 AD) was a Greek medical practitioner and philosopher who travelled widely in his youth before making his reputation in Rome. Here he became doctor to the official heir of the Emperor Marcus *Aurelius and the pre-eminent 'society' physician of his day. Much of his prodigious written output is lost to us, but versions of some of his works were the standard texts on illness and health in Europe and the Arab world until at least the 15th century, for at least three reasons: a) their rigorous medical logic; b) their elaborate — even fanciful — theoretical constructs; and c) the concentrated attacks Galen makes in them on rival systems.*

Galignani, Signor

An Italian violinist (PC 3).

> *This reference may perhaps be a conflation of two artistic names: the Gagliano family were a well-known Neapolitan family of violin-makers in the 17th and 18th centuries; the Galignani family were English-Italian publishers and booksellers in 18th and 19th century Paris.*

Gall

A phrenologist referred to by Maturin (COM 4).

> *Franz Josef Gall (1758–1828) was a German physician who, from about 1796 onwards, developed the 'holistic' medical theory — phrenology — that personality was determined by the relative sizes of parts of the brain. It could therefore be diagnosed by feeling their outward, physical manifestation, the bumps on the surface of the skull. Gall*

lived in Paris from 1807 onwards and published his major treatise on the subject between 1810 and 1819.

Gambier

An extremely religious British Admiral (M&C 2; HMS 5), who had been embroiled in controversy over his actions in the Battle of the Basque Roads (TMC 6). Jack Aubrey had served in his Baltic fleet (HD 5).

James, Lord Gambier (1756–1833) was commissioned Lieutenant in 1777; a well-connected man, he was promoted Commander and made Post just a year later, in 1778. A Rear Admiral of 1795, Vice Admiral of 1799, he was promoted full Admiral in 1805. Gambier also served as an Admiralty Commissioner in 1795–1801, 1804–1806 and 1807–1808, and was Governor General of Newfoundland from 1802 to 1804; in 1807 he was raised to the peerage. James Gambier was as much Admiralty politician as active warrior and only ever served afloat for six years before rising to flag rank. Although personally brave and active, he was famously court-martialed in 1809 for having failed, as Commander-in-Chief of the Channel, to press home the attack in the previous year on the French lying in the Basque Roads, having ordered his inshore commander, Thomas *Cochrane, to withdraw his squadron of gun-boats, apparently on the grounds that they were not really a 'gentlemanly' way of going about warfare. Cochrane complained about Gambier's conduct and threatened to raise the matter in Parliament; the Admiral in turn demanded a court-martial to vindicate his decisions and was honourably acquitted by a carefully selected, indulgent panel. Although after 1811 he never again held a sea-command, he rose by seniority to Admiral of the Fleet in 1830. As Jack *Aubrey indicates, Gambier was also well known — and often not especially well liked (see *Harvey # 5)— for his assertive, evangelical Christianity. In 1794 at *Howe's Battle of the Glorious First of June, Gambier's HMS Defence was first to cut the French line and was soon reduced to a battered hulk. As HMS *Invincible passed close by, her Captain *Pakenham called across, "I see you've been knocked about a good deal: never mind, Jimmy, whom the Lord loveth he chasteneth!" (see the similar exchange between Jack and Heneage *Dundas in WDS 10). The reference by Jack *Aubrey to Gambier's command in the Baltic looks like a slip for the equally religious Admiral *Saumarez.

Game Chicken
see **Pearce, Henry**

Game Chicken
A cannon in HMS *Diane* (TGS 5).

The cannon is named for the prize-fighter Henry *Pearce.

Gammon
Referred to by Maturin as a name associated with Shakespeare and Bacon (FSW 5: 197).

Gammon is of course both the bottom cut of a flitch of bacon — and other pork joints too — and slang for 'rubbish' or 'nonsense.'

Gamo
The ship famously captured by Thomas Cochrane in 1801 (FSW author's note).

Commander Thomas *Cochrane captured the Spanish 32-gun xebec frigate El Gamo with his 14-gun brig HMS *Speedy on May 6th 1801, just off Barcelona. The action forms the basis for Jack *Aubrey's capture (in M&C) of *Cacafuego with his little HMS *Sophie, O'Brian closely following Cocrhane's own account of the fight. Gamo was commanded by Don Francisco de Torres, who was killed during the action; once captured she was sent into Port Mahon under the command of Cochrane's younger brother, Midshipman Archibald Cochrane (d.1829 as a Post Captain of 1806), and later sold.

Ganges
An East Indiaman in Muffit's China Fleet, protected by HMS *Surprise* from Admiral Linois' French squadron (HMS 9).

Ganges, 1200 tons, made 4 round trips from India to England between 1796 and 1804; she was named for the great Indian river. The action is based on the defence of a Honourable East India Company merchant fleet against *Linois' attack in February 1804. However, no Royal Navy ship was present during the fight, the squadron being organised by the senior Master, Nathaniel Dance of *Earl Camden. On this occasion William Moffat (sic; see **Moffit, William***) was Ganges' Master.*

Ganymede
Jupiter's cup-bearer, to whom Maturin compares Abdul (TGS 6).

In classical myth Ganymede, the son of Tros, was a Trojan prince selected by *Zeus/*Jupiter to be his attendant (thus replacing the girl *Hebe) on account of his great beauty. In Greek and Latin literature Ganymede very often personifies homosexual love, with the Latin version of his name, Catamitus, giving the modern 'catamite.'

Ganymede, HMS
A corvette at Madeira (YA 10) and in Jack Aubrey's Mediterranean squadron under her Captain Cartwright (HD 1,2). She is later detached to the Eastern Mediterranean (HD 4).

HMS Ganymede, 26-gun post-ship, was the ex-French *Hébé, launched in 1808 and captured by the Royal Navy in the following year. Having been reduced to a convict ship in 1819, she was wrecked and broken up in 1838. She was named for *Jupiter's attendant, *Ganymede.

Garciá
One of the Chileans who interviews Jack Aubrey for a high position in their new navy (YA 10).

The character to some degree echoes Juan Garciá del Rio (1794–1856), a Peruvian (sic) diplomat and politician active in the independence movement in the 1820s and, as Foreign Minister, one of his country's chief negotiators for European financial and military support. Curiously GRAHAM & HUMPHREYS note that Garciá was an opponent of any attempt to secure *Cochrane's services for the Peruvian Navy after his recent service in Chile.

Garcio, don
see **Ignatio, don**

Gardner
William Babbington's uncle, newly ennobled as Lord Meyrick (LM 6,7).

Garland
A seaman in HMS *Surprise* who has scurvy (HMS 5).

Garrick
The famous actor referred to by James Dillon (M&C 7).

> *David Garrick (1717–1779), the friend and protégé of Doctor *Johnson and the Duke of *Devonshire, was a noted author and letter-writer as well as being part-owner of the Drury Lane Theatre and the leading stage performer of his age. Garrick is buried alongside *Shakespeare in Westminster Abbey, London.*

Garron, Lord
A Lieutenant in Jack Aubrey's HMS *Lively* (HMS 2), later twice met (by now as Lord Narborough, his father having recently died) as the Commander of the brig HMS *Staunch* (TMC 7) and the Captain of HMS *Boyne* (IM 5). His son, William Blakeney, serves as a Midshipman in Jack's HMS *Surprise* (FSW 3).

> *N.B., in TMC 7 Garron/Narborough is mistaken recalled by Jack *Aubrey and Stephen *Maturin as having been Third Lieutenant of HMS *Surprise rather than HMS *Lively. The Narborough title recalls a famous naval family of a past age. Rear Admiral Sir John Narborough (1640–1688) enjoyed great successes from 1674 to 1679 against Algerine pirates and occupied a number of important administrative posts ashore. Two of his sons entered the Navy but both were drowned in the 1707 loss of HMS* Association, *the flag-ship of Sir John's relative and protégé, Admiral Sir Cloudisley Shovell.*

Garter, the
see **Habachtsthal, Duke of**

Gauden
A divinity author referred to by Martin (LM 3).

> *Dr John Gauden (1605–1662), sometime Bishop of Worcester, is widely believed to have been the true author of* The Royal Image *(or 'Eikon Basilike' in Greek), a book of meditations supposedly written by King Charles I shortly before his execution in 1649.*

Gay-Lussac
A prominent French scientist at Maturin's Paris lecture (SM 5,10).

> *Joseph-Louis Gay-Lussac (1778–1850), the distinguished French chemist and naturalist, made in 1804 the first ever balloon ascent—to 13,000 feet—for scientific purposes, studying the composition and temperature of the atmosphere. Later the same year he ascended to over 23,000 feet, a record height for the next 50 years. Gay-Lussac made many fundamental contributions to the physical sci-ences, especially in the fields of the chemistry of gases and meteorology, and was also a noted practical, chemical engineer in respect of industrial processes.*

Gayongos, Pascal de
A Catalan merchant living in Peru who conspires with Maturin against the Spanish and French (WDS 7+).

Geary, Francis
A medical man of Maturin's acquaintance, encountered by him in Peru. He is currently the surgeon of *Three Graces*, a Liverpool merchantman (WDS 6).

Geary, Frank
The Captain of HMS *Phoebe* (DI 4) and later, perhaps, of HMS *Royal Oak* (COM 10).

> *The name may perhaps be inspired by that of Admiral Sir Francis Geary (1709–1796), famous amongst other things for his capture in 1745–1746 of a series of French ships all carrying immense sums of money.*

Gelijkheid
A Dutch-built 20-gun ship, offered by Governor Raffles to Jack Aubrey to replace the lost HMS *Diane*. Having been temporarily sunk to 'clear an infection,' she is now raised for further service, with Jack soon renaming her HMS *Nutmeg of Consolation* (NC 3,5).

> *A 64-gun HMS* Gelykheid, *64-gun, was captured from the Dutch at the Battle of Camperdown in 1797; taken into service, she became a prison ship in 1799 and was sold in 1814.*

General, the
see **Aubrey, General**

General Washington
An American whaler that had called at Desolation Island under her Master, William Hyde (DI 10).
see **Washington, President** *for name derivation.*

Généreux, HMS
At the opening of *Master and Commander, Généreux* is moored with the British Fleet in Port Mahon (M&C 1+). According to Stephen Maturin's later account, she had been captured by HMS *Foudroyant* and brought in as a prize by that ships' then Second Lieutenant, Jack Aubrey (PC 8). Yet Jack himself says only that *Généreux* had taken HMS *Leander*— in which he had served at the Battle of the Nile — and that a combination of his wound in the action and his being the only surviving Lieutenant are the occasion for his promotion to Commander (M&C 2).

> *The 74-gun* Généreux, *launched in 1785, was one of only four French ships to escape from *Nelson's great victory at the Battle of the Nile of August 1798. A few days later she engaged and took the smaller, 50-gun HMS *Leander, a*

*ship that Nelson had sent from Egypt with his victory dispatch. Généreux was finally captured by Nelson's squadron off Sicily in February 1800 and brought in to Minorca with Lieutenant Thomas *Cochrane as prize-master. Having become a prison ship in 1805, she was broken up in 1816. As regards in which of HMSS Leander or *Foudroyant Jack Aubrey served, it is of course amply possible that Stephen *Maturin's memory is at fault or even that he never really understood Jack's account of the affair at all. Alternatively, Jack may have been taken prisoner in the Généreux—Leander action, soon been released/exchanged and appointed to HMS Foudroyant, and then later re-encountered Généreux. Certainly the officers of Leander were badly treated by their French captors, just as alluded to by Jack in M&C 12. Amongst the Englishmen was Captain Edward *Berry, travelling as a passenger; he then commanded Foudroyant when she eventually took Généreux.*

'Gentlemen's Relish'

A young actress and singer who sneaks onto HMS *Ariel* in the hope of seducing the dashing Captain Jagiello (SM 5).

'Patum Peperium, the Gentlemen's Relish,' is a well-known savoury spread, favoured at the breakfast table by many generations of Englishmen; it consists primarily of pounded anchovies, butter and spices. Although the commercial product (still available today) itself was not invented, by John Osborn, until 1828, there is no reason to suppose that the term was not in common, earlier use for delights of the table and elsewhere.

Geoghegan

1: an Irish Midshipman in HMS *Bellona*, a splendid oboe player (YA 4) and a very distant relation of Stephen Maturin via the Fitzgerald connection (YA 5). Immediately after a musical session with Stephen and Jack Aubrey, Geoghegan races a friend up the rigging, falls and is killed (YA 5).
2: an Irish speaking seaman in HMS *Surprise* (HD 8,9).

Geoghegan, Reverend Mr

A parson in Ireland, known to Jack Aubrey and Stephen Maturin, whose Midshipman son is killed on HMS *Bellona* in an accidental fall (YA 5,6).

Geordie

Lord Keith's servant in HMS *Royal Sovereign* (HD 1).

George

1: a Marine sentry in HMS *Sophie* (M&C 3).
2: the name by which some of HMS *Sophie*'s crew refer, on one occasion, to Barret Bonden (M&C 9).
3: a British sailor, a prisoner of the French, encountered by Aubrey and Maturin on their escape route from France to Spain (PC 4).
4: a seaman in HMS *Polychrest* (PC 11).

5: a cousin of Barret Bonden who had once sailed in HMS *Bombay* (TMC 9).
6: a seaman in HMS *Surprise* related to Grainger (WDS 3,5).
7: a Catholic priest, Maturin's confessor (COM 4).
8: *see* **Aubrey, George**

George, HMS

A ship in which Ellis' father had once served under Captain the Honourable Byron (COM 1).

*The Royal Navy had many HMS Georges, without exception small gunboats and the like. Perhaps the reference is to one of the several HMS *Royal Georges, two of which were 100-gun first-rates, the first in service from 1756 to 1782 and the second from 1788 to 1822.*

George III, King

The King of England (referred to and toasted *passim*).

*George III (George William Frederick, 1738–1820) reigned as King of Great Britain and King of Ireland from 1760 to 1800; as King of the United Kingdom of Great Britain and Ireland from 1800 to 1820; as Elector of Hanover from 1760 to 1815; and as King of Hanover from 1815 to 1820. George III, the first of the German Hanoverian monarchs to be born in Britain and have English as his mother tongue, continued his grandfather, George II's, practice of close reliance on the Prime Minister's advice, seldom acting as any form of 'absolute King.' Consequently, his reign saw the consolidation of the British system of 'constitutional monarchy'; yet he was so stubbornly opposed to reform of political and economic relations with the American colonies that he must share direct responsibility for their consequent loss to the Crown with his Prime Minister of the time, Lord North (see also *Franklin). George III also suffered from repeated bouts of mental disability (see *Wallis # 3) from the early 1780s (possibly the result of the excruciating and debilitating physical illness, porphyria) and these too tended to place even more power into the hands both of his ministers (especially William *Pitt the Younger) and the elected parliamentarians. The King's permanent insanity after 1811 resulted in his eldest son, the Prince of Wales, assuming the title and somewhat limited powers of Prince *Regent until his own succession to the throne, as George IV, in 1820.*

George-a-Green

A reference to Maturin's shabby dress (COM 9).
George-a'-Green was the cheerful 'Pinder' (or cattle-pound keeper) of Wakefield who, in the Robin Hood legends, defeated all-comers at fighting with the quarterstaff.

Ghoul, The

A reference to Stephen Maturin, possibly made by Jack Aubrey (NC 6).

Gibbon

The great historian (TH 2; RM 7), one of whose works is owned by Captain Yorke of HMS *La Flèche* (FW 2).

Edward Gibbon (1737–1794), an eminent English scholar, historian, literary figure and sometime Member of Parliament, published his monumental History of the

Decline and Fall of the Roman Empire *in multiple volumes from 1776 to 1788. Although widely acclaimed for its intellectual acumen and fine prose style, the book was highly controversial in its own day for its most unfavourable treatment of early Christianity.*

Gibbs, Jr., Wolcott

The dedicatee of *The Far Side of the World*, who first encouraged O'Brian to write sea-tales (FSW dedication).

Wolcott 'Tony' Gibbs, Jr (b.1935), son of the famous New Yorker writer and critic of the same name, worked as a publisher's editor until 1968 and then became a full-time writer on yachts and boating. Since 1979 he has been the editor of Yachting magazine.

Gideon

A biblical character greatly admired by Arthur Mould for his polygamy. Mould's shipmates nickname their friend 'Gideon' for his own many, temporary lovers (COM 5).

In the Old Testament Book of Judges, Gideon, the saviour and de facto ruler of Israel (he had refused the title of King), is said to have had seventy-one sons by many wives and a single concubine.

Giffard

The surgeon of HMS *Stately* (COM 7).

Gijon, Archdeacon of

A Spanish Prelate (YA 1).

Gilkicker

A landmark at Portsmouth Harbour (COM 5).

Gilkicker (or Gillkicker) Point lies on the eastern or Gosport side of Portsmouth Harbour. From about 1650 to 1780 a white tower known as the Gilkicker Sea Mark stood on the point, serving as a navigational aid; in the latter year the dilapidated tower was pulled down and Fort Monkton built on its site. The origin of the name Gilkicker is obscure, but does not appear to stem from that of a person: a 1994 article in the Mariner's Mirror suggests it may perhaps have been sailors' slang for the sand-bank that the tower helped ships avoid.

Gill

1: HMS *Raisonable*'s carpenter (TMC 4).

2: the gloomy Master of Jack Aubrey's HMS *Worcester*. In former times he had been a Master's Mate in HMS *Hannibal* at the Battle of Algeçiras, being later treated by Stephen Maturin for an injury (IM 1–9). He next follows Jack to HMS *Surprise* (IM 10,11; TH 2+) before being promoted into HMS *Burford*, 74-gun (FSW 1,2).

Gill, Caleb

An officer in USS *Norfolk*, the nephew of her Captain Palmer (FSW 5,6,10). As prize-master of the captured British whaler *Acapulco*, he is taken prisoner on her re-capture by HMS *Surprise* (FSW 6).

Gillow

A helmsman in HMS *Surprise* (LM 1).

Giovanna

Laura Fielding's maidservant (TH 1,3,10).

Gittings

The official in charge of the Royal Navy postal office in Halifax (SM 1,2).

Giuseppe

A spy in the pay of the French in Malta whose cousin had been murdered by the British whilst held prisoner in HMS *Ocean* (TH 1).

*N.B., Although Guiseppe suspects Stephen *Maturin of the deed, it had in fact been carried out by Admiral *Thornton's confidential secretary, Mr *Allen.*

Glave

A seaman in *HMS Polychrest* on Lieutenant Parker's punishment list (PC 7).

Gloag

The faint-hearted Master of the East Indiaman *Abergavenny* (HMS 9).

*On the occasion that inspired this incident (see *Earl Camden), Earl of *Abergavenny was commanded by one John Wordsworth.*

Gloire

A Toulon privateer hired by Mateu to protect his smuggling craft, *Pardal* and *Xaloc* (M&C 7).

Gloucester, HMS

A ship, Captain Lewis, in Admiral Ives' Mediterranean fleet (FSW 1).

HMS Gloucester, 74-gun, was launched in 1812, cut down to a 50-gun in 1832, sent for harbour service in 1861 and sold in 1884. She was named for a cathedral city in western England.

Glover

The surgeon of HMS *Pomone* (YA 10; HD 1,2).

Gluck

A composer referred to by Stephen Maturin (M&C 2; RM 1) and played by Jack Aubrey (IM 6).

Christoph Willibald von Gluck (1714–1787), a German composer, is remembered chiefly for his many operas. These helped to establish a new form of 'music-drama,' making for the first time almost as many demands on the acting abilities of the cast as on their pure vocal skill. Gluck also wrote a number of symphonies and chamber works.

Gmelins, the

A family of naturalists (M&C 2), amongst whom is the ornithologist George John Gmelin (FSW 10).

*The Gmelins, a German family, were famed for prodigious accomplishments in the sciences over several generations. Best known to *Maturin and his circle may have been Johan Friedrich (1748–1804), a botanist, physician, chemist, and editor of *Linnaeus, and Johan Georg*

(1709–1755), a botanist, naturalist, geographer and explorer of Siberia (his Flora of Siberia of 1747 is probably the source of the note Maturin mentions). Other Gmelins with strong connections to natural history, medicine and exploration were Karl Christian (1762–1837), Philip Friedrich (1721–1768), and Samuel Theophilis (1744–1774).

Goadby

1: a builder employed by the Aubreys for work on Ashgrove Cottage (TMC 2,3).
2: Mrs Goadby, the keeper of the Marchelsea prison coffee-house (RM 9).

Goate

A friend of Aubrey, recently promoted Post Captain (TMC 1).

William Goate (d.1844) was commissioned Lieutenant in 1790, promoted Commander in 1799 and made Post in August 1809, a reward for having distinguishing himself (operating from his HMS *Mosquito) during a small-boat, cutting out expedition in the Baltic.

God

The Christian deity, used as a oath or exclamation *passim.*

God is the Supreme Being, the ruler and begetter of the universe in the Christian and other monotheistic religious traditions. Roman Catholics, *Maturin amongst them, often combine the name of God with that of *Mary or St *Patrick in their outbursts or greetings.

Godfrey's Cordial

A patent medicine (HMS 4).

Thomas Godfrey (d. shortly before 1722) produced a cordial of opium, sassafras and treacle in Hertfordshire. Its manufacture continued long after his death, the concoction remaining popular, addictive and sometimes deadly until the early years of the present century. The recipe was imported to America during the mid-18th century, with its local variant apparently becoming known as Dr Benjamin Godfrey's Cordial (see James Harvey Long The Medical Messiahs, *Princeton: Princeton University Press, 1967).*

Godoy

A military politician, referred to by Maturin as having betrayed Spain to France (PC 14) and also known as the 'Prince of Peace' (YA 5).

Manuel de Godoy (1767–1851), Principe de la Paz y Basano, was a royal favourite of humble origins who twice served as Prime Minister of Spain. Godoy obtained the title 'Prince of Peace' in 1795 for disentangling his country from the financially ruinous war against France. After a period of uneasy neutrality, in 1804 he was then either blackmailed or bribed into joining France in her war with England. In 1807 Godoy negotiated a secret, long-term pact with France which, although grossly to his own country's disadvantage, would have rewarded him personally with the Kingship of Algarve in Portugal: the true French intention was in fact to seize much of northern Spain (*Maturin's beloved Catalonia included), placing it under the direct control of Paris. When Godoy's duplicity became known, it led to the collapse of King *Charles IV's reign, his short-lived replacement by his brother King Ferdinand VII and the consequent occupation of Spain by *Buonaparte's armies (with Joseph *Buonaparte becoming King). Godoy, Charles and Ferdinand were all held prisoner by the French prisoners from 1808 until the first *Bourbon restoration but, on his release in 1814, the Prince of Peace never again visited his home country, wary of arrest or murder by his many enemies.

Godwin

An occasional, literary member of Louisa Wogan's circle in London (DI 6).

William Godwin (1756–1836) was the author of a number of novels, histories and political tracts arguing for man's perfectibility. A dissenting minister turned atheist and anarchist, Godwin believed that, as people were imbued with an overriding power of reason, no laws or institutions were necessary for their governance or social tranquillity. In 1797 he married the proto-feminist author Mary Wollstonecraft but she died in the same year, soon after giving birth to their daughter, also Mary, the future wife of the poet Shelley. Godwin's step-daughter by his second marriage, Claire Clairmont, bore the poet Lord *Byron a daughter, Allegra.

Godwin, Earl

Stephen Maturin refers to the legend of 'Earl Godwin's Bread' (M&C 2).

Godwin (d.1053), Earl of the West Saxons, was the father of that King Harold of England slain in 1066 at the Battle of Hastings. Legend has it that, during a banquet, Earl Godwin swore a sacred oath that he had not been responsible for the murder in 1036 of a rival, Aelfred the Aetheling. Having loudly invited God to strike him dead if he lied, he promptly choked to death on his next mouthful of bread. Although the historical record—such as it is—suggests that Godwin had simply died of a sudden stroke, trial by 'corsned'—the swallowing of a very large chunk of consecrated bread to determine guilt or innocence—was an established feature of Old English law and the legend has perhaps conflated sudden illness and bread-trial for dramatic effect. The Goodwin Sands off the coast of Kent (see SM 9) are also named for Earl Godwin.

Goffin, Captain 'Horseflesh'

The commander of the privateer *Triton*, a former Royal Navy Post Captain dismissed the service for keeping a false muster. In 1793 Jack Aubrey had known him as the Second Lieutenant of HMS *Bellerophon* (NC 6,7).

Golden Flower of the Day

A Batavian friend of one of the little girls encountered by Stephen Maturin on the HMS *Diane* shipwreck island (NC 2).

Goldilocks

The semi-affectionate name amongst his various crews for Jack Aubrey, at least whilst his hair remains a youthful yellow (M&C 8+; PC 7,9; HMS 8; TMC 9; NC 5).

Golding
A member of Black's club (YA 7).

Goldsmids
Cousins of Richard Canning and Mrs Canning's family by birth (HMS 1).

*In the 1770s the Goldsmid family had moved, as wealthy Jewish refugees, from Holland to England, where they rapidly rose to the centre of the London banking world. They also became tirelessly active, over several generations, in the cause of Jewish emancipation from restrictive legislation and social practices (finally achieved in 1859). Both of the brothers Benjamin (1753–1808) and Abraham (1756–1810) Goldsmid, heavily involved in the financing of British and Allied war-debt, made and lost colossal fortunes and each in turn committed suicide when spectacular collapse loomed. Abraham was also both financial backer and close friend of William *Pitt and Lord *Nelson.*

Goldsmith
A well-known poet (M&C 9; TH 4; NC 9), also referred to for his wandering life (TGS 3).

*Oliver Goldsmith (1730?–1774) was an Anglo-Irish writer of plays, poems and novels. In his youth he had studied both theology and medicine in Dublin and Holland but, from 1755 to 1756, then wandered penniless and unemployed around Europe before moving to London, initially in very great poverty. The brilliance of his pen soon won him influential friends — *Johnson, *Boswell and *Garrick amongst them — although financial success did not come until the 1773 production of his still-popular comedy,* She Stoops to Conquer. *Critical success also came from his novel* The Vicar of Wakefield *(1764) and his poem* The Deserted Village *(1770). Goldsmith was a very popular figure in London literary society, although regarded by some as impossibly vain, extravagant and dissolute.*

Goliath
A reference to enormous size (IM 1; FSW 7).

*In the Old Testament of the Bible, Goliath of Gath was the Philistine giant slain by the young *David, later King of all Israel.*

Goliath, HMS
A ship that makes several fleeting appearances in the series: Heneage Dundas takes passage in her to Deal (PC 10); her Second Lieutenant, Mr Smith, had once served in HMS *Lively* (HMS 7); she is flagship of Admiral Harvey and Jack Aubrey had served in her as a youngster (FW 7); and, finally, she is encountered at Gibraltar (IM 3).

HMS Goliath *was launched as a 74-gun in 1781. In 1797 she fought in the great victory at the Battle of Cape *St Vincent under Captain Sir Charles *Knowles and in 1798 she was in the van of *Nelson's fleet at the Battle of the Nile, her new Captain Thomas Foley (d.1833 as Admiral Sir Thomas Foley) leading four other ships between the head of the anchored French column and the shore batteries. The British ships were thus able to concentrate their fire on *Brueys leading ships from two sides at once whilst the French rear, straight downwind, was entirely unable to come up to their colleagues' assistance. The ship, named for *Goliath of Gath, was reduced to a 58-gun in 1812 and broken up in 1815*

Golovnin, Vasily Mikhailovitch
A Russian Lieutenant, commander of the Imperial Sloop *Diana*, who had arrived at the Cape not knowing war had been declared between England and Russia and been detained there, something of an embarrassment to Admiral Bertie (TMC 3). Later *Diana* is seen at sea, presumably having slipped quietly away from the Cape as Bertie had hoped (TMC 5). At some past time Golovnin had served as a volunteer in HMS *Seahorse* under Captain Corbett (TMC 3).

*Vasily Mikhaylovich Golovnin (1776–1831) entered the Russian Navy in 1788 and in 1803 was sent to England to study Royal Navy organisation and practice, serving with distinction under both *Nelson and *Collingwood as well as on *Corbett's frigate. On his return to Russia in 1806 he was commissioned by the *Czar to build the survey ship *Diana for the charting of the various coasts of the Russian empire, a task that he commenced in the following year. In 1808 he briefly visited England, obtaining there a permission to call at various Royal Navy ports on his continuing survey work but, by the time that he arrived at Cape Town in May of that year, war had broken out between the two countries. Admiral *Bertie, refusing to accept Golovnin's protection papers, detained him on parole for a little over a year whilst awaiting further instructions from London. When Golovnin eventually slipped Diana's anchors and escaped to sea no attempt at pursuit seems to have been made by the powerful British squadron at hand. Later in his voyages, Golovnin was held prisoner by the Japanese from 1811 to 1813 and his later book,* My Captivity in Japan *(1816), was widely translated, stimulating great interest in the still-mysterious land. From 1817 to 1819 Golovnin completed a circumnavigation for his government and then published well-regarded accounts of his voyages, including an account of his explorations of the Cape during his period of detention.*

Gomes, Father
A saintly priest on the Cape Verde Islands (DI 4).

Gomez
An intelligence agent, the object of Sir Joseph Blaine and Stephen Maturin's attentions in Minorca (HMS 1), whose reports are later nearly lost through Stephen's carelessness (DI 2).

Gomez, Father Inigo
A half-Inca, Catholic priest in Peru (WDS 7).

Gongora
A slave-ship referred to by Mr Whewell (COM 7).

Gonzalez
A Spanish government official referred to by Sir Joseph Blaine (YA 1).

González, don José
The Spanish commandant of Minorca (HD 1,3).

Gooch
The owner of a horse-and-cart in Boston (FW 8).

Good Samaritan
A biblical reference by Jack Aubrey (HD 3).

The Samaritans are a tribe of Jews (now a mere handful of families) who claim that their ancestors were not deported to Babylon by the conquering Assyrians in 722 BC. The Jews who later returned from exile refused assistance from the Samaritans (who may in fact have been settlers who arrived in Israel after the conquest), and long regarded them with outright suspicion. Hence, in the New Testament Gospel of Luke, the parable of the 'Good Samaritan,' the only man to aid an injured traveller, is given added point by his being motivated purely by brotherly love even though he stands as something of an outcast from 'proper' religious society.

Goodridge, Mr
The irascible Master of HMS *Polychrest* (PC 7–11), who had once been dismissed from the service for brawling with the chaplain of HMS *Bellerophon* over the significance of Halley's comet (PC 10). Ordinarily a prime seaman, who had once been a Midshipman and Master's Mate under Captain Cook (PC 10), his navigational error leads to *Polychrest*'s running aground in the attack on *Fanciulla*: yet he sails the now-captured *Fanciulla* safely out of the harbour (PC 11). Later in the series we find him in the naval section of the Marchelsea Prison in London, once again dismissed the service, now for biting an Admiral's finger (RM 7).

Goodwin
see **Godwin**

Goole, Captain and Mrs Harriet
The Captain of HMS *Irresistible* and his new wife. Once a Midshipman with Jack Aubrey in HMS *Resolution*, he had been party to the theft of the Captain's tripe, one cause of Jack's temporary demotion to the lower decks (RM 1).

Gordon
1: the fomenter of the 'Gordon Riots' (M&C 6; RM 2).

Lord George Gordon (1751–1793), a younger son of the 3rd Duke of Gordon, served briefly as a Royal Navy Lieutenant from 1772 to 1773 before resigning due to lack of sufficiently rapid progress. Having in 1774 then become an MP under family patronage, from 1779 onwards he established a reputation as a virulent agitator against any suggestion of Catholic emancipation in England. In 1780 a series of anti-Catholic riots broke out in London and in 1781 Gordon was tried for high treason for his supposed role in their organisation. However, as his exact involvement had been ambiguous, he was acquitted for lack of unequivocal evidence. In 1786 Gordon converted to Judaism and in 1788 — by now renowned for highly eccentric views and behaviour — was sentenced to a long prison term for libelling both British justice and the French monarchy.

He died in gaol, an enthusiastic and a half-mad supporter of the Revolution then occurring in Paris.
2: Fanny Wray's doctor (LM 2).

Gore, Captain John
see **Collins**

Gorges
A seaman in *Surprise*, probably sent as prize crew to Batavia in the recaptured whaler *Truelove* (C/T 9).

Gorges, William
A seaman of HMS *Diane* whose foot Maturin accidentally spears with a pick-axe (NC 1).

Gorgon
A reference to especially curly hair (HMS 9).

In classical myth, the Gorgon sisters, Stheno, Euryale and *Medusa, were beautiful sisters turned into monsters by the jealous goddess *Athena. They then bore writhing, entwined serpents instead of hair, their awful appearance supposedly turning to stone all who gazed on them.

Gorgonzola
An attempted classical reference by Jack Aubrey (YA 5).

Jack is presumably trying for the *Gorgon sisters rather than the northern Italian cheese-making town.

Gormanston
The title of an aristocratic Irish family, the Prestons, to whose death-ritual Maturin alludes (COM 9).

The Preston family arrived in Ireland from England in the late 13th century and soon became lords (and, from 1478, Viscounts) of Gormanston, near Dublin. The family arms show a fox, and legend has it that foxes gather at the doors of Gormanston House shortly before the death of the head of the family.

Gosling
A seller of prints and illustrations in London (LM 4).

Gouges, Henry
An elderly loblolly-boy in HMS *Sophie* who dies suddenly (M&C 5).

Gough, Robert
A former member of the United Irishmen, greatly disliked by Stephen Maturin for his pro-French bias. Stephen now sees him on the deck of a French ship chased by *Surprise* and, utterly dismayed at the role of 'informer' he may be compelled to adopt, contemplates active sabotage of *Surprise*'s pursuit. Fortunately, by morning Gough and his ship are nowhere to be seen (TGS 2). However, after Gough is taken by another English warship and later hung, the earlier incident gives rise to an unfounded suspicion amongst Irish emigrés that Stephen must indeed have been an informer (NC 10).

Gourin

A French violin-repairer aboard the *Franklin* who transfers to *Surprise* (WDS 3).

Gower, Joe

A carpenter's mate of HMS *Diane*, killed in the pirate attack on the shipwreck island (NC 1,2).

Gower, Leveson and Charlotte

The Captain who had wrecked the predecessor of Philip Broke's HMS *Shannon* (FW 7). His fashionable wife is living in Halifax, Nova Scotia (SM 1,2).

Edward Leveson-Gower (b.1776) had been made Post in 1795. On a very stormy night, in December 1803, his HMS Shannon *ran aground on the French coast near Barfleur and was burnt by her crew a few days later to prevent her being of any use to the enemy. At the time of SM, Leveson-Gower was by now a very senior Post Captain, the commander of the 74-gun HMS* Elizabeth, *but serving off the coast of West Africa and in the Mediterranean rather than on the North American station. He was promoted Rear Admiral in 1814 but resigned from the Royal Navy in 1821. The Leveson-Gowers were one of the wealthiest and most powerful families in Britain, being variously Dukes of Sutherland, Earls of Granville, admirals, generals and senior statesmen. Although the biographies are unclear, Edward may have been a son or nephew of that Admiral John Leveson-Gower (1740–1792) who had married a sister of Edward *Boscawen.*

Gowers

A doctor who treats the injured Jack Aubrey in England (COM 2).

Graaf

The scholar who had told Schlendrian of Ponsich's death at sea (SM 5).

The reference is perhaps to Eberhard Gottlieb Graff (sic; 1780–1841), a leading student of Old German language and literature.

Grace, Your

A member of Black's club (YA 1).

At the time only a Duke, Duchess or Archbishop would have been addressed as 'Your Grace.'

Graham

1: the Captain of HMS *Indefatigable*, Commodore of the squadron, including Jack Aubrey's HMS *Lively*, that captures Bustamente's Spanish treasure ships (PC 14; IIMS 1).

*The reference is to Sir Graham Moore (1764–1843), the son of an Archbishop of Canterbury and the younger brother of that famous General Sir John Moore (1761–1809) killed at the Battle Corunna in Spain. Made Post in 1794, promoted Rear Admiral in 1812, Vice Admiral in 1819, and Admiral in 1837, Moore was knighted in 1815 and served as an Admiralty Commissioner from 1816 to 1820. On October 5th 1804, Moore was the senior officer of the squadron of HMSS *Indefatigable, *Medusa (Captain Gore; see *Collins, Captain), *Lively (Captain *Hamond) and *Amphion (Captain *Sutton) that took*

Bustamente's Spanish treasure frigates off Cape St Mary, very much as described in PC.
2: a Lieutenant in HMS *Raisonable* (TMC 4).
3: the Captain of HMS *Bombay* who had the mortification of striking his colours to the sloop *Victor*, after having mistaken her for a frigate (TMC 10).
4: the surgeon of HMS *Ariel*, a well-read drunk (SM 7,11).
5: Mrs Graham, whose ball Fanny Wray had attended with William Babbington (LM 2).
6: the surgeon of HMS *Diane*, left behind in England when his ship makes a sudden departure (TGS 4,5,10).
7: a Colonel in New South Wales, an acquaintance of Jack Aubrey (C/T 1).

Graham, Professor Ebenezer

A Scottish moral philosopher and oriental linguist who travels to Minorca in Jack Aubrey's HMS *Worcester* (IM 2+). Before leaving the ship he tries to interest Stephen Maturin, whom he has not previously met, in becoming an intelligence agent (IM 3). Later Stephen, ashore in France on his own clandestine mission, discovers the accidentally wounded Graham and, astonished, gets him safely back to the English fleet (IM 7,8). Graham is in fact a British intelligence agent, meddling in Stephen's province of French and Spanish Catalonia. Yet his credentials are substantial, he having formerly induced the French garrison at Colombo, Ceylon, to surrender (IM 8). Graham now sails as a political advisor on Jack's mission to the Ionian Sea (IM 9–11), where, although his local expertise is very great, he is not consulted over which alliance will best suit British interests, leading to a furious quarrel with the Captain (IM 11). Recovering his composure, Graham acts as a sharpshooter in HMS *Surprise*'s successful battle with the rebel Turkish frigates, *Torgud* and *Kitabi* (IM 11). Arriving back in Malta, he remains there for a while (TH 1–4,8,10), even though ousted by a rival, Figgins Pocock, as an advisor to Sir Francis Ives, the new Admiral (TH 3). Graham does manage to identify the dangerous French agent, Lesueur, but then unfortunately confides in Andrew Wray, whom he does not know to be a traitor (TH 3). At curiously short notice, he is ordered to return to Britain aboard HMS *Sylph* (TH 4).

*For a note on Professor Hugh Cleghorn, the partial model for Graham, see the entry for Hercule de *Meuron.*

Grainger

An expert able-seaman in *Surprise*, promoted by Jack Aubrey to replace the dead Lieutenant Davidge (WDS 1+).

Grampus, HMS

A ship referred to as one of the very few 50-gun ships still in service, Jack Aubrey's HMS *Leopard* being another (DI 5). Years later, under her Captain Faithorne, she joins the Brest blockade squadron (YA 9) and, with Jack's *Bellona* and others, prevents two French 74-guns from slipping out (YA 9). Following Buonaparte's abdication, *Grampus* is sent home to be paid off (YA 10).

> *HMS* Grampus, *50-gun, had been laid down as HMS* *Tiger *but was renamed shortly before her launch in 1802; according to LAVERY there were only 14 50-gun fourth-rates in service by 1812. The ship, named for a type of northern dolphin, was sent for harbour service in 1820 and sold in 1832.*

Granby, Marquess of

The General after whom an inn near Shelmerston is named (LM 1).

> *John Manners (1721–1770), 1st Marquis of Granby, was a leading British general of the Seven Years' War and the heir of his father, the Duke of Rutland, whom he predeceased. From 1766 until his death he held the post of Commander-in-Chief of all British armies.*

Grand Master

The title of the head of the religious order that had ruled Malta (TH 2).

> *The full title of the 'Knights of Malta' is the 'Sovereign Military Hospitaller Order of St John of Jerusalem of Rhodes and of Malta.' The quasi-monastic order was founded in Jerusalem at the end of the 11th century and in 1530 moved its headquarters to Malta, which it held as sovereign territory until dispossessed by the French in 1798, the last Grand Master to rule Malta itself being Baron Ferdinand von Hompesch (1744–1803), a German. The Order has been based in Rome since 1834.*

Grand Mufti

A religious leader referred to by Maturin (HD 1).

> *The Grand Mufti, or sheikh al-Islam, was the chief canonical lawyer of the Ottoman Empire, delivering formal opinions—fatwas— in response to queries from judges or private individuals.*

Grand Turk

see **Turkey, Sultan of**

'Grandison'

A book by Samuel Richardson (FW 2; NC 9).

> **Richardson published his* Sir Charles Grandison *in 1754. In the novel Sir Charles, a man of equally great wisdom and virtue, eventually solves every problem that afflicts the various other characters, a daunting list— at least to a lesser fellow— including abduction, near-rape, religious bigotry, insanity, avarice, and unrequited love.*

Granny

see **Williams, Mrs**

Grant

1: a Lieutenant in HMS *Raisonable* (TMC 4).
2: initially the Second Lieutenant of Jack Aubrey's HMS *Leopard* (DI 3+), Grant becomes her Premier when Tom Pullings is left in Brazil to recover from fever (DI 6). A prime seaman and navigator, he nevertheless has a history of awkwardness as a subordinate, having once been demoted to the bottom of the Lieutenant's list (DI 3). Grant's relations with Jack are stiff and distrustful throughout the book as he resents Jack's dashing reputation and successful career (DI 4+) whilst Jack regards him as sorely deficient in fighting experience, hide-bound and no commander of men (DI 6+). Although his technical abilities during the iceberg collision crisis do much to keep the ship afloat, Grant eventually forms the view that the crew should abandon ship and take their chances in the boats. Although Jack does not agree, he allows him— and those many men who chose to follow— to leave the foundering *Leopard* in the launch (DI 8,9). The Lieutenant reaches the Cape, having 'trouble with his people' on the long journey (FW 1,2,8), and tells Sophie Aubrey that Jack must almost certainly have been lost (SM 5). Following Jack's safe return, Grant, now both unemployed and unemployable, complains at length about his former Captain's behaviour (SM 5,6). Some years afterwards, still blaming his subsequent lack of promotion on the soon-to-be-disgraced Jack, he appears as a prosecution witness at his fraud trial (RM 8).
3: a sick seaman in HMS *Surprise* who dies (WDS 4,6).

Grapes, the

A reference to Mrs Broad's husband, the landlord of the Bunch of Grapes Inn (PC 12).

Grappler, HMS

A brig taken by the French, now part of their Indian Ocean squadron (TMC 3). She is retaken by Jack Aubrey during his raid on Réunion (TMC 4) and given to Commander Dent (TMC 5).

> *VICHOT states that* Grappler *had been captured from the British in 1806 before being re-taken by the Royal Navy at Réunion in late 1809. As CLOWES, COLLEDGE and NORIE note, no HMS* Grappler *served in the Royal Navy after 1803, so the 16-gun brig captured in 1806 was probably a British privateer; her fate after 1809 is unknown.*

Gratipus, Madame

Diana Villiers' French waiting woman (DI 2).

Graves

1: the bosun of HMS *Ariel* (SM 9).
2: the loblolly-boy in HMS *Bellona* (YA 9).

Gray

1: HMS *Polychrest*'s carpenter (PC 9,11).
2: a member of the barge-crew of Captain Baker's HMS *Iris*, chosen for his colourful surname (FSW 2).
3: a quartermaster in HMS *Nutmeg of Consolation* killed in the action against *Cornélie* (NC 5).

4: the First Lieutenant of HMS *Bellona* who, operated on by Maturin for gall or bladder stones, later dies of sepsis (COM 6,7).

Gray, Alfred and Mrs

HMS *Leopard*'s carpenter (DI 5+) and his wife (DI 5).

El Greco

An artist referred to by Maturin for the emaciated, bearded faces typically found in his paintings (DI 5).

> *Domenikos 'El Greco' Theotokopoulos (1541–1614), a Cretan-born painter and sculptor, studied in Venice and Rome before moving, in about 1577, to Spain and there making his reputation in what became his home city of Toledo. His distinctive use of bold colour, elongated body forms and semi-abstract composition — the latter two more pronounced as his career progressed — somewhat limited his appeal during and immediately after his own life-time, yet he was always recognized as a most distinctively individual artist, especially in his dramatic — almost expressionist — portraits.*

Green

A member of the barge-crew of Captain Baker's HMS *Iris*, chosen for his colourful surname (FSW 2)

Green, Billy

A seaman in HMS *Surprise* (HD 6).

Green, Vivien

see **Simon, Richard**

Green Headcloth

The name given by Mr Welby to the Dyak pirate who takes command of the attacking force after Kesegaran's death (NC 2).

Greene

A Midshipman in HMS *Diane* (TGS 5).

Gregory

1: the author of *Polite Education* (FW 2; SM 11; IM 10; FSW 2).

> *The vicar and miscellany writer George Gregory (1754–1808) published in 1800 and 1807 Elements of a Polite Education, carefully selected from the Letters of the late Right Honourable Philip Dormer Stanhope, Earl of Chesterfield, to his Son. Lord Chesterfield (1694–1773) himself had been a statesman, writer and wit who became the touchstone of high-society taste in his own life-time. The letters that form the basis of Polite Education were written almost daily, over a number of years, to his somewhat diffident natural son — also Philip — and contain advice on behaviour in all manner of situations as well as the full compendium of cultural acumen thought to be necessary in making one's way in good society. They were first published by the younger Philip's widow shortly after Chesterfield's death, achieving instant popularity and soon appearing in various editions, Gregory's amongst*

> *them. Dr *Johnson — at various times both friend and enemy of the Earl — once famously remarked that the letters' elegant cynicism taught 'the morals of a whore and the manners of a dancing-master.'*

2: a manufacturer of quack medical remedies (WDS 7; COM 9).

> *The name is perhaps suggested by the early Christian Church father St Gregory the Thaumaturge (d.270?), whose Greek surname 'thaumaturgos' ('wonder-worker') comes from his reputation for performing miraculous cures.*

Grenville, Tom

A Captain who, having congratulated Jack Aubrey for the victory of *Cacafuego* (M&C 11), is later one of the officers who court-martials him for HMS *Sophie*'s subsequent loss (M&C 12).

> *The reference may possibly be to William Fulke Greville (sic; d.1837) who was made Post in 1783, retiring from the list in 1804. Both the 'Tom' and the spelling may be borrowed from Thomas Grenville (1719–1747), a famous young fighting Captain, killed in action during *Anson's defeat of the French fleet off Cape Finisterre.*

Grey

The pseudonym used by Wray in his dealings with Duhamel (RM 10).

Grey, Sir Charles

A gentleman to whom Lord St Vincent addressed a letter on the subject of Lieutenant Beresford (PC 3).

> *Charles Grey (1764–1845; 2nd Earl Grey from 1807) entered Parliament in the Whig interest in 1786, becoming a notable friend and supporter of the radical *Fox and a constant opponent of the Tory *Pitt. Under his courtesy title of Lord Howick (his father being an Earl), he served as *First Lord for just a few months in 1806, until Fox's death enabled him to become Foreign Secretary and Leader of the House of Commons. In this new position he was thereafter a leading supporter of the abolition of the slave trade (see also *Wilberforce). Grey was then out of office from 1807 until 1830 (although a vociferous supporter in the House of Lords of the Catholic Emancipation Act of 1829), in which year he succeeded *Wellington as Prime Minister, finally retiring in 1833. In HMS 1 it is presumably to the civilian Grey, not Admiral Barham (see* **First Lord # 4**), *that *Blaine refers as being a political, rather than naval, successor to *Melville.*

Greybeard

A servant at Vizier Hashin's camp (HD 7).

'Grey Melancholy'

Maturin's name for a monoglot Welsh seaman in HMS *Worcester* (IM 5).

Griffiths

1: the Captain of HMS *Charwell*, in which Jack Aubrey and Stephen Maturin are travelling as passengers (PC 1).
2: the Captain of HMS *Dolphin* (LM 6).
3: a relatively recent neighbour of the Aubreys at Woolcombe House, Griffiths — a.k.a. 'Black Whiskers' — is the MP for Carton and the heir

of Jack Aubrey's immediate superior, Admiral Lord Stranraer. The organiser of a scheme to enclose common land near Woolcombe (a change that Jack dislikes as much as he dislikes the man himself: YA 2–9), Griffiths appears to be plotting with the Admiral to have Jack recalled to HMS *Bellona* before he can voice opposition to the plan in Parliament (YA 3). Nevertheless Jack, aided by Stephen Maturin and others, both thwarts and humiliates his opponent (YA 3), who then sells up and moves away (YA 9,10). Griffiths is said to have been known, in their Mediterranean days, to both Jack and Stephen as Commander of the sloops HMSS *Espiègle* and *Argus* and later as Post Captain of HMS *Terpsicore* (YA 2).

Griffiths, Edward 'Judas'
A traitor in Gibraltar (HMS 4).

Griffiths, John
An elderly Lieutenant whose obituary is read by Maturin (DI 6).

Grim
The ferocious stable dog at Woolcombe House (YA 3).

Grimble
1: the author of a mathematics text, hence a favourite author of Jack Aubrey (HMS 2).
2: a seaman in HMS *Diane*, a cousin of the dying Arthur Grimble (TGS 5).

Grimble, Arthur
1: Arthur or Art Grimble, Preserved Killick's mate and a former butcher (WDS 1,9; COM 6,7,10; YA 9; HD 4,6,8).
See also William/Bill *Grimshaw, who often appears to be the same character.
2: a seaman in HMS *Diane* who dies of syphilis (TGS 5).

Grimmond
1: the Master of HMS *Ariel* (SM 6–9), a prime seaman (SM 8).
2: a 20-year-old, useless Midshipman in Jack Aubrey's HMS *Worcester* (IM 4,8).

Grimshaw, William or Bill
An old shipmate of Jack Aubrey (supposedly from HMS *Lively* days: NC 5) who, having been left ill in Batavia by HMS *Thunderer*, joins HMS *Nutmeg of Consolation*, and later *Surprise*, as Preserved Killick's helper (NC 4,5; WDS 2+; COM 1).
See also Arthur/Art *Grimble, who often appears to be the same character.

Groats, John O'
The man after whom a Scottish village is named (FSW 2).
According to a story first recorded in 1793, Jan de Groot was a Dutchman who had settled on the tip of Scotland with his two brothers and eight sons in the late 15th century, eventually giving his name to the village traditionally regarded as the northernmost inhabited point of the British mainland. In fact it is the nearby (rival) hamlet of Dunnet's Head that sits the furthest north, although for a very long time the highway ran out at John o'Groats.

Grobian, Slendrian & Co.
The company to which Jack Aubrey is in debt following the failure of his prize agent, Jackson (PC 12).

Groper, Saint
'Saint Groper' is referred to by Jack Aubrey as the 'patron saint of topers' (RM 4).
The phrase is rhyming slang for 'an excuse for a drink.'

Groper, HMS
A transport ship commanded by Lieutenant Pullings who, under orders, runs her aground at Réunion to provide a temporary breakwater (TMC 6).

Gros, Madame
An influential French politician's wife of who is seen wearing the Blue Peter stone that Diana Villiers appears to have used as a bribe in order to secure Stephen Maturin's safety (SM 11).

Gross, Thomas
A seaman in HMS *Sophie* (M&C 2).

Grotius
A famous lawyer referred to by Maturin (SM 4).
Hugo Grotius or de Groot (1583–1645) was a Dutch legal thinker, historian and theologian, precociously talented as a scholar and linguist from a very early age. In 1618 he was sentenced to life imprisonment in his native country after being unjustly accused of treason but in early 1620 managed, with the help of his wife, to escape confinement. He lived the rest of his life, apart from one brief and unsuccessful visit back to Holland in 1631, as an exile in Sweden and France and from 1634 to 1645 served as the Swedish Ambassador to Paris. His most important legal work was The Laws of War and Peace, *a treatise on international law.*

Grundy, Mrs
A literary reference to prudishness (TH 4).
The lawyer and comic playwright Thomas Morton (1764?–1838) introduced the rigidly moral Mrs Grundy in his Speed the Plough *of 1798.*

Guanerius or Guarnieri
The maker of Jack Aubrey's precious shore-fiddle (HMS 2; WDS 1; COM 3).
This stringed-instrument making dynasty was founded by Andrea Guarneri (sic; 1626?–1698) who, with the great Antonio *Stradivari, had been a pupil of Nicola *Amati. Bartolomeo Guiseppe Guarneri del Gesù (1698–1744), Andrea's nephew, was the most celebrated maker of the

clan and is today regarded as second only to Stradivari himself, although pieces by several other family members are very highly prized.

Guerrier *or* Guerrière, HMS

1: the ship in which Lieutenant Stapleton serves (M&C 1).

HMS Guerriere, 74-gun, was the French Peuple Souverain, launched as Souverain in 1757, democratically renamed in 1793 but then captured by the Royal Navy at the Battle of the Nile in 1798. Guerriere, French for 'warrior,' became a sheer hulk in 1800 and was broken up in 1810.

2: a 38-gun frigate, Captain Tom Dacres, taken and sunk (FW 4) by the 44-gun USS *Constitution* (FW 3+; FSW 3). She was sometimes known simply as the '*Guerry*' (FW 9).

*HMS Guerriere, 38-gun, had been launched in France in 1798 and was captured by the Royal Navy in 1806. Under her Captain James Richard *Dacres, she was taken by Isaac *Hull's USS *Constitution in August 1812 and, having been so badly damaged in the action, immediately burned. Although Constitution both threw a much greater weight of metal than Guerriere and was of far superior construction, in the brief, fierce action she was also better handled and enjoyed much superior gunnery, causing a disproportionately great loss and damage to her—undoubtedly valiant— British opponent.*

Guerry
see Guerrier *or* Guerrière, HMS

Guido

The artist thought by Jack Aubrey to be the painter of the *Magdalene* on display at the Keith's Ball (PC 6).

*Of many possible great Italian artists called Guido, this is probably a reference to Guido Reni (1575–1642), a prolific painter of great religious scenes, with several versions of the Mary *Magdalen story amongst them. A particularly fine Magdalen of his today hangs in London's National Gallery.*

Gulliver, Captain

The fictional hero associated with Lilliput (TMC 1).

Lemuel Gulliver, a naval surgeon and merchant seaman, is the central character in the 1726 satirical novel, Gulliver's Travels, of Jonathan Swift (1667–1745). In his various adventures Gulliver is shipwrecked amongst the tiny Lilliputians, abandoned to the enormous Brobdingnagians, visits both the brilliantly idiotic Laputans and the wretchedly immoral Struldbrugs, and finally encounters the pure, simple and rational Houyhnhnm horses and their debased enemies, the Yahoos. He then returns home to confront, with disgust, his own species.

Gully

A famous prize-fighter (YA 3).

*John Gully (1783–1863) was one of the most successful and colourful of all the great English prize-fighters. In 1805 he was beaten in a famous 59-round encounter with Henry *Pearce, and thus may well have been the man the 'Game Chicken' was on his way to meet when he shared a coach with Stephen *Maturin. After his career in the ring,*

Gully eventually became a very wealthy businessman and sports promoter, also serving from 1832 to 1837 as MP for Pontefract.

Gunner, Mrs

The wife of HMS *Lively*'s gunner, Mr Armstrong (PC 12).

Gunter

1: Jack Aubrey refers to Gunter's Scales, a mathematical tool (HMS 7).

Edmund Gunter (1581–1626), a distinguished English mathematician and inventor, was especially interested in problems of navigation and topographical representation. His 'Scale' is a logarithmic device for the use of draftsmen and map-makers.

2: the supplier of temporary servants to Blaine's dinner in honour of Aubrey (LM 7).

This is possibly a reference to the London confectionary and catering business run by the chef, Robert Gunter (1783–1852).

Gurney

A Quaker family referred to by Ellis Palmer (RM 4).

*The Gurney family of Norfolk were leading Quakers, or *Friends. The best-recalled is Joseph John Gurney (1788–1847), a wealthy philanthropist and anti-slavery activist.*

Gustav

A servant of Diana Villiers in Sweden (LM 9).

Guy of Warwick

A figure whom the captured Midshipmen of HMS *Ariel* claim for a parent (SM 10).

Guy of Warwick was a popular medieval romance, dating in manuscript from about 1300 but clearly based on an earlier original. Guy, son of the Earl of Warwick's steward, engages in heroic exploits to win the hand of Fenice, the Earl's daughter. After doing so, he undertakes further adventures in the Holy Land and, once back in England, against assorted Danish invaders. The tale remained popular in various versions for many centuries, exemplifying as it did English resistance to foreign influence.

Guy's

A hospital in London (RM 7; LM 4; TGS 4; COM 3).

The hospital, which still exists today, was founded by Thomas Guy (1645?–1724), a book-seller, printer, speculator and enormously wealthy philanthropist. From 1704 Guy was a Governor of St Thomas' Hospital, from whom he later bought nearby land to build a complementary institution, the construction of which was started in 1722.

Guzman

A member of the pro-independence forces in Chile (YA 7).

Guzman, Jaime

A Spanish merchant captured and held prisoner in *Merlin* (LM 3).

H

Haase

A seaman in HMS *Ariel* (SM 8).

Habachtsthal, Duke of

A Dutch Duke and minor member of the British Royal Family (COM 2), a.k.a. 'Pillywinks' (C/T 7) or, from his membership of the chivalric order, as 'the Garter' (COM 4). The patron of the traitors Wray and Ledward, he is himself an active spy for the French (COM 2+). Discovering that Stephen Maturin had killed his traitor friends and that Clarissa Oakes had identified him to Sir Joseph Blaine (C/T 6,7), he becomes their vigorous, though still secret, enemy (COM 4+). Stephen later learns that the Duke, now on the point of exposure, has killed himself in London (COM 10; YA 1). It is possible that, very early in the series, the Duke makes a fleeting, unnamed appearance at the theatre in the company of Diana Villiers and others (PC 14).

Haddock, Admiral

A retired, or 'yellow,' Admiral, a neighbour of the Williams family in Sussex (PC 1+). On the renewal of war after the collapse of the Peace of Amiens, he is given a shore command (PC 8,14; HMS 6).

The name, somewhat unlikely on its face, is probably inspired by that of the Haddocks, a famous English naval family that boasted two Admirals, Sir Richard (1629–1715) and his son Nicholas (1686–1746).

Hadley, Mr

HMS *Diane*'s carpenter (TGS 5,9,10), killed in the shipwreck island battle (NC 1,2,4).

Hafiz

A Turkish desert guide who accompanies Maturin and Jacob (HD 7).

Hafsa, Sultana

The wife of the Sultan of Pulo Prabang. Perhaps bribed by Maturin, she and her family act in league with the British mission in bringing about the downfall and deaths of Abdul, Wray and Ledward (TGS 7,8; NC 3).

Hahnemann

A naturalist after whom a petrel is named (WDS 2,3).

Hailes *or* Hales

HMS *Surprise*'s gunner (HMS 6,11).

Haines

1: a seaman in HMS *Polychrest* who had been pressed from the *Lord Mornington* Indiaman (PC 7,9,11).

2: a mutineer from HMS *Hermione*, now serving in USS *Norfolk*. On Old Sodbury Island he tries to desert to Jack Aubrey's HMS *Surprise* but is murdered by his fellow fugitives, to whom he is a 'Judas' (FSW 10).

Hairabedian

An Armenian dragoman, sent as a political advisor on Jack Aubrey's Mubara expedition, who is in the pay of the traitor Andrew Wray (TH 4–8). A keen and careless swimmer, he is eaten by sharks in the Red Sea and then discovered to have stolen Jack's diamond *chelengk*, soon found in his belongings (TH 5,6). In the past, Hairabedian had twice dined with Lord Byron, the poet (TH 4).

Hake

The chaplain of HMS *Charwell* (PC 1).

Hakluyt

An author of a book of voyages (HD 6).

Richard Hakluyt (1552?–1616; his surname is pronounced 'Hacklit') was an English parson and historian who spent his life collecting tales and accounts of journeys by sea, first publishing his Principall Navigations, Voiages, Traffiques and Discoveries of the English Nation *in 1589. This great work ran to many subsequent editions and is still quite easily available. Hakluyt also published several smaller volumes concentrating on English discovery and settlement in North America, a cause very dear to his heart. The Hakluyt Society, founded in 1847 by Sir John *Barrow and others, is dedicated to publishing scholarly reprints of the classics of the great age of discovery.*

Hal

see **Henry # 3**

Halde, Père du

An author referred to by Maturin (NC 3).

Jean Baptiste du Halde (1674–1743) was a French Jesuit priest, geographer, and anthropologist. He edited and published a collection of reports from Jesuit missions around the world and also compiled a major descriptive work on China, the first of any significance by a European. The reference by Maturin and Herapath to 'Père Bourgeois' (DI 6) may echo du Halde.

Hale

A Lieutenant in HMS *Queen Charlotte* at the Battle of the Glorious First of June. Although he was struck by the furious Admiral Howe for supposedly ignoring an order, he was soon forgiven (C/T 4).

Hales *or* Hailes

HMS *Surprise*'s gunner (HMS 8,11).

Hales, John

A sick seaman in HMS *Surprise*, secretly treated by the quack Higgins (FSW 3).

Halim Shah

The keeper of a brothel in Pulo Prabang (TGS 7).

Halkett

A Shelmerstonian seaman in *Surprise* (NC 7).

Hall

1: the Master of HMS *Boadicea* (TMC 9).
2: the Commander of the brig-sloop HMS *Skate*, thought by Aubrey to be a fine seaman (IM 2).
N.B., HMS Worcester's ex-Skates *later say that their Captain was a Mr* *Allen *(IM 7).*
3: the American Captain of *Spartan*, killed in the engagement with the Spanish privateer *Azul* (LM 3).
4: the owner of a school in Bath attended by the Christy family (NC 7).

Hallam

A Midshipman in HMS *Surprise* (HD 9), killed in action against Murad Reis' galley (HD 10).

Halley

The great Astronomer Royal and comet-discoverer (PC 10; RM 1), who had also written *The Art of Living Under Water* and invented the type of diving bell owned by Maturin (TH 3,4). As a Royal Navy Post Captain (HMS 1), he had commanded HMS *Paramour* on a scientific expedition (TH 3).
*Edmund, or Edmond, Halley (1656–1742) was the immensely influential astronomer, scientist and author who, in 1721, succeeded Flamsteed as the second *Astronomer Royal. The comet (with a 76-year appearance-cycle) named for Halley was first identified by him in 1705. His invention of the first practical diving-bell, constructed of wood and lead, came in 1717 and operated very much as Maturin describes: however, as early as 1780, pumped — rather than barreled — air was common for the many bells then in use. In PC 14 there is a reference to a temporary commission as a Post-Captain awarded to Sir Joseph *Banks, an appointment for which there is no historical evidence. However, Halley had been given a Royal Navy Post Captaincy in 1698 when he took command of the pink-sloop *Paramour for both exploration and the development of scientific navigation methods. The appointment seems to have lapsed on completion of the voyage in 1700 but, in 1729, King George II awarded Halley a non-serving Captain's half-pay for life: it is perhaps this set of events that O'Brian had in mind for Banks' honour.*

Halliwell

A Royal Navy Captain briefly encountered in Port Mahon by Jack Aubrey (M&C 2).
*The reference is perhaps to Sir Benjamin *Hallowell.*

Hallowell

A Captain who dines with Jack Aubrey and Admiral Snape. There is some suggestion that he had been present at the Battle of Cape St Vincent (DI 2).
*The reference is probably to Sir Benjamin Hallowell (1760–1834; known as Hallowell-Carew after his 1829 marriage) who was made Post in 1793 and then served extensively in the Mediterranean as a protégé of *Nelson, becoming one of his famous 'Band of Brothers' (see *Tigre, HMS). Although not at *St Vincent, he commanded HMS *Swiftsure at the Battle of the Nile in the following year (1798). Hallowell was promoted Rear Admiral in 1811, Vice Admiral in 1819 and Admiral in 1830.*

Hallows

1: the Captain of HMS *Frolic*, referred to in a letter from St Vincent to the Duchess of Kingston (PC 3).
2: a Marine in HMS *Polychrest* (PC 7).
3: a Marine sentry in HMS *Lively* (HMS 2).
4: a captured merchant seaman, now forced to serve in Murad Reis' galley (HD 10).

Hamad, Suleiman bin

A resident of Sierra Leone (COM 8).

Hamadryad, HMS

A frigate newly arrived in the Mediterranean under Captain Heneage Dundas (HD 9).
HMS Hamadryad, *36-gun, was the ex-Spanish* Matilda, *captured off Cadiz in 1804. She was sold out of the service in August 1815. In classical myth, a hamadryad was a tree-nymph.*

Hamel, du

The author of a nautical work referred to by Mr Scriven (PC 6).
The reference is probably to Henri Louis Duhamel de Monceau (1700–1782), the French botanist and naval engineer who had published his influential Principles of Naval Architecture *in 1758.*

Hamelin

The Commodore of the French squadron in the Indian Ocean (TMC 5–9), killed in action when his pennant-ship, *Vénus*, is taken by Jack Aubrey's HMS *Boadicea* (TMC 8,9).
Jacques-Félix-Emmanuel, Baron Hamelin (1768–1839) entered the French navy in 1792 as a Sailing Master after having had a career in the merchant service. In 1794 he became a Lieutenant and in 1796 was promoted Captain, later conducting, from 1800 to 1803, a voyage of exploration to the Australian coasts. Given Vénus *in 1806, Hamelin led a small squadron to the Indian Ocean and here became a successful commerce and coastal raider, until being forced to surrender to Commodore Josias Rowley's HMS *Boadicea in September 1810. Freed in 1811, he was immediately made both Baron and Rear Admiral, commanding at Brest until the end of the war. From 1818 he served under King *Louis XVIII, remaining in important sea- and shore- posts until his death. His nephew, François*

Alphonse Hamelin (1796–1864), had served as a cabin-boy in Vénus *and later rose to great distinction as an Admiral himself.*

Hames, Abel
The captain of the maintop in HMS *Surprise*, promoted bosun into the gun-brig HMS *Fly* (FSW 2).

Hamilton
1: a carriage horse from the stables of the Royal William Inn (COM 5).
2: the new British envoy to the Pasha of Barka (IM 6,7).

Hamilton, the Duchess of
A lady who, together with the Countess of Coventry, is said by Sir Joseph Blaine to have been one of the society beauties of his youth (HMS 4).

*Elisabeth Gunning, Duchess of Hamilton (1734–1790), came from a family of impoverished Irish gentry: on their arrival on the London scene in 1751, she and her sister Maria immediately became celebrated for their great beauty. In 1752 Elisabeth married James, 6th Duke of Hamilton (1724–1758), just a few weeks before Maria married the Earl of *Coventry. After her first husband's early death, Elisabeth married the Duke of Argyle and in 1766 she was also created Baroness Hamilton in her own right: no less than four of her sons, by her two marriages, became Dukes. N.B., *Blaine elsewhere indicates that he was not born until 1762 or 1763, some little time after the Gunning girls had been in their fullest bloom.*

Hamilton, Sir Edward or Ned, and Charles
The former commander of HMS *Surprise* who had cut out and re-taken the mutinous HMS *Hermione* (HMS 6; FSW 10; CT 2,5). Once dismissed the service for flogging his gunner, he had soon been reinstated (C/T 5). Sir Edward has a service brother, Charles (C/T 2).

*Sir Edward Hamilton (1772–1851), having first served at sea under his father, Captain Sir John Hamilton (d.1784), was in 1793 commissioned Lieutenant into a ship commanded by his elder brother, Sir Charles (1767–1849). Made Post into HMS *Surprise in 1797, Edward was knighted in 1800 for his dashing re-capture of *Hermione from the Spanish in the previous year, a bloody, small-boat action in which he was several times wounded. In 1801 he was appointed to the frigate HMS *Trent but in 1802 was court-martialed and dismissed the service for tying his elderly Gunner, William Bowman, into the rigging following a furious dispute (the Gunner, being appointed by Admiralty warrant, was in theory protected from such peremptory treatment). Hamilton's fame—and the likelihood that some of his eccentric behaviour was due to the head-wounds he had received in 1799—enabled him to be restored to the service, by King *George III himself, within a few months. From 1806 to 1819 Hamilton commanded the Royal Yacht and in 1818 received a baronetcy; he was promoted Rear Admiral in 1821, Vice Admiral in 1837 and Admiral in 1836. Sir Charles Hamilton had a long and very successful sea-career before being promoted Rear Admiral in 1810 (holding the position of Commander-in-Chief, Thames until the end of the war), Vice Ad-*

miral in 1814 and Admiral in 1830; from 1818 to 1825 he served as Governor General of Newfoundland.

Hamilton, Sir William and Lady Emma
Lady Emma Hamilton's eccentric marriage arrangements are much admired by Amanda Smith, who proposes something similar with Jack Aubrey (SM 2), and Diana Villiers later refers to the resentment by Lady Nelson of her husband's affair with Emma (RM 5).

*Sir William Hamilton (1731–1803) was the British Minister to the Kingdom of Naples, and a noted archeologist and antiquarian. In 1791, after an affair lasting several years, he had married Emma Hart (1766–1815), a well-known beauty with a background as paid mistress for several leading society figures in London. In 1793 she met *Nelson and by 1798 they had commenced a long and often scandalous affair, resulting in his eventual separation from his wife Fanny, Lady *Nelson. In 1801 Emma bore Nelson an illegitimate daughter, Horatia, who lived until 1881. Despite all this, Sir William always remained a firm friend and admirer of Nelson and bore the affair with fortitude, never publicly breaking with his wife: indeed, both Emma and Nelson were at his bedside when he died. After Nelson's death in 1805, Emma lived in considerably reduced circumstances until her own death in Calais shortly after the end of the war.*

Hamish, Dr
A medical doctor who dines at Barham House (COM 5).

'Hamlet'
O'Brian notes that Hamlet's going to school at Wittenberg is an anachronism (SM author's note) and the Prince is later referred to by Maturin, for his mother's forwardness, and by Jagiello, for his supposed grave at Elsinor Castle (SM 7). Somewhat later, the play is to be performed by HMS *Worcester*'s crew, Hamlet himself being given by the senior Master's Mate (IM 5,6,8). However, the event has to be postponed when 'Ophelia' (Midshipman Williamson) goes down with mumps (IM 8).

*Shakespeare wrote the tragedy of Hamlet, Prince of Denmark between 1599 and 1601, basing the play on a character dating from the 12th century or even earlier. Wittenberg University was not founded until 1502 and Kronborg Castle in Helsingør (Elsinor) not built until the end of that same century. As for presumptuous mothers, Queen Gertrude knowingly marries her late husband's brother and murderer, Claudius. Her son Hamlet slowly has his revenge but loses everything else, his life included (see also *Ophelia and *Polonius).*

Hamlyn, Mr
A surgeon in New South Wales (NC 8,9).

Hammersley
A distinguished entomologist (YA 1).

Hammond
1: referred to by the Master of *Alkmaar* as sometime

Captain of HMS '*Billy Ruffian*' (*Bellerophon*) (NC 5).

2: a member of Black's Club (TGS 4).

Hammond, G.

The MP for Hatton and a former lover of Louisa Wogan. He was also a friend of Horne Tooke (DI 4,6).

> *The reference is possibly to George Hammond (1763–1853), a diplomat and statesman who served from 1791 to 1795 as first ever British minister to the United States. From 1795 to 1809 he was an Under Secretary at the Foreign Office but he never sat as an MP.*

Hamond, William

The long-time Captain of HMS *Lively*, who wishes to attend Parliament in his capacity as a Whig MP for Coldbath Fields. Jack Aubrey accepts temporary command of the ship as his own first commission as Post Captain (PC 12,13; HMS 1,2; IM 4).

> *Admiral Sir Graham Eden Hamond (1779–1762) was made Post in 1798 and became Captain of HMS *Lively in 1804, later that year participating in the capture of *Bustamente's four Spanish treasure frigates in an action on which the final chapter of PC is partly based. He was promoted Rear Admiral 1825, Vice Admiral in 1837, Admiral in 1847, becoming Admiral of the Fleet in the year of his death. Although Sir Graham was never an MP, his father, Captain Sir Andrew Snape Hamond (1738–1828), served in Parliament from 1796 to 1806, supporting Whig interests. The elder Hamond had been made Post in 1770 and then served with distinction at sea before going, in 1794, permanently ashore as Comptroller of the Navy, responsible to the Admiralty for the technical and financial administration of the whole service, until his retirement in 1806.*

Hampole, Lieutenant

An officer refused an interview by Lord St Vincent (PC 3).

Hanbal, Ahmed ben

The under-secretary to Vizier Hashin (HD 7).

Handel

The composer (PC 12; RM 1; TMC 2), a performance of whose *Messiah* is attempted by HMS *Worcester*'s musical crew (IM 5,6,8). The event is cut short by the arrival of HMS *Surprise* with the news that the French fleet has slipped out of Toulon (IM 8).

> *George Frederick Handel (1685–1759), the great German composer, resided in England from 1712 until his death. Although in his youth he had been a virtuoso harpsichordist and a composer in the Italian style, his immense reputation rests primarily on his somewhat later sacred and celebratory music. He was, in 1720, the founding Director of the Royal Academy of Music and in this post composed many extremely popular operas until turning solely to oratorio in 1739, his Messiah being first given in 1742. After 1751 his eyesight began to fail, eventually leaving him wholly blind, yet still actively composing with the aid of amanuenses.*

Handley, Thomas

The maker of Diana Villiers' coach (YA 8).

Hanmer

1: a cousin of Admiral Haddock (PC 1).

2: a Post Captain met by Aubrey and Pullings on the island of Gozo (TH 2).

Hannibal, HMS or *Annibale*

A Royal Navy ship, Captain Newman, in which Fifth Lieutenant Jack Aubrey had challenged the more senior Lieutenant Carrol to a duel, resulting in a reprimand (M&C 4). Later she is a 74-gun ship of Saumarez' squadron, Captain Ferris, taken by Linois' squadron after running aground (M&C 12; IM 1,3). She is then seen as the French *Annibale*, anchored in Toulon harbour (PC 4; HMS 2).

> *HMS Hannibal, 74-gun, was launched in 1786 and captured at Algeçiras, almost exactly as described by O'Brian, on July 5th 1801; she then served the French Navy until 1823. Hannibal (247–183 BC) was the great Carthaginian general who conducted a long war with Rome. Despite his tactical brilliance and inspirational leadership, his conduct of the war was strategically unsound and he was finally defeated in 190 BC. He poisoned himself shortly before being handed over to Rome by his exile host, King Prusias of Bithynia.*

Harbrook

A nobleman referred to by General Aubrey as being Harry Tennant's father (RM 4).

Harden, John

A seaman in HMS *Sophie* (M&C 6).

Harding

1: the father of a boy Aubrey has taken into HMS *Leopard* as Captain's servant (DI 3).

2: according to Blaine, the best London lawyer for prize-money disputes (SM 4).

3: a seaman, or perhaps Midshipman, in HMS *Diane* (TGS 5).

4: the game-keeper at Woolcombe House (YA 1,2,3,6,10).

Harding, William and Eleanor

Once a Master's Mate in Sir Edward Pellew's HMS *Indefatigable* (YA 5) and a Lieutenant of HMS *Active* in Hoste's Adriatic squadron (HD 5), William Harding is initially Second Lieutenant of Jack Aubrey's pennant-ship HMS *Bellona* (COM 6) and then promoted Premier on the death of Mr Grey (COM 7,8; YA 4+). At the end of the war he volunteers to join Jack on *Surprise*'s semi-private mission to Chile (YA 10), remaining in her when she is diverted to become Jack's Royal Navy pennant-ship in the Mediterranean following Buonaparte's escape from Elba (HD 2–10). His wife, Eleanor, gives birth to a daughter (YA 6) and later inherits a small estate in Dorset near the Aubrey's Woolcombe House (YA 9).

Hardy

A seaman in *Surprise* (C/T 2).

Hardy, William

The Master of the whaler *Truelove*, detained by Kalahua and his French allies at Moahu Island (C/T 5) and later reported murdered (C/T 9).

Hare, Admiral

A neighbour of the Aubreys in Hampshire (DI 1).

Harlow

A man killed by Canning in a London duel (HMS 10).

Harlowe, Clarissa

The heroine of a novel by Richardson (DI 5; FW 2; NC 9).

> Clarissa: or, The History of a Young Lady, *an episto-lary novel by Samuel *Richardson, was published in eight volumes from 1747 to 1749, being translated into French, as* Lettres Anglaises, *by Abbé *Prévost in 1751. Clarissa Harlowe, an innocent, refuses to marry the wealthy Solmes and is in consequence locked up by her grasping family. Her sister's suitor, the rake Lovelace, 'rescues' her, installs her in a brothel and, when she repeatedly resists his advances, drugs and rapes her: Clarissa, gradually sent mad, soon falls into a debtors' prison. From here she is rescued—genuinely this time—by Lovelace's friend, Belford, who cares for her both during her recovery from madness and subsequent decline into physical illness and tranquil Christian death. Lovelace, now full of remorse, is killed in a duel by Clarissa's avenging cousin, Colonel Morden.*

Harper

1: a quartermaster in HMS *Surprise* (TH 10).
2: a Midshipman in HMS *Diane* (TGS 5–7; NC 1–4), killed in the Dyak attack on the shipwreck island (NC 2). Curiously resurrected, he then serves on HMS *Nutmeg of Consolation* (NC 5,6) only to be severely wounded in the *Cornélie* action, from which he struggles to make a recovery (NC 6).
3: a Treasury official who has fallen into the power of the spy Diego Diaz (YA 7).

Harrier, HMS

A small vessel under Admiral Pellew's command in Barbados (RM 2).

> HMS Harrier, *18-gun brig-sloop, was built in 1813 and sold in 1829.*

Harriet

see **Goole, Mrs Harriet**

Harrington

1: the Physician of the Fleet in the Mediterranean command, well known to Maturin (IM 4,9; FSW 1,2).

2: the newly appointed Governor of Bermuda, present at the King's Birthday Levée (RM 5).

Harris

1: the name of several seamen in Jack Aubrey's HMS *Surprise* (HMS 9; FSW 3; COM 1). Amongst them is the ship's butcher (HD 2) and a man killed in action against *Ardent* (HD 5).
2: the author of a nautical volume (FW 2; HD 6).

> *Joseph Harris (1702–1764) was a highly regarded Welsh author on optics, trigonometry and navigation who, in addition to his own several works, published a revised version of an earlier navigational volume by an unrelated namesake, John Harris (1667–1719). Joseph Harris also served as Assay-Master of the Royal Mint.*

3: a gunner's mate in HMS *Ariel* who had once served with Jack Aubrey in HMS *Surprise* (SM 7).
4: the heavy-drinking Marine Captain of Jack Aubrey's HMS *Worcester*, the cousin of the Marine officer James Macdonald of HMS *Polychrest* days (IM 1–7). After the fiasco at the neutral port of Medina, he forms the view that Jack could have acted more boldly in trying to provoke a fight with the French (IM 7).
5: a seaman in HMS *Irresistible* whose cousin had served with Aubrey in HMS *Sophie* (RM 1).
6: a purveyor of herbal remedies in New South Wales consulted by Aubrey (C/T 1,2; WDS 7).
7: Mrs Harris, a commoner in Woolcombe (YA 2).
8: an Admiralty official who has fallen into the power of the spy Diego Diaz (YA 7).
9: the Captain of HMS *Briseis* (HD 2).

Harris, Joe

A seaman from Manton who tows the stranded HMS *Leopard* off a sand-spit (LM 8).

Harris, John

A seaman in HMS *Boadicea* (TMC 9).

Harris, Snow

The designer of *Surprise*'s lightning conductor (WDS 10).

> *Sir William Snow Harris (1792–1867) was an English army surgeon and inventor, especially interested in electricity and meteorology. His invention—but not until 1820, well after WDS—of a system of lightning conductors to route energy from the masts to the sea by a permanently embedded, low-resistance, metal rod was thought to have saved many a ship from severe damage (such as sails and rigging catching fire). Harris, who later invented a new form of steering compass, less subject to magnetic disturbance, was knighted in 1847.*

Harrison

A draper in London's Royal Exchange buildings (PC 2).

Harrison, Dick

The sometime Captain of HMSS *Euterpe* and *Topaz* (COM 7).

Harrod, John

A banker and member of Louisa Wogan's circle in London (DI 6).

Harrowby

The Master of HMS *Surprise*, thought by Jack Aubrey to be not up to his job (HMS 8). A very religious man, who really owes his position to the influence of Admiral Gambier (HMS 5+), he is killed by fire from Linois' *Marengo* (HMS 9).

Hart, Ned

A gardener at Ashgrove Cottage engaged to Nan Pengelley. A former seaman, he had lost a foot in action aboard Aubrey's HMS *Worcester* (COM 6).

Harte

1: In the first half of the series Captain — then Admiral — M. Harte is Jack Aubrey's principal service enemy. As the senior Captain at the British Mediterranean base of Port Mahon he develops a great enmity for Jack, who is conducting a semi-open affair with his wife, Molly (M&C 1+). Harte delays communicating the news of Jack's promotion into HMS *Sophie*, causing many crewing and refitting difficulties (M&C 1,2), and, when Jack wins a dashing victory over the much larger Spanish *Cacafuego*, Harte plays down its significance, sending the victory dispatch to England by the slowest means he can contrive (M&C 11,12). Promoted Rear Admiral and member of the Admiralty Board, he continues to do all he can to block Jack's career (PC 6+; HMS 1; DI 1; SM 1). Some few years later, Harte is Sir John Thornton's second-in-command of the Mediterranean fleet (IM 3+), with the unhappy HMS *Thunderer*, Captain Fellowes, as his flagship (IM 4). Wishing to marry off his daughter, Fanny, to the politician — and secret traitor — Andrew Wray rather than to her beloved Commander William Babbington (IM 5), Harte takes the opportunity to send William and his sloop HMS *Dryad* into the midst of a French squadron moored in the neutral port of Medina, whilst ordering his old foe Jack to keep HMS *Worcester* out of the affair (IM 6). The plan, part of an attempt to provoke the French into breaching Turkish neutrality by seizing the prize offered, goes badly wrong in that William escapes and Harte has to bear Admiral Thornton's opprobrium for incompetent execution of the scheme (IM 6,7). However, Thornton's increasing debility and consequent death leave Harte as acting Commander-in-Chief, overwhelmed by his respon-

sibilities (IM 9–11; TH 1,4,10). He soon has a furious row with the newly arrived commanding Admiral, Ives, and is sent back to England in HMS *Pollux* (TH 10). This ship accompanies Jack's HMS *Surprise* on the Zambra mission, Harte showing an unexpected side of his personality by intending to redeem, out of his own pocket, Christian slaves held in the Muslim port (TH 10). However, *Pollux* is engaged just off Zambra by a powerful French squadron led by the 74-gun *Mars* and, after a short, brave fight, explodes with the loss of all aboard (TH 10; FSW 1; RM 6). Later in the series, we learn the curious fact that, on receiving a large inheritance, Harte had changed the family name (TGS 4); the complexities of this situation are discussed under the main entry for the new name of *Dixon.

*Although the character of Harte may be in part inspired by the poor relationship between Captain Manley *Dixon and Lord *Cochrane, a George Hart (sic; 1752–1812) was made Post in 1790 and promoted Rear Admiral in 1808, dates that fit O'Brian's Harte reasonably well.*

2: General Harte, a Dorset neighbour of the Aubreys (YA 3).

Harte, Fanny

A very rich heiress whom her father, Admiral Harte, wishes to marry off to an influential Admiralty politician, Andrew Wray, rather than to her beloved Commander William Babbington (IM 5). Her marriage to Wray — a secret traitor — does not diminish her ardour for William (TH 1,8; RM 5,6,9) and, with a maid as chaperone, she later sails in his HMS *Tartarus* (LM 2–6). On one occasion she refers to William as 'Charles' (RM 9), later elaborately explaining her confusion (LM 2).

Harte, Molly

The wife of Captain Harte, the Commandant of Port Mahon, and Jack Aubrey's occasional lover (M&C 1–11; IM 5,7). A lady with an indifferent reputation for virtue, she probably gives Jack a mild venereal disease (M&C 11).

Hartley, Admiral

A retired officer living in diminished circumstances on the island of Gozo, where he is visited by Jack Aubrey, his former Midshipman from their HMS *Fortitude* days. Hartley had also been a friendly examiner on Jack's promotion board to Lieutenant and later had once again been his commanding officer. He is one of the many men Jack has saved from drowning over the years (TH 2).

Harvey or **Hervey**

1: Harvey, an officer referred to by Purser Ricketts as having rapidly exchanged out of HMS *Sophie* (M&C 3).

2: Harvey, an officer who congratulates Aubrey on his victory over *Cacafuego* (M&C 11).

3: Harvey, a Midshipman in HMS *Lively* (PC 14).

4: Hervey, the First Lieutenant of Jack Aubrey's HMS *Surprise*, a man from an influential naval family full of Admirals (HMS 5,6,7; YA 2) who, although no great seaman, is popular with the officers and crew. On arrival at the East India station, he is immediately promoted Commander by his uncle, the Admiral (HMS 5,7). He is perhaps the same Captain Billy Harvey/Hervey who commands HMS *Arethusa* (IM 1), who loyally attends Jack's pillorying and is later met by Maturin at Durrant's hotel (RM 9,10) and who, years afterwards, is a guest at Woolcombe House (COM 3).

Hervey and Harvey were spellings often interchanged, but the former was the usual surname of Augustus John Hervey (1724–1779), Earl of Bristol, who rose to Admiral in 1775 and one of whose sons became a Post Captain. The very large, unrelated Harvey family, with branches in Essex and Kent, supplied at least six Admirals, and many other more junior officers, to the Royal Navy.

5: Captain Hervey, who had quarrelled with Admiral Gambier (TMC 6).

Sir Eliab Harvey (sic; 1758–1830) was made Post in 1783 and later commanded HMS Téméraire, *98-gun, at the Battle of Trafalgar in 1805 (the ship whose final journey to the breaker's yard in 1838 is the subject of J.M.W. Turner's great painting,* The Fighting Téméraire*). Harvey was promoted Rear Admiral by seniority very soon after *Nelson's great victory. In 1808, as one of *Gambier's subordinate commanders in the Channel, he took great exception to the appointment of *Cochrane — a mere Post Captain — to command the inshore operations and quarrelled furiously with his Admiral, disparaging him to other officers (Cochrane and *Neale amongst them) as an incompetent, hypocritical, canting, avaricious Methodist. For this he was court-martialled in 1809 and, although full of apologies for his insulting outbursts, dismissed the service. However, being both a very well-connected man and far from the only officer roundly to dislike both Gambier and Cochrane, he was restored in 1810 and promoted Vice Admiral shortly afterwards, although he was never again given a command. In 1819 he rose by seniority to full Admiral.*

6: Admiral Harvey, in whose flagship HMS *Goliath* Aubrey had served as a youngster (FW 7) and perhaps the same Admiral Hervey, later commanding the East India station, whose nephew serves on HMS *Surprise* (HMS 5,7,9).

7: Harvey, a Mate in *Diligence* (SM 3).

8: Captain Harvey of HMS *Antiope*, who had passed up the chance of capturing a prize in the southern Mediterranean in order to avoid any suggestion of a breach of the complex neutrality laws of the various Turkish outposts along the north African coast (IM 6).

9: Hervey, the Senior Naval Officer at Trieste (TH 9).

10: Harvey, a seaman in HMS *Surprise*, formerly a smuggler (LM 1; TGS 2; NC 7).

Harvey, Billy
see **Harvey** or **Hervey**, **# 4**

Harvey, George
A Midshipman in HMS *Caledonia*, a grand-nephew of Admiral Sir Francis Ives (TH 4).

Harvey, Moses
A seaman in HMS *Leopard* (DI 9).

Harvill, Clarissa
see **Oakes, Clarissa**

Harwood
A Quaker family referred to by Ellis Palmer (RM 4).

Hashin
The Vizier to Omar Pasha, Dey of Algiers (HD 6). A closet Buonapartist, he is in league with Ibn Hazm, Sheikh of Azgar, to ensure the passage of gold from Morocco to the Adriatic (HD 7,8).

Hassan
1: Hassan Bey, the man on whose horse Sir Sydney Smith had been mounted when, according to Clonfert, he shot a unicorn (TMC 3; *also* HD 7).

*Hassan Bey (dates unknown) was *Djezzar Pasha's chief military and naval commander at the siege of Acre in 1799 and, in that capacity, was highly regarded by Sir Sidney *Smith.*

2: the Arab gentleman who is to be installed by Aubrey as the new ruler of Mubara (TH 6).

3: the new Dey of Algiers after the overthrow of Ali Bey, who agrees that the Moroccan gold captured by Jack Aubrey at sea is the lawful prize of the Royal Navy (HD 10).

Hassan, Mulei
see **Mulei Hassan**

Hastings
see ***Warren Hastings***

Hastings, Sir William
A Royal Marine officer encountered in New South Wales by Stephen Maturin, who had saved his leg after Saumarez' action off Gibraltar in 1801. Sir William tells Stephen that he had seen the newspaper announcement of Diana Villiers' delivery of a daughter sometime in 'April last,' leaving Stephen utterly overwhelmed by the news (NC 10).

Hautboy
A racehorse owned by Jack Aubrey (DI 1).

Haverhill

A quarter gunner in HMS *Surprise,* sent to *Lushington* for the battle with Linois (HMS 9).

Hawke

A famous British Admiral referred to in Mowett's poem (M&C 3).

> *Edward, 1st Baron Hawke (1705–1781), was one of the Royal Navy's most distinguished commanders of any age. Hawke came from an influential political family and rose to Post Captain in 1734, at the rather early age of 29; promoted Rear Admiral in 1747, Vice Admiral in 1748, and Admiral in 1757, he rose to Admiral of the Fleet in 1768. A bold, quick-thinking officer — his coat-of-arms bore the single word 'Strike' as its motto — Hawke was responsible to a large degree for replacing the old, rigid Admiralty 'Fighting Instructions' with more flexible and aggressive tactics (especially the 'general chase') that allowed initiative to individual commanders when fleets closed together. Hawke also combined his own attacking spirit with considerable tactical patience, most clearly seen in his great victory at the Battle of Quiberon Bay (1759) during the Seven Years War. Knighted in 1747, he served as an MP from that same year until 1776, was First Lord of the Admiralty from 1766 to 1771 and was made Lord Hawke in 1776.*

Hawker

1: Miss Hawker, a dancing teacher in Portsmouth (C/T 2).
2: a groom at Ashgrove Cottage (COM 1).

Hawkins, Mrs and **Tom**

The sister of the inn-keeper Andrews, and her son (YA 3).

Hawley, Jacob

A ship's boy in HMS *Leopard* who dies of the gaol fever (DI 5).

Hay, Miss

A tutor of the various children at Woolcombe House (YA 8).

Haydn

The great composer, a favourite of both Aubrey and Maturin (M&C 11; TMC 2; IM 7; FSW 6; NC 9; COM 5; HD 9), the latter writing a set of variations on one of his themes (LM 6).

> *Franz Joseph Haydn (1732–1809), the Austrian composer, was famous for his prodigious output of operas, symphonies, oratorios and all forms of chamber music. He spent much of his life from 1761 onwards as Kapellmeister to the Esterházy family in Vienna but lived in London from 1791 to 1794, during which time he wrote the last 12 of a lifetime total of 104 symphonies. The Symphonie Funèbre whose score is bought by Stephen Maturin (COM 5) is not a work associated with either Joseph or his brother, Michael Johan (1737–1806), although of course it is later — in 1840 — a great work of the French composer Hector Berlioz. However, given the enormity of their joint output and the doubtful authenticity of many other works attributed to them, it is perfectly possible that Stephen either thought he was buying a Haydn or was perhaps looking at a version of Michael's unfinished final work, the requiem mass Pro Defunctis.*

Hayes, Abel

A young Shelmerstonian seaman, eager to join Aubrey in HMS *Surprise* (LM 5), who later falls ill (NC 7).

Haynes

A seaman in *Lord Nelson* who had once served with the young Jack Aubrey in HMS *Resolution.* He is killed in the action with *Bellone* (PC 5).

Hayter, John

A Marine in HMS *Sophie,* killed in action (M&C 7).

H.E.

Short-hand for His Excellency the British Envoy, Mr Stanhope (HMS 5,8).

Head, Mr

The chief of ordnance stores at Port Mahon (M&C 2).

Healy, Terence

A deceased tenant of Dillon's grandfather in Ireland (M&C 10).

Heartsease

A British whaler, Master John Trumper, detained for a brief period at Moahu by Kalahua and his French allies (C/T 5).

Heath

A Lieutenant in USS *Constitution* (FW 4).

Heatherleigh, Christine
see **Wood, Christine**

Heatherleigh, Edward

A naturalist and Fellow of the Royal Society well known to Maturin. His sister, Christine, is the wife of Captain James Wood, Governor of Sierra Leone (COM 9).

Heaven, Mr and **Mrs**

A quartermaster in *Surprise* and his unofficial 'wife' (TGS 1).

Hébé

A prize taken by Jack Aubrey's HMS *Boadicea.* Once the 28-gun HMS *Hyaena,* aboard which Admiral Bertie had once served as a Midshipman, she had been taken by the French when Jack was a boy (TMC 2, 3; YA 8). She is now commanded by Lieutenant Bretonnière, her Captain having been killed when she took the merchantman *Intrepid Fox* (TMC 2). *See also* ***Ganymede,*** **HMS** and ***Hyaena,*** **HMS**

Hebe, HMS

A ship now commanded by Captain Rowlands (IM 10), formerly a command of the Governor of Sierra Leone, Captain James Wood (COM 7; *also* HD 2).

The references could be to either of two HMS Hebes: a) an ex–French 38-gun, captured in 1782, re-named HMS Blonde in 1805, and broken up in 1811; or b) a 32-gun, launched in 1804 and sold out of the service in 1813. Hebe served as female cup-bearer to *Jupiter before being replaced by the beautiful young man, *Ganymede. See also **Hyaena, HMS**.

Hébert

A keeper of a country inn outside Toulon, favoured by Christy-Pallière (PC 4) and perhaps referred to some years later by Maturin when he recalls dining with the French Captain (FW 4).

Hecate

An 'HM Hired Vessel' referred to by Aubrey (NC 10).

At the time of NC, an HMS Hecate, 18-gun brig-sloop, was in full service; launched in 1809, she was sold in 1817, and may have ended up in the Chilean navy. In classical myth Hecate was a minor goddess of sorcery and dark crossroads, met again in *Shakespeare's *Macbeth.

Hecla, HMS

A bomb vessel in which Charles Fielding arrives at Gibraltar (FSW 1).

HMS Hecla, 10-gun bomb, was the ex-merchantman Scipio, purchased in 1797. In 1801 she played a small role, under Commander Richard Hatherill (d.1805 in the rank of Post Captain), in *Nelson's victory at the Battle of Copenhagen. Hecla, named for a volcano in Iceland, was broken up in late 1813.

Hector

1: one of the heroes of the Trojan war (FSW 2; C/T 8; COM 8; YA 10).

In *Homer, the Trojan Hector, the son of King *Priam and the husband of *Andromache, is the greatest of the warriors fighting the Greeks, bold, even brash, in his attitude to the invaders and to any lesser mortals. Usually at the centre of the fight, he often challenges his enemies to single combat, although he does not always get the better of the exchanges. After Hector kills *Patroclus, the enraged *Achilles pursues and kills him in turn, dragging the corpse behind his chariot in contemptuous triumph.

2: the name (*see* 1 *above*) given by Maturin to one of his interrogators for his loud, 'hectoring' voice (SM 11).

Hedges

A seaman in *Surprise* who carries no immunity to smallpox (NC 8).

Heliogabalus

A famous lecher referred to by Aubrey (YA 3).

Marcus Aurelius Antoninus (203?–222) ruled as the Roman Emperor Elagabalus from 218 until his death, his imperial name being taken from the god of the Syrian cult that he favoured, infamous for its orgiastic ceremonials. Public outrage at Elagabalus' peculiar ways and complex marriage arrangements resulted in his murder in a coup.

Hell, the Duke of

A curse used by Maturin (PC 14).

Heller

A secretary at the Admiralty (COM 2).

Helmholtz

A man to whom Jack Aubrey sends marine surveying data (C/T 4).

In the wider context the reference looks like a slip for Jack's more usual correspondent on matters hydrographic, Alexander *Humboldt. Hermann Ludwig Ferdinand Helmholz (1821–1894) was a distinguished physiologist and natural scientist of a later generation.

Hemmings

Aubrey's joiner (*or 'finish carpenter'*) in HMS *Bellona* (YA 6).

Hemmings, Bill

A colleague of Pratt the thief-taker (RM 7).

Hempson

A harpist from whom Maturin had once learned a lament (RM 3).

Denis Hempson (1695–1807), a famously long-lived Irish bard and harpist from Cork, is still often considered to be the greatest ever exponent of his art.

Hen

see **Dundas, Heneage** or **Hen**

Henderson

The Madeira associate of Jack Aubrey's prize agent (HMS 11).

Heneage

see **Dundas, Heneage** or **Hen**

Henry

1: HMS *Sophie's* sailmaker (M&C 2).
2: a lunatic in HMS *Surprise* (RM 3).
3: a retired Admiral now writing medical pamphlets (LM 1).

John Henry (1731–1829) entered the Royal Navy in about 1744, rising to Post Captain In 1777. After a long and active career, he served briefly in HMS *Irresistible at the start of the French wars in 1793, but his sea-service ended with his promotion to Rear Admiral in the following year. He became Vice Admiral in 1799 and Admiral in 1804. *Marshall notes that in 1816 he published a short pamphlet on his self-devised treatments for both gout and eye cataracts, the latter detailing the surgical instruments and procedures he himself had used.

4: Henry or Hal, an assistant blacksmith, badly beaten by the game-keeper Black Evans (YA 3).

Henry, Richard
A seaman in HMS *Sophie* (M&C 3).

Henry VI, King
Treason's Harbour opens with a quotation from Shakespeare's *Henry VI, Part 2* (TH frontispiece).

> *Henry VI of England (1421–1471) became infant King in 1422. During his long and troubled reign England both lost her possessions in France and then experienced at home the vicious 'Wars of the Roses,' in which Richard, Duke of York, vied with Henry's Lancastrian supporters for the Crown. The deceased Richard's son, Edward, took the title of King Edward IV in 1461, with he and Henry both intermittently ruling England and fighting each other for the next ten years, until Henry's final capture at the Battle of Tewkesbury in 1471. Henry—who seems himself to have had little interest in the momentous events taking place around him—soon died in prison, perhaps murdered by Edward himself or perhaps, as in *Shakespeare's play, by his younger brother, the Duke of Gloucester, later to rule as King Richard III.*

Henry VIII, King
The English king referred to by Stephen Maturin as having introduced mass Protestantism to England (RM 2).

> *King Henry VIII of England (1491–1547; ruled from 1509) was the initiator of the English religious Reformation, in part to facilitate his divorce (and sometimes execution) of a series of wives unsatisfactory to him for failing to produce male heirs. In 1533 legislation was introduced which made Henry the head of the English Church, now declared quite independent from Rome. The point of Stephen's remark is that, before Henry's introduction of near-compulsory Protestantism, almost everyone in England was of course a Roman Catholic and presumably equally loyal to both Pope and King.*

Henslow
A Lieutenant in Jack Aubrey's squadron, the senior of his inshore brig-commanders (COM 9).

Herapath, George
An elderly, wealthy merchant in Boston, the father of Michael Herapath. In his youth he had been a Tory loyalist who had fought in the Revolutionary War on the side of the British General Burgoyne (FW 4,7). Still somewhat sympathetic to this past cause, he agrees to help Aubrey, Maturin and Villiers escape from Boston but, during the mission itself, panics and takes off with the horses (FW 8,9).

Herapath, Michael
A young U.S. citizen who had been one of Louisa Wogan's lovers in London, occasionally working as her secretary (DI 2,4,6). Remaining loyal after her arrest and conviction for spying, he stows away in Jack Aubrey's HMS *Leopard* for the voyage to Australia (DI 3+). Discovered, he is put into Barret Bonden's mess as a common seaman, although he is clearly an educated gentleman (DI 3). Michael, by gaining access to Louisa's cell, again becomes her lover (DI 4+). After a fall from the yards, he is saved from downing by Jack (DI 4) and during the outbreak of fever in *Leopard* acts as an effective assistant to Stephen Maturin, eventually being rated Midshipman and temporary sick-bay attendant (DI 5). Michael's position as a free member of the ship's crew enables Louisa to use him as an unwitting sender, by letter, of coded information to the USA (DI 5) but Stephen in turn lays his own plot to feed the spy false intelligence via her naïve lover (DI 7). Having done so, Stephen subtly encourages Michael and Louisa to escape from Desolation Island aboard the American whaler *La Fayette* (DI 7–10). Before we first meet him, Michael had briefly served with the U.S. Army under General Washington, to whom he is related through his mother (DI 5). He had then moved to Europe to become a student of Chinese poetry under the great Sinologist, Père Bourgeois, meeting Louisa during a voyage from France to England (DI 6). Reduced to despair in London by the intermittent nature of their relationship, Michael had become an opium addict until being taken up again by Louisa and weaned off the drug (DI 6). We next hear of him living in Boston with Louisa and their baby daughter, Caroline (FW 2,4,5–8), with Stephen strongly recommending that Michael should follow his natural gifts and become a physician (FW 5). Out of a sense of personal obligation, Michael later agrees to help Stephen, Jack Aubrey, and Diana Villiers escape from the USA (FW 8).

***Hercules*, HMS**
A ship briefly seen by *Ringle* (COM 5).

> *The reference may perhaps be to one of two 74-guns: a) HMS l'Hercule, launched by the French in 1797, captured by the Royal Navy in 1798 (see *Hood) and broken up in 1810 (before COM); or b) HMS Hercules, launched in 1815 (after COM), sent for harbour service in 1853 and sold in 1865. In Greek myth Hercules or Heracles, son of *Zeus and *Alcmene, was offered a choice of the paths of Virtue or Pleasure. Choosing the former, he accomplished great deeds on behalf of his home city of Thebes but was then required then by the gods to serve his elder brother, Eurystheus, for a further twelve years. Heracles was now set an arduous sequence of tasks, the 'Twelve Labours' and, after accomplishing all of these, as well as meeting several other obstacles put in his path, he then sought a voluntary death, and was immortalised as one of the gods themselves (but see also *Nessus for an alternative telling of his fate).*

Hermenegildo
A Spanish ship engaged in the great action that concludes *Master and Commander* (M&C 12).

> *In the action on the night of 12th September 1801 San Hermenegildo, 112-gun, Captain José Emperran, ran foul of her blazing consort, *Real Carlos, and herself caught fire and blew up. The ship was named for Saint Hermenegildo, a son of one of the Visigothic kings of Spain who converted from his father's religion of Arianism to Christianity and started an armed rebellion. When cap-*

tured in about 585, he refused to renounce his new faith and suffered martyrdom.

Hermias

A famous eunuch referred to by Maturin (IM 8).

Hermias, Tyrant of Atarneus (d.341? BC), was a former student at *Plato's academy and a close friend of *Aristotle, who indeed married Hermias's adopted daughter, Pythias. By his astute diplomacy and statesmanship his city became virtually free of foreign control but his developing closeness to King *Philip II's Macedonia resulted in his eventual murder by the King of Persia.

Hermione, HMS

A ship that, some time after her crew had mutinied, was recaptured by Sir Edward Hamilton's HMS *Surprise*, being soon re-named HMS *Retribution* (HMS 6; IM 7; FSW 10; C/T 2,5; *also* HD 2). Many years later, Jack Aubrey finds some of the mutineers serving in USS *Norfolk* and they are eventually captured, tried and hanged (FSW 9,10; RM 1,2). The pressed gardener, Yeats, had once served in the ship (IM 2) and Allen's brother had deserted from her to the USA (DI 10).

The 32-gun frigate HMS Hermione, launched in 1782, was commanded on the West Indies station from February 1797 by the notoriously callous Captain Hugh *Pigot. In October of that same year her crew mutinied, slaughtered Pigot together with nine of his officers, and handed the ship to the Spanish authorities. In October 1799, Sir Edward *Hamilton's HMS *Surprise retook the now-Spanish ship in a dashing cutting-out action (in which surgeon John *M'Mullen played a leading role) and over the next several years many of the mutineers were hunted down, tried and executed (the last of the 24 who were hung meeting his fate in 1806). Hermione, first re-named HMS Retaliation, became HMS Retribution in 1800 and was broken up in 1805. In Greek mythology Hermione, daughter of Menelaus and Helen, became the wife of the hero *Orestes.

'Hero of the Nile'

see ***Nelson**

Herod

Jack Aubrey compares Stephen Maturin's regard for children to that of Herod (TMC 10); Stephen himself later remarks on both Herod's hubris and his being eaten by worms (TGS 9).

King Herod the Great of Judea (73?–4 BC) was appointed to his position by General Mark Anthony and the Roman senate. By skilful administration and financial management, he soon became one of the wealthiest men in the Empire, lavishing money on schemes all over the Mediterranean area and building fine monuments and public facilities in his own kingdom. Having engaged in a series of astute and successful border wars, he then became increasingly savage in his dealings with his court at home, murdering his eldest son and heir just a few days before his own death. In the New Testament (Matthew, II), the birth of *Jesus during his reign impelled him to order the slaughter of all new born babes in the hope of eliminating divine opposition to his own rule. Herod was

succeeded by one of his sons, Herod II Antipas (dates uncertain) who executed John the Baptist but then refused Pontius *Pilate's attempt to have him, as Judean King, put Jesus on trial. King Marcus Iulius (Herod) Agrippa I (10?BC – 44 AD; he was the nephew of Antipas and is called 'Herod' in the Bible alone) made great contributions to the reconciliation of Jews and Romans but seems to have been an implacable opponent of the Christian apostles, whose persecution he continued. In the New Testament he has himself proclaimed as divine and, promptly stuck down by an angel of *God, is consumed by worms (Acts XII). 'Herod' in fact died quite suddenly whilst hosting a spectacular series of games at Caesarea, held in honour of the Emperor Claudius.*

Herodotus

The ancient historian referred to by Maturin (FSW 7).

Herodotus of Helicarnassus (modern Bodrum in Turkey) lived from about 480 to 420 BC, although almost nothing is known of his life. He is the first of the Greek historians whose work — an account of the Greek-Persian wars of the 70 years immediately before his birth — has survived in its entirety. This great work shows an astonishing breadth of research — he undertook lengthy travels in search of key personalities and documents — and, in a break from past traditions, presents the variety of human experiences that had gone into making and conducting the wars on their own terms, rather than purely from the standpoint of the eventual Greek victors. Herodotus, as fine a narrative writer as he is historian, has been highly regarded from the very earliest times, although there has always co-existed a minority view that he is both superficial and perhaps even a wholesale inventor of his tales.

Herold

1: a seaman in HMS *Africaine* who had served in Jack Aubrey's HMS *Sophie* when she took *Cacafuego* (TMC 8).
2: one of Dr Redfern's assistants at his infirmary in New South Wales (NC 9).
3: Hérold, a French intelligence agent in the pay of the English (RM 5).

Heron, Robert

The author of *The Comforts of Life* (RM 3).

Robert Heron (1764–1807) was a prolific Scottish miscellany writer and journalist who spent long periods in jail for debt, eventually dying there of a fever. His final work, composed in prison, was The Comforts of Human Life, or Smiles and Laughter of Charles Chearful (sic) and Martin Merryfellow.

Hersant

A gentleman who had attempted to persuade Maturin to carry a secret message from Paris to London (SM 11).

Herschel

The great astronomer, whose sister Caroline had helped Jack Aubrey with the design and construction of his telescope (TMC 1; COM 3).

Sir Frederick William Herschel (1738–1822) was a German-born astronomer who in 1759 moved from Hanover to England, where he spent the rest of his career. From a family of musicians, Herschel first made a name for himself as a virtuoso organist before turning, from about 1768 onwards, his considerable mathematical talents to astronomy and optics (although until 1782 he remained dependent for his income on musical performance). From 1774 to 1779 he concentrated on designing and building his own large telescopes, helped by his sister Caroline (see following entry) and his brother Alexander; he then began his systematic examination of the heavens. Having discovered in 1781 the planet Uranus (originally named by him Georgium Sidus for King *George III) to great acclaim, he was appointed private astronomer to the King and elected Fellow of the Royal Society. With royal financial backing, he continued his discoveries of planetary objects — including the satellites of Saturn and Uranus — and began to construct a telescope 40 feet in focal length, the largest then in existence and regarded as a technological wonder of the world. With this instrument he now began detailed observations of the deep-space stars, making fresh discoveries almost every year, theorising boldly and effectively founding the modern science of astronomy. Knighted In 1816 for his life's work, both his son and grandson also later became highly regarded astronomers.

Herschel, Miss Caroline

The elderly sister of Herschel the astronomer, who has helped Jack Aubrey in the construction of his telescope and observatory (TMC 1; DI 2; COM 3,9).

Caroline Lucretia Herschel (1750–1848) achieved fame both as the life-long amanuensis of her brother, Sir William *Herschel, and as the discoverer in her own right of at least eight comets and three nebulae. Like her brother she was a noted musician, singing to his accompaniment in public concerts until 1782. As astronomers, she and William made observations throughout each night and, during the day, whilst he attended to the building of larger and more sophisticated instruments, she then carefully catalogued the notes of their previous labours, made many of the long mathematical calculations necessary for later theorising, and often set to grinding and polishing her brother's new mirrors (biographies often wonder at quite how little rest the pair seemed to need). Caroline's abilities and publications as a cataloguer (she also made sophisticated inventories of the observations of Flamsteed, the First *Astronomer Royal) brought her the Gold Medal of the Astronomical Society in 1828 and an enduring reputation as a founder of modern astronomy as a systematic science. After William's death in 1822, Caroline retired to her native Hanover, residing and cataloguing there until the age of 98.

Hertford, Lady

A friend of both the Prince Regent and Andrew Wray, whom Mrs Fitzherbert advises Stephen Maturin to consult over a possible pardon for Jack Aubrey (RM 9). Later, after she is rude to Diana Villiers, Jack makes an insulting remark about her, borrowed from the poet Dryden (TGS 1)

Isabella Anne, Marchioness of Hertford (d.1836), was the enormously wealthy wife of Francis Seymour, 2nd Marquis Hertford (1743–1826). A close confidant of the Prince *Regent, she exercised great influence over him for several decades.

Hervey
see **Harvey** or **Hervey**

Hervey, William

A gentleman possibly connected to Army intelligence (YA 1).

Hesiod

A Greek author referred to by Sam Panda (WDS 9).

Hesiod is regarded as the founder, with *Homer, of the epic tradition of Greek poetry; which of the two was earlier, or whether they were contemporaries, is uncertain and much debated. We know only a little of Hesiod's life from his extant works: he was the son of an unsuccessful sea-captain, became a shepherd, and later, having heard the voices of the Muses calling him to sing and compose, entered public poetry competitions with considerable success. *Plutarch recounts that he was murdered at Locris out of revenge for a crime he had not in fact committed. His surviving works are the Theogony, *an account of the origins of the gods;* Works and Days, *a poetic treatise on morality, hard work, agriculture and corruption; and — of doubtful authenticity — the* Shield, *a narration of *Hercules' battle with Cycnus.*

Hetty

A relative or fellow employee of Mrs Pearce, the Woolcombe House cook (YA 3).

Heywood, Peter

The former commander, in 1804 or 1805, of Jack Aubrey's HMS *Leopard*, remarkable for being the only Post Captain to have once been condemned to death for mutiny (for his role in the rebellion on Bligh's HMS *Bounty*). Once pardoned, he had been favoured in his subsequent career by 'Black Dick' Howe (DI 1). Heywood is well known to Jack, they having served together in HMS *Fox* and dined in HMS *Lively* (DI 1). He now dines at Ashgrove Cottage, giving a reticent account of his early adventures before collapsing in a drunken stupor (DI 1).

Peter Heywood (1773–1831), a nephew of Admiral Sir Thomas Pasley (1734–1808), joined the Royal Navy in 1786 as a Midshipman on *Bligh's exploration ship HMS *Bounty. When the infamous mutiny broke out off Tahiti in 1789, Heywood took little, if any, part in the affair but did remain on Bounty after Bligh's departure: indeed it has often been suggested that the Captain deliberately did not take him in the open boat on account of his youth. In 1791 Heywood and another Midshipman rowed out to the approaching HMS *Pandora and surrendered to Captain *Edwards (the leaders of the mutiny, Fletcher *Christian chief amongst them, having already fled Tahiti in Bounty, thus escaped capture). After the horrors of the journey back to England (accurately recounted in DI), Heywood and nine others were put on trial for mutiny. In late 1792 six were convicted (by a majority verdict) and sentenced to death, although almost all were certainly innocent, including the three men actually executed (the court chose to ignore that fact that the mutineer ringleaders had only allowed a single boat to leave Bounty, and that many men given no choice but to remain on the frigate had played no active part whatever in what had, in any case, been a bloodless rebellion). However, several of the senior mem-

bers of the panel, including its President Lord *Hood, were utterly convinced of Heywood's innocence, as was *Chatham, the *First Lord. They soon arranged for a pardon to be granted him, on account of his tender age, 16, at the time of the events (one other 'mutineer' was pardoned too and the other only briefly imprisoned). In 1793 Heywood was appointed Midshipman in Lord *Howe's HMS *Queen Charlotte (both Howe's *Captain of the Fleet and *Flag Captain had sat on the court-martial, voting with Hood for acquittal) and thenceforth enjoyed a successful and distinguished career. He was promoted Lieutenant in 1795 (serving on HMS *Fox from 1796 to 1798), Commander in 1800 and Post Captain in 1803; his period on the East Indies station in HMS *Leopard (in which he surveyed the coast of Ceylon) seems to have been an acting-command held either side of this promotion. At the time of his dinner with Jack Aubrey, Heywood was in command of HMS Nereus, 32-gun, which he held from 1809 to 1813. Heywood's his sea-career ended in 1816, with his death in 1831 coming well before he could have expected further promotion by seniority.

Hibernia, HMS

A ship distinguished for the beauty of her great cabin (TMC 3).

HMS Hibernia, 110-gun, was laid down in 1792 but not launched until 1804. She became the permanently moored flagship at Malta in 1855 and was not sold out of the service until 1902. Hibernia, the Latin name for Ireland, served for a great deal of the French wars in the Channel and Mediterranean as the flagship of Sir Sidney *Smith.

Hick, Mr

A neighbour of the Aubreys in Hampshire (TMC 2).

Hickey, William

A man whose description of a storm is borrowed by O'Brian (FSW author's note; the passage is in FSW 9).

William Hickey (1749?–1830) was a lawyer and miscellany writer whose Memoirs, 1749–1809 (not published until 100 years later) contain entertaining accounts of his many travels — including several trips to India — and his great weakness for debauchery.

Hicks

According to Sir Joseph Blaine, the best London lawyer for matrimonial disputes (SM 4).

Higgins

An expert tooth-drawer whom Maturin takes as his assistant surgeon in HMS Surprise (FSW 2–6). Soon developing a private practice as a quack (FSW 3), he performs a clumsy abortion on Mrs Horner (FSW 5) and, when discovered to have done so by her husband, the ship's gunner, is tossed overboard at dead of night (FSW 6).

High Bum

A Chinese seaman in HMS Lively, at one time almost certainly a pirate (HMS 2).

Hildebrand, Governor Sir

The British Civil Commissioner of Malta, a somewhat unintelligent soldier (TH 1–8).

Lieutenant-General Sir Hildebrand Oakes (1754–1822) was the Civil Commissioner for Malta from 1809 to 1813. However, his title of 'Sir,' in his case a baronetcy, did not come until his resignation from the post. He had succeeded a far more popular and effective man, Rear Admiral Sir Alexander Ball (1757–1809), Commissioner from 1800 until his death in office.

Hill

1: an Army major on board the Lord Nelson Indiaman, the uncle of the Misses Lamb (PC 5).
2: Jack Aubrey's clerk in HMS Boadicea (TMC 2,3)
3: the Captain of Three Graces, an English merchantman (WDS 6).
4: the owner of a musical instrument shop in London (YA 10).

The family business was founded in London by Joseph Hill (1715–1784), several of whose sons and nephews opened their own sales premises over time and also expanded into music publishing.

Hill, John

The Captain of HMS Leviathan (YA 5).

Hillier

A Midshipman in HMS Leopard (DI 7).

Himmelfahrt

An HMS Surprise seaman, once hospitalised in Malta (TH 8), who later serves in HMS Irresistible (RM 1).

Himmelfahrt, Ludwig

The name under which Casademon disguises himself as one of HMS Ariel's captured Royal Marines, thereby successfully eluding detection by the French authorities in Brest (SM 10).

Hinckley

A Sethian seaman in HMS Surprise (LM 5; NC 7).

Hincksey, Charles
see Hinksey, Charles

Hind, HMS

The 18-gun ship commanded by Ellis before his dismissal from the Royal Navy for fraud (RM 3).

An HMS Hind, 28-gun, was launched in 1785, rebuilt in 1800 and broken up in 1811.

Hinkman's

A Plymouth shipyard of indifferent reputation, the builders of HMS Polychrest (PC 6,7).

Hinksey or Hincksey, Charles and Mrs

The new rector of Swiving Monachorum (HMS 4) and his mother (HMS 7). Mrs Williams has Charles in her sights as a husband for her daughter Sophie, despite the young woman's attachment to Jack Aubrey (HMS 6). As vicar, he performs the marriage ceremonies of both Frances and Cecilia Williams (HMS 7) and turns out to have been well-known to Mr White during their time at Magdalen College (HMS 11). Many years later Hinksey has a parish close to the Aubreys' Ashgrove Cottage (COM 3), with Jack becoming intensely jealous of the attentions he still pays to Sophie (COM 3–6) until learning, with relief, that his 'rival' is soon to be married to a Miss Lucy Smith and given a Bishopric in India (COM 6,7).

Hipolito

Sam Panda's servant (WDS 7).

Hippocrates

The famous ancient doctor referred to by Maturin, the origin of the Hippocratic oath sworn by physicians (HMS 5,8; DI 3; FW 4; IM 4).

Hippocrates of Cos was probably a contemporary of the great philosopher Socrates (469–399 BC), although nothing certain his known of his life or work other than that he was regarded as one of the foremost of all medical practitioners from his own lifetime onwards. Hippocrates' enduring fame rests especially on the commentaries on his supposed career written by *Galen a few centuries after his death. The 'Hippocratic Oath' is ancient in origin — although we have no way of knowing whether or not it was actually associated with Hippocrates himself — and in its various forms sets out both the general duties of the physician to the profession of medicine and the 'first principle' of doing no harm to any patient. At various times the oath has explicitly excluded the performance of any invasive surgical procedure by a physician and has contained outright bans on both abortion and euthanasia.

Hislop, General

The Governor of Bombay, a passenger in HMS *Java*, who had once known General Aubrey (FW 3). After the disastrous battle with USS *Constitution*, he is put ashore in Brazil with the other prisoners (FW 4).

Lieutenant General Sir Thomas Hislop (1764–1843) was on his way in HMS *Java from England to his new post as Commander-in-Chief (not Governor) of Bombay when the action with USS *Constitution occurred. Having played a brave role in the fight, he was released on parole very soon afterwards, in due course presenting *Bainbridge with a handsome sword in commemoration of his most gentlemanly treatment of Java's captured crew and passengers. In 1813 Hislop was made a baronet and appointed to the military command of Madras and the Deccan (Bombay having been given to someone else in the meantime), a post that he retained for many years.

Hitchcock

Diana Villiers' groom (TGS 3).

Hoarehound, Roger

The sometime First Secretary at the Admiralty,

nicknamed 'Jolly Roger,' who had been investigated for corruption (RM 5).

The 'Jolly Roger' is the flag popularly supposed to have been flown by pirate ships, being either a skull-and-crossbones or a skeleton on a black background. There is no contemporary evidence that such flags were ever really used.

Hoare's

A London banking house used by General Aubrey (M&C 4) and subsequently by Jack Aubrey himself (M&C 8; HMS 6; RM 1,4; TGS 4,6; NC 4; COM 1), who deals on the premises with young Mr Hoare, a junior partner (RM 5).

Hoare's was founded in London in 1672 by the bullion dealer and Lord Mayor of London, Sir Richard Hoare (1648–1718). By Jack's day the bank was headed by Charles Hoare (1767–1857), a noted philanthropist as well as financier, and still employed many family members.

Hoath, Mrs

A convicted abortionist being transported to Australia in HMS *Leopard* (DI 3).

Hobbes

An author quoted by Maturin (C/T 8).

Thomas Hobbes (1588–1679) was an influential English philosopher who, having in his early years acted as assistant to Francis *Bacon, later became an intimate of many of the great thinkers of his age. Hobbes conceived of man as inherently dedicated to self-preservation, a view reflected in his extensive treatises on political theory, chief amongst them Leviathan (1651; revised 1668). His writings are distinguished not only for their intellectual brilliance but also for their language, at once clear, direct and full of highly memorable metaphors and phrases.

Hobbs

A Midshipman in HMS *Bellona* (COM 10).

Hobden

The Royal Marine Captain in HMS *Surprise* who argues and nearly duels with Maturin over the theft of a preserved hand by Naseby, his dog (HD 4). He later falls into an alcoholic coma (HD 6).

Hobson

1: a Master's Mate in HMS *Néréide* who, wounded in action, later dies in the French hospital on Mauritius (TMC 10).

2: a reference to water 'as pure as Hobson's Conduit' (C/T 2).

Thomas Hobson (1544?–1631), a prosperous carrier, was one of a group of Cambridge citizens and university dons who, in 1574, proposed a scheme to divert a nearby stream through the centre of the city to provide both fresh water and clean-scented air. 'Hobson's Conduit'— in fact a system of several connected conduits — still exists today, though lying mostly underground. The popular saying 'Hobson's Choice'— i.e., no choice at all— comes from Thomas' business practice of insisting that customers simply take the next available horse from his stables, what-

ever their own preference might have been, or take their custom elsewhere.

Hoche

The commander of the French invasion of Bantry Bay (COM 10; YA 5).

Louis-Lazare Hoche (1768–1797) rose from humble origins as a royal stable-lad to become a leading French military officer. Having entered the army in 1784 as a fusilier, he became a sergeant in the National Guard in about 1790 and by 1793, in the turmoil of the Revolution, had risen to General. Although very successful on the battlefield, he regularly seemed to pick the losing side in wider political affairs and was several time imprisoned. In 1796 Hoche was given the command of an army destined for Ireland but December storms prevented him from ever disembarking his 20,000 troops at Bantry Bay (on the extreme southwest corner of the island) and the plan was soon abandoned, with most of the ships and men returning unscathed to Brest. Once back in France he resumed successful command of armies in the northeast before dying of a sudden illness.

Hogg

1: Captain Latham's steward in HMS *Surprise* (IM 9).

2: a seaman from the destroyed whaler *Intrepid Fox* who, once aboard HMS *Surprise*, takes some time to come to terms with Royal Navy discipline (FSW 7). Wounded when *Surprise* intercepts the all-female crewed *pahi* (FSW 8), he later breaks his arm during a storm (FSW 9).

La Hogue, HMS

A ship referred to in Philip Broke's letter of challenge to Captain Lawrence (FW 9).

HMS Hogue *(or Hague), 74-gun, was launched in late 1811 and then sent to Canada, under Thomas *Capel, with large numbers of supernumerary seamen to bolster the North American squadrons. Converted to a screw ship in 1848, she was broken up in 1865 (N.B., COLLEDGE's '1965' is a typo). Her name commemorates the location of an English victory in 1692 over the remnants of the French fleet just recently beaten at the Battle of Barfleur.*

Holden

1: an Royal Navy officer dismissed the service for protecting Greeks from the forces of Britain's Turkish allies (TH 1).

2: an officer in HMS *Implacable* (HD 10).

Holden, Frank

The Captain of HMS *Pyramus* (COM 3).

Hole, James

A seaman in HMS *Leopard* (DI 9).

Holland

A fishmonger in Portsmouth (DI 1).

Holland, James

The Master of the captured and burned British whaler, *Intrepid Fox* (FSW 7).

Holland, Lady

A London socialite and sometime admirer of Buonaparte (C/T 7).

Elizabeth Vassal Fox (1770–1845) married Henry Richard Fox, 3rd Lord Holland (1773–1840), in 1797 after a scandalous affair lasting several years, being divorced by her first husband only three days before her second wedding. Lord Holland, a radical Whig like his uncle, Charles James *Fox, and his new wife were great admirers of *Buonaparte, whom they had met in Paris in 1802 during the Peace of Amiens. Lady Holland sent notes of commiseration to the Emperor on his first abdication in 1814 and corresponded fulsomely with him until his death in exile. Renowned for her peremptory manners and savage wit, she ran a dinner table in London that was envied and loathed in equal measure, with even *Talleyrand thinking her a formidable hostess.

Hollar

The bosun of Jack Aubrey's HMSS *Worcester* (IM 4+; TH 4+) and *Surprise* (IM 10+; FSW 2–9).

Holles

A Midshipman in HMS *Leopard*, beaten by Jack Aubrey for lecherous spying on Mrs Wogan (DI 4,6,7). He follows Jack home to England in HMS *La Flèche* (FW 1,2) and, when that ship accidentally takes fire, escapes in the cutter with his Captain (FW 3).

Hollis

A Principal Secretary present at the King's Birthday Levée (RM 5).

Hollom

An unemployed Midshipman, now desperate for a ship, who had briefly served under Jack Aubrey in HMS *Lively* and had most recently been in HMS *Leviathan*. Having encountered Jack ashore in Gibraltar, he obtains as a position in HMS *Surprise* but is immediately regarded by Jack and the rest of the crew as an unlucky man, a 'Jonah,' being old for his position and never having received advancement (FSW 1,3–6). A handsome man with a beautiful singing voice, he starts an affair with Mrs Horner, the pretty young wife of the gunner, leading to pregnancy and a secret abortion (FSW 3–6). When the crew are later allowed ashore on Juan Fernandez Island, Mr Horner murders the adulterous pair (FSW 6; RM 3).

Holroyd

A lawyer mentioned by Blaine (RM 7).

The reference is perhaps to Sir George Sowley Holroyd (1758–1831), a renowned courtroom pleader and, from 1816, judge.

Holroyd, Billy

The Captain of HMS *Tromp*, a boyhood shipmate of Jack Aubrey in HMS *Sylph* (NC 8).

Holy Father

see **Pope, the**

'Holy Joe'

A reference to ostentatiously strict religious observance (WDS 3).

Home

A naturalist referred to by Maturin (NC 10).

*The reference is possibly to Sir Everard Home (1756–1832), a surgeon friend of the great naturalist Sir Joseph *Banks, who published extensively on human comparative anatomy. He was the brother-in-law of John *Hunter, some of whose works he edited, and became President of the Royal College of Surgeons.*

Home, Sir George and Miss

A late Vice Admiral whose deceased daughter's obituary is read by Maturin (DI 6).

Sir George Home (d.1803) was made Post in 1779, promoted Rear Admiral in 1797 and Vice Admiral in 1802.

Homer

The great poet of ancient Greece (M&C 9; IM 10; TH 9; FSW 3,4,9; WDS 9; HD 3). Maturin queries whether the same man could have written the very different *Iliad* and *Odyssey* (FSW 4).

Through his Iliad *and* Odyssey, *the Greek epic poet Homer has had the most profound influence on Mediterranean and later Western culture. Yet nothing is known of his life and there is no certainty even as to the century in which his works were produced (the notion of him as an 'illiterate, blind bard' is a much later gloss). Currently scholars put the composition of the* Iliad *at about 750 BC and of the* Odyssey *at about 725 BC (i.e., about 450 years after the wars they describe), but these dates are part-inference and part-guess. It is also uncertain whether the works were composed purely orally or with the aid of the then-nascent written Greek, the earliest reference to some sort of written versions being in about 550 BC. There has long been debate over whether one man composed both works — the* Iliad *is a highly sophisticated, heroic tragedy of the Trojan Wars, the* Odyssey *a more straightforward (at least on its surface) adventure story of the returning Greek warriors — or even whether each is the product of several contributors. Current scholarship suggests that one genius is at the heart of both poems, a view that has always had its strong adherents and equally strong opponents.*

Honey, Joseph or William

As Joseph Honey, a young Master's Mate in HMSS *Worcester* (IM 3,7) and *Surprise* (IM 10+; TH 2+), he is encouraged by Jack Aubrey to sit his Lieutenant's examination (TH 9). As William, he continues on *Surprise* (FSW 2) and is soon made an acting Lieutenant by Jack (FSW 3–9; RM 2,6), al-though, much later, he seems once again to be a Master's Mate (C/T 8).

Hood

One of the Captains who court-martials Aubrey for the loss of HMS *Sophie* (M&C 12). He is also said to be the officer whose HMS *Centaur* had taken and fortified the Diamond Rock (HD 10).

*The first reference here must be to Sir Samuel Hood (1762–1814), a Post-Captain in the Mediterranean up until 1803, who commanded HMS *Venerable in Sir James *Saumarez' actions of 1801. As a Commodore in the West Indies in January 1804, Hood and his HMS *Centaur took and fortified the Diamond Rock, off the island of Martinique, by a prodigious feat of daring and creative rigging. The 600-foot high island was held, as an HM 'sloop-of-war,' until being surrendered in May 1805 by Lieutenant James Wilkes Maurice (d.1857 in the rank of retired Rear Admiral) to a determined French assault. Sir Samuel, made Post in 1788, was promoted Rear Admiral in 1807 and Vice Admiral in 1811. His elder brother, Captain Alexander Hood (1758–1798), had sailed as a young man with *Cook and had later been killed in action commanding HMS *Mars, 74-gun, when she took Hercule in January 1798. The brothers were cousins of the Admirals Samuel, Lord *Hood, and his brother Alexander, Viscount Bridport (1726–1814).*

Hood, Lady

Mrs Goole had once met Sophie Aubrey at Lady Hood's reception (RM 1).

*'Lady Hood' could perhaps refer to the wife of any one of three titled members of the distinguished naval Hood family who were also married men; Samuel, Lord *Hood, his younger brother Alexander Hood, Viscount Bridport (1726–1814), or their cousin Sir Samuel *Hood.*

Hood, Lord

A great admiral (SM 5) who in past times had ordered an attack by HMSS *Juno* and *Fortitude* on the Mortella tower on Corsica (SM 6).

*Samuel, Viscount Hood (1724–1816), a member of the distinguished Hood family of senior naval officers, was made Post in 1756 and promoted Rear Admiral in 1780. a baronet of 1779, in 1782 he was raised to the Irish peerage as Lord Hood for his most distinguished service as Captain, Commodore and Admiral. Promoted Vice Admiral in 1793, on the outbreak of war with France in that year he was given command of the Mediterranean fleet, a somewhat thankless and trying task given the British lack of either preparation or clear strategy. Hood was unable to hold onto Toulon (up until then in the hands of his French royalist allies) and conceived instead a plan to take Corsica as the British Mediterranean base. The attack on the Mortella fortress occurred in early 1794 but the British ships were beaten off by fire from the high tower, HMS *Fortitude being set ablaze and suffering over 60 casualties; the fort itself was soon taken by a land assault, but only after a fierce battle. Later in the campaign to secure the island, *Nelson — one of Hood's senior Captains and a great admirer of the Admiral — lost the sight of an eye in a shore-assault. In late 1794 Hood, suffering indifferent health and at odds with his army colleagues, was recalled to England and, although he expected to re-assume com-*

mand, he and the *First Lord, *Spencer, could not agree on the thrust of future operations: by May 1795 Hood's sea-career had formally ended. Having been promoted full Admiral in April 1794, in 1796 Hood was made a Viscount in the English peerage. In the same year he was appointed Governor of Greenwich Hospital, a position he held until his death. Despite his lack of clear-cut success in his final command, Lord Hood is regarded as one of the Royal Navy's greatest commanders.

Hooper

1: an army major, travelling from Madras to England, met by Jack Aubrey at Suez (TH 6).
2: a seaman in HMS Surprise (NC 8).

Hope

1: the Captain successively of HMSS Bulldog, Eclair and Romulus, in each of which Philip Broke had served (FW 7).
Sir George Johnstone Hope (1767–1818) was promoted Commander of HMS *Bulldog in 1790, made Post into HMS *Eclair in 1793 and given HMS *Romulus in 1795. At the Battle of Trafalgar in 1805 he commanded HMS Defence with great distinction and, from 1808 to 1811, was the Captain of HMS *Victory herself, now *Saumarez' flagship in the Baltic. During that time he several times acted as the Admiral's *Captain of the Fleet until his own promotion to flag rank in 1811. From 1812 until his death he served in London as an Admiralty Commissioner, although in 1813 he held a final sea-command, assisting the Russian fleet to shift to England during *Buonaparte's invasion of their country.
2: a Mate in Diligence (SM 3).
3: a gentleman met in Torbay by Maturin (YA 4).

Hope

An East Indiaman in Muffit's China Fleet, protected by HMS Surprise from Admiral Linois' French squadron (HMS 9).
Hope, 1200 tons, made 9 round trips from India to England between 1796 and 1814. The action is based on the defence of a Honourable East India Company merchant fleet against *Linois' attack in February 1804. However, no Royal Navy ship was present during the fight, the squadron being organised by the senior Master, Nathaniel Dance of *Earl Camden. On this occasion James Pendergrass was Hope's Master.

Hopkins

A seaman in Surprise who attempts to smuggle a girl aboard ship at Sydney Cove (NC 10).

Horace

The great Latin poet, much admired by Stephen Maturin and others (FW 2; SM 6; FSW 5; COM 1; YA 8). According to Stephen, he was either homo- or bi-sexual (TH 8).
Quintus Horatius Flaccus (65–8 BC), one of the greatest of all classical poets, came from a moderately prosperous family of small landowners and public auctioneers. Having studied at the finest institutions Rome and Athens had to offer, he seemed destined for a brilliant public career. However, in the Civil War, he joined *Brutus' forces and,

after witnessing his leader's defeat at Philippi, was deprived of the family property by the victorious Augustus, *Caesar's heir. Horace was fortunate both to escape exile and then to be able to support himself by becoming a minor civil servant. He now began to write poetry, coming to the favourable notice of both *Virgil and the Emperor Augustus's enormously wealthy friend Maecenas, who soon became his financial and literary patron. From 38 BC onwards Horace enjoyed wealth and fame, developing in his poetry a novel form of satire directed as much at his own foibles as at those of others. This clever self-mockery, combined with a very keen insight into the many facets of human nature and relationships, is a constant theme in all of his relatively modest output and has had an enormous impact on European literature. Similarly, his elegant and vivid phrasing—not especially difficult to understand, but notoriously difficult to translate from the Latin with any degree of faith—finds echoes in poets through the ages, but perhaps especially in those of 17th and 18th century England. In his Odes (published in 23 BC), Horace departs from the then-dominant theme of obsessive love for a single individual (e.g., see *Catullus) and muses on the company of a variety of partners, male and female, each enjoying physical consummation as a happy release from ever-present worries and cares.

Hordsworth

A rick-yard owner near Woolcombe (YA 3).

Horner

1: a Lieutenant in HMS Ajax at the time when that Jack Aubrey was a boy aboard. He was shortly afterwards made Post and is also somehow known to Jack's cox'n, Barret Bonden (FW 3).
2: Mr and Mrs Horner, the gunner of HMS Surprise and his pretty 19-year-old wife, who, as is the custom of the service, sails with him in the ship (FSW 2–6; HD 2). Horner, the former gunner of HMS Belette, had once served under Sir Philip Broke (FSW 2). A formidably ill-tempered and dangerous man, he confesses to Maturin that he is impotent (FSW 3). This affliction appears to lead his wife into an affair with Midshipman Hollom, resulting in both her pregnancy and a clumsy abortion by the quack Higgins (FSW 3–5). Ashore on Juan Fernandez Island, Horner murders his wife and her lover and, soon afterwards, tosses Higgins overboard from Surprise at dead of night before hanging himself (FSW 6; RM 3).

Hornet, USS

A 20-gun ship, Captain Lawrence, that had sunk HMS Peacock, killing her Captain Billy Peake during the action (FW 4,6; SM 1).
USS Hornet, 18-gun, was launched as a brig in 1805 and in 1811 converted to a 20-gun sloop. In February 1813, under *Lawrence, she was engaged by *Peake's brig, HMS *Peacock, near the mouth of the Demerara River. Dismal British gunnery led to the fight being a short one, of less than 15 minutes, before the badly holed Peacock surrendered, with Peake already dead. Hornet suffered only one

dead and two injured during the action but a further three men, sent across as prize crew, were drowned when the English ship promptly sank. Hornet was wrecked off the coast of Mexico in 1829.

Horridge
An unreliable builder used by the Aubreys for extensions to Ashgrove Cottage (DI 1,3).

Horsburgh
A well-regarded hydrographer (TGS 6; NC 6).
James Horsburgh (1762–1836), a Scottish sailing Master and naval surveyor, was Hydrographer to the East India Company from 1809. He was the author of The East India Directory *(a compendium of navigational information) and other similar works.*

Hortense
A lady referred to by two of Maturin's captors in Paris (SM 11).

Horton, Admiral
A deceased officer whose widow, the former Miss Isobel Carrington, Admiral Lord Barmouth has recently married (HD 9,10).

Hosier's Ghost
A tune improvised on by Aubrey and Maturin (PC 6).
The tune is named for Admiral Francis Hosier (1673–1727), whose fleet blockading Porto Bello in Central America was struck by a yellow fever epidemic in 1726–1727, resulting in the deaths of over 4,000 seamen, including Hosier himself; his body was returned to England buried in the bilges of his flagship. In 1739, the poet Richard Glover (1712–1785) wrote a famous ballad, 'Admiral Hosier's Ghost,' contrasting Hosier's horrible fate with Admiral Edward Vernon's (1684–1757) more recent success in the same vicinity. Hosier had been made Post in 1697, promoted Rear Admiral in 1719 and Vice Admiral in 1723. Vernon's own career and curious fate could also have made a good subject for a ballad with an especial appeal to Jack Aubrey. Made Post in 1706, promoted Vice Admiral in 1739 without having ever been a Rear Admiral, he rose to full Admiral in 1745, having been throughout his career pugnaciously outspoken both in the Royal Navy itself and in Parliament (where he served as an MP for 28 years). In 1745 he wrote a series of letters to the Admiralty, complaining in the liveliest terms of his supposed poor treatment by them whilst holding the Downs command. Replaced just before he could resign his flag, he commenced vitriolic public pamphlet attacks on the Admiralty Board, for which he was dismissed the service in 1746 despite his long record of valiant and effective service.

Hoskins, Colonel and Mrs
Neighbours of the Maturins in England. Sophie Aubrey's mother, Mrs Williams, believes the Colonel to be Diana Villiers' lover (COM 2).

Hoskins, William
A seaman in the whaler *Truelove* who had once

served as an armourer's mate in HMS *Polychrest* (C/T 9).

Hoste
A Royal Navy officer, famous for his fighting spirit (DI 5), of whose recent successes (TH 5; HD 5) and showy ways (TH 9) Jack Aubrey takes a somewhat dim view.
*Sir William Hoste (1780–1828), a brilliant young protégé of *Nelson, served as a Lieutenant on HMS *Theseus at the Battle of the Nile and was promoted into HMS *Mutine as Commander shortly after the great victory. Made Post in 1804, he soon made a reputation in Admiral Sir Sidney *Smith's Mediterranean squadron as a most enterprising and brave officer, capturing several hundred small enemy vessels over the next ten years. Yet, rather like Smith and even Nelson himself, the bold declarations by Hoste of love for country, profession, material rewards, honours and himself, often seemingly in reverse order, grated on the nerves of many colleagues. From 1808 to 1814 he led a squadron of frigates in the Adriatic (some of his adventures finding their way into Jack *Aubrey's Ionian mission) and in 1811, with just four of them, won a great victory off Lissa against a combined force of 10 French and Venetian ships. A baronet of 1814, at the end of the war Hoste returned to England, his health broken by malaria and other illnesses contracted early in his career. He now saw only a little further service — including command of the Royal Yacht from 1825 to 1826 — before his relatively early death.*

Hotham, Henry
A rigid disciplinarian appointed to the troubled HMS *Blanche*, whose crew then refused to accept him until the intervention of Nelson (COM 9).
*This incident is recorded only in the journal of Jacob Nagle (see note under *Nagel), an American seaman in HMS *Blanche. He tells that, when Hotham was appointed to the troubled Blanche by Commodore *Nelson in early January 1797, the ship's petty officers refused to accept him aboard because of his reputation as a 'tartar' in his previous ship, HMS Dido (there is no other evidence that Hotham had acquired such a reputation), and even turned the forecastle guns, loaded with canister-shot, on him. Hotham returned to the ship a little later with Nelson's First Lieutenant, who promptly threatened to hang every third petty officer unless they came to order, an outburst that of course only served further to inflame passions (Nelson at the time was flying his pennant in the frigate HMS *Minerve, whose Premier was Thomas Hardy, later Captain of HMS *Victory at the Battle of Trafalgar). Nelson himself now came to Blanche, saying that, although they must accept Captain Hotham, he himself would support them in any legitimate complaint about tyrannical behaviour. Nagle recounts that this intervention drew both three cheers from the Blanches and some tears from Hotham. Henry Hotham (1777–1833), born into a large naval family, was made Post in 1795, promoted Rear Admiral in 1814 and Vice Admiral in 1825. In 1815 it was to a ship in his Channel squadron, HMS *Bellerophon, that *Buonaparte surrendered after his defeat by *Wellington at Waterloo.*

Houmouzios

A Greek banker in Sierra Leone, an intelligence contact of Stephen Maturin (COM 8,9).

Howard

1: HMS *Surprise*'s Marine officer (FSW 3–9; RM 2).

2: an HMS *Surprise* youngster, the son of an old colleague of Jack Aubrey (RM 3).

Howard, Francis

The Captain of HMS *Aurora* and a noted scholar of ancient Greece (COM 3+).

Howard, John Condom

The junior Marine Lieutenant in HMS *Leopard* (DI 3–7), whose flute playing is compared by Maturin to that of the great Albini (DI 6). Aubrey, however, declines to play with him, having had cause to reprimand him most severely for lecherous intentions towards the prisoner, Louisa Wogan (DI 4,6). Later, just as he is about to play his instrument in the ward-room, Howard is murdered by the drunk and raving Mr Larkin (DI 7).

Howards, the

A family said by Sophie Williams to be Roman Catholic (PC 10).

The Howards, a leading English Roman Catholic family with many branches and influential members, were and are Dukes of Norfolk. At the time of PC, Charles Howard (1746–1815) sat as 11th Duke of Norfolk, having succeeded his Catholic father in 1786; however, the new Duke himself had converted to the Protestant faith as a young man. On his death, the title then passed to his cousin, the Catholic Bernard Edward Howard (1765–1842).

Howarth, Sir Alan

A Captain with whom Collins had once sailed, famous for his devotion to hoisting large expanses of sail (IM 7).

Howe, Earl

A name used by Mr Whewell for a Krooman tribesman in Sierra Leone (COM 8).

Howe, Earl 'Black Dick'

A famous British Admiral, referred to in Mowett's poetry (M&C 3), who had fought and won the Battle of the Glorious First of June in his flagship HMS *Queen Charlotte* (PC 9; IM 4,10; C/T 4). Known as 'Black Dick,' he was a very testy, elderly officer who had beaten Lieutenant Hale and Midshipman West for supposed errors in the action (C/T 4). Howe was also known as a supporter of Peter Heywood after the latter's conviction for mutiny (DI 1).

Richard, Admiral Earl Howe (1726–1799), was born into an influential political family; made Post in 1746, he was promoted Rear Admiral in 1770, Vice Admiral in 1776, Admiral in 1782 and Admiral of the Fleet in 1796. As active in politics (an MP from 1757 to 1782; *First Lord of the Admiralty from 1783 to 1788) as in war, he was brilliantly successful in both, amongst his many successes being the defeat of the French fleet at the Battle of the Glorious First of June in 1794. Known as 'Black Dick' for his complexion and dark whiskers, Howe was revered by his superiors (such as *Hawke), his juniors (such as *St Vincent and *Nelson) and by ordinary seamen alike. He was also well known for an intimidating taciturnity, maintained in almost all circumstances (the attack on his juniors seems most out of character and is not found in the biographies). In 1797, although by then a very weak invalid in Bath, he struggled back to Spithead to resolve the mutiny of the Channel Fleet, doing so on terms that were widely perceived by all parties as honourable and fair. Howe, who had inherited an Irish Viscountcy in 1758, was made an English Earl in 1782 and in 1797 became the first man ever to receive the prestigious Knighthood of the Garter for purely naval accomplishments. Always a martyr to gout, in the year of his death Howe underwent the then highly popular electrocution therapy but this seemed merely to hasten his end, bringing on what reads like a stroke.

Howell

A Midshipman in HMS *Charwell* (PC 1).

Howlands

A seaman in HMS *Leopard* who contracts a venereal disease from Peggy Barnes (DI 6).

Hoyle

The author of a treatise on games and tactics (PC 3).

Edmond Hoyle (1672–1769) was a prolific and influential English writer on the calculation of probabilities in games such as whist, piquet and backgammon.

Huascar Inca

One of Eduardo's Inca ancestors, the son of Huayna Capac (WDS 9,10).

Huascar Inca (1490–1533), the son of *Huayna, was half-brother to *Atahualpa, with whom he engaged in a civil war after their father's death, a conflict that enabled the Spanish conqueror *Pizarro to divide and conquer the Inca lands and peoples. Huascar was later captured by Atahualpa, who, shortly before his own execution by the Spanish, gave orders for his brother's murder.

Huayna Capac

The 'Great Inca' (WDS 9,10).

Huayna Capac (d.1525), the 11th Inca Emperor, was father of both *Atahualpa and *Huascar. Having ascended the throne in about 1473 as a very young boy, once he came to rule in his own right, he then travelled widely about his domains, suppressing minor rebellions and greatly improving both administration and prosperity. Huayna died rather suddenly during an epidemic (perhaps smallpox or measles, introduced by Spanish coastal settlers) and his failure to have indicated which of his sons was to be his heir then sparked off ruinous civil wars.

Hubble

A former school-mate of William Reade (HD 8).

Huber, Monsieur

A naturalist, and correspondent of Maturin, who specialises in the study of bee behaviour (PC 12,13; RM 7).

> *François Huber (1750–1831) was a blind Swiss naturalist whose* Observations on Bees *was published in 1792 to great acclaim. Since losing his sight in about 1785, he had been assisted in his immensely detailed work by carefully chosen and briefed amanuenses.*

Huge, Mr

A builder used by Mr Martin (TGS 1).

Hughes

The Port-Admiral at Gibraltar (FSW 2).

Hughes, Robert

The author whose *The Fatal Shore* provided O'Brian with much of the detail for his portrait of New South Wales in the early 19th century (NC author's note).

> *Robert Hughes (b.1938), the distinguished Australian art critic, journalist and historian, published* The Fatal Shore *in 1986.*

Hull, Captain

The Captain of the USS Constitution (LM 3).

> *Isaac Hull (1773–1843) joined the U.S. Navy in 1798 as a Lieutenant in USS *Constitution after having had a successful career as a merchant Captain. He soon distinguished himself in the short wars against France and Tripoli and, in 1806, was promoted Captain. When war with Britain broke out in 1812, he had already been in command of his old Constitution for two years and soon demonstrated his great seamanship by avoiding capture by a squadron of five British ships during a three-day chase. In August of the same year he brought one of them, Captain *Dacres' HMS *Guerrière, to battle and, by superior ship-handling and gunnery, soon reduced her to a sinking hulk; the British ship was burned by the Americans once her crew had been taken off. This first action of the war was also the first in a series of American victories against the hitherto all-powerful Royal Navy and brought Hull great acclaim, although he did not again hold a sea-command during the conflict (there being available for service many more ambitious and able Captains than frigates). In administrative positions from 1813 to 1824, he then commanded the Pacific fleet until 1827, the Washington Navy Yard from 1829 to 1835 and the Mediterranean fleet from 1839 to 1841.*

Hulme

The author of a naval medical text lent to Maturin by Florey (M&C 2).

> *Nathaniel Hulme (1732–1807) was an English physician who had once served in the Royal Navy as a surgeon's mate. He published his* Libellus de Natura Scorbuti *(A Handbook on the Nature of Scurvy) in 1768 and subsequently produced a number of other influential works on gout, bladder stones and similar complaints. His book follows *Lind in advocating lemon-juice as a specific but also unfortunately follows Lind's error of advocating preservation*

> *of the juice in a form reduced by long boiling, a process that destroys most of the essential ascorbic acid.*

Humboldt, Alexander

A gentleman referred to by Jack Aubrey as a polymath friend to whom he communicates hydrographical measurements (RM 8; TGS 1+; NC 4; C/T 1,3; WDS 2,10; COM 9). Gayongos adds that he is a highly respected opponent of slavery (WDS 7).

> *Friedrich Heinrich Alexander, Baron von Humboldt (1769–1859), was a famous Prussian naturalist and explorer of South America who, between 1799 and 1803, traced the Orinoco to its source, established its connection to the Amazon, and crossed the high Andes down to Quito. As well as publishing his scientific results from this great expedition, Humboldt had an active wider interest in geography and hydrography: the cold, north-running current off the west coast of South America is named for him. During his lifetime Humboldt enjoyed the highest reputation as a scientist, publishing many highly regarded works on a whole range of botanical, geographic and philosophical issues. In his general writings on South America (especially those of 1810 and 1811), he excoriates the practice of slavery. His younger brother Karl William, Baron von Humboldt (1767–1835), a celebrated philologist, educator, diplomat and statesman of similarly liberal political views, founded the University of Berlin on the then-novel principle of 'academic freedom' (at the time, primarily freedom from religious control). N.B., The reference in C/T 4 to *'Helmholz' as Jack's correspondent is probably a slip for Friedrich Humboldt.*

Humbug, HMS

A small hermaphrodite brig captured by the Royal Navy from the Russians (SM 8,9). Her new name causes some embarrassment and discomfort to Midshipman Jevons when he is forced to call it out to Captain Jack Aubrey (SM 8).

Hume, Davy

A philosopher referred to by Professor Graham (TH 1).

> *David Hume (1711–1776) was a Scottish lawyer, thinker and historian whose contributions to learning brought him great acclaim in his own lifetime (in part because of his graceful literary style; the ideas themselves were hotly disputed) and have ever since been a central part of the Western, philosophical canon. Although Hume thought of himself principally as a moralist, his contemporary reputation was chiefly as a controversial constitutional historian. Yet his enduring claim to attention is a systematic, empirical epistemology in which he forcefully argues for experience, through the physical senses alone, being the sole foundation of what humans call 'knowledge.'*

Hummel

A composer favoured by Jack Aubrey and Stephen Maturin (PC 2,5,6,12; HMS 11; SM 4; IM 5), also played by their wives, Sophie and Diana (LM 9).

> *Johann Nepomuk Hummel (1778–1837), a Hungarian pupil and protégé of *Mozart, became a noted composer and is commonly regarded as the founder of modern*

pianoforte technique. He was later one of the pall-bearers at Beethoven's funeral and performed at that great man's memorial concert.

Humphrey

A merchant Captain present at a dinner in Java (TGS 6).

Humphreys

A well-connected Lieutenant who carries the duplicate copies of Broke's victory dispatch from Canada to England in *Diligence* (SM 3,4).

Humphreys, Salusbury 'Buck'

The sometime Captain of HMS *Leopard* who, in 1807, had fired three controversial broadsides into USS *Chesapeake* (DI 10; FSW 9).

*Sir Salusbury Pryce Humphreys (1778–1845; took the surname Davenport in 1838 when his wife received a large inheritance) was made Post in 1804 after a very successful career as an enterprising Lieutenant. In 1807 Vice-Admiral the Honourable George *Berkeley, the British commander at Halifax, ordered that any Royal Navy deserters suspected to be in U.S. warships should be seized, even though no state of war then existed between the two countries. *Humphreys, in his 50-gun HMS *Leopard (the Admiral's flagship, to which Humphreys had been appointed in 1806; Berkeley seldom went to sea in her), intercepted USS *Chesapeake off Norfolk, Virginia and demanded the right to search the ship; Chesapeake's Captain, James Barron, was astonished at the temerity of the order and determined to resist. However, he was at the disadvantage of his ship being wholly unprepared for any such hostile encounter with the Royal Navy and, before he could get his guns free, he received three full broadsides from the British ship, compelling him to strike. As alluded to several times in the series, this incident caused great resentment in the U.S. and was a contributing factor to war eventually breaking out in the Spring of 1812. After the action, the political row led the Admiralty to recall Admiral Berkeley, whilst still insisting on the right to stop U.S. ships. Humphreys himself paid the price of vigorously following his clear—and only subsequently unpopular—orders by being deprived of his ship and placed on the half-pay list from 1808 to 1840. In 1838 he was appointed, by usual seniority, a 'yellow' Rear Admiral but, two years later, some of the previous injustice was reversed by his restoration to the active list as a full-pay Rear Admiral of the Blue, although he never went to sea in this rank. In the same year, 1840, he was also knighted for his services ashore as a magistrate.*

Hunks

Jack Aubrey's financial agent (M&C 1).

Hunt, Captain

The commander of HMS *Sirius* when she was wrecked on Norfolk Island (C/T 1).

*The reference is to John Hunter (sic; 1738–1821), a Scottish officer who joined the Royal Navy as a Midshipman in 1754 and from 1769 to 1778 served as a Sailing Master under many influential officers, such as *St Vincent and *Howe. Yet, although his reputation for seamanship was great, it was not until 1780 that he managed to obtain a Lieutenant's commission, the only path to positions of higher command. With Howe as *First Lord of the Admiralty, Hunter was in 1786 made Post into HMS *Sirius, part of Commodore Arthur Phillip's expedition to colonise the coast of New South Wales, earlier discovered by Captain *Cook. After successful arrival in Australia in 1788, Hunter continued to explore other locations thought to have potential as colonies but, in 1790, Sirius was wrecked on Norfolk Island during a great storm. Having returned to England in 1793, he failed to secure another ship but nevertheless served as a volunteer under Howe in the following year at the Battle of the Glorious First of June. In 1795 Hunter returned to Australia as Governor of New South Wales, a position he held until 1801. By 1804 he was back in active service in the Channel fleet but, after being promoted Rear Admiral in 1807, held no further sea-command. In 1810 Hunter was promoted, by seniority, Vice Admiral.*

Hunter, John and family

The author of a medical text consulted by Stephen Maturin (C/T 3,4; WDS 4). An expert anatomist (PC 12), he is a member of a distinguished medical family (FW 2).

*John Hunter (1728–1793), the great Scottish anatomist, worked first as a cabinet-maker before moving to London in 1748 as an assistant to his successful elder brother, the anatomist, lecturer and society physician, William Hunter (1718–1783). John soon became famous both for his skill in dissection and, after 1754, as a lecturer at his brother's private medical school. Having served as an army surgeon from 1760 to 1763 (greatly enhancing his already good skills with knife and saw), he then returned to London to set up what soon became a highly lucrative private practice. In 1767 his writings and lectures on comparative anatomy, physiology and natural history brought him a Fellowship of the Royal Society (William also being elected Fellow in the same year). Of Hunter's many books, Stephen *Maturin may have been best familiar with his Treatise on Venereal Disease, posthumously edited in 1810 by his pupil Sir Everard *Home, and his Treatise on the Blood, Inflammation and Gun-shot Wounds. Familiar too may have been the work of another (unrelated and less well-known) John Hunter (d.1809), who published books on military diseases of the West Indies, especially hepatitis and yellow fever.*

Hurst

A seaman in HMS *Surprise* under particular obligation to Maturin for treating him for past disease (LM 5).

Hurtado, General

Stephen Maturin's primary contact amongst the disaffected military in Peru (WDS 7,8; COM 2).

The reference may be to Don Manuel Hurtado de Mendoza, a Peruvian brigadier active from 1813 to 1815.

Hussar, HMS

The 'old *Hussar*,' a frigate once commanded by Admiral Russell, in which he had fought Kergariou's

La Sybille (LM 1). She is later referred to as a splendid sailer (C/T 8).

> *Thomas MacNamara *Russell commanded HMS* Hussar, *the third Royal Navy ship of that name, in her action with *Kergariou of January 1783. His ship was the 26-gun, ex–Massachusetts Colonial Marine ship* Protector, *captured by the Royal Navy in 1780 and sold out of the service later in 1783. By the time of Russell's remarks three more* Hussars *had come and gone, with the currently serving ship — probably the one referred to in C/T — being a 38-gun, launched in 1807 and eventually destroyed by fire in 1861. A 'hussar' is a member of a light cavalry regiment, usually deployed for skirmishing or rapid attack and withdrawal.*

Hyaena, HMS

The former name of the French *Hébé*, recaptured by Jack Aubrey in HMS *Boadicea* (TMC 2; YA 8). Forty-five years previously, Admiral Bertie had served in her as Midshipman (TMC 3).

> *O'Brian here seems to have conflated several, often-renamed ships. The first HMS* Hyaena *in the Royal Navy was launched in 1778 (13–14 years after *Bertie says he served in her), captured by the French in 1793 and renamed the privateer* Hyène, *and then retaken and restored to her original name in 1797; she was broken up in 1802. In 1809, at about the time of Jack's cruise, the French *Hébé was taken (for the first time in her own career, although she was not the first French ship of that name to be captured) by HMS* Loire *off the coast of Spain and soon re-named HMS *Ganymede. In 1804 a new HMS* Hyaena *had been purchased by the Royal Navy as the merchantman* Hope; *she became a store ship in 1813 and was sold out of the service in 1822.*

Hyde

The First Lieutenant of HMS *Ariel* (SM 6), regarded by Jack Aubrey as a good ship-manager but no great seaman (SM 8). In very foul weather, when HMS *Ariel* finds herself nearly on the rocks off Brest, Jack Aubrey is knocked down at a crucial moment and Hyde, who routinely confuses left and right (SM7), then issues a catastrophically muddled helm command (SM 9). HMS *Ariel* is wrecked, although all her men are saved and taken prisoner (SM 9,10). We later learn that, as a senior Midshipman, Hyde was once before a French captive and had escaped from the prisons at both Verdun and Bitche (SM 10).

Hyde, Ned

A seaman in HMS *Surprise* (HMS 7).

Hyde, Reuben

The First Mate of the American whaler *La Fayette* and the brother of William Hyde (DI 10).

Hyde, William and Martha

The Master of the American whaler *General Washington* and his wife. William is the brother of Reuben Hyde (DI 10).

Hydrographer of the Navy
see both Dalhousie *and* Dalrymple

Hyperion, HMS

A ship commanded by Captain Cobbold (WDS 10).

> *HMS* Hyperion, *32-gun, was launched in 1807 and broken up in 1833. In classical myth, Hyperion was a Titan who married his sister, Theia, and fathered the Sun, Moon and Dawn; indeed, often the word simply means 'the sun'.*

Hypothesis

The name by which Maturin refers to himself in a discussion with Duhamel (SM 11).

I

Ibn Haukal

A traveller referred to by Omar Pasha (HD 7).

> *Kasim Mohammed Ibn Haukal (fl. 943–975) was probably a native of Bhagdad and commenced a great series of travels in about 943. In 975 he published his* Book of Ways and Provinces, *a work containing maps and illustrations as well as basic geographical and ethnographic material.*

Ibn Hazm

The Sheikh of Azgar, in Morocco, who intends to finance the Moslem intervention in South Eastern Europe, sending his gold via Algiers (HD 1,5,7), with whose Vizier Hashin he is in league (HD 8).

Ibn Khaldun

A Muslim authority on ancient Andalusia (TH 2; HD 3).

> *Wali-aldin Ibn Khaldun (1332–1406), a member of one of the leading Arabic families of Muslim Spain, is one of the greatest of all medieval historians and social philosophers. Ibn Khaldun himself was born in North Africa about a century after the Christian reconquest of most of his family's home country. After a promising early career at the court of the King of Morocco, he fell out of favour and moved to Granada, one of the remaining Arab possessions in Spain. Here he served as a diplomat for its Sultan and, somewhat later (after a period of roving service in the sultanates of North Africa), as Prime Minister. In 1375, Ibn Khaldun took a four year 'sabbatical' in Algeria to write his* Muqaddimah *('Introduction to History'), a work that sets out a highly sophisticated theory of*

societal cohesion, growth and transformation, an approach to the discipline quite unlike anything that had either gone before or would appear for many centuries after his death He later also produced his Kitab-al-'ibar, a substantive history of the Arabs of North Africa. A controversial scholar and statesman in his own time, in 1382 Ibn Khaldun was forced to leave the western regions and seek his fortune in Cairo, then the leading city of the Arab world. Here he achieved great renown as a professor and as a judge (whose strictness in a hitherto rather free-wheeling city left him only intermittently popular). Late in life, his travels took him to Damascus, Syria and, when in 1400 that city was besieged by Timur (a.k.a. *Tamerlane), Ibn Khaldun spent several weeks in the Tartar army's camp as a hostage-cum-negotiator, a period he described in detail in his autobiography. Ibn Khaldun eventually retired to Cairo, where he is buried.

Ibrahim

1: a potentate in the Eastern Mediterranean (TH 4).
The reference is probably to Ibrahim Ali (1789–1848), the son of Mohammed *Ali, Pasha of Egypt, who, after making a career as a fighting man in his father's service, achieved high command from 1818 onwards. Ibrahim's reputation was that of a very able field commander, although exceptionally ruthless in his treatment of the inhabitants of captured towns. In 1848 he ruled in place of his very elderly father as Pasha, but died of illness only a few months later.
2: a guide given by Vizier Hashin to Maturin and Jacob (HD 7).

Icarus

The classical figure, famous for his death by falling from the sky (DI 4; LM 4).
In Greek myth Icarus, the son of the inventor *Daedalus, flew too close to the sun on wings of feathers and wax. The wax melted, the wings disintegrated, and Icarus fell to his death in the sea. His father, more prudent, survived the flight.

Icarus, HMS

A ship at Bombay to which HMS *Java* is carrying fresh crew (FW 3).

Ignatio, don

The Captain of the Spanish *Clara*, who surrenders his ship to Jack Aubrey's HMS *Lively*, Jack then referring to him as 'don Garcio' (PC 14).

Ignatius, St.

Maturin refers to the poisonous 'St. Ignatius' beans' (IM 4).
The bean is the strychnos ignatii, the source of the poison strychnine (the bean was long known as deadly; the alkaloid poison was isolated in 1818). It is not known for which of the several possible Saints Ignatius the bean is named, or why.

Iles, Billy

A villager in Woolcombe (YA 3).

Illegible, Mr

When Sophie Aubrey refers to Sam Panda in a letter, Jack is unable to read the actual name she has written (RM 1)

Illustrious, HMS

Admiral Bertie's new flagship at the Cape (TMC 10), in which Rogers had once served (C/T 9). Some years later, William Mowett becomes her First Lieutenant (LM 2).
HMS Illustrious, 74-gun, was launched in 1803 and broken up in 1868. In 1810 she was sent as temporary flagship to the Cape squadron—a command usually dominated by frigates and elderly 60-guns—for the coming assault on Mauritius and went onto to take part in the capture of Java in the following year.

Imam

see **Mahdi**

Immortalité, HMS

A frigate whose Captain Carlow wishes to attend Parliament as an MP. Lord Melville contemplates her as a first, temporary, post-command for Jack Aubrey (PC 12).
HMS Immortalité, 42-gun, was launched as the French Immortalité in 1795. In 1798 she was part of the abortive French invasion of Ireland, being then taken by HMS Fishguard whilst trying to return to her home waters. She was broken up in 1806.

Impétueux, HMS

A ship that had been near HMS *Magnificent* when the latter was wrecked (YA 5).
HMS Impétueux, 74-gun, was launched in 1788 as the French l'America and, in 1794, was taken by *Howe's fleet at the Battle of the Glorious First of June. Initially renamed HMS America, she became the Impétueux in 1795 and was finally broken up in 1813.

Implacable, HMS

The ship of Mr Jeavons, James Dillon's second in a duel at Port Mahon (M&C 7). Later Mr Brand serves in her, possibly as Captain (PC 6). Many years afterwards she is Lord Barmouth's flag-ship at Gibraltar, Captain Henry James (HD 9).
The first HMS Implacable, 74-gun, was the French *Duguay-Trouin, launched in 1800 but not captured until 1805, some time after both M&C and PC (she had fought at Trafalgar, being captured shortly after that battle by Sir Richard *Strachan's squadron). In 1855 she became a training ship and in 1912 was loaned out for preservation, being finally scuttled as late as 1949.

Impregnable, HMS

A ship in Plymouth harbour (PC 7).
A 98-gun HMS Impregnable, launched in 1786, had been wrecked at Spithead in 1799 (well before PC). Her similar replacement was not launched until 1810 (well after PC), being finally sold in 1906 (having been renamed HMS Kent in 1888 and HMS Caledonia in 1891).

Inchiquin

Maturin refers to an 'Inchiquin pistole' coin (COM 1).

Morrogh O'Brien, 6th Baron and 1st Earl Inchiquin (1618?–1674) was an Irish Protestant aristocrat and soldier who fought in the English civil war, sometimes for Charles I and sometimes for *Cromwell, depending on the party from which he could secure the best protection for both his lands and co-religionist tenants in Munster. For his conduct against Charles' Catholic supporters, he became notorious as 'Morrogh of the Burnings' and it was during this time that copper coins were minted under his name to pay his impoverished soldiery. By 1650 he had fallen out of favour with Cromwell and so left Ireland for the Continent to join the English royalists in exile there. He soon became a General in the French army and served as Governor of French Catalonia until the restoration of *Charles II to the English throne in 1660. Lord Inchiquin, who had been made an Earl by the King in 1654, served as an English General in Portugal from 1662 to 1663 before returning to a relatively quiet retirement in his native land. His hatred for both Cromwell and his Puritan regime had led Inchiquin to convert to Catholicism in 1656 (resulting in a separation from his Dutch Protestant wife) and it was in this faith that he died.

Indefatigable, HMS

1: a frigate that, in company with HMS *Amazon*, had driven the 74-gun *Droits de l'Homme* onto rocks off Brest (PC 1; YA 5). Under Commodore Graham, she later leads the squadron of HMSS *Medusa*, *Amphion* and *Lively* that captures Bustamente's Spanish treasure ships (PC 14; HMS 1). Years afterwards, Jack Aubrey believes she will be ordered to the North American Station, now that war with the USA has been declared (FW 1,2).

HMS Indefatigable *was launched as a 64-gun in 1784. One of the first British razees, she was cut down to a 44-gun frigate in 1795 and finally broken up in 1816. In the famous running fight of 1797 with *Droits de l'Homme she was commanded by Sir Edward *Pellew and, in the 1804 action against *Bustamente, was commanded by Graham Moore (see *Graham, Captain).*

2: Admiral Byron's flagship, of which Pulling's grandfather had been bosun (DI 3).

The first HMS Indefatigable *was not launched until 1784 (see 1 above), some years after *Byron's retirement from active command. His final flagship (in 1779) was HMS *Princess Royal.*

Indienne

A French ship in the great fleet action that concludes *Master and Commander* (M&C 12).

Indienne, 40-gun, was launched in 1795 and in 1809 burned by her own crew to avoid her being taken by *Gambier and *Cochrane's squadrons at the inconclusive Battle of the Basque Roads. In the actions with *Saumarez off Algeçiras in 1801, Indienne arrived on the scene shortly after the first French victory. She then attempted to tow the captured HMS *Hannibal out to sea in order to take part in the second battle but, as the joined ships were un-

able to keep up with their colleagues, they soon returned to port.

Indomptable

A French 80-gun ship, part of Linois' squadron, whose Captain Moncousu is killed in action (M&C 11). She is much later seen in Toulon Harbour (PC 4).

Indomptable, 80-gun, was launched in 1790. *Moncousu was severely wounded (dying of his injury in the following year) in the first of the two actions between *Linois and *Saumarez. Captain Jean-Jacques-Etienne *Lucas, at that time still a frigate commander, was then given temporary command of the ship for the second action. In 1805 she took part in the Battle of Trafalgar, escaping capture but being wrecked on the coast of Spain in the great storm that followed the action.

Indomptable, HMS

A ship at the Nore (SM 6).

Inflexible, HMS

A ship in which John Daniel had once served (HD 3).

HMS Inflexible, *64-gun, was launched in 1780; from 1793 until her break-up in 1820 she served mostly as a store- and troop-ship.*

Insurgent

A French ship taken by USS *Constellation* in 1799 (FW 2).

The 40-gun frigate Insurgente *(sic) was launched in 1793 and taken by USS *Constellation in February 1799 off the Caribbean island of St. Kitts (French depredation of U.S. commercial shipping having led to a quasi-war between the two countries from mid-1798 to early 1801). Renamed USS* Insurgent, *she was lost in a storm in late 1800.*

Intrepid Fox

1: a valuable merchantman, Master A. Snape, captured by *Hébé* and then re-taken by Jack Aubrey's HMS *Boadicea* (TMC 2; YA 8).

2: a British whaler, Master James Holland, taken and burned by USS *Norfolk* (FSW 7).

Intrépide

A French 74-gun in Toulon Harbour (PC 4).

Intrépide, 74-gun was launched in 1799 as the Spanish Intrepido *and handed to the French navy in 1800. In October 1805 she was taken by *Nelson's fleet at Trafalgar, being burned as useless a few days after the battle.*

Invincible, HMS

1: a ship in Earl Howe's fleet at the Battle of the Glorious First of June, that the Admiral had at one point mistaken for a Frenchman (C/T 4).

HMS Invincible, *74-gun, was launched in 1765 and wrecked on the Norfolk coast in 1801. She had fought in *Howe's great 1794 victory under Captain Thomas *Pakenham, who received a medal for especially valiant work during the action (and who delivered the bon mot about *Gambier during the fight). In the smoke and confusion,*

Invincible *was for a time mistaken by Howe and many others for the—entirely dissimilar—French* Juste.

2: an old ship from which Jack Aubrey obtains some replacement spars for HMS *Worcester* (IM 2).
The reference may possibly be to to materials salvaged from **1** *above many years before, for her replacement was not launched until 1808 (being broken up in 1857), only a very few years before* IM *is set.*

Iphigeneia

O'Brian refers to Sophie Williams as being akin to 'Iphigeneia before the letter' (PC 1).
*In Greek mythology, Iphigeneia was the daughter of *Agamemnon and Clytemnestra. The goddess Artemis demanded her sacrifice in exchange for a fair wind for the Greek fleet heading to Troy and her father then tricked her into attending court by sending her a letter announcing she was to be married to the hero *Achilles. Some tellings of the legend then have her sacrificed, with others having her snatched to safety by Artemis herself.*

Iphigenia, HMS, and Iphigenie

A 36-gun frigate that arrives at Capetown, under her Captain Lambert, after having delivered reinforcements to Keating on Rodriguez Island. She then becomes part of Jack Aubrey's squadron (TMC 5,6) but is taken by the French at the Battle of Port South East, then becoming *Iphigenie*, her original name (TMC 7,8). Under this name, and in company with *Astrée*, she takes HMS *Africaine* but immediately abandons her to Jack's approaching HMS *Boadicea* (TMC 8,9).
HMS Iphigenia *was launched in 1808, not having been a prize taken from the French. Captured, as described in* TMC, *in late August 1810, she was then re-taken by Admiral *Bertie's squadron at the fall of Mauritius in December of that year.* Iphigenia *was lent to the Marine Society from 1833 to 1848 and finally broken up in 1851. For her name derivation, see* **Iphigeneia** *above.*

Irby

The influential Captain to whom HMS *Blackwater* has been given in place of Jack Aubrey (TH 8; FSW 1). His brother, Major Pollack, gives the unwelcome news to Jack (TH 9).
*The Honourable Frederick Paul Irby (1779–1844), the second son of Lord Boston, was made Post in 1802. From 1807 to 1813 he commanded the frigate HMS *Amelia, being involved from 1811 onwards in the suppression of the slave trade in West Africa (somewhat recalling *Aubrey's adventures in COM). Irby saw no further sea-service after this campaign but in 1837 rose by seniority to Rear Admiral. His younger brother, Charles Leonard Irby (1789–1845), was made Post in 1814 and later became a famous traveller in Asia Minor. 'Major Pollock' may perhaps be intended as a brother-in-law rather than a brother.*

Iris, HMS

A ship whose Captain Baker likes her barge-crew to have surnames taken from colours of the rainbow (FSW 2).

HMS Iris, *44-gun, was an ex-Danish frigate, taken as part of the fleet that surrendered to the Royal Navy at Copenhagen in 1807; she was sold out of the service in 1816. COLLEDGE states that she was taken as* Marie; *other sources say she was already called* Iris. *In classical myth, Iris was goddess of the rainbow, a servant of *Juno/Hera and a messenger from *Jupiter/*Zeus to mortals.*

Irresistible, HMS

The ancient flagship of Admiral Pellew, commanded by Captain Goole (RM 1,2).
The 74-gun HMS Irresistible *was launched in 1787 as HMS *Swiftsure. Captured by the French in 1801 and then named* le Swiftsure, *under this name she was re-taken by the Royal Navy at Trafalgar in 1805. As there was a replacement* Swiftsure *already in service—indeed she too fought at Trafalgar—the older ship was renamed HMS* Irresistible, *serving only as a prison hulk until her break-up in 1816.*

Isaacs, Isaac

A seaman in HMS *Sophie* (M&C 6+).

Isabella

Aubrey makes a reference to an 'isabella-coloured' girl (TMC 6).
'Isabella' is a greyish-yellow or light buff colour; the origin of the reference is obscure.

Iscariot

see **Judas Iscariot**

Isidore of Seville, Saint

A saint (TH 8), the protector of travellers (WDS 9).
Saint Isidore (570?–636), a Spanish scholar, was Bishop of Seville from 600 until his death. Amongst his many works is a Chronicle of the World from the Origin to 626 AD.

Isis, HMS

A ship in which Burnet currently serves (M&C 1), in which Bonden and Ezekiel Edwards had once served together (IM 10), and in which Jack Aubrey had also spent time (TGS 4).
HMS Isis, *50-gun, was launched in 1774. She fought in *Duncan's victory at Camperdown in 1797 under Captain William *Mitchell and, by now under Captain James Walker (d.1831 in the rank of Rear Admiral; see also* **Monmouth, HMS**), *at *Nelson's crushing of the Danes at Copenhagen in 1801.* Isis *was broken up in 1810. In Egyptian mythology, Isis was the wife of the god Osiris; her cult—which spread into later Greece and Rome—centres on healing, birth and re-birth. Isis is also the name given to the upper Thames River in and around Oxford, and this may equally be the source of the ship's name.*

Ismael

A predecessor referred to by Emperor Suliman of Morocco (IM 4).
*The reference is probably to the Ishmael of the Book of Genesis, the son of *Abraham and Hagar and the founder of the sect of the Ishmaelites or Arabs.*

Ismail Bey of Mesenteron

A Bey who covets the rule of the Greek mainland town of Kutali and seeks British help vis-à-vis his two rivals Mustapha, Captain-Bey of Karia, and Sciahan, temporarily Bey of Kutali itself (IM 9–11). An elderly and somewhat evasive man, he fails to impress Jack Aubrey at their meeting (IM 10) but later a rumour circulates that he has been appointed Governor of Kutali by the Sultan of Turkey, a tale that, although untrue, has its desired effect of provoking Mustapha to outright rebellion (IM 11).

Ives, Admiral Sir Francis

A Vice Admiral of the Red (TH 10), the taut, efficient successor to Sir John Thornton as Commander in Chief of the Mediterranean station (TH 1+; FSW 1). Following the unhappy events at Zambra, his new, long-awaited, peerage puts him in a generous frame of mind and he declares himself content with the somewhat anxious Jack Aubrey's actions (FSW 1,2).

Ixion, HMS

A crack frigate in which Malloch had once been a bosun's mate (PC 7)

> No ship of this name is recorded in the Royal Navy, and perhaps for a good reason. In Greek myth, Ixion, King of Thessaly, was the world's first parricide, who then he went on to attempt to rape *Zeus' wife, Hera. For this outrage, he was condemned to be forever crucified on a fiery wheel, becoming a sun in Zeus' heavenly mechanism.

Izibicki

A man who had once given a disastrous lecture at the *Institut* in Paris (SM 5).

J

J.

Stephen Maturin's short-hand for his close friend, Sir Joseph Blaine (C/T 7).

J.A.

An abbreviation for Jack Aubrey often used by Stephen Maturin in his diary (PC 3).

Jabal, Sheikh
see al-Jabal, Sheikh

Jack

1: a common slang term for a sailor (PC 1; HD 2).
2: 'Jack of the bread-room,' one of the few accurate gun-aimers in HMS *Boadicea* when Aubrey first assumes command (TMC 2).
3: Mr Jack, HMS *Shannon*'s surgeon (FW 8).
> *Alexander Jack (d.1841) was responsible both for saving the life of the critically injured Captain *Broke and for a careful catalogue of all wounds received by HMS *Shannon's crew during the brisk action, details later used by the Reverend *Brighton in his meticulous account of the fight.*
4: *see* Aubrey, Jack or John

Jack-in-the-Dust

The usual ship-board name for the Purser's steward's assistant (M&C 5,10; TH 4; TGS 3; NC 4; C/T 4,6).

Jack-in-the-green

A reference to the best, fancy dress of the common seamen (M&C 8; TMC 6; DI 3).
> *Jack-in-the-green is a term used for the wicker-and-leaf covered characters at an English May-Day celebration.*

Jack Pudding or Pudden

Common slang for 'a fool' (HMS 2; TMC 3,5; RM 6; C/T 2; COM 7; YA 4,6,8), also used for a mountebank's assistant at a fair-ground (TH 4).
> *BREWER notes that each nation names their traditional fool for their favourite dish: Jean Potage in France, Hans Wurst in Germany etc. As O'Brian himself has noted, England is the land of the pudding, a dish seldom encountered elsewhere in its right, true form.*

Jackie or Jacky

A reference to Jack Aubrey by his close friend Queenie Keith (M&C 2,4; HD 1).

Jackruski or Jackruckie, Jan

A Polish seaman in HMSS *Sophie* (M&C 3) and *Polychrest* (PC 10). Later, in HMS *Leopard*, Maturin finds him in a deep, alcoholic coma (DI 4) but he appears to recover enough to go on serve in HMS *Surprise* (FSW 10).

Jackson

1: Maturin's predecessor as surgeon of HMS *Sophie*, who has followed Captain Allen into HMS *Pallas* (M&C 2).
2: Aubrey's prize agent and man-of-business, who crashes and absconds (PC 3) also causing loss to Robert Dundas (PC 12).
> *A Mr Jackson was an Admiralty prize court official in Malta, famously corrupt and revealed as such by Thomas *Cochrane.*
3: a reference by Aubrey to a man in very awkward circumstances (TMC 6).
> *This reference, at p.218, remains utterly opaque to me.*
4: an officer in Aubrey's HMS *Worcester* (IM 3).

5: a secretary to Governor Raffles (NC 3).
6: William Sadler's cousin (WDS 10).
7: a supplier of high quality coffee (YA 9).

Jackson, 'Gentleman'

A famous pugilist whose boxing establishment had been frequented by Aubrey (FSW 9). In 1797 he had beaten his rival, Mendoza, in a famous bout (YA 3).

> 'Gentleman' John Jackson (1769–1845) ran London's foremost boxing-gym, at No.13 Bond Street, from about 1797 onwards. The club had a very distinguished clientele, with the poet Lord *Byron being just one of Jackson's close friends and admirers. The fight with *Mendoza for the Championship of England (which took place in 1795) ended when Jackson seized his opponent's pigtail and then battered him senseless, a scene somewhat reminiscent of Barret *Bonden's defeat by Black *Evans in YA. Curiously Jackson then never defended his crown in the ring itself, being in 1803 displaced as Champion by the active, young Jem *Belcher. In later life Jackson became a republican and appears to have died in sadly reduced circumstances.

Jacob

1: a reference to Jacob's ladder, in both the sense of a heavily manned ship (TH 4) and to the certainty of further promotion once made Post (YA 1).

> In the Book of Genesis, the Jewish patriarch Jacob saw, in a dream, a ladder stretching up to heaven, with angels climbing up and down in orderly profusion.

2: a waiter at the Ship Inn, Dover (RM 4).

Jacob, Dr Amos

A Spanish Jew, both a physician and a long-time British intelligence agent, who is to accompany his old colleague Stephen Maturin on the new mission against the return of the Emperor Napoleon, contributing not only his linguistic abilities but also his special knowledge of the various heretical Jewish and Moslem sects around the Mediterranean rim (HD 1+). From a family of jewel-dealers, Jacob retains a keen private interest in the trade throughout his adventures (HD 3+). Thoroughly trusted by Stephen, Jacob acts as his right-hand-man for the entire operation, on one occasion visiting Kutali in *Ringle* on Stephen and Jack Aubrey's behalf, learning there that the scheme of Ibn Hazm of Morocco to ship gold to Moslem Buonapartists in the Adriatic is very well advanced (HD 4,5) and later discovering the complicity of Vizier Hashin of Algiers in the plot (HD 7). He is present aboard *Surprise* when the treasure is finally intercepted (HD 10).

Jacobin

A term of insult used for revolutionaries, radicals and similar troublesome souls (HMS 6,9; TMC 6,7; LM 4).

> The Jacobins were the French extreme radical republicans, active from 1790 to 1794 and particularly associated with Robespierre and St Juste. Their name derives in a somewhat roundabout way from the revolutionaries' holding their early meetings in a former monastery of the Dominican Order, whose original base in Paris was dedicated to St Jacques ('Jacobus' in Latin, St *John the Divine in English).

Jacobin

A French 80-gun ship at the Battle of the Glorious First of June (C/T 4).

> Jacobin, 80-gun, was launched in 1778 as Auguste; she was renamed Jacobin in 1793 and fought under that name in the great battle with *Howe's fleet of the following year. Shortly after the action she was re-named Neuf Thermidor and, under that name, was lost in a storm in January 1795. For her 1794 name derivation, see preceding entry.

Jaffar

The ex-Pasha of Barka, an English ally who has been deposed by his brother Mohammed, a situation that Admiral Thornton wishes to reverse (IM 4).

> N.B. that the competing Pashas of Barka are later said by Jack *Aubrey to be *Esmin and his son *Muley (IM 7).

Jaggers

A member of the carpenter's crew in HMS La Flèche (FW 2).

Jagiello, Gedymin

A Lithuanian hussar in the Swedish service, attached to Jack Aubrey and Stephen Maturin's Grimsholm mission (SM 6+), who rapidly gains a reputation in HMS Ariel for being cheerful, brave, beautiful and popular (SM 7). When the ship is later wrecked on the French coast, he is imprisoned with Jack and Stephen Maturin, first in Brest (SM 10), and then in Paris where he soon charms the pretty widow, Lehideux, into smuggling escape tools into his cell (SM 10). However, he is eventually released as part of a political deal and then travels to England with Jack, Stephen and Diana Villiers (SM 11). Later, now attached to the Swedish Embassy in London, Jagiello becomes a very close friend of Diana (IM 1), with Stephen — now her husband — starting to receive anonymous notes that the pair are lovers (IM 5; TH 8). Jagiello and Diana eventually abscond to Stockholm (RM 5,10; LM 4,8,9) but, despite his natural suspicions, Stephen learns that they are not in fact lovers and reclaims Diana from her self-imposed exile (LM 4,9). Jagiello, now a full Colonel, intends to marry the pretty Lovisa (LM 6,9).

Jaime

1: a wealthy card-sharp and condemned rapist with whom Stephen Maturin had been imprisoned in Spain in his youth. He had taught Stephen many useful techniques of both discovery and deception (TH 8).

2: a monk at a Capuchin monastery high in the Andes (WDS 9).

Jakes

The gunroom steward in HMS *Worcester* (IM 1).

James

1: according to O'Brian, the best of the contemporary naval historians (M&C author's note; FW author's note).

William James (d.1827) was a British Admiralty lawyer in Jamaica who spent much of his time writing immensely detailed histories of the Royal Navy. By far the largest and most important of these is the Naval History of Great Britain from the Declaration of War in 1793 to the Accession of George IV, published in five volumes from 1822 to 1824 and reprinted in six volumes in 1826. Although a chronicle rather than an interpretive history, its level and accuracy of detail on the many hundreds of actions fought make it an invaluable research source to this day. N.B., the sections (in his main work and elsewhere) dealing with the war between Britain and the USA of 1812–1814 are much less reliable than the work as a whole, given James' agenda of attempting to demonstrate that American victories were due to superiority of crew numbers and broadside weight alone, a most dubious proposition (e.g., see the account of the war in CLOWES, Vol.VI).

2: an Admiral who is a guest at Aubrey's Ball (PC 2).

3: Mr James, an army officer killed by Captain Macfarlane in a duel at Bombay (HMS 7).

4: an officer cheated at some time in the past by Admiral Bertie (TMC 3).

5: Sir James, a doctor who examines Mrs Williams (DI 1).

6: Aunt James, who keeps house for her brother George Herapath (FW 5).

7: Mr and Mrs James, the Marine sergeant of HMS *Surprise* and his wife (FSW 2–4).

8: the inventor of the anti-scorbutic 'James' Powder' (FSW 3).

Dr Robert James (1705–1776) was a successful and influential physician who patented his hugely popular powder as a general febrifuge: indeed LLOYD & COULTER regard its contemporary status as roughly equivalent to that of modern aspirin as a general reliever of minor distress. Unfortunately the powder's secret formula was a mixture of antimony and phosphate of lime, often deadly in substantial doses on already weakened constitutions as one of its main effects was to cause profuse 'laudable sweating.' Although widely touted as an anti-scorbutic, it was wholly ineffective as such, and later—in 1757—James himself advocated the more effective sauerkraut as a treatment for the complaint.

9: a waiter at Button's club in London (RM 4).

10: Sir James, the Admiral whose finger Mr Goodridge had bitten, leading to his imprisonment (RM 7).

11: a seaman in *Surprise* (LM 2; NC 8).

12: an attendant at the Admiralty offices (COM 2).

13: a waiter at Black's club (YA 10).

14: *see* **Dillon, James**

15: Sir James: *see* **Saumarez, Sir James**

James, Henry

1: an officer, a friend of Pullings, Babbington and Mowett, who is said by Jack Aubrey to have served under him in the past (SM 5).

2: the Flag Captain of Lord Barmouth's HMS *Implacable* (HD 9).

James, King

1: a King of England in whose time Jack Aubrey's Woolcombe House had been built and to whom Jack's ancestor of the time had paid a large sum to avoid being made a baronet (TMC 7; SM 5).

*King James VI of Scotland and I of England (1566–1625), the only son of Mary Queen of Scots, was a great-grandnephew of King *Henry VIII. In 1567 Mary abdicated her Scottish crown and was replaced by James, who, in 1603, then also succeeded the childless Queen Elizabeth I to the throne of England, establishing the House of Stuart (see 2 below) as rulers of all of the British Isles (although the thrones remained constitutionally separate until 1707: see *Anne, Queen). The ardently Episcopalian Protestant James (see *Fawkes, Guy) had a complex set of policies, foreign and domestic, and a perpetual shortage of cash with which to pursue them. In 1611 he instituted the order of baronetage (a form of hereditary knighthood, ranking above all other knights except those of the Order of the Garter; its style would be 'Sir John Aubrey, Bart.'), requiring a very large cash payment from those who sought it and a somewhat lesser sum from those who wished to avoid the ruinous expense of having it conferred on them, whether or no.*

2: a King of England who had also been an Admiral (C/T 5).

*King James II of England (also James VII of Scotland; 1633–1701), son of Charles I, was created Duke of York shortly after his birth. On his father's deposition and execution (see notes under entries for his elder brother *Charles II and *Cromwell) he fled to Europe, there pursuing a successful career in the French and Spanish armies. On his brother's restoration to the English throne in 1660 James became his *Lord High Admiral, seeing considerable active service, albeit with indifferent success. James, who had been raised as a Catholic, in 1672 made an open declaration of faith but, as the Test Acts of 1673 soon prohibited Catholics from holding public office, he was thereby compelled to resign from the Royal Navy. He was able to regain the post towards the end of his brother's reign and retained it when he succeeded him to the throne in 1685. Thereafter, with the assistance of his Secretary for Admiralty Affairs, Samuel Pepys, he became an effective naval reformer. However, James was a deeply unpopular King, partly on account of his faith (England having been assertively Protestant since the days of *Henry VIII) and partly because of his extremely conservative political views. In the 'Glorious Revolution' of 1688, he was soon deposed from both of his thrones, although by a Whig-led Parliament rather than by military force, and replaced by his Protestant daughter and her Dutch husband, who there-*

after reigned jointly as Queen Mary II and King *William III. In 1690 James, now something of a broken man, invaded Ireland with French support but was routed by William at the Battle of the Boyne, the ex–King then retiring to France. Some of James' sons and grandsons—the Stuart dynasty—continued the fight to reclaim the thrones they had lost: see *Young Pretender and *York, Cardinal.

James, Saint
The saint after whom the city of Santiago di Compostela in Spain is named (HMS 2).

The city, in northwestern Spain, is named for Saint James the Great, one of *Jesus' Apostles in the New Testament, who was supposedly martyred in 44 AD on the orders of *Herod Agrippa. Spanish legend has it that his bones were discovered near Santiago in 813.

Jameson
A gentleman who unsuccessfully writes to Aubrey in the hope of getting him to take his son to sea in HMS *Worcester* (IM 2).

Jansenists
A sect referred to by Maturin as condemning the use of wine and opiates (LM 2).

The name refers to the rigorous doctrines developed by Cornelius Jansen (1585–1638), Bishop of Ypres. A man of austere religious views, he followed St *Augustine in regarding direct divine intervention as a necessary condition for individual human salvation.

Jarvey or Jarvie, Old
see St Vincent, Admiral Lord

Jason, HMS
A ship, Captain Middleton, met by HMS *Ariel* at sea off Brest in close pursuit of the French 74-gun *Méduse* (SM 9; *N.B., we later learn that* Méduse *was taken by HMS* Ajax: SM 11). Now under Captain Berry, she is later seen at Bridgetown, Barbados (RM 1,2).

HMS Jason, 32-gun, was launched in 1804 and broken up in 1815. In classical myth, the Greek hero Jason sailed in his ship, *Argo, to the island of Colchis in search of a golden fleece guarded by a dragon. He later married the goddess *Medea, who had helped him to success in his quest. In one version of the Jason legend, the hero was killed in his ship by a rotten plank that fell on his head as he slept.

Jaswant Rao
A reference is made to his palace in Bombay (HMS 7).

The reference is perhaps to Jaswant Rao Holkar (d.1811), a warrior and leader of the Maratha Confederacy of Western India that fought for a time against the expansion of British rule. In 1804 he was heavily defeated by the forces of General Lake and, in 1806, forced to make peace on very unfavourable terms.

Jaume, En
The French Catalan uncle of En Pere, visited by

Maturin (PC 4). A nationalist leader, he is later reported to have been killed by the French (FW 2).

Java, HMS
A frigate commanded by Harry Lambert, *en route* from England to Bombay (FW 3–9). Off the coast of Brazil she picks up the shipwrecked Jack Aubrey and his followers—including Stephen Maturin—who have all abandoned the burning HMS *La Flèche* (FW 3). She soon encounters USS *Constitution* but is heavily defeated by her Amercian rival, being burned and blown up after her crew have been taken off as captives (FW 3; SM 1,2,4,11; FSW 3,9; COM 6,10; WDS 10).

HMS Java, 38-gun, was the ex-French Renommé, *launched in 1805 and captured by the Royal Navy off Madagascar in 1811. In late December 1812, the frigate USS *Constitution took and burned her off San Salvador. In the action, *Lambert's Java not only displayed inferior gunnery technique to *Bainbridge's ship (probably the deciding factor in the encounter) but also failed properly to exploit a speed advantage she enjoyed in the prevailing conditions to attempt to get across the heavier and slower American's bow or stern.*

Java Dick
A seaman in HMS *Lively* (HMS 2), a member of the party that rescues Maturin from torture on Minorca (HMS 3).

Jay
The head of the U.S. diplomatic mission in London (DI 2,6), on whose staff Louisa Wogan's former husband had served (DI 4).

John Jay (1745–1829) was a distinguished statesman and lawyer who, having been part of *Franklin's delegation that negotiated the ending of the Revolutionary War with Britain, later served as American Plenipotentiary-Extraordinary to London in 1794, negotiating there a treaty between the two nations that assured peace and some considerable prosperity until the outbreak of war in 1812. A strong Federalist, Jay was one of the Founding Fathers of the USA, serving as Secretary for Foreign Affairs from 1784 to 1790 and as first-ever Chief Justice from 1789 to 1795. When first agreed, the 'Jay Treaty' of 1794 was controversial in America and extreme opposition to it by *Jefferson's Republicans (its ratification was only narrowly passed in Congress) wrecked the chances that Jay was thought to have to succeed President *Washington. He then served as Governor of his native New York from 1795 until his retirement in 1801.

J.B.
Initials scratched on the wall of the nunnery/prison in Brest where HMS *Ariel*'s officers are held (SM 10).

Jean-Paul
A seaman in the French privateer *Bellone* (P 5).

Jean-Pierre
see Dumesnil, Jean-Pierre

Jeannot
One of Captain Christy-Pallière's orderlies (PC 4).

Jeavons, William
A member of the carpenter's crew in HMS *Sophie* (M&C 2).

Jeeze
see **Jesus**

Jefferson, President
A former President of the USA (DI 10; FW 5).

> *Thomas Jefferson (1743–1826),a lawyer, scholar, states-man and scientist, had been primarily responsible for the wording of the Declaration of Independence of 1776. In 1785 he succeeded *Franklin as Resident Minister in Paris, returning to America in 1789 to serve as *Washington's Secretary of *State until 1793. An ardent Republican, he contested the succession to the Presidency with his Feder-alist rival, John *Adams, and, on losing, he became under the system then prevailing Vice President in 1797. In 1800 he again stood for the highest office, this time assuming the Presidency in the following year, the third man to hold the office. Under Jefferson the U.S. Navy fought and won small wars in the Mediterranean against Morocco and Tripoli (whose semi-pirate fleets were disrupting Ameri-can trade) but suffered a humiliating insult at the hands of the Royal Navy when *Humphreys' HMS *Leopard virtually 'arrested' USS *Chesapeake not far off the Vir-ginia coast. The ensuing political row resulted in Jefferson's 'Embargo Act'— a somewhat timid response that hurt the USA far more than it hurt Britain— and gradually led in 1812 to war breaking out under *Madison, the fourth Pres-ident. On leaving office in 1809, Jefferson retired to his native Virginia where, amongst other things, he founded the great University of that state, the first ever such insti-tution to be free of religious affiliation.*

Jefferson P. Lowell
An American barque met at sea by HMS *Boadicea* (TMC 10).

Jeffreys
A helmsman in HMS *Sophie* (M&C 10).

Jeffries
The famous hanging judge, referred to by Lawrence (RM 7).

> *George, 1st Baron Jeffreys (sic; 1648–1689), was appointed Lord Chief Justice in 1682 and Lord Chancellor in 1685. In 1685–1686 he became notorious for his treatment of the captured participants of Monmouth's rebellion against King *James II with little justice and less mercy. On the assumption of the throne by *William III and Mary II in 1688, Jeffreys was imprisoned in the Tower of London, remaining there until his death from illness the following year.*

Jehu
A reference by Maturin to a prodigious coach dri-ver (IM 1: 31).

> *In the Old Testament Book of Kings, Jehu is chosen as king of Israel by an agent of the prophet *Elisha. He first*

> *has to kill the reigning King, Jehoram, which he does in the course of an encounter in their respective chariots, a conveyance of which Jehu is already known as a furious driver.*

Jelks
A cousin of Heneage Dundas (TH 10).

Jelly-Belly, Horatio
A Chinese seaman in HMS *Lively*, at one time al-most certainly a pirate (PC 12; HMS 2).

Jemmapes
A French 74-gun referred to by Lord Keith (SM 4) and later engaged inconclusively by Jack Aubrey's HMS *Worcester* (IM 2)..

> *Jemmapes, 74-gun, was launched in 1794 as l'Alexan-dre. She was renamed in 1793 to commemorate the first real French victory of the Revolutionary Wars, over the Austrians at Jemmapes, Holland, in the previous year. Jemmapes served in the French Navy until 1822.*

Jemmy, Mrs
The supposed wife of Jemmy Ducks (COM 1).

Jenkins
1: a seaman, possibly the senior gunner's mate, in HMS *Polychrest* (PC 11).
2: a seaman in HMS *Surprise* badly injured in a storm (FSW 5).
3: the temporary — and only semi-competent — Captain of HMS *Bellona* during Jack Aubrey's attendance in Parliament (YA 2,3,4).

Jenkins, Moses
A maker of ship-models from whom Aubrey has obtained a miniature of the refurbished HMS *Leop-ard* (DI 1).

Jenkins, William
A seaman in HMS *Surprise* wounded in the action with *Berceau* (HMS 9).

Jenkins, William or **Bill**
A quartermaster manning a signal station on Réu-nion (TMC 9).

Jenkinson
Admiral Sir Francis Ives' Flag Lieutenant in HMS *Caledonia* (FSW 2).

Jenks
A government functionary in New South Wales (NC 9).

Jenks, Fat-Arse
A seaman in HMS *Surprise* (FSW 5).

Jenning
A member of the carpenter's crew in HMS *Diane* (NC 2).

Jennings

1: the supercargo officer in the *Lord Nelson* Indiaman (PC 5).

2: Mrs Jennings, a lady with whom Lord Clonfert
had carried on a public affair that ended in an
ugly court case (TMC 2,5).

3: a servant at Ashgrove Cottage (COM 1,3).

Jenyns

A wealthy card player at Craddock's gaming house
(DI 1,2).

Jep

A waiter in Joselito's coffee house in Port Mahon
(M&C 1).

Jersey, Lady

A Villiers cousin by marriage, Lady Jersey is thought
by Stephen Maturin to be the Prince of Wales' mistress, a view that Diana Villiers rejects (PC 6,10,14).
Diana continues as a member of Lady Jersey's social circle (SM 4; IM 1; TH 2) and there first meets
Louisa Wogan (DI 4,6).

*Frances Twysden (1753–1821), Countess of Jersey, was from
1770 the wife of George Bussey Villiers, 4th Earl of Jersey
and 7th Viscount Grandison. As a leading hostess especially
associated with the 'fast set,' popular gossip, probably ill-
founded, had her as the *Regent's mistress.*

Jervis, Admiral Sir John

see **St Vincent, Admiral Lord**

Jessup, Robert

A seaman and cook's mate in HMS *Sophie* (M&C
6,11).

Jesus or Jesus Christ

The name of the son of God, used throughout the
series as an oath especially by Roman Catholic characters, when it is frequently seen in combinations
such as 'Jesus, Mary and Joseph' or 'Jesus, Mary and
Patrick.'

*In the Christian tradition of the New Testament, Jesus
Christ is the Son of *God, sent to Earth as the redeemer
of mankind, and there born to *Mary after an 'Immacu-
late Conception.' Outside the Bible itself there are no contemporary sources for Jesus' life or ministry, although it is
now usually estimated that he lived in Palestine from
about 8 BC to 33 AD and suffered death by crucifixion
as a political rebel under Roman law after having first
been condemned by the supreme Jewish tribunal for religious offences. (N.B., the usage of 'AD' and 'BC' is not seen
until over a thousand years after Jesus's era and was itself
the result of attempts to pin down the exact date of his
birth—the year 'zero'—by reference to other known
events.)*

Jevons

1: an officer of HMS *Implacable* who had acted as
James Dillon's second in duel in Port Mahon
(M&C 7).

2: a Midshipman in HMS *Ariel* (SM 7,8), suspected
of insolence for calling out the name of HMS
Humbug (SM 8).

3: a seaman in HMSS *Diane* (TGS 9) and *Nutmeg
of Consolation* (NC 6).

Jezabel

1: a reference by Diana Villiers to a bold temptress
(HMS 7).

*The Biblical Jezabel, daughter of Ethbaal, King of the
Zidonians, and wife of Ahab, King of Israel, was famous
for her ill-temper and wanton faithlessness. She was put
to death by being tossed from a window.*

2: the ship's goat in *Surprise* (C/T 2).

3: a race-horse once owned by Jack Aubrey (RM 6).

Jezzar Pasha

see **Djezzar Pasha**

Jo

A name uttered by Colley as he is being operated
on by Maturin and Cotton (TMC 9).

Joan of Arc

Pullings refers to the Misses Lamb as 'Joans of Arc'
after they act as powder 'boys' in the action between
the *Lord Nelson* Indiaman and the French privateer
Bellone (PC 5).

*Saint Jeanne d'Arc (1412?–1431; canonised 1920) was the
great French patriot who persuaded her compatriots to follow her religious vision and raise the English siege of Orleans. Her success, both military and moral, enabled
Charles VII to be crowned King of France in 1429. However, after her subsequent failure to take Paris, she was
captured by England's Burgundian allies, who tried and
burned her as a heretic.*

Joanna

The name that Amanda Smith intends for the child
she says she is bearing by Jack Aubrey (SM 5).

João

The owner of tavern in Lisbon (TGS 3).

Job

The Biblical patriarch to whom Jack Aubrey once
compares Stephen Maturin (NC 8) and who is also
used as a figure for misery (TGS 5).

*Job, a Patriarch of Uz, is considered an archetype of both
patience and destitution, characteristics both plentiful in
the Old Testament book that bears his name and recounts
his arduous and troubled life.*

Jobling

A bosun's mate in HMS *Worcester* (IM 2).

Jocasta, HMS

A ship the significance of whose name had once
been explained by Maturin to Aubrey (SM 11).

*As might be expected from the following tale, neither the
British, nor even the more liberal French, had ships named
Jocasta or *Oedipus. In Greek legend Jocasta, the wife of*

King Laius of Thebes, gave birth to Oedipus, a son un-wanted by his father, who promptly had the baby tossed out of the city. Nevertheless rescued and preserved by peas-ants, Oedipus returned to Thebes after a life in wander-ing exile, neither he nor the city knowing anything of his past. Here, at a chance meeting at a cross-roads, he slew Laius (without knowing he was either father or King) and then married his own mother, the newly widowed Queen (neither of them knowing that Oedipus was her son or that he had slain the King). In *Homer's Odyssey, Jo-casta (there named Epicaste) hangs herself when she dis-covers what has come about but in some later tellings of the awful tale this realisation and suicide only occur after she has given birth to Oedipus' children.

Jock
A sentry at Governor Macquarie's house (NC 9).

Jocko
An animal kept by the French naturalist, Buffon (M&C 6).

Joe
1: an HMS *Sophie* seaman sent aboard *Citoyen Du-rand* after her capture (M&C 5).
2: a seaman in HMS *Polychrest* (PC 8).
3: a tipstaff's mate who helps to arrest Jack Aubrey for debt (HMS 4).
4: a seaman in HMS *Leopard* who follows the new fashion of wearing his hair short rather than pig-tailed (DI 4).
5: George Herapath's boat-keeper in Boston (FW 5,8).
6: a seaman in *Diligence* (SM 3).
7: a seaman in HMS *Worcester* (IM 1).
8: a seaman in the *Dromedary* transport (TH 3).
9: a seaman in HMS *Surprise* (FSW 4).
10: a seaman in *Surprise* (LM 2; NC 6; C/T 6,8) and perhaps HMS *Nutmeg of Consolation* (NC 6).
11: a young seaman in HMS *Bellona*, temporarily in *Ringle*, her tender (COM 5).
12: a porter at Black's club (LM 7; YA 10).
13: a servant at the King's Arms in Dorchester (YA 8).
14: Sir Joe: *see* **Poer, Sir Joe** and **Lady Le**
15: *see* **Plaice, Joseph** or **Joe**

John
1: the Williams' butler (PC 1,2; HMS 1,4).
2: the 'acting deputy-assistant-master-attendant' in the harbour at Batavia (NC 3).
3: a seaman aboard HMS *Surprise* who assists Ma-turin in tending to the ill Martin (WDS 5).
4: a groom in the Aubrey household (YA 3).

John B. Christopher
An American merchantman thought to be carrying the fugitive United Irishmen, Mangan and Roche (M&C 7).

John Busby
A prize taken by Aubrey in HMS *Surprise* (LM 4).

'John Company'
The common personification of Honourable British East India Company (HMS 10; TGS 6).

John the Divine, Saint
A saint referred to by Stephen Maturin (DI 8; YA 1).

In the New Testament, John was, with his brother *James, one of *Jesus' first apostles, and the author of three books of Epistles, a Gospel and a Book of Revelations. He is supposed to have died at Ephesus in 99 AD after a long career promulgating the gospels, during which time he is supposed once to have been boiled in oil but, by heavenly intervention, survived unscathed. Saint John is often known as 'the Evangelist' or 'the Divine.'

Johns, Mr
The senior Marine Lieutenant in HMS *Shannon* (FW 9).

Johns and his fellow Royal Marine Lieutenant Law (the latter being the man who shot Captain *Lawrence) were both especially commended in *Broke's dispatches for their conduct in HMS *Shannon's great victory.

Johnson
1: a seaman in HMS *Polychrest* believed by Aubrey to be on the point of mutiny (PC 11).
2: the ship's cook in HMS *Surprise*, who had lost both his legs at the Battle of the Glorious First of June (HMS 5).
3: a Master's Mate in HMS *Boadicea*, made an act-ing Lieutenant by Aubrey (TMC 2+). His pro-motion is later confirmed by Admiral Bertie (TMC 3).
4: a seaman in *Surprise* who carries no immunity to smallpox (NC 7,8; *possibly William 'Darky' *Johnson*).

Johnson, Harry or Henry *(N.B., in HMS his name is spelt 'Johnstone')*
In Calcutta, Johnson is the wealthy American suitor, and lover, of Diana Villiers, who accompa-nies her homeward in the *Lushington* (HMS 10; 11). At Madeira, he and Diana then take ship to the USA, she leaving a note for Stephen Maturin revealing that they intend to marry (HMS 11). Later we learn that Johnson was already married, al-though separated from his wife, and is thus unable to wed Diana until a divorce is finalised (DI 1,2,5). In the meantime, the pair have recently spent time together in London (DI 2). Soon, Johnson and Diana are once again in Boston, openly living to-gether and awaiting the long-delayed divorce (FW 1, 5–9). Here too he is closely connected with the American intelligence system (FW 5) and has formed the erroneous belief that it was Jack Aubrey, not Stephen, who had perpetrated the intelligence

coup against Louisa Wogan (FW 5), a fellow South-
erner with whom he now becomes intimate (FW
5,6,8). Initially he tries to enlist Stephen to the anti-
British cause (FW 6), realising just too late that it
is the Doctor who is in fact the British agent (FW
7). Johnson, who has by now gradually fallen out
with Diana, partly because of his many other lovers
and even though she turns out to be pregnant by
him (FW 8; SM1+), still jealously pursues her,
Stephen and Jack after they have escaped from
Boston, first to HMS *Shannon* (FW 6,9) and onwards from Canada to England (SM 3). He has also
no doubt realised that Stephen has purloined many
of his private intelligence papers before fleeing (FW
8; SM 1+). When Stephen is later a captive in Paris,
Johnson arrives to denounce him — fortunately to
little effect — as a spy and killer (SM 11).

Johnson, Matthew
An HMS *Sophie* seaman referred to in Captain
Allen's log as having been lashed (M&C 2+).

Johnson, Sam
An armourer's mate in HMS *Surprise* (FSW 10).

Johnson, Dr Samuel
The friend of Queenie, Lady Keith, and a man
much admired by Maturin (M&C 4; PC 8; FSW
3; TGS 4; NC 3). Captain Yorke of HMS *La Flèche*
owns at least one of his works (FW 2).

> Dr Samuel Johnson (1709–1784) was the great English
> author, lexicographer and wit. Amongst many books and
> thousands of magazine pieces, he was the author of A Life
> of Mr Richard *Savage (1744) and A Dictionary of the
> English Language (1755). Much of what we know of his
> deep, if eccentric, humanity and sparkling conversational
> talents comes from The Life of Samuel Johnson by James
> *Boswell (1791) and from other earlier works by that same
> biographer, recounting his travels of 1773 with the Doc-
> tor in northern Scotland. In 1765 Johnson first made the
> acquaintance of the *Thrale family, giving the nick-name
> 'Queeney' to the precocious young daughter of the house-
> hold, who, many years later, was to become Lady *Keith.

Johnson, William 'Darky'
A seaman in *Surprise* (LM 6; WDS 3+; *see also*
Johnson # 4, *above*).

Johnstone
1: the First Lieutenant of the *Lord Nelson* Indiaman, a former whaler (PC 5).
2: a Judge from Java attached with his colleagues
Loder and Crabbe to Mr Fox's Pulo Prabang
mission. From their loud pomposity, the three
become known to HMS *Diane*'s crew as the
'Old Buggers' (TGS 6+). Johnstone is later
facetiously referred to by Aubrey by one of the
Sultan of Pulo Prabang's titles, Nutmeg of
Consolation, Rose of Delight or Flower of
Courtesy (TGS 9). He accompanies Fox and

his party in the small boat in which they hope
to return to Java but they are all believed lost
in the typhoon that then sweeps the area (TGS
10).
3: *see* **Johnson, Harry** or **Henry**

Johnstone, Commodore
An officer referred to in a letter from Lord Nelson
to Admiral Russell (LM 1).

> George Johnstone (1730–1787) was an exceptionally quar-
> relsome Scottish Royal Navy officer of famously doubtful
> competence yet considerable personal bravery. He was
> made Post in 1762 even though he had been found guilty
> in 1757 of killing his Captain's clerk in a duel, his only
> punishment having been a reprimand for insubordina-
> tion and disobedience. However, Johnstone never then held
> a sea command until his political influence (he had served
> from 1763 to 1767 as Governor of West Florida) won him
> a Commodore's appointment in 1779, he having preferred
> during the intervening years to develop a reputation both
> as a Parliamentary 'brawler' on Naval matters and en-
> thusiast duellist on matters of personal honour. In 1781,
> off the Cape Verde Islands and Cape Town, he led a sham-
> bles of a campaign against the Dutch, although one not
> entirely without military success. During the course of these
> events, he arrested Captain Evelyn Sutton of HMS *Isis
> for supposed dereliction of duty and confined him for a very
> long period without recourse to any form of trial. In 1784
> Sutton eventually returned to England to demand a court-
> martial, which soon acquitted him with honour of all
> charges. Sutton proceeded to sue Johnstone for false im-
> prisonment, being eventually awarded a very substantial
> damages settlement. However, Johnstone's declining health
> and chaotic financial affairs prevented Sutton ever re-
> ceiving his money.

Johnstone & Graham
Jack Aubrey's prize-agents in Gibraltar (M&C 1).

Johnstones, the
A Highland family referred to by Macdonald (PC
8).

Joliffe
A Midshipman in HMS *Surprise*, one of the members of the larboard mess who stole and ate Maturin's experimental rats (HMS 6).

'Jolly Roger'
see **Hoarehound, Roger**

Jonah
A reference to anyone on a ship thought to be a
bearer of bad luck (M&C 6; DI 7,9; IM 5; FSW
1–6; RM 3; TGS 3; COM 8). A 'Jonah's lift' refers
to the practice of quietly tossing him overboard
(FSW 6).

> In the Old Testament, the minor prophet Jonah is tossed
> overboard for supposedly bringing on a storm by incurring
> *God's wrath. He is then miraculously rescued from
> drowning by being swallowed by a whale (although the
> Hebrew original does not specify the exact sea-creature)
> and spewed up three days later.

Jonathan

Slang for an American citizen (FW 8).

The usage supposedly derives from General *Washington's habit of saying that all needs of the army would eventually be supplied by his good friend, 'Brother Jonathan,' a.k.a. Jonathan Trumbull (1710–1785), the Governor of Connecticut.

Jones

1: Miss Jones, the sister of Mrs Dockray, had acted as a powder-boy in James Dillon's action against French privateers in the hired cutter *Dart* (M&C 3).

2: Mr and Mrs Jones, the Purser of Aubrey's HMS *Polychrest*'s and his wife (PC 7,8).

3: a flashy, radical friend of General Aubrey (SM 5).

Jones, Griffi

A dealer in stuffed animals to whom Evan Evans intended to sell the head of his dead ape, Andrew Masher (PC 12).

Jones, Paul

A derisive cry uttered by the American crew of *John B. Christopher* to the crew of HMS *Sophie* (M&C 7).

John Paul Jones (1747–1792) was born (as plain John Paul) in Scotland and joined the British merchant marine at an early age, soon making a reputation as a prime seaman. In 1773 he emigrated to the colony of Virginia (now taking Jones as his surname), joining in 1775 the proto-typical U.S. Navy on the first stirrings of the Revolutionary War. He was soon appointed Captain and enjoyed a number of very notable successes against the British forces, often against superior odds. In 1782 he fell out with Congress over their seeming unwillingness to support a peace-time navy and moved to France in the hope of there obtaining a command. Unsuccessful in this, in 1788 he accepted a Rear Admiral's rank in the Russian Navy, a post he held with some élan until political intrigue ousted him in the following year. Jones spent the rest of his life in France, being given a state funeral in Paris. In 1905 his body was exhumed and taken to its final resting place in the U.S. Naval Academy Chapel at Annapolis.

Jones, Thomas

A seaman in HMS *Sophie* (M&C 3+).

Jones, Tom

A character who had been paid to sleep with a lady (PC 10).

The reference is to the leading character in Tom Jones, *or the* History of a Foundling, *a novel published in 1749 by Henry Fielding (1707–1754). Mr Macdonald's reference is to the manner in which the cheerful, but impoverished, young rake Tom is ensnared by the wealthy and ardent Lady Bellaston: Tom receives fifty pounds as reward for fours hours' labour.*

Jordan, Mrs

The mistress of the Duke of Clarence (NC 6) and a client of the banker Ellis (M&C 8).

Dorothy, or Dorothea, Jordan (1761–1816), a well-known Irish actress, had a 16-year liaison with *Clarence from 1790 onwards, bearing 10 of his children. All were surnamed Fitzclarence and many of them made brilliant marriages, although Mrs Jordan herself died in much reduced circumstances after the Duke broke with her.

José, don

see **González, don José**

Joselito

1: Maturin's mule in Peru (WDS 8).

2: the owner of a coffee house in Port Mahon (M&C 1+; IM 7).

3: the owner of a landmark warehouse in Callao, Peru (WDS 6).

Joseph

Used throughout series, especially by Roman Catholic characters, as part of the oath 'Jesus, Mary and Joseph.'

In the New Testament, Saint Joseph was the husband of *Mary, the mother of *Jesus. Finding her to be already pregnant when they had married, he intended immediately to divorce her but was told by an angel of *God that the child was the Divine Son and thus to be cherished. Although descended from the royal house of *David, Joseph worked in Nazareth as a humble carpenter.

Joseph, Saint

Aubrey's mis-reading of the tortured Maturin's handwriting of 'Sir Joseph' (HMS 3; *i.e.,* Sir Joseph **Blaine*).

see **Joseph**, *above*

Joseph, Sir

see **Blaine, Sir Joseph** *or, far more rarely,* **Banks, Sir Joseph**

Josephus

An author referred to by Maturin (YA 2).

Flavius Iosephus (37AD–95?AD) was a Greek-Jewish historian of royal descent who became an important statesman and rabbi in his native Jerusalem. A strongly pro-Roman Pharisee, he nevertheless accepted the Governorship of Galilee from the Jewish leaders of Judea and then defended the city of Jotapata against Roman legions for over a month. On his capitulation, he grew even closer to the Latin leadership and, after the fall of Jerusalem in 70 AD, accepted both Roman citizenship (adopting the appellation 'Flavius,' the family name of the Emperor Vespasian) and financial rewards. He then wrote, in Greek, his Jewish War, *based on his own experiences and other eye-witness accounts, and went on to produce a 20-volume* Jewish Antiquities, *again in Greek. N.B., the sections of this work purporting to deal with *Jesus' ministry are almost certainly a much later interpolation.*

Joshua

According to Maturin, the only man who could stop the sun in the sky (HMS 7).

In the Old Testament, Joshua succeeded *Moses as com-

mander of the Israelites. In defeating the Amorites, he—with *God's aid—stopped the movement of the sun and the moon across the heavens for an entire day.

Josiah

An associate of Bill Hemmings (RM 7).

Jospin

A wherry-man in Portsmouth (RM 8).

Jove or Jovian

see **Jupiter**

Joyce

The Lieutenant in command of HMS *Kite* (TMC 7).

Joyce, Maura

An Irish nurse at Choate's hospital in Boston (FW 6,7).

Joyce's Country

An Irish geographical reference by Maturin (SM 5: 135).

'Joyce's Country' lies in the in the far west of Ireland, north of Galway. It takes its name from a family of 12th century Welsh settlers who rose to become one of the leading 'Tribes of Galway,' a region where Joyce is still a common surname.

Joyful Surprise

The service nick-name of HMS *Surprise* (TH 5).

J.S.

1: initials scratched, with a Latin phrase, on the wall of the nunnery/prison in Brest where HMS *Ariel*'s officers are held (SM 10).

N.B., Aetat. 47 is Latin for 'age 47.'

2: a reference by Admiral Ives to a colleague eager for a peerage (FSW 1).

The reference is probably to Sir James *Saumarez.

Judas or Judas Iscariot

A reference, usually serious (M&C 8; PC 6; HMS 4; SM 6; IM 4; TH 10; FSW 10; LM 9; C/T 2,6; COM 5) but occasionally light-hearted (DI 7), to treacherous betrayal.

The Judas of the New Testament was one of *Jesus' disciples and ultimately his betrayer, for just thirty pieces of silver, to the Jewish chief priests. He later returned the money to his master's enemies and then hung himself.

Judas Priest

A oath by Pullings (HMS 9) and Aubrey (FSW 6).

The oath is supposedly a euphemism for '*Jesus Christ.' N.B., the earliest literary usage recorded by the Oxford English Dictionary *dates from 1914.*

Judd

A minor Admiralty official in London (COM 4; YA 3).

Jules

A London shopkeeper who acts as a French secret agent (RM 10).

Jules is described in a note as a 'traiteur,' a French word that means not what it seems to the English eye, but rather 'the owner of a ready-prepared food business.'

Julian the Apostate

A reference by Aubrey to the discomfort of being rigorously examined by one's peers and superiors (TH 3).

Iulianus Flavius Claudius (331–363) ruled as Roman Emperor from 361 until his death. By the time of his birth Emperors had espoused the Christian faith but, in about 351, the young Julian—a highly educated man—reverted to a neo-Platonic paganism, a highly controversial apostasy from the new 'true faith' that he publicly acknowledged in 361, immediately after being appointed Emperor by the army. He was an active and ambitious ruler who, whilst preferring pagan associates at court, did not encourage widespread persecution of Christians. Whilst on campaign in Persia, Julian received a fatal javelin-wound in a skirmish.

Julibrissim's

A coffee house in Lima, Peru (WDS 8).

Juliot

A French intelligence agent whose organisation had nearly been wiped out by Maturin's intelligence coup against the Americans (TH 2).

Jumping Billy

A cannon in HMS *Surprise* (RM 3; LM 2).

Juno

Maturin compares Queen Puolani to Juno in all respects, excepting only the goddess' hot temper (C/T 9).

Juno was one of the oldest of the Roman goddesses, worshipped as the patron of women, maternity and associated civic virtues. She is usually represented as a majestic, crowned figure, being the wife of *Jupiter and hence the Queen of Heaven. Juno is also often identified with the Greek goddess Hera, the wife of *Zeus. In *Homer and *Virgil, Hera/Juno is portrayed as subject to violent jealousies and as a relentless enemy of the Trojans.

Juno, HMS

A ship that had taken part in an unsuccessful attack on the Mortella tower on Corsica, ordered by Lord Hood (SM 6). Later, under Aubrey's old friend Captain Maudsley, she is an ancient frigate in the Baltic fleet (SM 9).

HMS Juno, 32-gun, was launched in 1780 and broken up in 1811 (a little before SM is set). The attack on the Mortella tower took place in 1794, with Juno then under Captain Samuel *Hood. She was named for the Roman goddess *Juno.

Junon

A French heavy frigate that slips out from Toulon, avoiding the British blockade (IM 4).

> *Although* Junon *(see* ***Juno**) *was a common name for French warships, 1812–1813 was one of the few periods that no vessel of the name was in service. However, at the time of IM, the 40-gun* Amélie *(launched in 1808) was stationed at Toulon; in 1814 she was re-named* Junon, *serving in the French forces under that name until 1842.*

Jupiter or Jove; also Jupiter Tonans and Jupiter Ammon

The supreme Roman god, a figure of great authority (TMC 9; FSW 1,2; TGS 6; NC 1; COM 2; YA 6). Aubrey refers to 'Jupiter Tonans' (DI 5) and Maturin to a statue of 'Jupiter Ammon' (FSW 3).

> *In Roman mythology and religious practice, Jupiter was King of all the Gods, identified with the Greek *Zeus. Jupiter, his wife *Juno and the goddess *Minerva were the patron deities of Rome itself. The appellation* Tonans— *'Thunderer'—comes from Jupiter's rule of all heavenly phenomena, his favourite way of indicating displeasure being a thunder-bolt hurled from on high. Ammon was the Greek form of the supreme Egyptian god, Amun or Amen, with* Zeus Ammon *being a way of uniting the two gods in one identity (used especially by *Alexander the Great, who claimed to be descended via *Hercules from the supreme god):* Jupiter Ammon *is a Roman reflection of this earlier Hellenistic practice.*

Jupiter, HMS

A 50-gun ship recently wrecked in Vigo Bay (TMC 1).

> *HMS* Jupiter, *50-gun, was launched in 1778 and, under her Captain the Honourable Henry Baker (d.1820), was wrecked on a sand-bar in December 1808 whilst anchoring—in calm weather but with a strong running tide—at the entrance to the Spanish port. She was named for the Roman god *Jupiter.*

Jussieu

A French scientist referred to by Maturin (COM 8).

> *Antoine Laurent de Jussieu (1748–1836) was the most famous member of a long dynasty of distinguished French botanists. After early training as a physician, in 1770 Jussieu was appointed to the* Jardin de Roi *and there developed, in 1774, a natural system of plant classification that for a while superseded that of *Linnaeus. Its immaculate observational foundations—best seen in his immensely influential* Genera Plantorum *of 1789—have since been incorporated into the revised Linnaean system used today. In 1793 Jussieu was appointed the first Professor of Botany at the newly named Museum of Natural History in Paris, a post he held until 1826 when he resigned in favour of his son, Adrien Jussieu (1797–1853).*

—— K ——

Kalahua

The chief of the northern part of the island of Moahu, in league with the Frenchman Dutourd against Queen Puolani and her British allies (C/T 5,8). He is defeated, killed and then eaten at the celebratory feast (C/T 9).

Kalim

A Lascar (*i.e. Bengali*) seaman in the *Lord Nelson* Indiaman (PC 5).

Kane

A warrant officer in HMS *Surprise* (LM 3).

Kant, Emmanuel

The great philosopher, referred to by Professor Graham (TH 1).

> *Emmanuel Kant (1724–1804) spent his entire life in his Prussian home town of Königsberg, first studying at its university, then becoming in 1755 an unpaid tutor at that same institution and finally, in 1770, being appointed its Professor of Logic and Metaphysics, a post he held until his death. Kant was a considerable natural scientist in his early years but his great reputation rests on his purely philosophical works, such as the* Critique of Pure Reason *(1781 and 1787), the* Critique of Judgement *(1790) and* Religion Within the Boundaries of Pure Reason *(1793). Kant's philosophy is profound, immense and relentlessly detailed on both the nature of knowledge and the imperatives that govern everyday life. His moral rule is to act as if one's own guiding principles were immediately to become universal laws governing everybody else's behaviour too (the problem of formulating such laws without encountering exceptions and contradictions has long been the greatest challenge to Kant's system). What Kant sees as our innate desire to act morally for the greatest good of all people—which he argues is a universal, logical duty—drives him to a belief in a supreme moral being—essentially, the Judeo-Christian *God—although he recognizes that proof of such existence is not available through human reason alone.*

Karouski, Andrew

A seaman in HMS *Sophie* (M&C 3).

Kate

see **Rowley, Mr** and **Mrs Kate**

Kaunitz, Prince

A man whom the con-man Kimber claims is anxious for his services (DI 1).

Kimber is presumably referring to the famous — and dead — Prince Wenzel Anton von Kaunitz (1711–1794), or perhaps some imaginary successor. Kaunitz was an Austrian statesman and diplomat who held such sway over Imperial affairs that he became known as the 'Coachman of Europe,' driving her wheresoever he pleased.

Kavanagh, Mrs

An Irish nurse at Choate's hospital in Boston (FW 4).

Kaway, Raja of

A cousin of the Sultan of Pulo Prabang (TGS 6).

Kearney

The First Lieutenant of HMS *Berenice* (COM 1).

Keating, Harry

A Lieutenant-Colonel in the East India Company Service who commands the relatively small British garrison on Rodriguez Island, near the French-held Réunion and Mauritius. He had previously met Jack Aubrey — now a Commodore — at the celebration dinner given him in Calcutta after his defeat of Linois' squadron (TMC 4+). Keating is an enthusiastic supporter of Jack's initial strategy of heavy raids against lesser French bases whilst awaiting reinforcements to assault Réunion itself (TMC 4). Once these have arrived he and Jack attack the island but, much to his disappointment, Stephen Maturin arranges a French surrender before his beloved set-piece battle can take place (TMC 6). Keating, having wished to press on against neighbouring Mauritius before he can be superseded by the approaching General Abercrombie, is thwarted — and left furious — by the latter's arrival from the Cape just in time to take the final glory (TMC 10).

*Henry Sheehy Keating (1777–1847), an Irish career soldier, was, at the time of TMC, the commander of the British garrison on Rodriguez Island (many of his troops being natives of the Indian sub-continent) and the most senior of some half-dozen Lieutenant-Colonels involved in the fall of Réunion and Mauritius. Keating later became Governor-General of Réunion itself once Sir Robert *Farquhar had moved on to Mauritius. According to the biographies of his son — a distinguished judge — the elder Keating also saw notable service in the West Indies and rose to the rank of Lieutenant-General before retirement.*

Keats, Captain

The Captain of HMS *Superb*, 74-gun, who offers assistance to Jack Aubrey in repairing the battered HMS *Sophie* (M&C 11). Having played a leading role in Saumarez' great victory, he is afterwards one of the Captains who court-martials Jack for his recent loss of HMS *Sophie* (M&C 12).

*Admiral Sir Richard Goodwin Keats (1757–1834) was a renowned fighting Captain whose quite remarkable actions of July 1801 in HMS *Superb are accurately recounted by O'Brian. These and other similar exploits led *Nelson to observe that, whilst Superb was a match for any French 74-gun afloat, with Keats in command she was a match for any two. Keats had been made Post in 1789, and was promoted Rear Admiral in in 1807; in that year he was also received a knighthood for his services in leading the evacuation the Marques de la Romana's Spanish troops from Denmark (see *Casademon, Ramon d'Ullastret), with his flag in his old *Superb. Keats was made Vice Admiral in 1811 and Admiral in 1825. Forced by ill-health to give up sea-commands in 1812, from 1813–1816 Keats served as Governor-General of Newfoundland. He was later Governor of Greenwich Naval Hospital, holding the position from 1821 until his death. Keats was a lifelong friend of William, Duke of *Clarence, who had served from 1779 to 1781 in HMS Prince George as a Midshipman on the then Lieutenant Keats' watch.*

Kehl

Captain Yorke of HMS *La Flèche* owns the Kehl edition of Voltaire (FW 2).

*In 1784–1789 the French entrepreneur and playwright Beaumarchais (1732–1799; *Mozart's *Marriage of Figaro is based on his play of the same name) published a 70-volume set of *Voltaire's works from his own printing works at Kehl, in Baden.*

Keith, Admiral Lord

Admiral Lord Keith is first met as the Commander-in-Chief of the Mediterranean Fleet (M&C 1+), an Admiral of the Blue (M&C 4). He not only promotes Jack Aubrey to his first independent post as Commander of HMS *Sophie* (M&C 1) but personally signs Stephen Maturin's warrant of appointment as a naval surgeon (M&C 4). Formerly known as Captain Elphinstone, Keith is only recently married to Jack's friend and former tutor Queenie (M&C 4). He remains Jack's patron throughout his career (PC 1,6; HMS 4; TMC 5; RM 1,4; LM 1; TGS 5; YA 2,10) and both Jack and Stephen regard him as a formidable commander, a man of great natural authority (DI 3,4; SM 5; IM 7). He is later encountered as commander of the Channel Fleet (SM 4) and then once again when about to become commander of the Mediterranean station, in which capacity he sends the 'retired' Jack news of Buonaparte's escape from Elba, immediately recalling him to the Royal Navy as a Commodore (YA 10). At Gibraltar Jack learns that Keith — now a Viscount — is intended to hold his new command only temporarily (HD 1), but the Admiral and his staff brief both him and Stephen on the Buonapartist activities in the Adriatic and the plot to finance anti-Allied activity with Moslem gold, issuing orders for the pair to act against these schemes (HD 1–8). Eventually superseded by Admiral Lord Barmouth, Lord and Lady Keith remain at Gibraltar, taking an active role in the events leading to the capture by Jack of the treasure-galley, and possibly thus sharing in the considerable prize-money (HD 8–10).

> *The Honourable George Elphinstone (1748–1823), Admiral Lord Keith, was one of the Royal Navy's foremost commanders of his age. The Scotsman Keith's reputation is that of a very sound—rather than a great—leader, widely admired for his considerable administrative skills, his fine appreciation of combined naval-military operations, his role in ending the mutinies at Sheerness and Plymouth in 1797 and also for his prodigious acquisition of prize-money (over the division of which he, *St Vincent and *Nelson all quarrelled when they were simultaneously Admirals in the Mediterranean: see FW 9). As George Elphinstone, he was made Post in 1775 but then spent the years 1780–1793 ashore. In 1794, soon after the start of the French Revolutionary War, he was promoted Rear Admiral and given a succession of important active commands. Knighted in 1794, he was raised to the Irish peerage as Lord Keith in 1797. Promoted Vice Admiral in 1795, and Admiral in 1801, Keith then held the Mediterranean command (in succession to St Vincent, and as Nelson's superior) from 1799 to 1803, the North Sea command from 1803 to 1807 and the Channel command from 1812 to late 1814. At the time of *Buonaparte's escape in February 1815 he was immediately re-appointed to the Channel, whilst Lord Exmouth (Sir Edward *Pellew as was) retained his Mediterranean station (hence the relationship between Keith and *Barmouth at Gibraltar in HD is fictional). When, three months later, the Emperor was finally defeated, Keith resigned and retired. In 1787 he had married a Jane Mercer and, after the wars, their daughter married the Compte de Flahaut, Buonaparte's former aide-de-camp. In 1808, by now a widower, Keith married Queenie Thrale (see following entry): their daughter eventually married into the *Villiers/*Jersey family (N.B., O'Brian takes the artist's liberty of having the Lord Keith—Queenie Thrale marriage take place in either 1800 or 1801). Having, in 1801, been made a Baron in the English peerage, in 1814 Keith was awarded a Viscountcy.*

Keith, Lady Queenie or Queeney

The new wife of Admiral Lord Keith (M&C 4), who had been Jack Aubrey's neighbour when he was a child and, being a great scholar, had tutored him rather as might an older sister. She remains Jack's close friend in later life (M&C 2+; PC 3,6,8,12; HMS 2,4; YA 10). At one point we learn that she is greatly upset at having a Roman Catholic foreigner as a step-father (M&C 4). Now a Viscountess, Lady Keith spends Napoleon's 'Hundred Days' in Gibraltar with her husband (HD 1+), especially attentive to advancing her friend Jack's career (HD 8,9).

> *Hester Marie Thrale Elphinstone (1762–1857), Viscountess Keith, was the daughter of the noted diarist Hester *Thrale Piozzi (1741–1821) and Mr Thrale, a wealthy brewer (see HD 9). Nicknamed 'Queeney' by her mother's friend Dr *Johnson for her imperious ways even when very young, she was indeed a great scholar, fluent in Latin and Greek when yet a child. The death of her elder brother in 1774 made Hester a rich heiress and, with her fondness for intelligent, enterprising company, she became a founding patron of *Almack's Club. In 1808 she became the second wife of George Elphinstone, Admiral Lord *Keith: their*

> *only daughter (Georgiana Augusta Henrietta, b.1809) eventually married into the *Villiers/*Jersey family. (N.B., O'Brian takes the artist's liberty of having the Keith—Queenie marriage take place in either 1800 or 1801.) Queeney's life, family and social circle offer O'Brian a number of inspirations: for example, in addition to the Villiers link, she had sisters called Cecilia (see *Williams, Cecilia) and Sophia (see *Aubrey, Sophie or Sophia) and another sister who lived 'in sin' in an *Ashgrove Cottage in Kent. In 1784, to the intense consternation of her family and friends, the widowed Mrs Thrale senior had married Gabriel Piozzi, a Catholic, Italian musician.*

Kelley, Joseph and Michael

Irish seamen in Jack Aubrey's HMS *Sophie* (M&C 3). Many years later, Michael again serves with Jack in HMS *Bellona* (COM 3).

Kelley, Sean

An Irishman abducted from home by corsairs and later sold in Algiers (HD 8).

Kelynach

A seaman in HMS *Surprise* suffering from scurvy (HMS 5).

Kemsley, Southdown

An acquaintance of Maturin who had taken Captain Macarthur to a Royal Society dinner in London (NC 8).

Kendrick

A gentleman friend of Serena Wesley (C/T 1).

Kenmare

A acquaintance of Dillon and Maturin in Ireland, involved in some way with issues of political and religious reform (M&C 5). According to Ellis he is Lord Kenmare, Dillon's uncle (M&C 8).

> *The references may perhaps be to either Thomas Browne, 4th Viscount Kenmare (1726–1795) or his successor Valentine Browne, the 5th Viscount and, from 1800, 1st Earl Kenmare (1754–1812). The Brownes were a leading Catholic family in the Irish aristocracy, noted for their conservatism and close connections to the British political élite.*

Kent, Duke of

The Duke, who is referred to by Lord St Vincent in his letter to Sir Charles Grey on the subject of Lieutenant Beresford, has also written to St Vincent in support of Jack Aubrey (PC 3).

> *Edward Augustus (1767–1820), Duke of Kent and Strathern and Earl of Dublin, was the 4th son of King *George III. He was also the father of Queen Victoria who, in 1837, succeeded the deceased Duke's childless, elder brother, King William IV (the former Duke of *Clarence) to the throne of the United Kingdom.*

Kent, William

An Admiralty intelligence official in Gibraltar (HD 1).

Keppel

A controversial Admiral referred to in passing (TMC 6). There are also several references to a public house named for him, the Keppel's Head (or 'Knob') in Portsmouth (SM 2; IM 1; TH 10; FSW 10; C/T 4; COM 3,5,9).

*Augustus, 1st Viscount Keppel (1725–1786), distinguished himself as a seaman from a very early age, being in 1744 promoted Lieutenant on *Anson's HMS *Centurion during her circumnavigation. Made Post later in the same year — still only 19 years old — he went on to enjoy a brilliant career as a fighting officer before being promoted Rear Admiral in 1762 and Vice Admiral in 1770. When war broke out with the American Colonies in 1775, Keppel, like many another committed political Whig (he served as an MP for 25 years), refused to serve his country in what he considered an unjust cause, only agreeing to accept command of the Channel when France entered the conflict in 1778. In July of that year — as a newly-promoted full Admiral — he led a large fleet against the French off Ushant. After an indecisive opening encounter the combatants separated, with both Admirals — the French led by d'Orvilliers — having the opportunity to renew the engagement if they so desired. Keppel ordered his lagging rear division, under the Tory Vice Admiral Sir Hugh Palliser (far more a politician than a fighting man), to bear up but they never quite did so, leaving the Admiral fuming on the quarterdeck of his HMS *Victory and the battle a 'draw.' After allegations later flew between Keppel's supporters and Palliser himself — each impugning the conduct of the other — both commanders were called to account. The accusation against Keppel — that he had failed to do all in his power to destroy the enemy — were serious, and were exactly those for which *Byng had been shot not so very many years before: indeed the Admiral, who had sat on Byng's court-martial, felt he was on trial for his life. The accusations against Palliser were of a lesser order — he being a subordinate commander — but had the potential to end his career summarily (in fact, Palliser's hearing was rather more a formal enquiry than a full trial). Keppel was completely exonerated but Palliser, although commended for activity in the opening stages of the battle, was censured for his failure to give proper regard to Keppel's crucial, later order. Keppel nevertheless resigned his command in disgust at his treatment by the Tory-led Admiralty; Palliser was disgraced in the public eye — he narrowly escaped with his life when the mob burned down his house — and never again served at sea. On a Whig election victory in early 1782, Keppel was appointed *First Lord of the Admiralty, a post that he held, with one brief political interruption, until the end of the war late the following year. The Keppel's Head — now a modest hotel rather than simply a pub — still stands on The Hard in Portsmouth.*

Keppel, Anne

A lady at the Colpoys' ball in Halifax (SM 2).

*The reference is possibly to Anne, Countess Keppel (d.1824) who in 1771 had married George Keppel, 3rd Earl of Albemarle, just a year before his death. The Earl was the elder brother of Admiral Augustus *Keppel noticed above; curiously, their father — the 2nd Earl, a career soldier of Dutch ancestry — was named William Anne Keppel (1702–1754), the family honouring the names of their*

*monarchs, *William III and his sister-in-law and successor, Queen *Anne.*

Kergariou de Socmaria

A French Captain whose *La Sybille* had been fought by Russell's HMS *Hussar* (LM 1).

*Thibaud René, Comte de Kergariou-Locmaria (sic; 1739–1795), was appointed Capitaine de Vaisseau in 1779 and given command of *Sibylle, 32-gun, in 1781. In 1783 he fought a controversial action in his only partly-armed ship with *Russell's 20-gun HMS *Hussar: Kergariou tempted Russell into battle by flying an upside-down Union Jack, often used in the Royal Navy as a distress signal. A furious fight ensued but, on the appearance of HMS Centurion, Sibylle surrendered. Russell felt that Kergariou's ruse de guerre was beyond the pale, and contemptuously broke his offered sword of surrender in two; he then ordered the Frenchman confined under strict guard. Kergariou later complained of this treatment and issued a duel-challenge to Russell; however, the two men never again managed to encounter each other. When revolution broke out in France in 1789, Kergariou went into exile, preferring to serve with the Royalist emigré forces allied to the British Crown. In 1795 he was a part of the English attack on Quiberon harbour but was captured by the Republican forces and soon shot as a traitor (as was his brother, and fellow Captain, Pierre-Joseph).*

Kerr, Robert

The Captain to whom HMS *Acasta* has been given in place of Jack Aubrey (SM 1). As a courtesy he sends Bonden and Killick ashore to Ashgrove Cottage, there to await Jack's return from captivity in America (SM 4).

*Alexander Robert Kerr (d.1831) was in command of HMS *Acasta from June 1813 to some time after 1815. He had been promoted Commander in 1802 and was made Post in 1806. Somewhat curiously, he had spent his early years as a Post Captain in command of 74-guns (principally HMS *Revenge from 1808–1810) before being given a series of frigates, beginning with HMS Unicorn in 1810, a reverse of the usual career path for officers other than *Flag Captains.*

Kesegaran

The young, female Dyak warrior who leads the attack on the HMS *Diane* shipwreck island and is killed in the ensuing mêlée (NC 1,2).

Kestrel

A 14-gun sloop, offered to Jack Aubrey by Raffles in support of HMS *Nutmeg of Consolation*, but declined by him as he wishes to draw the French *Cornélie* into single-ship combat (NC 4).

Kevin

1: a saint referred to by Padeen Colman (COM 3).

Saint Caemgen or Kevin (d.618) was an Irish hermit who founded an important monastery at Glendalough. In Irish legends he is often portrayed as a protector of animals.

2: an uncle of Midshipman Geoghegan (YA 5).

3: see **Fitzgerald, Kevin**

4: see **FitzPatrick, Kevin and Mona**

Keyne

With Mr Abel, a Royal Navy lieutenant held on pa-role in Boston, who rescues Maturin from Pontet-Canet's attack (FW 7).

Khaled, Yahya ben

The Algerine corsair who is to take Sheikh Ibn Hazm's gold from Morocco to the Adriatic (HD 7,9).

> N.B., at p.256 ben Khaled's name changes quite abruptly to '*Murad Reis,' under whose entry the rest of his short career will be found.

Kiernan

A Master's Mate in HMS *Africaine* who leads a party of volunteers to HMS *Boadicea* (TMC 9).

Killick, Preserved

Jack Aubrey's steward from his first command, a shrewish, yet loyal, personal servant and cook of strictly limited range, and often also a retainer in the various Aubrey households ashore (M&C 3+; PC 1+; HMS 2+; TMC 1, 3+; DI 1, 3+; FW 2–4,9; SM 4; IM 1+; TH 1+; FSW 1–9; RM 1+; LM 1+; TGS 1+; NC 1+; C/T 1+; WDS 1+; COM 1+; YA 1+; HD 1+). His curious forename *(suggesting a non-conformist religious background?)* is first given in PC 8. During the few periods away from Jack, Killick serves under Captain Collard in HMS *Ajax* (TMC 1), under Heneage Dundas on the West Indies station and then, in order to rejoin Jack at the Cape, in the awful Captain Corbett's east-bound HMS *Néréide* (TMC 3). Finally, for a very brief period he is in Robert Kerr's HMS *Acasta*, a ship to which he had expected Jack to be appointed (SM 1). On one occasion, whilst in domestic service at Ashgrove Cottage, Killick buys a wife at a local fair and is then ordered by Jack to marry her, with full Church process, before she can join him in the establishment (DI 1). Somewhat later, we hear that as soon as Killick had gone back to sea, his new wife had run off with her former husband, attempting to take all the seaman's worldly goods with her (SM 4).

> Aspects of Killick's cantankerous character and frequent over-familiarity are perhaps inspired by the relationship between *Nelson and his servant, Tom *Allen. His surname perhaps stems from nautical parlance, in which a 'killick' is a term for both an anchor and, by extension, a leading seaman (whose rank badge is an anchor sewn on the jersey).

Kimber

A mining speculator and fraudster who enmeshes the Aubreys in a scheme to extract silver from lead dross (DI 1,2,4; FW 1,2; SM 1,2,4).

King, the

1: *almost always see* **George III, King**; *but in French contexts see* *****Louis XVI, King** *or* *****Louis XVIII, King**

2: a monarch for whose execution his own brother, a member of Maturin's club, had voted (HD 3).

> Although *Maturin's remarks are somewhat ambiguous, the reference to the 'brother' recalls the curious career of Louis-Philippe-Joseph, Duc d'Orléans (1747–1793), an enormously wealthy, distant cousin of King *Louis XVI. After first pursuing a successful career as a soldier and naval commander, the Duke later made his Palais-Royal the leading political salon in Paris, a venue famed as much for its raffish social habits as its radical opinions. Here Orléans and his mistress, Madame de Genlis, hosted the opposition to the King and his court: the Duke, for reasons still not wholly understood, having come to loathe his cousin and all he stood for, with Queen Marie Antoinette returning the enmity with especial vigour. Espousing fashionable revolutionary positions (although he was an avowed admirer of the 'constitutional monarchy' of King *George III, as well as a frequent and lively member of the *Regent's set in London), Orléans joined the Estates-General in 1789, gradually changing his own name first to 'Monsieur Orléans' and later to 'Philippe-Egalité.' After perhaps contemplating his own bid for the crown, in January 1793 he voted for the death of Louis but, sliding rapidly into a political irrelevance, then fell victim himself to the guillotine during the bloody turmoil at the end of that same year. It has often been thought, though never quite proved, that the Duc d'Orléans and Madame de Genlis (1746–1830) were the natural parents of Lady Pamela *Fitzgerald.
>
> Orléans' legitimate son, Louis-Philippe (1773–1850), served in the Revolutionary army until 1793 but then fled for his life, living in exile in both the USA and England before returning home at the *Bourbon restoration of 1814. In 1830 Louis-Philippe became the first fully constitutional King of France—the 'Citizen King'—but was ousted in the popular uprisings of 1848, once again going into exile in England, this time until his death.

King

A Royal Navy Captain and the Governor of New South Wales, who in this capacity had pardoned Dr Redfern. Mr Adams interjects that he had served under King in HMS *Achilles* (NC 9).

> Mr Adams seems to have confused two unrelated Captain Kings. The Governor of New South Wales was Philip Gidley King (1758–1808) who had sailed out to Australia in 1787–1778 as a Lieutenant in HMS *Sirius, under Captain Arthur Philip and First Lieutenant John Hunter (see *Hunt, Captain). Captain Philip became the first Governor and Hunter the second. In 1788 King, still a Lieutenant, became Commandant of the harsh penal outpost of Norfolk Island. Promoted Commander in 1791 and made Post in 1798, he served as the third Governor-General from 1802–1806 (he pardoned *Redfern in 1803). The unrelated Sir Richard King (1774–1834) was made Post in 1794 and commanded HMS *Achilles from 1805 to 1811, fighting that ship with great distinction at the Battle of Trafalgar in 1805. Having inherited a baronetcy in 1806 (from his Admiral father, also sir Richard (1730–1806)), he was promoted Rear Admiral in 1812 and Vice Admiral in 1821. Sons of both Captain Kings became Admirals in the Royal Navy.

King, Alfred

A mute, black seaman who accompanies Mr Richards to HMS *Sophie* as part of Aubrey's price for his clerkship (M&C 2+). He is later rated bosun's mate (M&C 11).

King Log

A character referred by Aubrey in terms of passivity (PC 12).

A 'King Log' is a king incapable of exercising power, the name being taken from the classical 'Fable of King Log and King Stork.' The frogs decide they should have a King and apply to *Jupiter to provide them one; not quite seeing their need, he sends them a log of wood to fill the role. They foolishly reject the log as lacking vigour and other kingly qualities, so Jupiter now sends them a fine, regal stork, who promptly eats every one of them.

King of the Two Sicilies

A monarch referred to in passing (TH 4).

Ferdinand IV of Naples (1751–1825), a son of King Charles III of Spain, from 1759 ruled most of Italy south of Rome together with the neighbouring island of Sicily (known together as the 'Two Sicilies'). In 1768 he married Maria Carolina, a daughter of the Empress Maria Theresa of Austria, Ferdinand rapidly becoming known as a weak and foolish ruler and Maria as a devious and cruel one. Nevertheless the strategic position of their domains led to sustained attempts by Britain, from 1777 onwards, to secure them as allies. Lord *Nelson was later a renowned supporter of their cause, although his association with their worst antics (see *Caraciolo) did little for his reputation. In attempting to hold on to the crown, Ferdinand and Maria swopped sides several times, twice losing Naples to the French and having to retire to Sicily under English protection. Restored to both of his thrones in 1814, in 1816 he re-named himself formally as King Ferdinand I of the United Kingdom of the Two Sicilies.

Kingston, Duchess of

The addressee of a letter from Lord St Vincent (PC 3).

The Duchy of Kingston had gone into abeyance in 1773 on the death of a Duke with no issue or relatives-in-line; hence at the time of PC there was no Duchess. There was, however, a contemporary Earl of Kingston, who may perhaps have had a Countess wife (if so, she is unnoticed in the biographies, as are any children). Also possible is that the last, very colourful Duchess of Kingston had sprung to O'Brian's mind. The beautiful Countess Elizabeth Chudleigh (1720–1788) had separated from her husband, the Earl of Bristol, and in 1769 went through a famous second marriage ceremony with the last Duke of Kingston. She adopted the style of Duchess but was soon convicted of bigamy by the House of Lords and stripped of the title.

King's Fisher, HMS

A Royal Navy ship in which Peter Edwards had once served (M&C 6).

The reference is probably to HMS Kingfisher, 18-gun brig-sloop, launched in 1782 and wrecked off Lisbon in 1798. Her commander at the time was Lieutenant Frederick Lewis Maitland, who in 1815, as Captain Maitland

of HMS *Bellerophon, accepted *Buonaparte's final surrender.

King's Messenger, the

A government official with whom Aubrey and Maturin travel from London down to HMS *Ariel* at the Nore and thence onto Sir James Saumarez' Baltic fleet (SM 6).

Kitabi

A 20-gun Turkish frigate in the Ionian Sea, part of Captain-Bey Mustapha's very small squadron (IM 9–11). With her larger companion *Torgud*, she is engaged and defeated by Jack Aubrey's HMS *Surprise* (IM 11), being taken as a prize (TH 1).
See also **Seahorse**, HMS

Kite, HMS

A small armed transport vessel in Jack Aubrey's squadron commanded by Lieutenant Joyce (TMC 6,7).

Klopff

A scientist and promoter of the 'vital principle' theory (TGS 7).

Klopstock

1: a Baltic seaman in HMS *Ariel* (SM 8).
2: a deceased naturalist of Sierra Leone (COM 8).

In having John *Square say, 'Mr Klopstock, he dead,' O'Brian is echoing the famous line 'Mistah Kurtz, he dead' from the pen of another great master of tales set on and around ships, Joseph Conrad (1857–1924). The line, from Heart of Darkness (1902), is also famously quoted by the poet T.S. Eliot (1888–1965) beneath the title of The Hollow Men (1925).

Kneller, John

An officer referred to by Lieutenant Thomas Edwards (HD 1).

Knight of the Glen

A Irish chivalric title referred to by Maturin (PC 8).

The Knight of the Glen appears in many Irish myths, chief amongst them the tale of The Black Thief of Dubhain who, under the influence of his impoverished step-mother, attempts to steal the Knight's great Horse of Glory. After being caught red-handed and then telling wondrous tales to preserve his otherwise forfeit life, he is given the beast as a gift.

Knipperdolling, Bernhard

A Munster Anabaptist referred to by Martin as the founder of the religious sect with many members aboard HMS *Surprise*. However, he regards the ship's Knipperdollings as really being descendants of the Levellers, a republican sect in 17th century England (WDS 2+; COM 1).

Bernhard Knipperdolling (1470–1536) was a German religious leader and martyr. An impetuous fanatic from an early age, he joined the Anabaptists—'re-baptisers,' a sect founded in 1521— whilst in exile in Sweden. Having even-

tually returned to Germany, in 1534 he became bur-gomeister of Münster, instituting a reign of anti-Catholic terror in the vicinity. In 1536 Knipperdolling and his associate John of *Leiden were taken prisoner by Catholic forces and, refusing reconciliation with the Church, were brutally executed.

Knittel
The Master of the slave-ship *Nancy* (COM 8).

Knowles, Admiral
An officer serving in the Admiralty in London (PC 14).
The reference is possibly to Sir Charles Henry Knowles (1754–1831) who was made Post in 1780 and fought his HMS *Goliath with distinction at the Battle of Cape *St Vincent in 1797. On his retirement from active service in 1798 due to ill-health, he then wrote extensively on technical, naval subjects. Promoted by seniority Rear Admiral in 1799, he advanced to Vice Admiral in 1804 and Admiral in 1810. His DNB entry does not mention specific service in the Admiralty after 1799.

Koop, Hanbury
see **Stranraer, Admiral Lord**

Korah
According to a heretical Jewish sect, a descendant of Cain (HD 4).
In the Old Testament Book of Leviticus, Korah the Levite revolted against the rule of *Moses and his brother Aaron and, after his ensuing defeat, he and his followers were then consumed by *God's earthquake and fire.

Krantz
A seaman in *Surprise* (C/T 1).

Kresimir
The man from whom a Croat regiment stationed in Malta take their name (TH 1).
Peter Kresimir (1058–1074) was one of the heroes and early rulers of the short-lived, independent Kingdom of Croatia.

Kreutzer
A great violinist referred to by Maturin (C/T 7).
Rodolphe Kreutzer (1766–1831), a French violinist and composer of great renown, had his career as a virtuoso performer cut short by an arm injury sustained in a coaching accident in 1810. Beethoven, an admirer of his pure musicianship rather than simply his undoubted technical abilities, dedicated his Violin Sonata in A major (Opus 47, 1803) to Kreutzer, although it seems that he never played the work in public.

Krishna *or* Krisnaji
The Indian God referred to by Dil (HMS 7).
In Hindu mythology Krishna is regarded as the greatest and most popular of all the manifestations of the god, Vishnu. He is usually portrayed as a beautiful, blue-skinned youth crowned with peacock feathers, famous for his playful antics and frequent amorous dalliances.

Kumar
1: a wealthy citizen of Calcutta (HMS 10).
2: a servant in the Canning household (HMS 10).

L

Lacanfra, Francis
A seaman in HMS *Sophie* (M&C 3).

Lachesis, HMS
A frigate carrying dispatches met by HMS *Surprise* (HMS 11).
Lachesis was one of the Fates of classical mythology who, with her sisters Clotho and Atropos, span, and eventually snipped, the thread of human life and destiny. No Royal Navy ship went by this name.

La Colonna
The singer whom Canning says is performing Susanna in the *Marriage of Figaro* (PC 8).

Lady, Our
Maturin observes to Mr Etherege that Our Lady was, of course, a Jewess (HMS 10).
'Our Lady' is the traditional Roman Catholic appellation for *Mary, the mother of *Jesus Christ.

Lady Albemarle
An English mail packet once taken by the American privateer *Liberty* (SM 3).
The ship may perhaps have been named for Anne *Keppel, Countess Albemarle, the sister-in-law of Admiral Viscount *Keppel.

Lady Nelson, HMS
A small brig, equipped with sliding keels a little like those of HMS *Polychrest*, that Lieutenant Grant had commanded in 1800 on a voyage of discovery to the Southern Ocean (DI 3,4).
HMS Lady Nelson, a 6-gun survey brig purchased in 1800 for coastal exploration of Australia, was destroyed by natives in the Timor archipelago in 1825. The ship was named for Frances, Lady *Nelson.

Laënnec
A doctor who promotes the auscultation technique of diagnosis (YA 8; HD 6).
René-Théodore-Hyacinthe Laënnec (1781–1826) was one

of the most distinguished Parisian physicians and professors of his age, a leader in promoting a scientific approach to medical diagnosis. The nephew of a physician to King *Louis XVI, Laënnec became interested from an early age in improving the methods of investigating the presence and characteristics of diseases of the chest organs. In particular he wished to reduce reliance on the patient's own account of his or her distress and move towards direct and systematic examination, either by palpitating or listening to—'auscultation' of—the thoracic cavity. In 1816, as Chief Physician of the Hôtel Necker, he invented the stethoscope, initially as a means of examining female patients without physical contact between ear and breast—he first used a rolled-up tube of paper—but very soon thereafter as in itself a superior method of accurate diagnosis.

Laetitia

A name scratched on the wall of the nunnery/prison in Brest where HMS Ariel's officers are held (SM 10).

Lafarge, Admiral

A flag-officer regarded as still being loyal to Buonaparte (HD 4).

La Fayette, Madame de

A French novelist referred to by Maturin (NC 9).

Marie-Madeleine de la Vergue, Comptess de La Fayette (1634–1693) was a niece of the prelate-statesman Cardinal Richelieu and the author of a number of passionate tragedies. She is often regarded as the creator of the style and format of the modern French novel.

La Fayette

An American whaler that arrives at Jack Aubrey's Desolation Island under her Master Winthrop Putnam and in which the Americans Louisa Wogan and Michael Herapath escape (DI 10).

The whaler is undoubtedly named for Général Marie Joseph Paul de Motier, Marquis de Lafayette (1757–1834), a wealthy French aristocrat who entered the army in 1771. In 1777 he arranged, via Benjamin *Franklin, an invitation to serve with his own volunteer force in the American revolutionary army, into which he was then commissioned Major-General. He served with considerable distinction in the war against British rule and in 1782 returned to a hero's welcome in France. Lafayette soon became involved in the reform movement, at first attempting to persuade *Louis XVI to accept change in political institutions but, in 1791, being the man who arrested the King as he attempted to flee the country to the Austrian Netherlands. Under extremist, *Jacobite pressure, Lafayette was himself forced to flee France in 1792 but was then arrested by the Austrians and imprisoned until 1797, only being released on General *Buonaparte's specific insistence as part of a peace treaty between the two nations. He took up residence again in France but, despite a number of offers to engage his still-revered name in public affairs, refused to participate in political life, believing that the lack of a constitution resembling that of the United States rendered the French revolution morally insupportable. Although at heart a republican, Lafayette re-entered public life on the *Bourbon restoration of 1814 and

played a central role in the continuing reform movements until the end of his life. In 1824–1825 he again visited America and made a triumphant tour of all 24 of the United States, being greeted as one of the heroes of the revolutionary age.

La Feuillade, Madame de

A French lady who operates as an English agent in the port of Lorient, Brittany (RM 5,10).

The d'Aubusson family, Comptes de la Feuillade, had many distinguished members in French military, clerical and political life especially in the 17th century. The only notable family member of the early 19th century was the politician Pierre Raymond Hector d'Aubusson de la Feuillade (1765–1848), married to one Agathe-Renée. He, however, was a devoted follower of *Buonaparte and there is nothing to suggest his wife was otherwise inclined. Given O'Brian's great regard for the English novelist Jane Austen (see *Canopus, HMS for a note on her naval brothers), an alternative source for the name may be Jane's cousin and close friend, Eliza Hancock (1761–1813), whose first husband, the French Count Jean François Capot de Feuillide (sic; d.1794), was executed in the Revolution.

La Hire, Captain

A French Royalist artillery captain who assisted Dillon in the recapture of Gloire (M&C 7).

Lakes, John

A seaman in HMS Polychrest, formerly of HMS Sophie (PC 8).

The name is probably a typo for '*Lakey,' as the character is more usually named in this chapter and elsewhere.

Lakey, John or Jno.

An HMS Sophie seaman referred to in Captain Allen's log as having been lashed (M&C 2+). Injured in HMS Sophie's first battle under Aubrey's command (M&C 4), he later serves in HMS Polychrest, grateful to Maturin for having earlier saved his 'private parts' (PC 7+).

Laleso, Guiseppe

A seaman in HMS Sophie (M&C 3).

Lalla

An Arabian mare belonging to the Maturins (COM 3–5), later kept at the Aubreys' Woolcombe House (YA 2).

Lalonde

The Captain of the French Formidable, killed in action against Saumarez' squadron (M&C 11,12).

Captain Laindet Lalonde (d.1801) was *Flag Captain of Admiral *Linois' *Formidable in this action on July 6th 1801, and was reported killed in the Admiral's dispatches. Formidable went into the second action on July 12th under Commander Aimable Gilles Troude (1762–1824) who had been *Christie-Pallière's second-in-command on *Desaix in the first engagement. Troude was promoted Captain shortly after his second encounter with *Saumarez.

Lamb

1: HMS *Sophie*'s carpenter (M&C 1+).
2: the Reverend Mr Lamb, a member of the London Entomological Society (HMS 1).
3: the carpenter of HMS *Surprise* (TH 5; FSW 2+) and his wife, who, as tradition allows, often sails with him (FSW 2–9).

Lamb, Misses Lucy and Susan

Two sisters sailing home from India in the *Lord Nelson* under the protection of their uncle, Major Hill, who act as powder 'boys' in the action with the French privateer, *Bellone* (PC 5,6).

Lamb, William

A seaman in *Surprise* (C/T 5).

Lamballe, Princess de

A lady who had once owned a grand house in Paris (SM 11).

*Maria-Thérèse Louise de Savoie-Carignan (1749–1792), Princess de Lamballe, was a great beauty from the royal house of Sardinia who married the Prince de Lamballe in 1767 and was left a wealthy widow in the following year. She became a close confidante of Marie Antoinette, the wife of King *Louis XVI, and was arrested and imprisoned for that association during the revolutionary turmoil. Required by an impromptu tribunal to swear hatred for the King and Queen, the Princess refused and was promptly hacked to death by the 'court's' attending mob (with one well-known account maintaining that she was also sexually assaulted and mutilated). Her head, mounted on a pike, was then displayed outside the window of the Queen's cell at the Temple prison (the same prison in which *Aubrey, *Maturin and *Jagiello are held in SM).*

Lambert

A secret agent in the USA, probably British but perhaps French, referred to by Harry Johnson (FW 7).

Lambert, Harry

The Captain of HMS *Iphigenia* in Jack Aubrey's Indian Ocean squadron (TMC 6). In the disastrous Battle of Port South East, he is later said by Stephen Maturin to have made a sound suggestion to achieve a victory but to have been ignored by Pym, the senior Captain present (TMC 7). He is then forced to surrender his ship following the heavy defeat (TMC 7,8). A few years later, Lambert is that Captain of HMS *Java* who, en route to Bombay, picks up the shipwrecked Jack Aubrey, Stephen Maturin and their colleagues (FW 3). He is known personally to Jack (*but see note below*), who recalls that he had been the Captain of HMS *Active* in 1801, that he had captured *Scipion* and that, after marrying Maitland's sister, he has become a poor man with a large family (FW 3). Lambert soon encounters the powerful USS *Constitution* but, to Jack's dismay, uses no suitable tactics to offset the American's superior fire-power (FW 3). Lambert is injured in the

disastrous defeat, later dying of his wounds and despair after being put ashore in Brazil (FW 3,4).

*Henry Lambert (d.1813) came from a distinguished naval family. The son of Captain Robert Lambert (d.1787), who had been the Commissioner of the Jamaica naval base from 1782 to 1784, Henry was the younger brother of another Robert Lambert (1772–1836) who was made Post in 1796, promoted Rear Admiral in 1819 and Vice Admiral in 1830 and who served as Commandant of St Helena at the time of *Buonaparte's death in 1821. Henry himself had been made Post into HMS *San Fiorenzo in 1804 and appointed into HMS *Iphigenia in May 1808. After her loss during the Mauritius campaign in late 1810, he was next appointed, in August 1812, to HMS *Java in her first commission as a Royal Navy ship. In the battle of December 29th 1812 with USS *Constitution, Lambert fought his ship—crowded with stores and passengers, and with a new and untrained crew—with great personal bravery but with tactics that failed to take make anything of the speed advantage he enjoyed over the American in the conditions of the day. Hit in the chest by a musket ball after about an hour's action, he died ashore in Brazil on January 4th 1813.*

*It is curious that, whilst in Java, neither Jack *Aubrey nor Stephen *Maturin recall that Lambert (and his First Lieutenant, *Chads) had recently been with them in the Mauritius campaign and doubly odd that Jack seems to confuse him with some other officer, as none of the Lamberts had ever commanded an HMS *Active nor taken a *Scipion (nor, so far as I have been able to ascertain, did Henry marry a Miss Maitland).*

Lampson

The Captain of HMS *Briseis* (TGS 3).

Lane

The corrupt, drunken bosun of HMS *Leopard* (DI 4–8) who heads the party of warrant officers supporting Lieutenant Grant in his contention to Jack Aubrey that the ship should be abandoned (DI 8).

Lane, John

A seaman in HMS *Sophie* (M&C 2).

Langara, don Martin de

The Spanish Captain of *Cacafuego*, killed in action against Jack Aubrey's HMS Sophie (M&C 11).

*There were two famous Lángara sea-captains from whom O'Brian may have borrowed this name: Admiral Juan de Lángara y Arizmendi (1700?–1781) and Admiral Juan Francisco de Lángara y Huarte (1730–1806), the later a sometime Minister of Marine. The Captain of El *Gamo, the ship on which O'Brian bases his *Cacafuego, was one Don Francesco de Torres, killed in the action.*

Laocoön

His fate of being entwined by serpents is referred to by Maturin (FSW 5).

*In Greek mythology Laocoön was a Trojan hero, a son of either Antenor or King *Priam himself. He was one of the warriors who most strenuously opposed the entry of the Wooden Horse into the city, assaulting it with his spear. Shortly afterwards, he and his sons were sacrificing to *Neptune when two enormous sea-serpents sprang up, en-*

twined them and crushed all three to death. This startling event became a favourite theme of artists down the ages.

Lao Tung

A Chinese firework manufacturer in Pulo Prabang (TGS 7).

La Pallice

Maturin refers to 'a generality worthy of La Pallice' (RM 6).

> *Jacques de Chabannes (1470?–1525), Seigneur de la Palice (sic; sometimes seen as La Palisse), was a famous Maréchal de France whose supposed capacity for stating the obvious became the subject of a well-known comic song by Bernard de la Monnoye (1641–1728), featuring the line 'a quarter of an hour before his death, he was still alive.' From this is derived the common French phrase une verité de la Palice (or une palissade), meaning a glaringly self-evident truth.*

Laplace

The author of a treatise on games and tactics referred to by Maturin (PC 3).

> *Pierre-Simon, Marquis de Laplace (1749–1827), rose from peasant origins, his prodigious mathematical gifts soon making him a prominent savant and politician under *Louis XVI's 'Ancien Régime,' *Buonaparte's rule and the *Bourbon restoration. Although he published extensively from 1777 onwards on both probabilities and astronomy, his two principle works on 'game theory' were not published until 1812 (Analytic Theory) and 1814 (Philosophic Essay), some time after PC is set.*

Larkin

The Master of HMS *Leopard* who, as well as being somewhat young for his position, is also a very heavy drinker (DI 3–9). In a drunken rage he murders Howard, the Marine Lieutenant, and is then confined as a lunatic (DI 7). Suspected of being a 'Jonah' by many of the crew, he is — by implication — drowned by some of them as he tries to scramble into one of the boats that later leave the badly damaged ship (DI 9). Curiously, when Jack Aubrey later reports on the whole ugly affair to Admiral Drury, he neglects to mention Larkin, the senior warrant-officer aboard, as one of those who abandoned ship with First Lieutenant Grant (FW 1).

Larkin, John

A seaman in HMS *Surprise* (RM 3).

Larrey

Buonaparte's doctor, known personally to Maturin (SM 5,10; YA 4).

> *Domenique-Jean, Baron Larrey (1766–1842), served as a surgeon in both the French navy and army, in the latter of which posts he invented the 'flying hospital,' the first mobile field-unit for evacuating the wounded. Larrey rose to be chief medical officer of *Buonaparte's armies and became famous and admired for his dedication to the care of the soldiery on many arduous campaigns, the retreat from Moscow of 1812 included. In 1809 he was made Baron for his services. Wounded in 1815 during the Emperor's final defeat at Waterloo, he was nevertheless invited to hold high medical office under the *Bourbon restoration and continued to build his reputation as a dedicated, practical surgeon until his retirement in 1836. Larrey was described in Buonaparte's will as 'the most virtuous man I have ever known.'*

Larsen, Bent

A ship's boy in HMS *Surprise* (HMS 9).

Latham

A naturalist and author (WDS 9; C/T 3,4,5). His *General Synopsis of Birds* is not admired by Stephen Maturin, who nevertheless retains a fondness for the physical book itself as, between its pages, he had located the missing Spanish bank receipt for his large fortune (YA 1).

> *John Latham (1740–1837) was an ornithologist, surgeon and physician who became one of the leading scientific figures of his age. He published extensively on bird life and comparative anatomy and was important promulgator of *Linnaeus' classification system. His Synopsis appeared in six volumes from 1781 to 1787.*

Latham, Francis

The Captain of HMS *Surprise*, a man with a reputation for poor discipline in his ships (IM 5–9). Later, with his crew on the point of mutiny, both he and his First Lieutenant are killed by a single cannon-ball fired from the fleeing *Robuste* (IM 9).

Latif

A servant of van Buren (TGS 6,8)

La Tour, Charles de

A French naval Captain, loyal to Buonaparte (HD 4).

Latreille

A French scientist at Maturin's lecture in Paris (SM 5).

> *Pierre-André Latreille (1762–1833) became known in his own time as the 'Prince of Entomology.' Before the Revolution Latreille had practised as a priest but soon abandoned that calling — always secondary to his love for science — to dedicate himself to the study of insects. From 1798 to 1729 he was the chief curator of insects at the Museum of Paris, being in the latter year appointed Professor of Zoology, a post he held until his death. In addition to his own monographs on beetles, ants and — extending himself — reptiles, Latreille contributed specialist sections to the great general works of *Buffon and *Cuvier.*

Laura

see **Fielding, Laura**

Laurel, HMS

1: a 22-gun ship, Captain Woolcombe, that had been taken by *Cannonière* before Jack Aubrey's arrival in the Indian Ocean (TMC 1,6).

HMS Laurel, *22-gun, was launched in 1806 and, under her Captain John Charles *Woolcombe, was captured by the 48-gun* Cannonière *in September 1808. Now named* Esperance, *she was re-taken by the Royal Navy in April 1810 and then served as HMS* Laurestinus *until her loss on a reef in the West Indies in October 1813.*

2: a 22-gun ship in Jack Aubrey's squadron, Captain Dick Richardson (COM 4+).

The post-1808 successors to #1 *above were all rather larger ships: a 36-gun — the ex-French* Fidelle — *in service from 1809 to 1812 and a new 38-gun in service from mid-1813 to 1885.*

Laurie

The head of a secret police organisation in the French Ministry of the Interior (SM 11).

Lavater

A famous physiognomist referred to by Maturin (TMC 1).

John Caspar Lavater (1741–1801) was a Swiss Protestant minister who produced many well-regarded moral histories and poems as well as his influential Physiognomic Fragments for the Promotion of the Knowledge and Love of Mankind, *a work in which he set out a general system for ascertaining character from the physical characteristics of the human head (1775–1778). He was a staunch opponent of the French-inspired revolutionary fervour that broke out in his home-town of Zurich in 1799 and, when the city was taken in September of that year by General Massena's invading army, the unarmed Lavater was shot in the street during a skirmish. He died of his wound a little over a year later.*

Lavinia, HMS

A heavy frigate in the Mediterranean (HD 10).

HMS Lavinia, *48-gun, was launched in 1806; sent for harbour service in 1836, she was sunk in 1868 after a collision in Plymouth harbour. In classical legend, Lavinia was the Italian wife of the Trojan hero *Aeneas.*

Lavoisier, M. de

1: the famous French scientist and *savant* who had fallen victim to the Revolution (LM 7), and to whose memory Maturin asks Paulton to dedicate his forthcoming novel (NC 9).

Antoine-Laurent de Lavoisier (1743–1794) was the highly distinguished French chemist, scientist and inventor who devised the modern, systematic scheme for naming compounds, after having first discovered the mechanism by which combustion occurs and heat is produced. In addition to his scientific work, Lavoisier was — via his wife's family — a leading member of the Farmers-General, the powerful, private tax collecting (or 'farming') institution that controlled much of the commerce in France and whose depredations did much to bring down eventual ruin on the monarchy, from which it obtained its licenses and freedoms. For his role in these activities, Lavoisier was guillotined in 1794, being denied after his trial even a few days respite in which to finish some final papers on his beloved chemistry. Curiously, when Paulton's novel appears in England, it is dedicated to Maturin himself rather than Lavoisier (COM 7).

2: the inventor of a trepanning device used by, and very nearly on, Maturin (FSW 5,9).

Law

A lawyer, known as 'the Just Judge,' whom Maturin had met in India (RM 7).

The reference is possibly to Thomas Law (1759–1834), who had been a zealously reforming tax-collector (but not a judge) in India from 1773 to 1791 and who then lived in the USA from 1793 onwards. He was the younger brother of Edward Law, Lord *Ellenborough, the model for O'Brian's awful Lord *Quinborough, whose son, also Edward (1790–1871), became Governor-General of India in 1841.

Lawrence

1: the Captain of USS *Hornet* who had sunk HMS *Peacock,* killing her Captain Billy Peake (FW 4). Promoted into USS *Chesapeake,* then refitting in Boston, he visits the wounded prisoner, Jack Aubrey, the two men quickly coming to a mutual respect and liking (FW 6,8; *also* FSW 5,9 *where no mention is made of his subsequent fate, in part at Jack's hand).* Lawrence soon takes his new ship out to meet HMS *Shannon* in single combat, clearly deciding to do so before he receives Broke's written challenge (FW 9). However, he is wounded almost as soon as the action commences and is not seen again on deck during the rapid defeat of his ship (FW 9). We later learn that he had died of his wounds and was buried in Halifax, Nova Scotia (SM 1).

James Lawrence (1781–1813) became a Midshipman in the U.S. Navy in 1798 and rapidly made a reputation both as a brave, enterprising young officer and a prime seaman. As a brig and sloop Commander, he clearly showed he was destined for higher command and his taking of HMS *Peacock with his USS *Hornet in February 1813 was rewarded with promotion to a full Captaincy. Yet USS *Chesapeake was a somewhat awkward 'plum' to be given, at least for immediate action, for she was an unhappy ship, wracked with disputes over prize-money, in consequence of which the majority of her experienced crew had declined to re-enlist following her refit. Her new hands, officers and men alike, were both wholly untrained, too few in number, and late in being drafted aboard. Furthermore, for a U.S. war-ship an unusual proportion of them were non-Americans, some 40 British subjects amongst them. One reading of Philip *Broke's challenge (the text given by O'Brian is, of course, accurate) is that, in asking Lawrence to specify the time and location of a meeting, he was offering the American some few days to work up his crew and ship before an encounter. But Lawrence, perhaps now displaying an over-confidence that had hitherto been the preserve of British commanders, had already stood out to sea on seeing HMS *Shannon — a crack frigate, intensely well prepared — at the entrance to Boston harbour, intending immediately to engage her. The ensuing battle — in the early evening of June 1st 1813 — was short, bloody and, for Lawrence and his ship, disastrous. The American Captain was shot by Royal Marine Lieutenant James Law as the already heavily damaged ships drifted together; as he was carried below, dying, Lawrence is said to have repeatedly cried the famous words, 'Don't give up the ship….' Sadly, his inexperienced, badly mauled crew could offer no disciplined resistance to Broke's boarders, although their attempts were undoubtedly ferocious, and Chesapeake stuck her colours only 15 minutes after the opening broadsides had been exchanged. After the battle, Lawrence was treated as a fallen hero in the USA but, whilst there can be no question concerning his fighting spirit on the day, later historians have speculated that, had he survived, his court-martial for the loss of his ship might well have proved for him a most uncomfortable occasion. Lawrence died either during or shortly after the battle and was buried by his British victors at Nova Scotia. Very soon afterwards his body was recovered by the Americans—under a formal flag of truce—and taken for reburial in New York City, where it lies to this day.

2: an artist well known for his portraits of naval officers (TH 2).

Sir Thomas Lawrence (1769–1830) was one of the leading portrait painters of his age, having been a prodigy from very early childhood. In 1792 Lawrence succeeded Sir Joshua Reynolds as portrait painter to King *George III, thus becoming one of the best-paid and most highly patronised artists in British society. Knighted in 1815, he was elected President of the Royal Academy in 1820, a post he held until his death. Although he painted relatively few sea-officers, Lawrence had strong naval connections, for his elder brother, Andrew, was at one stage in his career a Royal Navy chaplain, serving under *Nelson himself for a time.

3: a man who dines at sea in HMS Surprise with Jack Aubrey after the re-capture of the British whaler, Acapulco. He is perhaps that ship's Master (FSW 6).

Lawrence, Brendan

Jack Aubrey's barrister at his trial for fraud, who had attended Trinity College, Dublin, with Stephen Maturin (RM 7,8). He later acts in various matters for both Stephen and Jack (COM 4,5,9; YA 1–6).

Although not associated with the *Cochrane trial upon which Jack *Aubrey's ordeal is modelled, a Sir Soulden Lawrence (1751–1814) was a contemporary and considerable rival of Lord *Ellenborough. Interestingly, one Charles Laurence (sic) was Chairman of the London Stock Exchange at the time of Cochrane's alleged fraud.

Lazarus

HMS Sophie's gunner, Mr Day, is nick-named 'Lazarus' after his miraculous recovery from open-brain surgery (M&C 5).

In the New Testament, Lazarus, the brother of *Mary and Martha, is recalled to life by *Jesus Christ after lying four days dead.

Leadbetter

The surgeon of Colnett's exploration ship Rattler (FSW 3).

Leake

A senior Midshipman in HMS Shannon (FW 9).

Leake in mentioned several times in accounts of HMS

*Shannon's great victory. He may be that Henry Martin Leake (d.1840) who was commissioned Lieutenant in 1814 but then received no further promotions.

Leander, HMS

A ship in which Jack Aubrey had served as a Lieutenant at the Battle of the Nile. Her taking by Généreux, and Jack's wound in that action, were the occasion for his eventual promotion to Commander (M&C 2+; PC 12). Some years later, in 1805, under her Captain Harry Whitby, she had allegedly fired into an unarmed U.S. merchantman (FW 4).

HMS Leander, 52-gun, fought at the Nile (August 1st, 1798) under Captain Thomas Boulden Thompson (d.1828 as Sir Thomas, in the rank of Vice Admiral). Following the great victory she was sent off to take the news to Lord *St Vincent, with *Nelson's *Flag Captain, Edward *Berry, carrying the dispatch as a passenger. However, on August 18th she encountered the much larger 74-gun Généreux, one of only four French ships to escape from the French defeat a few weeks earlier. After a long and furious resistance, Leander was compelled to surrender, with Thompson and Berry both wounded, along with many more of her crew. Following the encounter, the Leanders were badly mistreated by their captors, with many of the injured being both robbed and denied medical treatment (see M&C 11). In 1799 the ship was re-captured by the Russian Navy at Corfu and returned to the Royal Navy. Leander had been launched in 1780; re-named HMS Hygeia in 1813, she was then used as a medical depot until being sold in 1817. (The incident with the American merchantman is discussed under Captain *Whitby's own entry below.) In classical myth, Leander was the lover of the beautiful Hero, to whom he swam across the Hellespont every night until being caught and drowned in a sudden storm.

Lebrun, Vigée

A female artist referred to by Maturin (HMS 7).

Marie-Louise-Elisabeth Vigée (1755–1842), born into humble stock, made an early reputations as an artistic prodigy, beauty and wit and in 1776 married the art critic and dealer, Jean Baptiste Pierre Lebrun (1748–1813). She soon became a leading figure in Paris society as an accomplished and prolific portrait painter, famous for her cult of the 'unaffected, rustic life.' In her long career, she produced over 600 works, including many studies of Queen Marie Antoinette (of whom she became a confidante) and, somewhat later, Lord *Byron. In her autobiography of 1835, Madame Vigée-Lebrun reveals that much of her considerable fortune was squandered before the Revolution by her gambler husband, a fact that, luckily, forced her to paint for her living long after she could otherwise have retired.

Leclerc

A Royalist intelligence contact of Maturin—code name 'Voltaire'—who attempts to guide him to a clandestine meeting in France. Fearing discovery, he soon panics and runs off (IM 7).

Leda

A reference is made to Leda and her swan (COM 9).

> In Greek mythology Leda was the wife of the King of Pleuron, and the mother of Castor, *Pollux, Helen and others. According to one popular version of the tale, Helen was born to Leda from an egg produced by her copulation with *Zeus, he being disguised for the occasion as a swan.

Leda, HMS

A 38-gun ship recently wrecked off Milford Haven (TMC 1).

> HMS Leda, 38-gun, was launched in 1800 and, under Captain Robert Honeyman (d.1848 in the rank of full Admiral), wrecked on rocks at the entrance to Milford Haven Bay, Wales, in January 1808. For her name derivation, see *Leda above.

Ledward

With Andrew Wray, a traitor in the British administration and thus an enemy of Stephen Maturin (RM 2,5; LM 2–8), to whom both are identified as a spies by the French defector, Duhamel (RM 10; WDS 7). Ledward and Wray escape capture in London (LM 2) and, revealed as lovers as well as traitors, flee together to Paris (LM 4; TGS 1). Having been brought up in the Malay islands, Ledward is then made the effective head of the French mission to Pulo Prabang (TGS 3,4): here he encounters Stephen, who is acting as a member of Envoy Fox's party (TGS 6–9). Although a formidably able man, Ledward is undone by Stephen's discovery of his (and Wray's) sexual liaison with Abdul, the Sultan's lover and, consequently, the mortal enemy of Hafsa, the Sultana (TGS 6,7,8). When this affair is revealed, both Ledward and Wray are banished from the Sultan's court and soon assassinated (TGS 8; NC 3) by Fox and his associates (TGS 9). The pair are then dissected by Stephen (who may also have had a hand in their demise) and his fellow anatomist, van Buren, as a means of quiet disposal of their bodies (TGS 8). In their London days, both traitors had frequented Mother Abbott's whorehouse and were thus known by sight to Clarissa Oakes (C/T 6,7,9). Through this connection, their secret patron is eventually revealed to have been the Duke of Habachtsthal (COM 2,4,5).

Lee

1: a Midshipman in HMS Surprise (HMS 9,11)
2: a Midshipman in HMS Boadicea (TMC 3,10).

Lee, Nehemiah

A seaman in HMS Polychrest (PC 8).

Leeuenhoek

A naturalist said by Maturin to have demonstrated the existence of asexual reproduction (TGS 5).

> Antoni van Leeuwenhoek (1632–1723) was a Dutch naturalist, anatomist and physiologist who specialised, particularly in his early years, in investigations with the microscope, of which instrument he was also a noted designer and fabricator. His observations on asexual reproduction in micro-organisms were made in 1676–1677. Many of his discoveries were first published by the Royal Society in London, of which he was elected Fellow in 1680.

Leguat

'Leguat's Voyage' is read by Maturin (TMC 3).

> François Léguat (1638–1735) was Protestant Hugenot refugee from France who conceived the idea of finding and settling a remote island as an 'earthly Eden.' In 1691 he set out for Réunion in the Indian Ocean but his ship made a first landfall on the nearby, deserted Rodriguez Island. Léguat was left here together with eight companions and all the supplies they thought necessary for their future, idyllic life. However, the settlers very soon began to suffer great privations and, in 1693, built a small boat and left for French Mauritius. Here Léguat, distrusted for both his religion and social views, was for a while tossed into prison, not returning to France, after further adventures en route, until 1698. Still finding the religious atmosphere uncongenial, he soon emigrated to England where, in 1708, he published an account of his earlier travels, Voyage et Avantures en Deux Isles Desertes.

Lehideux, Madame B. 'Poupette'

A pretty young widow —veuve— who supplies Aubrey, Maturin and Jagiello with food and laundry services in the Temple prison (SM 10,11). Soon becoming enamoured of Jagiello, she smuggles in escape tools for the friends' use (SM 10).

Leibnitz

The great philosopher referred to by Professor Graham (TH 1).

> Gottfried Wilhelm, Baron von Leibnitz (1646–1716), was a philosopher and mathematician who became one of the leading figures in the German Enlightenment (although publishing many of his major works in French). Although his massive, complex metaphysical system was ridiculed by *Voltaire (see **Pangloss**) and others especially for its systematic 'Optimism' (his view being that the world is perfectly and harmoniously designed by *God), his mathematics remain profound and his closely connected system of formal logic is still of the first importance.

Leiden, John of

An early associate of Knipperdolling referred to by Martin (WDS 3).

> Jean Bockleson— or Bockold— of Leyden (1510?–1536), after an earlier career as an author, actor and bon vivant, arrived in Munster in 1533 and there became a fanatical Anabaptist, making his reputation as a fiery orator and becoming regarded as a new prophet of *God. In 1534 he was declared by his followers to be 'King of Sion' and ruler of the Anabaptist population. He then led the defence of Munster against its Catholic besiegers, putting to death anyone who lost heart or tried to desert. Eventually betrayed, he was horribly executed along with *Knipperdolling and others.

Leigh

The Commander of HMS Camel (LM 6).

Leland

An author on antiquarian, religious matters in England, referred to in relation to HMS *Surprise*'s Shelmerstonians (WDS 4).

> *John Leland (1503?–1552) was a renowned antiquary, later Royal Chaplain to King *Henry VIII. Leland was a prodigious traveller in search of English antiquities and, although a supporter of Henry's Protestantism, made great (if largely unsuccessful) efforts to save rare manuscripts from theft or destruction during the dissolution of the great Catholic monasteries. Sadly, by 1550 he had become incurably insane and was thereby prevented from publishing his many collections of observations. Editions of his material proliferated after his death, with an influential version of his* Itineraries *appearing from 1710 onwards.*

Lemmon

An officer in HMS *Euryalus* (HMS 11).

Lemon

A seaman in HMS *Néréide*, once a lawyer's clerk (TMC 7).

Lennox, Major

A guest at the Keith's Ball (PC 6).

Leon, Ponce de

A writer who held that the 'Fountain of Youth' was located in North America (SM 1).

> *Juan Ponce de Leon (d.1521) was a Spanish adventurer and explorer who sailed with *Columbus on his second voyage (1493) to the Americas, afterwards serving under various Generals in their campaigns of conquest and discovery in the Caribbean islands. In 1508 he led the subjugation of Puerto Rico and then, in 1512, went onto search for the 'Fountain of Youth' of Indian legend, first in the Bahamas and then in Florida, being the first European to visit that part of the American mainland. In the year of his death Leon was wounded in a skirmish with Florida natives, later dying in Cuba of his injuries.*

Leopard, HMS

Jack Aubrey's 'horrible old *Leopard*' (e.g., DI 1; FW 1; FSW 10; COM 3) is first mentioned in the series as a ship recently at Gibraltar (HMS 5) and makes her first appearance — ancient and decrepit (TMC 5) — temporarily attached by Admiral Bertie to Jack's Mauritius squadron (TMC 6,7,10). Jack's suspicion is that her only purpose is to secure a share in any prize money for her Captain, a relative of the Admiral (TMC 6; *perhaps Tom *Andrews:* DI 1). She is soon sent back to the Cape with the good news of the capture of Réunion (TMC 7). Some time later, she has been extensively overhauled in England (DI 1,5) and is given to Jack for a journey to Australia; although, to his great dismay, she is also to carry convicts to the colony (DI 1+). During the voyage, gaol fever spreads from the convicts to the crew, resulting in over 100 deaths and leaving many men as invalids (DI 4,5). In this weakened state *Leopard* is soon pursued through monstrous seas by

the Dutch 74-gun *Waakzaamheid*, a ship she nevertheless dismasts and sinks with a single shot (DI 6,7). The pursuit has driven her far south into the ice-fields and, whilst attempting to take on water from a berg, she is holed and left rudderless. After long efforts to save her, First Lieutenant Grant leads many of her crew away in the boats amid drunken and desperate scenes (DI 8). Jack and the remaining crew manage to ease the old ship eastwards to the remote and inhospitable Desolation Island, where they attempt to repair the damage (DI 9,10). The arrival of a well-equipped American whaler, *La Fayette*, is both welcome and awkward: the USA and Britain are on the brink of war; and in the recent past *Leopard*, under Captain Buck Humphreys, had most controversially fired into the semi-armed USS *Chesapeake* whilst in search of Royal Navy deserters (DI 4,10; FSW 9). However, Jack secures the supplies and tools that *Leopard* requires and her crew begin the repairs necessary to continue their voyage (DI 10). The work accomplished, she arrives at Admiral Drury's base on Java, via a brief visit to the Australian colony (FW 1–6). Jack and his immediate followers take leave of her to travel in HMS *La Flèche* back to England, where his new HMS *Acasta* supposedly awaits. *Leopard*'s intended new Captain, Mr Burrel, has died of dysentery, and Drury decides to relegate her to a transport 'sloop' under the command of a Lieutenant (FW 1). The memory of *Leopard* soon causes some concern to Jack when, as a prisoner in Boston, he is wrongly accused of firing from her into the American merchant brig *Alice B. Sawyer* (FW 4). A few years later *Leopard* is met as a transport ship operating in home waters and Stephen Maturin takes passage in her from the Nore to Sweden, a voyage during which she runs aground off the Norfolk coast (LM 8; also SM 2,4,6; FSW 5,10; LM 7; RM 8; TGS 5; NC 1+; COM 3,7; WDS 10; YA 5).

> *HMS* Leopard, *50-gun, was launched in 1790 and served most of her career as the flagship of small, out-of-the-way squadrons, the usual fate of 50-guns. In 1812 she was reduced to a troopship and in 1814 — under Captain Edward Lowther Crofton (d.1818) — was wrecked in the Gulf of St Lawrence. The *Chesapeake incident of 1807, which caused great fury in the USA, is detailed under the main entry for her then Captain *Humphreys. Her iceberg encounter and the subsequent dramas are closely based on a similar accident in late 1789 to Lieutenant Edward *Riou's HMS* Guardian, *a transport and temporary convict-ship en route from the Cape to New South Wales.*

Leopardina

see **Boswell, Salubrity** and **Leopardina**

Le Poer, Sir Joe and Lady

A recently promoted Admiral and his wife, friends of the Aubreys (YA 1). Sir Joe is also an expert on the economics of land enclosure (YA 2).

Lesueur

1: the senior French officer on Grimsholm island. A mere Major, his authority is not accepted by the Catalan troops actually holding the fort (SM 6).

2: a clerk, originally from the French possessions in India, now working for Duplessis's mission to Pulo Prabang. He becomes one of Maturin's intelligence sources (TGS 7) but is murdered as the French plans collapse (TGS 8).

3: the head of the Bourbon marine ministry (HD 4).

Lesueur, André

A French intelligence agent on the island of Malta who knows of Stephen Maturin's importance to British naval intelligence (TH 1+). He is perhaps a member of Thévenot's organisation (TH 3) and his principal contact is the English traitor, Andrew Wray (TH 2+). Lesueur enlists Laura Fielding to spy on Stephen but the Doctor manages to turn this trick against the Frenchman, feeding him false information (TH 3+). Later warned by Wray that his network had been compromised, he had managed to escape from the island even though many of his minions were soon captured and executed (FSW 1; RM 5).

Lethargy

The name by which Maturin addresses his captive Brazilian sloth (HMS 6).

Lettice

Jack Aubrey's great-aunt, of whom the rather ineffectual Mr Stanhope puts him in mind (HMS 6).

Lettsome, Dr

A doctor who examines Mrs Williams (DI 1).
John Coakley Lettsom (1744–1815) was an English Quaker physician, born in the West Indies. From 1769 onwards he built a very large practice in London, being elected as a Fellow of the Royal Society in 1771. He achieved some considerable note as a naturalist, travel writer and biographer as well as publishing several well-regarded medical texts.

Lever, Mr

A neighbour of Aubrey and Maturin in Sussex (PC 1).

Leveson-Gower

see **Gower, Leveson**

Leviathan

A fishing vessel, under Master William, met at sea by *Diligence* (SM 3).

Leviathan, HMS

A ship mentioned several times in passing (IM 8; FSW 1; YA 5; HD 8).
*HMS Leviathan, 74-gun, was launched in 1790. Known as a particularly fine sailer, she took part in a number of great fleet actions, notably under Lord Hugh Seymour (d.1801 in the rank of Vice Admiral) at *Howe's Glorious First of June (1794) and under Captain Henry Bayntun (1766–1840; a full Admiral of 1837) at *Nelson's Trafalgar (1805). Leviathan— her name is that of a sea-monster, or whale, often referred to in the Bible (see e.g., HMS 6)— was reduced to a convict ship in 1816 and a gunnery target ship in 1848, before being sold in 1848.*

Lewin

A naturalist referred to by Martin (NC 10).
John Lewin (1770–1819) was a noted English painter of natural history subjects whose best-known works are the illustrated Birds of New Holland (1808–1822) and the Prodromus Entomology of the lepidoptera of New South Wales (1805). His brother, William (d. 1795), wrote two quite successful, if subsequently poorly regarded, natural history works, The Birds of Great Britain (1789–1795) and The Insects of Great Britain (1793).

Lewis

1: a cook in HMS *Sophie* (M&C 11) who later works for Jack Aubrey ashore (PC 1).

2: Mr and Mrs Lewis, Stephen Maturin's senior assistant surgeon in HMS *Worcester* and his wife (IM 3–7).

3: the Captain of HMS *Gloucester*, to whom Admiral Ives addresses an angry letter of rebuke (FSW 1).

4: an Admiralty official who has replaced the deceased Mr Smith and whom Maturin assaults for his off-hand rudeness (RM 5).

Lewis, M.

A seaman in HMS *Leopard* (DI 9).

Lewis XIV

Captain Yorke quotes the King's famously imperious remark, '*J'ai failli attendre*' (FW 2).
King Louis XIV (1638–1715) ruled France from 1643 onwards, becoming known as 'Louis the Great' for his expansion and consolidation of French power and prosperity. He also became known as the 'Sun King,' for the magnificence of his court at Versailles and for his positioning of the monarch as the absolute fount of all power and authority in the land, a view summed up in his famous pronouncement, L'Etat, c'est moi! ('I am the State'). However, it is often argued that his absolutism, coupled with military and diplomatic reverses in the last years of his reign, sowed the earliest seeds of the revolution that was to erupt some 75 years after his death. The remark quoted by Yorke means 'I nearly had to wait.'

Lexell

A comet studied by Goodridge (PC 10).
Anders Johann Lexell (sic; 1740–1784) was a Swedish/ Finnish mathematician, from 1769 Professor of Astronomy in St Petersburg, Russia. The celestial object named for

him was first discovered by Messier in 1770 but its orbit was analysed and confirmed as that of a comet by Lexell himself in 1776.

Liberty

A Boston privateer, Master Mr Henry, that, under Johnson's orders and in company with a sister-ship, pursues the mail packet *Diligence* across the North Atlantic in order to capture Jack Aubrey, Stephen Maturin and Diana Villiers. During the chase she runs onto an ice flow, sinking as she is being abandoned (SM 3).

Liebig, Dr von

An Austrian doctor whom Maturin had known in Spain (YA 2).

Ligier, Colonel

An artillery Colonel and former Commander of the Grimsholm garrison, now due to return there with General Mercier. He is killed by cannon fire from Jack Aubrey's HMS *Ariel* as he tries to escape from the captured *Minnie* (SM 7,9).

Lille, Compte de
see **Louis XVIII, King**

Lily

An author referred to by Mr Standish (TGS 3).
William Lily (or Lilly, Lyly; 1468?–1522) was a leading English scholar of Latin and Greek who became the first headmaster of the famous St Paul's School in London. Lily's Grammar was long the basis of schoolboy education in the Latin language.

Lima, Bishop of

A prelate referred to in a letter to Maturin as a possible source of support for an anti-Spanish uprising in Peru (NC 9).

Lind, Dr

A famous naval doctor referred to by Stephen Maturin and his various medical colleagues (M&C 2; DI 4; WDS 4; COM 9).
*The Scotsman James Lind (1716–1794) is regarded as the 'Father of Nautical Medicine,' having himself served as a naval surgeon under Admiral *Haddock in the 1730s and 40s. He became a physician in 1748, first published his Treatise on Scurvy in 1754 and issued its most important, expanded edition in 1772. Lind also published standard texts on seamen's general health from 1757 onwards and on tropical medicine from 1768 onwards. Although Sir Gilbert *Blane who later popularised fresh fruit and vegetables as anti-scorbutics, it was Lind who first clearly demonstrated their efficacy, himself building on largely forgotten work from the late 16th century. Sadly, the stigma of having been a 'mere naval surgeon' meant that, in his own lifetime, Lind was neither well regarded nor well rewarded for his work, yet, without his methods of preventing scurvy, the long and successful blockades of the French fleets by the Royal Navy during the wars following his death could scarcely have*

*been possible. Curiously, there was another contemporary James Lind (1736–1812) of some note, this gentleman being an ex–East Indies surgeon who later became a naturalist, Royal physician and explorer-colleague of Sir Joseph *Banks: it is this Lind who is briefly noticed in O'Brian's* Sir Joseph Banks: a Life.

Liberator, the

A reference to Jean Dutourd by one of his crew (C/T 9).

Lin Liang

A banker and merchant in Pulo Prabang associated with Shao Yen (TGS 6,7).

Linnaeus

The great naturalist, often referred to as the leading authority in his field (M&C 2; FW 2; SM 3; RM 3; LM 9; TGS 5; NC 5; WDS 9; COM 9).
Carl von Linné (in Latin, Linnaeus; 1707–1778) was the great Swedish polymath and leading classifier of species whose system and nomenclature is used to this day. A man of quite astonishing energy, ambition and capacity for work, his influence in his own lifetime on the development of his chosen fields — botany and natural history — has scarcely been equalled in the history of any science. After an early career of outstanding accomplishment in these disciplines, he then reverted to his first training as a medical doctor and, in 1739, became Physician to the Swedish Admiralty. In 1741 he accepted the Chair of Medicine at Uppsala but in 1742 exchanged this for the Chair of Botany, spending the rest of his life as a brilliant teacher, scholar and writer. His three most important works regarding the classification system are the Systema Natura *of 1735, the* Genera Plantarum *of 1737, and the* Species Plantarum *of 1753.*

Linois

The French Rear Admiral whose squadron takes Jack Aubrey's little HMS *Sophie* and who then inflicts the initial defeat on Saumarez' fleet before being himself beaten (M&C 11+; PC 4). Shortly afterwards, he is command of a small French squadron harassing trade in the Indian Ocean (HMS 6–8) where Jack, using his HMS *Surprise* and some of Muffit's merchant fleet, fights a running action with the Frenchman's poorly supplied ships over several days, eventually beating him off (HMS 9–11; also TMC 2; IM 6; TGS 6; FSW 4).
*Charles Alexandre Léon, Compte Durand de Linois (1761–1848), had the unusual distinction of being taken prisoner at least four times by the Royal Navy during his career. As acting Captain of l'*Atalante, he was first captured in May 1794. On his release early the following year, he was immediately promoted full Captain into the 74-gun *Formidable but, in June of that same year, both he and his ship were again taken by the Royal Navy, Linois himself losing an eye in the encounter. After about two months in captivity in England, Linois was exchanged and, once back in Paris, then had his promotion to Captain back-dated to January 1794; he was also promptly appointed Commodore into* Nestor, *74-gun, taking up this position in late May 1796. At this point*

there is a curious discrepancy between British and French sources: both *James and CLOWES state that in mid–April of 1796 Linois was in command of the 36-gun Unité (see *Surprise, HMS) when she was taken by Francis Cole's HMS Révolutionnaire, yet no French biographical note on Linois makes any mention of this incident. French sources maintain that the Captain of Unité was in fact one M. Durand, and perhaps this is how a confusion arose. Certainly, Linois and Nestor took part in Hoche's abortive invasion of Ireland at the end of 1796, returning safely to France in the early months of the following year. A Rear Admiral of April 1799, Linois hoisted his flag in Formidable (the new replacement for his former command) whilst defeating *Saumarez' squadron off Algeçiras in 1801; during the second phase of that battle, he adopted the Spanish practice of shifting his flag to a frigate, Sabina, from which he then witnessed his squadron's heavy defeat.

From 1804 onwards Linois enjoyed some limited success at disrupting British trade in the Indian Ocean in his flagship *Marengo (see *Earl Camden for a note on the origins of his brush with Jack *Aubrey). However, in 1806 he was defeated, wounded and captured by a British squadron off North Africa just as he was returning to France and then held in England until 1814. Freed following *Buonaparte's abdication in that year, Linois was now appointed Royal Governor of French Guadeloupe. During the '100 Days' of Buonaparte's restoration in 1815, he refused to surrender his new command to the British fleet sent to take possession of the island and was defeated and taken prisoner to England once again. On Buonaparte's final defeat at Waterloo, Linois was released and, in 1816, went into an honourable retirement.

Lion

A dull-sailing French ship in Emeriau's fleet (IM 8).

Although Lion was a frequent name for French warships, none served in the Napoleonic wars after 1809, some years before IM is set.

Lion, HMS

The ship in which the seaman-boxer Jack Thorold had served (YA 3), later found dismasted by Jack Aubrey's HMS Surprise and Ringle (HD 8).

HMS Lion, 64-gun, was launched in 1777. From about 1798 until 1800 she sailed under Captain Manley *Dixon in the Mediterranean command and, despite her increasing age and old-fashioned rating, she saw much active service throughout her later career, being as late as 1811 part of the fleet that took Java. Lion was reduced to a sheer-hulk in 1816 and finally sold for break-up in 1837.

Li Po

1: a Chinese poet translated by Michael Herapath (FW 5).

Li Po (701–762) was, with his younger contemporary Tu Fu, one of the two leading poets of his age, noted for his romanticism and celebration of the joys of drinking. According to Chinese legend, Li Po was drowned when, drunk in a boat, he leaned out too far to grasp the reflection of the moon glinting on the water's surface.

2: the father of Mai-mai and the owner of the Chinese junk that visits the HMS Diane shipwreck island (NC 2,3).

Lisbon, Patriarch of

The Portuguese prelate who assists Stephen Maturin in enabling Sam Panda to enter the Roman Catholic priesthood (TGS 1,3).

Litchfield, HMS

A ship mentioned in a ballad sung and improvised on by Aubrey and Maturin (PC 6).

HMS Lichfield (sic), 50-gun, was launched in 1746 and wrecked off the Moroccan coast in late 1758 with heavy loss of life. The few survivors were held for ransom by the Sultan for some considerable time.

Littlejohn

1: a seaman in HMS Leopard suffering from a hernia (DI 6).

2: a Midshipman in HMS Shannon whose father, the one-time Captain of HMS Berwick, had served with Jack Aubrey in HMS Euterpe (FW 9).

Adam Littlejohn (d.1795) was made Post in early 1795 and appointed to the temporarily-disabled 74-gun HMS *Berwick, whose former Captain William Smith had just been dismissed the service—together with his First Lieutenant and the ship's Master—for incompetence during a refit. Whilst proceeding jury-rigged and alone, as per Admiral Hotham's orders, from Corsica to Italy, she was taken by a French squadron of frigates, with Littlejohn being the only man killed in the brief action. His son, Midshipman David Littlejohn, served under *Broke in HMS *Shannon but nothing is known of his subsequent career.

Lively, HMS

A frigate whose Captain William Hamond, an MP, wishes to attend Parliament. Lord Melville consequently gives her to Jack Aubrey as a temporary, first appointment as Post-Command (PC 12+). Under Jack, she helps take Admiral Bustamente's Spanish treasure ships, including Clara and Fama (PC 14). The action, however, takes place before war is formally declared and consequently the Spanish ships are not legitimate prizes but rather droits of the Crown, a fact that much reduces the various financial rewards available for their capture (HMS 1). Jack remains in command of Lively for a little while longer on the blockade of Toulon, awaiting Hamond's imminent return (HMS 1,2; also HMS 6,8; TMC 2; DI 1; IM 4; NC 5; YA 9).

HMS Lively, 38-gun, was launched in 1804 and commissioned by Captain Graham Eden *Hamond. One of her very first actions was the capture of *Bustamente's ships in October of that same year. In August 1810, whilst under the command of Captain George Mckinley (d.1852 as an Admiral of the Blue), she was wrecked on rocks off the coast of Malta.

Liverpool, Lord

A politician referred to by Maturin and Blaine (RM 7,9).

Robert Banks Jenkinson (1770–1828), a leading English politician, was known as Lord Hawkesbury from 1796 and as the 2nd Earl of Liverpool from 1808. As a young man on his Continental tour, he had been an eye-witness in Paris of the fall of the Bastille in 1789. He went on to become a central figure in the Tory political establishment, holding high government office continually from 1793 to 1827 (with the exception of a few months in 1806), being Foreign Secretary (1801–1804), Home Secretary (1804–1806 and 1806–1809), Secretary of War (1809–1812) and finally, following the assassination of Spencer *Perceval, Prime Minister (1812–1827).

Livy

The Latin author referred to by Maturin (TMC 10).

Titus Livius (59 BC–17 AD), a Latin historian, was a protégé of the Emperor Augustus and the leading celebrator of Rome's greatness, past and present. His Ab Urbe Condita Libri *('Books from the Foundation of the City,' often simply known as his* Annals*) tells the story of his city-state from the very earliest times down to 9 BC; it was produced in 142 volumes, of which 35 have survived. Livy's claim to greatness lies less in his analytical power or depth of research — neither of which is really evident in the work — but in his eloquence of expression and his descriptive abilities as applied to both events and personalities.*

Liza, Miss

A dinner guest at Ashgrove Cottage, probably a member of the Fanshaw family (COM 3).

Llers, Dr

A Catalan specialist in the mental development of children (COM 3,5) consulted by Stephen Maturin in the case of his own daughter, Brigid (YA 1).

Lloyd

1: a scientific and medical acquaintance of Maturin (PC 3).

The name may perhaps be inspired by that of Bartholomew Lloyd (1772–1837), who would have been a contemporary of Stephen Maturin at Trinity College, Dublin, in the late 1780s. Lloyd was an Irish scientist and mathematician of very wide learning who held Chairs in Greek, in Natural and Experimental Philosophy and in Divinity before coming Provost of Trinity in 1831. However, he did not become a Doctor (and of Divinity, not Medicine) until 1808, well after PC is set.

2: an officer in HMS *Raisonable* (TMC 4).

Lloyd, Professor Christopher

A biographer of Lord Cochrane referred to by O'Brian (RM author's note).

Charles Christopher Lloyd (1906–1986) was a prolific author and scholar of the 'Age of Sail' and, from 1945 to 1966, a leading member of the History Faculty at the Royal Naval College, Greenwich. The work mentioned is Lord *Cochrane: Seaman, Radical, Liberator; a Life of Thomas, Lord Cochrane, 10th Earl of Dundonald, *published in 1947. Amongst his many other works, of particular interest to admirers of Stephen *Maturin would be Volume III of* Medicine in the Royal Navy, 1200–1900 *(with J.L.S. Coulter; 1961).*

Lloyd, Evan

A cook's mate in the tender *Ringle*, injured in an accident (YA 4).

Lloyd's

The London insurance market whose members had given Jack Aubrey a Presentation Sword in recognition of his services in preserving merchant ships and their cargo (RM 2).

The institution is named for Edward Lloyd (fl.1688–1726) who originally kept a coffee house in Tower Street, London. In 1692 he moved his shop to Lombard Street, where it soon became a centre for the transaction of insurance business, especially that of marine coverage. The institution has a continuous history of insurance provision to the present day. From 1803 onwards, Lloyd's ran a 'Patriotic Fund' that not only rewarded heroic deeds, with swords, medals, plate etc., but also supported various Naval charities.

Llull, Ramón

A Catalan man of letters (COM 5).

Ramón Llull (a.k.a. Raymond Lully; 1233–1316), a mystic, poet and intellectual, was reared in the style of a troubadour at the royal court on the Catalan island of Majorca. In about 1263, after early success as an elegant entertainer, Llull took up life as a missionary, attempting to convert Muslims in Spain and North Africa to Christianity and often using complex and subtle arguments closely based on Arabic and Greek philosophy to make his case. According to legend, he was stoned for his faith in Tunis and died of his injuries at sea whilst trying to return to Majorca. His mystical and philosophical works — mostly in Latin — are still closely studied in the Roman Catholic faith, whilst his earlier Catalan poems and romances play an important role in that language's literary traditions.

Locatelli

It is during a performance of a Locatelli work in Port Mahon, Minorca, that Jack Aubrey and Stephen Maturin first meet (M&C 1); many years later, they again encounter his music (HD 3,4).

Pietro Antonio Locatelli (1695–1764) was an Italian violinist and composer, famous as a great virtuoso and technical innovator. Although many of his works for both solo violin and string quartet survive, the 'great C major quartet' of the opening of the Aubrey-Maturin series is not among them, appearing to be a happy invention by O'Brian (as it the trio of HD 3).

Locker

The author of a medical text unavailable to Maturin and Martin (WDS 4).

The name may perhaps be borrowed from that of Edward Hawke Locker (1777–1849) who became Secretary to

Greenwich Naval Hospital in 1819 and its Civil Commissioner in 1824. The son of a distinguished Royal Navy Captain (William Locker, d.1800), Locker took up a career as a naval administrator, serving as civil secretary to Admiral Sir Edward *Pellew from 1804 to 1814. He was also an author and naturalist of some note, being elected a Fellow of the Royal Society for this work.

Lock's

A hat-maker (RM 4; C/T 4).

Established in London in 1676, James Lock & Co. today still operates from premises in St James's Street.

Loder

A civil servant from Java attached, with his colleagues Crabbe and Johnstone, to Mr Fox's Pulo Prabang mission. From their loud pomposity the three become known to HMS *Diane*'s crew as the 'Old Buggers,' although Loder himself is regarded as the least disagreeable of the three (TGS 6+). Jack Aubrey later facetiously refers to him by one of the Sultan of Pulo Prabang's titles, probably that of 'Nutmeg of Consolation' (TGS 9). A good amateur sailor (TGS 9,10), he accompanies Fox and his party in the small boat by which they hope to return to Java after *Diane*'s wrecking. However, they are all believed lost in the typhoon that then sweeps the area (TGS 10).

Lodge, Mr

A Bostonian friend of Louisa Wogan in London (DI 6).

Lomax

A Midshipman in HMS *Néréide* who had lost his arm at the battle of Port South East (TMC 10).

Lombard

An officer mentioned by Jack Aubrey as a possible replacement for the very ill Admiral Sir John Thornton (IM 4).

Long, Edward

The Captain of the recently sunk HMS *Aeolus* (TH 1).

Long Tom Turk

A cannon in HMS *Surprise* (TH 10).

Lopez

The owner of a ship-yard in Brazil, a friend of Mr Allen (FSW 4,5).

Lord, the

see God

Lord Clive

An East Indiaman in which Pullings had once sailed (HMS 8) and which later calls at Madeira (HMS 11).

Although Pullings may simply be referring to a 'country

ship' (i.e. a private merchantman) rather than an HEIC vessel, the only 'official' Clive was a 500-tonner that completed four round trips for the Company from 1761 to 1770. She was named for Baron *Clive.

Lord High Admiral

A title used in Jack Aubrey's letter of appointment to HMS *Diane* (TGS 4).

The office of Lord High Admiral was created in 1391. In 1628 its then holder, the Duke of Buckingham, was assassinated and the office then devolved to a committee known, in full, as the 'Lords Commissioners for Executing the Office of Lord High Admiral,' gradually shortened in everyday usage to 'the Board of Admiralty' or even just 'the Admiralty.' The 'First Commissioner' soon became known as the '*First Lord.' Lord High Admirals were occasionally appointed — King *James II twice in his career and Prince William, Duke of *Clarence, once — but mostly the Board continued to exercise its jurisdiction in the name of the Crown. When, in 1964, the Board was itself abolished and replaced by a Ministry of Defence, the title — though not the power — of Lord High Admiral reverted to the Crown and is thus currently held by Queen Elizabeth II. In order to preserve a long tradition, those senior members of the Ministry of Defence — both civil service and military personnel — dealing with the Royal Navy are still known as the 'Admiralty Board.' The serving head of the Royal Navy is now known as the *First Sea Lord; his chief operational deputy, the Second Sea Lord, by tradition flies his flag in HMS *Victory at Portsmouth.

Lord Mayor

References are made to 'Lord Mayor's Men' (PC 7; FSW 4) and the Lord Mayor himself is a bye-word for sumptuous feasting (FSW 3,7).

Technically the 'Lord Mayor's Men' were fellows arrested in London for only minor offences — such as public inebriation — who could then be offered, by the Mayor's magistrates, service in the Navy as an alternative to the 'disgrace' of fines or imprisonment. Seamen themselves tended to use the term for any young landsmen who ended up in the Navy by means other than being pressed or volunteering. As to the feast reference, each year the incoming Lord Mayor of London — an office first established in 1192, but almost entirely ceremonial for most of its existence — holds a great parade and banquet.

Lord Mornington

An East Indiaman in which Pullings had once served (PC 7) and which later calls at Madeira just ahead of HMS *Surprise* (HMS 11).

The Earl of Mornington, 241-tons, completed just one round trip, in 1799, between India and England for the East India Company. She was named for Richard Colley Wellesley (1760–1842), 2nd Earl of Mornington (from 1781) and 1st Marquis Wellesley (from 1799). He was the elder brother of General Sir Arthur Wellesley, 1st Duke of *Wellington. The Earl was appointed Governor General of India in 1797 but, after achieving notable military and diplomatic successes, constant disputes with the directors of the East India Company led to his forced retirement in 1805. In 1809 he served briefly as ambassador to Spain before holding, until 1813, the office of Foreign Secretary. He *later served as Lord Lieutenant of his native Ireland from 1821 to 1828 and from 1833 to 1834.*

Lord Nelson

An East Indiaman, Captain Spottiswood, in which Jack Aubrey and Stephen Maturin sail homewards from Gibraltar following their escape from France, finding Tom Pullings to be serving in her. *En route* she is captured by the French privateer *Bellone,* despite putting up a spirited resistance (PC 5).

*Lord Nelson, 818-ton and 26-gun, made five round trips for the British East India Company between 1799 and 1807; she was of course named for the great hero, Horatio *Nelson. In August 1803, having been taken off Brest by the privateer *Bellone, she was immediately pursued first by the small English privateer, Thomas and John, and then by HMS *Seagull, an 18-gun brig under Commander Henry Burke (d.1804, drowned at sea). Seagull, although much damaged by Lord Nelson's heavier broadside, kept hounding her until, by good fortune, a powerful squadron led by Sir Edward *Pellew's HMS *Tonnant came into sight. Burke then had the honour of accepting Lord Nelson's surrender and seeing her restored to HEIC service.*

Lord of the Isles

A romantic Highland title referred to by Maturin. Mr Macdonald belongs to the family (PC 8).

The isles in question are the Hebrides and the title was held by the MacDonald Earls of Ross from the mid-14th to the late 15th century. In 1815 it became the title of a popular romance by the novelist Sir Walter Scott.

Lord Warden

An official with whom Jack Aubrey is invited to dine following the *Fanciulla* action (PC 12).

*The reference is to the Lord Warden of the Cinque Ports (Hastings, New Romney, Hythe, Dover and Sandwich) on the southeast coast of England. Ships from these five towns (of which today only Dover retains a significant harbour) formed the nucleus of the Royal Fleet until the 14th century. Their association dates from the reign of Edward the Confessor (King of England from 1042 to 1066) and, in 1278, they were granted liberties by Royal Charter. The Lord Warden, an honorific title, serves as Constable of Dover Castle and has Walmer Castle, Kent, as an official residence. The present Lord Warden is Her Majesty Queen Elizabeth, the Queen Mother, and famous past holders of the office have included the Duke of *Wellington.*

L'Orient
see **Orient**

Lorraine, Claude

The famous painter, referred to by Maturin (FW 2; WDS 1).

Claude Lorraine (properly Claude Gallée; 1600–1682) was the great French painter of the formalised landscape or harbour scene, almost always set near Rome, where he spent most of his artistic life. Claude — as he is often simply known — is one of the most distinguished masters at

painting the effects of sunlight, especially in combination with water. His chosen subjects also led him to be an important innovator in the development of perspective.

Louis

The Captain of Admiral Lord Keith's flagship (M&C 4).

*Sir Thomas Louis (1759–1807) was made Post in 1783 and commanded HMS *Minotaur from 1794 to 1802. In March 1800, Lord *Keith lost his flagship HMS *Queen Charlotte to fire and briefly shifted his flag to Louis' ship. Louis, promoted Rear Admiral in 1804, raised his flag in HMS *Canopus as one of *Nelson's subordinate commanders, his first *Flag Captain being Francis William Austen (1774–1865; see **Canopus, HMS** for a note on the naval and literary Austens). Louis and his ship were unlucky enough to miss Battle of Trafalgar of October 1805, having been sent into Gibraltar to re-supply. The Rear Admiral was made a baronet in 1806 but in May of the following year died of illness on board Canopus whilst cruising off Egypt.*

Louis XIV, King
see **Lewis XIV, King**

Louis XVI, King

The King of France, held in the Temple prison after the Revolution and then executed (SM 5,10).

*Louis XVI (1754–1793) ruled France from 1774 until his death by guillotine in 1793. By no means an unintelligent or uncaring man, Louis lacked confidence in himself and was consequently both indecisive and easily swayed by favourites, perhaps chief amongst them his strong-willed wife of 1770, Marie-Antoinette of Austria. From the very beginning of his reign France was wracked by successive financial crises, opposition to all attempts at reform being led by entrenched aristocratic interests who, with the Queen's help, usually soon won the vacillating King to their side. The strength of this opposition to a fresh reform proposal of 1787 led Louis in 1789 to summon, for the first time in 200 years, the States-General, composed of clergy, aristocrats and commoners. At this convention were unleashed all the frustrations, hatreds and ambitions — noble and depraved — of the various classes and all power to control events rapidly slid away from the King and his court, with violent revolution breaking out in July of the same year. Louis and his family effectively became hostages of the competing power-brokers and, fearing for their own safety, attempted in 1791 to escape to the Austrian Netherlands. This act, seen as a betrayal of France by almost all parties, especially as the country was on the verge of war with Austria, effectively sealed Louis' fate, even though he continued as nominal ruler, paraded as a dismal figurehead, for a little while yet. By the second half of 1792 the extremist *Jacobins were in the ascendant — at least in Paris — and the royal family were consigned to the gloomy Temple prison. In September of that year the King was put on trial for 'counter-revolution' and condemned to death (by 387 votes to 334, the minority being for banishment or confinement). Conducting himself with great dignity, Louis was led to the guillotine on January 21st 1793. In August of that year Marie Antoinette — enormously hated for her arrogance and intransigence — was moved from the Temple to the* even more awful Concièrgerie. On October 12th she was given a brief and humiliating trial (with a nasty concentration on her supposed sexual depravity, including accusations of incest with her young son, Louis-Charles), condemned and taken in an open tumbril to 'shake the hot hand' (as the leading Jacobin newspaper of the time put it). The fate of the son himself, Louis XVII as he was styled by royalists and some foreign governments, was perhaps worse. Never a robust child from his birth in 1785, young Louis was often ill whilst confined with his mother in the Temple and politically dangerous rumours slowly began to spread of her tender, motherly care and concern for him. This would not do, and a decision was soon taken to make the young boy a ward of the Republic, thus separating him from what had routinely been portrayed as Marie-Antoinette's 'malign influence.' Yet the manifestation of this policy was simply to have the boy tossed, alone, into a squalid cell immediately below hers — for days on end, she could hear his sobbing — where he remained until his death, probably by simple neglect, sometime before June 1795.

Louis XVIII, King, or the Compte de Lille

The current *de jure* King of France, living in exile in England (SM 5,11; RM 10) where Diana Villiers had once been presented to him (SM 5). On Buonaparte's first abdication in 1814, he assumes his throne in Paris but is forced to flee in the following year during the Emperor's 'hundred day' restoration (HD 1,3,4,5).

Louis-Stanislas-Xavier, Compte de Provence (1755–1824; 'Compte de Lille' was not one of his titles) was de jure *King Louis XVIII of France from 1795, and* de facto *King from the *Bourbon restorations of 1814 and 1815. He was a younger brother of the executed *Louis XVI and thus the uncle of the short-lived Louis XVII (see preceding entry). From 1789 to 1791 he was a public supporter of the reformist aspects of the Revolution — possibly in the hope of being asked to assume the crown in place of his brother — but fled the country as turmoil increased. Having declared himself King in June 1795, he then established a small court in various parts of Prussia and northern Italy but, by 1807, *Buonaparte's advances led him to seek refuge in England, where he remained at Hartwell (north of London) until the end of the war in 1814. On his taking possession of the throne — with a brief interruption for Buonaparte's '100 day' return in early 1815 — he found it impossible to reconcile the desires of the populace for genuine reform with either the desires of the — often very grasping — ex-emigrés for triumphalist revenge or the desires of the other European powers to exploit France's defeat and weakness. Louis died a sick, frustrated and unhappy man and was succeeded by his own younger brother, Charles X.*

Louisa
see **Wogan, Louisa**

Lou-mêng
A young Chinese girl, a friend and colleague of Mai-mai (NC 2,3).

Lovage, Harry
A friend of Jack Aubrey, popularly known as 'Old Lechery' (YA 3).

Lovelace
A character in Richardson's novel *Clarissa* (DI 5). see **Harlowe, Clarissa**

Loveless, Charles
The ailing Captain of HMS *Boadicea*, originally appointed to lead the Mauritius expedition. Deeming him unsuitable for the task, Stephen Maturin, by chicanery part political and part medical, arranges for his replacement by Jack Aubrey (TMC 1,2).

Lovisa
Jagiello's fiancée (LM 9).

Low, William
The lob-lolly boy in HMS *Diane* (TGS 5).

Low Bum
A Chinese seaman in HMS *Lively*, at one time almost certainly a pirate (HMS 2; PC 12).

Lowe, Captain
A wealthy landowner in New South Wales with whom Stephen Maturin quarrels after the two have traded insults about each other's friends, John Macarthur and Sir Joseph Banks. In an impromptu sword-fight, Lowe is rapidly wounded and compelled to apologise to Stephen (NC 8+).

Lowestoffe, Captain Lord
The Royal Navy officer originally intended for the Mubara expedition. Being somewhat ill, he is replaced by Jack Aubrey (TH 2,4).

Lowndes
1: the mad cousin of Diana Villiers and the Williams family, a.k.a. 'The Teapot' (PC 2,8,10,13; SM 5).
2: a Foreign Office official in London (RM 10).

Lowry
A ship's boy in HMS *Diane* (TGS 9).

Lowthers, the
A very rich family from the North of England, one of whom is a Lord of the Admiralty (DI 1).

The Lowther family were Viscounts and Earls of Lonsdale, vastly rich. The Earldom was created in 1784 for James Lowther (1736–1802), a widely detested landowner and devious politician, known in the north country simply as the 'Bad Earl.' The title went into abeyance on his death but was later revived for a distant branch of the family. William Lowther (1787–1872), an altogether more reputable statesman, served as an Admiralty Lord from 1809 to 1813 and be-

came 2nd Earl (of the second creation) on his father's death in 1844.

Loyola

The founder of the Jesuit religious order (M&C 6,10).

Inigo Lopez de Recalde (1491–1556), called St Ignacio de Loyola, was a Spanish religious reformer and the founder of the Jesuit order. After an early life as a wealthy soldier and diplomat, Loyola was severely wounded in 1521 at the siege of Pamplona. During and after his recovery, he turned to an ascetic life as a beggar, pilgrim, student and, eventually, priest. From 1534 onwards, he established an arduous religious community with like-minded colleagues and, in 1540, Pope Paul III approved the 'Society of Jesus,' with Loyola as its head or 'General.' The Jesuits are renowned for both their assertive missionary activity (especially, during Loyola's own lifetime, in Brazil, India and Central Africa) and their dedication to scholarship and teaching. Loyola was canonized by the Roman Catholic church in 1662.

Lucan

A French intelligence official (RM 10).

Lucas, Jean Jacques

The Captain, known personally to Jack Aubrey, of the French *Redoubtable* at Trafalgar (IM 6), whose brother later commands *Diane* (LM 4).

*Jean-Jacques-Etienne Lucas (1764–1819), Captain from 1803 of the 74-gun *Redoubtable, is commonly thought to have been the best fighting man amongst the French and Spanish commanders at Trafalgar in 1805, being awarded membership of the Legion d'Honor for his conduct on that day. Efficient, brave, fiery (and of tiny stature), he was known for his preference for musket-work and boarding over longer range exchanges of cannon-fire and it was one of his well-trained sharpshooters who downed Lord *Nelson in HMS *Victory. Although Redoubtable was taken in the great battle, on his release Lucas continued to serve his country until his retirement in 1816 (although, on the *Bourbon restoration of 1814, his recently gazetted Rear Admiral's rank was denied him). His acquaintance with Jack *Aubrey probably stems from his time in the Mediterranean in 1800–1801, when he served on *Linois' Formidable as a staff officer to the Admiral, being made acting Captain of *Indomptable after *Moncousu's fall in action. I have not found mention in the standard biographies of a brother of Lucas being in the naval service.*

Lucas, Joe

A seaman in Captain Corbett's harsh HMS *Néréide* who, according to Bonden, repeatedly tried to desert (TMC 3).

Lucatellus

'Lucatellus' Balm,' a medical treatment referred to by Maturin (PC 14; TMC 4; DI 3; IM 3).

Lucifer

see **Devil, the**

Lucock, George

A foretopman in HMS *Sophie*, Barrett Bonden's cousin, who is rated Midshipman by Jack Aubrey, following Bonden's refusal of such promotion for himself (M&C 8+). Later, ship-less, he had been pressed into HMS *York* and lost, with all other hands, when she foundered in the North Sea (PC 7).

Lucretius

An author referred to by Maturin (IM 5).

Titus Lucretius Carus (94?–51? BC) was a great Latin poet, of whose life almost nothing is now known. His claim to enduring fame lies in his De Rerum Natura ('On the Nature of Things'), a six-book work of philosophical enquiry — in stylish verse — into the rational scepticism of Epicurus, whose teaching he followed.

Lucullus

A reference to splendid dining (HMS 7; IM 1; LM 5)

Lucius Lucinus Lucullus (110?–55? BC), a Roman senator and general, was devoted in his retirement years to entertaining and living in the most sumptuous imaginable manner.

Lucy

The niece of Mrs Broad of the Grapes Inn (DI 2; SM 6; LM 4,8; TGS 4; COM 2; YA 8).

Ludolphus

The name of two people who had studied the rabies infection (PC 14).

Luigi

A Maltese spy in the pay of Lesueur (TH 1,10).

Luisa, Sor

A Dominican nun, from a 'respectable' branch of the Torquemada family of Inquisitors, who had been a childhood guardian of Stephen Maturin in Spain (NC 1).

Lumley

1: Miss Lumley, a language pupil of Laura Fielding in Malta (TH 1).

2: a British infantry Colonel in northern Spain who offers Mr Standish a post as his secretary (TGS 4).

Lushington, Alexander

A Royal Marine Captain, known personally to Jack Aubrey, who has recently married Amanda Smith (SM 11).

Lushington

An East Indiaman in which Tom Pullings had twice served. Under Commodore Muffit, she heads the merchant fleet protected by HMS *Surprise* (HMS 9,10) and, in the battle with Linois's squadron, has *Surprise*'s Pullings, Collins, Haverhill and Polly-blank aboard her as she flies Royal Navy colours as a *ruse de guerre* (HMS 9). Johnstone and Diana Villiers later take passage in her from India to Madeira (HMS 11; also FSW 4; TGS 4).

> Lady Lushington, *594-ton, made four round trips for the British East India Company between 1808 and 1817. However, she was not part of the squadron, led by Commodore Dance's *Earl Camden, that saw off *Linois attack in 1804. The ship was named for Hester, wife of Sir Stephen Lushington (d.1807), Chairman of the East India Company from 1790 until his death.*

Lycum

A boy mentioned in the Latin poem quoted by Broke and Maturin (FW 8).

> *The character Lycus is found in *Horace's first book of Odes and some lines, crucial for an outsider's understanding of the overall sense, are skipped by the very Latinate pair. A very literal translation follows, with the additional lines enclosed in brackets: (It was Alcaeus, the stout patriot from Lesbos, who used to tune his lyre) / when he had just been in the fighting at war / or had anchored his storm-tossed ship at the water-lapped shore / (he sang of the Muses, of *Bacchus and fair *Venus / and of Cupid, still her page-boy) / and also to Lycus, with black eyes and black / hair adorned.*

Lydgate

The Chaplain of HMS *Lively*, a cousin of her regular Captain Hamond. Usually the Perpetual Curate of Wool, he is aboard purely for the sea-air and his health (PC 12).

Lygdamus

The father of Artemesia, Queen of Cos (SM 8).

> *Lygdamus is usually represented as either the son or nephew of Queen *Artemesia, whom he succeeded to power, then ruling from about 465–450 BC.*

Lynch

An Irish seaman in HMS *Sophie* (M&C 3).

Lyra, HMS

A ship met by HMS *Surprise* at Rio de Janeiro (HMS 6).

> *The first HMS* Lyra, *10-gun brig-sloop, was not launched until 1808, some few years after HMS is set; she was sold for break-up in 1818. She was named for one of the constellations in the northern sky.*

Lysander

A classical figure referred to by Marine Lieutenant Willoughby (COM 8).

> *Lysander (d.395 BC) was a great Spartan general and admiral who, after long service, destroyed the Athenian fleet at the Battle of Aegespotami in 405 BC, accepting the surrender of the rival city in the following year. After this resounding victory, he was worshipped as a god on the island of Samos (HORNBLOWER & SPAWFORTH suggest he was the first living Greek so honoured) and soon acquired considerable autocratic power in the areas he subdued. Initially the lover of Agesilaus, the younger son of the Spartan King Archidamus, the pair became rivals, after 396, for political and military leadership. On campaign against Thebes, Lysander was ambushed and killed by skirmishers.*

M

M., Lord
see **Melville, Lord**

McAber

The First Lieutenant of HMS *Thunderer* (COM 1).

McAdam, William

The often-drunken surgeon of Lord Clonfert's HMS *Otter*, formerly a distinguished mad-doctor in his native Belfast, whose reduced financial circumstances have compelled him to go to sea (TMC 3+). He consults with Stephen Maturin over Clonfert's violent stomach cramps, agreeing with the view that his Captain's problems lie rather more in the mind than in the body (TMC 4). On Clonfert's promotion, McAdam follows him to HMS *Néréide* (TMC 5) but, in the disastrous Battle of Port South East, succumbs to a drunken coma and is relieved by Stephen (TMC 7). McAdam then becomes a pris-

oner-of-war of the French on Mauritius, caring for the severely injured Clonfert and part-blaming Jack Aubrey for the latter's eventual suicide (TMC 10).

M'Alister

The Scottish assistant surgeon in HMS *Surprise* (HMS 5+) who acts as medical attendant for Stephen Maturin's duel with Canning (HMS 10).

MacAlpine

A Scottish clan referred to by Professor Graham (TH 3).

McAnon

The pseudonym by which Maturin refers to a French official in the power of British intelligence (COM 5).

Macarthur, Captain and Mrs

A sometime officer in the New South Wales 'Rum Corps,' who had been court-martialed in London for duelling with Colonel Paterson. Stephen Maturin had once met him at a Royal Society dinner (NC 8,9) and it is an offensive remark Stephen makes about Macarthur's character that is a cause of his impromptu duel with Captain Lowe (NC 8). Mrs Macarthur is later reported to have given an important party in New South Wales (C/T 1).

John Macarthur (1767–1834), a famous New South Wales soldier, farmer and entrepreneur, was the son of a Scot who, having in 1745 been a supporter of the *Young Pretender, had then spent several subsequent years in exile before settling in southern England. In 1790 the penniless young John arrived in New South Wales as a newly commissioned Lieutenant in the 102nd Foot—the 'Rum Corps'—and rapidly amassed a great fortune through ruthless entrepreneurial skills. Notoriously quarrelsome, he was recalled and tried in England between 1801 and 1805 for duelling with his superior officer, Lieutenant-Colonel *Paterson. Macarthur was eventually acquitted on the grounds that technically Paterson had issued the challenge, albeit under extreme provocation. Macarthur had been promoted Captain in 1795 but appears to have resigned his commission in 1804. In 1807–1808 he was one of the leaders of the rebellion against *Bligh's governorship and from 1809 to 1817 was then embroiled, in England once again, in legal disputes over these events. His snub by *Banks over the merino sheep issue—alluded to in NC 8—was a real incident but it was Macarthur, from his base at *Camden, who was in fact responsible for the eventual huge expansion of sheep-farming in New South Wales and he is usually today given great credit for his role in the economic transformation of the colony. In 1788, whilst still in England, he had married a Devonshire neighbour, Elizabeth Veale (1767–1850), who accompanied him to the colony and became a leading light in its social world.

Macaulay

1: a seaman in *Surprise* who hails from the Orkney islands (TGS 1; C/T 8).
2: an anti-slavery activist in Britain (COM 8).

Zachary Macaulay (1768?–1838) was a noted Scots-English philanthropist and colonial administrator who, after serving as an accountant on a plantation in Jamaica, became an ardent opponent of slavery. When the West African colony of Sierra Leone was founded by William *Wilberforce and others as a refuge for freed slaves, Macaulay was chosen as its governor, serving from 1784 to 1799. Once back in England, he then played a leading role in Wilberforce's campaign to abolish the trade. Zachary was the father of the great historian and essayist, Thomas, Lord Macaulay (1800–1859).

Macaulay, Alexander

The junior assistant surgeon in HMS *Bellona*, formerly a dresser at Guy's Hospital (COM 3,4,6,9; YA 5,8,9).

McBean

Maturin's very unsatisfactory London banker (TGS 2).

Macbeth

A seaman in HMS *Surprise* who imagines himself to have been addressed by Jack Aubrey, grasping for a Shakespearean quotation (FSW 2,4).

'Macbeth'

A play read aloud by Jack Aubrey to his daughters (COM 3).

Shakespeare's five-act tragedy Macbeth was first performed in 1605–1606 in London. The historical Macbeth—or Macbéda—ruled Scotland from 1040 (when he defeated King Duncan I in open battle) until his own death on the battlefield at the hands of Malcolm (thereafter King Malcolm II) in 1057.

Maccabe, Simon

The owner of a Buonapartist ship-yard in the Adriatic destroyed by fire (HD 5).

MacCarthy

The employer of the father of the FitzPatrick twins (HD 8).

McCarthy Mor

A Irish chivalric title referred to by Maturin for its romantic sound (PC 8).

Mor is Irish Gaelic for 'Chieftain' and 'McCarthy Mor' is the traditional title for the head of that clan, who were also sometime Lords of Desmond and, until 1596, Kings of Munster.

Macchiavel, Macchiavelli, Macciavel or Machiavelli

The Italian political author, usually referred to for his reputation for ruthless cunning (PC 10; FW 2,5; RM 5; LM 5; C/T 6).

Niccoló Machiavelli (1469–1527) was a Florentine statesman and political theorist who served from 1499 to 1513 as Chief Secretary to the city-state's foreign affairs council and from 1520 to 1526 as a diplomat and official historian of the city. Out of favour from 1513 to 1520 (and briefly imprisoned and tortured by the newly all-powerful Medici family), he used his enforced retirement to write treatises and histories. The best known of these is The Prince (1513) in which he argues that the acquisition and effective use of power for the promotion of the public good will usually necessitate methods highly undesirable in themselves. His name has consequently become a synonym for cunning and perfidy, although all he does in this work is lay bare—in trenchant, memorable terms—the mechanisms often used, but usually concealed, by effective governments through the ages.

McClure

An assistant surgeon in HMS *Java* (FW 3).

MacCoul, Finn

References are made to the fables of Finn MacCoul, including those of his salmon (LM 9) and his military prowess (C/T 8).

The legendary Irish hero Finn MacCool placed himself as a young man under the tutelage of wise old Fineglas, who lived on the banks of the River Boyne. Fineglas had spent his life fishing for the 'Salmon of Knowledge' (see *Ceasoir) but, although he eventually caught the fish, it was Finn who first tasted it and acquired its magic powers.

Finn, the father of *Ossian/Oisín, later went on to lead the elite band of warrior-poets, the Fianna Éireann *(referred to in C/T 8).*

Macdonald

A French General (SM 6).

Jacques-Etienne-Joseph-Alexandre Macdonald (1765–1840), the French-born son of a Scottish Jacobite exile (see *James II, King*), joined the army in 1784 and in 1786 transferred to *Dillon's regiment. Here, and elsewhere, he soon made a brilliant reputation as a staff officer and by 1793 had risen to Brigadier General, with a further promotion in the following year. Macdonald commanded in the field with considerable success between 1795 and 1801 and thereafter undertook important diplomatic missions. Although in 1804 he fell from *Buonaparte's favour and lost his command, in 1807 he was re-appointed to field service in the Italian and Austrian campaigns. In recognition of his decisive contribution to the great victory of 1809 at Wagram, Macdonald was appointed Maréchal on the field of battle itself, the only commander ever so honoured by the Emperor. Created Duke of Tarentum later that same year, he went on to brilliant service in Catalonia, Russia and Germany but began—with many other French generals—to suffer heavy reverses in 1813 and 1814. In that latter year, after the fall of Paris to the Allies, Macdonald was active in pressing Buonaparte to abdicate, becoming a supporter of the *Bourbon restorations of 1814 and 1815 and later holding important military and political positions under King *Louis XVIII.*

Macdonald, James

The Hebridean Marine Lieutenant in Jack Aubrey's HMS *Polychrest* (PC 7–10,14), who receives a severe arm injury in the action against *Bellone*, and then undergoes an amputation by Stephen Maturin (PC 9, 10). Years later, we learn from his cousin, Marine Captain Harris of Jack's HMS *Worcester*, that he had made a good recovery (IM 1).

Macduff, Sawney

A seaman in HMS *Surprise* who is thought to have been addressed by Jack Aubrey, attempting a Shakespearean quotation (FSW 2). He may be the same man who later falls ill on the private vessel *Surprise* (WDS 4,6).

The line from *Macbeth that Jack is grasping for is the King's final cry of 'Lay on, Macduff, and damn'd be him that first cries, "Hold, enough!"' Macduff, a supporter of Malcolm's cause, thereupon kills and beheads the usurper.

Macedonian, HMS

A 38-gun frigate taken by the 44-gun USS *United States* (FW 3+; FSW 3).

HMS Macedonian, *38-gun, was launched in 1810 and captured by USS *United States in October 1812. She was then taken into the U.S. Navy under her British name and served until being broken up in 1829. A few months into the war, Macedonian, Captain John Surman Carden (1771–1855; made Post 1806, Rear Admiral 1838, Vice Admiral (on retired list) 1848 and Admiral 1853), had met Stephen Decatur's United States to the west of the Canary Islands and willingly engaged her; indeed, the two Captains had once met and joked about the—then—ut-*

terly unlikely prospect of a hostile encounter between them. As was typical of the early encounters of the conflict, Macedonian—a crack frigate, though one with a reputation for harsh discipline—had a speed advantage but threw a broadside inferior to her foe in both weight and, crucially, accuracy. After a fierce, 60-minute action she was battered, bloodied and disabled by the almost untouched American and compelled to strike. Such was Carden's unpopularity with his crew that, although they fought their ship furiously, most managed to evade ever being returned to England or the Royal Navy, enlisting instead in the American merchant service or remaining as immigrants to their captors' land.

McElwee

The East India Company Red Sea pilot in Jack Aubrey's temporary command, *Niobe* (TH 6).

Macfarlane, Captain

An officer who had killed Mr James in a duel at Bombay (HMS 7).

Machaon and Podalirius

Famous surgeons referred to by Maturin (IM 2).

In Greek legend Machaon and Podalirius, sons of the great doctor Asclepius (see *Asclepia), were physicians and warriors who took a notable part in the siege of Troy. In some accounts of the war Machaon died in battle during the taking of the city, after perhaps being one of the soldiers concealed inside the great Wooden Horse, whilst Podalirius survived the war and settled in Italy.

Machiavelli

see **Macchiavel**

Macintosh, Captain

An officer whom Jack Aubrey recalls having captured the French *Sibylle*. Later, he had suffered a shipwreck and fallen foul of the Admiralty over missing ship's papers (NC 4).

McKay or Mackay

1: Mr McKay, the Master of HMS *Royal George* (HMS 10).

2: the author of 'Mackay on Longitude' (DI 3).

Andrew Mackay (1760–1809), a Scottish mathematician, was the long-time Keeper of Aberdeen Observatory. He published a number of works on navigational issues and problems, including The Theory and Practice of Finding the Longitude at Sea or on Land *(1793 and several subsequent editions) and* The Complete Navigator *(1804 onwards).*

McLean or Maclean

1: Mr McLean, the Scottish surgeon of HMS *La Flèche*, a keen naturalist who had studied at Jena. A heavy smoker, he is careless in the proximity of his pipe or cheroot to the alcohol he uses to preserve his specimens and, by implication, is responsible for the outbreak of fire that destroys his ship. It is not revealed whether he survives the disaster (FW 2).

2: Mr Maclean, the new Marine officer of Jack Aubrey's HMS *Surprise* (TH 10).

McLeod

1: Colonel McLeod, one of Colonel Keating's subordinate officers (TMC 6,7).

A Lieutenant-Colonel M'Leod (sic) is given in *James and CLOWES as active in the Mauritius campaign but I have been unable to find any further details of his life or career.

2: a Scottish seaman in *Surprise*, an expert rock-climber, who had been in HMS *Centaur* when her Captain Hood had taken the Diamond Rock. He now helps Jack Aubrey to accomplish a similar feat at Cranc/Fortnight Island (HD 10).

Macmillan

Stephen Maturin's assistant surgeon in HMS *Diane*, on the shipwreck island and in HMS *Nutmeg of Consolation* (TGS 5+; NC 1,4,5,7). He returns to Batavia in *Nutmeg* when Stephen rejoins *Surprise* (NC 8).

M'Mullen

The Lieutenant in command of the dispatch cutter HMS *Eclair*, the son of John M'Mullen, a former surgeon of HMS *Surprise* (C/T 2).

M'Mullen, John

The father of that Lieutenant M'Mullen who commands the cutter HMS *Eclair*. In 1799 he had been the surgeon of Edward Hamilton's HMS *Surprise* when she cut out *Hermione*, commanding a boat in the expedition (FSW 10; C/T 2).

John M'Mullen (dates unknown) led the first boat of the second division attacking *Hermione from HMS *Surprise. Especially singled out for praise in *Hamilton's victory dispatch, he was later presented with a commemorative sword by Surprise's officers for his role in the action. There is no record of a son later serving as an officer in the Royal Navy, although two Lieutenants M'Millan (sic) were active at the approximate time of C/T.

McPhee, Michael

The Master of the whaler *Cowslip* (C/T 5).

MacPherson, Colonel

Governor Macquarie's regimental second-in-command and his Deputy Governor of the colony of New South Wales. He had once served under General Aubrey (NC 8+).

Macpherson, William

The senior Marine Lieutenant in HMS *Leopard*, who later dies in the goal fever outbreak (DI 3,4,5,7).

M'Quaid

An East India Company Captain, previously known to Jack Aubrey from their Indian Ocean days, who dines aboard HMS *Surprise* in the Atlantic Ocean (FSW 4).

Macquarie, Governor and Mrs

1: the Governor of New South Wales (NC author's note, 8+; C/T 1,2) and his wife (NC 8+).

Lachlan Macquarie (1762–1824), a Scot, served the Crown as a junior officer in Canada and America before extended service — primarily administrative — in India. Back in Britain, he rose to Lieutenant-Colonel of his 73rd Foot Regiment in 1807 and in 1809 he was sent to New South Wales with that force to re-establish order after the deposition of Governor *Bligh. Having taken the title of Governor in January 1810, the first non–Royal Navy man to hold the post, he was promoted full Colonel later in that year and General in 1811. Although Macquarie is credited with doing much to remove the stigma of the penal origins of the colony and with making substantial improvements in its infrastructure, his relationships with the London government were often uneasy, resulting in his recall in 1821.

Elizabeth Henrietta Campbell (1778–1835) became the second wife of her distant cousin Lachlan Macquarie in 1807. In the colony of New South Wales she was a lively and effective consort to her Governor husband, taking a special interest in social welfare and agricultural improvements.

Macrea

The surname of two Scottish Highland Marine soldiers in HMS *Polychrest* (PC 8).

McWhirter

A Scottish clan referred to by Professor Graham (TH 3).

Mad Anthony

A cannon in HMS *Surprise* (RM 3).

'Mad Willy'

A lunatic aboard HMS *Sophie* (M&C 11).

Madison

The President of the USA (FW 4,5).

James Madison (1751–1836), a distinguished American lawyer and statesman, served as 4th President of the United States from 1809 to 1817, having served for the eight years immediately prior to his election as *Jefferson's Secretary of *State. It was during Madison's Presidency that war was declared on Britain, in mid–1812, as a consequence of the running dispute over disruption of American trade by the Royal Navy and the frequent 'arrests' of American ships on the high seas. This 'War of 1812' (which in fact lasted until early 1815) is occasionally known in the USA as 'Mr Madison's War,' in part because of the strong domestic opposition to its declaration on the part of those merchants who considered that active hostilities would be even more disruptive than occasional skirmishes.

Maelsechlinn

According to Maturin, an Irish ruler, the son of Erc (TGS 9).

Maelsechlinn II 'The Great' (949–1022; a.k.a. 'Malachy Mor') established himself by force of arms as Chieftain of the southern branch of the Ui Neill clan and soon became a rival of *Brian of the Tributes for dominance over the whole island. The two were also several times allies against the Danish settlers in their newly built stronghold of

Dublin. Maelsechlinn held the title of High King from 980 until 997 (when Brian wrested it from him) and again from 1014 (when Brian was killed by a Danish war-band) until his death. Neither he nor his predecessor, Maelsechlinn I (d.863), were sons of *Erc.

Magdalene

The subject of a painting on display at the Keith's Ball (PC 6,12).

Mary of Magdala (fl.1st century AD), a follower of *Jesus, was cured by him of 'seven demons' and then became a leading disciple and the first person to see the Lord after his resurrection. Her later reputation as a saved prostitute, although frequently the theme of the many artistic works inspired by her life, is not directly biblical in origin.

Magellan

The great Portuguese seaman and explorer, after whom a foul-weather jacket is named (FSW 5; WDS 10; YA 5).

Ferdinand Magellan (1480?–1521), a great and enterprising navigator, travelled extensively between Portugal, India and Africa between 1505 and 1515. In 1519 he set out, under Spanish patronage, to discover a westerly route to the riches of the East Indies and, although Magellan himself was killed in the Philippines in 1521, a sole surviving ship of his squadron eventually arrived back in Spain, completing the first recorded circumnavigation of the globe.

Maggie

1: a servant at Woolcombe House (YA 8).
2: *see* **Cheale, Maggie**

Magicienne, HMS

A ship under Admiral Bertie's command, yet not immediately available to Jack Aubrey's squadron (TMC 3–7). Under her Captain Lucius Curtis, she later joins Jack and retakes the valuable East Indiaman *Windham* from the French (TMC 5). However, during the disastrous Battle of Port South East she runs aground and, devastated by French fire, is set ablaze by her own crew to prevent her capture (TMC 7).

HMS Magicienne, *32-gun, was launched as a French ship of the same name in 1778 and was captured by the Royal Navy in 1781. She was burned by her crew, as described in the text, in late August 1810.*

Magliabechi

A man said by Maturin to have spoken one hundred languages and thought by Aubrey probably to have been Pope (NC 5).

Antonio Magliabechi (1633–1714), the great Italian bibliophile, lay scholar and linguist, was said by the Jesuit savant Jean Mabillon (1632–1707) to have been 'a walking museum, a living library' on account of his prodigious memory and immense learning.

Magnificent, HMS

A ship recently wrecked off Brest (YA 5,7).

HMS Magnificent, *74-gun, was launched in 1766 and in 1782 took part in *Rodney's victory at the Battle of the Saintes. After long, yet somewhat uneventful further service, she was wrecked off Brest in March 1804.*

Mahdi

The title of a legendary 'hidden Imam,' whom a Muslim sect now believe to be Buonaparte (HD 1).

mahdi is Arabic for the 'guided one,' a messianic figure who will supposedly deliver the world from evil. No mention of the Mahdi is found in the Koran and only a hint in the hadith ('attributed sayings') of *Mahomet; hence the status of the figure is a matter of considerable disagreement between the various Islamic traditions, with Mahdis tending to come forward at times of social or political turmoil. During *Buonaparte's invasion of Egypt, a supposed Mahdi did appear in Lower Egypt but attracted little support and credence.

Mahmud

The lion hunted and shot, together with his mate, by Omar Pasha and Stephen Maturin (HD 7).

Mahomet

The Prophet and founder of Islam (IM 4; RM 3; COM 10; HD 1). Jack Aubrey makes a wild attempt at the name of his wife (RM 3).

Mahomet (many variant Western spellings are seen; 570?–632) was the founder of the Moslem religion, Islam. After a career in his family trading business, at about the age of 40 Mahomet abandoned the traditional idolatry of his birthplace, Mecca, and became the prophet of a one, true god, *Allah. His evangelism—deeply influenced by a study of Judaism and Christianity—soon became highly unpopular in his home city and, in 622, he took flight to the neighbouring community of Medina (the Moslem calendar takes this year of the 'Hijrah' as its basis). From his new base he combined evangelism with aggressive war in order to spread the new faith, Islam (Arabic for the act of surrender to God's will), before dying of a fever whilst on campaign in Syria. The spiritual and social revelations that Mahomet received are preserved in the Q'uran or Koran, which he asserted had been dictated to him by Allah; many sections of the work are in the form of ecstatic poetry of the very highest order. Jack and General *Aubrey's entertaining attempt at the Prophet's wife's name confuses the bird 'ptarmigan' with the word 'termagant,' a term for a violently abusive woman. This in turn is derived from 'Tervagaunt,' a brawling female character featured in medieval Christian morality plays as a supposed object of Moslem worship. For the prophet Mahomet marriage was primarily a means of cementing economic or political alliances and he married Khadija (taking no other wife before her death, even though a member of a polygamous society), Aishah, Hafsah, Umm Habibah, and Maymunah.

Mahommed ibn Rashid

A Bedouin tribesman met by Jack Aubrey in northern Egypt (TH 5).

Mai-mai

The daughter of the merchant Li Po (NC 2,3).

'Maiden'

The mild-mannered Tom Pullings' nickname in the Ionian port of Kutali (IM 11).

Maimonides

A philosopher referred to by Maturin (M&C 10).

Moses ben Maimon or Maimonides (1135–1204), a Spanish Jew, became at an early age the outstanding intellectual figure in early medieval Judaism and was also soon widely revered in the Arabic world. His many works on religious philosophy, law and medicine remain influential to this day. Driven out of both Spain and western North Africa by extremist Islamic persecution, from 1165 onwards Maimonides lived mostly in the far more secular Egypt, making his living as chief physician to the Sultan Saladin and his heirs.

Maimonides, Moses

A glass seller in Malta (TH 2).

Mainwaring, Captain

The subject of a letter written to his sister, Mrs Paulett, by Lord St Vincent (PC 3).
see **Paulett, Mrs**

Maistral, Esprit-Tranquil

The Commodore of the French squadron engaged by Jack Aubrey off the Irish coast who, in 1796, had been a Captain in Hoche's Bantry Bay invasion fleet. His ship, engaged by HMS *Bellona*, strikes on rocks and surrenders (COM 10).

Esprit-Tranquille (sic) Maistral (1763–1815), the son of a naval surgeon, joined the French navy in 1775 and saw a very great deal of active service before being promoted Lieutenant at the age of 20. He was promoted Commander in 1792 and full Captain in the following year, soon becoming one of his country's leading naval officers. The commander of Fougueux *for *Hoche's abortive 1796 invasion of Ireland, he went on to to command* Neptune, *as a Commodore, at the Battle of Trafalgar in 1805. However, Maistral had then retired from service at sea in 1806 — well before COM is set — and had left the Navy itself, in the rank of Rear Admiral, in mid-1814. His younger brother, Désiré (1764–842), was also a distinguished naval Captain, although he appears never to have seen any service off Ireland that could be the source of *Aubrey's engagement.*

Maitland

1: the man whose sister Harry Lambert had married (FW 3).
2: a Midshipman in Jack Aubrey's HMS *Worcester* (IM 2) who follows his Captain into HMS *Surprise* and is promoted Master's Mate (IM 10; TH 2,4,9; FSW 2) and then acting Lieutenant (FSW 3–9; RM 2,3,6).

Majestic, HMS

A ship in which Philip Broke had served as a very young Midshipman (FW 9).

HMS Majestic, *74-gun, was launched in 1785 and played a part in two famous fleet victories, *Howe's at the Glorious First of June, 1794, and *Nelson's at the Nile in 1798, her then commander, George Blagden Westcott, being the only British Captain killed in the action. In 1813 she was reduced to a 58-gun and in this form — supposedly now a heavy, if unwieldy, 'frigate' — she played a role in the War of 1812 against the USA, being leader of the squadron that took Stephen Decatur's USS *President just before the end of the war in early 1815. Majestic was broken up in 1816 after running aground on a sand-bar. I have not found a record of *Broke ever having served in her.*

Majesty, His
see **George III, King**

Majesty, His Imperial
see **Buonaparte, Napoleon**

Majesty, His Most Catholic

The King of Spain, in whose army Stephen Maturin's father had served (FW 1).

*The reference may be to either Charles III of Spain (1716–1788), King from 1759 until his death, his son *Charles IV, or both.*

Maker, the

A reference to God (TMC 1).

Mallet

A member of the carpenter's crew in HMS *Lively* and previously a receiver of stolen property ashore (PC 14).

Malloch

The bosun of HMS *Polychrest*, formerly bosun's mate of the crack HMS *Ixion* (PC 7–11).

Malpighi

An author whose works are owned by Sir Joseph Blaine (SM 4).

Marcello Malpighi (1628–1694), a renowned Italian natural historian, physician and anatomist, held a series of medical professorships and, in 1691, became chief physician to the Pope. In addition to books on human anatomy (of the tongue, lungs and brain, the first studies of their kind to be informed by microscopy), he published a seminal work on the anatomy of plants, starting a whole new field of scientific endeavour.

Mama
See usually **Williams, Mrs**

Mammon

The personification of the corrupting influence of wealth (C/T 5).

Mammon is used in the New Testament as a term for material riches. By the Middle Ages the term had come to refer to a supposed evil deity who corrupted by means of money and possessions.

Manby

Admiral Saumarez' Captain of the Fleet in the Baltic, an old enemy of Jack Aubrey (SM 7).

Thomas Manby (d.1834) never served in the Baltic fleet and had retired from sea-service on health grounds in 1808, well before SM is set; he had been made Post in 1799 and was promoted Rear Admiral in 1825. Indeed, according to Captain Sir John Ross (1777–1856; the author of the memoir mentioned in SM author's note), the reduced size of Saumarez' fleet during 1812, his final year in command, meant that no *Captain of the Fleet was necessary. However, at various times during the Admiral's time in the north he had as one of his subordinate flag-officers Manley *Dixon, to some extent the model for Jack's enemy, *Harte. Furthermore, Dixon's *Flag Captain on his HMS Vigo was his own son, Manley Hall *Dixon, a man also greatly disliked by Jack. 'Manby' may therefore well be a hint at one of the two 'Manleys.'

Manche

A new French 40-gun frigate destined for service in the Indian Ocean (TMC 1+) where, in company with Vénus, she takes the merchantmen Windham, United Kingdom and Charlton (TMC 5). During the Battle of Port South East, her arrival at a crucial moment enables the French to secure victory (TMC 7).

> Manche, 40-gun, was launched in 1806 and captured by the Royal Navy on the fall of Mauritius in December 1810; her fate thereafter is unrecorded. La Manche is the French term for the English Channel.

Mandeville

An author who had written on the subject of the 'Earthly Paradise' (DI 10; FSW 2).

> Sir John de Mandeville (perhaps 1300?–1372) was the supposed Anglo-Norman author of a famous travel book, Voyages, written in French. However, the volume is in fact a compendium of fabulous tales from other authors and there is no certainty that a Mandeville actually existed or produced the work. On its face a guide to the Holy Land, Voyages contains diversions to China, India and other far-flung parts and, in its entertaining digressions into tales of marvels and riches, provided a model for the later travel tales and segments of both *Chaucer and *Shakespeare. The work remained highly popular, in many editions and versions, for several hundred years.

Mangan

A Catholic priest and United Irishman, discovered aboard the John B. Christopher, who threatens to denounce James Dillon if the latter arrests him (M&C 7+).

> A name perhaps jointly inspired by: a) Francis Magan (sic), a young barrister and United Irishman who, in 1798, first betrayed the Society to the conservative Irish newspaper editor and British intelligence agent, Francis Higgins, and next betrayed Lord Edward *Fitzgerald to Major *Sirr before fleeing to the USA; and b) Chaplain Edward Mangin (sic), who served aboard HMS *Gloucester, 74-gun, in 1812 and left a fascinating, illustrated journal of ship-life.

Mangold

One of Diana Villiers' coach-horses (YA 8).

Manichaean

A reference by Maturin to a heretical sect (TMC 8).

> Manichaeus (or Mani/Manes) (216–277?) was a Persian scholar and religious leader who, following a 'revelation by an angel' in about 240, started preaching a new dualist religion. His distinctive mixture of Christian and Magi doctrines was based on a belief that the world is enmeshed in a struggle between two eternal and equally balanced forces of spirit and matter that manifest themselves as light and darkness, good and evil. Having attracted many converts in Persia and India, he then fell out of favour with a new Persian king, Bahram I, and died in prison after a long trial for heresy and sedition. The prophet's own writings, containing some elements of autobiography, had a wide and long-lasting influence. Manichaean sects flourished in the old Roman Empire until the end of the 6th century and enjoyed a resurgence in Western Europe in the 7th, 10 and 12th centuries (they were usually eventually persecuted out of existence by the established Catholic church). The faith also spread eastwards into China, where it lasted until finally suppressed in the 14th century, and, in Persia itself, Manichaeism lasted until about the 10th century before being pushed northwards into obscurity and decline. A renewed interest in Manichaean mysticism came in the 20th century with the discovery, in Egypt and southern China, of fragments of long-lost scriptures, possibly attributable to Mani himself or to his earliest followers.

Mann

An HMS Surprise seaman ill in hospital in Valletta (TH 8).

Mannering

A Midshipman in HMS Bellona (YA 7).

Manners, Colonel

The soldier commanding the 43rd Regiment in Malta (TH 1).

Manton, Joe

A famous gun-maker (PC 9; HMS 6; FW 7; TGS 5; NC 1,3; YA 2).

> Joseph Manton (1766?–1835), perhaps the most celebrated maker of high-quality sporting guns of his age, was from 1792 onwards established in premises just off Berkeley Square in London. His brother, John (d.1834), ran a separate business of almost equal reputation from his shop on Piccadilly.

Manu

One of the younger members of the crew of the pahi that picks up Aubrey and Maturin in the South Seas. She and her companion Taio save the pair from the fate intended for them, emasculation and death, and have them cast away on a small, deserted island (FSW 7,8).

Mapes or Mapes Court

> An occasional generic reference to the *Williams family, whose home it has long been.

Maragall, Joan

1: a Catalan alias used by Maturin in France (PC 4).
2: Maturin's Minorcan-Catalan associate (HMS 2,3).

Marengo

Admiral Linois' flagship in the Indian Ocean (HMS 9,11).

> Marengo, 80-gun, was launched in 1795 as Jean-Jacques *Rousseau but in 1802 was renamed for *Buonaparte's great, and somewhat improvised, victory of 1800 at the

*Battle of Marengo in northern Italy. In early 1806, on his way back to France from his cruise in the Indian Ocean, *Linois and his flagship were taken by HMSS London and *Amazon. Taken into the Royal Navy under her French name,* Marengo *became a prison ship in 1809 and was broken up in 1816.*

Margaret

A young street urchin encountered by Jack Aubrey in Dover (RM 4).

Maria Theresa

A reference is made to 'Maria Theresa dollars' (TH 2).

Maria Theresa (1717–1780), the daughter of Emperor Charles VI of Germany, became a central figure in European dynastic politics of the 18th century. A woman at once pious, charming, stubborn and traditionalist, she was often a pragmatic reformer of the unwieldy, domestic institutions she had inherited. Charles had designated Maria as heir to all his hereditary Habsburg kingdoms but, on his death in 1740, her succession to many of them was disputed, with only Austria and Hungary welcoming her as Empress to their joint throne, and a long series of wars followed her assumption of power. In 1745 Maria Theresa arranged for her beloved husband, Francis, to be elected Emperor of Germany — a traditional Habsburg fiefdom, available only to a man — and by 1748 the 'War of the Austrian Succession' was over, leaving Maria Theresa in possession of most of her inheritance, with the crucial exception of the extremely valuable Silesia, unwillingly ceded to Prussia. In 1756 war again broke out between Prussia and an alliance of Austria, France and Russia. This 'Seven Years' War' was concluded in 1763, again with Maria Theresa's Empire substantially intact but now much reduced in influence, saddled with monstrous debts and still without Silesia. Francis I died in 1765 and was succeeded to the German throne by his and Maria's son, Joseph II. She continued to exert a powerful influence over the young man until the end of her life but was much troubled by his desire to extend his limited reforms into a complete, rational re-thinking of the notion of statehood itself (the 'Enlightenment,' as his program became known). Of her large number of children, her (extremely unenlightened*) daughter, Marie Antoinette (1755–1793), married King *Louis XVI of France and, like him, was executed in the Revolution. High-quality gold 'thalers — or 'dollars' — had been minted in Austria since the 15th century, and those with Maria Theresa's head became the leading trade currency in the south-east Mediterranean and along the Red Sea for well over a hundred years after her reign, the coins always showing 1780, the date of her death.*

Mariae Sacrum

see **Mary # 1** *below*

Marie-Paule

A French privateer, Master M. François, that unsuccessfully pursues *Ringle* (COM 5).

Mark, Saint

The Patron Saint of Venice (IM 10) and the subject of a *Passion* by the elder Bach, a score that is owned by Jack Aubrey (IM 2).

Saint Mark the Evangelist is traditionally regarded as the

author of the second *Gospel of the New Testament (although other authorships have also been suggested). Mark accompanied Saint *Paul on several of his missions, including one to Rome, and is also thought to have acted as Saint *Peter's interpreter for a time. He is believed to have founded the Christian Church in Upper Egypt and to have been martyred there in about 68 AD. In the 9th century Saint Mark's body was supposedly taken to Venice and reburied where the great cathedral named for him now stands.*

Markham, Admiral

An officer famous for his design of a new sick-bay (COM 3).

*John Markham (1761–1827), a younger son of the Archbishop of York, made a reputation from about 1800 onwards — when still a Captain — as a reformer of conditions for sick and injured seamen on his HMS *Centaur. Although, in a previous command on the West Indies station, Markham had lost over one quarter of his crew to fever in 1795 and had himself come close to death, his immediate spur to a dramatic improvement of conditions on Centaur may have been the admonishment he received from Lord *St Vincent in 1798 (a year in which the ship also briefly mutinied under him), following allegations from his then surgeon of filthy conditions on the lower decks. Curiously, after a furious exchange of letters, St Vincent soon withdrew the reprimand and thereafter became an assiduous promoter of Markham's career. On Centaur itself Markham now built a relatively spacious, well-ventilated sick-bay between the two forward guns under the forecastle (in most ships of the time the traditional location of the pig-sty!), equipping it with beds and settees, its own head and washing facilities, a simple kitchen and access to special food. This design was privately adopted by a few fellow-Captains and, in 1801, was taken up and commended by St Vincent (now Commander-in-Chief of the Channel) on the advice of his Fleet Physician, *Trotter, both men rightly thinking that the control of sickness would play a crucial role in enabling ships to stay at sea on blockade duty for far longer than had been the case in the immediate past. Markham had been made Post in 1783 and went on to serve as an Admiralty Commissioner between 1801–1804 and 1806–1807, being promoted Rear Admiral in 1804, Vice Admiral in 1809 and Admiral in 1819. Between 1801 and 1826, with a short gap from 1818 to 1820, he was also MP for Portsmouth.*

Marlborough, HMS

A ship in which Jack Aubrey and Captain Seymour had once been shipmates (PC 3).

HMS Marlborough, *74-gun, was launched in 1767. She took part in *Rodney's victory at the Battle of the Saintes in 1782 and in *Howe's defeat of the French fleet at the Glorious First of June in 1794, being commanded in the latter engagement by Captain the Hon George *Berkeley. Under Captain Thomas Sotheby (d.1831 in the rank of full Admiral)* Marlborough *was wrecked off the French coast in late 1800. The ship was named for the Duke of Marlborough (see* **Marlbrouk,** *below).*

Marlbrouk

The subject of a song enjoyed by Frenchmen in Boston (FW 8).

The reference is probably to General John Churchill (1650–1722), 1st Duke of Marlborough, who made his *military reputation as British Commander-in-Chief during the War of the Spanish Succession, winning great victories at Blenheim (1704), Ramillies (1706), Oudenaard (1708) and Malplaquet (1709). His wife, Sarah (1660–1744), was a long-time confidante of Queen *Anne, over whom she exercised enormous power until falling from grace in 1711. At this point Marlborough too was dismissed from the army and even charged with embezzlement of military funds, remaining wholly out of favour until the accession of King George I in 1714. Some later versions of the song also include references to the Duke's grandson, Charles Spencer (1706–1758), 3rd Duke of Marlborough and 5th Earl of Sunderland, who fought against the French in the 1740s and 1750s, enjoying much less military success than his illustrious ancestor.*

Marno, Edward
Marno and his fellow transported convict, Robert Smith, die of sea-sickness in HMS *Leopard*, the only two such deaths Stephen Maturin has ever encountered (DI 3).

Maro
see Virgil

Maronite Patriarch, the
A religious leader who had once given a scimitar to Lord Clonfert (TMC 3).
The Maronite Christian sect live largely in the Lebanon, with the Patriarch having his See at Antioch.

'Marriage of Figaro'
Stephen Maturin sings Jack Aubrey a short passage from Mozart's *Marriage of Figaro* to illustrate the possibility of sexual congress between Queenie and her rather older husband, Lord Keith (M&C 4). Canning had heard the work performed in London (PC 8) and, some years later, Blaine intends shortly to do so (SM 4). The young Jack had also heard the piece in about 1792 (C/T 3).
Mozart's opera—in Italian, Le Nozze de Figaro—was first performed in 1786 but was then not performed in England until 1812, long after *Canning's outing but only shortly before *Blaine's remark (although Jack *Aubrey does not say where he heard the piece, the strong implication is that it was in England). Characters from the work mentioned in the series include: **Conte/Count Almaviva (LM 8,9) and his wife the **Contessa/Countess** (PC 8; LM 8; C/T3); her desirable young maid, **Susanna** (M&C 4; PC 8; C/T 3), who is engaged to Almaviva's valet, **Figaro** (M&C 4; HMS 2; LM 8); the young page **Cherubino** (SM 4; LM 8: a male role, but always sung by a woman); and Figaro's scheming enemy, **Dr Bartolo** (SM 4).*

Marriot, Captain
The Captain of the unhappy HMS *Defender* in Admiral Thornton's Mediterranean fleet (IM 4).

Mars, HMS
The ship into which Clonfert had transferred from HMS *Agamemnon* (TMC 2). Years later she visits Torbay under her Captain Henry Woolton (YA 4).
*HMS Mars, 74-gun, was launched in 1794. In 1798 Cap-*tain Alexander *Hood was killed aboard her whilst taking the French Hercule (see *Hercules, HMS) and, in 1805, at Trafalgar, her then Captain George Duff was decapitated by a ball whilst engaged against Pluton. After a spell in the Baltic, Mars served in the Channel fleet from 1809 to 1813, when she was paid off at Portsmouth, acting as a hulk until her break-up in 1823. She was named for Mars, the Roman god of war.

Mars
The French ship-of-the-line that leads the French squadron at Zambra, where she engages and destroys Dawson's HMS *Pollux*, with Admiral Harte aboard (TH 10; FSW 1).
VICHOT notes that a ship-of-the-line Mars was launched in 1813 but provides no further details of her career.

Marsden
An odious parson, sheep farmer and magistrate, known as the 'Flogging Parson' and 'Parson Rapine,' who is encountered by Stephen Maturin in New South Wales (NC 8,9; C/T 8).
The Reverend Samuel Marsden (1764–1835) emigrated to Australia in 1794 as a Chaplain appointed by Royal Warrant and soon acquired land, sheep and great wealth. From 1814 he was especially active in New Zealand as an enthusiastic and very effective promoter of Christianity, being known to this day as the 'Apostle' of that country. Robert *Hughes describes Marsden as 'a grasping evangelical missionary,' virulently anti–Catholic and anti–Irish, who became widely known as the 'Hanging Parson.' He was certainly the object of sustained attack by Governor *Macquarie for his harshness as a magistrate but he eventually cleared his name, at least to his own satisfaction.

Marshall
A naval historian referred to by O'Brian (M&C author's note).
John Marshall (1784?–1837) went to sea at the age of 10 and later served in the Royal Navy as Midshipman and Master's Mate; in 1815 he was promoted Lieutenant and promptly beached for life. Between 1823 and 1835 Marshall published his 12 volume Royal Naval Biography, a compendium of all contemporary commissioned officers, largely based on contributions by the men themselves but also containing the text of many valuable reports and official letters (see also *O'Byrne).

Marshall, William
The homosexual Master of Jack Aubrey's HMS *Sophie* (M&C 1+), on one occasion threatened and blackmailed by Lieutenant James Dillon (M&C 7). Absent in a prize, he misses the capture of *Cacafuego* (M&C 11).
When Jahleel *Brenton commanded HMS *Speedy (the real-life model for the fictional HMS *Sophie) in 1799, a Mr Marshall was her Master. He remained in the sloop under Commander Thomas *Cochrane but it was his absence taking a prize into Minorca that allowed the ship's surgeon, Mr Guthrie, to take the helm as Speedy closed with El *Gamo, an incident that O'Brian borrows for Stephen *Maturin.

Marsham

The First Lieutenant of HMS *Briseis* (HD 1).

Marsyas

A man defeated in a contest by Apollo (SM 8).

In Greek myth, Marsyas challenged *Apollo to a contest in skill at playing a flute that had been discarded by the goddess *Minerva, the victor to do what he would with his vanquished opponent. Apollo triumphed and promptly flayed the presumptuous Marsyas alive, then using his skin for a wine-flask.

Martens

A seaman in HMS *Worcester* who had previously sailed with Jack Aubrey (IM 7).

Martha

The widowed sister of Mrs Broad of the Grapes Inn (YA 8).

Martial

The great Latin poet referred to by Maturin (HMS 5).

Marcus Valerius Martialis (40?–101? AD) was a Spanish-born, Latin poet of whose personal life and career little is known for certain. He appears to have lived in Rome from about 60 to 95, making his living as a poet-for-hire under the patronage of wealthy families, often with Spanish connections. He became celebrated — though, by his own account, never wealthy — for his many books of Epigrams, *short, elegant and striking poems commemorating important public events or private celebrations. Using fairly conventional forms, Martial extended the art of epigram both by his brilliance of concise description or comment and by his biting wit, all heightened by his clear — if somewhat affected — sense of being a quasi-rustic outsider in a subtle, devious, cosmopolitan city. Of his own writings he famously wrote: 'Some are good, rather more are mediocre and a lot are terrible!'*

Martin

N.B., almost all references in the present book to 'Martin' or 'Mr Martin' are to Stephen Maturin's close friend and colleague, Nathaniel *Martin.

1: a doctor — presumably French — at the military hospital on Mauritius where Lord Clonfert is being treated as a wounded prisoner (TMC 10).
2: the Port Admiral at Portsmouth (TGS 4,5).

Martin, Betty

The subject of the catch-phrase 'all my eye and Betty Martin' (TH 2).

The origins of the phrase — meaning 'nonsense' — are obscure. OED notes it as a popular naval expression from 1781 onwards and BREWER offers as a possible source an improbable, complex tale involving the misunderstanding — by a sailor — of a Latin prayer to Saint Martin containing the line '...mihi, beate Martine,' ('...to me, O blessed Martin.').

Martin, Mrs Deborah

The Reverend Nathaniel Martin's new wife, who visits HMS *Surprise* shortly after their wedding cer-

emony for a celebration dinner (LM 5) and later spends time in Shelmerston with Sophie Aubrey (LM 8). Curiously, Martin had earlier (RM 6) said that his intended wife was 'Polly' (*a familiar form of 'Mary'*), soon reporting that the ceremony had taken place (RM 10; *also* C/T 3).

Martin, Nathaniel

Mr Martin is first met as a one-eyed, newly appointed naval parson, travelling out to the Mediterranean in Jack Aubrey's HMS *Worcester* to join his own ship, HMS *Berwick*, after having tried unsuccessfully to live by his pen. The delayed arrival of *Berwick* enables him to form strong friendships in *Worcester*, especially with his fellow-naturalist Stephen Maturin, to whom he reveals that he had lost his eye to an owl that was protecting its chicks (IM 3–8). Soon given a leave of absence from *Berwick* by her Captain Bennet (who finds a parson cramps his amorous propensities), Martin now accompanies Jack and Stephen on the Mubara expedition (TH 4–6) and here assists in Stephen's clumsy attempts to recover supposed treasure chests by diving bell (TH 6). On their return from the mission, Martin remains ashore in Malta (TH 7–10). At first much liked by both Stephen and Jack (FSW 1), he is soon invited to join HMS *Surprise* as schoolmaster and chaplain (FSW 2+). However, Jack quickly begins to feel constrained in his social behaviour by the presence of a man of the cloth, whom he in any case doubts has a useful role on a fighting ship (FSW 4). On the subsequent journey to the Pacific, Martin and Stephen have splendid opportunities to indulge their mutual passion for natural history in Brazil (FSW 5) and off the Galapagos Islands (FSW 7), although Nathaniel is later wounded when *Surprise* intercepts the female-crewed *pahi* that had rescued Jack and Stephen after their fall overboard (FSW 8). When Stephen later receives a severe concussion in a fall, Martin — by now also an informal assistant in the sick-bay — is encouraged by Jack to operate but remains most reluctant to do so, at least whilst still at sea. He soon lands with his sinking friend on Old Sodbury Island but is there saved from having to attempt surgery first by the presence of the ship-wrecked American surgeon, Mr Butcher, and then by Stephen's own sudden recovery (FSW 9,10). On his eventual return to England (RM 1–4), Martin announces his intention to wed (RM 6) but soon falls severely ill, being successfully operated on by Stephen (RM 7). He then marries (RM 10; LM 5,8; *see* **Martin, Deborah**) but promptly wrecks his Royal Navy career prospects by publishing an intemperate attack on ship-board disciplinary practices (RM 10). Unemployable in the service, Martin joins *Surprise* — now Jack and Stephen's private letter-of-marque — as assistant surgeon (LM 1+; TGS 1,2,9). Most usefully, he is able to explain to the pair the origins of the many strange religious sects amongst the new crew (LM 5; WDS 3). In New South Wales (NC

7+) Martin and Stephen enjoy the natural riches of the colony and here also, together with an old university friend Paulton, they plan the escape of the transported, former sick-bay attendant, Padeen Colman (NC 9,10). Martin is now increasingly sensitive to Jack's strong dislike of his presence in the ship, as both ordained parson and the close confidant of Stephen (NC 8; C/T 1+), and only with considerable misgivings does he accept Jack's generous offer of a number of modest livings in England that lie in his gift (C/T 3,4). After performing the marriage ceremony of the run-away convict Clarissa Harvill and Midshipman Billy Oakes (C/T 2), Martin himself becomes the victim of an unhealthy infatuation with the young stowaway and thus contributes to the tense, disagreeable atmosphere that spreads through the ship (C/T 4+). Continuing for the time being in *Surprise* and her prize *Franklin* (WDS 1–5), Martin begins to behave strangely in Jack's, and even Stephen's, company and to exhibit signs of physical illness. Having convinced himself that he has contracted a venereal disease from Clarissa, he is now poisoning himself with excessive mercury treatment, even though he is suffering only from salt-sores, guilt and a overwrought imagination (WDS 3,4,5). Stephen, now feeling that his friend would be better away from Jack, the spectre of Clarissa and the sea, arranges for him to return home to England in a merchantman putting out from Peru (WDS 6; *also perhaps* YA 3).

Martin, Paul

The assistant surgeon in HMS *Leopard*, a noted anatomist recommended to Stephen Maturin by his French colleague, Dupuytren. Martin falls ill during the gaol fever outbreak and, after making some initial recovery, dies of a pneumonia (DI 3–5). As part of a plan to pass false intelligence to the spy Louisa Wogan, Stephen later claims to have discovered suspicious documents in the belongings of the dead man, who conveniently hailed from the Channel Islands, English possessions lying just off the French coast that are easily represented as a hotbed of Parisian plot (DI 7; FW 1).

Martineau

A Bourbon supporter with whom Maturin intends to hold a clandestine meeting in France (IM 7).

Martinez

A Spanish merchant whose house in Port Mahon serves as both the British (M&C 1+) and, later, French (HMS 3) headquarters. In this latter role, the house is the scene of Stephen Maturin's imprisonment and torture (HMS 3). Martinez has other interests on the island, owning the mail-packet *Ventura* (M&C 11) and a landmark warehouse (HMS 3).

Mary

1: The dedicatee of 14 of the Aubrey-Maturin novels, in English (PC, DI, FW, RM, CO/T, COM, YA, HD) and Latin (M&C, SM, IM, TH, LM, NC).

Mary, Patrick O'Brian's wife of over half a century, died in March 1998. The several Latin dedications to her may be rendered in English as follows: 'I present and dedicate (this book) to Mary, the Commander and Mistress of our yacht' (M&C); 'Dedicated to Mary' (SM, IM, TH, NC); 'Dedicated twelve times over to Mary' (LM, the 12th book of the series).

2: a religious greeting or oath uttered by Maturin and other Catholics many times in the series, often in combination with God, Joseph and/or Patrick.

In the New Testament tradition, Saint Mary is the natural mother of *Jesus by divine conception from *God, her earthly husband being Saint *Joseph. The 'Blessed Virgin Mary, Mother of God' is especially venerated in the Roman Catholic faith, even being sometimes elevated to 'Queen of Heaven.'

Mascara, Dey of

A potentate on the North African coast, to whose port of Zambra Jack Aubrey is sent by Admiral Ives to resolve a dispute (TH 10). That the Dey has become a French ally is known only to the traitor Andrew Wray, who intends to use the situation to bring about Stephen Maturin's death (TH 2,8). Jack and Stephen, sent into this trap, manage to escape, but only after a fierce encounter with the waiting French warships (TH 10). We later learn that Mr Consul Eliot and the Admiral's secretary, Pocock, had soon arranged for the Dey's murder and replacement by one of his sons (FSW 1).

Masher, Andrew

A deceased female ape, whose dried head belongs to Evan Evans (PC 12).

The name is naval slang for *Andromache, just as *'Billy Ruffian' is naval slang for *Bellerophon and *'Wheel'em Along' for Ville de Milan. The Royal Navy term most often encountered for any HMS Andromache is 'Andrew/ Andy Mack,' with O'Brian's 'Masher' reflecting different possible ways of pronouncing of the Greek original.

Master Attendant

An official at Plymouth harbour (PC 7).

The Master Attendant was the senior bosun of naval service installations.

Mateu

An intelligence agent in Catalonia linked to the British (FW 2).

Mateu, Jaime

A Barcelona merchant, the owner of *Pardal* and *Xaloc*, who hires the privateer *Gloire* to protect his ships from Jack Aubrey's HMS *Sophie* (M&C 7).

Matthew

A seaman in the French privateer *Bellone* (PC 5).

'Matthew Walker'

A type of knot (PC 7; LM 8).

The 'Matthew Walker' is a form of stopper-knot worked into the end of a line to prevent its running through a block or eye. First mentioned, as an already well-known name, by Darcy Lever in his Sheet Anchor *of 1808, the current* Ashley Book of Knots *suggests Walker may have been a master rigger in a British naval dockyard.*

Matthews

1: a seaman in HMS *Surprise* who had been ashore at Gibraltar as an 'Abraham-man,' falsely claiming to be a lunatic in order to avoid work (FSW 2).

2: Paulton's cousin, a landowner in New South Wales, who refuses to participate in the customary mistreatment of convicts and aboriginals (NC 9+).

3: a member of the Foreign Office who has fallen into the power of the spy, Diego Diaz (YA 7).

Matthews, John

A seaman in HMS *Néréide* (TMC 7).

Maturin, Brigid (*also* Brigit, Bridie, Brideen *or* Breen)

Whilst in the colony of New South Wales, Stephen Maturin learns of the birth of a daughter to his wife, Diana Villiers (NC 10; *anticipated in* TGS 1,2,9). He later discovers, by letter, that little Brigid's birth had been a sad trial to Diana and that subsequently very little, if any, bond has formed between mother and baby, whose mental development also seems slow. Jack Aubrey has received a similar report about the situation from his own wife, Sophie, Diana's cousin (C/T 3). Stephen finds that these unhappy circumstances at home play on his mind during the long voyage home (C/T 9; WDS 5,9) and he approaches his first meeting with his child with some trepidation (COM 2), especially having learned she has been deserted by her mother and left in the hands of his old ship-mate and current house-guest, Clarissa Oakes (COM 1–4). Brigid's taciturn, withdrawn strangeness greatly disturbs Stephen, but fortunately the girl soon forms a bond with the servant Padeen Colman, who teaches her to speak Irish and gradually draws her into a more normal childhood world (COM 2–5). When Stephen's political affairs take a turn for the worse, he takes Brigid to Spain and leaves her, together with Clarissa and Padeen, in the care of his aunt Petronilla, an Abbess (COM 5,9,10). A little later Brigid — now quite out-going and well developed — is re-united with her mother, Diana, and the two achieve a happy relationship before returning with Stephen to live, once again, in England (YA 1+). However, the girl soon suffers the loss of her mother in a coaching accident: fortunately, she is said to be still too young fully to comprehend what has happened (HD 1,2).

Maturin, Mrs Diana

see Villiers, Diana

Maturin, Stephen (*often referred to by his full Spanish name of* Don Esteban Maturin y Domanova *and occasionally by the French version of his name,* Etienne Maturin; *also very often simply* 'the Doctor')

Master and Commander opens late in the evening of 18th April 1800. Stephen Maturin is sitting next to Lieutenant Jack Aubrey Maturin during a Locatelli concert at the Governor's House in Port Mahon, Minorca: the pair quarrel and appear to be intent on a duel the following day (M&C 1). Before the encounter can be arranged, Jack receives promotion to Commander of HMS *Sophie*, reconciles himself to Stephen and invites him to celebrate the joyous news over dinner (M&C 1,2). Stephen, an Irish physician *(who had trained at Trinity College, Dublin—RM 7; LM 6—and later in Paris—RM 5; WDS 3; COM 1)*, accepts the post of surgeon on his new friend's command, revealing that he was returning from Ireland to his boyhood home of Catalonia in the hope—thwarted by sudden impoverishment—of pursuing his passion for natural history (M&C 2). He soon learns that one of his new shipmates is to be a fellow-countryman, Lieutenant James Dillon (M&C 2), with whom he had once been active in the United Irishmen, a political society, dedicated to Catholic emancipation and Irish self-rule, that had staged an unsuccessful armed rebellion in 1798 against English dominance (M&C 3,5). Stephen, never in favour of revolutionary violence, had distanced himself from the subsequent, awful events but both he and James—who had been absent at the crucial time—are deeply affected by the resulting turmoil in their country (M&C 5; *Stephen had also somehow lost* *Mona, his first love, in the rebellion: TGS 4). James' confusion and unhappiness spill over into his relationships with the assertively English Jack Aubrey and Stephen—a Catholic by upbringing *(strongly suggested in, e.g.,* M&C 5; *confirmed in* PC 3,10)—spends much time trying to mediate between the two (M&C 5–10). In *Sophie* the Doctor receives—from William Mowett—the first of many long and detailed lessons in what will always remain to him the impenetrable mysteries of the seaman's craft (M&C 3). Yet he is also the first to alert the distracted Jack to the attack on a merchant convoy by an Algerine galley and, in the ensuing action, treats his first-ever wounded, naval patients (M&C 4). After the battle, he trepans the ship's gunner, Mr Day, for a depressed fracture of the skull, an operation that firmly establishes his reputation in the fleet as a medical miracle-worker: Admiral Lord Keith even personally signs the warrant formally appointing him a Royal Navy surgeon (M&C 4). Stephen, whilst ashore for a spell in mainland Catalonia, learns from friends that frustrated merchants have engaged the frigate *Cacafuego* to hunt down *Sophie* (M&C 7,8) and, when Jack later attacks and captures the much larger Spanish ship, Stephen is at the British sloop's helm (M&C 10; *as was *Cochrane's surgeon, Mr Guthrie, in the action upon which O'Brian bases his tale*). *Sophie* is soon captured by the French *Desaix*, with whose surgeon, Dr Ramis, Stephen strikes up a professional friendship (M&C 11,12; *N.B. much later Stephen claims to have participated in the Battle of Algeçiras, which in truth he could only witness from his captivity:* IM 3). When the British crew are exchanged on parole, Stephen gives evidence at the court-martial of Jack — by now his firm friend — for the loss of his ship (M&C 12).

Post Captain opens in late 1802 with Stephen and Jack taking passage back to England. *En route* they hear that a peace treaty between France and England has just been signed (PC 1; *the Peace of Amiens was agreed in October 1801 and signed in March 1802 — O'Brian conflates these dates and then delays the signing until October 1802*). The pair take a house in Hampshire and soon meet their neighbours, the beautiful — and moderately wealthy — Sophie Williams and her equally beautiful — but rather poor — widowed cousin, Diana Villiers (PC 1,2). Stephen admires Sophie and encourages her and Jack as partners. He himself falls for Diana but she too, though certainly reciprocating his friendship with her customary dashing spirit, sees Jack as having the better of the two sets of prospects and commences some sort of affair with him, causing Stephen great distress and confusion, turning him to laudanum for relief (PC 2,3; *the start of his series-long affair with the narcotic*). Another cause, of a different but no less passionate kind, is revealed as close to Stephen's heart, that of Catalan independence. We learn that he is — and has been for some time — a valued, volunteer intelligence adviser to Sir Joseph Blaine of the Admiralty (PC 3; *Stephen had a Catalan mother and an Irish father, an officer in the service of Spain — e.g., HMS 1; RM 1,5; WDS 1 — and, throughout the series, loathes what he sees as *Buonaparte's brutal tyranny over Europe; see also* ***Somerville, John**). During a peace-time visit to France with Jack, he is able to engage in a little spying in partnership with his old medical friend, Dr Ramis, now revealed as another Catalan nationalist (PC 3). When war again suddenly breaks out (*May 1803*) Stephen and Jack escape on foot to Spain, there taking refuge for a while in Stephen's own large, though dilapidated, family estate (PC 4) before returning to England (PC 5). Here Stephen again strikes up his tortured friendship with Diana Villiers — and also her wealthy, Jewish merchant friend, Canning — before taking to the sea again in Jack's new HMS *Polychrest* (PC 6,7. *Stephen is by now a naval doctor of great renown:* PC 3,6. *Yet he never acquires any great skill at ship-board dentistry:*

FSW 2). Service in home waters enables both Stephen and Jack to keep up their troubled relationships with Sophie and Diana but their mutual desire for the latter eventually results in a furious quarrel and, for the second time in their short friendship, an arrangement to fight (PC 8,10). Soon however, Stephen, out of a sense of both professional obligation and residual amity, feels compelled to warn Jack that the *Polychrest*s are on the point of mutiny. Jack's answer is to take the ship straight into action and the glory of his subsequent victory, together with some severe wounds in the fight, facilitate a silent reconciliation between the two friends (PC 11). Jack's long-awaited promotion into the frigate HMS *Lively* enables him — after much dithering — to make an offer of sorts to Sophie, thus in theory leaving a clearer path to Diana's affections. Yet, to his dismay, Stephen finds her both gone from home and now the scarcely concealed mistress of Canning (PC 12–14). Stephen's intelligence affairs are faring better, for he has learnt that Spain is to join France in her war against England. With Blaine, he arranges for Jack and others to intercept one of her valuable treasure squadrons, heading homewards from the New World colonies (PC 14). He himself is awarded a secret, temporary Post Captaincy in order that he may share in the valuable prize money certain to be won as the Spaniards are taken. The book ends (*October 1804*) with Stephen nominally wealthy and successful, yet broken-hearted (PC 14).

As **HMS Surprise** opens, the action against Bustamente's squadron should have made both Jack Aubrey and Stephen Maturin wealthy men. Yet events turn out otherwise, for the pair are denied prize money, the battle having occurred just before war with Spain was formally declared (HMS 1). Even worse, at an Admiralty Board meeting Stephen is inadvertently revealed as an important intelligence agent (HMS 1), a leak that soon leads, whilst he is on a further mission to Minorca, to his capture and torture by the French (HMS 2; *the island having been handed to Buonaparte under the terms of the Treaty of Amiens*). Not far from death, he is rescued by Jack and a raiding-party from HMS *Lively* (HMS 3). Both wanting and needing to get away from Europe, Stephen now joins Jack's new HMS *Surprise* for a voyage to India (HMS 5+), during which passage he learns to swim (HMS 5), teaches Bonden to write (HMS 6), famously brings aboard a Brazilian sloth (HMS 6) and reveals his continuing, passionate attachment to Diana Villiers (HMS 6). Their complex friendship is renewed in Bombay, where she is now living openly if uneasily with Richard Canning, and Stephen soon asks for her hand in marriage, an offer over which she prevaricates (HMS 7). Here too Stephen meets the lively street-urchin, Dil, but his ill-considered gift to her of silver bangles immediately results in her murder by thugs: Stephen has then to arrange her immolation (HMS 7). A little later—by now in Calcutta—Stephen and Diana are found kissing by Canning, resulting in a furious quarrel and pistol-duel. Canning badly injures Stephen with the opening shot but is, in turn, dropped dead by the second despite Stephen's intention to miss or merely wound (HMS 10). The Doctor now operates on himself to remove his opponent's ball and is then briefly nursed by the shocked and penitent Diana before the pair take separate passage home to England (HMS 11). Before they part, Stephen gives his beloved a ring, although it is clear to neither party exactly what mutual obligations, if any, have been exchanged. To Stephen's shock, the 'engagement' lasts scarcely any time at all, the ring being returned by letter when Diana runs off to the USA with a rich new lover, Harry Johnstone (HMS 11).

The Mauritius Command opens some years later (*probably in mid–1809*): Stephen has recently returned to England from Spain (TMC 1) and we see him examining the new Aubrey babies (for Jack and Sophie have married), revealing that, in his student days, he had delivered many infants (TMC 1; *curiously, in DI 7 he denies such experience*). Continuing as an advisor to the Admiralty on political issues, he is able to use his influence to obtain for Jack the command of the expedition to Mauritius, using—perhaps misusing—his medical authority to confine the previously chosen, but somewhat ailing and in any case unsuitable, Captain Loveless to England (TMC 1). Accompanying the mission as surgeon in Jack's HMS *Boadicea*, Stephen is confirmed at the Cape by Admiral Bertie as official political advisor to the campaign (TMC 3). On the next stage of the voyage he treats Lord Clonfert, one of Jack's junior commanders, for violent stomach cramps, coming to the view that his illness lies more in the mind than the body (TMC 4); in his diaries he goes on to analyse subtly Clonfert's extreme need for reassurance and esteem (TMC 5+). In the political role, Stephen lays plans to suborn the loyalty of the strongly Catholic inhabitants of French Mauritius (TMC 5) and, much to the disappointment of the army Colonel Keating and his officers, arranges the surrender of the nearby island of Réunion before a set piece battle is necessary (TMC 6). Following a close brush with death by drowning whilst attempting to board HMS *Néréide*, he resumes his laudanum habit (TMC 7). Present during the disastrous Battle of Port South East, Stephen witnesses what he later reports to Jack as Clonfert's initial gross folly and comes to regard Pym, the senior Captain present, as deficient in leadership (TMC 7,8). As the battle ends, Stephen escapes to Réunion by launch, carrying the news of the heavy British defeat (TMC 7,8). He successfully continues his job of the subversion of Mauritius (TMC 8–10) but later reveals to his colleague Dr McAdam his current lack of zest for life: although Diana Villiers is mentioned only once by name in the book—and then only as a past love (TMC 7)—it is clear that her abandonment of him left a deep wound (TMC 10).

Desolation Island opens (*sometime in 1811*) with Stephen now both a distinguished author and activist on the improvement of naval health (DI 3,9; *see also* TH 1) and an active, if jaded, intelligence agent (DI 2). He visits the Aubreys at Ashgrove Cottage to examine, with other leading physicians, the hypochondriac Mrs Williams (DI 1). Part of his emotional unease lies in renewed rejection by Diana Villiers, whom he has recently met in London (DI 1,2), and his consequent slipping back into laudanum abuse (DI 1+). Indeed Stephen has recently operated on a friend, the naturalist John Deering, whose death under the knife he hints may have been partly due to his clouded judgement (DI 1). Although at first Stephen does not intend to travel with Jack Aubrey and his HMS *Leopard* to the penal colony in Australia, he is persuaded to do so by Sir Joseph Blaine in order secretly to interrogate the convicted American spy, Louisa Wogan, during the voyage (DI 1,2). As ship's doctor, and still a friend to the cause of Irish independence (DI 4; *as well as his activities in the United Irishmen (e.g.* M&C 2+) *Stephen had spent his boyhood as a native Irish speaker (*NC 10*) in Cahirciveen (*PC 10*))*, he wins her unwitting confidence (DI 3+), not only discovering further details of spies in London but achieving the *coup* of passing false intelligence to her, via her lover Michael Herapath, and effecting her 'escape' back to the USA from Desolation Island, where *Leopard* has been wrecked (DI 7,10). During the voyage, Stephen deals with an horrific outbreak of fever in the ship (DI 4,5) and tends to the birth of Leopardina Boswell by caesarian section (DI 8), curiously stating that he has no great experience of midwifery (DI 7; *but see* TMC 1).

At the opening of **The Fortune of War** (*in early 1812*) Stephen has remained in HMS *Leopard* all the way from Desolation Island to Java. Here he meets his intelligence colleague, Wallis, on whom he had performed an adult circumcision some time previously (FW 1). Eager to return to Catalonia, where he sees fresh opportunities to discomfort the French, he accompanies Jack Aubrey on his return to England in HMS *La Flèche*, but not before demonstrating an entertaining confusion between the rules of English cricket and Irish hurling (FW 1,2). When *La Flèche* takes accidental fire, Stephen escapes with Jack and other colleagues in a small boat: eventually picked up by HMS *Java*, they soon after experience her defeat and destruction by USS *Constitution* (FW 2,3). Taken prisoner, Stephen loyally accompanies the sick and wounded Jack to Boston: yet he approaches the USA with some considerable misgivings, arising from his recent intelligence *coup* against Louisa Wogan (FW 4; *see* DI 7,10). Furthermore, he reveals to the American surgeon, Evans, that, although he was indeed once a republican who cheered the fall of the Bastille (*see also* WDS 3), he is now a good, British monarchist, if only on pragmatic grounds (FW 4). In Boston Harry Johnson (*see* HMS 11; *the spelling of his name has changed*), now the lover of both Louisa Wogan and Diana Villiers, tries to recruit Stephen to serve American interests, thinking that it is Jack rather than the Doctor who is the dedicated British intelligence agent. Stephen soon sees that Johnson himself is very closely connected with both American and French secret networks, especially through the sinister agents Pontet-Canet and Dubreuil (FW 5,6). To complicate matters further, Stephen has again encountered Diana, again fallen hopelessly in love with her and again turned to laudanum (FW 6). This time she agrees to his proposal of marriage, an arrangement that, although initially intended simply to help her to escape from both the USA and Johnson, soon takes a mutually heartfelt turn (FW 6,9). Eventually the American and French agents see Stephen for the spy he is and try to abduct him. He saves himself by fleeing and hiding in Diana's bed while she goes to summon help from Jack Aubrey; during her absence Stephen is forced to kill both Pontet-Canet and Dubreuil, still hot on his trail (FW 7). All three friends then escape by small boat to the British frigate HMS *Shannon*, conveniently cruising just outside the harbour, but not before Stephen has seized many of Johnson's private intelligence records (FW 8; *also* SM 4). The Doctor soon asks *Shannon*'s Captain Broke to perform a shipboard marriage between himself and Diana but the great battle with USS *Chesapeake*, and Broke's own severe wounding at the moment of victory, prevent the ceremony from ever taking place (FW 9; *this action took place in June 1813*).

(*N.B., all books from this point in the series until **The Yellow Admiral** remain notionally set in the second half of 1813, even though each occupies about one calendar year.*)

The Surgeon's Mate finds Stephen in Canada, attending the celebrations of HMS *Shannon*'s great victory. He reveals that he has been invited to address the *Institut* in Paris, purely in his capacity as a naturalist of international reputation (SM 1; *in* IM 1 *Stephen is confirmed as being long-standing Fellow of both the Royal Society and Royal College of Surgeons*). Returning to England in the mail packet *Diligence*, Stephen, Jack Aubrey and Diana Villiers narrowly escape capture by Harry Johnson's determined privateers (SM 3,4). Diana, having found herself to be pregnant by her former lover, has now refused to marry Stephen whilst carrying another man's child (FW 8; SM 1,2). He in turn rejects the suggestion of an abortion, suggesting she accompany him to Paris and remain there for her confinement (SM 2–5). The pair arrive in France, where Stephen prepares for his lecture, rejecting all the while many requests to carry secret messages back to the Bourbon exile court in England. The address is well attended by the great and good but Stephen suffers such bad stage-fright that its impact is somewhat dulled (SM 4,5). Learning immediately afterwards that the Catalan patriot Ponsich has been killed during an English-sponsored secret mission to the Baltic, Stephen hurries back to London to offer his services as a replacement (SM 4,5,6). He tells Sir Joseph Blaine that, as the Commandant of the Catalan troops holding the island of Grimsholm is his own godfather, Casademon, he believes that he will easily be able to subvert their allegiance from France to England. He will then persuade them to abandon their fortress, provided always that Casademon and his troops can be offered free passage to Spain, there to join Wellington's army (SM 6,7). The mission is accomplished without great difficulty and Stephen and his Catalans sail southwards on Jack Aubrey's HMS *Ariel* (SM 7,8,9; *see the entry for *Casademon *for a note on the origins of these events*). However, when *Ariel* is wrecked on the French coast, the Doctor is taken prisoner and escorted to Paris, together with Jack Aubrey and their dashing new colleague, the Lithuanian cavalryman Jagiello, by the secret policeman Duhamel (SM 9,10). Here, Stephen is interrogated over his past activities by members of various French intelligence services (SM 10,11) and soon learns that his immediate safety has been secured both by an enormous bribe paid by Diana Villiers (using her 'Blue Peter' diamond) to an influential politician, and by his being in the immediate hands of Prince Talleyrand, a man who wants to make use of the Doctor in contacting the Bourbon exiles (SM 10,11). Just as Harry Johnson arrives in Paris to denounce Stephen, and just as Jack Aubrey's gaol-break plans are coming to fruition, all three prisoners are released by Talleyrand's man Duhamel. They are joined in their flight to the coast by Diana, who has recently miscarried her baby (SM 11). On the cartel ship, HMS *Oedipus*, Stephen and Diana are now married by their old friend Commander William Babbington, with Jack and Jagiello in attendance (SM 11).

At the opening of **The Ionian Mission**, Stephen and Diana have agreed to maintain separate dwellings in London in order to accommodate their rather different social habits (IM 1). The Doctor wishes to add to their ship-board, civil marriage a Catholic ceremony — for in the eyes of his Church he remains a bachelor — but Diana steadfastly refuses (IM 1). Stephen now plans to travel to the Mediterranean in Jack Aubrey's HMS *Worcester*, both to visit Barcelona and to conduct intelligence operations in Southern France (IM 1+). Painfully injured en-route in a short action with the French *Jemmapes* (IM 2), he takes again to laudanum in order to aid his recovery (IM 3). Having visited Spain (IM 3), Stephen is soon delivered by Jack to the southern coast of France (IM 7) where, when his rendezvous with royalists is aborted in chaos, he comes across a wounded British intelligence agent, Professor Graham, and effects his rescue (IM 7). With Graham, Stephen is appointed as an advisor to Jack on HMS *Surprise*'s mission to the Ionian Sea (IM 9–11). *En route* he takes a swim, finds himself left behind in *Surprise*'s wake, but fortunately is spotted by an alert seaman and rescued, somewhat embarrassed (IM 9). Stephen plays little active part in the Ionian adventure but is present at the great victory over the rebel Turkish frigates, *Torgud* and *Kitabi* (IM 11). During the course of events, Stephen comes to suspect that Diana may be pregnant (IM 1) but is later told by his wife that he was mistaken (IM 5). He is also told, in an anonymous letter, that Diana and Jagiello are lovers, an allegation that he dismisses out of hand (IM 5)

Treason's Harbour opens with Stephen now in Malta, wary of the attentions paid to him by Laura Fielding, the pretty Sicilian wife of Lieutenant Charles Fielding, a prisoner-of-war in France (TH 1+). He immediately suspects a plot, soon confirmed by the distraught Laura herself, who is a victim of blackmail by the French intelligence agent Lesueur; Stephen then makes use of Laura to feed false information to his enemy (TH 3+). In the meantime, the Doctor's natural science interests are concentrated on his new Halley diving-bell, in which he makes a descent with his friend, Captain Heneage Dundas (TH 3). Soon Stephen is sent to the Red Sea as an advisor to Jack Aubrey on his Mubara expedition (TH 4). There the Halley device is used to recover supposed treasure chests from a galley sunk by Jack's hired ship, *Niobe*, but only lead ingots are recovered, together with a note indicating that the mission has been betrayed from the outset (TH 6). Back in Malta, it becomes widely, though wrongly, thought that Stephen and Laura Fielding are lovers: crucially, Lesueur also accepts the rumour (TH 8+). The Doctor now travels in HMS *Surprise* to Trieste, learning here that Laura's husband, Charles, has escaped from captivity and been rescued by HMS *Nymphe*. Indeed Stephen even operates on him for an old wound, discovering that the Lieutenant in fact believes a service rumour that his wife is Jack Aubrey's lover (TH 9). Realising that Fielding's escape spells doom for Laura — Lesueur now having no power over her, and she able to identify him and his colleagues — Stephen returns to Malta and snatches her from immediate danger, taking her to safety aboard Jack's *Surprise*. Although entirely innocent, neither Jack nor Stephen relish a further meeting with Laura's husband once he arrives home in Malta (TH 10). Before this can happen, *Surprise* is dispatched to the African port of Zambra in order to resolve difficulties with the rebellious Dey of Mascara (TH 10) but, once again, the mission is betrayed and, following a brisk battle with a waiting French squadron, Stephen advises Jack to withdraw to Gibraltar for consultation and reinforcements. At no point does the Doctor suspect that the traitor is Andrew Wray, a senior British administrator with intelligence responsibilities (TH 2,10; *N.B., Stephen, in*

TH 1, *curiously understates his knowledge of the earlier dispute between Jack *Aubrey and *Wray over cards, for he himself warned Jack of the first cheating incident and had a direct account from his friend of the second:* DI 1,2. *Stephen's own gaming expertise comes from a period of his youth when he endured a long spell in a Spanish prison for debt, there sharing a cell with *Jaime, a card-sharp from whom he had learnt many useful techniques of discovery and deception:* TH 8).

In **The Far Side of the World** Sir Joseph Blaine, in view of the mixed intelligence triumphs and fiascos in the Mediterranean, arranges for Stephen to accompany Jack Aubrey and HMS *Surprise* on a relatively minor mission to the South Atlantic. They are also under orders to pursue and take the marauding American frigate, USS *Norfolk* (FSW 1+). Before leaving Gibraltar, Stephen again receives an anonymous letter about Diana and Jagiello and himself sends a letter to her via Andrew Wray — still unsuspected as a traitor — refuting the rumours of his own supposed affair with Laura Fielding (FSW 1,2). The political element of the new journey is soon accomplished when Jack re-takes the mail-packet *Danaë* from the Americans. Hidden on board is an enormous fortune, intended for the subversion of governments in South America, of which Stephen takes reluctant custody (FSW 5). With his new friend and colleague Nathaniel Martin, he has an extended opportunity during the long voyage to indulge their passion for natural history whilst at sea, during a stop in Brazil (FSW 5) and off the Galapagos Islands (FSW 7). Stephen also now swops his long-time laudanum habit for the chewing of coca leaves (FSW 4,5). Once in the Pacific, Stephen manages to fall into the warm sea whilst leaning far out of the stern windows in order to net sea organisms by night. Jack follows, in order to rescue his friend, but *Surprise* stands on, blithely unaware of events in the great cabin (FSW 7). The pair are eventually picked up by a South Seas *pahi* crewed entirely by women warriors and narrowly escape emasculation and death (FSW 7). Eventually abandoned on a desert island, they are rescued by HMS *Surprise*'s searching launch (FSW 7,8). Soon, during a storm, Stephen receives a severe concussion in a fall and, in order to stabilise his friend's condition, Jack sails *Surprise* to the remote Old Sodbury Island, here discovering the crew of the long-sought *Norfolk*, their ship wrecked on the reef (FSW 9). On dry land, Stephen awakes from his coma — just before an intended brain operation by Martin and the American surgeon, Mr Butcher — and makes a rapid recovery (FSW 9). However, *Surprise* is forced away from the island by sudden bad weather, leaving her shore party in near-open warfare with the Americans. Just as matters come to an ugly head, the ship re-appears in hot pursuit of an American whaler, which she then easily takes (FSW 10).

The Reverse of the Medal opens a little while later

with Stephen safely back on board HMS *Surprise*, now arriving at Barbados on the way home to England. On the Caribbean island he strikes up a friendship with Jack Aubrey's natural, black son, Sam Panda, who wishes to become a Catholic priest (RM 1). Stephen, newly rich from an inheritance (RM 4,7; *also* LM 1. *The inheritance is from his mother's Spanish connections; on his father's Irish side Stephen is a Fitzgerald from the wrong side of the blanket:* RM 5), is anxious to return to his wife Diana, hoping that the letter he sent to her via Andrew Wray (FSW 1,2) has assured her that rumours of his supposed affair with Laura Fielding were unfounded (RM 2–4). However, on arrival in London, he discovers that Diana has already run off to Sweden with Jagiello, never having received his explanation (RM 5). He again takes to his laudanum bottle (RM 8). Stephen also finds the political situation at home much changed, for he and Sir Joseph Blaine are being treated with increasing disrespect — Stephen assaults a particularly insolent official — and there is a plot afoot to lure him into a trap in France, a scheme in which Wray seems to play a role (RM 5). When Stephen receives the sudden news of Jack Aubrey's arrest for fraud, he uses his contacts and wealth to try and unearth exculpatory evidence, but to no avail. Yet he and Blaine do discover that Jack is the innocent victim of a deeper, traitorous conspiracy (RM 7,8). Seeing that Jack's Royal Navy career is doomed, Stephen uses all his remaining influence to secure approval for a scheme to send them both on a private mission in support of the independence movement in Chile and Peru, a voyage for which Stephen buys *Surprise* from the service (RM 7–10). Whilst she is fitting out, he receives a note from the disillusioned French agent Duhamel indicating that Diana's 'Blue Peter' diamond (*see* SM 10,11) may yet be restored to them. Stephen meets Duhamel, obtains the gem and learns that Andrew Wray, together with his Treasury colleague Ledward, are the long-sought traitors, news he urgently communicates to Blaine (RM 10).

At the opening of *The Letter of Marque*, Stephen is making his way with his friend Nathaniel Martin to join the recently disgraced Jack Aubrey in *Surprise*; the Doctor's ownership of the frigate has been kept secret (LM 1). Jack's job of working up the ship and her new crew is eased by Stephen's having obtained a general letter of exemption from impressment for her hands. Furthermore, Jack's troubled mind is somewhat eased by Stephen and Sir Joseph Blaine's discovery of important details of the plot that brought about his downfall, even though the traitors Wray and Ledward have both escaped to France before they could be taken and interrogated (LM 2,4). The short training cruises that *Surprise* undertakes as a private letter-of-marque offer Stephen and Martin a number of opportunities to pursue their natural history interests (LM 3–5). Spells ashore in London enable the

Doctor to plan with Blaine how Jack might earn restoration to the Royal Navy list by capturing a French frigate, *Diane*, currently being fitted out for a mission to South America (LM 4+). Stephen, having learned that his wife is almost certainly not Jagiello's lover, also intends to track her down in Sweden before leaving for the Pacific; he is much affected by a colourful poster he is shown of Diana performing spectacular hot-air balloon ascents, perhaps in order to raise cash to support herself (LM 4,8). Jack's attack on *Diane* is a triumphant success during which Stephen not only gets the chance to display his considerable powers of swordsmanship (LM 6) but also to seize valuable intelligence information regarding French intentions in Chile and Peru (LM 7). However, his plan to get Jack back into his beloved Royal Navy goes awry, for both the friends and Blaine himself still seem to have mysterious enemies in high places, whilst Jack himself is intransigent over unacceptable conditions in the restoration offer he receives (LM 7). Stephen, taking with him the 'Blue Peter' diamond, now heads to Sweden (LM 8). Here he meets Diana but is initially unable to bring about any more than an uneasy friendship (LM 9). Opium-ridden (*from* LM 4 *onwards*), he takes a fall and breaks his leg and a period confined to his bed — when he returns to coca leaves as his drug of choice (*see also* COM 1+) — does enable the full reconciliation with his wife that he desires. The couple then joyously set off back to England in Jack's *Surprise* (LM 9).

The Thirteen Gun Salute finds Stephen at home in England, wealthy by inheritance, properly Church-married to Diana (TGS 1) and expecting the birth of their first child (TGS 1,2,9). Very dissatisfied with his London bankers, he decides, on Jack Aubrey's recommendation, to shift his money to Tom Smith's new office (TGS 1,4). The friends are later much concerned to hear that Smith's bank is experiencing difficulties (TGS 6). On the intelligence front, the Doctor had obtained from the captured *Diane* coded documents regarding French plans to disrupt Spanish rule in South America and, consequently, Sir Joseph Blaine now wishes to push ahead with the delayed scheme of sending Stephen, Jack and *Surprise* to Peru and Chile (TGS 1–3). However, the mission is somehow betrayed to Britain's Spanish allies, who naturally want no foreign meddling in their territories whether by friend or foe. Blaine therefore temporarily diverts Stephen to the South China Sea as intelligence advisor to Mr Fox's treaty negotiations with the Sultan of Pulo Prabang (TGS 3+). Stephen sails east with Jack — now restored to the Royal Navy — in his new HMS *Diane* and, on arrival, once again encounters the spies Wray and Ledward, they having fled England and have thrown in their lot with their French masters (TGS 1,3–9). Both by the collection of information and the distribution of large bribes, Stephen enables Fox to secure a treaty with the Sultan and, in the process, brings about the final downfall and death of the English traitors (TGS 6–9; *Stephen's exact role in their demise is left ambiguous*). As a means of quiet disposal, Stephen then dissects the two bodies with his anatomist colleague, van Buren (TGS 8). Natural history is not neglected, for during a break in the negotiations Stephen is able to visit the remote Buddhist temple at Kumai, finding there a paradise of unmolested animal life (TGS 7). On the political front, Stephen and Jack's plan is now quietly to resume the South American mission by meeting *Surprise* at sea and transferring into her. However, *en route* to the rendezvous, *Diane* strikes on an uncharted reef and is totally wrecked in an ensuing typhoon (TGS 9,10). Stephen, Jack and most of the crew are saved but remain stranded an small, uninhabited island (TGS 10).

The ***Nutmeg of Consolation*** opens with Stephen still ship-wrecked with the crew of HMS *Diane* on a remote island (NC 1). After a series of fierce battles with raiding Dyak pirates, the Doctor contrives to arrange passage to Java for himself and his shipmates in a passing Chinese merchant junk (NC 2). In Batavia he learns with dismay that his English bankers, Smith and Clowes, have certainly gone under and that his fortune must therefore be lost: apart from other considerations, Stephen does not relish the prospect of becoming financially dependent on his wife, Diana (NC 3,5). At sea again in Jack Aubrey's temporary, new command, HMS *Nutmeg of Consolation*, the Doctor is anticipating both the long-delayed rendezvous with *Surprise* and the resumption of the mission to South America, to take place after a short a refit and resupply in Australia (NC 4–7). After the meeting takes place, *Surprise* visits Sweeting's Island in search of anti-scorbutics and here Stephen rescues two little native girls, the sole survivors of a smallpox epidemic, whom he names Emily and Sarah (NC 8+). On arrival in Sydney he attends an official dinner and there, in a generally unpleasant atmosphere, quarrels with the wealthy and influential Captain Lowe over disobliging remarks each make about mutual acquaintances, John Macarthur and Sir Joseph Banks. The pair fight an impromptu duel, which Stephen easily wins (NC 8), leading to endless difficulties for Jack with the work he needs done on *Surprise* (NC 9,10). Whilst in the colony, Stephen receives several items of news, some far more welcome than others. His fortune had never in fact been transferred to Smith and Clowes and is safe (NC 9) and Diana has recently given birth to a daughter (NC 10). Yet his former servant, Padeen Colman, is now a convict in Sydney and is being severely mistreated (NC 9,10) and transported United Irishmen prisoners have come to believe Stephen to be a traitor and informant (NC 10; *we also learn here that his own first language was Irish*). Whilst ashore, Stephen and Martin take several opportunities to ex-

plore the natural riches of the colony, the pair also laying plans to help Padeen escape in *Surprise* (NC 9,10). Jack, however, refuses to countenance such a direct breach of the law, occasioning a serious row between him and the Doctor (NC 10). The awkward situation is resolved by Stephen's near death ashore from a platypus sting. As Padeen helps bring him aboard the departing *Surprise*, Jack appears to accept the *fait accompli* of his presence (NC 10).

As ***Clarissa Oakes*** (published in the USA as ***The Truelove***) opens, the recovered Stephen is *en route* to resuming, at long last, the South American mission. At some point he has sold his ship, now HM Hired Vessel *Surprise*, to Jack Aubrey (C/T 1). Having given a vigorous demonstration of Irish dancing for the wedding of the stowaway convict, Clarissa Oakes (C/T 2), Stephen then treats her for a deep-seated venereal infection, gaining her close friendship in the process (C/T 3+). Having learned from Clarissa her history of sexual abuse and of her later employment at Mother Abbott's society brothel in London, Stephen achieves the long-awaited *coup* of identifying the secret patron of his old foes, the now-deceased traitors Wray and Ledward, who had all been frequenters of the house (C/T 6,7). He helps to arrange Clarissa's journey back to England so that she might give further valuable information to the intelligence chief Sir Joseph Blaine (C/T 9). During the course of *Surprise*'s cruise, Stephen learns by letter of the strangeness of his new baby daughter, Brigid, and senses Diana's probable severe post-natal depression (C/T 3). *(N.B. later, in* COM 2, *Stephen and Clarissa mis-recall the sequence of events in their Pacific cruise together, especially confusing the roles of the ships* *Surprise *and* *Nutmeg.)*

At the opening of ***The Wine Dark Sea*** Stephen is still in *Surprise*, heading towards the coast of Peru in pursuit of *Franklin*, a privateer owned by the French social revolutionary Jean Dutourd. During the long chase they encounter a curious, violent volcanic eruption from the sea-bed (WDS 1). When *Franklin* is finally taken, Stephen is somewhat concerned that Dutourd may recognize him from their days in Paris and guess at his intentions for Peru: this does indeed happen, but only slowly and uncertainly (WDS 2–5). During the remaining voyage, Stephen treats Nathaniel Martin for self-inflicted mercury poisoning (WDS 5) and, on arrival in Lima, arranges for him to take passage home in a merchantman (WDS 6). In Peru, the Doctor meets his various political contacts and begins to arrange a rebellion against Spanish rule, being aided in this by Jack Aubrey's natural son, Sam Panda, now a Catholic priest (WDS 6–8). Yet, the political situation has changed since the plans were first laid in London — indeed Chile now seems to offer better opportunities than does Peru (WDS 7) — and French agents are also present. Stephen presses ahead, but with less confidence than he might earlier have possessed (WDS 7,8). At a crucial point, Dutourd escapes from Jack's custody at sea (WDS 7), arrives in Lima and denounces the English plot (WDS 8). Stephen flees across the high Andes to Arica (WDS 8,9) and thence to Chile, where he rejoins *Surprise* off Valparaiso, eventually heading home to England in company with Heneage Dundas's HMS *Berenice* (WDS 10). Throughout the adventure he has endured a feeling of great apprehension about his wife, Diana, and his unseen daughter, Brigid (WDS 1+).

The Commodore opens with Stephen still homeward-bound in *Surprise* (COM 1). On arrival in London he is asked by Sir Joseph Blaine to support the newly appointed Commodore Jack Aubrey, first in suppressing the slave trade in West Africa and in then intercepting a planned French invasion of Ireland (COM 2+). For this second mission Stephen assures Blaine that he has always dreaded French, especially *Buonapartist* French, interference in Irish affairs even more than he longs for his country's self-rule (COM 2,7,10; *see also* M&C 5). Before departing anew, Stephen has first to attend to important domestic matters. He meets his daughter Brigid for the first time, being much disturbed by her withdrawn strangeness (COM 2+), and renews his friendship with the now-widowed Clarissa Oakes, who is looking after the girl (COM 2–5). He then searches unsuccessfully for Diana, who has once again left home, this time partly because of her daughter's condition and partly because she is convinced that Stephen and Clarissa have been lovers at sea (COM 2+). At least Stephen still possesses his fortune, never having properly signed the documents that would have transferred it to the now-broken bank of Smith and Clowes (COM 2). Blaine soon reveals that Wray and Ledward's hitherto-secret, traitorous patron, the powerful Duke of Habachtsthal, has discovered both Stephen's role in his minions' deaths and Clarissa Oakes' role in his own exposure (COM 4). The intelligence chief advises Stephen to transfer his money and loved ones temporarily out of the country and Brigid, Clarissa and Padeen Colman all go with the Doctor to Spain (COM 4+), the gentle Padeen slowly drawing the child out of her shell (COM 3–5). Blaine also reminds his friend that, because he could even now be prosecuted for his long-past role in the 1798 United Irishmen uprising, a general pardon has been quietly obtained for him. However, the Duke's enmity means that its validity might yet be questioned (COM 4). Nevertheless, Stephen can now join Jack's HMS *Bellona* for the West African mission (COM 6–9), towards the end of which he contracts a near-fatal dose of yellow fever (COM 9). Following Jack's subsequent defeat of the French squadron off the coast of Ireland, Stephen goes ashore and there prevents a potentially disastrous – for the local popu-

lation – rebellion against the Crown (COM 10). To his joy, he finds his wife staying with an elderly relative nearby and is reunited with her, soon learning with great relief that Habachtsthal, on the point of exposure, has killed himself in London (COM 10).

(N.B., from an aside in the book, at COM 7, we learn that Stephen's birthday is probably Lady Day, the Catholic Feast of the Annunciation that falls on March 25th.)

At the opening of *The Yellow Admiral* Stephen has been in Spain with Diana and Brigid, in part to recover the fortune he had deposited there on Sir Joseph Blaine's advice. However, having carelessly left the crucial bank receipt in England and too embarrassed to visit the bank in question without it, he has been forced to return empty-handed (YA 1). This foolishness had nevertheless been a stroke of great fortune, for Jean Dutourd (*see* WDS 8) has turned up in Spain and denounced Stephen as a spy: the Maturins – unknowingly – have avoided a trap laid for them at their bank in Corunna by instead taking a leisurely family holiday before returning to England to find the precious docket (YA 1). Although his fortune is now seized by the Spanish authorities, Stephen has the compensation of finally receiving his pardon for the events of 1798 (*see* COM 4) and being invited to live with his family and retainers at the Aubrey's Woolcombe House (YA 2+). His political attentions have once more turned to South America and the possibility of Chilean independence from Spain, with he and Blaine also seeing a possible future role for Jack Aubrey in training a new Chilean navy (YA 4,8+). In the meantime, Stephen continues service aboard HMS *Bellona* (treating the seriously ill Admiral Lord Stranraer, Jack's naval superior and political enemy: YA 4,7+), goes ashore in France on an intelligence mission (YA 4) and exposes the spy Diego Diaz in London (YA 7). As the war with Buonaparte draws to its close, Stephen receives Admiralty support for the Chilean proposal (YA 7+) and obtains a senior position for Jack in the purely naval aspects of the scheme (YA 8,10). He also recovers – by some method unspecified – his impounded fortune from the Spanish authorities (YA 8). Following Buonaparte's abdication *(April 6th, 1814)*, Stephen and Jack are sent home to refit *Surprise* – which now appears once again to belong to the Doctor – for South America (YA 10). Once this task is complete, the pair sail with their families to Madeira to enjoy a short holiday *en route* to Chile. However, whilst on the island, they receive news of Buonaparte's escape from Elba *(early March, 1815)* and Jack's immediate recall to the Royal Navy as a Commodore (YA 10).

The Hundred Days opens with Stephen Maturin about to arrive at Gibraltar aboard Jack Aubrey's HMS *Pomone*: yet much has happened since the happy days on Madeira (HD 1). Diana has returned to England and there immediately been killed, along with her cousin Cholmondeley, Mrs Williams and others, in a coaching accident: Stephen, who has returned to England to deal with the catastrophe, seems emotionally numb, using his loathing of the restored Buonaparte to distract him from his personal grief (HD 1). At Gibraltar he is briefed on the complex political situation in south-eastern Europe, where certain Moslem sects, strongly Buonapartist, are trying to finance both the building of new warships and guerrilla-like activity aimed at preventing the union of Russian and Austrian armies against the Emperor. With an old intelligence colleague, Dr Amos Jacob, Stephen is to work with Jack Aubrey to disrupt these plans (HD1,2). After arranging both the subversion of some loyalties in the Adriatic and the destruction of the local Buonapartist ship-yards by fire (HD 3–5), Stephen travels to Algiers, hoping there to persuade the Dey to prohibit passage of the Moroccan gold of Sheikh Ibn Hazm to the eastern militants (HD 6). After consultations with the British consul, Stephen and Jacob set off into the hinterland to meet, first, Vizier Hashin and then the new Dey himself, Omar Pasha (HD 6): the Algerian Sahara of course stimulates Stephen's abiding interest in the natural world (HD 7). Although Stephen is successful in securing Omar Pasha's co-operation — at least in part because he saves the Dey's life during a nocturnal lion hunt — he learns, via Jacob, that the Vizier is in league with Ibn Hazm (HD 7). Once back in Algiers itself, Stephen finds that Omar has been deposed and murdered and that the treasure is now to be transported by sea direct from Morocco's Atlantic coast to the Adriatic, news that he must urgently communicate to Jack Aubrey at sea (HD 8). Accompanied by Jacob and the two young Irish children, the FitzPatricks, he has redeemed from slavery, Stephen returns to Gibraltar in *Ringle* and lays his information before the naval authorities (HD 8). Jack Aubrey is given the task of intercepting the treasure-galley, successfully doing so after a long chase (HD 9,10). On their triumphant return to Gibraltar, Stephen and Jack learn that Buonaparte has finally been defeated at Waterloo and soon receive orders to resume their mission to South American waters (HD 10).

> The name Maturin (which is pronounced with the stress on the first syllable), usually thought to indicate French Huguenot— i.e., Protestant— origins, is not especially uncommon in France or Ireland, yet it is an intriguingly unusual name for a Catholic such as Stephen to bear. As to possible inspirations for the name, a Charles Robert Maturin (1782–1824) of Dublin's Trinity College was a successful writer of Gothic novels of the 'Napoleonic' period and in O'Brian's own 1952 novel, Testimonies (not a sea-tale), there is a passing reference to a Mr Maturin, a former university colleague of the narrator, Joseph Aubrey Pugh.

Maudsley, Captain
The Captain of HMS *Juno*, an old friend of Jack Aubrey (SM 9).

Maule, Serjeant
The lawyer defending Jack Aubrey's supposed co-conspirator, Cummings, at their trial for fraud (RM 8).

> The Serjeants were a superior class of lawyers from whose ranks the Common Law judges were drawn. The name here may perhaps be borrowed from the barrister, publisher and legal commentator, George Maule (1776–1851).

Maurya
see **Joyce, Maurya**

Mausolus
A classical figure married to Artemesia (SM 8).

> Mausoleus became King of Caria in about 377 BC and then embarked on an ambitious series of conquests in both Persia and Greece. After his death, in about 353 BC, his sister *Artemesia, with whom he had also made an incestuous marriage, completed as his tomb the great shrine that he had earlier begun for himself, the 'Mausoleum' at Haliacarnassus.

Maxwell
A seaman in HMS *Irresistible* who had once served with Jack Aubrey (RM 1).

Mead, Dr
The maker of a patent medicine (HMS 4).

> The name may perhaps be inspired by that of the leading society doctor Richard Mead (1673–1754) who, from 1727 onwards, was physician to King George II, a role that game him an influential voice in all aspects of public medicine. He had also been a pupil and friend of *Booerhaave and was a translator of *Rhazes. Mead became especially interested in the prevention of contagious fevers and was a leading advocate of both inoculation and the benefits of well-circulated, fresh air. This focus on transmittable diseases, though admirable in many circumstances, led him into error on the origins of scurvy on long-distance sea-voyages, believing as he did that the complaint was associated more with cramped and fetid conditions that dietary deficiencies. Mead was also a strong advocate of treating certain fevers with a copious, forced inhalation of tobacco smoke.

Meadows
1: a volunteer in HMS *Surprise*, one of the members of the larboard Midshipman's mess who steal and eat Maturin's experimental rats (HMS 6).
2: a General referred to in a letter from Nelson to Admiral Russell (LM 1).
> Sir William Meadows (1738–1813) served as a full Colonel under Commodore *Johnstone on the Cape of Good Hope expedition of 1781–1782 and between 1783 and 1792 was Commander-in-Chief of Bombay and, subsequently, Madras. Promoted General in 1793, he briefly held the position of Commander-in-Chief, Ireland, in 1801.

Meadows, Henry
A young relative of the Commissioner of Plymouth Dockyard, Captain Fanshaw, whom Jack Aubrey enters on HMS *Worcester*'s books as captain's servant (IM 2).

'Mealy-Mouth'
see **Firkins**

Meares
1: a Midshipman in HMS *Ariel* (SM 9).
2: a Royal Navy Commander met by Aubrey and Pullings on the island of Gozo (TH 2).
3: the gunner of HMS *Bellona* (COM 6,9,10; YA 9).

Medea
The classical figure to whom Maturin compares the dangerous side of Clarissa Oakes' personality (C/T 3,4,6).
*In Greek myth, Medea is always portrayed as a scheming woman, capable of the greatest ferocity in pursuit of her interests. In the renowned Euripides setting of her tale, she is the wife the Argonaut *Jason who, when abandoned by him for a younger bride, slaughters both her rival and her own children in an act of terrible revenge.*

Medea
The 40-gun Spanish frigate leading Admiral Bustamente's bullion squadron from South America to Spain. She is captured by Commodore Graham's squadron (PC 14; HMS 6).
*Following the October 1804 action, Medea was taken into the Royal Navy as HMS *Iphigeneia. In 1805 she was renamed HMS Impérieuse and was for a time famously commanded by Lord *Cochrane. Sent for harbour service in 1818, she was sold in 1838.*

Medusa, HMS
A member of the squadron that takes Bustamente's Spanish treasure ships (PC 14), by implication she is commanded by Captain Collins (HMS 1).
*HMS Medusa, 32-gun, was launched in 1800 and broken up in 1816. In the 1804 action against the Spaniards she was commanded not by the fictional *Collins but by John Gore (a brief note on whom may be found in Collins' main entry). In classical myth, Medusa was the youngest of the *Gorgon sisters, hideous maidens whose hair was made of writhing serpents and who turned into stone anyone who gazed on them. Medusa was eventually decapitated by the hero Perseus.*

Méduse
A new French 74-gun, pursued by Jack Aubrey's HMS *Ariel*, in company with HMS *Jason* (SM 9). Jack later learns that she was taken by HMS *Ajax*, in sight of HMSS *Ardent* and *Swiftsure* (SM 11).
*At the time of SM the Méduse in French service was a frigate, rather than a ship-of-the-line, that had been launched in 1810, serving until being wrecked in 1816. She was named for the *Gorgon *Medusa.*

Meiklejohn
The official who manages Jack Aubrey's Sea-Fencibles office (DI 1).

Meilhan, Sénac de
see **Sénac de Meilhan**

Mela, Pomponius
The author of *De Situ Orbis*, seen here in a printing by Elzevier (COM 9).
Pomponius Mela (fl. 50 AD) was a Roman geographer from southern Spain who produced an influential work (descriptive and without a drawn map, although he suggests he may have had one available to him), tracking the known coasts of the world and remarking on what demographic, ethnographic and fabulous details were known of them. The work is various known as De Situ Orbis ('On the Situation of the World') or De Chorographia ('On Geography').

Melampus, HMS
A frigate mentioned several times in passing (DI 5; SM 7; IM 6; COM 5).
HMS Melampus, 36-gun, was launched in 1785 and, after rather an uneventful career, sold to the Dutch navy in 1815. In Greek myth, Melampus was said to be the first mortal to practise medicine.

Melbury, Captain
A name by which Joan Maragall, Stephen Maturin's Minorcan associate, addresses Jack Aubrey (HMS 2).
The name, obviously suggested by Stephen in order to establish Maragall's bona fides with Jack, is taken from 'Melbury Lodge,' the Sussex home that the pair shared in PC.

Meleager, HMS
A frigate recently wrecked on Barebush Cay (TMC 1).
*HMS Meleager, 36-gun, was launched in 1806 and wrecked, following a misjudgement by her Master, off Jamaica in July 1808. In Greek myth, Meleager is primarily portrayed as the hero of the Calydonian boar-hunt but is also sometimes given as one of *Jason's Argonauts.*

Mellish
A seaman in HMS *Surprise* (HMS 8).

Mellows
A doctor and Fellow of the Royal Society who is regarded by Maturin as a quack (DI 2).

Melon
A gunner's mate in *Surprise* (C/T 4).

Melpomène, HMS
A frigate in Admiral Harte's squadron (PC 7), said to be a poor sailer (HMS 2). Barret Bonden had once served in her (HD 9).
The 38-gun Melpomène was launched by the French in 1789 and captured by the Royal Navy in 1794. Taken into service under the same name, she was eventually sold in 1815. In classical myth, Melpomene was the Muse of Tragedy and mother of the Sirens.

Melsom, John
A seaman in HMS *Sophie* (M&C 10).

Melville, Lady
The wife of the First Lord of the Admiralty (PC 12).
*Lady Jane Hope (d.1829) was the second wife of Henry Dundas, 1st Viscount *Melville, having married him in*

*1793. She was not the parent of Robert, 2nd Viscount *Melville (nor therefore of the younger, fictional Heneage *Dundas), whose mother, Elizabeth Rennie, had married Henry in 1765. After her first husband's death in 1811, Lady Jane was remarried in 1814 to Thomas, Lord Wallace.*

Melville, Lord or Viscount

1: the First Lord of the Admiralty, of whom Jack Aubrey is something of a protégé (PC 5+). Lord St Vincent is trying to have him impeached for financial irregularities (PC 10) and he is later said to be nearly out of office, in part because he is unable openly to discuss his disbursement of the secret intelligence funds (PC 14; *also* HMS 1; IM 10; *a reference in DI 2 could be to either Melville, but is probably to the elder*).

*Henry Dundas (1742–1811), 1st Viscount Melville, was a leading member of a very large and influential Edinburgh family of lawyers, Tory politicians, soldiers and sailors. In the 1780s he served as Treasurer to the Navy before becoming Home Secretary in 1791 and Secretary of War in 1794. Created Viscount Melville in late 1802, he became *First Lord of the Admiralty in May 1804. However, in 1805 he was forced to resign following allegations of financial scandals in his early Navy Treasurer days; impeached before the House of Lords in 1806, he was acquitted yet never again held office. In 1809 Melville was offered, but declined, an Earldom. In the series Henry is always referred to as 'Lord Melville' or simply 'Melville.' References to 'Viscount Melville' are always to his son, Robert (see below), although he too is occasionally spoken of simply as 'Lord' ('Lord' being a perfectly correct form of informal address to a Viscount).*

2: Robert Dundas, the elder brother of Heneage (PC 6) and the son of Lord Melville, the First Lord of the Admiralty (PC 12). In due course Robert succeeds his father as both Viscount Melville and First Lord (SM 4,6; IM 1,4; TH 1; RM 5,8; LM 4–7; COM 1; YA 3,7,8). In this latter capacity he appears as a defence witness for Jack Aubrey at his fraud trial (RM 8) and later reinstates the now-cleared Jack to the Royal Navy in return for his support in Parliament (LM 8; TGS 1,4). Robert and Heneage are seldom on good terms, not least because of the elder brother's disapproval of the younger's siring of so many children out of wedlock (e.g. RM 8; WDS 5,10; COM 1).

*Robert Sanders Dundas (1771–1851), 2nd Viscount Melville, was the only son of Henry Dundas, 1st Viscount (see above), whose title he inherited in 1811. In 1812 he too became *First Lord of the Admiralty, a position he then occupied for 16 years with only a few short gaps. Like his father, Robert was a Tory politician and statesman who never served as a sea officer (despite the implications of the first Lord Melville's remark in PC 12 about his son's problems with a prize-agent). His own second son, Sir Richard Sanders Dundas (1802–1861), did enter the service, serving with considerable distinction and rising to Rear-Admiral in 1853.*

Mendoza

1: a Barcelona merchant (PC 6).
2: a professional intelligence agent working for the British Admiralty, recently captured in Spain (PC 14).
3: a famous prize-fighter (FSW 9), beaten in 1797 by his rival Gentleman Jackson (YA 3).

*Daniel Mendoza (1765?–1836) was the first British Jew to gain fame and acceptance as a professional fighter, eventually becoming Champion of England. In 1795 (sic) he defended his title against Gentleman *Jackson but the bout ended when the challenger seized Mendoza's much-prized pigtail and then battered him senseless, a scene somewhat reminiscent of Barret *Bonden's defeat by Black *Evans in YA.*

4: a General in Peru who had been a potential rebel against direct Spanish rule until his recent accidental death (WDS 7).
5: a member of the independence movement in Chile (YA 7).

Menhasset

A seaman in HMS *Lively* (PC 12).

Mennonites

A religious sect mentioned by Mr Martin (WDS 3).

The sect is named for the Dutch priest Menno Simonsz (1496–1561), a leading member of the peaceful wing of the Anabaptist movement who wrote extensively on the religious controversies of his day, emphasising the virtues of hard work, a love of neighbours and a simple, open belief in scriptural doctrine.

Menoglu Bey

A potentate in the Ionian region involved in violent disputes with his neighbours (IM 9).

Mentor, HMS

A ship anchored at Portsmouth whose paid-off crew then burn an effigy of her unpopular First Lieutenant (DI 1).

Mercedes or Mercy

A pretty chambermaid at the Crown Inn, Port Mahon, to whom Jack Aubrey is very strongly attracted (M&C 1+). She is also a useful source of intelligence on local shipping movements (M&C 8,9). Many years later, now married to the Crown's owner, she and Jack come close to renewing their former intimacy (IM 7).

Mercedes

A 34-gun Spanish frigate, part of Admiral Bustamente's treasure squadron, that explodes in the action against the British squadron including Jack Aubrey's HMS *Lively* (PC 14; HMS 6).

*In this action of October 1804, Mercedes blew up alongside Samuel *Sutton's HMS *Amphion within minutes of the start of the fight.*

Mercier, General

The officer sent by General Oudinot to take command of the garrison on Grimsholm island. Whilst trying to escape from the captured *Minnie*, he is killed by cannon-fire from Jack Aubrey's HMS *Ariel* (SM 7,9,11).

Mercy
see **Mercedes**

Merlin
An American merchant schooner, Master Mr Dupont, the first prize taken by Jack Aubrey and *Surprise* after his dismissal from the Royal Navy (LM 3).

Merry-Andrew
A reference to the generic name for fairground assistants (TH 4), often gaily dressed (COM 5). The term is also used as a reference to foolish sailors (TMC 3; YA 8).

> BREWER gives Dr Andrew Borde (1500–1549), a physician to King *Henry VIII, as a possible source for the term. He took to addressing fairground crowds on medical matters, holding their attention with his clowning wit and bright clothes.

Mersennius, Dr
The doctor who treats Maturin's broken leg in Stockholm (LM 9).

Messiah
The great oratorio by Handel, performed by the musical crew of Jack Aubrey's HMS *Worcester* (IM 5–8; FSW 3).

> 'Messiah'— Hebrew for 'anointed'— refers to the anticipated saviour of the Jewish people. In Christianity, the term refers specifically to *Jesus Christ. *Handel's work was first performed in 1742.

Metcalf
1: a young relative of Admiral Hughes (FSW 2).
2: a shipping agent in Valparaiso (FSW 6).

Methusalem
1: a reference to great age (SM 1; TGS 1; C/T 8; YA 9).

> In the Old Testament, Methusalem (the common spelling in French; Methusalah in English), a son of Enoch, was supposed to have died at the age of 969, shortly before the great flood.

2: a seaman in either *Surprise* or HMS *Nutmeg of Consolation* (NC 6).

Metrodorus of Lampsacus
An author who had argued that Homer's Gods were simply personifications of natural phenomena (FSW 4).

> Metrodorus was a pupil of Anaxagoras (500?–428? BC), the first recorded philosopher to settle in Athens. The master later moved his 'school' to Lampsacus, where his pupil then produced his work on Homer's epic poetry. A later, and better-known, Metrodorus of Lampsacus (331?–278 BC) was a close associate of the moral philosopher Epicurus and a founder with him of the famous retreat, the Epicurean Garden.

Meuron, Hercule de
A Swiss officer who had commanded the Dutch garrison at Colombo, Ceylon, and whose loyalty had later been subverted by Professor Graham (IM 8).

> The private Régiment Meuron was established in Switzerland in 1781 by Charles-Daniel, Comte de Meuron (1738–1806), and was often commanded in the field by his brother Pierre-Frédéric (1746–1813) or other members of the family (which did not include an Hercule). The regiment's first client was the Dutch East India Company, which it served at the Cape of Good Hope and, from 1788, Ceylon. By 1791 the Comte, a deeply conservative man, had grown most unhappy at political developments in Europe and consequently visited London to make contact with the British government. Here he also encountered (for the second time) the Scotsman Hugh Cleghorn (1751–?1837), a Professor of History at St Andrew's University, who for some years had been a member of the British secret service, being especially active in Switzerland (where the Chargé d'Affaires was William Wickham [1761–1840], a man described in his DNB entry as the British government's "principal spy on the continent"). De Meuron and Cleghorn became firm friends and, over the next few years, kept up a political correspondence. In early 1795 William *Pitt and Henry Dundas, Lord *Melville, devised a scheme to seize Ceylon from Dutch/French control, intending thus to secure British operations in India. Cleghorn was sent to Switzerland and there persuaded his friend the Comte to agree to transfer his regiment to British control, the price for which was to include Generalships for both of the de Meuron brothers. Cleghorn and Charles-Daniel now travelled to Southern India (encountering en-route many adventures and hardships that find an echo in Stephen *Maturin's professional career as an intelligence agent). Here it was necessary to get a message to Pierre-Frédéric, commanding the regiment on the ground: a tricky task, accomplished, according to Cleghorn, by smuggling a note to him in a cheese under the very noses of the Dutch authorities (the Regimental History of the de Meuron casts doubt on the authenticity of this ruse)! With the Swiss forces now standing aside, the army of the British East India Company was able to easily oust the Dutch administration, Ceylon coming largely under British control in 1796, becoming a Crown colony in 1798 and, in 1803, being formally ceded to London by Holland. (N.b., Maturin makes a slip of the tongue when he says the 1795–1796 operation was prompted by *Buonaparte's seizure of Holland. At the time, the French general was commanding in Italy and was still some years from seizing political power; it was, however, his defeat of the Austrian rulers of Holland that led to London's rupture with the authorities in the Low Countries themselves.)
>
> In 1798, Hugh Cleghorn became Chief Secretary to the first British Governor of Ceylon, but was dismissed in 1800 (probably for financial irregularities) and returned, a wealthy man, to retirement in Scotland. The de Meuron regiment went on to serve under *Wellington in India (where they formed the 'Forlorn Hope' assault battalion on *Tippoo Sahib's Seringapatam) and the Iberian Peninsula. In 1813 they were transferred to the British army operating in Canada for the war with the U.S., being eventually disbanded in 1816.

Mexico, Emperor of

A madman at Choate's hospital in Boston, also known as the Duke of Montezuma (FW 4,5,6).
see **Montezuma, Duke of**

Meyer

The banker Nathan's younger brother (RM 5).
See ***Rothschild, Nathan** *for the derivation of the name.*

Meyrick, Lord

Babbington's newly ennobled uncle, until recently plain Mr Gardner (LM 7).

Michel

A supplier of medical glassware in Paris (SM 10).

Middleton

A Royal Navy officer promoted Commander into the desirable HMS *Vertueuse* at the same time as Jack Aubrey's promotion into the less desirable HMS *Sophie* (M&C 2).

Middleton, Jo

The Captain of HMS *Jason* (SM 9).

Midhat Bimbashi

The commander of the Turkish forces attached to Aubrey's Mubara expedition (TH 6).

Migueletes

The family name of a group of Spanish bandits (PC 4).

Miller

1: Mrs Miller, the vivacious, married sister of Lieutenant Dashwood of HMS *Lively*, who travels briefly in the ship as a passenger, together with her young son, Brydges (PC 13,14).

2: the Captain of HMS *Euryalus*, met at sea by Jack Aubrey's HMS *Surprise*. He roundly berates Jack, his junior, for approaching his ship in the dark, fully cleared for action and showing no lights (HMS 11).

3: 'One-eyed' Miller, the captain-of-the-foretop in Aubrey's HMS *Leopard* and Barret Bonden's cousin (DI 4).

4: a seaman in Aubrey's HMS *Worcester* (IM 3).

5: a Lieutenant in HMS *Goliath*, a published poet (IM 3).

6: Mrs Miller, a ferocious lady of Aubrey's acquaintance (RM 3).

7: a Midshipman accidentally left behind in Batavia by HMS *Clio* who then joins Aubrey's HMS *Nutmeg of Consolation*, initially as an ordinary seaman. Soon re-rated Midshipman, he is killed in the *Cornélie* action (NC 4,5; C/T 7).

8: the Third Lieutenant of HMS *Bellona* (COM 7,8,10; YA 6).

Milo of Crotona

A classical figure, famous for strength, to whom Maturin and Graham compare the puny Mr Calamy (IM 4,8).

Milo, or Milon, of Croton (fl. late 6th century BC) was a champion athlete and wrestler who was supposed to have carried a bull around the arena before killing it with a single blow and eating it for dinner at a single sitting. Milo, having later become stuck fast in the cleft of a tree he was trying to split with his bare hands, was devoured by wolves.

Milton

The great poet referred to by Jack Aubrey (TMC 6).

John Milton (1608–1674), the author of Paradise Lost *(published 1671), was also a prolific author of elegant, shorter verse in a variety of languages and the writer of many influential pamphlets on the political and moral controversies of his day; from 1654 onwards, he was completely blind. Following the execution of King Charles I, Milton—a wealthy man who did not otherwise pursue any public career—acted as Latin Secretary to the republican Council of State until the restoration of *Charles II in 1660.*

Mindham

Philip Broke's coxswain in HMS *Shannon* (FW 9).

There seems to be a little confusion in the sources over who acted as *Broke's coxswain on HMS *Shannon on the day of the battle with USS *Chesapeake. *Brighton's memoir states in its narrative that Billy Mindham (dates unknown) had the job but, in a table of the wounded, gives the title to one William Stack. Peter Padfield's Broke and the Shannon *(Hodder and Stoughton, 1968) states that William Stack was indeed cox'n, being wounded by grape and musket fire in both arms sometime after cutting down one of Broke's assailants. Padfield gives Mindham as the captain of the aftermost maindeck gun, who later tended to the wounded Broke on* Chesapeake's *deck.*

Minerva or *Minerve*

A Portuguese frigate taken by *Bellone* and her prize, the ex–HMS *Victor*. Taken into French service, she becomes *Minerve* (TMC 5+). One of the many ships that run aground during the Battle of Port South East (TMC 7), she is later rumoured to have recently been damaged by disaffected Papists or Royalists on Mauritius (TMC 10).

The Portuguese 40-gun Minerva, *launched in 1807, was taken by* Bellone *in November 1809. According to *James, the French squadron in the Indian Ocean was so short-handed that they were forced to crew her with a large number of Irish Catholics captured from British ships; perhaps *Maturin somehow then subverts his countrymen's new allegiance.* Minerve *was taken by *Bertie's squadron when Mauritius finally fell in late 1810 and, although her fate thereafter is unrecorded in British and French sources, she was probably returned to Portugal, Britain's ally.* Minerva *was the Etruscan and Roman*

Goddess of handicrafts, often identified with *Athena/Pallas.

Minerva, HMS

Referred to by Jack Aubrey as a ship, Captain Soules, in which he had served when very young (WDS 1).

HMS Minerva, 38-gun, was launched in 1780 and, in 1797, fought under Captain George *Cockburn at the Battle of Cape *St Vincent. Renamed as the troopship HMS *Pallas in 1798, she was broken up in 1803.

Minerve, HMS

A 38-gun frigate encountered by HMS *Polychrest* at sea (PC 5,7).

The 38-gun Minerve was launched by the French in 1794, captured by the Royal Navy in 1795 and then, whilst under Jahleel *Brenton, stranded and recaptured by France in August of 1803. In 1809, now re-named Canonnière, she was sold into commercial service as Confiance. In 1810 she was once again taken by the Royal Navy and, as HMS Confiance, then served until at least 1814.

Minnie

A Danish merchantman and privateer in which Jack Aubrey suspects that the French officers, Mercier and Ligier, are en route to Grimsholm (SM 8). Trying to run, *Minnie* grounds on a sandbank and is taken, with the escaping Frenchmen then being killed by HMS *Ariel*'s canon fire (SM 8,9). Under the temporary command of Mr Wittgenstein, she now takes Stephen Maturin into Grimsholm (SM 8).

Minotaur, HMS

A ship present at the Battle of Trafalgar (FW 2).

HMS Minotaur, 74-gun, was launched in 1793 and first commanded by *Nelson's friend, Thomas *Louis. Under him, she fought at the Battle of the Nile in 1798 and in 1800 spent time as one of Lord *Keith's several flagships. At Trafalgar in 1805, by now under Captain Charles Mansfield (d.1813), she had a relatively easy time, coming through the fight with only 3 fatalities and little damage. However, in 1810, under John Barrett, she was wrecked off the Dutch coast in thick fog, her Captain and some 400 others losing their lives in the disaster. Minotaur was named for the legendary half-man, half-bull slain by the Greek hero, *Theseus.

Mirza

A troop transport, Master Mr Smithson, in Jack Aubrey's convoy to Spain (SM 9).

Mirza Shah

A retired potentate in Calcutta (HMS 10).

Miss

A reference to Sophie Aubrey (*then still Miss Williams*) by Killick (HMS 2).

Missus

A pronunciation of 'Mrs,' and itself British slang for 'wife' (passim).

Mitchell

The present Captain of Jack Aubrey's old HMS *Boadicea*, now on the Brest blockade (SM 9).

Mitchell, Aaron

A seaman and mutineer from HMS *Hermione*. Captured by Jack Aubrey from USS *Norfolk*, he is court-martialed in HMS *Irresistible* and sentenced to hang (RM 2).

Mitchell or Mitchel, Admiral William

Admiral Sir John Thornton's third-in-command in the Mediterranean (IM 3) who leads the inshore squadron as Rear Admiral of the Blue (IM 4–8). A former pressed seaman, Jack Aubrey says he was once flogged round the fleet for repeated desertion (IM 4; *also* WDS 1, *where he is said now to have risen to Vice Admiral*). A very fit man, he races Jack up and down a mast of his flagship, HMS *San Josef* (IM 4; *also* YA 5).

Sir William Mitchell (1745?–1816) served from 1766 to 1768 as an able seaman on *Wallis' HMS *Dolphin. He became a Midshipman in about 1777 and in 1781 was commissioned Lieutenant. A Commander of 1782 and a Post Captain of 1790, in 1797 he commanded HMS *Isis at the Battle of Camperdown and in 1803 became the Flag Captain of Admiral *Saumarez' HMS Zealand. Captain Sir John Ross (1777–1856), in his memoir of his days as a Lieutenant and Commander under *Saumarez, remarks in passing that Mitchell was known for having been flogged round the fleet but provides no further details. In 1807 Mitchell was appointed to a Sea Fencibles command ashore in England and, in 1808, promoted Rear Admiral; he rose to Vice Admiral in 1813 and was knighted in 1815. Sir William also enjoys a later distinction, for his DNB entry (in the 'Missing Persons' supplement) is written by Patrick O'Brian himself.

Mnason

The Aubrey family butler at Woolcombe House (COM 4; YA 1,3,10).

Mocatta

A Jewish family closely connected with the Cannings and the Goldsmids (HMS 1, 7)

The Mocatta family were a leading family of British Jews, famous for using the wealth and influence they derived from their activities as financiers to promote both understanding of Jewish history and culture as well as the political and religious emancipation of their faith. Originally named Lumbrozo, the family had been driven from Spain in 1492 with one branch arriving in England in about 1670. The name Mocatta — officially adopted in 1790 — was taken from a maternal ancestor and it was under this title that, in about 1780, Abraham Lumbrozo de Mattos helped found the important *firm of Mocatta and *Goldsmid, London bullion brokers.*

Mocenigo

The keeper of a tavern on the island of Gozo (TH 2).

Moghul

The scent bought by Stephen Maturin for Diana Villiers reminds her of the 'Moghul's harem' (PC 8) and the name is later used by Admiral Dommet as a figure for pride (SM 6). The name is also guessed at by Stephen for Diana's great 'Begum' diamond before he — wrongly — recalls the gem as the 'Blue Peter,' the name by which it is henceforth known (SM 3).

> *'Moghul' (or 'Mogal'/'Mughal') is the name of the Muslim dynasty, descendants of the Mongolian Ghengis Khan, who ruled North India from 1526 to 1761 and who then remained in some diminished power, under British rule, until 1858. An enormous diamond called 'The Great Moghul,' now long disappeared, was discovered in India in the 17th century and named for Shah Jehan, the builder of the Taj Mahal.*

Mohamet

A guide used by Maturin in Calcutta (HMS 10).

Mohammed Pasha of Barka

Sir John Thornton states that Mohammed has deposed his brother Jaffar, an English ally, as Pasha of Barka, a situation that the Admiral wishes to see reversed (IM 4,6).

> *Note that the competing Pashas of Barka are later said by Jack Aubrey to have been *Esmin and his son *Muley (IM 7).*

Molina

1: an author recited in his delirium by Maturin (HMS 11).

> *The reference is presumably to Luis Molina (1535?–1600?), a Spanish Jesuit theologian who in 1588 made a famous and controversial attempt to reconcile the seemingly opposed doctrines of free-will and predestination.*

2: the llama used by Maturin and Eduardo in their crossing of the Andes who then dies of exposure in a storm (WDS 9).

Molly

1: a servant in the Williams household (PC 1; YA 6).

2: an imaginary person referred to by the mad Mr Lowndes (PC 8).

Molter

A composer referred to by Stephen Maturin (PC 14) who, many years later, forgets he has ever heard of him (FSW 4).

> *Johann Melchior Molter (1696–1765), a prolific German composer, spent his early years in Venice and Rome before becoming Kapellmeister at Baden and then Eisenach.*

Mona

1: a former love of Stephen Maturin, lost to him in the sad events of 1798 (TGS 4).

2: *see* **FitzPatrick, Kevin and Mona**

Monarch, HMS

The ship aboard which Jack Aubrey is court-martialled and acquitted for the loss of HMS *Polychrest* (PC 12).

> *HMS* Monarch, *74-gun, was launched in 1765 and, in a 48-year long career, had the distinction of participating in no less than 13 significant campaigns and great fleet actions. Amongst these were *Rodney's victory at the Saintes in 1782, *Duncan's at Camperdown in 1797 and *Nelson's at Copenhagen in 1801. At the time of PC, she was Admiral Lord *Keith's usual flagship in the Mediterranean.* Monarch *was finally broken up in 1813.*

Moncousu, Captain

French Captain of *Indomptable*, killed in action against Saumarez' squadron (M&C 11).

> *Pierre-Augustin Moncousu (1756–1801) entered the French navy as an ordinary seaman in 1773 and by 1777 had risen to Sailing Master. Captured by the Royal Navy in 1778, he escaped from England in the following year and returned to France, soon becoming a highly respected Master in the merchant service. In 1794 he was offered a senior Captaincy in the new French revolutionary navy. Appointed in 1800 to* Indomptable, *80-gun, he was killed by a cannon-ball in the first of the two battles of July 1801 against *Saumarez' squadron.*

Monmouth, HMS

A ship on the Brest blockade (YA 6).

> *HMS* Monmouth, *64-gun, was the ex–East Indiaman* Belmont, *purchased by the Royal Navy whilst on the stocks and launched in 1796. She then fought under an acting–Captain, Commander James Walker (d.1831 in the rank of Rear Admiral; see also *Isis, HMS), at *Duncan's victory at *Camperdown in 1797. After a somewhat uneventful career thereafter on blockade duty, she was sent for a sheer-hulk in 1815 and broken up in 1834.*

Monserrat, Abbot of

A Prelate visited by Stephen Maturin in Catalonia (PC 10,14).

Montagne

A French 120-gun ship at the Battle of the Glorious First of June (C/T 4).

> *This 120-gun ship was launched in 1780 as* Etats de Bourgogne *and in 1793 she was renamed* Montagne *after spending a few months under the name* Côte d'Or. *At the Battle of the First of June, in 1794, she was the flagship of Rear-Admiral Villaret de Joyeuse (1748–1812), her Captain Bazire being killed in the action but his ship escaping capture by *Howe's victorious fleet. In 1795 she was renamed* Peuple *and later that year was once again renamed — this time finally — as* Ocean, *continuing in service until 1855.*

Montague

1: a member of the British government's intelligence co-ordinating committee (COM 2).

2: a naturalist after whom a harrier is named (YA 10).

The bird is named for George Montague (1751–1815), a natural scientist who in 1802 published his highly regarded Ornithological Dictionary of British Birds.

Montague, Drogo

A relative of Pellew whose cousin was a Midshipman in HMS *Hermione*, murdered by the mutineers (RM 1).

The only Midshipman killed on HMS *Hermione was a thirteen year old named Smith (1784–1797), who was first struck down by a 19-year-old maintopman, David Forester (already one of *Pigot's killers) and then hacked to death by a mob of other mutineers. His body was tossed overboard by Forester and John Fletcher, an able seaman who had been flogged at Smith's instigation a few days beforehand. Forester was arrested in 1802, having, oddly, rejoined the Royal Navy as a bargeman in the sloop HMS Bittern: he was tried and hanged in the same year. Fletcher was never found and his subsequent career and fate are unknown.

Montague, Lady Mary Wortley

A lady referred to by Mrs Williams as a great traveller (PC 6).

Lady Mary Wortley Montague (1689–1762), a well-known wit, lady of letters, poet, author and correspondent, was a daughter of the 1st Duke of Kingston and a distant cousin of the novelist Henry Fielding. Her husband, Edward, having been appointed Ambassador to the *Supreme Porte at Constantinople in 1716, Lady Mary accompanied him, writing hundreds of letters, later published, to her many friends about her travels to, within, and from Turkey. On her return to London in 1718 she became a leading society hostess (as well as a strong proponent of the Turkish practice of inoculation against smallpox) and from 1739 onwards travelled extensively in Europe, again writing many letters to the great and good of her age.

Mont-Blanc

A French 74-gun in Toulon Harbour (PC 4).

Mont Blanc was launched in 1791 under the name *Pyrrhus; she was then re-named Trente-et-un Mai in 1794, Républicain in 1795 and Mont Blanc in 1796. In 1805 she fought at, and escaped from, the Battle of Trafalgar but was captured by Sir Richard *Strachan's squadron some two weeks later, soon becoming HMS Mont Blanc. She was sent for a powder hulk in 1811 and sold for breakup in 1819.

Montezuma, the Duke of

A madman at Choate's hospital in Boston, also known as the Emperor of Mexico (FW 4).

The name is borrowed from that of Montezuma (1446–1520), the last Aztec Emperor of Mexico. Although a successful warrior on his own local terms, he was no match for the Spanish conqueror Cortés, with whom he was forced to reach an uneasy, and humiliating, accord in

1519. After sending an immense quantity of gold to Spain as a tribute, he was pelted to death by rebels amongst his own people.

Montgolfier

A type of balloon (LM 4).

The balloon is named for the Montgolfier brothers, Joseph-Michel (1740–1810) and Jacques-Étienne (1745–1799). The younger brother is credited with the actual invention of the untethered hot-air balloon but the two first demonstrated the device together, in June 1783. This first flight was 'unmanned' but, a few months later, they safely sent aloft a duck, sheep and rooster and, in November of the same year, *Rozier and a colleague ventured upon the first ever human, untethered ascent. Both brothers were talented mechanical innovators and entrepreneurs in many related fields of endeavour.

Moon

1: Aubrey's drunken coxswain in HMS *Boadicea* before the arrival of Bonden from the West Indies (TMC 3).

2: Mrs Moon, the owner of the Mayfair building where Diana Villiers had recently maintained an apartment (DI 2).

Moore

The Marine Captain in HMS *Leopard* (DI 3+) who fires the single ball that dismasts *Waakzaamheid*, causing her to founder (DI 7). During the voyage he had been reprimanded by Jack Aubrey in the strongest possible terms for failing to prevent his Lieutenant Howard from making lecherous advances to the prisoner Louisa Wogan (DI 4). Remaining with *Leopard* after her collision with the iceberg, he eventually arrives safely in Java and plays in his ship's cricket match against HMS *Cumberland* (FW 1).

Moore, Old

A reference to Jack Aubrey by the prostitutes gathered outside the Keith's Mayfair house (PC 6) and later a reference to a popular prophet (TGS 1, COM 10).

Francis Moore (1657?–1715) was an astrologer and writer who published the enigmatically prophetic 'Old Moore's Almanack' from 1701 onwards. The almanack is still published to this day.

Morales, Juan

A servant or monk at a Capuchin monastery high in the Andes (WDS 9).

Moreira

A gentleman in Brazil, a friend of Mr Allen (FSW 4).

Morgan, John

A bosun's mate in HMS *Sophie* (M&C 6), disrated for drunkenness (M&C 11).

Morgan and Levy
London money-lenders who had rejected Louisa
Wogan as a bad financial risk (DI 4).

Morley, Robert or **Bob**
The Captain of HMS *Blanche*, formerly of HMS
Semiramis, who, having returned home to find his
wife pregnant by another man, is consoled by his
old friend, Jack Aubrey (COM 5).

Mornington
see **Lord Mornington**

Morocco, Emperor of
see **Suliman, Emperor of Morocco**

Moroni, Paulo
A Venetian merchant, an agent of the French spy
Lesueur, who delivers the captive Charles Fielding's
letters to his wife Laura (TH 3).

Morris, the Honourable Mrs Selina
The friend and companion of Mrs Williams (WDS
10; COM 1–3) who, with her and the manservant
Briggs, begins to run an illegal betting business
(COM 2,3). Later we learn that she had afterwards
run off and married Briggs (YA 6), who is soon arrested for bigamy (YA 8).
> N.B., although this seems likely to have ended the friend-
> ship between the two ladies, Mrs Williams and her com-
> panion' later die in the same coaching accident that kills
> Diana Villiers (HD 1).

Morton
1: a man after whom a surgical retractor is named
   (PC 13).
2: the erstwhile best friend of the Bombay ornithologist Mr Norton, with whose wife he has
   absconded (HMS 7).

Morton, John or **Charles**
The Flag Captain of Admiral Lord Stranraer's HMS
Queen Charlotte, said to be named both John (YA
4) and Charles (YA 6).

Moses
1: A reference by Queenie Keith to early antiquity
   (HD 1) and, somewhat earlier, the name for a
   small flat-bottomed boat used for conveying
   produce around harbours (RM 2).
   *In the Old Testament Book of Exodus Moses, a Hebrew
   child, was saved by his mother from the decreed murder of
   all the male infants of his people by being floated off in a
   basket amongst the reeds of the Nile. Found by Pharaoh's
   daughter, he was adopted and rose to great eminence.
   However when he later became active in the concerns of
   his captive native race, he was forced to flee to Midian and
   live as a humble shepherd. After many years Moses received *God's command to lead his Jewish people from op-
   pression in Egypt to the promised land of Canaan. Having
   taken them through the Red Sea and across the Wilder-*

*ness to Israel, he then laid down the set of theocratic laws
that were to govern Jewish society. Despite his obvious and
considerable strength of character and purpose, Moses was
famed for his meekness.*
2: an elderly, meek horse belonging to Sophie
   Aubrey (RM 6).

Moses, Awkward
A seaman in HMS *Ariel* (SM 7).

***Mosquito*, HMS**
A ship referred to by Jack Aubrey for its tiny size
(YA 4).
> Although Jack seems to be referring to tiny, rather in-
> consequential ships in general, an HMS Mosquito, 18-
> gun brig-sloop, was launched in 1804 and served until
> being sold in 1822. For a period up until late 1809 she
> was commanded, with great distinction, by William
> *Goate.

Moss
1: Mrs Moss, the landlady of the Crown Inn,
   Portsmouth (HMS 4).
2: two brothers, quarter-gunners in HMS *Surprise*,
   who are sent to the Indiaman *Royal George* for
   the battle with Linois' squadron (HMS 9).

Mothe, Adhémar de La
A wealthy, influential and homosexual friend of
Stephen Maturin in Paris with whom Diana Villiers
stays during her pregnancy (SM 5,10,11). He is then
influential in securing, via his friend d'Anglars, the
release from prison of Stephen, Jack Aubrey and
Captain Jagiello (SM 11; LM 9).

Mother of God
see **Mary, # 2**

'Mother Williams'
see **Williams, Mrs**

Mould, Arthur (or **'Gideon'**) and **Mrs**
An elderly, highly experienced ex-smuggler who
serves with Jack Aubrey in the letter-of-marque
Surprise (LM 5; NC 7) and HMS *Bellona*, his wife
remaining in Shelmerston (COM 5,6). Mould is
also nicknamed 'Gideon' by his ship-mates for his
preference for multiple sexual partners (COM 6).

Moussa
A servant in the Clifford household in Algiers (HD
8).

Mowett, William (or **James**)
A Master's Mate in HMS *Sophie*, a little under 20
years old, who has recently failed his examination
for Lieutenant (M&C 1,2). He nevertheless becomes a valued member of Jack Aubrey's crew, especially popular for his poetic gifts (M&C 2+).
Away as a prize-master, he misses the great victory
against the much larger Spanish frigate *Cacafuego*

(M&C 10,11). Some time later, he attends the ball given by Jack and Stephen Maturin (PC 2). Years afterwards, Jack hopes to call at the Cape of Good Hope in his HMS *Leopard* to substitute the now-promoted Mowett for his incompetent Lieutenant Turnbull (DI 1) but is prevented from doing so when *Waakzaamheid* pursues the ship far to the south (DI 8). Months later, Captain Lawrence of USS *Chesapeake* tells Jack that Mowett is now in hospital in New York, an injured prisoner-of-war from the defeat of HMS *Peacock* by USS *Hornet* (FW 6,7). He is soon returned to England (SM 5,8) and now becomes Second Lieutenant of Jack's HMS *Worcester* (IM 1+), later following his Captain to HMS *Surprise* (IM 9–11). Here, continuing as an enthusiastic amateur poet 'in the modern style,' he engages his rivals Rowan and Driver in a gun-room verse competition (IM 6,9; TH 4). Following the promotion of Tom Pullings to Commander, Mowett becomes First Lieutenant of *Surprise* (TH 2+), accompanying Jack on the Mubara expedition (TH 4–7) and on the mission to Zambra (TH 10). On the next long voyage, to the far side of the world, he agrees to share the duties of Premier of *Surprise* with Tom Pullings, who has been unable to get a ship for himself (FSW 2–9). After many adventures, Mowett arrives at Barbados en route home to England (RM 1) and here learns that Tom, gone ahead to England in a prize, has secured a publishing contract, on as-yet-unknown terms, for his verse (RM 2,7). Once in London, he loyally attends Jack Aubrey's public ordeal in the pillory following his conviction for fraud (RM 9). A little later Mowett has been appointed First Lieutenant of HMS *Illustrious* and is being given a lift to his new ship in his old friend William Babbington's HMS *Tartarus*. He has also just begun to see quite how rapacious and unreliable his publisher has turned out to be (LM 2; TGS 1).

The name of this cheerful character may perhaps have been inspired by that of William Mowatt (sic), a Lieutenant of 1803, who served in HMS Neptune, 98-gun, at Trafalgar in 1805 and who died, without further promotion, in 1833. Curiously, on three occasions Stephen Maturin calls Mowett 'James' rather than 'William' (FSW 4; RM 2; LM 2): as a result of this confusion some later printings of The Reverse of the Medal *'correct' the initials 'WM,' intended to appear on Mowett's volume of poetry, to 'JM,' thus giving the impression that the young man has himself mis-recalled his own first name (RM 2). Our William Mowett's verse is taken by O'Brian from the works of William *Falconer.*

Mozart

The famous composer, often referred to, heard and played by Stephen Maturin and Jack Aubrey (M&C 2; PC 14; TMC 2; DI 9; IM 3; LM 2,8; TGS 3,4; NC 9; C/T 7; YA 5). As a boy he had played for King George (C/T 3).

*Johann Chrysostom Wolfgang Amadeus Mozart (1756–1791), very often regarded as the greatest composer of his own or any other age, was also prodigiously talented as a keyboard player, violinist and conductor. Born in Salzburg, Austria, he started playing at the age of three and composing at the age of five. His output was immense, his craft infallible, his musical and psychological insight simply breath-taking; these talents, combined with an exquisite lightness of touch, enabled him continually to produce pure musical gold, often from seeming trifles. After travels round Europe with his parents (his father, Leopold (1719–1787), was a Vice-Kapellmeister at Salzburg) and his older sister (Anna Maria (1751–1829), also brilliantly talented at piano and harpsichord), Mozart returned to Salzburg in 1778, having failed to obtain a post in any of the courts he had visited. The boyhood meeting with King *George III had taken place in 1764 and, whilst in London, the 8-year-old Mozart composed the first three of his many symphonies. Once back in his home city, he did obtain a musical post in the Archbishop's household yet, even though he now achieved many musical triumphs, he came to loathe his rather worldly employer and, in 1781, resigned his position and moved to Vienna. Here, in 1782, he married Constanze Weber and obtained a small allowance from the Emperor Joseph II. From then until his rather early death in December 1791, Mozart poured forth music of the most sublime character, despite being almost continually plagued by both money and health problems. His burial in an unmarked, communal grave was a consequence not, as is often suggested, of his own financial disarray but rather of municipal regulations for sustained periods of freezing, deadly weather.*

M'puta, Sally

The young black woman concealed by the young Midshipman Jack Aubrey in HMS *Resolution*, an offence for which Captain Douglas had turned him before the mast for six months (M&C 4). Sally is the mother of Jack's son, Sam Panda, although the two parents seem never again to meet after their early liaison (RM 1).

Muffit or Muffitt

The Master of the *Lushington* East Indiaman and the Commodore of the merchant fleet protected by Jack Aubrey's HMS *Surprise* (HMS 9,11; TMC 3). Many years later, still in the same ship, he dines aboard *Surprise* in the Atlantic Ocean (FSW 4). Afterwards, and now retired in England, he is visited by Jack, giving him valuable South China Seas navigational charts (TGS 4,5,6,9).

*In the action against *Linois of February 1804, William Moffat (dates unknown) commanded *Ganges, with the fleet's Commodore being Nathaniel Dance of *Earl Camden (see that ship's entry for a note on the events and personalities involved).*

Mufti
see **Grand Mufti**

Muggletonians

A religious sect referred to by Martin (LM 5; WDS 1).

The sect was founded in England in about 1651 by Lodow-icke Muggleton (1609–1698) and John Reeve (1608–1658), who claimed to be the final and greatest of *Jesus Christ's prophets. The pair denied the Trinity, held matter to be eternal and taught that 'Reason' was the *Devil's creation.

Muiron

A French 38-gun frigate, part of Admiral Linois' squadron, that captures the mail packet *Ventura* (M&C 11).

Muiron was captured by the French in 1797 whilst on the stocks in Venice and survived until 1850. She was named for a favourite aide-de-camp of General *Buonaparte who had been killed at the Battle of Arcola in late 1796. It was in Muiron that, in 1799, Buonaparte himself escaped from the fiasco in Egypt, narrowly avoiding capture by British squadrons whilst en route back to France.

Mulei Hassan

A potentate of a past age (HD 10).

Mulei Hassan (d.1545) reigned as King of Tunis from 1533 until his death, supported in his rule by Emperor *Charles V of Germany.

Muley

The son of Esmin Pasha of Barka (IM 7).

Mulgrave

1: General Mulgrave, a First Lord of the Admiralty (TMC 1) who had introduced reforms in the system of prize-money (YA 3)

Henry Philip Phipps (1755–1831), Lord Mulgrave, was a younger brother of the arctic explorer Captain Lord Mulgrave (see 2 below), inheriting his Irish title in 1792 and then being created Baron Mulgrave in the English peerage in 1794. Having entered the army in 1775 (and Parliament in 1784), he rose to Major General in 1797 but then saw no active service after 1801, spending his remaining years as a determined and effective statesman. In 1805, as Foreign Secretary, it was Mulgrave who had to defend the controversial decision of the previous year to attack and seize *Bustamente's treasure squadron before war on Spain had been formally declared. As *First Lord, from 1807, he was a strong proponent of the view that the Royal Navy should take an aggressive role in pursuing the war and not remain merely as the defender of home waters. It was also under his administration that, in 1808, the Captain's share of prize-money was reduced from 3/8 to 1/4. Mulgrave resigned from the Admiralty in 1810 on health grounds but later served several times as Master of the Ordinance, also a Cabinet position. In 1812 he was created Earl of Mulgrave and Viscount Normamby.

2: Captain Lord Mulgrave, the some-time commander of HMS *Racehorse*, in which Fielding's father had once served. Mulgrave, under his previous name of Captain Phipps, was also a famous Arctic explorer (LM 9; NC 7).

Constantine John Phipps (1744–1792), Baron Mulgrave, was Commodore, in his HMS *Racehorse, of a Arctic expedition that unsuccessfully attempted to find a north-west passage from the Atlantic to the Pacific in 1773. The young Horatio *Nelson served in the second ship of the small squadron, HMS *Carcass. Phipps, a Post Captain of 1765, saw no active service after 1778, having been a supporter of Sir Hugh Palliser in his dispute with Admiral *Keppel. Having already inherited his father's Irish title of Lord Mulgrave, he was given the same title in the English peerage in 1790. On his death, the Irish title passed to his younger brother, General Henry Philip Phipps (see 1 above), but the English title was for a while extinct until being revived in a second creation in 1794.

Muller

A scholar referred to by Martin as the author of a great work on religious sects (WDS 3).

Of many scholarly Mullers only two seem to fit this reference, although both are a little anachronistic. Samuel Müller (1785–1875) was a German-Dutch historian of the Anabaptist sects of the 16th century, though he published little before 1820. Friedrich Max Müller (1823–1900), known as the 'father of the comparative study of religions,' was the author of The Science of Religion *amongst many other related works. However, in addition to being born somewhat too late, he is chiefly recalled for his massive series of volumes on* The Sacred Books of the East *rather than as a student of Christian sects.*

Mullins

The maker of a patent balm referred to by Stephen Maturin (FSW 3).

Mungo's

The name of a patent cordial used by the ailing Admiral Thornton (IM 4).

Munoz, Juan

A Spanish government agent in Peru (WDS 7).

The name may be inspired by that of Juan Bautista Munoz (1745–1799), a Spanish historian and ethnographer who, in 1793, published a History of the New World, *a volume highly regarded by Alexander *Humboldt.*

Muong

A well-educated and well-socialised female orangutan met by Stephen Maturin at the Buddhist temple of Kumai (TGS 7,9).

Murad Bey

The local ruler of the Egyptian port of Tina who tells Jack Aubrey of his exploits at the Battle of Acre with Sir Sidney Smith (TH 5).

This character may be in part inspired by Murad Bey (1750–1801) who was, with Ibrahim (1735–1817; not the *Ibrahim mentioned in TH 4), the leader of the ruling Marmelukes of Egypt. He opposed the French invasion of Egypt in 1798 but then suffered several defeats at the hands of General *Desaix. Having then made an accommodation with *Buonaparte's replacement in Egypt, General Kléber, he may have been about to switch sides and throw in his lot with the British forces when he died in a outbreak of the plague. This Murad Bey did not fight at Acre.

Murad Reis

A renowned sea-captain who commands Sheikh Ibn
Hazm's treasure-galley (HD 9). Murad leads Jack
Aubrey and *Surprise* on a long chase before taking
shelter in the shallow bay of a deserted Mediterranean island (HD 10); here he is publicly beheaded
by his own crew in an act of surrender to the Royal
Navy (HD 10).

> *N.B., Somewhat oddly, the vessel had just a few lines pre-*
> *viously been under the command of the Algerine corsair,*
> *Yahya ben Khaled.*
>
> *Reis or rais is Arabic for Captain (or, in political con-*
> *texts, Governor) and the title was usually given to the High*
> *Admirals of the largely pirate fleets operating from the*
> *various, small Ottoman protectorates along the North*
> *African coast: two different Admiral Murads may per-*
> *haps have inspired O'Brian's choice of name for his char-*
> *acter. A famous Murad Reis had been an Algerine corsair*
> *of the late 16th and early 17th centuries (he may have been*
> *a Dutchman by birth), and his name was later borrowed*
> *by the Bashaw of Tripoli's naval commander of the early*
> *19th century, a renegade Scot called Peter Lisle (fl.1796–*
> *1815). After a most unhappy career in the American mer-*
> *chant marine, Lisle ended up taking service in an Arab*
> *privateer operating out of Tripoli. Once he had risen to a*
> *position of some wealth and prominence in his new call-*
> *ing, he married Bashaw Yusuf Karamanli's daughter and,*
> *in 1796, was awarded the official position of Reis. His*
> *particular pleasure in taking American ships drew down*
> *the attentions of the U.S. Navy but he proved an able and*
> *tenacious opponent, taking Commodore *Bainbridge's*
> *USS Philadelphia in 1803, after she had run aground in*
> *adverse weather, and then avoiding or beating off several*
> *subsequent attempts to capture him. By 1815, when the*
> *USA once again sent a squadron to deal with the corsair*
> *fleets, Lisle had lost favour with his father-in-law and, re-*
> *cently returned from a period of exile in Egypt. was now*
> *employed only as an official translator in negotiations with*
> *the American officers, after which time he vanishes from*
> *notice.*

Muratori, Count

A musical friend of Laura Fielding in Malta, a very
able flautist (TH 3).

Murd, Douglas

A sick seaman in HMS *Surprise* (WDS 5).

Murphy, Thomas

An able seaman in HMS *Sophie* (M&C 3+).

Murray, John

The publisher of Lord Byron (IM 9; RM 2).

> *John Murray (1778–1843), the son of the founder of the*
> *family firm, was a close friend of Lord *Byron as well as*
> *his publisher. In 1807–1809 he founded the influential*
> Quarterly Review *and became a very effective promoter*
> *of many important British authors, Byron amongst them.*
> *The publishing company of John Murray & Co. exists in*
> *London to this day.*

Murray, Wm

The deceased surgeon of Woolwich Dockyard
whose obituary is read by Stephen Maturin, an acquaintance (DI 6).

Musgrave

A member of the London Entomological Society
(HMS 1).

Musgrave, William

A seaman in HMS *Sophie* referred to in Captain
Allen's log as having been lashed (M&C 2). Later
injured in her first battle under Jack Aubrey, he becomes Stephen Maturin's first naval patient (M&C
4).

Mustapha

1: the Capitan-Bey of Karia who, coveting the rule
   of the Greek mainland town of Kutali, seeks
   British help vis-à-vis his two rivals, Ismail, Bey
   of Mesenteron, and Sciahan, Bey of Kutali itself (IM 9–11). As senior Turkish naval officer
   in the Ionian, he has his own small squadron,
   consisting chiefly of the frigates *Torgud* and
   Kitabi (IM 9). Mustapha visits HMS *Surprise*
   but Jack Aubrey rejects him as an ally, in part
   because he is reported to be on excellent terms
   with the French (IM 10). When another local
   potentate, Ali Pasha of Iannina, starts a false rumour that Ismail of Mesenteron has been appointed Governor of Kutali by the Sultan of
   Turkey, Mustapha throws off his allegiance and
   sets out to attack both Jack and the town (IM
   11). His frigates are defeated by *Surprise* and he
   is then forced by his own officers to surrender
   (IM 11; TH 1).

   Mustapha Bey's fierce character and eventual defeat are
   somewhat reminiscent of Scandril Kichuc Ali, whose
   *Badere-I-Zaffér was taken by HMS *Seahorse in 1808.*

2: an ally of Vizier Hashin who had hoped to replace Omar Pasha as Dey of Algiers. Defeated
   by Ali Bey, he is now thought to be doomed to
   execution (HD 8).

Mutine, HMS

A ship at the Battle of the Nile (PC 12).

> *Mutine, 16-gun brig-sloop, was launched by the French*
> *in 1794 and captured by the Royal Navy in May of 1797*
> *in a small-boat attack led by First Lieutenant Hardy of*
> **Cockburn's HMS* *Minerve. Hardy, already a protégé of*
> **Nelson, was then promoted Commander into her as re-*
> *ward. Although Mutine was in fact a rather small ship*
> *for a Commander to be given, a sloop only by a stretch of*
> *the imagination, Nelson was always short of 'eyes of the*
> *fleet' in the Mediterranean, and she was a weatherly lit-*
> *tle craft, now under a prime seaman. Under Hardy she*
> *went on to take part in the Battle of the Nile (playing the*
> *role described in PC), with her commander being pro-*
> *moted to Nelson's *Flag Captain immediately after the*
> *victory. She was then was given successively to Comman-*
> *ders *Capel and *Hoste, until being sold out of the service*
> *in 1807. In French, the word 'mutine' is usually intended*

to convey 'revolt' or 'revolution' rather than 'mutiny' in its strict, military sense.

Thomas Masterman Hardy (1769–1839) himself, a man renowned for taut discipline and meticulous attention to detail, went on to serve as Nelson's Flag Captain in a series of ships and, at the Battle of Trafalgar of 1805, was alongside the great man in HMS *Victory when he was struck down. For his part in the triumph, Hardy was in early 1806 awarded a baronetcy. Always remaining in active service, he became Commodore and Commander-in-Chief of the South American Station from 1819 to 1823, being promoted Rear Admiral in 1821. Hardy then became *First Sea Lord (i.e., the senior naval member of the Admiralty Board) from 1830 to 1834, in which year he re-

tired to become Governor of Greenwich Naval Hospital. He was promoted Vice Admiral in 1837.

Mutton

An able-seaman in HMS *Lively* (PC12).

'Myrtle Bough'

A prize-fighter referred to by Barret Bonden (YA 3).
The reference by *Bonden is somewhat anachronistic, for 'the Myrtle Bough/Sprig' was Simon Byrne (1806–1833; thus about 7 at the time of YA), a well-regarded Irish pugilist killed in a bout with Deaf James Burke (see *Burke, Dumb).

— N —

Nabob

A name for Diana Villiers' 'Begum' diamond guessed at by Stephen Maturin before he — wrongly — recalls it as the 'Blue Peter,' the name by which it is thenceforth known (SM 3).

Also see *Nawab

Nabonidus

A king, the dates of whose reign are, according to Mr Goodridge, ambiguously given in Ussher (PC 10).
Nabonidus, or Nabu Na'id, ruled as King of Babylon from 556 to 539 BC, when the city was taken by the Persian King, Cyrus. Nabonidus was thereupon exiled and nothing further is known of his fate.

Nagel

A troublesome seaman from HMS *Defender*, now serving in HMS *Surprise*. He had once served under Pullings in HMS *Ramillies* (FSW 2,3).
The name Nagel recalls that of an American-born seaman, Jacob Nagle (sic; 1762–1841), who left a fascinating journal describing his life and career (a work from which O'Brian takes the tale of Captain *Sawyer's penchant for molesting young seamen). Amongst many other adventures in his long life, Nagel served in the Royal Navy as a pressed man from 1782 to 1794 (including a voyage to Australia in HMS *Sirius of the 'First Fleet') and as a volunteer from 1795 to 1802. After a subsequent career as a merchant sailor, he finally retired from the sea in 1824. The diary came to light in 1982 and is now available in print as The Nagel Journal (ed. John C. Dann; New York: Weidenfeld & Nicholson, 1988).

Naiad, HMS

A ship referred to by Jack Aubrey as one of several very desirable frigates into which he would like to be made Post (M&C 11). She is later mentioned several times in passing (PC 5; HMS 2; LM 9; YA 4,9).
HMS Naiad, 38-gun, was built in 1797. In 1799, under

Captain William Pierrepoint (d.1813 as a Rear Admiral) she helped capture the extremely valuable Spanish treasure frigate *Santa Brigida and at the Battle of Trafalgar in 1805 she was commanded by Captain Thomas *Dundas. Naiad became a store ship in 1847 and was sold in 1866; she was finally broken up in Peru in 1898. The Naiads are some of the *Nymphs of Greek mythology, spirits of nature always represented by beautiful young girls.

Namur, HMS

A ship in which William Mowett (M&C 3) and Jack Aubrey had once served, the latter as a Midshipman (FSW 10). At one point she is encountered at Gibraltar where a Captain Ponsonby is to be a temporary substitute for her usual commander, Billy Sutton, an MP who wishes to attend at Westminster (FSW 1).
HMS Namur, 90-gun, was launched in 1756. In 1782 she fought in *Rodney's victory at the Battle of the Saintes under Captain Robert *Fanshawe and, in 1797, was at Cape *St Vincent under James Whitshed (d.1849 as Admiral of the Fleet Sir James Hawkins Whitshed), later serving briefly as Lord St Vincent's own flag-ship in the Channel command during 1800. Reduced to 74-gun in 1804–1805 (when *Seppings' method of her adaptation set the fashion for solid, round bows in all subsequent wooden ships of the Royal Navy), in November 1805 she was, under Lawrence Halsted (d.1841 in the rank of full Admiral), part of Sir Richard *Strachan's squadron that took four French escapees from the great victory at Trafalgar some two weeks previously. Namur, like her predecessor of 1697 named for a Belgian fortress taken from the French by King *William III in 1695, was finally broken up in 1833.

Nan

see **Pengelleys, the**

Nancy

A serving girl at Mrs Broad's Grapes Inn (TGS 4).

Nancy

An illegal slaver, Master Mr Knittel, taken by Jack Aubrey's squadron. As a demonstration of force, Jack then destroys her by cannon-fire in full view of shore (COM 7,8).

Nancy Dawson

A cannon in *Surprise* (C/T 8).
For the name derivation see **Dawson, Nancy**

Nancy's Fancy

A cannon in HMS *Surprise* (RM 3).

Nanny

The ship's goat in HMS *Nutmeg of Consolation* (NC 5)

Napier

The inventor of 'Napier's Bones,' a mathematical tool (HMS 7; YA 5).
John Napier (1550–1617), Lord of Merchiston, was a Scottish mathematician (as well as a theological controversialist and weapons-inventor), famed for the invention of the logarithmic method of simplifying complex calculations, especially those needed in the burgeoning science of astronomy. In the year of his death he published a method of using small, calibrated rods—'Napier's Bones'—to further aid and speed calculation, a semi-mechanical device that was the fore-runner of the slide-rule.

Napoleon

see **Buonaparte** *or* **Bonaparte, Napoleon**

Narborough, Lord

see **Garron, Lord**

Narcissus, HMS

The former ship of Mr Stourton, HMS *Surprise*'s new First Lieutenant. (HMS 8).
HMS Narcissus, *32-gun, was launched in 1801, reduced to a convict ship in 1823 and sold in 1837. In Greek myth,* Narcissus *was the beautiful youth who, having fallen in love with his own glorious image, reflected in a pond, then died of an unrequited passion and was transformed into the pretty, eponymous flower.*

Narses

A famous eunuch referred to by Maturin (IM 8).
Narses (478–573), a eunuch general and diplomat under the Roman Emperor Justinian I, led the re-conquest of Italy south of the Alps from the Ostrogoths and then established for himself an Imperial governorship of these territories, once again based in Rome (the city having been lost to the Empire in the mid–5th century).

Naseby

The dog belonging to Captain Hobden of HMS *Surprise*'s Royal Marines. He is the cause of a quarrel, and near duel, between his master and Stephen Maturin when he steals and eats a preserved hand (HD 4,5).
The hound is named for one of the decisive battles of the

English Civil War, fought in 1645 at Naseby, Leicestershire. Here the army of Charles I, led by Prince Rupert, was routed by the Parliamentary forces led by Fairfax and *Cromwell.*

Nasmyth, Captain

The Captain of the frigate HMS *Alexandria* (YA 6).

Nastyface, Jack

A cook's mate in HMS *Surprise* (C/T 1,7; NC 10).
Jack Nastyface (a common sailors' nickname, especially for a cook's mate) was the name under which William Robinson published his 1836 memoir, Nautical Economy. *Robinson volunteered for the Royal Navy in 1805, soon serving at the Battle of Trafalgar aboard HMS* *Revenge (although not in the galley). In 1811 he deserted his ship, an embarrassing fact that his memoir passes over in silence.*

Nathan

Diana Villiers' banker, a man especially admired by Stephen Maturin for his dedication to the overthrow of Buonaparte. He has a younger brother, Meyer (IM 1; RM 5,8).
The name is clearly inspired by that of the great financier Nathan Meyer *Rothschild.*

Nathaniel

see **Martin, Nathaniel**

Nawab

An Indian potentate who had once given Diana Villiers pearls (SM 1), some of which she later sells in Paris to defray her expenses (SM 5).
Nawab—anglicised to Nabob—was the North Indian Moslem term for the deputy governor of a province. By transference, it became used in England to designate anyone who had accumulated great wealth or power through connection with the sub-continent.

N'Diaje, Amandu

A resident of Sierra Leone (COM 8).

Neale, Sir Harry

The Captain of HMS *San Fiorenzo*, who had been First Lieutenant of HMS *Resolution* when Jack Aubrey was a Midshipman. He had later commanded HMS *Success*, also with Jack aboard (M&C 7).
Sir Harry Burrard (1765–1840) was made Post in 1793, adopting in 1795 his wealthy new wife's surname of Neale. In that latter year he was appointed to the 42-gun HMS *San Fiorenzo (never having served in either HMSS* *Resolution or* *Success). In 1797 his ship was present at the Nore mutiny but was one of those few that refused to join the rebellion, slipping out from her anchorage under fire from other ships. In 1801 Neale was appointed to HMS* *Centaur, 74-gun, but almost immediately transferred to command of the Royal Yacht. Having returned to more active duty in 1805, in 1809 Neale was James* *Gambier's* *Captain of the Fleet at the Battle of the Basque Roads, and thus, a little later, a key witness in the court-martial of the Admiral, held under pressure from Lord* *Cochrane,*

the inshore squadron commander. Neale was then promoted Rear Admiral in 1810, Vice Admiral in 1814 and Admiral in 1830. Sir Harry, a baronet by inheritance in 1791, also served as an MP for a total of 37 years.

Neave

A quartermaster *in Surprise* (TGS 2).

Nebuchadnezzar

The legendarily rich King of Babylon (NC 7), several times referred to as a model of fame and pride (TMC 7; LM 8; NC 7; COM 1).

Nebuchadnezzar (630?–562 BC), who ruled Babylon from 605 until his death, had a court legendary for both its opulence and idolatry. Probably the most powerful monarch of his age, the King supposedly became excessively proud, was struck mad by *God and then deposed. Shortly before his death, and by now a pious follower of the God of the Jews, he was restored to his throne by divine intervention.

Ned

1: a servant of Admiral Haddock (PC 1).
2: a seaman in *Surprise*, captain of the cannon *Spitfire*'s gun-crew (C/T 8).
3: *see* **Brenton, Edward**

Needham

1: Jack Aubrey's clerk in HMS *Leopard* (DI 3), who later dies in the fever outbreak (DI 5).
2: an intelligence official in London, possibly connected with the Army (YA 1).

Needham, Helen

A friend of the Aubrey children, the daughter of a General (COM 3).

Nellie or Nelly

A servant at the Maturins' Barham House (COM 2,3).

Nelson, David

The botanist who had sailed with Captain Bligh in HMS *Bounty* (DI 1).

David Nelson (d.1789) was a member of the staff of Kew Gardens, an expert practical botanist and plant-tender who had sailed on *Cook's third voyage of exploration in 1776–1780. Appointed in 1787 to care for the breadfruit plants on HMS *Bounty's expedition, he remained loyal during the mutiny and was one of the very few men commended by *Bligh for his behaviour. Shortly after arriving in Timor in the launch he contracted a fever and died, but not before he was reported to have warned a colleague against ever again serving under Bligh, stating that he had been the source of all the ship's woes.

Nelson, Lady

The wife of Admiral Lord Nelson, who had been famously deserted by her husband (PC 14; RM 5). Amanda Smith clearly takes the side of Nelson and his lover Lady Hamilton in the quarrel, hoping that

her lover Jack Aubrey will follow their example (SM 5).

Frances, or Fanny, Nisbit (1758–1831) was a young widow (original maiden name, Woolward) who, in 1787, married the then Captain *Nelson in the West Indies (being given away by Horatio's friend and colleague, William Duke of *Clarence). Their union (which had no offspring) was eventually wrecked by her husband's long, public association with Lady Emma *Hamilton and the couple effectively separated in 1800. Viscountess Nelson's marriage to Horatio did endure as a legal fact and she was thereby his main heir, living out her life in reasonable affluence in England, both cherishing his memory and being always somewhat bitter at her desertion (N.B., it was however her husband's brother, the Reverend William Nelson [1757–1835], who, quite undeservedly, reaped most of the rewards for Trafalgar itself, being made an Earl and given a huge state pension). In 1797, Fanny's son by her first marriage, Josiah Nisbit (1780–1830), had become a Commander (of HMS *Dolphin, hospital ship) under his step-father's patronage. Although made Post at the end of the following year and soon given the frigate HMS Thalia, his reputation for drunkenness and indifferent seamanship meant that his naval career was never destined to be a success and he seems, wisely, to have left the service in about 1801. Not, however, entirely without talent, he later became a prosperous businessman.

Nelson, Lord

Lord Nelson is mentioned several times over in every book of the series. Very often the occurrences are simply remarks of warm praise, such as Jack Aubrey proudly relating that he has twice dined in his company, being spoken to on each occasion (M&C 3; SM 2; COM 10). As it would prove neither practical nor useful to list every reference to the great man, in this short biography I have simply added cross references to remarks by O'Brian's characters on specific events in his career.

Vice Admiral Viscount Horatio Nelson (1758–1805), Duke of Brontë, is undoubtedly Britain's greatest naval hero. The son of a Norfolk parson, Nelson first went to sea in 1770 in his uncle Maurice Suckling's HMS *Raisonnable. After an adventurous career as Captain's servant and Midshipman — later including an Arctic voyage in HMS *Carcass under Captain Skeffington Lutwidge — he was commissioned Lieutenant in 1777. During the American War of Independence he served in the West Indies fleet under Admiral Sir Peter Parker, who gave him several independent cruises, promoting him Commander in 1778 and Post Captain in 1779 (PC 12). In 1787 Nelson married Francis Nisbit, the widowed niece of the President of Nevis, becoming step-father to her small son, Josiah (see *Nelson, Lady).

The end of the American war left Nelson ashore in England on half-pay from 1788 until 1793, when the start of the French Revolutionary War saw him given HMS *Agamemnon, 64-gun. In 1794, during a shore attack on the port of Calvi, Corsica, he was blinded in the right eye by sand and debris thrown up by a cannon-ball (FW 9). By 1796 he had risen to be a Commodore in the Mediterranean fleet and, in 1797, played a decisive role in Sir John Jervis' great victory at the Battle of Cape *St Vincent where, in the 74-gun HMS *Captain, he engaged and boarded the Spanish *San Nicolas, 80-gun, and *San Josef, 112-gun, crossing from the one to the other with San Nicolas being his 'Patent Bridge for Boarding First-Rates' (FW 9; IM 3,11). In the same year he was promoted Rear

Admiral (purely by seniority), became 'Sir Horatio,' a Knight of the Bath, and also lost his right arm in an attempt to take a Spanish treasure ship at Tenerife (FW 9).

As a flag-officer Nelson now led a detached squadron in the Mediterranean whose captains soon became known as his 'Band of Brothers.' In 1798, with his flag in HMS *Vanguard, he won a decisive victory over the French Admiral *Brueys at the Battle of the Nile (M&C 3; DI 5; COM 10; also known as the Battle of Aboukir Bay), receiving during the action a scalp wound that for a short while made him fear that he had been totally blinded (DI 8; TH 4). Following this triumph, Nelson was made a Baron (thus now being addressed as 'Lord Nelson') and became popularly known as 'the Hero of the Nile' (HMS 11). Continuing as a squadron commander (FW 9; TMC 2; COM 7), he based himself in Naples and there again met Emma, the wife of the British consul Sir William *Hamilton, whom he had first come to know in late 1793: the two commenced a long and often scandalous affair, leading in 1800 to Nelson's effective separation from his wife (PC 14; TH 9; RM 5). In 1799 his successes in and off southern Italy gained him the Dukedom of Brontë (in Sicily) from Ferdinand, *King of the Two Sicilies (NC 7). However, as part of these campaigns, he had accepted the surrender in Naples of Commodore *Caraciolo, a republican rebel. Under pressure from the Neapolitan royalists, Nelson was then instrumental in having him hanged, without proper trial, from the yardarm of a Sicilian frigate (PC 14).

Promoted Vice Admiral in January 1801, his next command was in the Baltic, as a subordinate to the somewhat ineffectual Sir Hyde *Parker. Later that year Nelson's squadron defeated the Danish fleet at the Battle of Copenhagen (DI 1; SM 4; TH 10), a victory for which he was made a Viscount and also given permission by King *George III to use his Sicilian Duke's title in England. It was at Copenhagen that Nelson chose to ignore Parker's recall signal, remarking that he had a right occasionally to use his blind eye.

Made Commander-in-Chief of the Mediterranean fleet in 1803, he hoisted his flag in HMS *Victory. On October 21st 1805 — in his final rank, as of April 1804, of Vice Admiral of the White (YA 1) — Nelson brought the combined French and Spanish fleets to battle just off Cape Trafalgar (FW 2). Although he defeated them comprehensively, during the battle was brought down by a sharpshooter operating from the tops of Captain *Lucas' *Redoubtable (LM 6). He died a few hours later, shortly after hearing from his Flag Captain, Thomas Hardy (see *Mutine, HMS), that a great victory had been secured. Lord Nelson, revered as much for his humanity (e.g. HMS 5) and inspirational qualities (e.g. DI 5; LM 1,2, WDS 1) as for his tactical brilliance, was given a state funeral and buried in St Paul's Cathedral, London.

Although regard for Nelson was wide-spread and deeply felt, many contemporaries also noted in him a streak of affectation and self-absorption that could irritate even those disposed to admiration. Lord St Vincent always treated his protégé as an awkward, touchy, yet brilliant, son; General Sir John Moore — the brother of a Royal Navy Captain, *Graham Moore — wrote that Nelson's bemedalled and be-ribboned dress at the Sicilian Court made a 'pitiful impression ... more like a Prince of an Opera than the Conqueror of the Nile'; and the future Duke of *Wellington, when still a relatively junior general, briefly met Nelson in London in early 1805, at first finding him almost disgustingly silly and vain, but soon — after Nelson was told to whom he was talking, and abruptly modified his conversation — seeing him as 'really a very superior man' with a impressive depth of insight into affairs of state, both military and political.

On board ship, although usually loved by his officers and crews, Nelson also had a reputation for falling into periods of morose tetchiness, especially when afflicted, as he often was during rough weather, with sea-sickness and intestinal upsets (at TGS 4 his cox'n appears loyally to have been down-playing the Admiral's affliction).

Nemesis

The service nick-name of HMS *Surprise* (HMS 6,7).
See **Surprise, HMS**

Neptune

The sea god (TMC 2; YA 9).
In Roman myth, Neptunus was the god of water and sometimes, with the Greek Poseidon, the patron of sea-journeys.

Nereid

An 18-gun privateer, owned by Canning, that had been captured by the French privateer *Bellone* (PC 6).

Néréide

A Buonapartist corvette destroyed at Bertolucci's ship-yard (HD 5).

Néréide, HMS

A frigate initially commanded by Captain Corbett (TMC 1+) and later by Lord Clonfert (TMC 4). Under the latter, she is very severely mauled at the Battle of Port South East, with the majority of her crew being killed or wounded (TMC 7). Having surrendered, she is taken into the French service (TMC 8).

*HMS Néréide, 36-gun, was launched by the French under that same name in 1779; she was captured by the Royal Navy in 1797 and later served, very much as described by O'Brian, in the Indian Ocean campaign of 1809–1810. In August of that latter year, under acting Captain Josiah Nesbit Willoughby (to some degree the model for *Clonfert), she was re-taken by the French. She returned to British hands on the fall of Mauritius to *Bertie's squadron a few months later, but was too badly damaged to be taken to sea. Long laid up in harbour, in March 1816 she was sold for break-up (N.B. MANNING & WALKER suggest she was broken up in 1812). In September of 1810 the captured French frigate *Vénus was also re-named Néréide, a replacement for Willoughby's lost ship; she too was broken up in 1816, although not until May of that year. In Greek myth, the Nereids — or Sea-*Nymphs — were the many daughters of the sea god Nereus.*

Nero

A reference by Maturin to tyranny (IM 2).
Nero Claudius Caesar (37–68 AD) was the step-son of the Roman Emperor Claudius, succeeding him in 54 AD. For

about the first five years of his reign, Nero was almost universally regarded as a fine ruler, presiding over peace, prosperity and good government. However, in 59, he then arranged for the murder of his domineering mother, Agrippina, an act that soon enabled him to indulge in grand artistic and sporting schemes that gradually began to undermine the imperial finances. These were dealt a further, severe blow by the fire that swept through Rome in mid-64, leaving much of the city in ruins. Although at first Nero was active in relief and re-construction plans, he soon decided to appropriate large, privately owned areas for the construction of parks and palaces, all at the public expense. Rumours soon spread that the Emperor started the fires deliberately in order to further these ambitions, an accusation to which he responded by blaming, and burning, the Christians. The costs of these construction enterprises, coupled with those of on-going border wars (especially *Boadicea's revolt in Britain), soon ended such popularity as Nero had enjoyed amongst the propertied, ruling classes. Conspiracies, both real and imagined, against the Emperor now led to assassinations, executions and all the usual paraphernalia of Imperial paranoia. In 68, Nero returned from an extended visit to his beloved Greece to find both his support and power slipping away. Soon the powerful and ambitious governor of Spain, Galba, rose against him and was declared Emperor by the Senate. Nero, denounced as a public enemy, committed suicide, supposedly crying at the last, 'What an artist dies with me!'

Nesbit or Nesbitt, John

A Midshipman in HMS *Surprise* who suffers a broken collar bone (FSW 5,7).

Nessus

Maturin refers to 'Nessus' shirt' (SM 6).

In one telling of the fate of *Hercules, the hero struck down Nessus, a *Centaur, with a poisoned arrow after the beast had tried to ravish his wife, Deianira. As he lay dying, Nessus gave his shirt— soaked in his contaminated blood— to the lady, telling her that it had always acted for him as a magical love-charm. Many years later Deianira, now deserted by Hercules, sent him the shirt in the hope of regaining his affections through its powers but, when her husband donned the garment, its old poisons were released into his skin, with Hercules then hurling himself on a burning pyre in order to end the agony. A 'Nessus' shirt' is thus a term for any poisoned gift.

Netley

A cutter which conveys Maturin from London to the Nore (LM 8).

The reference may perhaps be to HMS Netley, 12-gun schooner, captured in 1807, as Nimrod, from the U.S. Navy, renamed and bought into the Royal Navy in 1808 and broken up in 1814. She was named for a small town on Southampton Water, near Portsmouth

Nevin

1: a Royal Navy Captain who consults Maturin on a medical matter at Molly Harte's party (M&C 6).
2: Jack Aubrey's clerk in HMS *Surprise* (HMS 9).

Newberry

The keeper of an inn in New South Wales (NC 10).

Newby, John

The seaman in HMS *Surprise* who notices that Stephen Maturin has gone swimming and been left behind in the ship's wake (IM 9).

Newman

1: the sometime Captain of HMS *Hannibal* who had reprimanded Lieutenant Jack Aubrey for petulance in challenging Lieutenant Carrol to a duel (M&C 4).
2: a neighbour and fellow astronomer of Jack Aubrey in Hampshire (TMC 1).

Newnham, Captain

An artillery officer who takes part in the capture of Ile de la Passe. However, he is separated from his men at a crucial stage of the battle, thus missing the opportunity to wreak havoc on the French squadron with shore-fire (TMC 7).

Newton

The great scientist (RM 7; HD 6).

Sir Isaac Newton (1642–1727) was one of the greatest of all English polymaths, a scientist, inventor, mathematician and philosopher. He spent much of his career in Cambridge, becoming Lucasian Professor of Mathematics in 1669 and also twice serving as MP for the University. Amongst the many honours showered on him, Newton became President of the Royal Society in 1703 and was knighted in 1705. He is best remembered both for the profundity of his mathematical thinking and exposition and for his development of the theory of gravitational attraction.

Ney

A general who has declared for the returning Emperor Napoleon (HD 1)

Michel Ney (1769–1815), Prince de la Moskowa, joined the ranks of the French army in 1787 and, after seeing considerable action, was commissioned as a cavalry officer in 1792. His boldness in attack brought him an extraordinarily rapid rise to field rank only four years later, in 1796, and he was promoted to Field Marshal just 8 years after that, in 1804. Continued success brought him the Dukedom of Elchingen in 1808, in which year he began a series of successful campaigns in Spain and Portugal under the overall leadership of Marshal Massena. Always a man of fiery temperament, Ney was sacked for insubordination in 1812 but was soon given command one of the army corps invading Russia, an adventure in which he was one of the very few French generals to enhance his reputation, earning for himself the soubriquet 'bravest of the brave' and the title Prince de Moskwa. In the campaigns of 1813–1814 against the newly-resurgent Allies, Ney fought in almost every eastern-front battle and was several times wounded. In mid-1814, when the Imperial armies had been pushed back to central France, he led the army call for *Buonaparte's abdication. Immediately entering the *Bourbon service, Ney became Commander-in-Chief of Cavalry and, when his old master escaped from Elba in early 1815, led the Royal advance southwards, vowing to bring Napoleon back to Paris 'in an iron cage.' Yet, on actually confronting the Emperor, he immediately fell under his old spell and transferred both his allegiance and army back to the Buonapartist cause. However, Ney's old spark appeared now not quite to re-ignite. Leading the French against *Wellington at the Battle of Quatre Bras he failed to get a grip on events, appearing slow and indecisive. At Waterloo, a few days later, the chief command of the battlefield given to him by Napoleon is often considered to have been one promotion too many, Ney's enormous personal valour — he had five horses shot from under him on the day — not quite disguising his lack of mastery on this grandest of scales. Following the defeat, Ney was soon arrested by the returning Bourbon authorities and, in December, tried and immediately shot for treason.

Ngobe, Kande

A resident of Sierra Leone (COM 8).

Nicholas of Pisa

An author referred to by Maturin (PC 4).

> Nicholas of Pisa (1206?–1278) was a famous Italian sculptor and architect. Maturin may perhaps have in mind Nicholas of Cusa (1401–1464), a Roman Catholic Cardinal and writer on philosophical and scientific matters, or even Nicholas of Padua, a 13th century author of romance verse.

Nicholl

A seaman in HMS Diane (NC 2).

Nicholls or Nicolls

The Second Lieutenant in HMS Surprise, previously of HMS Euralyus, who had been known to Stephen Maturin some years ago in Gibraltar (HMS 5). Following a very unhappy marriage, he is now a changed man, profoundly depressed and seen drunk and dirty on duty (HMS 5). When a squall hits the small island where he and Stephen have landed on an expedition, he disappears and is presumed drowned (HMS 5,6; FSW 4).

Nicholls, Edward

A former First Lieutenant of HMS Arethusa (HD 3).

Nicholson

The gunroom cook's mate in Surprise (WDS 4).

Nicomachean Ethics

A work recited by Maturin in his delirium (HMS 11).

> *Aristotle's Nicomachean Ethics takes its name from the great philosopher's son, Nicomachus (dates unknown), who may have been either the editor or simply the dedicatee of the work. Aristotle's father, a physician, was also named Nicomachus.

Niger, HMS

A ship referred to as being famous for the black dress of her bargemen (RM 2).

> HMS Niger, 32-gun, was launched in 1759. In 1794,

under Captain the Honourable Arthur Kaye Legge (d.1835 in the rank of full Admiral), she fought in *Howe's victory at the Glorious First of June and in 1797, now under Edward James Foote (d.1833 in the rank of Vice Admiral), she was present at the Battle of Cape *St Vincent. Niger (Latin for 'black' and the name of a great African river) became a prison ship in 1810 and, having been renamed HMS Negro in 1813, was sold in 1814. Her replacement, a 38-gun HMS Niger, was launched in 1813 and broken up in 1820.

Nightingale, James

A seaman in HMS Sophie, wounded in action (M&C 7).

Nilus

Martin refers to 'old Nilus' flood' (TH 5).

> Nilus is the Latin name for the River Nile in Egypt, famous for its annual flooding of a broad, fertile valley. The term is also used for the god of the Nile, said to govern its activities.

Nimble, Harry

A name used by Mr Whewell for a Krooman tribesman in Sierra Leone (COM 8).

Nimble, HMS

A large cutter commanded by Lieutenant Michael Fitton (TGS 4; COM 3,4,10), at one point employed on the blockade of Brest (YA 5). At some past time, Jack Aubrey and Stephen Maturin had travelled in her from Spain to England (COM 3).

> Between 1778 and 1816 four 10- or 12-gun cutters named HMS Nimble served in the Royal Navy for various periods.

Niobe

The Honourable East India Company sloop that Aubrey commands on the unsuccessful expedition from Suez to Mubara and back (TH 6–7).

Niobe, HMS

A frigate docked at Port Mahon (M&C 1) that, years later, joins Admiral Thornton's Mediterranean fleet (IM 6).

> The first HMS Niobe of the Royal Navy was the 38-gun ex-French Diane, launched in 1796 but not captured, off Malta, until August 1800 (several months after M&C 1); she was broken up in 1816. In Greek myth Niobe, the wife of King *Amphion of Thebes, had many children, all of whom were murdered by *Apollo and Artemis, the offspring of her jealous rival, Leto: 'Niobe Weeping' (even after being turned to stone in her grief) was consequently long a favourite topic for painters.

Nizam, the

A potentate visited by Richard Canning (HMS 7), who had once given Diana Villiers a large and valuable emerald (HMS 11).

> 'Nizam' was the title of the Ruler (the meaning of the word in Arabic) of the Indian state of Hyderabad from the early 18th century until the mid–20th. In 1798, Nizam Ali

Khan (ruled 1762–1802) was forced to place Hyderabad under British protection, establishing an alliance that lasted until the state was forcibly absorbed by the newly-independent India in 1948. Ali's son, Nizam Akbar Ali Khan, ruled in Hyderabad from 1802 to 1829 (it is presumably he who is visited by *Canning but *Villiers could have received her gem from either ruler).

Noah

The commander of Noah's Ark (SM 3; TH 9; TGS 4; WDS 10; COM 3).

*In the Old Testament, the six hundred year-old patriarch Noah, a descendant of *Seth, was, some 10 generations after *Adam's creation, one of the few remaining virtuous men on earth. *God, having decided to cleanse his creation with a great flood, allowed the old man to build an ark to save himself, his family and pairs of each animal. Noah, his offspring and companions now re-populating the world, died at the age of nine hundred and fifty.*

Noakes, Joe

A seaman in HMS *Surprise*, spied by a creditor amongst HMS *Irresistible*'s crew (RM 1).

Norfolk, USS

A light frigate in the U.S. Navy for which Jack Aubrey believes his somewhat out-of date HMS *Surprise* to be an even match (TH 8). Having been sent to the Pacific, under her Captain Palmer, to disrupt the British whaling trade, Jack and his ship are soon given the task of hunting her down (FSW 1+). After a very long chase, *Norfolk* is eventually found wrecked on a reef off the remote Pacific island of Old Sodbury, with a number of mutineers from HMS *Hermione* then found to be among her marooned crew (FSW 9,10; RM 1; TGS 10).

*As mentioned in FSW author's note, the fictional USS Norfolk is based on the USS *Essex (although both ships are mentioned in TH 8). A Norfolk, 18-gun brig, had briefly served in the U.S. Navy, being launched in 1798 and sold in 1800.*

Norie

The author of a navigational text (TH 9; FW 2).

John William Norie (1772–1843) was a mathematician, hydrographer and publisher whose Epitome of Navigation, *a set of nautical tables, was long the standard work in its field. In addition to this work (and many related charts and books), Norie published several editions of a very useful biographical and geographical compendium of the wars of the period (see **Bibliography** section, below).*

Norman

A carriage horse from the stables of the Royal William Inn (COM 5), later used by Diana Villiers on her coach-team (YA 8).

Normand

A French soldier in Port Mahon (HMS 3).

Norrey

HMS *Lively*'s Master (PC 13; HMS 2).

Norris, Edward

A whaler who had once sailed with Mr Allen (FSW 3).

Norris, George

A mutineer, a gunner's mate, from HMS *Hermione*. Captured by Jack Aubrey from the crew of USS *Norfolk*, he is court-martialed in HMS *Irresistible*, by Jack amongst others, and sentenced to hang (RM 2).

Northcote

A naval medical tome consulted by Maturin (M&C 2,4).

William Northcote (d.1783?) was a naval surgeon of great practical experience, if little formal training, who published a number of influential works, amongst them The Marine Practice of Physic and Surgery *(2 vols, 1770; with an appendix on 'Operating Under Fire') and* The Anatomy of the Human Body for the Use of Naval Practitioners *(1777).*

Northumberland, HMS

A ship seen at Port Mahon (M&C 11) and Gibraltar (HD 2).

HMS Northumberland, *74-guns, was launched in 1798, reduced to a hulk in 1827 and finally broken up in 1850. In 1815, as the flag-ship of Sir George *Cockburn, she conveyed *Buonaparte to his final exile on St Helena.*

Norton

An ornithologist in Bombay whose wife has run off with his erstwhile best friend, Mr Morton (HMS 7).

Norton, Edward

A considerable landowner near the Aubrey family estate, known to Jack as 'Cousin Edward,' though only very distantly related to him (LM 8; C/T 1; COM 3). Himself an MP (WDS 3), Norton offers Jack the late General Aubrey's Parliamentary seat of Milford, which lies in his gift (LM 8,9). A few years later he has died, leaving Jack a large fortune (C/T 3).

Norton, Sam

An able seaman in HMS *Surprise*, promoted Midshipman by Jack Aubrey to replace the departed Oakes (WDS 1+).

Norton, William

A Marine Lieutenant in HMS *Nymphe*, a relation of the Northumberland Collingwoods (TH 9).

Nossa Senhora das Necessidades

A old Portuguese merchant vessel (RM 2).

Nostradamus

A sooth-sayer referred to by Jack Aubrey (PC 6).

Michel Nostradamus (1503–1566), a French physician of high reputation, was also a popular astrologer who, in

1547, started to make prophesies later published in verse form as Centuries (1555).

Nova Scotia, HMS

The sloop that is to take Philip Broke's dispatch on the capture of USS *Chesapeake* from Canada to England (SM 2–4).

HMS *Nova Scotia*, 14-gun brig, (the ex-American privateer *Rapid*, taken in October 1812) arrived, under Lieutenant Bartholomew Kent (d.1841 in the rank of Commander), in Plymouth on July 17th 1813 with *Broke's victory dispatch. Later that year she was re-named HMS *Ferret*, being sold in 1820.

Nugent

The family name of friends of Charlotte and Fanny Aubrey (YA 6).

Numps

The brother of HMS *La Flèche's* purser (FW 2).

Nutmeg of Consolation

One of the many titles of the Sultan of Pulo Prabang (TGS 6), later used by Jack Aubrey both as a facetious reference to one of the 'Old Buggers,' probably Loder (TGS 9), and then as the name of his new ship (NC 7; *see following entry*).

Nutmeg of Consolation, HMS

The name given by Jack Aubrey to the re-floated Dutch 20-gun *Gelijkheid*, given to him by Governor Raffles to replace HMS *Diane* (NC 3–7). Her new name is one of the Sultan of Pulo Prabang's

many fine titles (TGS 6,9). Later, having made her rendezvous with Jack's private ship *Surprise*, she returns to Batavia under Lieutenant Fielding's command (NC 7; C/T 1,4).

> *N.B., curiously, both Stephen *Maturin and Clarissa *Oakes later state that they first met in *Nutmeg, with Stephen even recalling that she carried out both the Australian and Moahu sections of his subsequent missions (COM 2): these events all happened in *Surprise.*

Nuttall

HMS *Ariel's* gunner, who had once served under Philip Broke (SM 8).

Nymph or Nymphe, HMS

A 32-gun frigate, Captain Fielding, that Jack Aubrey meets at Recife after she has been badly damaged in a brief encounter with a Dutch 74-gun, *Waakzaamheid* (DI 5,6; SM 6). A few years later, now under Captain Henry Cotton, she is met by Jack's HMS *Surprise* at Trieste (TH 9), where she has just picked up Charles Fielding, once her Third Lieutenant, following his escape from captivity in France (TH 9,10; FSW 1). Even later still, she forms part of the small inshore squadron blockading the harbour of St Martin (LM 4).

> HMS *Nymphe was launched in 1812 (COLLEDGE suggests that, on the stocks, she had been named HMS* Nereide), sent for harbour service in 1836, re-named HMS *Handy in 1871 and finally broken up in 1875. The* Nymphs (sometimes *Naiads or *Nereids) of Greek mythology are spirits of nature, always represented by beautiful young girls.

O

O., Mr

see **Oakes, Billy**

O., Sir

see **Floode, Sir Oliver**

Oakes

1: a physician at the hospital on Gibraltar (FSW 2).

2: a Marine sentry in HMS *Surprise* (FSW 9).

Oakes, Billy

A Midshipman, left behind in Batavia by HMS *Clio*, who joins Jack Aubrey's HMS *Nutmeg of Consolation*, initially as an ordinary seaman (NC 4–7); he then follows Jack into *Surprise* (NC 8+; C/T 1+). Whilst in New South Wales he conceals a young, transported convict, Clarissa Harvill, aboard the ship. When she is soon discovered by Jack (C/T 1),

the young couple decide to marry, in a ceremony performed by Mr Martin (C/T 2). Oakes seems largely unaffected by, or perhaps is not even wholly aware of, the sexual relations Clarissa begins to have with other of the ship's officers (C/T 3+), although Martin later angrily reports that he beats her (C/T 5). Although Jack is at first furious with Oakes for ever bringing Clarissa aboard (C/T 2+), he soon rates him Master's Mate (C/T 3) and later gives him an order as acting Lieutenant to sail the re-taken whaler *Truelove* to Batavia (C/T 9; *also* WDS 1,2). Once he eventually returns to England he obtains, under the patronage of both Stephen Maturin and Sir Joseph Blaine, a full Lieutenant's commission. However, he is soon reported to have been killed in action (WDS 10; COM 2).

Oakes, Clarissa

A young, well-educated convict from New South

Wales who, although at one time condemned to death in England for shooting a Mr Caley, had won a commutation of the sentence to that of transportation to the penal colony through the offices of one Harry Essex (C/T 7). Under her maiden name of Clarissa Harvill, she is found in Jack Aubrey's *Surprise*, having been concealed there by Midshipman Billy Oakes (C/T 1). Now discovered, Clarissa and Oakes announce their intention to marry, with Jack then making her a gift of some scarlet silk, properly intended for his wife Sophie, in order to make a respectable dress for the ship-board ceremony (C/T 2). Clarissa soon enters sexual relationships — utterly meaningless to her and perhaps intended to secure favours for Billy — with other *Surprise* officers, resulting in deep jealousies and divisions throughout the ship (C/T 3+). Although it is left unclear whether Billy himself is fully aware of his wife's behaviour, at one point Mr Martin angrily reports to Stephen Maturin that he beats her (C/T 5). Clarissa, treated by Stephen for an unspecified, chronic venereal infection, becomes firm friends with the Doctor (C/T 3+) and tells him of a childhood of sexual abuse followed by a descent into prostitution at Mother Abbott's society brothel (C/T 6). From her, Stephen now discovers the connection between the traitors Ledward and Wray and their hitherto secret patron, all some-time clients of the whore-house (C/T 6,7). He is then able to help to arrange for Clarissa and Billy to return to England so that she can give further useful information to Sir Joseph Blaine (C/T 9; *also* WDS 1–3, 5; COM 2, *where she and Stephen mis-recall all these incidents as having taken place on HMS *Nutmeg of Consolation*). Although the pair do return safely home, Oakes himself is soon thereafter killed in action, with the widowed Clarissa then moving in with Stephen's wife, Diana, in part to care for Brigid, the Maturins' strange young infant daughter (WDS 10; COM 2–5). Unfortunately both Diana and Sophie Aubrey now become convinced, wrongly, that Clarissa had been mistress to each of their respective husbands whilst at sea (COM 2,5,6). In the meantime, Clarissa's expected pardon has been delayed by political machinations in England (COM 2+), the traitorous but powerful Duke of Habachtsthal having come to know of her role in his exposure (COM 4,9). It soon becomes necessary for her to flee to Spain — under Stephen's protection and in company with Brigid and the servant Padeen Colman (COM 4,5,10) — but, eventually, she is able to return to England with the Maturin family (she is no longer at odds with Diana) and receive her pardon via the good offices of Blaine (YA 1). Clarissa then moves with the family to the Aubreys' Woolcombe House, where Sophie initially continues somewhat jealous of her supposed relationship with Jack (YA 1+). Later, she helps Diana

to persuade Sophie to forgive the adulterous affair Jack did once have with Amanda Smith (YA 8) and, now on good terms with both families, travels with them to Madeira (YA 10). When the news of Buonaparte's escape from Elba arrives, Clarissa then travels back to England with the families, remaining there as Brigid's guardian after Diana is killed in a coaching accident (HD 1,2).

Clarissa Oakes, *the British title of the fifteenth novel of the series, was afterwards published in the USA as* The *Truelove.

Oakhurst

A former Master of HMSS *Arethusa*, *Euryalus* and *Inflexible* (HD 3).

Oaks, Captain

A Captain whose bargemen are beaten by HMS *Sophie*'s crew in Port Mahon in a dispute over naval precedence (M&C 6).

Oates

A man referred to by Blaine as having been pilloried (RM 9).

*Titus Oates (1649–1705) was an infamous English agitator and perjurer. During the reign of King *Charles II, Oates concocted evidence of Jesuit plots (largely to line his own pockets with bribes and rewards), resulting in the execution of at least 35 innocent Roman Catholics. Shortly after the accession to the throne of the Catholic King *James II in 1685, Oates' extravagant claims and ruthless use of downright lies soon led to his own downfall. Accused and convicted of perjury, he was sentenced to imprisonment, flogging and annual stints in the pillory. Whilst he was enduring this last punishment, a combination of the Protestant fervour of the mob and the unpopularity of King James himself are said to have protected Oates from physical harm. In 1689 the new King, the Protestant *William III, released Oates, who then took up a somewhat less scandalous and deadly variant on his former career of paid informant.*

O'Brien, Thurlough

A King of Thomond who had sacked Clonmacnoise (COM 2).

*There is a little confusion between two separate Irish Kings here. Clonmacnoise Abbey, a renowned centre of learning lying on the banks of the Shannon, was infamously robbed in 1073 by King Turlough O'Brien of Munster (1009–1086), a grandson of *Brian of the Tributes, who thereafter suffered the divine retribution of permanent ill-health for his sin. His later namesake, King Turlough O'Brien of Thomond (d.1306) seems carefully to have avoided any such desecrations.*

O'Byrne

A naval biographer referred to by O'Brian (M&C author's note).

William Richard O'Byrne (1823–1896) published his Naval Biographical Dictionary, *containing a note on every living Royal Navy officer, between 1845 and 1849; a later edition, begun in 1859, was never completed (although many of its entries can be found in BANK: see below). Like the earlier* Biographia Navalis *by John Charnock (1756–1807), the dictionary relied for the most part on officers writing their own contributions, leading to an impression of seamlessly successful careers, occasionally thwarted by lack-lustre superiors, jealous colleagues or an ungrateful government. (Extracts from both of these works, which are undoubtedly useful sources, can now conveniently be found in BANK's* British Biographical Archive*).* RALFE's *Naval Biography of Great Britain (1828) is problematic for the same reason. A similarly conceived work, the* Royal Naval Biography *of John *Marshall, suffers from the same basic defect yet does include much valuable information reproduced from letters and reports, both private and official.*

Ocean

An East Indiaman in Muffit's China Fleet, protected by HMS *Surprise* from Admiral Linois' French squadron (HMS 9).

Ocean, 1200 tons, made 5 round trips from India to England between 1800 and 1810. The action is based on the defence of a Honourable East India Company merchant fleet against *Linois' attack in February 1804. However, no Royal Navy ship was present during the fight, the squadron being organised by the senior Master, Nathaniel Dance of *Earl Camden. On this occasion John Christopher Lochner was Ocean's acting Master.

Ocean, HMS

Admiral Sir John Thornton's flag-ship in the Mediterranean (IM 3,8,9), in which the cousin of the Maltese spy, Giuseppe, had been murdered (TH 1).

HMS Ocean, 98-gun, was launched in 1805, becoming a depot ship in 1841, a coal hulk in 1853 and being finally broken up in 1875. She long acted as one of the chief flagships of the Mediterranean fleet, especially favoured by Admiral Lord *Collingwood.

O'Connor

A member of the barge crew in HMS *Surprise* (HMS 6).

O'Connor Don

A romantic Irish chivalric title referred to by Maturin (PC 8).

This is the traditional title of the head of the clan O'Connor, also sometime High Kings of Ireland.

O'Connors, the

A Protestant, United Irish Society family. In the vain hope of diffusing a growing tension between James Dillon and his Captain, Stephen Maturin tells Jack Aubrey that many United Irishmen were well-educated Protestants and not merely 'Catholic rebels,' as Jack might have supposed (M&C 3).

The two best-recalled O'Connors of the period are Arthur (1763–1852) and his brother Roger (1762–1834), both dedicated Irish nationalists. Arthur was the chief editor of the United Irishmen Press from 1796 to 1798, when he went into exile in France. There, having been made a non-serving, army general by *Buonaparte, in 1807 he married Eliza, the daughter of *Condorcet, becoming a

French citizen in 1818. Roger was also a member of the United Irish Society, being imprisoned from 1797 to 1804 for his activities. He, however, is best remembered as an important writer on early Irish mythology.

Odabashi, the

A Turkish janissary, met by Jack Aubrey's Mubara expeditionary force. He is fluent in English, his mother having been born in Tower Hamlets, a district in London's East End (TH 5).

Oedipus

Jack Aubrey refers to the oddity of both Oedipus' family relationships and his feet (SM 11).

In Greek legend, Oedipus (the name means 'swollen foot' but the reason for the appellation is obscure) was the unwanted son of King Laius of Thebes and his wife *Jocasta, tossed out of the city by the King as a baby. Nevertheless rescued and preserved by peasants, Oedipus returned to Thebes after a life in wandering exile, neither he nor the city knowing anything of his past. Here, at a chance meeting at a cross-roads, he slew Laius (without knowing he was either father or King) and then married his own mother, the newly widowed Queen (neither of them knowing that Oedipus was her son or that he had slain the King). There are, however, many variant accounts both of the tale thus far and of subsequent events. Most have the gods revealing the awful tale to the royal couple (some only doing so after the birth of children), with Jocasta promptly killing herself and Oedipus suffering torments until the end of his life. Several accounts have Oedipus blinding himself with pins from the dress of his dead mother/wife and going into either retirement or exile and most include Thebes itself being ravaged by either plague or war as a consequence of the unhappy events.

Oedipus, HMS

The cartel-ship, plying between England and France, in which Diana Villiers and Stephen Maturin are married by her captain, Commander William Babbington (SM 11; IM 1; RM 5).

Ogle, James

A seaman in Jack Aubrey's HMS *Surprise* who follows his Captain into his temporary command, *Niobe* (TH 6).

Ogle, Paul

see **Palmer, Ellis**

O'Hara

1: Colonel O'Hara, a guest at one of Laura Fielding's musical evenings (TH 3).

2: a man after whom a tower on Gibraltar is named (FSW 2).

General Charles O'Hara (1741?–1802), a career soldier, served as Governor of Gibraltar from 1795 onwards. In 1793, wounded and taken prisoner by General *Buonaparte at Toulon, he was confined in Paris during the worst period of the *Jacobin terror, once exclaiming during an argument with a fellow prisoner, a Frenchman, that, 'In England we can say King *George is mad; you dare not say here that Robespierre is a tiger!'

3: Miss O'Hara, the governess of the Aubrey children (COM 3).

Given the intimate name-derivation of the more usual Miss *O'Mara, 'O'Hara' must surely be a printer's typo.

O'Higgins

The Vicar-General of Peru, whose confidential assistant is Father Sam Panda, Jack Aubrey's natural son (WDS 6,8+).

O'Higgins, Bernardo (*also* 'the younger O'Higgins')

A Chilean General in favour of independence from Spain (RM 9; WDS 8; COM 2; YA 4,7).

Bernardo O'Higgins (1778–1842) was the natural son of Ambrose O'Higgins Ballenary (1720–1801), an Irishman in the Spanish service who, in 1788, had been appointed Captain-General of Chile and, in 1796, Commander-in-Chief (and, very briefly, Viceroy) of Peru. Bernardo, Chilean-born, was sent to London and Madrid in 1795 for his education. Whilst in Europe he came under the influence of the exiled Venezuelan nationalist, Francisco Miranda, and began to entertain hopes of independence for his own native country. He returned home in 1801 and by 1810 had become an influential politician and part-time soldier. In 1808 *Buonaparte's invasion of Spain resulted in the New World colonies being largely left to their own devices and O'Higgins was soon part of a Nationalist junta that replaced the Spanish Governor-General. In 1814, however, the Viceroy of Peru sponsored a loyalist invasion of Chile and O'Higgins fled to Argentina. In 1817 O'Higgins then led another liberation expedition back to Chile, this time successfully, and was soon elected Supreme Dictator (recruiting Lord *Cochrane as his Admiral). Forced to resign this office in 1823, he thereafter lived as an exile in Peru.

O'Higgins, Jaime

One of Maturin's potential protectors in Chile (WDS 9).

Oken

The Professor under whom McLean had studied at Jena (FW 2).

Lorenz Oken or Ockenfuss (1779–1851) was a zoologist, physician and somewhat eccentric philosopher of prodigious output in each field, who in 1807 moved from Göttingen to Jena as Professor of Medical Sciences, a post that he held until moving to Geneva in 1832.

Old, William

A volunteer landsman in HMS *Worcester* who had been an impoverished 'trifler' beforehand (IM 2).

N.B., a 'trifler' was a maker of medium-hard pewter-ware.

Old Bald Peg

A famous racehorse, descended from both Flying Childers and the Darley Arabian (DI 1).

Old Bald Peg (fl.1650), one of the 43 original 'taproot mares,' was an ancestor (not descendant) of the mare to which the *Darley Arabian's son, *Flying Childers, was born. She is regarded as the single most influential mare of the British thoroughbred line.

'Old Buggers'

The name given by HMS *Diane*'s crew to the three pompous members of Mr Fox's Pulo Prabang mission, Crabbe, Johnstone and Loder (TGS 6–9). Later, Jack Aubrey also facetiously refers to them by the Sultan of Pulo Prabang's ritles of Rose of Delight, Flower of Courtesy and Nutmeg of Consolation (TGS 9).

'Old Chucks'

The nick-name of *Surprise*'s bosun, Mr Bulkeley (C/T 1,5).

'Old Fart'

A name by which HMS *Sophie*'s crew refer to Captain Harte (M&C 11).

Oldfield

A seaman in HMS *Polychrest* (PC 9).

'Old Groan'

see **Simmons, Joshua**

Oldham

The Post Captain immediately below Jack Aubrey on the Navy List (TGS 4).

'Old Harry'

A slang term for the Devil (PC 1; HMS 5; TMC 2; DI 10; FW 8; SM 7; IM 2; RM 1; NC 7; COM 10; HD 6).

The term may be derived from 'the one who harries or harasses' or may perhaps be a corruption of 'old hairy,' from a Biblical reference to *devils as 'hairy ones.'

Old Ironsides

see ***Britannia***, HMS *and* ***Constitution***, USS

'Old Jarvey or Jarvie'

see **St Vincent, Admiral Lord**

'Old Lechery'

see **Lovage, Harry**

'Old Man of the Mountains'

see **al-Jabal, Sheikh**

'Old Man of the Sea'

A name given by Jack Aubrey to Awkward Davies (TH 4).

In the Arabian Nights *tale of Sinbad, the Old Man of the Sea clung to the young sailor's shoulders and could only be dislodged by being made drunk.*

'Old Moore'

see **Moore, Old**

'Old Nick'

A reference to Earl St Vincent (COM 5)

'Old Nick' is a slang term for the *Devil, derived from the Scandinavian nik or nicor, an evil spirit especially associated with water.

'Old Pagan'
see **Pagan, Old**

'Old Parr'
see **Parr, Old**

'Old Purchase'
see **Schank, Admiral**

'Old Reliable'
A quarter-gunner in HMS *Surprise* who, although sent to the *Bombay Castle* for the first brush with Linois' squadron, appears to have returned to HMS *Surprise* for the following morning's fight (HMS 9).

'Old Saturnino'
A nickname for Stephen Maturin amongst certain seamen (COM 8).

'Old Subtlety'
A name used by Blaine for a senior intelligence figure (HMS 4).

'Old Thomas'
A former school-mate of William Reade (HD 8).

Oliver
1 a London sausage-maker referred to by Killick (NC 7).

2: part of the catch-phrase 'a Roland to your Oliver' (NC 7).

> *In the King Charlemagne legends, set in the 8th century, Oliver is the very close friend of the hero *Roland, their relationship having been cemented in a long-running, always indecisive duel over a matter of honour.*

Olivia
see **Raffles, Olivia**

Olivier
A naturalist referred to by Sir Joseph Blaine (TGS 3).

> *Guillaume-Antoine Olivier (1756–1814) was a French naturalist and explorer of Persia, Turkey and Egypt. As well as accounts of his travels, he published from 1789 onwards a seven-volume* Dictionary of the Natural History of Insects, Butterflies and Crustaceans.

Ollard, Richard
The dedicatee of *The Thirteen Gun Salute*.

> *Richard Laurence Ollard (b.1923), a distinguished historian and writer on the age of sail, taught at the Royal Naval College, Greenwich, from 1948 to 1959. From 1960 to 1983, he was a staff Senior Editor at Patrick O'Brian's UK publishers, Collins Books and acted as O'Brian's own editor from 1969 until 1987. In his contribution to CUNNINGHAM, Ollard recalls that he accepted O'Brian's manuscript of* Master and Commander *when it had already been rejected by its original, commissioning publishers.*

Omar
A Moslem leader, a mosque bearing whose name lies in Pulo Prabang (TGS 8).

> *Umar/Omar ibn ul Khattab (586–644) was a distant cousin of *Mahomet who, after being his bitter rival, converted to the new faith of Islam in about 615; in 625 the Prophet married Hafsa, his new ally's daughter. After Mahomet's death in 632, his close associate Abu-Bekr founded the Moslem Caliphate and, in 634, he was succeeded to this position by Umar. A brilliant, expansionist general and ruler, Caliph Umar I took the great cities of Damascus and Jerusalem and conquered much of Syria, Persia and Egypt before being assassinated in Medina by a Persian slave. Umar is the object of special veneration by the Sunni sect of Muslims, amongst whom he enjoys a reputation for great wisdom, piety and moderation as well as for the huge expansion of the faith under his rule.*

Omar Pasha
A nephew of Djezzar Pasha who, having fought against the French at Acre in 1799, later became Agha of the Dey of Algiers' janissaries and has now become Dey himself following a *coup* (HD 6,7). After Stephen Maturin saves his life during a nocturnal lion hunt in the desert, he agrees to prohibit the passage of Moroccan gold through his country onwards to eastern Mediterranean Buonapartists (HD 7), but is almost immediately overthrown and (reportedly) murdered, being replaced by Ali Bey (HD 8).

> *Omar Pasha (d.1817), *Agha of the janissaries, became Dey of Algiers in April 1815 following a series of coups that had seen two of his predecessors murdered in a fortnight. After *Buonaparte's final abdication in 1815, the British authorities used their new-won freedom of policy and action to attempt to secure, by forceful negotiation, the release of Christian captives and abolition of slavery in Algiers. When diplomatic pressure failed, the Royal Navy resorted to a fierce bombardment of the city by the combined fleets of Lord Exmouth (see *Pellew, Sir Edward) and his Dutch allies, bringing about a rapid settlement on London's terms. In September 1817, Omar Pasha was murdered by his own Turkish palace guards and replaced by Dey Ali-Khodja.*

O'Mara, Miss
The daughter of an officer killed at the Battle of the Nile, soon to arrive as the governess of the Aubrey children (LM 4; TGS 4), to whom she teaches history, geography and French (C/T 2).

> *In CUNNINGHAM's collected volume, O'Brian says that 'dear Miss O'Mara' was his own childhood governess. Also see* **O'Hara, Miss**

Ommaney
Jack Aubrey's prize agent (TMC 2,6).

> *The Ommanney (sic) family is a distinguished one in British naval history, contributing several admirals and other officers (as well as soldiers, lawyers and politicians) over many years. The reference here is to Sir Francis Molyneaux Ommanney (1774?–1840), a leading prize agent and, from 1818 to 1826, the MP for Barnstaple. He was the son of Rear Admiral Cornthwaite Ommanney (d.1801) and the brother of Admirals Sir John Acworth (1773–1855) and Henry Maneton (d.1857) Ommanney.*

O'Neil, Major

One of Lieutenant-Colonel Keating's officers (TMC 4).

Ophelia

As a Midshipman in the West Indies, Jack Aubrey had performed the singing elements of the role of Ophelia (SM 7). In HMS *Worcester*'s production, the entire role is to be given by Midshipman Williamson until his bout of mumps forces a cancellation (IM 8).

> In William *Shakespeare's *Hamlet, Ophelia is the daughter of the courtier *Polonius and the sister of Laertes. At first Prince Hamlet's lover, she is cruelly spurned as his mind fills with confusion and conspiracy. She herself is then driven to madness and death by Hamlet's killing of her father, twin spurs to Laertes' later revenge on the Prince.

Orbilio, Plagoso

A nickname for 'Old Pagan,' Jack Aubrey's sometime classics master (TGS 7).

> Lucius Orbilius Pupillus (fl. 63 BC) was a grammarian and teacher, famous for his severe views and habits. The poet *Horace, one of his unhappy pupils, recalls him as Orbilius plagosus, 'Orbilius the Flogger.'

Orcus

A reference in a Latin poem translated by Clarissa Oakes (C/T 8).

> In classical mythology, Orcus is another name for Pluto, ruler of the infernal regions.

O'Reilly

The owner or founder of an hotel in Boston (FW 4,5).

Orestes, HMS

A brig-sloop in Jack Aubrey's squadron, Commander Carlow (COM 3,4,10).

> HMS Orestes, 16-gun, was launched in 1805 and sold in 1807. In Greek myth Orestes was the son of King *Agamemnon and Queen Clytemnestra, and the eventual killer (with the help of his sister, Electra) of both his mother and her lover as revenge for their murder of the old king. Orestes later married *Hermione and became King of Argos.

Orient

A ship that Jack Aubrey had seen blow up at the Battle of the Nile (M&C 12; TH 4; *see also* PC 12; HMS 2).

> The French 120-gun Orient was launched in 1791 as Dauphin Royale, re-named Sans-Culotte in 1792 and Orient in 1795. At the Battle of the Nile of August 1798 she was anchored in the centre of the French line as the flagship of Admiral *Brueys, with Honoré Ganteaume aboard as *Captain of the Fleet and Luc-Julien Casabianca as her *Flag Captain. Orient was hotly engaged during the course of the action by four of *Nelson's ships in succession and at about 9.00pm — shortly after Brueys had been killed by a cannon-ball — she took fire. Ganteaume

> and his immediate staff escaped in one of the few remaining undamaged boats, but Casabianca and all but about 70 of his crew were killed in the mighty explosion that utterly destroyed her at about 10.00pm. Contemporary accounts record that the physical shock and emotional horror of the blast produced a pause in the battle lasting several minutes. Captain Casabianca had on board his 11 year-old son, Jacques, who refused to leave his wounded father when the fire took hold: his conduct later inspired the well-known lines by Felicia Hemans (1794–1835), 'The boy stood on the burning deck, whence all but he had fled....' N.B., in both PC 12 and HMS 2 Jack Aubrey makes a verbal slip, saying he saw *Orion, not Orient, destroyed in the action.

Origen

A man who had cut off his own penis in order better to focus his mind (SM 6).

> Origen Adamantius (186?–253?), an Egyptian-born father of the early Christian Church, wrote an edition of the Old Testament in several languages and a number of highly influential commentaries on the scriptures. Very little of his original work has survived, being known today primarily via later commentaries. An extreme ascetic, Origen followed what he took to be the divine exhortation to self-emasculation found in the Gospel of St Matthew, 19:12.

Orion

1: *see* **Orient**
2: a merchant vessel belonging to George Herapath (FW 5,8).

Orion, HMS

The ship in which Jack Aubrey had been Third Lieutenant at the Battle of Cape St Vincent (PC 2; *but see* **Colossus, HMS**), perhaps at the time being ship-mates with Theobald, Wilkins and Blodge (HMS 8). Jack's friend, Yorke, had then been her Second Lieutenant at the Battle of Trafalgar (FW 2). Now said to be merely a receiving ship at Plymouth, she is offered to Jack as a temporary command but, even though this would involve few duties and command full pay, he declines to accept the position (SM 5,6). Restored to her status as a warship, she then serves under her Captain Wodehouse in Admiral Thornton's Mediterranean fleet (IM 8). Later she is commanded by Heneage Dundas (TGS 4) and later still, and presumably now under a different commander, is briefly seen by *Ringle* (COM 5).

> HMS Orion, 74-gun, was launched in 1787 and broken up in 1814 after a very distinguished career as a participant in major battles: *Howe's 1794 victory at the Glorious First of June, the Battle of Cape *St Vincent in 1797, and *Nelson's victories at the Nile in 1798 (on these latter two occasions under Captain Sir James *Saumarez) and Trafalgar in 1805, when she was commanded by Sir Edward *Codrington. She continued to see active service until 1809, when she was gradually retired. In Greek myth, the hunter Orion was slain by the goddess Artemis/Diana and turned into a great cluster of stars.

Orlando and Angelica

The subjects of a love-song given by Laura Fielding (TH 8).

In a number of medieval romances, Orlando (or *Roland), one of King Charlemagne's Christian heroes, falls deeply in love with Angelica, a daughter of the infidel King of Cathay. After many attempts to win her from various rivals, Orlando is driven into a mad fury when he discovers that she has married the young Moorish warrior, Medoro.

Orloff

The name of a great diamond compared by Stephen Maturin to Diana Villiers' 'Blue Peter' (SM 3).

The Orloff diamond is reputed to have been long set as the eye of a Hindu god in the temple of Sri Rangen and then stolen by a French soldier in about 1700. In 1774 the great stone (which some suppose to have been cut from the vanished Great *Moghul) turned up in Amsterdam, being bought there by Prince Gregory Orloff (1734?–1783) as a gift for his lover, Empress Catherine II of Russia.

Orpheus

A musical reference by Maturin (PC 14).

In Greek myth, Orpheus was the greatest of all singers and musicians. In one telling of his tale, he followed his deceased lover, *Eurydice, to the underworld in order to rescue her but, by disobeying a command not to look on her face until they reached the surface-world, then lost her forever.

Orrage

The ship's cook, and a keen singer, in HMS *Surprise* who had lost an arm at the Battle of Camperdown (FSW 3,4).

Osborne

A British intelligence official aboard HMS *Indefatigable* who tries, unsuccessfully, to negotiate Admiral Bustamente's surrender (PC 14; HMS 1,4).

According to *James, the negotiator sent across by Captain *Graham Moore was one Lieutenant Thomas Arscott. A Lieutenant of 1802, he was promoted Commander in 1814 and died in that rank in 1827.

O'Sionnach the Fox

A romantic Irish chivalric title referred to by Maturin (PC 8).

N.B., Sionnach is Gaelic for 'fox' itself.

Osman Pasha

A potentate in the Eastern Mediterranean (TH 4).

In the context this reads as if it were a reference to the Sultan of *Turkey. Although Osman was a common name for the Sultans (indeed, 'Ottoman' comes from the same stem), at the time of TH the throne was held by Mahmood II. The man best known as 'Osman Pasha' was a Turkish general and statesman of a later generation, who lived from 1832 to 1900.

Osman the Smyrniot

An advisor to Sciahan Bey and a friend of Professor Graham (IM 10,11).

Ossian

An ancient author, the subject of much controversy (PC 8).

Ossian — or Oisín — is a famous character in Gaelic literature, the son of Fingal and the father of the hero Finn *MacCoul, supposedly active in the 3rd century. Many of tales and poems ascribed to him are first found in manuscripts dating from about 1400 onwards. In the early 1760s, James MacPherson (1736–1796) published to great acclaim Fingal, verses which he claimed to have translated from newly-discovered, original Ossian manuscripts. In 1775 Dr *Johnson disputed both Ossian's existence and MacPherson's honesty, thus joining in a lively controversy which had already been running since 1762 and which then lasted until at least 1807, when a committee of learned Scots carefully debunked MacPherson's manuscripts. Whether MacPherson had invented the verses or not, his Fingal was hugely influential on the whole 'Romantic Movement' in Europe.

Ota

A Danish Queen who had sacked Clonmacnoise (SM 7).

Othello

George Herapath refers to Othello's blackness (FW 8) and Stephen Maturin to his jealousy (TH 4).

William *Shakespeare's Othello, the Moor of Venice was written between 1602 and 1604. Othello himself is a Moorish (i.e., originally a North African Arab) general, a hero in the service of the city-state of Venice. His marriage to Desdemona, the daughter of a senator, is wrecked by the machinations of his subordinate commander, Iago, who has been passed over for promotion in favour of Cassio, a rival. Iago then induces Othello to believe Desdemona has become Cassio's lover, resulting both in her death at her husband's hands and Othello's own suicide when he realises that he has been duped.

Otter, HMS

An 18-gun sloop initially commanded by Lord Clonfert (TMC 1,3). When he is given HMS *Néréide*, Jack Aubrey promotes *Otter*'s First Lieutenant, Tomkinson, to be her Commander (TMC 4,8).

HMS Otter, 18-gun, was launched in 1805, sent for harbour service in 1814 and sold in 1828. During the Mauritius campaign she was at first under Commander Nesbit Willoughby, the partial model for *Clonfert. She was given to *Tompkinson in March 1810.

Ottoboni

A lady whom Canning says is singing the *Contessa*

in a London performance of *The Marriage of Figaro* (PC 8).

> *The name is perhaps borrowed and adapted by O'Brian from two well-known musical figures, the great artistic patron Cardinal Pietro Ottonboni (1667–1740) and the tenor Gaetano Ottoni (1736?–1827).*

Oudh, Nawab of

An Indian potentate referred to by Colonel Mac-Pherson (NC 8).

> *Given that MacPherson seems to be telling a tale of his long-past service in India, the reference could be to one of several *Nawabs of Oudh (later known as Lucknow): Shuja-ud-Dawlah, ruler from 1754 to 1775; his successor, Asafuddaula (1749–1797); or his successor (in 1798, after a brief, disputed period), Sa'adat Ali, who then ruled until the greater part of the state was annexed by Sir Arthur Wellesley (later Duke of *Wellington) in 1801.*

Oudinot

A French General (SM 6,7).

> *Nicolas Charles Oudinot (1767–1847), Duc de Reggio was a career soldier who rose through the ranks, becoming famous for his personal valour and for the 22 serious wounds he received in his career; *Buonaparte indeed likened him to the Chevalier *Bayard. He was first promoted General in 1794, rising to Maréchal in 1809 and being made a Duke in the following year. Loyal to the Emperor until the collapse in national morale of 1814, he was instrumental in arranging the subsequent armistice with the Allies. Briefly exiled during Buonaparte's 'Hundred Day' return, Oudinot later became Commander of the *Bourbon Royal Guard and Governor of the Invalides, the Parisian hospital for retired soldiers.*

Our Lady of Consolation

Laura Fielding has a devotional picture on this topic hanging in her house (TH 10).

> *In the Roman Catholic religion, 'Our Lady of Consolation' is one of the traditional titles of *Mary, the mother of *Jesus.*

Ovart

A name mentioned by Sir Joseph Blaine to Stephen Maturin in connection with an intelligence plot (RM 5).

> *This may possibly be a reference to Gabriel Julien Ouvrard (1740–1846), a wealthy French financier associated with naval matters from 1797 onwards. From 1808 to 1813 he was imprisoned on unspecified charges and he was certainly a character who played all ends against the middle under both *Buonaparte and the *Bourbon restoration.*

Overly

A seaman in HMS *Bellona* who recovers from yellow fever (COM 9).

Overreach, Sir Giles

A character in a play to whom Jack Aubrey compares the somewhat grasping Admiral Bertie (TMC 3).

> *Sir Giles Overreach is the villain of* A New Way to Pay Old Debts *(1625–1626) by the English playwright, Philip Massinger (1583–1640). After tricking and robbing his young nephew of the family estate, Overreach attempts to marry off his own daughter, Margaret, into the higher echelons of society. Various worthy figures combine to do Sir Giles down by enabling Margaret to marry her true love, the young Tom Allworth. The cruel father now discovers that he is to be deprived both of his hopes and, by a legal judgement, his ill-gotten property: he goes mad and is consigned to *Bedlam, to the joy of all around him.*

Ovid

The Latin poet quoted by Maturin (RM 3).

> *Publius Ovidius Naso (43BC–18AD) was a leading Roman poet and society figure, suddenly and permanently banished in by the Emperor Augustus in 8AD for reasons that remain obscure (although he may have been a minor accomplice in the adultery of Augustus' daughter, Julia, either by some direct action or by the provision of poetic encouragement). Much of his prodigious output consists of sophisticated, witty love poems of great charm and insight but his grandest work is the* Metamorphoses, *a collection of tales blending myth, history and sheer imagination in which the poet so artfully represents the twists and turns of the human condition that the verses have remained popular and provocative for nearly 2000 years. His powers of detailed description have also made Ovid one of the foremost inspirations for visual artists down the centuries. In exile, the poet produced* Sorrows, *a somewhat elegiac, melancholy work in which he both pleads for Imperial forgiveness and resolutely defends his artistic integrity.*

Owen

1: a seaman in *Surprise* who had once been abandoned on Easter Island (C/T 1) by the fur-trader *Proby* (C/T 2). He is a fluent Polynesian speaker (C/T 1+).
2: an apothecary in Hampshire (COM 3).

Owen, Bill

A seaman in HMS *Lively* killed when the nearby Spanish *Mercedes* blows up (PC 14).

Owner, the

A reference to Mr Dalgleish of *Diligence*, the literal owner of the vessel (SM 3), and later to Jack Aubrey, the figurative 'owner' of his ship, HMS *Diane* (DI 8).

P

P., Lieutenant
see **Pullings, Tom**

P., Mr
see **Palmer, Ellis**

P., Mrs
see **Pullings, Mrs**

Pablito
A servant at Thompson's Hotel at Gibraltar (HD 1).

Pachacutic Inca
The first great Inca conqueror (WDS 9).
> *Pacacuti Inca Yupanqui (fl. 15th century; Inca Emperor 1438–1471) was initially the leader of the Cuzco Inca. He then rapidly extended his empire from southern Peru northwards into Ecuador, unifying all the Inca under his rule. In 1471 Pacacuti abdicated in favour of his son, Topa Inca Yupanqui.*

Padeen
see **Colman, Padeen**

Pagan, Old
Jack Aubrey's classics master when a boy (M&C 1), a.k.a. '*Plagoso Orbilio*' for his propensity to flog (TGS 7).
See also **Orbilio, Plagoso**

Paganini
A renowned violinist (SM 4).
> *Niccolò Paganini (1782–1840), a native of Genoa, is often regarded as the greatest of all violin virtuosi, usually playing works of his own composition designed to display his extraordinary technique. He was also an exceptionally talented guitarist. Paganini made his reputation from about 1795 onwards with his greatest successes coming from 1805 until about 1834, when ill-health eventually forced him to retire. His showmanship, his debauched, satanic appearance, and his instrumental ability (unrivalled in his own lifetime) all stimulated tales that he had sold his soul to the devil.*

Page
A famously cruel judge referred to by Lawrence (RM 7).
> *Sir Francis Page (1661?–1741) was a judge notorious amongst his contemporaries for harshness and brutality (a verdict that his DNB entry regards as somewhat unjustified on the facts), being famously ridiculed by leading authors such as Alexander *Pope (as 'the Hanging Judge'), Henry Fielding and Dr *Johnson.*

Paget, General
A passenger in HMS *Charwell* (PC 1).
> *This may be a reference to the career soldier Sir Edward Paget (1775–1849), a younger brother of that General the*

Earl of Uxbridge (1768–1854) who lost his leg alongside *Wellington at the Battle of Waterloo. Sir Edward Paget spent much of his career closely associated with joint military/naval operations and had been present at the battle of Cape *St Vincent in 1797 as a Lieutenant-Colonel. However, he was not promoted from full Colonel to Brigadier-General until October of 1803, a year or so after PC 1 is set. In 1809 Paget lost an arm at the Battle of Oporto and from 1811 to 1814 was held prisoner-of-war in France. The younger brother of the family, Sir Charles Paget (1778–1839), served in the Royal Navy, becoming Post Captain in 1797, Rear Admiral in 1823 and Vice Admiral in 1837.

Paine, Thos.
A seaman in HMS *Leopard* (DI 9).

Paine, Tom
The radical writer (WDS 4).
> *Thomas Paine (1737–1809) was a famous radical of English Quaker origins who spent much of his political career in America and France. Between the ages of 16 and 19 he served at sea, aboard English privateers, but, by about 1768 and now back in England, he had become a moderately successful tradesman (a corset-maker), a vociferous and active Whig, and a publisher of political poetry. From 1774 to 1787 Paine lived mostly in America as a writer, an editor, an intelligence officer in the Revolutionary Army and then as a cantankerous politician in the new USA, of which he became a citizen. His pamphlet* Common Sense *(1776) was extraordinarily influential on the development of revolutionary ideas in his newly adopted home. In 1787 he returned to London (in order to indulge another passion, the promotion of schemes for building iron bridges) and in 1790 travelled to Paris. Under the influence of French revolutionary fervour, and as a riposte to the Irishman Edmund Burke's conservative* Reflexions on the Revolution, *Paine wrote his famous* Rights of Man *(1791). A huge success, the book inevitably embroiled him in legal actions in England, where he narrowly escaped imprisonment. In Paris once again, he soon became opposed to the violent excesses of the Jacobins and in 1793 was imprisoned. For a while in grave peril of his life, he was released on U.S. intervention in the following year, whereupon he published his* Age of Reason *(1795). On his return to the USA in 1802, Paine resumed his controversial and disputatious career as a polemicist and agitator, although now in growing obscurity and failing health.*

Painter
1: the Commander of the sloop HMS *Victor*, one of the judges at the trial of the HMS *Hermione* mutineers (RM 2).
2: a released convict in New South Wales, now a clerk to Firkins (NC 9).

Paisley
The Purser of HMS *Bellona*, an accomplished viola player (YA 5).

Pake, Kitty

A popular singer referred to by Etherege (HMS 6).

Pakeea

A Polynesian warrior, met by Jack Aubrey at Annamooka Island and said to be the under-chief of Tiaro (C/T 5,6).

Tiaro may be a village, or may be a slip for *Tereo, said elsewhere to be Chief of Annamooka and King of the Friendly Islands.

Pakenham

The designer of an emergency rudder system (DI 8; IM 3; COM 1).

The jury rudder — consisting of three spars lashed together, with planks fixed either side of the sea-end — was invented and advocated by one of a large family of distinguished Irish military- and sea-officers, Captain Edward Pakenham (d.1798); the design was still in use in the 1820s. Pakenham was lost off Sumatra in July 1798 when his HMS Resistance, 44-gun, blew up after being struck by lightning (see also *Harris, Snow). Very few of his crew survived the explosion itself and only one lived long enough to tell his tale.

Palestrina

A composer whose *Missa Brevis* is heard by Maturin in Tarragona (M&C 8).

Giovanni Pierluigi da Palestrina (1525?–1594) was born in Palestrina, near Rome. In 1550 the Bishop of Palestrina was elected Pope Julius III and summoned the young organist, singer and teacher to Rome as a choirmaster, the calling which he thereafter followed under a number of patrons, in various important churches. During his career, Palestrina composed about one hundred masses (including the Missa Brevis of 1570) as well as many other vocal works, both sacred and secular.

Pallas

A naturalist referred to by Maturin (M&C 2).

Pyotr Simon Pallas (1741–1811) was a German naturalist, geographer and traveller who originally trained as a physician. From 1767 to 1810 he was associated exclusively with the development of Russian natural science and during his lifetime enjoyed a reputation equal to that of *Buffon and even, in some minds, *Linnaeus.

Pallas, HMS

The ship into which Captain Allen is promoted from HMS *Sophie*, leaving a vacancy for Jack Aubrey (M&C 1).

HMS Pallas, 38-gun, was launched in 1780 as HMS *Minerva. Renamed in 1798, she was then reduced to a troopship, being broken up in 1803. In classical myth, Pallas was another name for the goddess *Athena, herself often associated with the Etruscan goddess Minerva.

Pallière, Captain

see **Christy-Pallière, Captain**

Palmer

1: Sophie Williams' uncle, a great traveller (HMS 1).

2: the Captain of USS *Norfolk* (FSW 5+) who, pursued into the Pacific by Jack Aubrey's HMS *Surprise*, is wrecked and marooned with his crew on Old Sodbury Island. After unsuccessfully trying to persuade Jack that the war has ended, he is eventually made prisoner (FSW 9,10; RM2). By implication, Palmer was an admirer of the social idealist, Jean Dutourd (C/T 6).

Palmer, Elliott

An elderly, learned gentleman whose name the fraudster 'Ellis Palmer' may have part-borrowed (RM 7).

Palmer, Ellis

The assumed name of the fraudster, an associate of Wray and Ledward, who gives Jack Aubrey the stock market tip that leads to his conviction for fraud (RM 4+; COM 4). He is also know as 'Black Coat.' When his disfigured body is later found in the Thames, we learn that his real name had been Paul Ogle (RM 7). 'Palmer' is soon revealed also to have been a secret agent of the French spy, Duhamel (RM 10; LM 2).

Pamela

see **Fitzgerald, Lord Edward** and **Lady Pamela**

'Pamela'

A novel by Richardson (FW 2).

Samuel *Richardson published his epistolary novel Pamela, or Virtue Rewarded in 1740–1741. The young Pamela Andrews is left destitute by the death of her employer, known only as Lady B_. Mr B_, the son of the family, has designs on her virtue and, by various oppressions and confinements, attempts to wear down her resistance. Yet it is her exquisite character that eventually wears down even his dishonourable lust and the two marry happily. In the second installment of the book (written by Richardson because forged sequels to the first soon appeared), Pamela is portrayed as an ineffably virtuous wife and mother, continuing the reform of her husband's somewhat wayward habits. The novel, vastly successful in the public eye, was parodied for its excessively high moral tone by Henry Fielding (the author of Tom *Jones, and, in this case, Shamela) and others.

Panda, Sam

Jack Aubrey's natural, black son from his youthful liaison with Sally Mputa. Looking for his father, he has visited Sophie Aubrey in England and now, *en route* to Brazil, meets Jack by chance in Barbados, where he strikes up a friendship with his fellow–Catholic Stephen Maturin, revealing his desire to be ordained priest (RM 1). Later Sophie confesses to a liking for Sam, although she stops short of specifically acknowledging him as her husband's son (RM 6). At first able only to enter minor orders owing to his bastardy (TGS 1), Sam is now about to be ordained full priest through Stephen's influence in Rome (TGS 3; NC 7). In this new capacity he moves from Brazil to Peru, where he becomes confidential secretary to the pro-independence Vicar-General, O'Higgins (WDS 6,7). Having helped Stephen to set up the planned rebellion, on its later collapse in disarray he is able to tell Jack of Stephen's escape and whereabouts (WDS 9; also COM 5).

Pandora, HMS
A ship that had been sent in search of the HMS *Bounty* mutineers, Peter Heywood amongst them. She was later wrecked, and the captive seamen nearly drowned, when her Captain Edwards refused to release them from their cage (DI 1).

> *HMS* Pandora, *24-gun, was launched in 1779 and lost under her Captain *Edwards on the Great Barrier Reef in August 1791, just as *Heywood describes. In classical myth Pandora was the first human woman, created on *Zeus' orders to punish the human race for having accepted the assistance of the 'rebel god,' Prometheus. Given a box, or jar, containing 'gifts' from all the gods, when she opened its lid there flew out all the evils that have since plagued humanity.*

Pangloss
A Royalist with whom Maturin intends to hold a clandestine meeting in France (IM 7).

> *The name is presumably a pseudonym taken from Dr Pangloss, the philosopher in *Voltaire's* Candide *who blithely maintained that 'all is for the best, in the best of all possible worlds,' despite all too clear evidence to the contrary. His position is intended as a satire on that of *Leibnitz.*

Panmure, Lord
A friend of Blaine, present at the dinner given to honour Aubrey (LM 7).

> *William Ramsey Maule (1771–1852), Lord Panmure of Brechin and Navar, was a well-known gambler, rake and radical-Liberal MP.*

Paon
A ship, commanded by Captain Penhoët in 1799, whose name Jack Aubrey pronounces as 'Pong' (PC 4).

> Paon *is French for 'peacock' and, although several French ships have held this name, none were in service in or around 1799.*

Papa
The father of Lady Queenie Keith (HD 9).
Also see **Thrale, Mrs**

Papadopoulos
The owner of a Buonapartist ship-yard in the Adriatic destroyed by fire (HD 5).

Papenburg or Pappenburg
A flag used by Aubrey as a *ruse de guerre* (PC 9; *also* HMS 1).

> *Papenburg is a town and district in Hanover, Prussia.*

Papin
The inventor of 'Papin's Digester' (LM 2).

> *Denis Papin (1647–1712?), a French medical doctor and physicist, was one of the inventors of the steam engine and, in 1679, developed his 'digester,' a pressure-cooker used to soften bones for stocks and stews. Elected a Fellow of the Royal Society in 1681, he spent much of his later life in London but eventually sank into obscurity and died unnoticed.*

Paquita
Mrs Thomas' Spanish maid (M&C 11).

Paracelsus
A medical authority referred to by Maturin (M&C 2; TMC 7; IM 2; TGS 1).

> *Theophrastus Phillipus Aureolus Bombastus von Hohenheim (1493–1541), called 'Paracelcus,' was a Swiss-born military surgeon, chemist, philosopher and mystic. His original and controversial thinking on the diagnosis of illness and the treatment of wounds was extremely influential, yet rather more so long after his death than during his own lifetime when he was often denounced as a charlatan.*

Paramour
Jack Aubrey refers to Halley's command of the *Paramour* pink (TH 3).

> *HMS* Paramour, *6-gun pink, was launched in 1694 and sold in 1706. She was commanded by *Halley on a voyage of exploration lasting from 1698 to 1700.*

Pardal
A Barcelona smuggling vessel, owned by Mateu and protected by the privateer *Gloire*, later captured by Jack Aubrey's HMS *Sophie* (M&C 7).

Parfit, Mr
The elderly, musical cooper of HMS *Worcester* (IM 5).

Parfitt
A seaman in HMS *Surprise* (NC 8).

Paris, Matthew
A servant aboard HMS *Polychrest*, an ex-framework knitter, who makes Maturin the infamous one-piece, woolen garment that so entertains the officers of HMS *Lively* (PC 12).

Parker
1: a man addressed by Molly Harte at her salon (M&C 1).
2: the elderly, somewhat deaf First Lieutenant of Jack Aubrey's HMS *Polychrest*, a member of the Duke of Clarence's circle (PC 6+). His harsh disciplinary regime, combined with his poor seamanship, bring HMS *Polychrest* to the point of mutiny, a situation that Jack defuses by taking the ship straight into action against *Fanciulla* in the heavily defended Chaulieu harbour (PC 11). Following the successful action, Jack

somewhat reluctantly recommends Parker for independent command and Lord Melville then gives him the captured and bought-in *Fanciulla*, rated a sloop for his new rank of Commander. Parker later visits Jack, now in HMS *Lively*, to express his gratitude (PC 12).

3: a Lieutenant in HMS *Africaine*, killed in action. With Forder and Tullidge, he had earlier asked Surgeon Cotton whether Captain Corbett might be relieved of command on the grounds of insanity (TMC 9).

Parker, Edward

A former shipmate, from a famous naval family (RM 4), who attends Jack Aubrey's ordeal in the pillory ordeal (RM 9).

Curiously, at least three separate Parker families contributed multiple Captains and Admirals to the Royal Navy, perhaps the most famous of them being those East Anglian Parkers often fore-named 'Hyde' (see below). However, the only Edward Parker in the Royal Navy of the time had been promoted Commander in 1799 and had then died in 1801, well before RM is set.

Parker, Hyde

The Captain of HMS *Tenedos* (FW 8; SM 1).

Sir Hyde Parker (1784–1854) was the son of that Admiral Sir Hyde Parker (1739–1807) whose recall signal at the Battle of Copenhagen was famously ignored by the one-eyed *Nelson and the grandson of Vice Admiral Sir Hyde Parker (1714–1782), a famous prize-taker and fighting commander who had been murdered by natives of the Malabar Islands following the wrecking of his HMS Cato on a reef. O'Brian's Hyde Parker had been made Post in 1807 and commanded HMS *Tenedos on the North American station throughout the War of 1812 (which in fact lasted until early 1815). In 1815 he accepted the surrender of Stephen Decatur's USS *President after she had been harried and crippled by a small British squadron. Parker was promoted Rear Admiral in 1841 and Vice Admiral in 1854, having become *First Sea Lord in 1853. His son, also Hyde (1824–1854), rose to a Post Captaincy but was killed in action just a few weeks after his father's death.

Parker, Nosey

A reference by Mowett to the interfering Admiral Harte (TH 10).

'Nosey Parker' is common British slang for one who intrudes into affairs not of his or her concern.

Parkin & Clapp

A firm who have issued a judgement summons against Aubrey (HMS 4).

Parkinson, Professor Northcote

O'Brian tells us that Parkinson edited the memoirs of Lieutenant Samuel Walters, RN, a volume not published until 1949 (IM author's note).

C. Northcote Parkinson (1909–1993; the 'C' is for Cyril), a historian and educator, is best remembered for his Parkinson's Law of 1958, a telling satire on the economics of work. Having once been a schoolmaster at Dart-

mouth Royal Naval College, Parkinson became Professor of Naval History at Liverpool University after service in World War II and later Professor of History at the University of Singapore. As well as his satires, Parkinson wrote many well-regarded volumes of naval history and biography (including The Life and Times of Horatio Hornblower, *a 'biography' of C.S. Forester's fictional naval hero) and a series of novels of the Napoleonic era featuring Captain Richard Delancy, RN.*

Parley

The surgeon of the *Lord Nelson* Indiaman (PC 5).

Parley, Jack

A servant of Mr Newman who assists in getting Jack Aubrey's new astronomical telescope aboard HMS *Boadicea* (TMC 1).

Parr, Admiral

A member of the Admiralty Board (HMS 1).

Parr, Old

A character referred to by Maturin as sexually active at age 122 and beyond (SM 6).

Thomas Parr (1483?–1635) was a Shropshire farmer, renowned for his longevity and vigour. In 1608 he married for the third time, taking a neighbouring widow, Jane Adda, as his wife (there appear to have been no offspring from the union) and continuing to work the land beyond his one hundred and thirtieth year.

Parslow

A Midshipman in HMS *Polychrest*, the son of a naval widow and a protégé of the Commissioner of Portsmouth dockyard (PC 7–11).

Parslow, 'Sleeper'

A seaman in HMS *Surprise*, a perpetual over-sleeper (IM 11).

Parsons

1: a seaman in HMS *Polychrest* (PC 9).
2: a Polynesian-speaking seaman in *Surprise* (C/T 5).

Parsons, William

The 'sea-daddy' who was the young Jack Aubrey's mentor on details of practical seamanship (YA 5).

Partholan

A character mentioned by Maturin as an early visitor to Ireland (TGS 4).

In Celtic legend, Partholan arrived in Ireland after the flood with his fellow-chieftains and their families, becoming the second wave of inhabitants of the island—after *Ceasoir—and the founders of its distinctive civilization.

Partre

A French gunner from *Bellone*, now in the captured *Lord Nelson* as prize-crew (PC 5).

Pascal

The great scientist and mathematician (NC 9; HD 5).

Blaise Pascal (1623–1662), the great French mathematician, philosopher and scientist, was one of the outstanding figures of the mid–17th century intellectual world. As is common in the field, he made his mathematical reputation early in life but, after 1654, then turned his talents almost entirely to religious questions, becoming an extreme ascetic said to wear a metal 'hair shirt' beneath his clothes as a penance. In France herself he was, and is, distinguished equally for the elegant wit of his prose style (especially in Provincial Letters *of 1656) as for the profundity of his mathematics.*

Pasiphae

A character referred to by Maturin as having loved a bull (SM 11).

In Greek myth, Pasiphae was the wife of King Minos of Crete, made by *Zeus to fall in love with a handsome bull that her husband had failed to sacrifice to the deity. From the bestial union sprang the *Minotaur, eventually slain by *Theseus.

Pasley

A Royal Navy hired brig at Gibraltar (M&C 12).

The Sir Thomas Pasley *hired brig, 16-gun, was active in the Mediterranean from 1801 to 1802, forming part of Sir James Saumarez' squadron. She was almost certainly named for Sir Thomas Pasley (1734–1808), a brave and popular Scottish officer who had risen to the rank of full Admiral in January 1801, having, as a Rear Admiral, lost a leg in *Howe's great victory at the Battle of the Glorious First of June in 1794. From 1799 until his 1801 promotion, Pasley was *Port Admiral at Plymouth.*

Paterson

An officer in New South Wales, wounded by Macarthur in a duel (NC 8).

William Paterson (1755–1810) had gone to New South Wales in 1791 as a Captain in the newly raised 'Rum Corps.' He was made Lieutenant-Governor 1794, being promoted Lieutenant-Colonel in 1798 and full Colonel in 1808. An easy-going, even indecisive man, Paterson fell out with his industrious subordinate, *Macarthur, and in 1801 fought with him, being very badly wounded in the duel. In 1808 he assumed temporary control of the colony on Governor *Bligh's deposition but left Australia in early 1810 following *Macquarie's arrival with a replacement regiment. He then died at sea during the voyage home. Colonel Paterson was a naturalist of some distinction, a friend of Sir Joseph *Banks and, from 1798 onwards, a Fellow of the Royal Society.

Patier and Honneur

Words spoken by a captured French officer that Jack Aubrey fails to understand, supposing them to be the names of people (HMS 2).

The Ensign has of course called in aid his notions of patrie *(homeland) and* honneur *(honour).*

Patrick

A cousin of Midshipman Geoghegan (YA 5).

Patrick, Saint

The patron saint of Ireland (PC 6; LM 2,9; YA 1,3).

St Patrick (373?–463?) was the son of a minor Romano-British official, the family residing somewhere in western Great Britain. At an early age Patrick was abducted by raiding pirates and taken into captivity on the neighbouring island of Ireland. After his release, or perhaps escape, some years later, he then studied in Gaul for the priesthood and later returned to Ireland to preach the Gospel. In the O'Brian series his name is very often compounded by Roman Catholic characters into religious oaths and greetings such as '*God, *Mary and Patrick be with you.'

Patroclus

A military figure referred to by Maturin as a famous paederast (COM 8).

In *Homer's Iliad, *Patroclus and his father Menoetius were offered refuge by King Peleus, the father of *Achilles, after the young man had accidentally killed a play-mate. In due course he became Achilles' personal attendant and fellow-warrior, until being slain in battle by the Trojan *Hector. The Greek dramatist Aeschylus later portrayed Achilles and Patroclus as lovers, a relationship not specified, but perhaps inherent, in Homer's treatment of the pair.*

Patterson

1: a Lieutenant whom Aubrey had wanted for HMS *Worcester* in place of the incompetent Somers (IM 2).
2: a one-armed Lieutenant in command of the armed transport ship HMS *Polyphemus* (IM 6). He thinks Aubrey not bold enough in his attempts to provoke the French into breaching the neutrality of Medina (IM 7).

Paul

1: a seaman in HMS *Shannon* (FW 8).
2: Mr Paul, Admiral Harte's secretary in the Mediterranean (IM 6).

Paul, Saint

A prodigious traveller (PC 6), eventually shipwrecked (HMS 8) off Malta (TH 2).

Saint Paul the Apostle (d.65 AD) was born as Saul of Tarsus, a Roman citizen and strict Pharisee. At first strongly opposed to the new Christian cult, he was even instrumental in its persecution. Then, whilst travelling to Damascus, he received a great vision from *God that led both to his conversion and to his joining the other Apostles of *Jesus Christ in Jerusalem. Thereafter he travelled extensively, preaching, writing letters, and energetically developing Christian doctrine. The New Testament Acts of the Apostles *recounts his shipwreck at Malta (Melita in Latin) whilst enroute to Italy and his subsequent conversion of *Publius and the island. Eventually, in about 59 AD, he was arrested in Jerusalem, initially for his own protection from the mob but soon on charges of sedition. As a citizen, he was entitled to trial in Rome, whence he was taken; but we know only that he was then held there for at least 2 years before his death (which may perhaps have been by execution during *Nero's persecution).*

Paulett, Mrs

A lady to whom Lord St Vincent addresses a letter on the subject of her brother, Captain Mainwaring (PC 3).

> *St Vincent's letter to Mrs Paulett (whom I have been unable to identify) was dated March 27th 1802. In the version of the letter printed in Edward *Brenton's biography of the great man, the Captain-brother is identified only as 'Captain M___y' (sic). Of the Royal Navy Mainwarings, none was either a Commander or Post Captain in 1802.*

Paulo

An assassin employed by the French agent Lesueur (TH 10).

Paulton, John (*on one occasion* Nathaniel)

A former university friend of Mr Martin now encountered in New South Wales, where he is a Catholic convert (*also* C/T 1) both writing a novel and working on his cousin's farm: John was once known as 'Anguish' Paulton for his melancholy love-verses (NC 9). He assists in Padeen Colman's escape from the penal colony in return for a passage back to England and help from Maturin with the publication of his book (NC 9; COM 7). Curiously, Nathaniel Martin on one occasion addresses his old friend as 'Nathaniel' too (NC 10).

Paunch's

The shop in Port Mahon where Jack Aubrey had bought his Commander's epaulette (M&C 9).

Pausanias

An author whose treatment of Pyrrhus is discussed by Professor Graham (IM 10).

> *Pausanias of Magnesia (fl.150 AD) was the author of* A Description of Greece *in which, amongst other things, he idolised the great heroes and patriots of the glory-days of his homeland.*

Pavelic

The owner of a Buonapartist ship-yard in the Adriatic destroyed by fire (HD 5).

Payne, Mrs

Admiral Russell's cook (LM 1).

Peacock, the

Satan, as referred to by Adi, the devil-worshipping cook in *Surprise* (LM 5).

Peacock, HMS

A ship sunk by USS *Hornet* (FW 4,8,9; SM 1; FSW 5). Mr Mowett was serving in her at the time, being wounded in the action (FW 6).

> *HMS* Peacock, *18-gun brig-sloop, was launched in 1806 and, under Captain Billy *Peake, sunk off Demerara by *Lawrence's USS *Hornet on February 24th 1813.*

Peake, Billy

The Captain of HMS *Peacock*, killed when she was sunk by USS *Hornet* (FW 4).

> *William Peake (d.1813) was made Lieutenant in 1797 and promoted Commander in 1806. In late February 1813 his sloop HMS *Peacock, a ship known on the North American station as 'the yacht' for her Captain's attention to the beauty of her deck and rigging, engaged *Lawrence's USS *Hornet. In a 15 minute action, the lamentable standard of Peake's gunnery left the American virtually unscathed whilst his own ship was reduced to a shambles — a third of her crew of 122 killed or wounded — and holed repeatedly below the water-line. Peake was killed by Hornet's second broadside and his ship soon surrendered. She then rapidly settled in the water, unfortunately leading to the deaths of three of the American prize-crew as well as nine more of her own men. Peake came from a large naval family, being the son of Sir Henry Peake, Surveyor of the Navy from 1806 to 1822 and the elder brother of both Thomas Ladd Peake (1785–1865; Post Captain of 1822) and Henry Frederick Peake (dates unknown) a Royal Navy Lieutenant of post–1815 who, in 1833, joined the Portuguese Navy under an alias and held command of* Donna Maria, *42-gun, until about 1836.*

Pearce

1: a seaman in HMS *Surprise* who had been confined as a lunatic on Gibraltar (FSW 6).

2: the prosecutor at Jack Aubrey's fraud trial (RM 7,8).

> *Given the description of the peculiar trial, the name is possibly inspired by that the London lawyer James Pearce (dates unknown) who in 1814 published a* Treatise on the Abuse of Laws.

3: Mrs Pearce, the cook at Woolcombe House (YA 3).

Pearce, George

A seaman in HMS *Sophie* (M&C 6).

Pearce, Henry

A famous prize-fighter, a.k.a. the 'Game Chicken,' who had once been met by Maturin on his way to fight Tom Cribb (FSW 9; YA 3).

> *Henry — or 'Hen,' whence his nickname — Pearce (1777–1809) was one of the leading English pugilists, retiring as undefeated Champion of England shortly before his early death from consumption. His most famous fight — a 59-round match with John *Gully — took place in 1805 and, as he never fought Tom *Cribb, *Maturin (in FSW) may be mis-recalling Pearce's intended opponent. See also* **Game Chicken**

Pearl or *Pearl of the Mascarenes*, HMS

An aviso given as a command to Lieutenant Richardson (TMC 8) and later used by Maturin to travel from Réunion to Mauritius and back (TMC 9).

Pedro

A waiter at an inn in Gibraltar (M&C 12).

Peg

1: Diana Villiers' Boston maid, whose loyalties are very much to her regular master, Harry Johnson (FW 7).

2: *see* **Barnes, Peggy**

Pegasus

A legendary horse (IM 6; HD 7).

*In Greek myth, Pegasus was the winged horse ridden by *Bellerophon.*

Pegasus, HMS

A ship once commanded by Prince William (WDS 10).

*HMS Pegasus, 28-gun, was launched in 1779 and sold in 1816; she was commanded on the West Indian station by Prince William (the Duke of *Clarence) from 1786 to 1788, setting a standard for beauty and rigorous discipline much admired *Nelson and *St Vincent. In 1794, now under Robert Barlow (d.1843 as Admiral Sir Robert Barlow), she took part in Lord *Howe's great victory at the Battle of the Glorious First of June.*

Peggy

1: a maid in the Williams' household (PC 8).

2: the title character of *Lovely Peggy,* a song given by William Babbington (HMS 10).

Pei T'sao

A friend and colleague of Mai-mai (NC 3).

Pelagian

The name of a heresy discussed by Grant and Fisher (DI 4).

Pelagius (fl. 380–418) was a British-born lawyer and theologian who settled in Rome and there became a protégé of certain aristocratic Christians. Under their protection he developed controversial doctrines that rejected the notion of original sin and, consequently, predestination. Forced to leave Rome by the Gothic invasion of 410, he gradually lost the support of his now-dispersed patrons and was relentlessly hounded by the Church hierarchy. Under their influence he suffered Imperial condemnation in 415, soon after which date he vanishes from notice.

Pelham or Pellew, Captain

A Royal Navy Captain officer ashore in Malta (TH 1).

*These fleeting references, presumably to the same man, could perhaps be to one of the two sons, briefly noticed below, of Sir Edward *Pellew.*

Pelham, Lord

Andrew Wray's cousin, for whom he had once worked in the Treasury (TH 1).

The reference is probably to the Irish statesman Thomas Pelham (1756–1826), Lord Pelham from 1801 and 2nd Earl of Chichester from 1805. Although he does not seem to have served in the Treasury, Pelham held a number of other senior positions including those of Irish Secretary from 1794 to 1798 and Home Secretary from 1801 to 1803. One of his younger sons, Frederick Thomas (1808–1861),

entered the Royal Navy, becoming Post Captain in 1840 and Rear Admiral in 1858.

Pellew

see **Pelham** or **Pellew, Captain**

Pellew, Sir Edward

The Captain of HMS *Indefatigable,* the ship that had driven *Droits de l'Homme* onto rocks off Brest (YA 5). Later, as an Admiral, he is due to arrive as the new Commander-in-Chief of the Mediterranean, replacing Lord Keith (HD 1).

*Sir Edward Pellew (1757–1833), Viscount Exmouth, rose rapidly through the ranks of the Navy, being several times promoted for gallantry. Made Post for this same reason in 1782, in the early years of the wars against France (1793 onwards) he established a reputation as the most dashing of Britain's frigate commanders, being knighted for achieving the first sea-victory of the conflict. In 1796 he was made a baronet for another, no less typical, example of resourcefulness and personal bravery when, on his way to a dinner engagement, he leapt from his coach to organise the rescue of the troops and passengers aboard the transport Dutton, then foundering in Plymouth Sound. In an act rather reminiscent of Jack *Aubrey (who, to some degree, resembles the early Sir Edward), this was one of the many occasions on which Pellew personally saved men from drowning. The famous defeat by his HMS *Indefatigable of *Droits de l'Homme (which see for a brief note on the engagement) took place in 1797. In 1804 Sir Edward was promoted Rear Admiral and, in this and his successive ranks of Vice Admiral (1808) and Admiral (1814; in which year he also became Viscount Exmouth), commanded in the East Indies, the North Sea and, as permanent successor to *Collingwood, the Mediterranean, this last post from 1810 to 1817 (with a short hiatus during *Buonaparte's exile on Elba, when the command was left vacant). In 1816 Pellew attacked and bombarded Algiers, forcing the Dey, *Omar Pasha, to release many thousands of Christian slaves, a feat that brought him many domestic and foreign honours. From 1817 he held the Plymouth command, finally retiring from the sea in 1821. Sir Edward's brother, Sir Israel (1758–1832), commanded HMS Conqueror at the Battle of Trafalgar in 1805 and was promoted Rear Admiral in 1810, Vice Admiral in 1819 and Admiral in 1830. Sir Fleetwood (1789–1861) and Pownoll (d.1833) Pellew, sons of Sir Edward, both became Post-Captains (neither achieving great service distinction), with the elder rising to Rear Admiral in 1846 and Vice Admiral in 1853.*

Pellew, Admiral Sir William

A homosexual Admiral, flying his flag in HMS *Irresistible* (RM 1,3; TGS 4).

*Pellew is a distinguished name in Royal Navy history (see *Pellew, Sir Edward above) but no 'Sir William' served in the Royal Navy of the time.*

Pellworm

The Baltic pilot sent on board HMS *Ariel,* well known to and respected by Jack Aubrey (SM 7–9). However, his portentous style of forecasting heavy weather begins to irritate both Jack and the crew, who are eventually rather glad to see him ashore in England (SM 9).

Penderecki

A seaman in *Surprise* (NC 7).

Penelope, HMS

A frigate on the Brest blockade (YA 9).

Penfao

The surname of some girls with whom Diana Villiers had been friendly whilst a youngster in Paris (SM 5).

Pengelleys, the

A family who are tenants of the Aubreys in Dorset: the father **Frank** has recently died, leaving as possible heirs his sons **William** and **Frank** and their cousin **Caleb** (whose daughter **Nan** is a maid at Ashgrove Cottage). The complexities of the situation are the occasion for a heated dispute between Jack and Sophie Aubrey (COM 6).

Penhoët, Captain

A French frigate Captain, once commander of 'Pong,' who dines with Christy-Pallière, Aubrey and Maturin in Toulon (PC 4).

> The name is possibly inspired by Armande Louis Bon Maudet (1764–1839), Compte de Penhouet. He had been a Lieutenant in the French Navy until emigrating to England in 1792 and, from 1796 to 1799, then served as a British soldier. In 1814 Penhouet returned to France and was appointed Post Captain in the new *Bourbon Navy; spent his later life as a noted historian and archeologist.

Penn

A Midshipman in HMS *Boadicea* (TMC 10).

Pennant

An authority on birds referred to by Fabien (WDS 6).

> Thomas Pennant (1726–1798) was an English traveller and prolific author who published his Genera of Birds in 1773 and a well-known monograph on the wild turkey in 1781. Although a considerable ornithologist, he is best remembered for his more general British Zoology (1776 onwards) and his History of Quadrupeds (1781).

Perceval

A politician who has recently made an economic speech in the House of Commons (DI 1).

> Spencer Perceval (1762–1812), a son of the Earl of Egmont, made his early career as a lawyer before becoming an MP in 1796. After service in the Government law departments, he became Chancellor of the Exchequer in 1806 and in 1809 succeeded the deceased Duke of Portland as Prime Minister. His subsequent ministry was rather reduced in effectiveness by the quarrels between *Canning and *Castlereagh over the Walcheren fiasco of 1809 (also see *Chatham and *Strachan). In May 1812 he was assassinated (the only British PM ever to meet this fate) in the lobby of the House of Commons by John Bellingham, a

semi-crazed bankrupt with a private grudge against members of the administration. The Perceval family also had many connections with the Royal Navy, either as Lords of the Admiralty or as active officers, with one of Spencer's nephews, George James Perceval (1794–1874; Earl of Egmont from 1840), serving as a Midshipman on HMS *Orion at Trafalgar in 1805 and eventually, in 1863, advancing to full Admiral.

Pere, En

The French Catalan nephew of En Jaume, godfather to little Ramón's sister (PC 4).

Pergolesi

A composer played by Admiral Russell's ward, Polly (LM 1).

> Giovanni Pergolesi (1710–1736), was a prolific Italian composer, violinist and organist. Although his output was undoubtedly vast, many works are falsely attributed to him.

Perkins

1: a reference by Diana Villiers to the impertinent Mr Atkins (HMS 7).
2: Miss Perkins, a young lady who frequently sails as the companion of Captain Bennet of HMS *Berwick* (FSW 2).

Péron

A former castaway on Amsterdam Island referred to by Maturin (TGS 5).

> Francois Péron (1775–1810) was a French naturalist and traveller who, after periods both as soldier and medical student, joined Baudin's 1800 expedition to Australia, New Holland and the Southern Ocean as a zoologist. In his subsequent account of his adventures, he relates how he and colleagues were abandoned for a time on a remote shore when their ship was driven off by a storm.

Pert, Miss

The name by which Mrs Williams chides Frances, her daughter (PC 3).

Peshwa, the

A Mahratta chief in Bombay (HMS 7).

> Peshwa, a Persian term in origin, was originally the title of the Chief Minister of the Princes of Mahratta (or Maratha) but, in 1749, the then Peshwa took complete power and turned himself into the hereditary ruler of the principality. At the time of HMS, the Peshwa was Baji Rao II who, in 1802, had sought British protection, an arrangement that by 1818 was effectively to end the history of his state as any sort of independent power.

Peter

1: Mr Peter, a cousin of Mr Shepherd, Admiral Bertie's secretary, recommended by him as Commodore Jack Aubrey's new secretary (TMC 3+). Stephen Maturin suspects that his loyalties remain more with his relative and patron than with Jack (TMC 6, 10). Badly injured in a fall during a storm, he then makes a full recovery (TMC 5).

2: Maturin's servant in HMS *Surprise* (HD 5).

3: Sir Peter: *see* **Clifford, Sir Peter**

Peter or Simon, Saint

The patron — as Saint Simon — of an abbey church in Malta, the rendezvous of the French agent Lesueur and his various contacts (TH 2,3,8). Later, when Martin is asked whether the Scthians are Christians, he replies that the precise religious affiliation some of the gnostic sects would puzzle even Saint Peter (LM 5).

> *Saint Peter (d.65?), originally named Simon, and his brother, Andrew, were the first of *Jesus Christ's Apostles. Simon was renamed* Petros *(Greek for 'rock') by the Lord and thus designated as the foundation stone of the coming Christian faith. Although he denied Jesus as his master at the time of the crucifixion, Peter later became the central figure in spreading the faith until his supposed death by martyrdom in *Nero's Rome.*

Peterborough or Peterbuggah, Lord

A Englishman, his name entertainingly mispronounced by Casademon, who had routed the Spanish with Catalan help some years previously (SM 6,9).

> *Charles Mordaunt (1658–1735), an English statesman, diplomat, admiral and general, was created Earl of Monmouth in 1689 and in 1697 inherited his father's title of Earl of Peterborough (pron. Pee-tah-buh-ruh). Having been made Post in 1687, in 1705, after a series of high commands, he was appointed Joint Admiral of the English Fleet with Sir Cloudisley Shovell (1650–1707). In that same year Peterborough had already been appointed General of the small British army in Spain and, during the War of the Spanish Succession, won a series of brilliant land victories, including the capture of Barcelona in 1706. A staunch Tory, he lost his power and influence on the accession of King George I to the British throne in 1714 and the consequent rise of the Whig party.*

Peters

1: a ship's boy in HMS *Surprise* (HMS 5).

2: one of Jack Aubrey's HMS *Leopard* Midshipman, now a passenger in HMS *La Flèche* (FW 2).

Peterssen, Peter

A seaman in HMS *Sophie* (M&C 3).

Petit

The author of a medical text, fruitlessly consulted by Maturin on the subject of Clarissa Oakes' illness (C/T 4).

> *The reference is probably to Antoine Petit (1718–1794), one of the most celebrated French doctors of his age and the author of numerous works on conception, child-bearing, child-birth and their associated illnesses and diseases. However, *Maturin may perhaps have only had access to one of his other works, a text on complaints of the male urinary tract.*

Petit-André

A seaman in the French privateer *Bellone* (PC 5).

Petronilla

An Abbess in Avila, an aunt of Stephen Maturin, to whose care Brigid Maturin, Clarissa Oakes and Padeen Colman are entrusted (COM 5,9).

Petty

A lawyer defending some of Jack Aubrey's supposed co-conspirators at his fraud trial (RM 8).

Petty, Sir William

A Cromwellian, according to Maturin a 'black thief,' who had invented a double-hulled vessel (FSW 7).

> *Sir William Petty (1623–1687), after an early career both in the merchant service and Royal Navy, went on to become a physician, inventor and influential political economist. In 1662 he was one of the founders of the Royal Society, an act for which he was knighted in the same year. Having in 1650 been appointed Professor of Anatomy at Oxford, in 1652 he became Chief Physician to Oliver *Cromwell's army in Ireland and from 1657 continued there as Chief Secretary to Oliver's son Henry, resigning when the Cromwellian regime ended in 1659. Whilst in Ireland, Petty was responsible for the detail of the scheme by which land was appropriated from its 'rebellious' owners and re-distributed amongst Cromwell's settler-soldiers; he afterwards wrote a number of economic tracts, including* A Political Anatomy of Ireland. *A man of many talents, he not only invented a double-keeled hull but also became, in his later years, a Professor of Music in London. By a curious co-incidence, the antiquarian John Aubrey (1626–1697) is noted as an especially close friend of Petty, writing after his death a memoir of his colourful life and personality.*

Petty-Bag

A newly appointed official present at the King's Birthday Levée (RM 5).

P.H., Dr

A pseudonym once used by Stephen Maturin (SM 4).

Phaeton, HMS

A Royal Navy vessel, some of whose crew Stephen Maturin had encountered in Port Mahon (M&C 3). She is later referred to by Jack Aubrey as one of several very desirable frigates into which he would like to be made Post (M&C 11).

> *HMS* Phaeton, *38-gun, was launched in 1782 and in 1794, under Captain William *Bentinck, took park in Lord *Howe's great victory at the Battle of the Glorious First of June. She was sold for break-up in 1828. In early Greek myth, Phaeton was allowed by his father, Helios, to drive the Sun's horses for the day: failing to control them, he was killed by a thunderbolt from *Zeus lest he set the heavens ablaze.*

Phaon

A man referred to as a lover of Sappho (DI 4).

In classical myth, Phaon was a ferryman, made permanently young and desirable by the goddess *Aphrodite/ *Venus. The tale of *Sappho's suicide on account of her unrequited passion for Phaon seems to have its origins in much later Greek comic plays.

Pheidias or Phideas

A Greek sculptor, referred to by Mr Atkins in his attempt to make a pass at Diana Villiers (HMS 7), and later compared by Jack Aubrey to Moses Jenkins, a model-ship maker (DI 1).

Phideas (fl.465–425 BC) was regarded by his contemporaries as the greatest of all Greek sculptors and was to become the greatest single influence on later Greek and Roman neo-classicism. Working either in bronze or in gold and ivory laid over a wooden base, he produced mainly statues and mythological groups (none of which survive except in later copies), famous for their opulence, size and complexity, both technical and iconographic.

Phelps

A seaman in HMS *Worcester*, formerly of HMSS *Circe* and *Venerable*, whose last ship had been *Wheel 'em Along* (IM 2). He may be the same man who, a little later, serves in HMS *Surprise* (FSW 6).

Phidias

see **Pheidias**

Philip

see **Aubrey, Philip**

Philip, Sir

see **Broke, Sir Philip**

Philips

1: a Polynesian-speaking seaman in *Surprise* who had served in HMS Sirius when she was wrecked on Norfolk Island (C/T 1,2).
2: an Admiralty official travelling in HMS *Thunderer* (COM 1).

Phillimore, John

The Captain of HMS *Eurotas*, who had taken *Clorinde* (YA 9).

Sir John Phillimore (1781–1840) was made Post in 1807 and in 1813 commissioned the new frigate HMS *Eurotas. The long action with *Clorinde took place on February 25–26th 1814, very much as described in the text, with Phillimore being several times severely wounded; yet another phase of the action took place some years later. William *James, in his Naval History of 1822, paid due homage to Phillimore's fighting spirit but severely criticised his poor handling of the guns. Sir John, still a serving officer, took violent objection to James' remarks and, whilst on leave in England, turned up at the author's house and gave him a thrashing with a cane on his own doorstep, an assault for which he later had to pay compensation of one hundred pounds. In the History's second edition of 1827,

James nevertheless repeated his allegations (as did CLOWES later still), now justifying them at great length.

Phipps, Captain

see **Mulgrave, Captain Lord**

Phoebe, HMS

A frigate that had successfully fought the heavily over-manned *Africaine* (PC 4) and whose later pursuit of USS *Essex* is echoed in *The Far Side of the World* (FSW author's note); she had also once nearly been cut out by the Buonapartist Captain Charles de La Tour (HD 4). She is also mentioned several times in passing (M&C 10,11; DI 4) and, although at one point said to be scrapped (RM 4), later appears on the Brest blockade (YA 5).

HMS Phoebe, 36-gun, was launched in 1795. In 1801 she took the 44-gun *Africaine (which see for an account of the fight) in the Mediterranean, an action that won a knighthood for her Captain Robert Barlow (d.1843 as a full Admiral). In 1805, under Thomas Bladen *Capel, she took part in *Nelson's final victory at Trafalgar and in 1810, now under James Hillyar (d.1843 as a Rear Admiral), was part of Admiral *Bertie's squadron that accepted the surrender of Mauritius and, later, Java. Hillyar's pursuit and capture in her of David Porter's USS *Essex took place in early 1814. I have been unable to locate details of the attack on her referred to in HD. Phoebe was paid off later that year, reduced to a slop-ship in 1826 and sold for break-up in 1841. In early Greek myth, Phoebe was one of the Titan race but later became known as the moon goddess and, as such, was an alternative name for Artemis/ *Diana.

Phoenix, HMS

A 36-gun frigate, Captain Tom Baker, that took the 44-gun *Didon* in 1805 (FW 2). Charles Fielding had at one time been her acting First Lieutenant (TH 3).

HMS Phoenix, 36-gun, was launched in 1783. In August 1805, under Tom *Baker, she took *Didon and went on later that year to discover the small French squadron that had escaped from *Nelson's victory at Trafalgar, conveying their whereabouts to Sir Richard *Strachan's force. Phoenix was wrecked in the Mediterranean in 1816, being commanded on that occasion by Captain Charles Austen (see *Canopus, HMS for a short note on the Royal Navy Austens, brothers of the novelist Jane). In classical myth, the Phoenix was a fabulous bird that regularly burnt itself on a pyre and then, renewed, rose from its own ashes.

Physician of the Fleet

A post several times referred to (PC 6,12; IM 1; TGS 4; HD 1,2)

This position was an appointment by an individual Admiral to be the Chief Physician to the fleet under his command. There being seldom more than two or three qualified physicians at any one time in the Royal Navy of the period (i.e., men such as *Blane, *Trotter or *Maturin himself, 'gentlemen' doctors holding the degree M.D.), the appointment was rarely able to be made.

Pierrot
see **Dumesnil, Jean-Pierre**

Pierson, Mr
A resident of Batavia (NC 3).

Pig, Ikey
A famous prize-fighter (YA 3).

Piggot
An author who advocated health nostrums (YA 5).
Robert Pigott (sic; 1736–1794) was a fervent supporter of the French Revolution and, as Jack *Aubrey remarks, an advocate of the supposed health-benefits of both radical vegetarianism and cap-wearing. He was also an associate, and later dupe, of the quack doctor James Graham (1745–1794), a proponent of the merits of mild (though, unfortunately, not always so: see *Howe) self-electrocution.

Piggott
An Admiral whose daughter had married Captain Henry Smith of HMS *Revenge* (TGS 1).

Pigot, Hugh
The Captain of that 'hell afloat,' HMS *Hermione*, later killed by his mutinous crew (HMS 6; RM 2; COM 5).
Hugh Pigot (1769–1797) was the son of Admiral Hugh Pigot (1721?–1792) and the younger brother of General Sir Henry Pigot (1750–1840). Being so well connected, he had been appointed Commander in early 1794 and Post-Captain later that year. Already carrying with him, from his HMS *Success, a reputation as a harsh disciplinarian, he was given the frigate HMS *Hermione in July 1797. On September 21st of that same year, after a short and intensely disagreeable cruise in the Caribbean, Pigot hurried two men off the mizen topsail yard: in the rush to avoid being flogged as 'last man down,' they both fell to their deaths. The Captain merely ordered the crew to 'throw the lubbers overboard' without further ceremony and that night the men mutinied, slaying Pigot and all his senior colleagues, with the exception of one Midshipman and three warrant-officers (see also *Montague, Drogo).

Pilate, Pompous
see **Pilate, Pontius**

Pilate, Pontius or **Pompous**
1: the Roman governor, referred to both in term of uneasiness of judgement and for his pride (PC 4, 13; IM 5; TGS 3; C/T 8; COM 3; YA 2). His name is several times altered to 'Pompous Pilate' (M&C 8; COM 8; YA 5).
Pontius Pilatus (d. after 36 AD) was the Roman Governor of Judea who, somewhat unwillingly, passed the death sentence on *Jesus Christ; he is reputed later to have been banished and taken his own life. The confusion of 'Pontius' and 'Pompous' is a well-known school-room 'howler.'
2: the gunroom cockerel in HMS *Surprise* (FSW 5).

'Pillywinks'
The code name used by the traitors Wray and Ledward for their secret patron, the Duke of Habachtsthal (C/T 7)

Pindar
A classical writer, referred to by Martin (TH 6) and renowned for his liberty with verse rhythm (TH 4).
Pindar (518?–438? BC) was one of the most widely celebrated of the early Greek lyric poets, especially famous for his celebrations of the moral virtues of great sporting events and victories; very little is known of his life. Of his surviving works, there are only two that employ exactly the same metrical pattern.

Pinto
An author on Japanese matters referred to by Maturin (C/T 8).
Fernão Mendes Pinto (1510?–1583) was a Portuguese traveller and adventurer who, having first arrived in India in 1537, then spent twenty years, at least according to his own account, visiting the whole of Asia, sometimes as a trader, sometimes a soldier. His popular and entertaining Voyages and Adventures of 1614 recounts his eventful life (including being '13 times a prisoner and 17 a slave'), although how much is true and how much invented or exaggerated has always been much debated.

'Pipes, Tom'
An HMS *Surprise* officer or petty officer whose behaviour is complained of by Compton, late of HMS *Defender*,(FSW 3).
Although this is presumably a reference to bosun *Hollar and his call-pipe, it could perhaps be to Tom *Pullings, the ship's First Lieutenant.

Pique, HMS
A ship in which Admiral Mitchell had once been a Lieutenant (IM 4).
The first HMS Pique of the Royal Navy was the French ship of the same name, launched in 1785 and captured by HMS *Blanche in 1795, some years after *Mitchell had last been a Lieutenant (1782). Pique was wrecked in 1798.

Piscator, Eusebius
A Swedish member of the London Entomological Society (HMS 1).

Pishan
A Lapp retainer of Jagiello, on loan to Diana Villiers (LM 9).

Pitt
1: Colonel Pitt, a friend and lover of Molly Harte (M&C 8).
2: the name of a great diamond (SM 3).
The Pitt or Regent Diamond was discovered in the rough in India in 1701 and bought by the Governor of Madras, Sir Thomas Pitt (1653–1726; the great-grandfather of 'Billy' *Pitt). In 1717 he sold the now-cut gem for the colossal sum of 135,000 pounds sterling to the Duc d'Orléans,

the Regent of France, after whom it was thenceforth named. The stone, long in the French crown jewels and later worn by the Emperor *Buonaparte in the pommel of his sword, is displayed to this day in the Louvre, Paris.

3: the surgeon of HMS *Niobe* (IM 6).

Pitt, Billy

1: the new Tory Prime Minister (PC 5,12,14), a sometime friend of Philip Broke's father (FW 7).

*William Pitt (1759–1806) was the younger son of the statesman William Pitt, 1st Earl of Chatham (1708–1778) and the great-grandson of Sir Thomas Pitt (see *Pitt # 2 above). 'Billy' Pitt first became an MP in 1781, making an immediate impact as an orator and in 1782 rose to high office, serving for a few months as Chancellor of the Exchequer. In 1783 — not yet 25 — he became Prime Minister, holding office until 1801, when he resigned over King *George III's opposition to Catholic emancipation in Ireland. When his friend and successor, Henry Addington (see *Sidmouth, Lord), showed himself incapable of managing the war, Pitt again became Prime Minister (in May of 1804, as referred to in PC), although his always delicate health was now failing badly. In 1805 he was a loyal supporter of Henry Dundas, Lord *Melville, during his impeachment proceedings, leaving Parliament in tears when a censure motion was passed against his friend. In 1805 his health was finally broken by two pieces of overwhelming news: *Nelson's victory at Trafalgar in October and an Allied defeat at Austerlitz in December at the hands of *Buonaparte. Pitt died in office in January of 1806. Like *Canning and *Castlereagh a little later, Pitt was also one of the Parliamentary fighting-men, having in 1798 fought an ineffectual duel with another MP, Tierny, the result of an exchange of insults in the House. His elder brother, John Pitt, entered the army in 1778 but, inheriting his father's title of Earl of *Chatham in that year, he then spent as much time involved in politics as in military affairs, serving as his brother's *First Lord of the Admiralty from 1788 to 1794 and in other high offices until 1801, when he rejoined the army. The younger brother of the family, James Charles Pitt (1761–1781), entered the Royal Navy and rose to command (as Lieutenant according to SYRETT & DiNARDO, as Commander according to DNB), the 14-gun HMS Hornet before dying of fever in the West Indies.*

2: A seaman in HMS *Bellona* (COM 4).

Pitt, Edward

A mutual friend of Diana Villiers and Colonel Aldington (SM 2).

Pius VII, Pope (*often simply* 'the Pope')

The head of the Roman Catholic Church (HMS 1,7; DI 10; FW 4; SM 5,7; IM 3; TH 1; C/T 3; COM 5) who had excommunicated Buonaparte and consequently been imprisoned (TMC 3,6,9; SM 7; TGS 2; COM 10).

Barnabas Luigi Gregorio Chiaramonti (1740–1823) became a Benedictine monk in 1756, a bishop in 1782 and a cardinal in 1785. Elected Pope in 1800, he immediately negotiated a treaty with Paris (the Concordat of 1801) that re-established Catholicism as the French state religion and secured, for the time being, the independence of the Papal

*States themselves. (As alluded to in TMC 3,6, his predecessor Pius VI (1717–1819) had allied himself with Austria and others against revolutionary France and had subsequently been attacked and deposed — in 1798 — by General *Buonaparte.) In 1804 Pius went to France to crown Buonaparte as Emperor Napoleon I but the new relationship soon deteriorated when the Pope both refused, in 1805, to annul the marriage to the Empress Josephine and declined, in 1806, to join the 'Continental System' of blockading the trade of France's enemies, Britain chief amongst them. Buonaparte thereupon occupied Rome in 1808 and the Papal States themselves in 1809. Pius retaliated by excommunicating the Emperor and his generals, but was promptly imprisoned for his pains and soon coerced into new treaties. Released on Buonaparte's first abdication of 1814, he returned to Rome and soon re-acquired the bulk of the Church's former territories. As well as negotiating treaties and settlements with all the Allied powers, Pius also now raised a permanent army to defend his earthly possessions.*

Pizarro

The Spanish conqueror of Peru (WDS 9).

*From some unknown time before 1510, Francisco Pizarro (1471–1541), the illiterate natural son of a Spanish colonel, led what was at first a largely unsuccessful career as an adventurer in the New World. Eventually securing Royal support for an expedition in search of gold, in 1531 he sailed from Panama to Peru. Here he exploited the civil war between *Huascar and *Atahualpa and by 1533 had much of the country under his control, as much by cunning and perfidy as by military conquest. Pizarro was eventually assassinated by associates of his defeated and executed Spanish rival, Almagro.*

'Plagoso Orbilio'
see **Orbilio, Plagoso**

Plaice, Joe, Joseph or 'Old'

An elderly able-seaman, Barret Bonden's cousin, first met in Jack Aubrey's HMS *Polychrest* (PC 7+; *although here he behaves and speaks as if he has previously sailed with both Jack and Stephen Maturin and is later said to have sailed on HMS Sophie*: COM 3; HD 1). Throughout the series he is a loyal follower of Jack on ship and shore (DI 3,10; FW 1; IM 2+; FSW 3+; RM 3,6; LM 3; TGS 1,3; NC 7+; C/T 6,7,8; WDS 1+; COM 1,3,4,7; YA 9,10; HD 1,4,5,8). Amongst many adventures, he falls overboard and is rescued by Lieutenant Pullings from a boat (LM 3) and, some years later, fractures his skull in an accident, is trepanned by Stephen and makes a full recovery (FSW 5; NC 7+).

*It is possible that William *Plaice is intended to be the same character.*

Plaice, William

A seaman in HMSS *Leopard* (DI 9) and *Surprise* (TH 4,6,8).

*It is possible that William is intended to be the same character as Joe *Plaice.*

Plato

The ancient Greek philosopher (M&C 8; FW 6; C/T 1; COM 6).

> *Plato (429?–347? BC), a high-born Athenian, is one of the most influential thinkers of all time, yet almost nothing is known of his personal life. As a young philosopher he studied under the great Socrates, before founding his own* Academia, *and almost all of his extant work — ethical, political, logical and metaphysical — is in the form of dialogues in which his old master is cast as the chief interlocutor. Plato's work offers two main challenges to its readers (which can here only be signalled rather than at all adequately described): a) understanding his approach to how true knowledge may — or may not — be properly acquired; and then b) establishing whether there is some definable 'Platonic system' of substantive knowledge itself. Both tasks remain as formidably difficult and elusive today as they were in his own life-time and it is a tribute to Plato's ambition and vigour that the challenge of engaging with his dialogues shows no sign of flagging after two and a half thousand years. As HORNBLOWER & SPAWFORTH remark, Plato is the consummate master of stimulating debate rather than a teacher of clear doctrine. Both creative and rigorous in his thinking, Plato also wrote in a Greek of exceptional clarity and purity.*

Plimpton

An American seaman in HMS *Sophie* who unsuccessfully petitions not to be flogged by the black bosun's mate, King (M&C 11).

Plover, HMS

A Royal Navy sloop referred to by Raffles (NC 3).

> *HMS* Plover, *18-gun sloop, was launched in 1796 and sold in 1819.*

Plumb

A member of the barge crew in HMS *Surprise* whose treasured pig-tail had to be cut free by Dick Turnbull after becoming tangled in the rigging (HMS 6).

Plutarch

A writer and historian (PC 4; IM 10; LM 2).

> *Mestrius Plutarchus (46?–126 AD) was a Greek biographer and essayist of prolific and highly influential output; his best remembered work is his* Parallel Lives *of pairs of eminent Greeks and Romans. In the mention of his work in LM 2, the character whose name cannot be recalled is Pheidippides, who ran from Athens to Sparta and back just before the Battle of Marathon (490 BC), covering the 150-mile distance in two days.*

P.M.

Initials scratched on the wall of the nunnery/prison in Brest where HMS *Ariel*'s officers are held (SM 10).

Pobst

A European *savant* at Maturin's Paris lecture (SM 5).

> *The reference may perhaps be to Johann Heinrich Pabst (sic; 1785–1868), a German historian and philosopher.*

Pocock

An artist whose work is owned by Aubrey (DI 1).

> *Nicholas Pocock (1741–1821) was a British marine painter who, in his early years, had commanded merchant ships. He has an unrivalled reputation for the technical accuracy of his many fine paintings of great sea battles.*

Pocock, Figgins

Admiral Sir Francis Ives' advisor on Oriental affairs, a great rival of Professor Ebenezer Graham (TH 3+; RM 5). He and Mr Eliot arrange for the Dey of Mascara to be murdered and replaced by one of his more amenable sons (FSW 1,2).

Podalirius

see **Machaon**

Poel, van der

A naturalist in Capetown, a friend of Maturin (TMC 5), who has later moved away (FW 2).

Poer

see **Le Poer, Sir Joe and Lady**

Poggius

An author referred to by Maturin and Martin (M&C 9; TH 6).

> *Giovanni Francesco Poggio Bracchiolini (1380–1459; in Latin, Poggius) was an Italian scholar and reviver of classical learning who searched out many lost manuscripts of the ancients (especially *Cicero, *Lucretius and Plautus) in monastery libraries. He was also an author in his own right of lively historical and social commentaries.*

Poirier

The very able French chef taken into Aubrey's HMS *Boadicea* from *Hébé* (TMC 2) and later left at Capetown as a prisoner-of-war (TMC 3).

Pola

A merchantman taken by HMS *Sophie* (M&C 10).

Pole, Charles

A Foreign office official in London, with an American mother. Louisa Wogan unsuspectingly lets slip to Maturin that he is a spy (DI 10; FW 1) and we later learn he has been hanged (FW 5).

Pole, William or Bill

A seaman in HMS *Surprise* (IM 11).

'Polish Giant'

see **Astley**

Polixfen

A Hampshire neighbour of the Aubreys (TMC 6).

Poll

see **Skeeping, Mrs Poll**

Pollack

A seaman in HMS *Surprise* (NC 8).

Pollard

1: the schoolmaster in HMS *Resolution*, much disliked by the then Midshipman Aubrey (M&C 4).

2: a seaman in HMS *Diane*, the keeper of the ship's livestock (TGS 10).

Pollock, Major

The brother of that Captain Irby who has been appointed to HMS *Blackwater* in place of Jack Aubrey (TH 9).

Pollux

Babbington's Newfoundland dog, his companion in HMS *Leopard* (DI 3,5,10). He is later reported to have been eaten by the natives of the Friendly Islands (FW 5).

> In classical myth, Pollux was the son of Leda and the brother of both Castor and Helen. Castor and Pollux became known as the guardians of sailors at sea.

Pollux, HMS

Captain Dawson's old, battered 64-gun ship in which Admiral Harte is to travel back to England. She accompanies HMS *Surprise* on the mission to Zambra, where she is destroyed, with the loss of all hands, by a powerful French squadron led by the 74-gun *Mars* (TH 10; FSW 1).

Polly

1: presumably 'Miss Christy,' the English cousin of Captain Christy-Pallière and a notable cook (PC 4).

2: a slave belonging to Johnson, who acts as one of Diana Villiers' maids (FW 6).

3: Mr Martin's intended wife (RM 6; *but see also* **Martin, Deborah**)

4: Admiral Schank's ward (LM 1).

Pollyblank

A quarter gunner in HMS *Surprise* sent to *Lushington* for the battle with Linois' squadron (HMS 9).

Polonius

The character in Shakespeare's *Hamlet* to be played by Midshipman Calamy in HMS *Worcester*'s production (IM 5,8).

> In William *Shakespeare's* *Hamlet, Polonius, a foolish advisor to King Claudius, is the father of *Ophelia, Hamlet's sometime lover, and of Laertes, Hamlet's eventual killer. Polonius is unintentionally slain by Hamlet when the latter, hoping to kill Claudius, thrusts his sword through the curtain, or 'arras,' behind which the interfering old courtier is hiding.*

Polwhele

1: a friend of General Aubrey and the donor of the Cornish 'rotten borough' of St Muryan to him as his Parliamentary seat (PC 13).

> The name may perhaps be inspired by that of Richard Polwhele (1760–1838), the Cornish vicar and miscellany writer.

2: a seaman in *Dromedary* whose tooth is extracted by Maturin (TH 4).

Polybius

An author whose treatment of Pyrrhus is discussed by Graham (IM 10).

> Polybius (200?–118? BC) was a Greek historian who produced a long and subtle account (only a little over a tenth of which has survived intact) of Rome's rise to dominance over the Mediterranean world. Polybius himself had an active career as a politician, diplomat and explorer (even undertaking a short voyage out into the blue-water Atlantic), initially serving his own Greek city-state and later, after its defeat by the Latins, his Roman patron Scipio Aemilianus. In the latter's company, Polybius witnessed the final destruction of *Hannibal's Carthage in 146.

Polychrest, HMS

HMS *Polychrest*, a sloop known as the 'Carpenter's Mistake,' being an experimental vessel designed by Mr Eldon and built by the unsavoury Hinkman's yard, is Jack Aubrey's second and final ship in the rank of Commander. Designed to carry a 'secret weapon,' she is consequently equipped with sliding keels and a pointed stern, considerably reducing her sailing abilities (PC 6+). Having run aground whilst attacking *Fanciulla* in Chaulieu Harbour, she eventually sinks under heavy fire (PC 11; *also* TMC 3,6; DI 3,5; FW 3; RM 7; C/T 9).

> Polychest is anglicised Greek for 'more than one peak,' a reference to her pointed bow and stern. Her peculiar design and sailing qualities may have been part-inspired by the experimental mortar-boat HMS Project, built to a design of the *Congreves that featured a flat bottom and rudders at each, pointed end (a horrible thought with any kind of sea running). She was launched in 1804 and commissioned in early 1806 but, owing at least in part to having been fir-built, she was unseaworthy by 1810 and broken up at the end of that year (see Ware, Christopher The Bomb Vessel, London: Conway, 1994).

Polyphemus, HMS

An armed transport ship, commanded by Lieutenant Patterson, that accompanies Jack Aubrey and HMS *Worcester* to Barka and Medina (IM 6). Years later she is seen at Gibraltar (HD 9).

> The reference may be to HMS Polyphemus, 64-gun, launched in 1782. In 1801 she took part in *Nelson's victory at Copenhagen and, in 1805, in his final victory at Trafalgar; after this battle she towed the disabled HMS *Victory to Gibraltar. From 1808 until being paid off in 1812 Polyphemus was commanded by William Pryce *Cumby. She was reduced to a powder hulk in about 1813 and finally broken up in 1827. In classical myth, Polyphemus was the one-eyed Cyclops of Sicily, defeated and blinded by *Ulysses.

Pomfret

1: the author of *To a Friend Inclined to Marry*, given by Driver as his entry to the HMS *Surprise* verse competition (IM 9).

John Pomfret (1667–1702) was a vicar and poet, most famous for his verse The Choice, *in which he celebrates the joys of a bachelor-vicar living, somewhat modestly, on a quiet country estate. The verse enjoyed great popularity (especially when later highly commended by Dr *Johnson) but embroiled Pomfret himself in controversy, with some people reading into his work a recommendation to take mistresses rather than a spouse. In* To his Friend, Inclined to Marry *(1699) Pomfret, who was in fact a married man, advocates taking a wife from the 'middle region' of life's classes and talents in order to secure '…the least disquiets, and the smallest cares.'*

2: an HMS *Surprise* quartermaster on Jack Aubrey's Mubara expedition (TH 7).

Pomfret, Hugh

The newly appointed Captain of HMS *Pomone* (HD 2). Deeply troubled at having killed Christian slaves whilst sinking an Algerine corsair (HD 2), he is later killed in an 'accident' in his ship, leading to speculation of self-murder (HD 3).

Pomone, HMS

1: a French-built frigate, famously swift (M&C 9).

*HMS Pomone, 44-gun, was an ex–French frigate of the same name, launched in 1785 and captured by the Royal Navy in 1794, at which time she was the most powerful frigate afloat, (though not especially swift). For a time around 1800 she was then commanded by Edward Leveson *Gower (Pomone in French), named for a minor Roman goddess of fruit trees (* poma*) later elevated and celebrated by the poet *Ovid in his* Metamorphoses, *was broken up in 1802.*

2: a swift-sailing frigate in Admiral Thornton's Mediterranean fleet (IM 8) that had been captured by Jack Aubrey from the French in his Mauritius campaign (YA 10). Admiral Lord Keith now orders Commodore Aubrey to take her for his pennant-ship at Madeira (YA 10). Jack travels in her to Gibraltar but there transfers his pennant to his old HMS *Surprise* (HD 1). Her new Captain, Hugh Pomfret, is soon killed in an accident (which may perhaps be suicide) and *Pomone* is then given to the newly promoted John Vaux (HD 2–5).

*This 38-gun HMS Pomone was the ex–French *Astrée captured in 1810, renamed in 1811 and broken up in 1816. At about the time she is given to Jack *Aubrey (May 1815), she was on her way back home from the North American Station where, under Captain John Richard Lumley (d.1821), she had just assisted in the capture of USS *President.*

Pompee, HMS

A 74-gun ship of Saumarez' squadron (M&C 12) aboard which Jack Aubrey is court-martialed for the loss of HMS *Sophie* (M&C 12). She is later referred to in passing (IM 5,6; LM 1).

*HMS Pompee, 80-gun, was an ex-French 3rd rate of the same name, launched in 1791 and captured by the Royal Navy in 1793. Under Captain Charles *Stirling she fought in the first of *Saumarez' two 1801 fleet actions but was too badly damaged to take part in the second. Lord *Cochrane's later court-martial aboard her for the loss of his HMS *Speedy is the model for Jack *Aubrey's trial. Pompee, broken up in 1817, was probably named for either Cnaeus Pompeius Magnus (Pompey the Great; 106–48 BC), the general who eventually came to oppose, unsuccessfully, Julius *Caesar's expanding power, or for his son Sextus Pompeius (80?–35 BC), a 'rebel' admiral in the ensuing civil wars of Augustus' reign.*

Pompeu, En
see **Ponsich Pompeu**

Pond
A seaman in HMS *Polychrest* (PC 9).

Pong
see ***Paon***

Ponsich, Pompeu

A Catalan patriot and scholar, entrusted by Sir Joseph Blaine with the Baltic mission (SM 4), who had been drowned when HMS *Daphne* was sunk by fire from Grimsholm island (SM 6). Stephen Maturin, originally intended for the mission had he been available (SM 4), learns of his death whilst in Paris (SM 5) and hurries to England to offer himself as a replacement to Sir Joseph (SM 6,7).

Ponsonby

The temporary commander of HMS *Namur* whilst her Captain Billy Sutton attends Parliament in England (FSW 1).

Pontet-Canet, Jean-Paul

A French intelligence official from Dijon (FW 4–7), whom Stephen Maturin recalls seeing with Captain Christie-Pallière some years earlier in Toulon, now travelling as a passenger aboard USS *Constitution* (FW 4). Later, he briefly meets Stephen at Harry Johnson's house (FW 6) and, once he is certain that Stephen is an intelligence agent, twice tries to abduct him before being himself killed by the Doctor (FW 7; also SM 1,4,11; TH 2).

Although a native Burgundian, Pontet-Canet is named for one of the great wines of Bordeaux, a Pauillac.

Ponto

Laura Fielding's Illyrian mastiff, rescued by Jack Aubrey from a well into which he has fallen (TH 1). Usually fiercely protective of his mistress, Ponto's ensuing devotion to Jack convinces many people that he and Laura are lovers (TH 2,3,8). Ponto is later poisoned by Lesueur's agents in preparation for their attempt on Laura's life (TH 10).

Pope, the

Although sometimes a general reference to the head of the Roman Catholic Church, see usually ***Pius VII, Pope**

Pope

1: Mr Lowndes' butler in Dover (PC 13).

2: The poet who had translated Homer (TH 9; FSW 4) and Horace (YA 8). He is also referred to by Maturin for his remarks on the London Monument (TGS 7).

Alexander Pope (1688–1744) was a precocious poet, largely self-educated, who rose great eminence in London literary society. Typical of both his many works and his approach to life and friendship is his Dunciad (1728 and revised versions thereafter), a brilliant and biting satire on dullness and dullards (among whom Pope from time to time seems to have included virtually everyone he knew, for, as was famously said of him, 'he hardly drank tea without a stratagem'). Pope made many translations of the classics, all of which enjoyed great commercial success, including *Homer's Iliad (1715–1720) and Odyssey (1725–1726, with the assistance of two colleagues), *Horace's Epistles and Satires and works by *Virgil and *Ovid. He also wrote many fine verses in explicit imitation of classical styles. Although his translations are widely admired on their own merits, as the critic *Bentley said of one of them, 'it is a pretty poem but not Homer.' Pope was raised a Catholic and, although later a rationalist, always retained a sympathy for his family faith. The London Monument, erected to commemorate the outbreak Great Fire of 1666, bore for a time (until as late as 1830) an inscription at its base blaming Catholic dissidents for the conflagration and, in his Epistle III, Pope condemns this as a bullying lie.

Pope, John

An armourer and mutineer of HMS *Hermione*. Captured by Jack Aubrey from USS *Norfolk*, he is court-martialed in HMS *Irresistible* and sentenced to hang (RM 2).

Porson

A man referred to as a model of prodigious learning (RM 3).

Richard Porson (1759–1808) was a distinguished classical scholar, from 1792 Professor of Greek at Cambridge University. In addition to his critical powers, he was renowned for an extraordinarily accurate and capacious memory, being able to recite verbatim entire sections of books only once read through.

Port Admiral

A senior Royal Navy officer at Plymouth about whom Tom Pullings sings a rude verse (PC 7).

Port Vice- and Rear-Admirals served at all the main naval bases and were usually older men with no great fighting distinctions. The Admiral's squadron consisted of all ships in the harbour or in the approaches (unless these latter were under the orders of a more senior sea-Admiral) and his somewhat ambiguous duties — for he had no power over the *Commissioner or his dockyard officials — were to ensure all such ships were ready for sea, particularly as regards crewing. In time of war, he could have frigates and smaller vessels under his direct command to secure the base from attack. *Pullings' song is somewhat anachronistic, for it is a near-quotation from a later verse by Frederick Marryat (1792–1848, a Post Captain of 1828), the famed early naval novelist who had entered the Royal Navy in 1806 as a Midshipman under Lord *Cochrane: 'Let's give him a piece of our mind, my Bet,/Port Admiral, you be damned.'

Porte, the

see **Sublime Porte, the**

Portugal, King of

Two of the King's massive guns are in Mustapha's *Torgud* (IM 10).

The reference is probably to some King of Portugal of past times, perhaps one of the several Johns (João) of the Braganza dynasty who ruled from 1640 onwards. At the time of IM, Portugal, Britain's long-time ally, was nominally ruled by Queen Maria I (d.1816) but her madness had resulted in her son, John of Braganza (1763–1826), ruling in her name from 1792 and being formally appointed Prince Regent in 1799. On his mother's death in 1816, the Prince took the title King John VI.

Potier

A French corporal in Port Mahon (HMS 3).

Potin, Jean

Jean Dutourd's servant (WDS 4).

Potooooooooo

A racehorse once owned by Carroll's grandfather (DI 1).

Potooooooo (usually pronounced, and often written, 'Pot-8-Os') was born in 1773 to the great racer Eclipse, himself a descendant of the *Darley Arabian via his son Bartlett's Childers (a brother of *Flying Childers).

Pott

A medical authority consulted by Martin when Stephen Maturin receives a severe concussion (FSW 9).

Percival Pott (1713–1788) was a very distinguished English doctor and medical-text writer, responsible, at *Barts Hospital, for many improvements in technical aspects of surgery. Amongst his several works on trauma was Observations on Injuries of the Head (1760).

Potto

The name used by Christine Wood for her own, deceased potto/lemur (COM 9).

Poupette

see **Lehideux, Madame B.**

Powell

A naval parson travelling out on board Jack Aubrey's HMS *Worcester* to join his new ship in the Mediterranean (IM 3).

Power, Father

An Irish priest who, together with Father Birmingham, had accompanied Sam Panda to England in order to find his father, Jack Aubrey (RM 1).

Pram, Christian

A Danish quartermaster in HMS *Sophie* (M&C 3), injured in the battle with *Gloire* (M&C 7).

*Cochrane in his HMS *Speedy made use both of his ship's resemblance to the Danish merchant brig *Clomer and his own possession of an (un-named) Danish quartermaster.*

Pratt

1: the sister of Mrs Williams (PC 6).
2: a thief-taker several times employed by Sir Joseph Blaine and Stephen Maturin (RM 7; LM 7; COM 3,4,5; YA 7).

*The 'Bow Street Runners,' of which Pratt had been a member, were a private police force founded in the mid–18th century London by the novelist and magistrate Henry Fielding (see *Jones, Tom) and his half-bother, Sir John, from their house in Bow Street, London.*
3: a seaman and drummer in *Surprise* (C/T 1).

Pratt, Ashley

A distinguished London surgeon known to Maturin (TGS 2).

Pratt, Ellen

A servant at Ashgrove Cottage (COM 1).

Pratt, Jamie

Maturin's lob-lolly boy in HMS *Surprise* (FSW 5–9).

President, the

When Stephen Maturin speaks slightingly of the President of the USA, HMS *Java*'s officers assume he is referring to a frigate, USS *President* (FW 3).
see *Madison

President, USS

A new 44-gun frigate, heavier than anything possessed by the Royal Navy (FW 2,3,5; TH 8; FSW 3).

*USS *President, rated 44-gun, was first authorised in 1794, re-authorised in 1798 and finally launched in April 1800. Not much smaller than slightly older British 74s, in the War of 1812 she in fact carried 57 heavy guns. In January 1815, towards the end of the conflict, President (under Stephen Decatur) slipped out of New York harbour during a storm. However, the adverse conditions held her back and she was soon engaged and taken by the sizeable British blockading squadron, including HMSS *Endymion, Majestic, *Tenedos and *Pomone. The battle itself was fought principally between President and Endymion and it is that latter ship to which the credit for the capture is usually given, even though she herself was battered to a standstill by Decatur's ship. President was taken into the Royal Navy and then served under that same name until being broken up in 1818.*

Preston

A Foreign Office official (COM 2).

Preston, D'Arcy

An Irish captain who had succeeded the disgraced Captain Sawyer into HMS *Blanche* (COM 9).

*D'Arcy Preston (1765–1847) was made Post in mid–1796, promoted retired Rear Admiral in 1819 but then restored to the active list as Vice Admiral in 1840 and Admiral in 1846. As HMS *Blanche was his third temporary post-ship in the few months since his initial promotion, his appointment to her by Commodore *Nelson was perhaps a quick and convenient way out of the latter's immediate difficulty with *Sawyer. Preston was soon (in January 1797) given longer-term command of HMS Dido. Although Preston is indeed the family name of the Irish *Gormanstons (as both *Aubrey and *Maturin remark), D'Arcy Preston seems to have been more closely associated with North Yorkshire in England, marrying there, commanding the local Sea-Fencibles from 1803 to 1810 and becoming a Deputy-Lieutenant of the County (which would be a most unusual, though not impossible, appointment for a man without a long family connection to the locality). Furthermore, both Preston and D'Arcy have a strong North Yorkshire ring, the former being a common place- and surname, and the latter also being the family name of the Earls of Holderness, themselves sometime Lord Lieutenants of the county. Amelia, the daughter of the last ever Earl, had married one of Admiral *Byron sons, a man who was later to become, by a second wife, the father of the poet, Lord *Byron.*

Pretender

see **Young Pretender**

Pretty Anne

A prize taken by Jack Aubrey in *Surprise* (LM 4).

Prévost, Abbé

A translator and travel-writer referred to by Scriven (PC 6), Yorke and Maturin (FW 2; NC 9).

*Antoine-François, L'Abbé Prévost d'Exiles (1696–1763), took monastic vows as a youth but soon gave up that life for one of a professional and prolific author. Prévost published his 20-volume Histoire Général des Voyages between 1746 and 1759; today he is chiefly remembered for a novel, Manon Lescaut (later the inspiration for operas by both Massenet and Puccini), and for his translations into French of the works of Samuel *Richardson.*

Priam

A reference to a leading character in Homer's *Iliad* (FSW 4).

*In *Homer, Priam is King of Troy at the time of its encirclement and destruction by the Greek forces led by *Agamemnon. In *Virgil's Aeniad, he is said to have been killed by Neoptolemus, the son of *Achilles, at the fall of the city. Priam is usually portrayed as a well-respected old man, known by friend and foe alike to have endured, with dignity, many great changes in fortune during his long life.*

Priapus

Mr Lowndes refers to 'priapic verses' (PC 8) and Sir Joseph Blaine refers to his own sexual reinvigoration by comparing himself to Priapus (RM 5).

Priapus was the classical fertility god, often portrayed as a symbol of semi-comic lust. In the pithily obscene, highly popular Priapea *verses, he is usually seen threatening to violate all intruders into his private garden, male or female.*

Price
A seaman in HMS *Surprise* (HD 8).

Prince of Peace
see **Godoy**

Prince of Wales, the
see **Regent, the**

Prince Regent
see **Regent, the**

Princess Royal, HMS
A ship in which Midshipman Ricketts had nominally served (M&C 2).
HMS Princess Royal, *90-gun, was launched in 1773, spending her career as a flag-ship, very often in the Mediterranean or Channel commands. Up-rated to 98-gun in 1800, she was then reduced to a 74-gun in 1807, shortly before being broken up in that same year. 'Princess Royal' is the traditional title of the eldest daughter of the British monarch and, in 1773, was held by Princess Charlotte (1766–1828).*

Pring
A gun-captain in HMS *Sophie* killed in her first battle (M&C 4).

Probus
An English mail packet taken in the past by the American privateer *Liberty* (SM 3).

Proby
The fur-trade ship that had stranded Owen on Easter Island (C/T 1,2).

Proby, John
A seaman in HMS *Surprise* who dies at sea (WDS 10).

Probyn
Jack Aubrey's temporary steward in HMS *Boadicea* before the arrival of Preserved Killick (TMC 2).

Prodgers
The owner of the Ship Inn, Dover (RM 4).

'Prolixity'
According to Stephen Maturin, the tedious Mr Sowerby's 'middle name' (NC 3).

Prote
Mr Farquhar's secretary (TMC 5).

Prudence
An English 12-gun privateer commanded by Mr Ellis (RM 3).

Prussia, King of
A monarch referred to in passing (FW 6; SM 6).
*King Frederick William III (1770–1840) succeeded his father to the Prussian throne in 1797 and soon established a reputation as a moderate reformer. Initially maintaining a policy of delicate neutrality between the warring European powers, in 1805, under the influence of his wife Queen Louise, he joined the coalition against *Buonaparte. The move was disastrous, with Frederick seeing his armies smashed in quick succession at Jena and Auerstädt (1806) and then having his country dismembered and reduced to a French client by the Treaty of Tilsit (1807). After the further disasters that befell the Prussian armies in 1812 whilst accompanying Buonaparte's invasion of Russia, Frederick again threw in his lot with the Allies and, from 1813, played a leading role in the Emperor's eventual defeat, being himself present at several major battles. At the Congress of Vienna of 1814–1815, Frederick regained most of the territories lost in 1807 but now abandoned almost all of his earlier moves to liberalise the traditional Prussian regime.*

Ptolemy the Third
A pharaoh whose reign Goodridge had studied in Tacitus (PC 10).
Ptolemy III Euergetes, King of Egypt (d.222 BC; King from about 247 BC), was the third member of the ruling Macedonian dynasty, a notable expander of his empire and patron of the arts (euergetes is Greek for 'benefactor'). He is reputed to have been poisoned by his son, Ptolemy IV 'Philipator' (an ironic Greek tag meaning 'father-lover').

Publius, Saint
The patron saint of a church in Valletta (TH 1).
*Saint Publius (d.125? AD) was the 'chief man' of Malta who first entertained the shipwrecked Saint *Paul and who seems then to have been converted by his visitor and made the island's first Bishop. Publius may later have become Bishop of Athens.*

Pufendorf
A famous lawyer referred to by Maturin (SM 4).
Samuel, Baron Pufendorf (1632–1694), a German who spent much of his career in Sweden, was the leading legal scholar of his day on constitutional and related political issues.

Pullings
1: Mr and Mrs Pullings, small farmers in Hampshire and the parents of Tom (PC 7; WDS 1).
2: Mrs Pullings, Tom's wife (HMS 4; TH 1) and presumably the former Miss Chubb (PC 7). The mother of John Pullings (TMC 10) and three other children, she is understandably annoyed at her husband's lack of a ship of his own (TGS 1).

Pullings, John
Tom Pullings' baby son (TMC 10).

Pullings, Thomas or Tom
Tom Pullings is one of Jack Aubrey's most loyal and

able followers, gradually rising through the ranks of the Royal Navy under his Captain's somewhat wayward patronage. We first meet him in HMS *Sophie* as a Master's Mate who had passed for Lieutenant some time previously *(N.B., in PC 6 this examination is said not to have occurred until 1801)* but failed to obtain a commission to a ship in this rank (M&C 1). He soon becomes a valued member of Jack's crew (M&C 2+), eventually being made acting Lieutenant (M&C 11). Yet, although he plays a most active role in the capture of the Spanish frigate *Cacafuego* (M&C 10; COM 4), Captain Harte — Jack's bitter enemy — refuses to confirm his rank (M&C 11). Lacking any real influence for promotion in the Royal Navy (*see also* IM 10), Tom becomes an officer in the *Lord Nelson* Indiaman and there, quite by chance, again encounters Jack and Stephen Maturin when they take passage from Spain to England; he is then wounded in her action against the privateer *Bellone* (PC 5). When Jack is given HMS *Polychrest* he finally secures Tom his commission (PC 6,7) and the young man soon follows his promoted Captain into HMS *Surprise* (HMS 4) as Third Lieutenant (HMS 5+).

Some years now pass (*until early 1809*) and we next find Tom in command of a transport ship (TMC 1), HMS *Groper*, still as Lieutenant (TMC 6). As part of Jack Aubrey's squadron during the assault on Réunion, Tom runs his ship aground as a temporary breakwater (TMC 6). Later, he obtains a replacement command from amongst the many small prizes taken at the island (TMC 7) and, in her, recaptures the Indiaman *Windham* from the French (TMC 8). To assist in the assault on Mauritius' defences, Tom then takes command on his own initiative of the transport HMS *Emma* (TMC 8,10). Just before the island falls he then has the happy task of passing on to Jack the news that Sophie Aubrey has given birth to a son, mentioning in the process that he and Mrs Pullings already have a baby boy, John (TMC 10; *his wife presumably being the Miss *Chubb met in PC 7*).

Once back in England Tom is appointed First Lieutenant of Jack's HMS *Leopard* and visits the Aubreys in Hampshire, his own native county (DI 1,3; also PC 7; WDS 10). Here he reveals that he was first inspired to go to sea by the tales of his grandfather, who had served with Midshipman Byron in HMS *Wager* and later become bosun of Admiral Byron's HMS *Indefatigable* (DI 3). However, during the subsequent voyage Tom contracts gaol fever and has to be put ashore in Brazil to recover his health, leaving the semi-competent Mr Grant as Jack's second-in-command (DI 5,6,8). A little while later, he is back in England, hale and hearty (SM 5,8). Appointed First Lieutenant of Jack's HMS *Worcester* (IM 1–9), Tom soon follows his Captain back to *Surprise* (IM 9–11). In the Ionian port of

Kutali, he becomes enamoured of a young lady, Annie, and earns the nick-name of 'the Maiden' in the town for his mild manners and appearance, before being hideously injured at the height of the battle with the rebel Turkish frigates *Torgud* and *Kitabi* (IM 11). We also learn that, in the past, Tom has often been ship-less, in part because he is not seen as enough of a 'gentleman' for many a quarterdeck, and that Lord Melville had once rejected him for promotion for his part in the cutting out of *Rosa* (IM 10; *an incident not elsewhere mentioned*). However, for his gallant part in the action against the Turkish rebels, Tom is at long last promoted Commander (TH 1). He is not, however, given a ship of his own and thus remains in Malta, cruelly scarred yet, for the time being, deliriously happy at his notional advancement (TH 1+).

Some time later, Tom arrives at Gibraltar in HMS *Berwick*, travelling home to England as a still ship-less passenger (FSW 1). To demonstrate his enduring zeal to the Admiralty, he now volunteers to serve in Jack Aubrey's *Surprise* as joint First Lieutenant with his good friend, William Mowett (FSW 2). When Jack re-takes the valuable mail-packet *Danaë*, Tom is given her to take back home (FSW 5; RM 1,9). Once in London, he then arranges for Mowett's poems to be published, although on commercial terms that seem far from satisfactory (RM 2, 7). Following Jack's later conviction for fraud, Tom helps Stephen Maturin buy the elderly *Surprise* from the Navy and starts to fit her out as a private letter-of-marque (RM 8; LM 2); naturally, he also loyally attends Jack's ordeal in the public pillory (RM 9).

After Jack's disgrace and dismissal from the Royal Navy, the ship-less Tom — still a half-pay Commander — joins *Surprise* as volunteer First Mate (LM 1+), a role he continues to fill at least in part to escape from the anxieties of Mrs Pullings and their four young children (TGS 1–9). He assumes temporary command of the ship when Jack, restored to the Navy List, is given HMS *Diane,* and then sails her towards a rendezvous with his old Captain off Java (TGS 3,4; NC 4). After long delays, Tom and *Surprise* meet Jack — now temporarily in HMS *Nutmeg of Consolation* — at sea (NC 6). Jack now shifts back into *Surprise* and offers Tom command of the departing *Nutmeg*. As this would probably be a very short-term job, he he chooses to remain as volunteer Premier in *Surprise*, her forthcoming South American mission offering him the best chance of eventual advancement (NC 7+; C/T 1+; WDS 1: *N.B., this was not an uncommon arrangement for otherwise unemployed officers in search of the elusive opportunity to shine in the Admiralty's eyes: indeed, in 1827 London officially approved Commanders as seconds-in-command to Post-Captains*).

Whilst cruising off Chile, Tom is given command

of the prize *Franklin* (WDS 2–5), narrowly avoiding capture by the French privateer *Alastor* (WDS 5) before again taking command of *Surprise* to run Stephen Maturin into Peru for an intelligence mission (WDS 6–8). When this scheme collapses in disarray, Tom and Jack run *Surprise* south to collect the escaped Stephen from Chile, before returning home to England (WDS 9,10; COM 1). Here Jack, appointed a first-class Commodore for a mission against the West African slave trade, is able to have Tom made Post as Captain of his pennant-ship, the 74-gun HMS *Bellona* (COM 1,2). In this glorious rank, he assists Jack both in suppressing the trade (COM 2–9) and in defeating a French squadron off the coast of Ireland (COM 10).

> *Tom's name is probably inspired by a Commander colleague of Lord *Cochrane (the model for Jack *Aubrey's early career) in his HMS *Speedy days, one George Christopher Pulling (sic; dates unknown) of HMS Kangaroo. He had been commissioned Lieutenant in 1790 and was then promoted Commander in 1798 and Post Captain in 1802.*

Pulo Prabang, Sultan of

The ruler of a state in the Malay islands, much given to piracy, to whom the French and British send competing envoys in order to negotiate a treaty (TGS 3–8; *also* NC 1,3,4,7; C/T 7; COM 2,3; WDS 7). Stephen Maturin discovers that the Sultan, a paederast, is strongly attached to his cup-bearer Abdul, much to the anger of his pregnant Sultana, Hafsa; Abdul himself is intimately involved with the traitors Ledward and Wray, present as part of the French mission (TGS 7). Their illicit troilism is exposed to the Sultan by Stephen and Mr Fox, the British envoy, using the good offices of Hafsa's family. The Sultan, shortly before signing a treaty with Fox, then effectively condemns the three to death by withdrawing his protection from them (TGS 8). Among his elaborate titles are 'Flower of Courtesy,' 'Rose of Delight' and 'Nutmeg of Consolation' (TGS 6), this last being later used by Jack Aubrey as the name of his new ship (NC 3).

Punch and Judy

The comic puppets (TMC 4; FSW 3).

> *Punch and Judy, the marionettes and (somewhat later) glove-puppets often seen at English fairs, have their origins in the festivals of ancient Rome and the fairs of renaissance Italy and France. The characters appeared in England after the restoration of King *Charles II in 1660, 'Pulcinella' or 'Polichinelle' soon being shortened to 'Punch,' with his wife being given the name Joan or Judy. Punch himself is traditionally a wretched, hook-nosed, wild brute of a man, cackling with delight (hence 'as pleased as Punch') as he beats the down-trodden, but often reciprocally violent Judy with his baton.*

Puolani

The Queen of the Polynesian island of Moahu who is in dispute with Kalahua, the chief of the northern part of the island, and his French allies (C/T 5+). With Jack Aubrey's aid she defeats and kills her rival, sleeping with Jack after a celebratory feast at which Kalahua has been one of the dishes served (C/T 9).

Purdey

A gun-maker, one of whose pieces is owned by Mr Fox (TGS 7).

> *James Purdey (1784?–1863), a pupil of Joe *Manton, became head gun-maker at the London firm of Alexander Forsyth & Co. in 1807. In 1818 he founded, under his own name, the firm that still operates today in South Audley Street (from later 1882 premises). Purdey was a fine craftsman and technical innovator whose weapons were highly prized from his early days with Manton onwards.*

'Purple Emperor'

see **Thomas, Captain**

Purvis

The inventor of a distilling machine (TH 6).

Puss

A name initially contemplated for Scourge, Mr Hollar's cat in HMS *Surprise* (FSW 3; *also* WDS 5).

Putnam, Aunt

George Herapath's insane sister, a resident at Choate's hospital (FW 5,7).

Putnam, Winthrop

The Master of an American whaler, *La Fayette,* that arrives at the scene of Jack Aubrey's shipwreck on Desolation Island. As Putnam's cousin had been killed in HMS *Leopard's* attack on USS *Chesapeake* some years previously, he is not inclined to help Jack to repair his ship. However, needing treatment for an acute tooth-ache, he eventually exchanges tools and materials for Stephen Maturin's aid (DI 10).

Pye, Admiral

An officer referred to by Jack Aubrey in terms of the oddities of promotion in the Royal Navy (YA 10).

> *Sir Thomas Pye (1713?–1785) was made Post in 1741 and, in 1752, appointed Commodore and Commander-in-Chief of the Leeward Islands station. Superseded in 1755 by a more senior officer, Rear Admiral Thomas Frankland (d.1784), he was almost immediately accused by the latter with fraud and neglect of duty during his period of command. Having been sent home to England, Pye there demanded a court-martial, only to be told that, as this could only properly be presided over by Frankland himself, he would either have to return to the West Indies or await the Rear Admiral's own return to London. As he feared a completely Frankland-dominated court in the Leeward Islands, Pye chose the latter course and was then suspended without pay for three years until being tried in 1758. Although eventually acquitted of most offences by a largely friendly panel (he*

being a man with important political patrons in London whom Frankland could not dominate), Pye was nevertheless admonished for poor account keeping and sentenced to a retrospective suspension on half pay from 1755 until the date of the trial (i.e., effectively a 'time served' punishment). Now, in the natural course of events Pye would have been promoted to Rear Admiral in mid–1756, simply by virtue of his 1741 seniority. However, his initial, pre-trial suspension had made this advancement impossible and he was therefore not actually advanced to flag rank until mid–1758, just after his court-martial ended. For most of the rest of his career, Pye therefore lagged two or three years behind the 'class of 1741' in his promotions, this despite his special elevation to Admiral of the Blue in 1773 by the King himself (this was done ahead of the strict due-date but not in advance of any other men on the list; he was knighted at the same time). However, Pye's final promotion, to Admiral of the White in 1778, was made in a general advancement of the 'classes of 1741–1743,' enabling him at long last to stand as the equal in rank of his 1741 colleagues.

Pym

The Captain of HMS *Sirius* in Jack Aubrey's Mauritius campaign (TMC 1+), said by Admiral Bertie to be reliable although lacking in initiative (TMC 3). Like most other members of the squadron, he is soon on bad terms with the showy, insecure Lord Clonfert (TMC 5). Given an independent command by Jack, Pym takes the fort of Ile de la Passe with Clonfert's assistance but fails to take a grip, as senior Captain present, on the subsequent Battle of Port South East, badly lost (TMC 7). His *Sirius* is stranded, abandoned and burned, with Stephen Maturin forming a very poor view of Pym's abilities, especially in his refusal to listen to Captain Lambert's sound plan to secure victory (TMC 7). At the end of the battle, Pym then moves to Lambert's HMS *Iphigenia* and, by implication, surrenders to the French with all the other British commanders and ships (TMC 7,8).

*Sir Samuel Pym (1778–1855) had become a wealthy man as a Lieutenant, being in HMS Ethalion when she helped take the hugely valuable Spanish prizes *Santa Brigida and *Thetis in 1798. Made Post in 1802, he commanded HMS *Sirius from 1808 until her loss at Mauritius in 1810 (N.B., the accounts of this last event in *James and CLOWES make no mention of Pym's supposed ineffectiveness and, at his court-martial for the loss of his ship, he had been most honourably acquitted, with no adverse comment being made on his role as Senior Naval Officer). Pym, knighted in 1815, was promoted Rear Admiral in 1837, served as *Commissioner of Plymouth Dockyard from 1841 to 1846 and was made Vice Admiral in 1847.*

Pyramus

A character used by Stephen Maturin to describe Michael Herapath's means of communication with his lover, the prisoner Louisa Wogan (DI 4).

*The tragic tale of Pyramus and Thisbe is first found in *Ovid's Metamorphoses. Banned from marrying by their families, the young Babylonian lovers communicate through a crack in the wall between their adjoining houses. Finally they agree to meet at a nearby tomb, where Thisbe, arriving first, is frightened by a lioness and, in effecting her escape, drops her cloak. The animal, bloodstained from a recent kill, mauls the garment before making off. Pyramus now happens across the bedraggled and besmeared wrap and, believing Thisbe to have been eaten, kills himself. The girl soon returns to the scene, sees her dead lover and follows him by taking her own life. The tale is famously repeated in *Shakespeare's A Midsummer Night's Dream.*

Pyramus, HMS

A frigate promised to Jack Aubrey for his squadron (COM 2). However, she and her Captain Frank Holden are diverted to other duties (COM 3).

*HMS Pyramus, 36-gun, was launched in 1810 after four years on the stocks; she was reduced to a receiving ship in 1836 and broken up in 1879. She was named for *Pyramus, above.*

Pyrrhic

A dance referred to by a Marine Lieutenant (COM 8).

The classical Greek pyrrhic dance (named for an otherwise unknown Pyrrhus) was performed by soldiers in full armour as a ritual preparation for battle.

Pyrrhus

A man whose life-story is found in several classical authors (IM 10).

*King Pyrrhus of Epirus (319–272 BC), who claimed descent from *Achilles' son Neoptolemus (see *Priam), first expanded his rule from northwest Greece into neighbouring Mesopotamia and then fought on behalf of the southern Greeks against the rising power of Rome. He defeated the Latins at Asculum in 279 but his losses were so heavy that he was soon forced to retreat from Italy (hence a 'pyrrhic victory,' won at too high a cost), arriving back in Greece in 275. In 272 he assaulted the town of Argos but was killed during the street-fighting by a tile thrown from the roof of a house.*

Pythagoras

1: a wayward reference by Jack Aubrey to stoicism (PC 12).

see **Damon**

2: the great Greek mathematician (IM 3; TH 10; YA 5).

*Pythagoras (fl.c. 530 BC) was a Greek-born philosopher and mathematician who spent his working life in Crotona, Southern Italy, where he seems to have founded a sect and an academy; however, almost nothing is known of his life. The Pythagorean ratios found in music, astronomy and geometry are known only through later thinkers and writers such as *Plato, *Aristotle, Euclid and even the poet *Ovid.*

Q

Quarles

An officer in HMS *Charwell* (PC 1).

Quayle

A seaman in HMS *Polychrest* who has informed against his shipmates (PC 9).

Queen, HMS

The ship into which Jack Aubrey was promoted in 1792 from unemployed Master's Mate to Fifth Lieutenant (WDS 3), having previously served in her as a youngster (IM 10).

HMS Queen, *98-gun, was launched in 1769. In 1794 she was one of the flag-ships in Lord *Howe's fleet at the Battle of the Glorious First of June (her Captain John Hutt being killed in action) and in 1805 she was unlucky enough to miss Trafalgar by being one of the squadron (led by *Louis' HMS *Canopus) sent by *Nelson to Gibraltar for supplies a few days before the great fight. When she rejoined after the battle, *Collingwood immediately took her as his flag-ship for the Mediterranean command that he had inherited on Nelson's death.* Queen *was reduced to 74-gun in 1811 and broken up in 1821.*

Queen Charlotte or *Charlotte*, HMS

1: A first-rate that had caught fire and been destroyed with heavy loss of life, witnessed by James Dillon. Some of her surviving crew are brought to Port Mahon in HMS *Burford* and transferred to Jack Aubrey's HMS *Sophie* (M&C 2,3). *Queen Charlotte* had been Lord Howe's flagship at the Battle of the Glorious First of June (IM 4; C/T 4) and is a former flag-ship of Admiral Sir Francis Ives (FSW 1).

HMS Queen Charlotte, *100-gun, was launched in 1790. At Lord *Howe's great victory in 1794 she was commanded by Sir Andrew Snape Douglas with Captain Roger Curtis (1746–1816; the father of Lucius *Curtis) aboard as Howe's *Captain of the Fleet. At the time of her accidental destruction off Livorno by fire and explosion (March 17th 1800) she was carrying the flag of Lord *Keith — himself not aboard, but a witness to the catastrophe from the shore — and was under the command of Andrew Todd (a Post captain of 1796). Todd perished in the disaster but not before writing several short accounts of the spread of the blaze which he then gave to escaping seamen to carry with them. Of* Charlotte's *complement of 859 men, 673 were lost in the disaster. The ship was named for Queen Charlotte (1744–1818), from 1761 the wife and consort of King *George III.*

2: The flag-ship of Admiral Lord Stranraer (YA 4+).

HMS Queen Charlotte, *104-gun, was launched in 1810 and in 1816 was the flag ship of Lord Exmouth (see *Pellew, Sir Edward) at the bombardment of Algiers. In 1859 she was renamed HMS* Excellent, *gunnery training ship, and finally sold in 1892. Like her predecessor above, she was named for Queen Charlotte, the wife of King George III.*

Queen of the May

A joking reference by Jack Aubrey to himself (FW 3; COM 3).

In English rural life, the Queen of the May is the local girl chosen to preside over the May-Day festivities.

Queeney or Queenie

see: **Keith, Lady Queenie**

Quinborough, Lord

The judge at Jack Aubrey's trial for fraud (RM 7,8; LM 8).

see also **Ellenborough, Lord**

Quincy

A nephew of Mr Evans of USS *Constitution* (FW 4).

Quincy, John

An associate of George Herapath in Salem (FW 8).

Quinn

HMS *Sophie's* Marine sergeant (M&C 4+).

Quinn, Dr Paddy

A London physician whom Stephen Maturin regards as a quack (RM 8).

Quixote

A reference by Sir Joseph Blaine to Stephen Maturin's holding of romantic notions (HMS 4).

Don Quixote de la Mancha is the hero of the novel of the same name published by the Spanish soldier and writer, Miguel de Cervantes Saavedra (1547–1616) in 1605 and 1615. Don Quixote is an impoverished gentleman whose deep attachment to old tales of chivalry turns him part-mad and leads him to wander the countryside in search of adventures appropriate to his imagined status as a knight of yore (amongst them tilting at windmills, seen by him as fearful giants). After some time one of his former neighbours, fearing for Quixote's sanity and safety in equal measure, disguises himself as an enemy knight, defeats his old friend in combat and, as 'penalty,' orders him to return home for at least a year. Sadly Quixote, newly resolved to abandon his romantic ways, dies of an illness almost immediately on reaching his village.

R

Rabbetts, Reverend Mr Cicero
The elderly parson of Yarell, a parish whose living is in the gift of Jack Aubrey (C/T 3).

Racehorse, HMS
A vessel in which Lieutenant Fielding's father had served as a Midshipman under Captain Lord Mulgrave (NC 7).

> HMS Racehorse, 8-gun bomb ketch, was the ex-French privateer Marquis de Vandrevil *captured in 1757; her Arctic expedition under *Mulgrave took place in 1773. In 1776 she was captured by the American* Andrea Doria *but in the following year was burned by her captors during a British raid. N.B., CLOWES, Vol. 3:58, is mistaken in identifying the* Racehorse *taken by the French in 1777 (and then renamed* Sénégal *until again being re-taken by the Royal Navy in 1780) as Mulgrave's ship; she was a 16-gun replacement for that vessel, bought into the Royal Navy soon after the loss of her namesake.*

Racoon, HMS
A small ship, recently returned to England from the North American station, whose entire crew had been drafted into HMS *Surprise* without any shore-leave. They are found to be much afflicted by scurvy (HMS 5,6).

> HMS Racoon, 16-gun sloop, was launched in 1795. Just prior to her return to England in HMS, she had established a brilliant fighting reputation in the Caribbean under her Commander Austin Bissell (d.1807), engaging and defeating several more powerful French ships. As a consequence, in 1804 (i.e., just before HMS opens) Bissell was made Post and soon appointed *Flag Captain of Sir Thomas *Troubridge's HMS Blenheim, 74-gun. Racoon was broken up in 1806.

Raffles, Mrs Olivia
The wife of Governor Stamford Raffles (TGS 6; NC 3–5,8).

> Olivia Mariamne (sic) Devenish (1771–1814) had married in 1793 one Fancourt, a military surgeon in India; he died in 1800 and, in 1805, the widowed Olivia married the young Stamford Raffles. From surviving accounts, it is clear that Mrs Raffles inspired admiration—and often passion—in all those men who knew her. She died in Java of a fever in 1814, leaving Raffles and others heart-broken.

Raffles, Stamford
The Lieutenant-Governor of Java, based in its capital, Batavia (TGS 3–10; NC 1–8; C/T 1).

> Sir Thomas Stamford Raffles (1781–1826) was born off Jamaica in his father's merchantman Ann and in 1795 entered the East India Company a very junior clerk. A young man of industry and quick intelligence, he soon made a reputation as an administrator and in 1806 was appointed Government Secretary at Pulo Penang. As well as confirming his political talents, Raffles began here to make a second reputation as an historian and naturalist of great

> ability. Having in 1811 become Lieutenant-Governor of the island of Java (newly acquired from the Dutch), he instituted many social and economic reforms but then gradually fell out of favour with the East India Company directors, who came to regard him as somewhat too generous with their profits. Broken both by constant ill-health and the death of his wife Olivia (see entry above), in 1815 Raffles was recalled to England to face charges of maladministration. Although he was only ever partially cleared of these allegations, whilst in London he was elected Fellow of the Royal Society and awarded a knighthood for his work as an Orientalist scholar. Soon after Java was returned to Dutch control in 1816, Raffles published a well-regarded history of the island, a work that confirmed him as a natural scientist of international importance. In 1818 he was appointed Governor of Bencoolen in Sumatra, an unpromising post from which he nevertheless organised, from 1819 onwards, the purchase and development of the island and port of Singapore, the enterprise for which he is perhaps now best remembered. In 1823 Raffles, now in very poor health, resigned and returned to England. On his voyage home during 1824 he lost everything he possessed (including all his manuscripts and collections) in a fire and explosion in the merchantman Fame. Although he spent his last years at home embroiled in controversies over his various administrations, he also helped found the London Zoological Society, of which he was chosen the first President.

Raghunath Rao
The man who had previously owned Canning's house in Bombay (HMS 7).

> Raghunath Rao (d.1783) was the uncle of the Maratha *Peshwa, Narayan Rao. On the latter's death in 1773, Raghunath was intermittently supported for the succession both by the Bombay (but not the more senior Calcutta) officials of the East India Company and elements of the London government. However, in 1782, after several military reverses, his cause was abandoned and he was pensioned into retirement.

Raikes
1: an HMS *La Flèche* seaman who escapes from her accidental burning in Jack Aubrey's cutter. After he later dies of starvation and exposure, he is partly eaten during the night by one or more members of the boat's crew (FW 3).

2: a gunner's mate in HMS *Ariel* who had once served with Jack Aubrey in HMS *Surprise* (SM 7).

3: a seaman in HMS *Diane* whose leg is amputated by Stephen Maturin following an accident (TGS 5).

Rainbow, HMS
A corvette at Madeira (YA 10) and, under her Captain Brawley, in Jack Aubrey's squadron (HD 1,2) until being detached to the eastern Mediterranean (HD 4).

HMS Rainbow, *28-gun corvette frigate, was the former French* Iris, *launched in 1806 and captured by the Royal Navy in 1809. She was sold out of the service in mid–1815.*

Rainier, Admiral

A commander referred to by Bonden for his success at Trincomalee (HMS 6).

Peter Rainier (1741?–1808) was made post in 1778, promoted Rear Admiral in 1795, Vice Admiral in 1799 and Admiral in 1805. In 1794 Rainier had been appointed Commodore and Commander-in-Chief of the East Indies Station, a post that he held in successively higher ranks until his retirement from active service in 1804. In 1795 he led the British naval forces that, together with East India Company troops, took Trincomalee, and eventually the whole island of Ceylon, from the Dutch. He went onto enjoy similar successes against other Dutch and French possessions in the Indian Ocean.

Raisonable, HMS

An ancient 64-gun ship, Captain Eliot, acting as Admiral Bertie's flagship at the Cape (TMC 1,3). She becomes Jack Aubrey's temporary flagship for the opening of the Mauritius campaign, with Eliot moving to HMS *Boadicea* (TMC 3), but soon returns to the Cape under her former Captain (TMC 3).

HMS Raisonnable *(sic; she was named for her ex-French predecessor), 64-gun, was launched in 1768. In 1770 she became the first ship of the young Horatio *Nelson, his uncle Maurice Suckling (d.1778) being her Captain. At the great victory at Copenhagen in 1801, Raisonnable was one of the squadron that remained at sea with Sir Hyde Parker whilst his one-eyed, insubordinate Vice Admiral, Lord Nelson, stood in to do battle. Under Captain Josias Rowley (in part the model for Jack *Aubrey's exploits in TMC), she took part in *Calder's famously indecisive pre–Trafalgar action of 1805. Sent soon thereafter to the Cape station, in late 1809 she led the squadron that took Réunion, her final action. Reduced to a receiving ship at Cape Town in late 1810, she was broken up in 1815.*

Raitt

A Commander made Post ahead of Aubrey (M&C 11).

*The only man of this name on the Royal Navy list of the time was one William Raitt (dates unknown), a Lieutenant of 1800, Commander of 1806 and Post Captain of 1809, an officer therefore considerably junior to Jack *Aubrey.*

Raleigh

The great English seaman (RM 7).

*Sir Walter Raleigh (1552?–1618), an Elizabethan adventurer, explorer, soldier and admiral, first took up a career of arms and colonial entrepreneurship at the age of 17, soon making and losing fortunes in France, Ireland and America. He was a great favourite of Queen Elizabeth I (although, disapproving of his marriage, she did find occasion to imprison him for several weeks in the Tower), serving as a naval Captain and Rear Admiral in her wars against Spain. On the accession of *James I in 1603, Raleigh fell rapidly from favour and was soon arrested and condemned to death for a supposed intrigue. The capital sentence was commuted, but Raleigh was imprisoned until 1615. On his release, he then set out on an expedition to Guyana where, in 1617, he fought an unauthorised battle with Spanish settlers. Not only did Raleigh lose his son, Wat, in this fight but he also brought about his own eventual death for, on his return to England, he found King James in an alliance with Spain and resolved to carry out the death sentence commuted, but never wholly withdrawn, in 1603. Raleigh was soon beheaded.*

Raleigh, don Curtius

A lawyer briefly encountered by Maturin in Peru (WDS 6)

Ralphe, Docteur

A coded greeting used by Maturin for a clandestine meeting (IM 7).

Rame, Isaac

A seaman in HMS *Surprise*, struck insensible by lightning (WDS 10).

Ramilles or *Ramillies,* HMS

The ship in which the then Lieutenant Clonfert had struck a fellow officer, leading to his being dismissed the service (TMC 2). She had also been served in by the very young Jack Aubrey, who had seen his first naval execution during this time (TMC 6), and, later, Tom Pullings (FSW 2). Some time afterwards, under Captain William Fanshawe, she is on the Brest blockade (YA 4–9) where, together with Jack's HMS *Bellona* and other ships, she prevents two French 74-guns from slipping out from Brest (YA 9).

HMS Ramillies, *74-gun, was launched in 1785. She fought at Lord *Howe's 1794 victory at the Battle of the Glorious First of June and was in Sir Hyde *Parker's offshore squadron at *Nelson's Copenhagen victory of 1801. During the War of 1812, the U.S. Navy made several attempts (during 1814) to attach a clockwork-driven mine to her hull by means of a primitive submarine, an endeavour only discontinued when it was realised quite how many American prisoners were held in her. The ship, sent for harbour service in 1831 and broken up in 1850, was named for the Duke of Marlborough's (see *Marlbrouk) victory over the French at the Battle of Ramillies in 1706.*

Ramis, Dr Juan

The surgeon of the French *Desaix* and a friend of Stephen Maturin (M&C 12; HMS 6). He is a secret supporter of the Catalan independence movement, to which he has been drawn by his Minorcan birth (PC 4,7).

Ramon (sometimes Ràmon or Ramón)

1: a small boy with an un-named sister, encountered in the Pyrenees by Aubrey and Maturin (PC 4).

2: Maturin's godfather and cousin, who has died leaving him a considerable fortune (RM 7; LM 1; NC 5).
This may be the same man as # 3 below.

3: *see* Casademon, En Ramon d'Ullastret

Ramsden

A source of navigational instruments in London (LM 4; TGS 1).

The business was founded in about 1764 by Jesse Ramsden (1735–1800), a Yorkshireman whose reputation rested on the fine optical, nautical and scientific instruments produced in his London workshop. He was elected a Fellow of the Royal Society in 1786. At the outset of his career, Ramsden had married a daughter of the *Dolland family of instrument makers.

Randall

The Master of the school attended by George Aubrey (YA 9).

Randall, Mr and Master Josiah

HMS *Lively's* widowed Second Lieutenant whose very young son, Josiah, sails as a bosun's servant in the care of Mrs Armstrong, the gunner's wife (PC 12+; HMS 2).

Ranelagh

A London pleasure garden (HMS 6; C/T 6) that, with Vauxhall Gardens, is a source of popular tunes (YA 5).

Ranelagh House, in Chelsea, was originally the newly-built London home and estate of the wealthy Irish peer, Richard Jones (1638–1712), 1st Earl of Ranelagh. About 1733, they were lost to his family in a complex legal dispute and soon came into the possession of a Mr Lacy, one of the owners of the Drury Lane Theatre. In 1742 he opened the Gardens as a venue of popular amusement: at their centre was a great Rotunda in which a centrally-placed orchestra entertained the circulating crowd. The gardens closed in 1804 (with the land returning to its pre–Ranelagh owner, the Royal Chelsea Hospital), though its earlier rival, the New Spring (or Vauxhall) Gardens, continued until 1859 as a pleasure-palace for all levels of society.

Ranger

A transport from Bombay taken by the French (TMC 8).

Ranger was taken by *Vénus in August 1810; her fate thereafter is unknown.

Rankin

1: Miss Rankin, a guest at the Keiths' Ball (PC 6).
2: a Colonel who acts as Jack Aubrey's second in arranging his duel with Stephen Maturin (PC 10).
3: the Marine Captain of HMS *Java* (FW 3).

Raphael, Archangel

Maturin makes a reference to Toby listening in awe to the Archangel Raphael (WDS 6).

In the Old Testament apocryphal Book of Tobit, Tobias (Toby) is the son of devout Jewish captives in Assyrian Ninevah, Tobit and Hannah. Following Tobit's prayers for *God's aid, the Archangel Raphael—often in human disguise as 'Azarias'—guides Tobias' every move, assisting him to overcome demons, to find a wife, Sarah, and to restore his old father's eyesight. In the Old Testament tradition, Raphael (a.k.a. Suriel) is one of God's seven senior (or

'arch') angels who present the prayers of saints to their Lord. He is also often associated with earthly healing.

Raphaelo

The artist referred to by Jack Aubrey (PC 14).

Raphael di Sanzio (1483–1520), one of the greatest of the Italian Renaissance artists, was born in Urbino, near Rome, and from about 1495 studied under the great master, Perugino. Raphael spent his almost his entire creative career in Rome and Florence, executing great religious scenes and bold architectural projects.

Rapine, Parson
see **Marsden**

Rattler

A private exploration sloop commanded by Colnett in the South Seas (FSW 2,3).

James *Colnett's Rattler was originally a 16-gun RN sloop, launched in 1783. In 1792 she was chosen for the forthcoming Pacific expedition but, when it was found that the necessary conversion would render her unsuitable as King's ship, she was sold to the commercial whaling side of the joint endeavour, in which Colnett was himself an investor. In 1795 she was replaced in the service by the slightly larger HMS *Rattler: as Colnett's ship had just recently returned to England, it is possible that the vessels are one and the same, re-built and re-adapted (see following entry).

Rattler, HMS

A brig at Port Mahon, docked next to Jack Aubrey's new command, HMS *Sophie* (M&C 1); many years later, she serves on the Baltic station (SM 8). John Daniel had once served in her (HD 6).

HMS Rattler, 16-gun brig-sloop, was launched in 1795 and sold out of the service in 1815.

Rattray

HMS *Surprise's* bosun, who had held this post when Jack Aubrey had been a Master's Mate in the ship (HMS 5+). He is taken ill in Bombay from a surfeit of work and sun (HMS 7,8).

Rawley, Dr

A medical friend of George Herapath (FW 5).

Ray

A naturalist, referred to by Stephen Maturin (M&C 2), whose books are owned by Sir Joseph Blaine (SM 4)

John Ray or Wray (1627–1705) was a blacksmith's son whose prodigious talents led him to a lectureship in Greek at Cambridge University at the age of 23. From 1660 he began to establish a reputation as a most distinguished botanist and zoologist and, in 1667, was elected a Fellow of the Royal Society. A protégé and colleague of Francis *Willughby, Ray was an early, influential developer and publisher of classification schemes based on detailed comparative work. Indeed, as great a man as *Cuvier thought him the most important zoologist of the previous age.

Reade, William

A Midshipman in Jack Aubrey's HMS *Diane* (TGS

5–9). Following the attack on her shipwreck island by Dyak pirates, he has his right arm amputated at the shoulder by Stephen Maturin but makes a good recovery (NC 1+; *even to the extent of having enough arm left to carry a splendid hook*: HD 2), eventually following Jack into HMS *Nutmeg of Consolation* (NC 3–7) and *Surprise* (NC 8+; C/T 1+; WDS 1+). When injured somewhat later in an accident and dosed with laudanum, he reveals to Stephen in his delirium that Clarissa Oakes has many secret visitors to her cabin (C/T 5). On arriving home in England (COM 1), he follows Jack into HMS *Bellona* and is often given command of *Ringle*, her tender (COM 5,6,7; YA 5–9). He and *Ringle* remain at home when Jack sails to Madeira in *Surprise* (HD 1) but both soon rejoin Commodore Aubrey's new squadron in the Mediterranean, taking a leading part in the various missions (HD 2+).

Real Carlos

A Spanish 112-gun ship engaged in the squadron action that concludes *Master and Commander* (M&C 12).

> In the action on the night of 12th September 1801, Real Carlos, *Captain José Esquerra, was engaged and set on fire by Richard *Keats' HMS *Superb. In her confusion she first fired into and then ran foul of her companion, *Hermenegildo. Both ships blew up, with the loss of about 1,700 lives.*

Réamur

An author whose books are owned by Sir Joseph Blaine (SM 4).

> *René-Antoine-Ferchault Réamur (1683–1757), a French entomologist, mathematician and inventor of industrial processes, is credited with the invention in 1731 of the thermometer. From 1734 to 1742 he published his* Notes Towards A History of Insects, *a work much admired by *Cuvier.*

Red Admiral, the
see **Ségura, Paul**

Redfern, Dr

A naval surgeon who, having become involved in the Nore mutiny of 1797, had been sentenced to hang, a penalty later commuted to transportation. In the penal colony of New South Wales he had been given a free pardon by Captain King of HMS *Achilles* and has now, under the Macquarie reforms, become an important and prosperous doctor. Redfern has also saved Padeen Coleman from potentially deadly punishment (NC 9+; C/T 1,3,8,9; *N.B., in* PC 10 *there is a passing reference to 'that man at the Nore,' a surgeon involved in a mutiny*).

> *William Redfern (1774?–1833) was (perhaps) born in Canada and then brought up in England. In June 1797 he qualified as a surgeon and joined, as surgeon's mate, HMS* Standard, *a ship that, only a few months later, was one of those that mutinied at the Nore. During the course of events, Redfern advised the men to 'be more united amongst them-*

*selves,' an offence for which he was soon arrested and sentenced to death as a leader of the rebellion. On the grounds of his youth and inexperience, this sentence was later commuted to life imprisonment and, in 1801, Redfern was transported to New South Wales. He soon made an impact as assistant surgeon to the outlying Norfolk Island colony and was consequently pardoned by Governor *King in 1803. Having returned to Sydney in 1808, he there made a great reputation and considerable fortune, becoming known as the 'Father of Australian Medicine.' In 1809 he was responsible for introducing to the prison colony the practice of widespread vaccination against smallpox. Redfern acted as family doctor to both the *Macquaries and *Macarthurs but, much to his irritation and dismay, his convict origins prevented his appointment to the most senior official posts. After retiring from medical practice in 1826, in 1828 he went to Scotland with his son to see him started on a career at Edinburgh University but, despite oft-repeated intentions so to do, Redfern never thereafter returned to Australia.*

Redoubtable

The French 74 gun, commanded by Captain Lucas, whose sharpshooters killed Lord Nelson at Trafalgar (IM 6; LM 4,6).

> *Redoubtable was launched in 1791 as* Suffren; *she was renamed* Redoubtable *in 1794 and at Trafalgar in 1805 was the principal opponent of *Nelson's HMS *Victory. Having eventually struck to the British flag-ship, she then became one of the several Frenchmen to sink in the great storm that followed the battle. Although her Captain *Lucas was known for his attention to brisk and effective musket-work from his fighting tops, it is usually not thought that the man who shot Nelson was necessarily aiming directly at the Admiral, his task being simply to sweep, through the smoke, the opponent's rather crowded quarterdeck. After hitting Nelson from a distance of about 45 feet, the sharp-shooter was himself supposedly shot by* Victory's *Signal Midshipman, John Pollard (d.1868 in the rank of retired Commander).*

Redwing, HMS

A ship whose surgeon watches Maturin operating aboard HMS *Nymphe* (TH 9).

> *HMS* Redwing, *18-gun, was launched in 1806 and in 1808, under Commander Thomas *Ussher, fought the final naval action of the war with Spain, attacking and dispersing seven small escort ships off Cape Trafalgar. In 1827 she was lost off West Africa, probably after being struck by lightning.*

Regent or Prince Regent (*also sometimes* Prince of Wales)

The 'acting monarch' of England (PC 3,6; FSW 2; RM 5,9; C/T 5; YA 10), to whose set Richard Canning and Diana Villiers were once connected (HMS 1; SM 4). A man for whom Jack Aubrey has never cared (PC 10), the Regent later opposes his restoration to the Royal Navy, especially as Jack has recently insulted Lady Hertford, his *confidante* (TGS 1).

> *George Augustus Frederick (1762–1830), the eldest son of *George III, was created Prince of Wales shortly after his birth. The bouts of disabling mania that the King suffered from about 1788 resulted in the Prince often ruling, in his father's name, as Regent. In 1811, when the sovereign's ill-*

*ness finally overwhelmed him, the title and powers of Prince Regent were passed into law by Parliament. On his father's death in 1820, the Prince then became King George IV of Great Britain and Ireland and King of Hanover. Always an extravagant gambler and rake, as Prince he had enjoyed a very long intimacy—and possibly even marriage—with the Catholic Mrs *Fitzherbert. In contrast, his poor treatment of his 'official' wife, Princess Caroline of Brunswick (1768–1821; m.1795), was notorious. The royal pair had separated almost immediately after the conception of their daughter, Charlotte (b.1796), and Caroline had eventually moved to Europe. In 1820 George, now King, sued the now–Queen (who was trying to claim the right to be treated as Consort) for alleged adultery as a prelude to an intended divorce, making a series of allegations whose scabrous nature so disgusted (but undoubtedly also thrilled) the nation that the case soon had to be abandoned. However, Caroline then died only a few weeks after George's coronation. When George IV died in 1830 he was succeeded by his younger brother, the Duke of *Clarence, as King William IV.*

Reid
A hotel-keeper on Gibraltar (FSW 1,2).

Reilly, Teague
A Catholic Irish seaman in HMS *Surprise* (FSW 3).

Reis
see **Abdul Reis** *or* **Murad Reis**

Relish, the
see **Gentlemen's Relish, the**

Rembrandt
The artist referred to by Aubrey (PC 14) and later, somewhat facetiously, by Blaine when enduring the intense, fire-lit gloom of Maturin's sick-room (HMS 4).

Rembrandt Harmenzoon van Rijn (1606–1669), the celebrated Dutch painter of portraits and historical scenes, was one of the very greatest masters of light and colour on the canvas. Although by no means the originator of the chiaroscuro *technique, he is perhaps its best known and best admired exponent. Rembrandt was also a prolific engraver and etcher of formidable skill and artistry.*

Renault, Mary
The dedicatee of TMC, where her name is followed by the Greek phrase, γλαῦκ᾽ εἰς ᾽Αθήνας.

*Mary Renault was the pseudonym of Mary Challans (1905–1983), a writer best known for her many historical novels set in ancient Greece and Asia Minor, who had written a number of glowing reviews of O'Brian's early Aubrey/Maturin novels. The Greek tag (pronounced 'glock eh-ees Athenas') means 'an owl to Athens': as the goddess *Athena's owl was the symbol of the great city, O'Brian's use of the tag modestly declares his book to be an almost inconsequential addition to an already well-supplied genre.*

Renommé
The former, French name of HMS *Java* (FW 3).
The name means 'Renown/Renowned'; see **Java, HMS.**

Renown, HMS
A ship, once commanded by Admiral Bertie (TMC 3), later in Admiral Thornton's Mediterranean fleet (IM 8).

*HMS Renown, 74-gun, was launched in 1798 (having been called HMS Royal Oak whilst on the stocks), being commissioned by the then Captain *Bertie. She was sent for harbour service in 1814 and broken up in 1835.*

Repulse, HMS
1: the 'old *Repulse*,' a ship in which Will Summers had served (YA 3).
The reference is probably to HMS Repulse, 64-gun, launched in 1780 and wrecked under her Captain James Almes (d.1816 in the rank of Vice Admiral) off Ushant in 1800. Her First Lieutenant and Master were later dismissed the service for their actions on that day.
2: a ship referred to by Pullings in a tale about lightning strikes (WDS 10).
*HMS Repulse, 74-gun, was launched in 1803 and broken up in 1820. In 1805 she took part, under Captain the Honourable Arthur Kaye Legge (d.1835 in the rank of full Admiral), in *Calder's indecisive pre–Trafalgar action.*

Resolution *or* Reso, HMS
(N.B., 1 and 2 below served simultaneously in the Royal Navy, there presumably being almost no chance of their being confused.)
1: a ship in which the young Jack Aubrey had served as Midshipman under Captain Douglas and First Lieutenant Sir Harry Neale (M&C 4,7; TMC 3; SM 9; IM 6; RM 1; LM 7; TGS 4). From time to time Jack's shipmates had included Charles Yorke (FW 2), Henry Cotton (TH 9) and Billy Sutton (FSW 1). In *Reso* Captain Douglas had turned Jack before the mast for six months as punishment for his lechery with Sally M'Puta (e.g., M&C 4) and, during this spell, he had served as topman and sail-maker's crew (FW 7).
HMS Resolution, 74-gun, was launched in 1770 and broken up in 1813. She is one of those ships occasionally referred to in the series that saw almost no action in her long career.
2: Captain Cook's exploration ship (FSW 3).
*Cook's famous HMS Resolution, rated a 12-gun sloop, was purchased in 1770 as the Yorkshire collier Marquis of Granby and briefly re-named HMS Drake. On being allocated to the South Seas expedition of 1771, she was then re-named Resolution and served as one of Cook's ships until 1779 (with William *Bligh as her Master). In 1782, whilst acting as an armed transport under the command of Lieutenant Robert Fitzhugh Hassard (d.1783), she was taken by the French Sphinx in the Indian Ocean and disposed of in the following year.*

Retaliation *and* Retribution, HMSS
Along with *Unité*, the former names of Jack Aubrey's *Surprise* (LM 8).
*Although O'Brian is right that HMS *Surprise was once the French *Unité, it was the mutinous HMS *Hermione*

that, after her re-capture by Surprise, *was re-named first HMS* Retaliation *(the only instance of the usage in the Royal Navy) and then HMS* Retribution. *However, following this famous incident,* Surprise *did take on the nick-name of* Nemesis, *which in Greek myth means something very like 'Retribution.'*

Retribution, HMS
see **Retaliation** *and* **Retribution, HMSS**

Revenge
A cannon in *Surprise* (C/T 8).

Revenge, HMS
A ship due at Bombay (HMS 7), many years later commanded by Captain Henry Smith (TGS 1).

HMS Revenge, *74-gun, was launched in early 1805 and later that year fought at Trafalgar under Captain Robert Moorsom (1760–1835; a full Admiral of 1830). Between 1806–1808 and 1812–1813 she was commanded by Sir John Gore (see* *Collins, # 1), who then also flew his new Rear Admiral's flag in her until the end of the war with *Buonaparte in 1814.* Revenge *was broken up between 1849–1851.*

Reynière
An intelligence agent operating in France for the British Government (IM 7).

Reynolds
A 'crooked' United Irishman referred to by Maturin (M&C 5).

*Thomas Reynolds (1771–1836) was a wealthy, dissolute Dubliner who, in 1794, married Harriet Witherspoon (1771–1851), the sister-in-law of Wolfe *Tone. In 1797 he joined the United Irishmen, soon becoming a confidant of Lord Edward *Fitzgerald. However, Reynolds was by now in some financial difficulties and, in 1798, approached British government agents with valuable information on the movements and plans of the activists, a move for which he was generously rewarded (he may also genuinely have dreaded the prospect in Dublin of the horrors he had witnessed in the streets of revolutionary Paris a few years earlier). Although he rapidly came under great suspicion in the United Irish Society, he seems to have remained in the confidence of Fitzgerald and was thus able, for a while, to continue his lucrative betrayals to Major *Sirr, the head of the Dublin police. Reynolds and Harriet (who had been complicit in the treachery) were soon forced to flee for their lives, moving first to England and Scotland and then— he having squandered the blood-money— holding minor British administrative and diplomatic positions in Portugal and Denmark (where Reynolds served as British Consul to Iceland). The couple eventually retired to Paris, reviled, when recalled at all, by foe and ally alike.*

Rhadamantine
An especially strict system of law (SM 2).

*In classical myth, Rhadamanthys was the famously fair-minded son of *Zeus and *Europa, sent as a judge to the blissful underworld refuge of Elysium. The tradition of his there being an especially severe arbiter is post-classical and seems to be derived purely from his connection with the underworld.*

Rhazes
A medical authority referred to by Maturin (M&C 2; HMS 5) and Martin (DI 5).

*Abu Bakr Muhammad ibn Zahariyya al-Razi (852?–932; called Rhazes in the West) was a great Arab physician of whose life little is known other than that he ran several important hospitals. His extensive writings reveal him to be both controversially irreligious and an opponent of the 'philosophical medicine' approach of, e.g., *Galen. As a strongly empirical practitioner, Rhazes was often attacked both during and after his life for being too much the practical doctor and not enough the theorist.*

Rhodes, Colonel and Mrs
Friends of Laura Fielding in Malta. Mrs Rhodes' brother, Captain Maclean, is to be the new Marine officer in Jack Aubrey's HMS *Surprise* (TH 8).

Richard
Captain Christy-Pallière's secretary in *Caroline*, preparing a comparative study of the various European navies (HD 4).

Richards, David
A cousin of the prize-agent Mr Williams' wife, taken by Jack Aubrey as his sea-clerk (M&C 1+) and, later, Midshipman (PC 11).

Richards, Dick
see **Richardson, Dick**

Richardson
1: a tavern-keeper on Gibraltar (FSW 2).
2: a quartermaster in HMS *Surprise* (FSW 4).
3: the family name of Admiral Lord Barmouth (HD 9).

Richardson, Arklow
Admiral Lord Barmouth's son, who had served as a Master's Mate under Jack Aubrey and been revealed as no seaman. After a short spell as a Lieutenant, with an independent command, he had then been left unemployed by the Royal Navy (HD 9).

Richardson, Dick (*often just* 'Dick' *or* 'Spotted Dick'; *on one occasion* 'William')
A young Midshipman, often called 'Spotted Dick' for his dreadful complexion, in Jack Aubrey's HMS *Boadicea* (TMC 2+), later given command of the aviso, *Pearl* (TMC 8). Soon promoted Lieutenant, he is wanted, but not obtained, by Jack for HMS *Leopard* (DI 4). Some years later, Dick (here a.k.a. William) is met as the now Apollo-like Flag Lieutenant of Admiral Pellew's HMS *Irresistible* (RM 1) but he afterwards re-joins Jack as Third Lieutenant of HMS *Diane* (TGS 4+; NC 1,2). After her shipwreck, he follows his Captain into HMS *Nutmeg of Consolation* (NC 4–6; C/T 4). His career soon takes a leap forward with promotion to Captain of HMS

Laurel, a 22-gun sixth-rate attached to Commodore Jack Aubrey's squadron (COM 4,7,8,10).

> *N.B., in C/T 4 and COM 4 Richardson is referred to as 'Richards.' Given that he is nowhere called Richard Richardson, 'Dick' may simply be his nick-name, with 'William' (RM 1) being his proper given name.*

Richardson, Samuel

The author of the novels *Clarissa* (DI 5; FW 2; NC 9), *Pamela* (FW 2) and *Grandison* (FW 2; NC 9). He had been translated into French by the Abbé Prévost (FW 2).

> *Samuel Richardson (1689–1761), the son of a relatively humble joiner, was apprenticed at age 17 to a London printer. In this business he made a great success, becoming a wealthy master-craftsman and important publisher in his own right; his first wife was the daughter of his former employer and his second the daughter of a fellow printer. From an early age Richardson had also dabbled in creative writing and, in 1740, published *Pamela to great acclaim. His most famous work, Clarissa (see *Harlowe, Clarissa) appeared in several volumes from 1747 onwards, with Sir Charles *Grandison following from 1753 to 1754. In 1755 he published a compendium of the chief moral lessons to be drawn from the three massive novels. As well as being one of the founders of the recognisably modern novel (although he used an 'epistolary'—i.e., letter-writing—technique, without authorial narration), Richardson was an important and popular figure in the London literary scene of his day, with his Fulham house being a famous salon.*

Ricketts, Mr and Master Charles Stephen

HMS *Sophie*'s Purser and his son, a Midshipman in the same ship (M&C 1+).

> *A Mr Ricketts was Purser aboard HMS *Speedy—the model for HMS *Sophie—under both Jaltleel *Brenton and Thomas *Cochrane.*

Rieu

A Royal Navy Captain, an old friend of Aubrey and Dundas (HMS 10).

Right

One of Canning's two domestic tigers, the other being Wrong (HMS 10).

Riley

The owner of a hotel in Sydney (NC 9+).

> *The reference may be to Alexander Riley (1778?–1833), one of the earliest free settlers to arrive in New South Wales, later a successful merchant, farmer and politician. However, in 1817, after suffering business losses, he returned to England, there becoming a successful exporter of sheep flocks to the colony, to which he himself never returned.*

Ringle

A Baltimore clipper, of prodigious sailing qualities, found abandoned at sea by Heneage Dundas and thereafter used as tender to his HMS *Berenice* (WDS 10). Dundas soon loses the ship to Jack Aubrey in a game of backgammon (COM 1; *where*

she is first named), she then becoming tender to the latter's HMS *Bellona* (COM 2+; YA 3–9). *Ringle* is left in England when Jack sets sail in *Surprise* for Chile (YA 10) under the command of William Reade (HD 1). Summoned back to duty in the Mediterranean (HD 2), she then plays an active role in Jack and Stephen's campaigns (HD 3+).

> *The ship was named by O'Brian for the Washington Post journalist Kenneth Ringle who, in 1992, had written in a review of Clarissa Oakes/The Truelove that O'Brian was 'the best writer you never heard of.' This notice precipitated in the USA a massive increase in the sales and popularity of the whole Aubrey/Maturin series.*

Riou

A Captain referred to by Maturin as the very ideal of a good sea-officer (HMS 5).

> *Edward Riou (1758?–1801) became one of the best-known sea-officers and frigate Captains of his day. Having been a Midshipman in HMS Discovery on *Cook's final 1777–1779 voyage of exploration, Riou was in 1780 commissioned Lieutenant and in late 1789 he found himself in command of the transport ship HMS Guardian, en route from England to the penal colony in Australia. In the far southern ocean Guardian approached an iceberg to take on water but ran foul of her and was badly holed. Having sent off many of the crew in the boats, Riou and his remaining 62 men managed to keep his ship afloat and nurse her to Cape Town, some 1,200 miles distant, a feat of seamanship and determination that won him great renown (N.B., this incident supplies the inspiration for Jack *Aubrey's similar adventure in HMS *Leopard). Riou was promoted Commander in 1790 and made Post in 1791, fast establishing a reputation for dash and efficiency combined. In 1801 he commanded HMS *Amazon, 38-gun, at the battle of Copenhagen, being given charge by *Nelson of all the frigates and small boats present. He was cut in two by a cannon-shot from one of the Danish shore batteries just after Admiral *Parker had given Nelson the famously ignored recall signal.*

Rivera, José

A man referred to by General Hurtado in connection with an act of treachery (WSD 8).

Rizzio

A tavern-keeper in Malta (TH 4).

Rob

A horse owned by George Herapath (FW 8).

Robarts, John

A seaman of the East Indiaman *Thurlow* who had become wealthy by finding a large lump of precious ambergris (FSW 3).

Robert

see **Lord Melville, # 2** (*formerly* Robert Dundas)

Roberto

see **Eduardo**

Roberts

1: an Admiralty intelligence clerk (PC 14).
2: a famous naval engineer with whose 'iron knees' HMS *Leopard* has been refurbished (DI 1,5).
*Iron 'knees,' massive right-angle brackets supporting the main beams, are more usually associated with Gabriel *Snodgrass.*
3: a seaman in HMS *Leopard* who contracts gaol-fever (DI 5).

Robertshaw

A curator at the Royal Society's London headquarters at Somerset House (HD 3).

Robin

A young member of the family that owns Maturin's bank, a heavy gambler (TGS 1).

Robinson

1: an Admiralty intelligence clerk (PC 14).
2: the author of *Elements of Navigation* (FW 2; TH 5; YA 6).
John Robertson (sic; 1712–1776) was a mathematician who, from 1755 to 1766, taught at the Royal Naval Academy at Portsmouth and from 1768 until his death was Librarian to the Royal Society. His Elements of Navigation *first appeared in 1754 and ran to many further editions over the next half-century.*
3: the author of the *Abridgement of Ancient History* (FSW 2).
The reference is perhaps to John Robinson (1774–1840), a vicar and scholar who wrote several successful compendia of historical and cultural knowledge for the popular market. His Easy Grammar of History, Ancient and Modern *first appeared in 1806 and in 1831 was expanded as his* Ancient History, *long a standard school text.*

Robuste

The rearmost ship in the French Admiral Emeriau's fleet. Being a dull sailer, she is briefly engaged by the extreme van of Sir John Thornton's fleet (IM 8), when one of her cannon-shots kills both HMS *Surprise*'s Captain Latham and his First Lieutenant (IM 9).

Rocco, Saint

The patron saint of a church in Malta (TH 2,3).
Saint Roche (or Rocco in Italian) (fl.1350–1380?) was a well-born Frenchman who dedicated his life to the relief of plague victims, especially in Italy and Rome. He is supposed to have been imprisoned as a heretic on his return to his native Montpellier and subsequently died of neglect.

Roche

A Lieutenant refused an interview by Lord St Vincent (PC 3).

Roche, Patrick

A fugitive United Irishman aboard *John B. Christopher* (M&C 7).
The name is possibly inspired by that of Father Philip Roche (d.1798), an Irish priest and rebel commander in the 1798 uprisings, hanged by the Crown forces following the massacre of Protestants at Wexford and elsewhere. Roche was clearly an able commander and it appears that he may in fact have been effective at preventing the forces under his immediate control from participating in the massacres. He nevertheless suffered the fate of many of those captured who had assumed any sort of leadership role in the vicinity of armed conflict.

Roche, Stanislas

A friend of Stephen Maturin and Diana Villiers in Ireland (COM 10).

Rochester, HMS

A decrepit ship commanded by Jack Aubrey's friend Captain Edward Calamy, lost with all hands in 1807 during a storm (IM 2).

Roderigo

A character in Blue Breeches's novel (LM 1).

Rodger

A Midshipman in HMS *Surprise* (HD 5).

Rodgers

1: an officer in HMS *Charwell* (PC 1).
2: a Commodore referred to in Philip Broke's challenge to Lawrence (FW 9).
*John Rodgers (1773–1838) served in the American merchant service from about 1787 until 1798, when he entered the U.S. Navy as a Lieutenant in USS *Constellation. After notable service from 1802 to 1806 as a Captain in the Mediterranean war against the Tripoli pirates, Rodgers was in 1810 appointed to command the heavy frigate USS *President and during the War of 1812 was, as the senior active sea-officer of the Navy, several times a squadron Commodore. In early 1814 he was superseded in* President *by Stephen Decatur and given charge of the defence of the port of Baltimore. From 1815 to 1837 Rodgers served as senior member of the Board of Naval Commissioners, with the exception of a short period from 1824 to 1827 when he was appointed Commander-in-Chief of the U.S. fleet in the Mediterranean.*

Rodham, Admiral

An admirer of Jack Aubrey (YA 1) and the tenant of Sophie Aubrey's Ashgrove Cottage (YA 2).

Rodney, Admiral Lord

A famous Admiral of a former age under whom several elderly seamen recall serving (FW 9; IM 4; RM 6).
George Brydges, 1st Baron Rodney (1719–1792), came from a well-connected family and rose rapidly through the ranks of the Royal Navy, becoming a Post Captain 1742 (one of the relatively few officers ever to be promoted directly from Lieutenant to Post rank). After service from 1748 to 1752 as Governor of Newfoundland, he was promoted Rear Admiral in 1759 and Vice Admiral in 1762, ranks in which he made an immediate impact on the naval operations of the Seven Years War (1756–1763). By 1775 Rodney's always complex financial affairs were in ruins, forcing him to flee to France to escape his creditors. He was unable to

return to England until 1780 (by which time he had already been advanced, in 1778, to full Admiral). In this year he won a key victory against the Spanish, both relieving the besieged Gibraltar and defeating a squadron off Cape St Vincent. In 1782, when England's fortunes in the protracted wars against France and Spain were at a very low ebb, Rodney inflicted a decisive defeat on the French at the Battle of the Saintes, fought off the Caribbean island of Dominica, a victory that won him both a peerage and sufficient financial reward to enable retirement in the style to which he had always aspired.

Roe, Dick

A seaman in HMS *Bellona* beaten by Barret Bonden for joking about Stephen Maturin's severe illness (COM 9).

Roger

1: a horse owned by George Herapath (FW 8).
2: a name given to rams in the West Country of England (WDS 5).

Rogers

An HMS *Surprise* seaman, ill in hospital in Malta (TH 8). He may be the same man who, badly injured in a storm, later has his arm amputated by Maturin (FSW 5,7)

Rogers, George

A seaman in HMS *Lively*, perhaps a bosun's mate (PC 7), accused by Evan Evans of the theft of the dried head of an ape (PC 12).

Rogers, Sam

A friend, long deceased, of Jack Aubrey when he was a young Master's Mate (C/T 3).

Rogers, Woodes

The author of a nautical volume owned by Captain Yorke of HMS *La Flèche* (FW 2).
Woodes Rogers (d.1732) was an English privateer Captain who, whilst engaged by British merchants to circumnavigate the globe and take prizes, in 1709 discovered the castaway Alexander Selkirk (the model for Daniel Defoe's 'Robinson Crusoe') on Juan Fernandez Island. On completion of his voyage, Rogers published his very popular A Cruising Round of the World (1712). From 1718 to 1721 and from 1729 until his death he served as Governor of the Bahamas, active, amongst other things, in suppressing his former trade.

Roke, Mr

The Master of HMS *Leopard* (LM 8).

Roland

1: a London gunmaker referred to by Killick (NC 7).
The Rowland (sic) family of gunsmiths enjoyed most of their fame in earlier times, producing weapons under their own name in London and Birmingham from 1629 to 1632 and from 1680 to 1718.

2: part of the catch-phrase 'a Roland to your Oliver' (NC 7).
In the King Charlemagne legends, set in the 8th century, the hero Roland is the very close friend of *Oliver, their relationship having been cemented in a long-running, always indecisive duel over a matter of honour. In the medieval chivalric chanson tradition, Roland, here said to be a nephew of Charlemagne, was killed during his uncle's defeat by combined Basque and Gascon forces at the Battle of Roncesvalles of 778.

3: Madame Roland, a Paris salon hostess (WDS 2,4).
Marie Jeanne Roland (1754–1793), a learned, eloquent and influential Frenchwoman, in 1780 married the lawyer and politician Jean-Marie Roland. In the crucial early days of the Revolution they both became supporters of the Girondin faction, which often then met in Madame Roland's salon. In 1792 M. Roland became Minister of the Interior but in 1793, when Robespierre's extreme *Jacobites seized power, he fled to the country. His wife remained in Paris, where she was soon arrested and executed. Although the two had recently fallen out over Mme. Roland's taking of a young lover, M. Roland nevertheless killed himself immediately on hearing the news of her death. Whilst in prison awaiting her fate, she had written a set of Mémoires, inspired by the ideas of her hero *Rousseau, and it is on these that her considerable literary reputation rests.

Rolfe

HMS *Polychrest*'s gunner, killed in the *Bellone* action (PC 7–9,11).

Rome, the Pope or Bishop of
see Pope, the

Romilly

An anti-slavery activist in Britain (COM 8).
Sir Samuel Romilly (1757–1818) was an English lawyer and statesman, the son of a French jeweller who had fled the persecution of his fellow–Protestants. A liberal Whig, he entered Parliament in 1806 and made an immediate impact on the House with a speech in condemnation of the slave trade but thereafter concerned himself largely with domestic penal reform. Long subject to depression and bouts of mania, he committed suicide in 1818, shortly after the death of his wife.

Romulus

A French ship at Brest (YA 5).
Romulus, a ship-of-the-line, was launched in 1812. Cut down to a frigate and re-named Guerrière in 1821, she then served until 1840. She was named for that Romulus who, with his twin Remus, is supposed in classical myth to have founded the city of Rome.

Romulus, HMS

A ship in which Philip Broke had served and in which Jack Aubrey had once taken passage (FW 7).
HMS Romulus, 36-gun, was launched in 1785, spending most of her career in the Mediterranean fleet. Reduced to a troopship in 1799, she was sent for harbour service in 1813 and broken up in 1816.

Rory
The cousin of the FitzPatrick twins (HD 8).

Rosa
A ship that had been cut out and captured sometime in the past by Tom Pullings. Although Jack Aubrey had hoped it would result in his protégé's promotion, Lord Melville had tersely rejected the suggestion (IM 10).

Rose of Delight
A title of the Sultan of Pulo Prabang (TGS 6), later used by Jack Aubrey as a facetious reference to one of the 'Old Buggers' (TGS 9).

Ross
The Captain of HMS *Désirée*, who has recently married a Miss Cockburn (SM 11).

Charles Bayntun Hodgson Ross (1774?–1849) is most famous as that Captain of HMS *Northumberland who conveyed the Emperor Napoleon *Buonaparte to his final exile on St Helena in 1815. On this occasion Ross' ship wore the flag of Rear Admiral George *Cockburn, whose sister-in-law and cousin he had married in 1803 whilst in command of the frigate HMS *Désirée, a ship he held from mid–1802 until late the following year; the only child of the marriage died as Royal Navy Commander C.W. de Courcy-Ross. Ross, a Post Captain of 1802, served as Cockburn's *Flag-Captain in several ships between 1812 and 1816 and went on to a distinguished, further career: a Commissioner of the Navy in 1822, he was Commissioner of Malta Dockyard from 1825 to 1828 and of Plymouth from 1829 to 1837. Ross, promoted Rear Admiral in that latter year, was then appointed Commander-in-Chief of the South American station. He retired from this post in 1841 and was then promoted, by seniority, Vice Admiral in 1847.

Rossall
A senior Master's Mate in HMS *Polychrest* (PC 7–11).

Rothschild, Nathan
A leading financier (HD 1).

Nathan Meyer Rothschild (1777–1836), the great German-born, Jewish financier, founded the London bank of N.M. Rothschild in 1804. During the wars against *Buonaparte he became the foremost negotiator of loans for the various allied powers and must be given considerable credit for enabling such a long conflict to be successfully sustained even after France was able to dominate mainland European trade. Nathan is reputed to have also made a fortune for himself when he received early news of *Wellington's victory at Waterloo via his private intelligence network. His four brothers — each with Meyer in his name for their father, the Frankfurt banker Meyer Amschel Rothschild (1743–1812) — headed or founded banks in Frankfurt, Venice, Naples and Paris, and were all leading participants in war-finance schemes. Nathan's direct descendant, Sir Evelyn Rothschild (b.1931), currently heads the London family business. See also **Nathan** *and* **Meyer**

Rousseau
The lugubrious prison guard at the Temple prison in Paris (SM 10,11).

Rousseau, Jean-Jacques
The renowned social philosopher, hated by Maturin (TH 1; WDS 2,4).

Jean-Jacques Rousseau (1712–1778), a Swiss by birth, is one of the dominant figures of French literature and political thought. Drawing proudly on his traditional Swiss background, Rousseau was a staunch opponent of the complexities and power-disparities of both agricultural 'advances' and early industrial development (e.g., in his Discourses on Science and Art *of 1751). He advocated the virtues of simpler and purer times, although he saw no prospect of a return to 'uncorrupted' society; instead he advocated new forms of mutually agreed living (e.g., in his* Social Contract *of 1762), based on somewhat traditional, small-family values. His striking imagery and his passionate condemnation of the ills of contemporary social organisation later turned Rousseau into a hero of the radical French revolutionaries. Yet his critics saw him as dogmatic, impractical and hypocritical, pointing out that he seemed unable to develop anything like satisfactory social relationships in his own tumultuous life.*

Rowan
A Lieutenant in HMS *Colossus* who exchanges into Jack Aubrey's HMS *Worcester* in place of the disgraced Mr Somers, later following Jack into HMS *Surprise* (IM 5–9). A keen poet in the modern style, he falls out with William Mowett over the precise definition of verse (IM 6) and later himself engages in *Surprise*'s poetry competition (IM 9). He is then sent to Malta as the prize-master of the captured French merchant brig *Bonhomme Richard* (IM 9). Following Tom Pullings' promotion out of *Surprise*, Rowan rises to Second Lieutenant (TH 2+) and accompanies Jack on both the Mubara expedition (TH 6,7) and on mission to Zambra (TH 10). After the Zambra battle, he is sent back to Malta in HMS *Surprise*'s cutter with dispatches (FSW 1). However, he is then unable to rejoin his ship before she sets sail for South America (FSW 2,3,7; *N.B., he is nevertheless once referred to by Maturin as if still aboard:* RM 1). Later, in London, he loyally attends the disgraced Jack Aubrey's ordeal in the public pillory (RM 9).

Mr Rowan's poem on the wrecking of HMS *Courageux is taken from the works of Lieutenant Samuel *Walters.

Rowan, Hamilton
A Protestant United Irishman. In the vain hope of diffusing a growing tension between the fiery Irishman James Dillon and the assertively English Jack Aubrey, Stephen Maturin tells Jack that many United Irishmen were well-educated Protestants and not merely 'Catholic rebels,' as Jack might have supposed (M&C 3).

Archibald Hamilton Rowan (1751–1834) joined the United Irish Society in 1791 under the influence of Wolfe *Tone and soon rose to be its Secretary. Tried for sedition in 1794, he managed to flee, spending his exile in France and the USA. Greatly disillusioned by the revolutionary *atrocities he had witnessed in Paris, Rowan refused to engage in the 1798 uprising in his home country. In 1803 he was pardoned by the British government and then returned to Ireland, where he continued as a strong supporter of Catholic emancipation by constitutional means. Three of Rowan's children later held commissions in the British Crown forces: one of them, William Rowan Gawen-Hamilton (1783–1834), was made Post in 1811 and in 1827 took part in *Codrington's victory at Navarino, the last fleet action fought wholly under sail. (N.B., some biographies of the elder Hamilton Rowan assert that his son was present at Trafalgar in 1805 as a Midshipman but, although his surname name is variously given in naval listings as Hamilton, Rowan or Gawen, he does not appear under any version in MACKENZIE as a participant in *Nelson's great victory.)*

Rowbotham
A Midshipman in HMS *Ariel* (SM 7,9).

Rowland
A seaman in HMS *Lively* (HMS 2).

Rowlands
The Captain of HMS *Hebe* who declined to give Tom Pullings a job, not considering him gentleman enough (IM 10).

Rowley
1: Admiral Haddock's butler (PC 10,14).
2: a supplier of naval uniforms in London (TGS 4).

Rowley, Mr and Mrs Kate
The gunner of HMS *Bellona*, formerly a gunner's mate in Aubrey's HMS *Worcester*. Kate, his wife, sails with him as tradition allows (COM 3).

'Royal Bird'
A reference by Admiral Ives to a Royal Prince (FSW 1).
*The reference may be either to that naval Prince, the Duke of *Clarence, or even to the *Regent himself.*

Royal George
An East Indiaman in Muffit's China Fleet, Master Mr McKay, protected by HMS *Surprise* from Admiral Linois' French squadron. She is joined for the battle by William Babbington and the brothers Moss. Flying a Royal Navy flag as a *ruse de guerre*, she is one of the ships that successfully engages *Marengo* (HMS 9,10).
*Royal George, 1333-tons, completed seven round trips for the East India Company between 1802 and 1817. The action is based on the defence of a Honourable East India Company merchant fleet against *Linois' attack in February 1804. However, no Royal Navy ship was present during the fight, the squadron being organised by the senior Master, *Earl Camden's Nathaniel Dance. During the action Royal George was under the command of Mr John Timins and was the only British ship to suffer casualties, with one seaman wounded and one killed.*

Royal George, HMS
The ship that sank *Superbe* in a very short action (YA 5).
*HMS Royal George, 100-gun, was launched in 1756 and in 1759 was Sir Edward *Hawke's flagship at the Battle of Quiberon Bay. During the early stages of this encounter, fought in heavy weather inside a confined bay, the 70-gun *Superbe sank after receiving two brisk broadsides from Hawke's ship. In 1782, whilst being heeled over for lower hull repairs at Spithead, Royal George herself suddenly rolled over and sank, resulting in the deaths of her Rear Admiral Richard Kempenfelt and 900 other men, women and children aboard at the time. Royal George was named for King George II. See also* George, HMS

Royal Oak, HMS
A 74-gun, Captain Geary, that appears during Jack Aubrey's action with Commodore Maistral's squadron (COM 10; YA 4).
HMS Royal Oak, 74-gun, was launched in 1809, sent for harbour service in 1825 at broken up in Bermuda in 1850. By tradition she is named for the tree in which King Charles II hid after his defeat by Cromwell's forces at the Battle of Worcester in 1651.

Royal Sovereign, HMS
The flagship of Admiral Lord Keith (YA 10) at Gibraltar, Captain Buchan (HD 1,2).
*HMS Royal Sovereign, 100-gun, was launched in Plymouth in 1786 (having been laid down in 1774); a sluggish sailor, she became known as the 'West Country Waggon.' In 1794 she fought in Lord *Howe's fleet at the Battle of the Glorious First of June and thereafter was commonly one of the main flagships of the Channel and Mediterranean fleets. At Trafalgar in 1805 she bore the flag of *Nelson's second-in-command, *Collingwood, and was one of the most hotly engaged British ships in the great battle, being reduced almost to a hulk. In 1812 she was briefly *Keith's flagship in the Channel and from 1813 to 1814 that of Sir Sidney *Smith. In April 1814 Sovereign carried King *Louis XVIII home to France from exile in England and from 1815 to 1816 was the flagship of Rear Admiral *Hallowell. Renamed HMS Captain in 1825, she was then sent for harbour service, being finally broken up in 1841.*

Royal William, HMS
An 110-gun ship, laid down in 1676 and yet still in service (NC 7).
*HMS Royal William was launched as HMS Prince, 100-gun, in 1670 (sic). In 1692 she was re-built and re-named HMS Royal William, after King *William III. In 1719 she was again re-built, this time as an 84-gun. By about 1790 she was serving only as a guard ship and was finally broken up in 1813 (at around the time of Jack *Aubrey's reference to her).*

Rozier, Pilâtre de
A French balloonist killed following a fire aloft, an event witnessed by Sir Joseph Blaine (LM 4).
*In 1783 Jean-François Pilâtre de Rozier (1756–1785) and the Marquis d'Arlandes (dates unknown) made the first-ever, untethered, manned flight in a *Montgolfier hot-air*

balloon. In 1785, whilst preparing an attempt to cross the English Channel from near Boulogne, Rozier and his new companion, Romain, were killed when their balloon (now a hydrogen-filled sphere mounted above a heated-air balloon) took fire at about 3000 ft. and fell from the sky.

Rubens

The artist referred to by Maturin for his famously full women's figures (NC 4).

Peter Paul Rubens (1577–1640) was perhaps the greatest artist of the Baroque period, producing religious epics, landscapes, portraits and intimate family scenes from his Antwerp studio.

Ruiz

The author of *Flora Peruvianae et Chilensis* (WDS 9).

Hipólito Ruiz (1754–1816) was a Spanish botanist who, from 1778 to 1785, joined an expedition to Peru. From 1798 to 1802 he then published his Flora Peruvianae et Chilensis *and other associated volumes. His work was somewhat controversial in that other Spanish botanists on the original mission claimed that he had stolen their discoveries.*

Ruiz, don José

The Director of the Bank of Commerce and of the Holy Ghost in Corunna (COM 5; YA 1).

Rumelia, Derwend-Pasha of

A Bey in the Ionian region involved in violent disputes with his neighbours (IM 9).

*Rumelia (consisting of a large part of the Balkan region) was one of the largest and most important Ionian provinces of the Sultan of *Turkey's Ottoman Empire. The illiterate brigand *Ali Arslan served as Lieutenant to the Derwend-Pasha of Rumelia until 1787 when he obtained the title for himself on the fall from grace of his master, blamed by Constantinople for depredations that had mostly been carried out by Ali himself.*

Russell, Admiral

A retired Admiral living near Shelmerston. Jack Aubrey had served under Russell as a Midshipman and had obtained his Lieutenant's commission via his good offices (LM 1,8).

*Thomas MacNamara Russell (1740?–1824) entered the Royal Navy in 1766, becoming Lieutenant in 1776 and Post-Captain in 1781. In 1783 he fought a controversial action in his 20-gun HMS *Hussar with *Kergariou's partly-armed 32-gun *Sibylle. Kergariou tempted Russell into battle by flying an upside-down Union Jack, often used as a distress signal: a furious fight ensued, but on the appearance of HMS *Centurion, Sibylle was compelled to surrender. The victorious Russell, feeling that Kergariou's ruse de guerre had been beyond the pale, broke the Frenchman's proffered sword in two and then ordered him confined under strict guard. Kergariou later complained of this treatment, issuing a duel-challenge to Russell: however, the two men were never able to arrange a meeting. Russell was promoted Rear Admiral In 1801 and Vice Admiral in 1805. In 1807 he became Commander-in-Chief of the North Sea Fleet, rising in 1812 to full Admiral.*

Rutherford, Dr

A naval doctor who holds Maturin's sick-bay design in HMS *Bellona* in high regard (YA 5).

Ruyter, De

A Dutch Admiral whose plans had been revealed to the British by the spy Aphra Behn (DI 2).

Michiel Adrienszoon de Ruyter (1607–1676) was the greatest Dutch naval commander of his age, renowned for his courage, his leadership qualities and his seamanship. He first went to sea in 1618 at the age of age 11 and, after long spells in both the merchant and fighting services, by 1641 had risen to Rear Admiral. In the following year de Ruyter turned once again to the merchant fleet but in 1652, on the outbreak of hostilities between England and Holland, he resumed high military command: although Britain had the better of the overall naval war, he rapidly inflicted a series of small defeats on English squadrons. On the cessation of the war in 1654, de Ruyter now remained as an Admiral, inflicting defeats on the Swedes and gaining a reputation as an effective suppressor of pirate fleets along trade routes. In 1665 conflict again broke out with England and, in 1666, de Ruyter now inflicted a considerable defeat on an English fleet in the Four Days Battle; in 1667 he then raided anchorages in the Medway and Thames (as referred to in DI), destroying or taking sixteen war-ships. The war ended in that latter year but erupted once again in 1672, with England now allied to France. Although de Ruyter was unable to achieve any decisive victories over the combined fleets, on several notable occasions (e.g., at the Battles of Solebay and the Texel) he showed himself the superior tactician and leader. Peace was finally achieved with England in 1674 but war with France continued. In early 1776, de Ruyter inflicted a decisive defeat on an enemy fleet off Sicily but was himself severely wounded in the engagement, dying a few days later.

S

Sabidi

A classical reference made by Stephen Maturin to illustrate James Dillon's dislike of Jack Aubrey (M&C 5).

*'non amo te Sabidi…' is the opening line of an epigram by the Latin poet *Martial: 'I don't like you Sabidius, though I can't tell you why. It's really as simple as this, I just don't like you.' A famous—and supposedly impromptu—translation by Thomas Brown (1663–1704) was addressed to Dr John Fell (1625–1686), the Master of his Oxford College: 'I do not love thee Dr Fell….' We know nothing of Sabidius himself.*

Sadducee

Jack Aubrey refers to himself as the 'righteous Sadducee' after having beaten some Midshipmen (TGS 7).

> *The Sadducees, a sect of Jewish priests noted for their aristocratic connections and their religious and political conservatism, flourished from about 150 BC until the fall of Jerusalem in 70 AD. Rejecting all but the Torah (i.e., the first five books of the Bible) as the foundation of religious practice, they were notoriously harsh in punishing crimes, believing, for example, quite literally in the admonition 'an eye for an eye.'*

Sadler, John

A seaman in HMS *Surprise* wounded in the action with *Berceau* (HMS 9).

Sadler, William

A seaman in *Surprise*. The brother-in-law of Grainger, he is promoted Mate by Aubrey following Vidal's departure (WDS 10).

Sadong

One of the Sultan of Pulo Prabang's Dyak bodyguards, temporarily assigned to Aubrey and Maturin (TGS 7).

'Sails'

The common nickname for a ship's sail-maker (IM 8; FSW 9).

Saint

> *N.B., entries beginning* **St** *are listed here as if spelled* **Saint** *in full; as usual the entries for persons precede those of ships. Entries beginning* **San** *or* **Santa** *etc. are listed under those exact spellings.*

Saint-Hilaire or St-Hilaire

A famous French naturalist (SM 4) who attends Maturin's lecture in Paris (SM 5).

> *Etienne Geoffroy-Saint-Hilaire (1772–1844; often indexed under 'Geoffroy') was one of the leading French zoologists and comparative anatomists of his age. In their early careers he and Cuvier worked as colleagues, jointly publishing five works in their field, but much later (from 1830 onwards) the two great men came to differ radically in accounting for the forms of animal life, with Saint-Hilaire favouring an early form of evolutionary theory. At the time of *Maturin's lecture, Saint-Hilaire held (from 1809) the Chair of Zoology at the University of Paris.*

St John, Mrs

A member of Mr Savile's hunt (PC 1).

> *In British English, the name is usually pronounced 'Sin-jen.'*

St Leger

A member of the British government's intelligence co-ordinating committee (COM 2).

> *In British English, the name is usually pronounced 'Sill-edger.'*

Saint-Michiel or St-Michiel, Captain

The commander of the French garrison at St Paul on Réunion, in dispute with his senior officer, General Desbrusleys. Following Jack Aubrey's successful raid and the suicide of his General, he sues for terms (TMC 4).

> **James gives St Michel (sic) as the surrendering commander of the St Paul garrison but I have been unable to find any further details of his career.*

Saint-Susanne, Colonel

The French commander of the forces on Réunion during Aubrey's second assault (TMC 6).

> *CLOWES names Colonel Ste. Susanne (sic; presumably the successor to *Desbrusleys) as the surrendering commander of Réunion but I have been unable to find any further details of his career.*

St Vincent, Admiral Lord

A British Admiral, famous, amongst many other things, for his savage temper (M&C 1), leading to a familiar name of 'Old Nick' (COM 5). From his former name of John Jervis, he is also known as 'Old Jarvie' (M&C 2+; PC 2; COM 5). Now the Whig First Lord of the Admiralty (PC 1+), he angrily refuses the Tory Jack Aubrey's claim to be made Post (PC 3) and even presses a Lieutenant Salt as a common seaman for his temerity in insisting on a ship (PC 5). Having later lost office on a change of Government (PC 5), he is soon involved in attempts to impeach his successor, Jack's patron Lord Melville (PC 10). As a fighting man, the Admiral's most famous action had been aboard his flagship HMS *Victory* at the Battle of Cape St Vincent (hence the name of his peerage), a great victory at which Jack himself had been present (PC 5,12; TH 10). His view that sea-officers should remain single is well known to both Sophie Williams (HMS 7) and Jack Aubrey (TMC 6). (*also referred to:* M&C 11; HMS 1; TMC 1,5; FW 5,7,9; SM 5; IM 3,7; FSW 2,3; C/T 2; COM 5,6; YA 4)

> *Sir John Jervis (1735–1823; baronet 1782, 1st Earl St Vincent 1797) was one of the most influential and successful naval officers of his age. From a relatively modest background without interest or influence, he ran away to sea at the age of 13 and rose on merit alone to Post Captain in 1760 at the age of 25 and merit again secured him a solid reputation as a effective fighting man over the next twenty-five years. Promoted by seniority Rear Admiral in 1787, Vice Admiral in 1793 and Admiral in 1795, in that last year he was given the job that was to make his reputation, Commander-in-Chief of the Mediterranean. In 1797 he engaged and defeated a Spanish fleet off Cape St Vincent, thus preventing their linking up with a French force for a planned invasion of England. In this battle, a crucial and dashing role was played by the Admiral's young protégé, Commodore Horatio *Nelson (with the Admiral's own HMS *Victory suffering only very light casualties in the engagement: PC 3). Made an Earl by his grateful King (and given a most handsome state pension of 3000 pounds per annum), he took in the following year the enormous strategic risk of splitting his fleet and sending the larger part of it off under Nelson (now a Rear Admiral, but by no means the most senior of the available flag-officers: see*

*Durrant) to find and destroy the French. The credit for the subsequent, decisive victory at the Nile must therefore in some large degree go to the boldness and determination of the Commander-in-Chief. In 1799, after his health had broken down completely, St Vincent struck his flag and returned to England. On his recovery, he briefly held the Channel command and then followed a career as a strategic politician, serving as *First Lord of the Admiralty from early–1801 to mid–1804. From 1806 to 1807 the great man then held his last sea-command, the Channel again, before retiring from the active list. Amongst many distinguished contributions to the well-being of his beloved Navy was his association in the Mediterranean command with the naval surgeon Andrew Baird (a somewhat elderly and otherwise obscure man) with whom he made great advances in improving the health of seamen, believing that ships full of fit men could not only remain at sea longer on blockade but could then fight well in all conditions. St Vincent also had spent a period in his early Royal Navy days messing with warrant officers (he could not afford to mess with his fellow Midshipmen after a bill drawn on his father's account was returned unpaid) and always retained a close interest in and sympathy towards the ordinary men of the service. Although O'Brian portrays the Earl as a veritable fire-eater (the incident in PC 3 is taken from a similarly over-wrought interview with *Cochrane), many of his contemporaries took a much kinder view of the man, finding him exceptionally convivial, uproariously witty and fiercely loyal to his intimates. Yet none doubted either his powers of sheer intimidation in pursuit of his duty or his devotion to very strict naval discipline, it being his firm belief that the ordinary seaman must fear his own officer more than he feared danger from the enemy. St Vincent married in 1782 (at the age of 48: it was youthful marriage that he objected to in Captains) and served as an MP from 1783 to 1794; he was elected a Fellow of the Royal Society in 1815. In 1821, on the promotion to Field Marshal of the Duke of *Wellington, that other great hero of the war against *Buonaparte, St Vincent was specially advanced to Admiral of the Fleet, a post he then held in tandem with the Duke of *Clarence (who had been given the title, ahead of strict seniority, in 1811). One final note: history seldom leaps vividly from the pages of official reports and correspondence but St Vincent was surely one of the greatest letter-writers of his, or any other, age. His several biographies (especially the early example by Captain Edward *Brenton) often print verbatim pages of them in succession, as entertaining as they are revealing of the man and his times.

Sal
see **Sweeting, Emily and Sarah**

Sally
1: a slave belonging to Herapath and Wogan in Boston (FW 5).
2: see **M'puta, Sally**

Sally, Aunt
see **Aunt Sally**

Salmon
A Master's Mate in HMS *Surprise* (HD 3).

Salt, Lieutenant
An officer pressed as a common seaman by Lord St Vincent for his temerity in insisting on a commission to a ship (PC 5).

A George Burgoyne Salt passed for Lieutenant in 1789, was promoted Commander in 1797 and made Post in 1807; there is no record of his having such a dispute with *St Vincent. The incident is perhaps based on the case of David Evan Bartholomew who, pressed out of a merchantman in 1794, was shortly afterwards made a Midshipman but then turned ashore in 1803. He wrote repeatedly to St Vincent advancing his claim to another ship and, on receipt of the eighth such letter, the irascible Earl ordered him to be pressed as a common seaman. In this lowly capacity he was sent to HMS Inflexible, where the Captain soon re-rated him Midshipman. The incident was picked up by St Vincent's enemies in Parliament, to his very considerable embarrassment, and, as a result of the fuss, Bartholomew was given in 1805 his commission as Lieutenant. Subsequent brave conduct won him promotions to Commander in 1812 and Post Captain in 1815. He died of fever whilst on active service in 1821.

Salterello, La
A singer who, together with her sister, had sung *sotto i pini* in a production heard by the young Jack Aubrey and a friend (C/T 3).

The salterello is an Italian folk-dance, somewhat similar to an English jig and perhaps Jack and his companion invented the musical-nautical nickname for an especially engaging singer. The duet enjoyed by the pair is from *Mozart's *Marriage of Figaro, where it is sung by the Contessa and Susanna, her young maid.

Sam
1: a slave belonging to Johnson in Boston (FW 7).
2: see **Panda, Sam**

Sammartini
A composer referred to by Maturin (LM 3).
Giovanni Battista Sammartini (1698?–1775), a prolific Italian composer, organist and choirmaster, is regarded as a pioneer of the sonata form, the basis of the construction of symphonic and chamber music.

San Antonio
A Spanish 74-gun engaged in the great fleet actions that conclude *Master and Commander* (M&C 12).
San Antonio was launched in 1797 and ceded by Spain to France in 1800. Although in *Saumarez' victory off Cadiz on July 12th 1801, she sailed under the French Captain Julien Le Roy as St Antoine, she is variously referred to by her Spanish and French names in accounts of the battle. Having struck to *Keats' HMS *Superb, she was taken to England and there employed, under the name HMS San Antonio, as a prison ship and powder-hulk until her break-up in 1828. The ship could be named for either of two great Saint *Anthonies of the Roman Catholic church.

San Carlo
A merchantman captured by HMS *Sophie*, part of whose cargo was later disallowed as lawful prize (M&C 9).

Sancy

The name of a great diamond compared by Stephen Maturin to Diana Villiers' 'Blue Peter' (SM 3).

The Sancy diamond, an Indian gem of great antiquity, takes its current name from Nicolas Harlay de Sancy (1546–1629), a French diplomat who bought the stone in 1570. At various times over the next three hundred years it was owned by French, English and Russian royal and aristocratic families, before being bought at the beginning of the present century by Lady Nancy Astor.

Sandby

The owner of a sail-loft in Shelmerston (COM 1).

Sandwich

A friend of Sir Joseph Banks who had invented the 'sandwich' (RM 7).

*John Montague (1718–1792), 4th Earl of Sandwich, was a British administrator, general and statesman who served three times as *First Lord of the Admiralty, in 1748–1751, 1763–175, and 1771–1782. In his early service Sandwich had supported Lord *Anson's naval reforms but his last period in office was marked by such gross corruption and ineffectiveness (despite his reputation for personal efficiency and diligence) that many leading Captains and Admirals simply refused to accept commands under his 'leadership.' He is nevertheless recalled as an enthusiastic promoter of Captain *Cook's great voyages of discovery. A patron of the arts, a famous rake and a notorious gambler, the Earl supposedly invented the 'sandwich' as a convenient means of eating without having to leave the card-table. One of his younger sons, Robert Montague (d. 1830), served in the Royal Navy, being made Post in 1781, Rear Admiral in 1799, Vice Admiral in 1805 and Admiral in 1810.*

San Fiorenzo, HMS

A frigate, Captain Sir Harry Neale, met by HMS *Sophie* at sea (M&C 7). She is referred to by Jack Aubrey as one of several very desirable frigates into which he would like to be made Post (M&C 11).

*Until her capture by the Royal Navy in 1794 the ship had been the French 38-gun *Minerve (launched in 1782), her new name of HMS San Fiorenzo being taken from the Corsican bay in which she had been found scuttled. Captain Sir Harry Burrard *Neale then commanded her from 1795 to 1801. A frigate that several times distinguished herself in single-ship actions, she was sent for harbour service in 1812 and broken up in 1837.*

San Josef or San Josef, HMS

A Spanish 112-gun ship taken by Nelson (M&C author's note). Later, as HMS *San Josef*, she is Admiral Mitchell's flag-ship in the Mediterranean (IM 4,5,8).

*San Josef was captured by *Nelson at the Battle of Cape *St Vincent in 1797, the only captured ship fit enough to be taken into active service in the Royal Navy. In 1813 (around the time IM is set) she was the Mediterranean flag-ship of Rear Admiral Sir Richard *King. A gunnery training ship from 1837, HMS San Josef was broken up*

*in 1849. She was named for Saint *Joseph, the husband of *Mary, mother of *Jesus.*

San Juan de Nepomuceno

The rear-most ship of the Franco-Spanish fleet at the Battle of Trafalgar (FW 2).

*San Juan de Nepomuceno, 74-gun, was launched in 1767. At Trafalgar in 1805, she brought up the rear of the Franco/Spanish fleet under her Captain don Cosme Churruca, killed in the action. The ship ultimately struck to HMS *Dreadnought (having already at one point briefly surrendered to HMS Tonnant) and was boarded by a prize-crew from HMS *Defiance. Although very briefly re-named HMS Berwick soon after the battle, it was as HMS San Juan that she served as a harbour ship at Gibraltar until about 1816, being sold for break-up in 1818. The ship was named for Saint John of Nepomuk (1340?–1393), a Bohemian lawyer and priest whose defence of church privilege supposedly led to his torture and drowning by King Wenceslas.*

Sankey's

A ship-yard of most indifferent reputation where HMS *Worcester* had been built (IM 1).

San Nicolas

A Spanish 80-gun ship boarded by Nelson (M&C author's note).

*San Nicolas was captured by *Nelson at Cape *St Vincent in 1797 and renamed HMS San Nicholas the same year. Sent immediately for harbour service, she became a prison ship in 1800 and was sold in 1814. Saint Nicholas (d.340), an early Christian bishop, is the patron saint of sailors, merchants and captives.*

Sans Souci

The ship in which Harry Johnson and Diana Villiers travel to America (DI 2).

Santa Brigida

A famously rich prize (HMS 1; IM 10), the source of a great double rope of pearls worn by Molly Harte (M&C 1).

*Santa Brigida, a Spanish 40-gun frigate laden with great quantities of treasure, was captured off the coast of Spain by a Royal Navy squadron (see *Collins # 1) in 1799; on the previous day, the same squadron had taken her companion, the 40-gun El *Thetis, a similarly rich prize. (N.B., the reference in HMS 1 to there being some doubt over the legitimacy of these actions remains obscure to me, as both ships were routinely condemned, making the capturing crews temporarily affluent and their officers wealthy for life). The ship was probably named for Saint Bridget (1302–1373), the Swedish nun and mystic writer, rather than that *Brigid who, with *Patrick, is one of the patron saints of Ireland.*

Santa Lucia

A Neapolitan merchantman carrying French Royalist refugees, first captured by the French *Gloire* and then re-taken by HMS *Sophie* (M&C 7).

Santisima or Santissima Trinidad

A Spanish warship of which Admiral Russell has a model (LM 1). She was taken by the Royal Navy, perhaps by Lord Barmouth himself (HD 9).

> *Launched in Havana in 1769, Santisima Trinidad (sic) was a four-decker, the biggest warship of her age and wonderfully ornate; however, her sailing qualities had largely been sacrificed to her massive, 130-gun armament. At the Battle of Trafalgar in 1805 she was the flag-ship of Rear Admiral don Hidalgo Cisneros. One of the first of the Franco/Spanish fleet to engage *Nelson's HMS *Victory, she eventually surrendered after being pounded to a hulk by smaller ships lying on her bow and stern and, during the great storm that followed the battle, *Collingwood ordered her to be scuttled. She was named for the Most Holy Trinity of the Catholic Church, the Father, Son and Holy Spirit.*

Sappho

A classical poet (PC 13; COM 7) who loved Phaon (DI 4).

> *Sappho was a celebrated Greek lyric poetess (625?–600? BC), of whose often erotic creations only one complete work and some fragments have survived. It is from a combination of her birthplace on the island of Lesbos and the homoerotic (though often enigmatically so) character of her verse that the term 'lesbian' is derived. According to much later legend, it was for unrequited love of *Phaon—a man— that Sappho supposedly committed suicide.*

Sara

A camel used by Maturin in the Algerian Sahara (HD 7).

Sarah

The daughter or servant of Mrs Moss, a Portsmouth inn-keeper (HMS 4).

Sarah or Sal

see Sweeting, Emily and Sarah

Sarastro

The 'Sarastro affair' is said to be an excuse for Spain to declare war on Britain (PC 14).

Satan

see Devil, the

Satisfaction, John

A Chinese seaman in HMS *Lively*, at one time almost certainly a pirate (PC 12; HMS 2).

Satterley, Admiral

A senior official at the Admiralty offices in London (TGS 4)

Satterly

The Master of HMS *Néréide* (TMC 5,7).

Saturnin

The name by which Admiral Colpoys imperfectly recalls Stephen Maturin (SM 1).

Saul, Captain

An officer who has an interview with Lord St Vincent (PC 3).

Saumarez, Sir James de

The British admiral (M&C author's note, 2+) who loses the first and then wins the second of the two great battles that conclude *Master and Commander* (M&C 12). Later, he is the Commander-in-Chief of the Baltic, a famously religious man (FW 4; SM author's note, 7,8,9).

> *James de Saumarez (1757–1836) was from a Guernsey family of French descent with a distinguished record of service in the Royal Navy. Having entered the service in 1770, he was made Post in 1782 and knighted in 1793. In 1797 Saumarez fought his HMS *Orion at the Battle of Cape *St Vincent and in 1798, still in the same ship, was one of *Nelson's 'band of brothers' at the Battle of the Nile. Promoted Rear Admiral in January 1801 (and shortly afterwards made a baronet), he then flew his flag in the Mediterranean aboard HMS *Caesar. The first, unsuccessful action described in* Master and Commander *was fought on July 6th 1801, with the second, a brilliant victory, taking place on July 12th. Promoted Vice Admiral in 1806, from 1808 until late 1812 Saumarez commanded the Baltic squadrons, establishing a reputation as an exceptional diplomat in an area of great political complexity. (N.B., as O'Brian notes in SM, DNB implies that Saumarez resigned in 1813 but ROSS shows that he left the Baltic on November 5th 1812, striking his flag in England a week later). A full Admiral of 1814, he served as Commander-in-Chief, Plymouth, from 1824 to 1827 and, in 1831, Sir James was raised to the peerage as Lord de Saumarez.*

Saumarez, Richard or Dick

Admiral James de Saumarez' brother, a doctor known to Maturin (SM 7).

> *Richard Saumarez (1764–1835) followed in the medical footsteps of his elder brother John, an army surgeon, and enjoyed great distinction as a London doctor from about 1785 until his retirement from a large and rich practice in 1818. He was also well known as a lively author on medical controversies of his day. His son, also Richard (1791–1866), chose the path of his uncle, Admiral James *Saumarez, and entered the Royal Navy. Made Post in 1824, DNB states he eventually rose to flag rank but this is not confirmed in SYRETT & DiNARDO.*

Saunders, Admiral

A neighbour of the Aubreys in Hampshire (IM 5).

Savage

1: Maturin refers to Dr Johnson's *Life of Savage* in glowing terms (M&C 4).

> *Richard Savage (1697?–1743) was a well-known poet and playwright whom Dr *Johnson recounts as having endured terrible hardships in pursuit of his literary vocation. Moreover, in 1727 Savage had killed a man in a drunken brawl and been condemned to death by the notorious judge Sir Francis *Page, only securing a pardon in 1728 following the intervention of his influential literary and political friends.*

2: a Midshipman in HMS *Worcester* (IM 2,8).

Saverien

The author of a nautical French-English dictionary referred to by Mr Scriven (PC 6).

> *Alexandre Saverien (1722?–1805), a French naval engineer, scientist and philosopher, published his* Dictionnaire de la Marine *in 1758.*

Savile, Edward

A Master of Foxhounds in Sussex (PC 1,2,3; HMS 1).

> *As Edward Savile is several times referred to as the 'young Mr Savile,' the rather ferocious 'Mr Savile' briefly encountered in PC 1 may perhaps be his father.*

'Sawbones Romeo'

Stephen Maturin, as thought of by Lady Forbes (HMS 10).

Sawyer

1: the Admiral on the North American Station (FW 8) who later is said to have met Sophie Aubrey and Harriet Goole at Lady Hood's reception (RM 1).

> *Sir Herbert Sawyer (d.1833) was made Post in 1789, promoted Rear Admiral in 1807, Vice Admiral in 1811 and Admiral in 1825. In 1811 he was Commander-in-Chief on the Leeward Islands station, moving to the North American post at Halifax on the outbreak of war in 1812. In early 1813 (i.e., a little before FW 8) he was superseded by Sir John Borlase Warren (see* ***Warne**) *but appears, from various sources, to have then remained in Halifax for some time. His father, also Herbert (1731?–1798), had become a Rear Admiral in 1787, Vice Admiral in 1793 and Admiral in 1795.*

2: the Captain of HMS *Blanche*, dismissed the service after accusations of ship-board buggery (COM 9).

> *The tale of Captain Charles Sawyer's predilections and subsequent downfall is mentioned in passing by the seaman Jacob Nagle (see* ***Nagel**). *According to DANN's summary of the court-martial proceedings, the habits of the Captain of HMS *Blanche were drawn to the attention of Captain George *Cockburn of HMS *Meleager in mid–1795 when the two ships were cruising in company. Cockburn — senior to his colleague as a Post Captain by only one month — made enquiries of the various parties, Sawyer included, and somehow managed to hush up the whole matter. However, in the following year, Sawyer's renewed activities — taking hold of young seamen 'about the privates' in the dark of his cabin by night and allowing insubordination from crewmen presumed to have been his lovers — caused a hot dispute with his First Lieutenant, who consequently requested a court-martial. Cockburn submitted to the court letters that damned Sawyer, who, on October 18th 1796, was dismissed the service (note, however, that this dismissal is not recorded in SYRETT & DiNARDO). Sawyer had been commissioned Lieutenant in 1785 and promoted Commander in late 1793. Having briefly held the 8-gun bomb vessel, HMS Vesuvius, he was made Post in March 1794 into the 74-gun HMS *Vanguard as Pennant-Captain to Commodore*

> *Charles Thompson (a position usually given to young protégé by a close patron). Sometime in 1795 Sawyer was given the frigate *Blanche and in her, before the unhappy events recounted above, made a good reputation for himself in the Caribbean. N.B., although DANN says Sawyer had Blanche in June 1795 (the date of the first complaint against him), both CLOWES and *James have him taking Superbe, 24-gun, with his Vanguard in October of that year. NORIE, however, has Vanguard commanded in that action by Simon Miller (d.1825 in the rank of retired Rear Admiral). Sawyer's fate after 1796 is unknown.*

Saxony, King of

An ally of Buonaparte (SM 4, 10).

> *Frederick Augustus I (1750–1827) had succeeded his father as Elector of Saxony in 1763. For most of the Napoleonic war he adopted a policy of neutrality, perhaps just slightly favouring the French. At the end of 1806, however, he declared himself King of Saxony and threw in his entire lot with France and *Buonaparte's new, enforced ally, the King of *Prussia. As a consequence, in the peace settlements of 1814–1815 Frederick lost about half of his traditional lands to rival German princes.*

Scanderberg

Maturin refers to the 'sword of Scanderberg' (IM 2).

> *George Kastrioto (1405–1468), a.k.a. Skanderbeg (sic; i.e., Iskander/Alexander Bey) is one of the great national heroes of the Albanian people. In 1444, after earlier illustrious service for the Ottoman Sultan (by whom he was given his title), Kastrioto renounced Islam, returned to the Christianity of his native Albania and there organised resistance to successive Turkish invasions. He soon became a hero of the Western Christian world and was even appointed Captain-General of Pope Calixtus III's Holy See in Rome. Although Kastrioto's personal resistance to the Eastern onslaught was effective for over 20 years, Albania succumbed to the Turks soon after his death. The usual meaning of the tag 'Skanderbeg's sword must have Skanderbeg's arm' is that the power of the weapon is nothing without its proper owner.*

Scanlan

A seaman in the American whaler *La Fayette*, recognised by Jack Aubrey as a deserter from HMS *Andromache* (DI 10).

Scanlon, Michael

A look-out in HMS *Lively* (PC 14).

Scarlatti

A composer whose works are often played by Aubrey and Maturin (IM 2,3,5,9; FSW 4,6).

> *Giuseppe Domenico Scarlatti (1685–1757) was one of the greatest Italian composers for the harpsichord and organ, on both of which he was also a famous virtuoso. Like both his father, Alessandro (1660–1725), and his own nephew, Giuseppe (1718–1777), Domenico also composed many operas and vocal works, both sacred and secular.*

Scarlet

A member of the barge-crew of Captain Baker's HMS *Iris*, chosen for his colourful surname (FSW 2).

Schank, Admiral

A retired Admiral and friend of Admiral Russell, Jack Aubrey and Stephen, known in the service as 'Old Purchase,' a nickname derived from his invention of a system of lines and pullies for hanging and moving an invalid's cot (LM 1; TGS 1).

John Schank (1740–1823), a Scottish engineer, inventor and naval officer, entered the Royal Navy as an able seaman in 1758, winning promotion to Midshipman in 1762 and Lieutenant in 1776 (being in this rank a mentor of Midshipman Edward *Pellew during the American Revolutionary War). In 1783, by now already widely known as 'Old Purchase,' he was made Post but in 1802 was forced to retire by his failing eyesight. Promoted Rear Admiral by seniority in 1805, he rose to Vice Admiral in 1810 and full Admiral in 1821. Schank is best remembered for his invention of a system of sliding keels, rather like a modern centre-board, for small craft.

Schikaneder

A man referred to by Maturin as a secret agent working for the British (HMS 1).

Schlendrian

A German philologist at Maturin's lecture in Paris (SM 5).

Schmidt of Gottingen

A man who had once given a disastrous lecture at the *Institut* in Paris (SM 5).

Scholey

A friend of Captain Howard of HMS *Aurora* and a Fellow of the Royal Society (COM 7).

Schwarzenberg

An Austrian general marching to join Wellington in the Low Countries (HD 1).

Karl Philip, Prince von Schwarzenberg (1771–1820) joined the Austrian army in 1788, made an early reputation against the Turks and then fought against the French in the campaigns of 1794 and (as a field officer from 1796 onwards), 1799 and 1805. After the heavy Austrian defeats at Wagram and Znaim, Vienna made peace with *Buonaparte in 1809 and Schwarzenberg went to Paris in the French service, leading his Austrian troops in the invasion of Russia of 1812. When Austria rejoined the cause against the Emperor in 1813, Schwarzenberg was appointed Allied Commander-in-Chief and, after an initial defeat at Dresden, inflicted the defeat of Leipzig on the French before marching to Paris in 1814, a campaign that led to Buonaparte's first abdication. During the latter's 'hundred day' return of 1815, Schwarzenberg led his Austrian army westwards again but did not arrive in the Low Countries in sufficient force in time to participate in *Wellington and *Blücher's great victory at Waterloo. After a short period in political office, the Prince suffered a total health break-down in 1817.

Sciahan, Bey of Kutali

A Bey currently in possession of the disputed Greek port of Kutali, now seeking British aid to hold it against his rivals, Ismail, Bey of Mesenteron, and Mustapha, Captain-Bey of Karia (IM 9). He is chosen by Jack Aubrey as an ally, in part because he had once fought alongside Sir Sidney Smith at Acre (IM 10). Sciahan is also an ally of Ali Pasha of Iannina (IM 10) and appears to benefit from a cunning trick played by that man on Mustapha, leading to the latter's defeat at sea by Jack (IM 10,11; TH 1,5). A little later, Sciahan is again briefly visited by Jack (TH 9) and, some years later, by Stephen Maturin's intelligence colleague Dr Jacob, when he is able to confirm the progress of Buonapartist Muslim plans in the Adriatic region (HD 4).

Scipion and *Scipion,* HMS

A French 74-gun in Toulon Harbour (PC 4), later captured by Harry Lambert in Strachan's action against the French (FW 3; YA 9).

Scipion, 74-gun, was launched in 1801 and in 1805 fought, under her Captain Charles Bellanger (or Berranger), in the French line at the Battle of Trafalgar. Although escaping immediate capture by *Nelson's victorious fleet, she was then taken by Sir Richard *Strachan's squadron a week later (but not by Harry *Lambert, who played no part in the action). Re-named HMS Scipion, she was eventually broken up in 1819. The ship was named for Scipio Africanus Major (234–183 BC), the famous Roman general and politician.

Scorpion

The Keiths' gardener at Gibraltar (HD 9).

Scott

1: the Captain's clerk in Jack Aubrey's HMS *Surprise*, one of the members of the larboard Midshipman's mess who steals and eats Stephen Maturin's experimental rats (HMS 6).

2: the Captain of HMS *Cambridge* (FSW 1).

Scotus, Duns

A philosopher referred to by Professor Graham (TH 1).

John Duns Scotus (1266?–1308), a Franciscan friar and scholar, born in Duns, Scotland, enjoyed a career as a scholastic philosopher that took him to the universities of Cambridge, Oxford, Paris and, finally, Cologne, the city of his death. In his own lifetime and for many centuries afterwards, his reputation for refined, speculative thought on the central mysteries of the Christian faith stood very high throughout Europe. However, his parallel defence of the temporal rights of the Papacy led English religious reformers of the 16th century to use his name as a term of abuse — a 'dunce' — for what they saw as idiotic subservience to a corrupt power.

Scourge

The cat belonging to bosun Hollar of HMS *Surprise*, as named by Stephen Maturin (FSW 3).

Screech, William

A seaman in HMS *Polychrest*, an ex–HMS *Sophie* (PC 9,11).

Scriven, Adam

The hack-writer turned unsuccessful foot-pad who is captured by Jack Aubrey whilst attempting a robbery. Having become Jack's temporary clerk, he soon betrays his master to the bailiffs (PC 6,7; HMS 9).

> *The name may well be inspired by a poem of Geoffrey *Chaucer addressed to his own copyist, 'Adam the scriveyn,' on whom the poet wishes a plague of lice for the poor quality of his work (I am grateful to Andrew Midkiff of the 'Gunroom' for bringing this connection to light). Another source of the name, contemporary to Jack, could possibly be one Edward Scriven (1775–1841), a noted engraver of portraits and illustrations for high-quality books.*

Scroby

A Polynesian-speaking seaman in *Surprise* (C/T 1).

Scroggs

The family name of Lord Clonfert (TMC 2,5).

Scutari, Bey of

A Pasha defeated and killed by his rival, Ali Arslan of Iannina (IM 9).

Scylla and Charybdis

A classical reference used by Aubrey (LM 2; YA 5).

> *In classical myth, Scylla was a great sea monster stationed at the foot of cliffs opposite the fearful whirlpool, Charybdis.*

Seagull, HMS

An 18-gun brig that engages the *Lord Nelson* Indiaman after her capture by the French privateer *Bellone*. On the approach of a powerful British squadron, *Lord Nelson* is forced to strike to her (PC 5).

> *HMS Seagull, 16-gun brig-sloop, was launched in 1795. In the August 1803 action described by O'Brian she was under Commander Henry Burke, presumed drowned when she was lost during a squall in the English Channel in the following year.*

Seahorse, HMS

A ship referred to by Aubrey as one of several very desirable frigates into which he would like to be made Post (M&C 11). Golovnin had once served in her as a volunteer under Captain Corbett (TMC 3).

> *HMS Seahorse, 38-gun, was launched in 1794. She spent most of her career in the Mediterranean, acting for some time as one of *Nelson's 'eyes of the fleet' in the blockade of Toulon. *Golovnin served on her under her newly-appointed Captain *Corbett in 1806. Seahorse's most famous action took place in July 1808 under her then Captain John Stewart (d.1811). In a fight strongly reminiscent of Jack *Aubrey's encounter with *Mustapha Bey's *Kitabi and *Torgud, she engaged the Turkish frigates Badere-I-Zaffér, 44-gun, and Alis Fezzan, 26-gun, taking the larger and driving off the smaller. Seahorse was broken up in 1819.*

Searle

A hotel-keeper in Valletta, Malta (TH 1,8,10).

Sebastian, Saint

A saint to whom there is a shrine on the island of Gozo (TH 2).

> *Saint Sebastian (d.288) was supposedly a native of France who went on to serve in the Emperor *Diocletian's Praetorian Guard. When he refused to renounce his Christian faith, he was tied to a tree and shot through with arrows.*

Secondary of the Poultry Compter

A minor government official with whom Theobald's erstwhile sweetheart has eloped (HMS 8).

Secretary, Mr *or* Secretary of State

see State, Secretary of

Ségura, Paul

An ex-naval, French intelligence officer, a.k.a. the 'Red Admiral.' Captured when *Diane* is taken by Jack Aubrey, he then escapes by a ruse (LM 7).

Seine, HMS

The ship that had captured *La Vengence* (FW 2).

> *HMS Seine, 48-gun, was launched as the French ship of that name in 1793 and taken by the Royal Navy in 1798. In 1800, under Captain David Milne (d.1845 as Admiral Sir David), she took the 50-gun *Vengeance, recently badly damaged by USS *Constellation, in a long, evening action fought off the coast of Puerto Rico. In 1803, still under Milne, she was wrecked near the Texel estuary and then burned by her crew to avoid capture. The two pilots who had brought about this disaster were each sentenced to two years imprisonment in the Marshalsea.*

Seldon

A lawyer referred to by Dillon and Maturin (M&C 5).

> *John Selden (sic; 1584–1654), a noted English jurist, politician and historian, published in 1636 his famous Mare Clausum, a work in which he argued that Britain should have exclusive use of the seas surrounding her shores: from 1645 he then served on the forerunner of the Board of Admiralty. From humble origins, Selden had risen in his career to a position of great wealth and influence, partly on his undoubted merits and partly through his close connection with the rich, widowed Countess of Kent, as whose financial secretary he acted. When she died in 1651, Selden was the main beneficiary of her estate and, indeed, the antiquarian John Aubrey (1626–1697) even suggested that they had secretly married.*

Selim

A potentate in the Adriatic/Ionian region (HD 5).

> *The reference may perhaps be to a Sultan of *Turkey.*

Sémillante

A 36-gun frigate of Linois' squadron (HMS 6,9), years later thought to be at Mauritius (TMC 1).

> *Sémillante ('lively') was launched as a 36-gun in 1791. From 1802 onwards, under her Captain Léonard Motard (1771–1852), she was one of the most effective commerce-*

raiders in the Indian Ocean. Eventually, in 1808, she was engaged by William Montague's HMS *Terpsicore and so badly damaged that, although she escaped capture, she was deemed unfit for further active service. Re-named Charles, she returned to France in 1809 as a transport ship and was disposed of the following year.

Semiramis, HMS

A former command of Captain Robert Morley (COM 5).

HMS Semiramis, 36-gun, was launched in 1808, reduced to a 24-gun in 1827 and broken up in 1844. She was named for a legendary Queen of Assyria (fl.c.1250 BC), a notable warrior and a builder of great monuments in Babylon, her capital.

Semple

One of Jack Aubrey's bargemen in HMS *Nutmeg of Consolation*, injured in action (NC 5).

Sénac de Meilhan

An author quoted by Stephen Maturin on the subject of women's supposed contempt for timidity or impotence in men (FSW 4).

Gabriel Sénac de Meilhan (1736–1803), the son of a celebrated French physician, spent most of his career as a senior civil servant. Later in his life, he turned to writing and produced the fictitious Memoirs of Anne de Gonzague, his Thoughts on Mind and Manners and L'Emigré, a novel about the Revolution, highly sympathetic to aristocratic concerns. He himself had fled France on the outbreak of the Terror, ending his days in exile.

Senhouse

A man whom Admiral Schank says went too high in a balloon, never to be seen again (LM 1).

Sennet, Geo.

An HMS *Sophie* seaman referred to in Captain Allen's log as having been lashed (M&C 2,6).

Seppings or Sepping, Robert and Thomas

The renowned naval architect (NC 3; C/T 1; YA 10) and his son, a Poole ship-yard owner (YA 10; HD 1,8).

*Sir Robert Seppings (1767–1840), the great British naval architect, was born into a large naval family, close Norfolk neighbours of the *Nelsons. From 1804 Seppings was Master Shipwright at Chatham Dockyard and from 1813 to 1832, Surveyor of the Navy. Elected Fellow of the Royal Society in 1814, he was knighted in 1819. Amongst many other innovations, Seppings was responsible for the introduction of diagonal bracing and trussing in ships' frames to prevent 'hogging,' the drooping of the bow and stern when the crest of a wave passes under the mid-point of the keel.*

Serapis, HMS

A ship in which William Smith had served (COM 3).

HMS Serapis, 44-gun, was launched in 1782, reduced to a floating battery in 1801 and a 20-gun transport ship in 1803, before being sold in 1826. She was named for Ser-

apis/Osiris, the Egyptian god of healing and the underworld.

Seringapatam

An East India Company ship met by HMS *Surprise* at sea. Her Master, Mr Theobald, is an ex-naval colleague of Jack Aubrey (HMS 8).

Serocold

A Royal Navy officer whose career had been wrecked by an arrest for debt (PC 6).

*The only officer of this name who served in the Royal Navy of the time was Walter Serocold (d.1794), commissioned Lieutenant in 1179 and promoted Commander in 1794. He was killed at the siege of Calvi, Corsica, in the same action in which *Nelson lost the sight of his eye.*

Serracapriola, Miss

Harry Bennet's Sicilian lover who, as a child, had been kissed by Nelson (IM 5).

Sesostris

A king whose reign Goodridge had studied in Tacitus (PC 10).

Sesostris, or Sesoosis, is better known as Rameses II, Pharaoh of Egypt c.1400 BC. His preserved mummy was discovered in 1881.

Seth

Surprise's Sethian seamen believe that Seth's elder brothers, Cain and Abel, were brought into being by angels, whereas Seth, born after Cain's murder of Abel, was God's own direct creation and thus a suitable object of direct reverence. Mr Martin observes that Sethians seem to be remote and vague descendants of Valentinus' Gnostic sects (LM 4,5; TGS 1; NC 7; WDS 1,2; COM 1,5; HD 10; *also seen as the adjective 'Sethian').*

*In the Book of Genesis, Seth is the third and youngest son of *Adam and the ancestor of *Noah.*

Seven Sleepers

A reference by Maturin to great depth of sleep (C/T 2).

In a very popular legend, both Christian and Moslem, of the Middle Ages, seven (or eight) young Roman soldiers, Christians all, had been saved from a religious persecution in about 250 AD by being sealed in a cave near Ephesus. When the cave was opened some two hundred and fifty years later, the Sleepers awoke, explained the religious significance of their survival and then died. In the Western version of the tale, the Sleepers were Constantine, Denis, John, Malchus, Marcian, Maximian and Serapion.

Seward, Miss

A lady whom Raffles recounts had debated with Dr Johnson (NC 3).

*Anna Seward (1747–1809), a poet and letter-writer, was often called the 'Swan of Lichfield' after the English town where she spent most of her life. Amongst other works, she wrote a Life of Dr *Darwin published in 1804. Miss-*

Seward was an important literary hostess, well known for her active dislike of her father's friend and frequent visitor, Dr *Johnson.

Seymour

1: the Second Lieutenant of HMS *Boadicea*, soon promoted Premier on the departure of Mr Akers in the *Hébé* prize (TMC 2+).

2: a Midshipman in HMS *Worcester* (IM 6,8).

3: a Master's Mate in HMS *Diane* and HMS *Nutmeg of Consolation* (TGS 5–9; NC 1–7) given an acting order as Third Lieutenant (NC 6).

Seymour, Sir Michael

A famous British Captain whose exploits inspired O'Brian (M&C author's note) and who is regarded by Stephen Maturin and others as the ideal type of a good sea-officer (HMS 5; DI 5; SM 5; TH 4). He now commands HMS *Amethyst*, having once been shipmates with Jack Aubrey in HMS *Marlborough* (PC 3,5,9) and remaining his good friend (HMS 10). On this account, he obtains a position in the *Lord Nelson* Indiaman for the unemployed Tom Pullings (PC 5).

Sir Michael Seymour (1768–1834), a member of the Irish gentry, entered the Royal Navy as a boy in 1780. Commissioned Lieutenant in 1790, from 1793 to 1794 he then served in HMS *Marlborough, losing an arm in 1794 during the Battle of the Glorious First of June. After a brilliant career, from the following year, as a Commander, Seymour was made Post in 1800 and, in June 1806 (i.e., a little after PC is set), given the 38-gun HMS *Amethyst. In her he fought several distinguished single-ship actions, being knighted in 1809. He was promoted retired Rear Admiral in 1829 and held the post of *Commissioner of Portsmouth Dockyard in that rank until 1832. At that time he was placed back on the active list and made Commander-in-Chief of the South American station, in which post he died of fever in Rio de Janeiro. Both his son and grandson rose to flag rank in the Royal Navy.

Shaddock

A seaman in HMS *Polychrest* (PC 11).

Shakespeare

The great playwright and poet (TH 2,5; FSW 5; HD 6), a copy of whose First Folio is owned by the Aubrey family (SM 5; YA 2). Direct references are made to his plays *Titus Andronicus* (FW 7), *Hamlet* (SM author's note, 7; IM 5,6,8), *Macbeth* (SM 2; COM 3) and *Henry VI* (TH frontispiece). O'Brian himself notes that Shakespeare scarcely ever invented his own basic plots (FSW author's note).

William Shakespeare (1564–1616) is widely regarded as the greatest of all dramatists, yet relatively little is known of his education, personality or career beyond bare facts and dates. Born to a moderately affluent tradesman in Stratford-on-Avon, he married a local woman, Anne Hathaway, in 1582 and had their children baptised in his home town in 1583 and 1585 (his last descendant, Elizabeth Hall, died in 1670). By 1592 he had established himself as a playwright in London (having probably started his writing career in the late 1580s) and in 1594 he became a key member of the leading theatrical troupe, the 'Lord Chamberlain's Men.' From 1599, this company resided at the Globe Theatre, taking the new name of the 'King's Men' on the accession of *James I in 1603. Clearly rather wealthy from at least 1597 (when he started to acquire substantial property), from about 1608 Shakespeare may have been attempting to retire from London back to Stratford (where his family had always remained). Certainly he died there and is buried in Holy Trinity Church (the likeness on his memorial dating from 1623). Relatively little of Shakespeare's work appeared in print during his own lifetime, with the 'First Folio' edition of his collected plays, assembled by his erstwhile theatrical colleagues, appearing in 1622–1623; about 250 copies of this publication have survived. The range of sources used and cultural allusions made by Shakespeare—who, like many great creative artists, was a man of limited formal education—led some mid–19th century authors to suppose that the works had in truth been written by the elegant scholar Francis *Bacon, but these theories are now almost entirely discounted.

Shannahan

A seaman in HMS *Sophie* (M&C 2+).

Shannon, HMS

A frigate, Captain Philp Broke, that is blockading Boston (FW 5+). Built at Brindley's ship-yard, she is the replacement for the ship wrecked under an earlier Captain, Leveson Gower (FW 7). Under Broke, and with Aubrey, Maturin and Villiers aboard, she engages and takes USS *Chesapeake* (FW 9). Later, under the acting command of Lieutenant Provo Wallis, she arrives victorious in Halifax (SM author's note, 1–4; *also* IM 10; FSW 3; TGS 9)

Philip *Broke commissioned the new HMS Shannon, 38-gun, in 1806 and over the next several years turned her into one of the most effective ships in the Royal Navy, yet one that never saw much action. On the outbreak of the War of 1812 (a conflict that lasted until early 1815), she was sent to the North American station, with Broke as the senior naval officer of a blockading squadron. After a series of calamitous reverses for the British, on June 1st 1813 Shannon engaged and took *Lawrence's USS *Chesapeake in a brief and bloody encounter. Shannon—named for a river in southern Ireland—continued in service for many years after her famous victory, but once again saw very little action. Reduced to a receiving ship in 1832, she was renamed HMS St Lawrence in 1844 and finally broken up in 1859. The earlier Shannon briefly mentioned was launched in September 1803 (having been named HMS *Pallas on the stocks) and in December of that year, having run ashore on the French coast during a gale, was burned by her Captain Leveson *Gower to avoid her being captured.

Shao Yen

A banker and merchant in Java used by Maturin (TGS 6; NC 1–4).

Shape

General Aubrey's disreputable stock-broker, now

used by Jack Aubrey in his controversial share dealings (RM 4).

Shark, HMS

The ship into which Philp Broke was first promoted Commander (FW 7; FSW 2).

HMS Shark, *16-gun sloop, was launched in 1779, reduced to a receiving ship at Jamaica in 1805 and foundered, whilst serving as a hospital ship, in 1818. From 1799 to 1801 she was commanded by Philip *Broke, his second (sic) and last ship as Commander.*

Shaw

A naturalist referred to by Maturin (NC 10).

George Shaw (1751–1813) was a vicar, physician and naturalist who published extensively in the field of zoology. Elected Fellow of the Royal Society in 1789, in 1807 he became Keeper of the Natural History Collections at the British Museum.

Sheba, the Queen of

The ruler referred to by Maturin for both her beauty and blackness (RM 2).

In the Old Testament First Book of Kings, *the fabulously wealthy Queen of Sheba (which lies in present-day Yemen) visited Jerusalem in order to test King *Solomon's wisdom with a series of riddles. In the Islamic version of the traditions, the Queen is named as Bilqis, whilst in Ethiopian traditions she is named Makeda and said to have born Solomon a son Menilek, the founder of the Ethiopian royal house.*

Sheehan

A seaman in HMS *Sophie* (M&C 7).

Sheffield, Lord

A friend of the writer Gibbon (RM 7).

*John Baker Holroyd (1735–1821), 1st Earl of Sheffield, was a statesman and expert on agriculture and commerce who became Lord Sheffield in 1781 and Earl in 1816. From 1764 onwards he was closely associated with Edward *Gibbon as best friend and patron and, after the writer's death, both edited Gibbon's manuscripts and wrote on his work and life.*

Shelton, Edward

A English seaman in an American whaler captured by Jack Aubrey who, having once served in Heneage Dundas' HMS *Euralyus*, now volunteers for *Surprise* (WDS 5).

Shelvocke

The author of a nautical volume owned by Captain Yorke of HMS *La Flèche* (FW 2).

George Shelvocke (1675–1742) served as a Royal Navy Lieutenant and Purser before being dismissed the service (for reasons unknown) in 1713. In 1719 he obtained command of a small privateering expedition but, having fallen out with his employers, slipped away in his Speedwell *to pillage the South Seas, acting more as free pirate than regulated privateer. During the voyage, Shelvocke's second-in-command, Simon Hartley, shot an albatross that was following the ship, an incident said to have later provided the inspiration for the* Rime of the Ancient Mariner *by Samuel Taylor Coleridge (1772–1834). After many adventures (including a claim to have discovered gold mines in California), Shelvocke returned to England in 1722 and was immediately imprisoned on charges of piracy and fraud. The first charge was dismissed for lack of evidence and, before the second could be pressed, Shelvocke then escaped to France. In his exile he wrote* A Voyage Around the World *(1726), a popular if somewhat fantastic account of his travels and, towards the end of his life, managed to return to England, dying at his son's house in London.*

Shepherd, Mr

Admiral Bertie's secretary, who recommends his cousin, Mr Peter, as Commodore Jack Aubrey's new secretary (TMC 3,10).

Sherman

A physician and naturalist, the author of the *Mental Health of Seamen*, who is the surgeon of Admiral Stranraer's flag-ship, HMS *Queen Charlotte* (YA 4,8–10).

The name recalls that of William Sherman/Shearman (1767–1861), a London physician who wrote extensively on epilepsy, brain complaints and nervous afflictions.

Shields

The Master of the whaler *Amelia* (FSW 3).

Shipton, Mother

The prostitutes outside the Keith's Mayfair house liken Jack Aubrey to Mother Shipton (PC 6), a well-known prophetess (TGS 1).

Mother Shipton was a reputed seer from Yorkshire (Shipton being near the city of York itself) who lived, if she lived at all, during the early 16th century, with published biographies and versions of her prophecies being widely influential for several centuries thereafter. She is usually portrayed as being remarkably hideous in appearance.

Sibbald or Sibyl

Two references by Lord Melville, presumably to a member of his family (PC 6).

Sibylle or Sybille, HMS

1: a ship referred to by Jack Aubrey as one of several very desirable frigates into which he would like to be made Post (M&C 11). Charles Yorke had been her First Lieutenant when she took *La Forte* (FW 2).

HMS Sibylle *(variously spelled), 44-gun, was an ex-French frigate of the same name, launched in 1791 and captured by the Royal Navy in 1794. In early 1799 she engaged the significantly heavier La *Forte in the Bay of Bengal, taking her after a fierce fight in which her Captain Cook was mortally wounded (dying in Calcutta a few months later) and the French Captain, Beaulieu, was killed. After many years of further distinguished service, Sibylle was sent to harbour duty in 1831 and sold in 1833. She was named for the classical Sibyl, initially a prophesier inspired by *Apollo and later a generic term for any seer (e.g., TGS 1).*

2: a former command of Captain Richardson (now Admiral Lord Barmouth), in which Jack Aubrey had been a Master's Mate (HD 9).

HMS Sibyl (variously spelled), 28-gun, was launched in 1779 and re-named HMS Garland in 1794 (after the capture of # 1 above). She was wrecked off Madagascar in 1798.

Sibyls
see **Sibylle** or **Sybille, HMS**

Sidi Hafiz
An acquaintance of Dr Jacob in Algiers (HD 8).

Sidmouth, Lord
A government minister (RM 7), originally known as Mr Addington (HMS 1), for whom Mr Yarrow had once been a speech-writer (FSW 1).

*Henry Addington (1757–1844) was a Tory statesman who served as Speaker of the House of Commons from 1789 to 1800 and followed his close friend William *Pitt as Prime Minister from 1801 to 1804, eventually resigning (in Pitt's favour) when it became apparent that he could not manage the pressures of war. Created 1st Viscount Sidmouth in 1805, he served as an unpopular and reactionary Minister for Home Affairs from 1812 to 1822.*

Sievewright, Admiral
The officer who is to be the nominal Head of Naval Intelligence in succession to Sir Joseph Blaine (HMS 4). As a consequence of a coarse remark he makes about Diana Villiers, the Admiral has a furious row with Stephen Maturin (DI 2). An unsubtle man, we later learn that he has been replaced (SM 4).

Simaika, Dr
A French-speaking, Coptic Christian physician, now living in Suez, who had been a childhood friend of Stephen Maturin (TH 7).

Simeon Stylites, Saint
A saint whose feast day is celebrated on the island of Malta (TH 1).

Saint Simeon Stylites (390?–459) was a Syrian monk who became the first of the ascetics to spend much of his life, from about 420 onwards, perched atop a pillar (stylos in Greek), at first only six feet, but eventually no less than 50 feet from the ground

Simmons
1: a family who attend Jack Aubrey and Stephen Maturin's ball (PC 2).
2: the First Lieutenant of HMS *Lively* (PC 12+; HMS 2,3) who takes command of the Spanish *Clara* after her surrender (PC 14).
3: Jack Aubrey's predecessor as Captain of HMS *Surprise*, who had died of an illness (HMS 5).
4: a Midshipman in HMS *Hamadryad* (HD 9).

Simmons, Arthur or Art
An elderly seaman in HMS *Polychrest* (PC 8).

Simmons, Joshua
A seaman in HMS *Surprise*, a.k.a. 'Old Groan.' He had served at Nelson's three great victories of the Nile, Copenhagen and Trafalgar (HD 3).

Simmons, Tom
A popular seaman in HMS *Sophie* who drinks himself to death on his birthday. He had once served with Mr Day in HMS *Phoebe* (M&C 1,10).

Simms
A seaman in HMS *Surprise* (IM 11; TGS 2).

Simon
A seaman in HMS *Surprise* who, having once been married in Nantucket, is familiar with Yankee ports (WDS 5).

Simon, Richard
The dedicatee, with Vivien Green, of *The Wine Dark Sea*.

Richard Simon and Vivien Green are Patrick O'Brian's long-time literary agents in London.

Simon, Saint
see **Peter** or **Simon, Saint**

Simpkin
Jack Aubrey's servant in HMS *Sophie* (M&C 3).

Simpson
1: the surgeon to HMS *Leopard*'s convict passengers, soon murdered by them (DI 3).
2: Jack Aubrey's temporary clerk in HMS *Worcester* (IM 2).
3: a naval parson who travels to Gibraltar in Jack Aubrey's HMS *Worcester* in order to join his own new ship, HMS *Goliath* (IM 3).
4: HMS *Surprise*'s barber (HD 8).

Simpson, George
A gentleman engaged to be married to the Williams' neighbour, Sophie Bentinck (PC 3).

Sims
A seaman in HMS *Surprise* (FSW 9).

Singleton, Jack
A man hanged near Shelmerston, along with seven accomplices (COM 1).

Sirius, HMS
1: a ship that had been wrecked on Norfolk Island under her Captain Hunt (C/T 1).

*Hunt's HMS Sirius, 22-gun, was bought as the store-ship Berwick in 1781 and renamed Sirius (for the Dog Star) in 1786. She was wrecked in early 1790, with many of her crew eventually transferring to the hired Dutch merchant snow *Waakzaamheid for the journey back to England.

2: a ship referred to by Jack Aubrey as one of several

very desirable frigates into which he would like to be made Post (M&C 11). Some years later she serves in Jack's squadron off Mauritius (TMC 1–7), becoming stranded under heavy French fire at the Battle of Port South East and being then abandoned and burned by her crew (TMC 7).

*HMS Sirius, 38-gun, was launched in 1797. Early in her career, in 1798, she captured the Dutch corvette *Waakza-amheid and in 1805 was present, under William Prowse (d.1826 in the rank of a Rear Admiral), at both Sir Robert *Calder's indecisive action and in *Nelson's great victory at Trafalgar a few months later. After further distinguished service she was lost, under *Pym, on August 25th 1810, just as described in TMC.*

Sirr, Major
A man referred to most disparagingly by Stephen Maturin in the context of the United Irishmen uprising (M&C 5), still active in Dublin many years later (COM 4).

*Henry Charles Sirr (1764–1841), an Irishman, served for some years in the British army before becoming in 1796 Chief of the Dublin Police, a post held by his father before him. In the 1798 United Irishmen uprising he became known as the city's '*Fouché,' after *Buonaparte's notoriously effective head of domestic security in Paris. In May of that same year he led the party that captured Lord Edward *Fitzgerald (betrayed to Sirr by Magan; see *Mangin), inflicting a fatal wound on him in the struggle. Loathed by his enemies and much admired by his friends, Sirr retired from the police in 1826. Curiously, he and Fitzgerald are buried no great distance apart at St Werburgh's Church in Dublin City.*

Sivaji
A religious reference by Diana Villiers (HMS 7).

Siva or Shiva (derived from Sanskrit for 'happiness/prosperity') is the 'great god,' or 'Mahadeva,' of the Hindu faith, presiding over the endless cycle of creation and destruction of both people and crops. At shrines, he is often represented by a linga or phallus.

Skate, HMS
A brig-sloop, Commander Hall, that arrives at Plymouth where many of her crew are immediately transferred to Jack Aubrey's HMS Worcester (IM 2,5). Later the Skates compare Jack unfavourably to their former leader, whom they now recall as Captain Allen (IM 7).

Skeeping, Mrs Poll
A female sailor drafted from HMS Leviathan to HMS Surprise as a nurse or 'loblolly-girl.' Poll had once before sailed with Jack Aubrey and had later worked at the Haslar Royal Naval Hospital (HD 2+).
See also **Defiance, HMS**

Skelton
A bosun's mate in HMS Leopard (DI 4).

Skinner, Wilbraham
A lawyer recommended by Sir Joseph Blaine to Jack Aubrey as the best man to handle the disputes with the fraudster Kimber (SM 4–6).

Slade, Nehemiah
A Sethian seaman in Surprise (LM 5; NC 7+; CT 1+) who seems to be sent to Batavia as prize crew in the recaptured whaler Truelove (C/T 9). He may be the same man who later serves in HMS Bellona and Ringle, her tender (COM 5).

Slaughter
The keeper of a dining-house in England to which Jack Aubrey had taken the unemployed Tom Pullings for an unsuccessful meeting with Captain Rowlands (IM 10).

Slocum
An American prisoner in HMS Shannon who takes Philip Broke's letter of challenge USS Constitution's Captain Lawrence. Lawrence, however, has already set sail before the note can be delivered (FW 9).

*Eben Slocum was the Master of a fishing boat stopped by HMS *Shannon the day before her great battle. So colourfully and at such length had he abused *Broke for tyranny, that he had been seized, clapped in irons overnight and his boat burned.*

Sloper, Aunt
Barrett Bonden's aunt, the mother of George Lucock (M&C 8).

Smailes, Aunt
A Sethian, and hence known to Surprise's Sethians, transported to New South Wales (NC 9).

Small, Captain
An officer refused an interview by Lord St Vincent (PC 3).

Smallpiece
A seaman in HMS Irresistible (RM 1).

Smectymnus
The first author to mention a particular deformation of the hand (HD 7).

Smectymnuus (sic) is the acronym under which five Presbyterian churchmen published a pamphlet in 1641 attacking the Episcopalian position, starting an often vicious literary controversy between leading thinkers of the time. The five co-authors were Stephen Marshall, Edmund Calamy, Thomas Young, Matthew Newcomen and William Spurstow.

Smith
1: Miss Smith, a young lady who accompanies the Captain of HMS Burford on his voyages (M&C 2).
2: a bosun's servant in HMS Lively (PC 12).

3: a former officer of HMS *Lively*, now Second Lieutenant of HMS *Goliath* (HMS 7

4: a Midshipman in HMS *Shannon* (FW 9).
William Smith (d.1862) fought well in HMS *Shannon's taking of USS *Chesapeake, leading the charge that cleared the American sharp-shooters from their fighting tops. As reward he was promoted Lieutenant shortly after the battle, eventually rising to Commander in 1826 and Post Captain in 1846.

5: a deceased Admiralty official replaced by Mr Lewis (RM 5).

6: a pseudonym used by Ledward in his dealings with Duhamel (RM 10).

7: *Surprise*'s gunner (LM 3; C/T 1+; WDS 2,6,10).

8: the very accomplished ship's cook of *Merlin* (LM 3).

9: a groom at the Maturins' Barham House (COM 2).

10: the Commander of HMS *Camilla* (COM 4,7).

11: an English army Captain whom Maturin had known in Spain (YA 2).

12: the Master of one of the East Indiamen rescued by Jack Aubrey from an attack by corsairs (HD 3).

13: Smith major, a former school-mate of William Reade (HD 8).

Smith, Amanda
An unmarried lady of nearly 30, living in Halifax, Nova Scotia, under the protection of her temporarily-absent soldier brother, Major Henry Smith (SM 1,2). She has acquired an indifferent reputation in both America and India, where she had earlier been known to Diana Villiers (SM 1,2). Undaunted, Jack Aubrey strikes up a sexual relationship with her and she, in turn, indicates her intention to emulate the relationship of Lady Hamilton, her heroine, with Lord Nelson, and likewise prise Jack away from his wife (SM 2). Once Jack has departed home to England, she writes many effusive love letters to him, including one stating she is carrying his child and asking for financial aid (SM 5,6). To Jack's great relief, he soon learns that Amanda has since married Alexander Lushington, a Royal Marine Captain known to him (SM 11). Many years later, Jack's mother-in-law, Mrs Williams, finds the old, compromising letters and immediately shows them to her daughter Sophie, occasioning a bitter dispute and temporary separation between the couple (YA 6,8).

Smith, Edward and **Mrs**
Jack Aubrey's former shipmate, now Captain of the 74-gun HMS *Tremendous*, and his wife (TGS 1). Edward, a guest at a dinner given by Jack (TGS 1), has brothers Captain Henry Smith of HMS *Revenge* and Tom Smith the banker (TGS 1).

Smith, Father
The maker of an organ pumped by Aubrey (PC 12).

Bernhard Schmidt (1630?–1708) the German-born builder of English organs following Charles II's restoration in 1666, was called 'Father' as he worked on his projects with his two young nephews. The organ blown by Jack Aubrey may be the still-extant 1684 instrument of the Temple Church in Fleet Street, London.

Smith, Henry
1: an army Major, the brother of Amanda Smith (SM 2).
2: the Captain of HMS *Revenge*, the brother of Captain Edward Smith of HMS *Tremendous* and of Tom Smith the banker. Henry had married the daughter of Admiral Piggott (TGS 1).

Smith, J.
The father of Amanda and Major Henry Smith (SM 11).

Smith, John
A seaman in HMS *Sophie* (M&C 3).

Smith, John and Peter
Two related seamen in HMS *Surprise* (NC 7).

Smith, Lucy
The intended wife of Mr Hinksey (COM 6).

Smith, Robert
Smith and his fellow transported convict, Edward Marno, die of sea-sickness in HMS *Leopard*, the only two such deaths Stephen Maturin has ever encountered (DI 3).

Smith, Sir or **Lord**
see **Smith, Admiral Sir Sidney** or **Sydney**

Smith, Admiral Sir Sidney or **Sydney**
A senior officer (M&C 8) who had once beaten the French at Acre (TMC 2,3,5,7; IM 10; TH 5,9; HD 7,8) and who also previously escaped from imprisonment in Paris (SM 11). Lord Nelson greatly disliked his use of a Swedish title (COM 7).
Sir William Sidney Smith (1764–1840) entered the Royal Navy in 1777 and in 1783 rose to Post Captain when still only 19 years of age. From 1789 to 1792, whilst England was at peace, Smith was in the service of the King of Sweden, receiving a local knighthood that King *George III then allowed him to use in England. A most quarrelsome man, Smith's many Royal Navy enemies thereafter referred to him with some derision as the 'Swedish knight.' In the British forces once more, he was then captured whilst conducting inshore operations in the mouth of the Seine and held captive from 1796 to 1798 in the Temple Prison, Paris, until he managed a dramatic escape (see also *Wright). As Commodore, he now went on to serve as *Nelson's second-in-command—a most uneasy relationship—in the eastern Mediterranean from 1799 to 1801 and in that first year enjoyed a great success at Acre against French forces commanded by *Buonaparte himself. At the opening of this period, he was appointed Joint Plenipotentiary to the Ottoman Court with his brother, John

Spencer *Smith. Captain Smith was promoted Rear Admiral in 1805 and commanded the South American station from 1808 to 1809, often at furious odds with the Admiralty. He rose to Vice Admiral in 1810 but bad health ended his sea-career in 1814. Yet, in 1815, he was present as an observer at the Battle of Waterloo, going on later that year to take up permanent residence in Paris where, in 1821, he rose by seniority to full Admiral. Sidney Smith was undoubtedly a brave and active officer, if always widely disliked and distrusted by the majority of his senior colleagues for his arrogant self-obsession and incessant self-promotion. (N.B., the occasional typo in the text of the Admiral's first name recalls his near contemporary, the renowned wit and conversationalist, the Reverend Sydney Smith (1771–1845).

Smith, Sir Spencer

A former British Minister at Constantinople, the brother of Admiral Sir Sidney Smith (HD 7).

John (sometimes seen as Charles) Spencer Smith (fl.1792–1839) was a younger brother of Sir Sidney *Smith and served as Ambassador to Constantinople from about 1792 to 1801, holding the post jointly with his brother in 1798 and 1799. Biographies of Sir Sidney note only that Spencer was a career diplomat who was still living, retired, in 1839.

Smith, Tom

The banker brother of the Royal Navy Captains Edward and Henry Smith. His establishment, Smith and Clowes, is recommended to Stephen Maturin by Jack Aubrey (TGS 1,4; NC 3,4) but later, in Java, the pair learn that the house has gone broke (TGS 6). Fortunately it later transpires that the transfer of Stephen's money to their care had never been effected, owing to a lucky act of carelessness on his part (NC 9; COM 2).

Although the Smiths are fictional, this incident recalls the similar predicament of the brothers of the novelist Jane Austen. Henry Austen (1771–1850) was partner in a bank—Austen, Maunde, Austen & Co—that crashed with heavy losses in 1815–1816, resulting in Henry's personal bankruptcy. TOMALIN identifies the second Austen in the firm's name with one of Jane's other brothers, Captain Francis Austen RN, who also lost heavily (see *Canopus, HMS for a note on the naval Austens' careers). One wonders if many of his naval friends had also been recommended to the bank.

Smith, William

1: the First Mate in the *Dromedary* transport (TH 4).

2: the senior assistant surgeon in HMS *Bellona*, formerly of HMS *Serapis* (COM 3–9; YA 5,8,9).

Smith and Clowes

see **Smith, Tom**

Smithers

An unreliable, Irish Marine in HMS *Polychrest*, unrelated to Lieutenant George Smithers (PC 11).

Smithers, George

The Marine Lieutenant who replaces the wounded Macdonald in HMS *Polychrest* (PC 10,11).

Smithson

The Master of the troop transport *Mirza* (SM 9).

Smollett

An author referred to by Maturin (RM 3).

Tobias George Smollett (1721–1771), the Scottish writer, historian, satirist and literary figure, served in the Royal Navy as the surgeon's mate of HMS Chichester *from about 1739 to 1744, afterwards setting up ashore as a surgeon and, on gaining his M.D. in 1750, physician. However, his main source of income always continued to be his writing. Numbers of his books, especially* The Adventures of Roderick Random *of 1748, contain biting satires on the Navy and, although accuracy in Smollett was usually the servant of effect, much of what we know of day-to-day conditions afloat in the first half of the 18th century comes from his works. Smollett's grand-nephew, John Rouett Smollett (d.1842), served in the Royal Navy, being made Post in 1802 and promoted retired Rear Admiral in 1837.*

Smyth

1: an Admiral met by Stephen Maturin outside his London club and asked by the Doctor to explain a naval term (RM 10).

William Henry Smyth (1788–1865) was a renowned naval surveyor and cartographer, work for which he was also elected Fellow of the Royal Society in 1826. Smyth was also the author of the invaluable Sailor's Word Book, *first published in 1867, shortly after his death. However, his appearance in* Reverse of the Medal *is somewhat anachronistic: he was commissioned Lieutenant in 1813 (i.e., at around the time of his meeting *Maturin), promoted Commander in 1815, made Post (on the retired list) in 1846 and not made Rear Admiral by seniority until 1853. Smyth rose to Vice Admiral in 1858 and Admiral in 1863.*

2: a sick seaman in HMS *Surprise* (WDS 5).

Smyth, Ahmed

Mr Stanhope's Oriental Secretary, who joins HMS *Surprise* in Bombay (HMS 8; FSW 7).

Snape

An Admiral, first met at Craddock's card house (DI 1), who later dines at Ashgrove Cottage with Jack Aubrey and Captain Hallowell. By implication, he had been at the Battle of Cape St Vincent (DI 2).

Snape, A.

The Master of *Intrepid Fox* (TMC 2).

Snodgrass

A famous naval architect TMC 1), with whose diagonal braces HMS *Leopard* has been newly equipped (DI 5).

Gabriel Snodgrass (fl.1790–1795), the Chief Surveyor to the East Indian Company and a strong advocate of improvements in the technical quality of Royal Navy ships, was the inventor of iron 'knees,' massive right-angle brack-

ets used to support the main beams. However, innovations in diagonal bracing are more usually associated with the name of Sir Robert *Seppings.

Snooks

A reference by Jack Aubrey to the typical, wretched man who first seeks the hand in marriage of one's beloved daughters (TMC 10).

Soames

1: one of the gaolers of HMS *Leopard*'s convict passengers who later assists Maturin in the sickbay (DI 4)

2: a civil servant at Blaine's dinner in honour of Jack Aubrey who subsequently mis-handles the proposal to have Jack reinstated to the Royal Navy (LM 7,8).

3: a Lieutenant in HMS *Bellona* (COM 7,10).

Soames, Eddie

A eunuch seaman in HMS *Surprise* (HD 5).

Socinians

A religious sect mentioned by Mr Martin (WDS 3).
Socinian doctrines, which reject predestination and original sin, were developed by the Italian theologians Laelius Socini (1525–1562) and his nephew Fausto (1539–1604). Both men were persecuted for heresy by Catholics and Protestants alike.

Socrates

The clerk to the banker Houmouzios (COM 8,9).

Sod, the Honourable

The derisive nickname in HMS *Worcester* for the disgraced Mr Somers (IM 5).

Sodbury, Reuben

A Nantucket whaler for whom a remote Pacific island is named (FSW 9,10).

Solander

A naturalist mentioned by Maturin (M&C 2).
Daniel Carl Solander (1733–1782), the Swedish physician, naturalist and early pupil of *Linnaeus, spent much of his life in England as the protégé and librarian of Sir Joseph *Banks, under whose patronage he was elected Fellow of the Royal Society in 1764. Having sailed with Banks and *Cook on their first voyage of discovery (1768–1771), he later became a keeper of the natural history collections at the British Museum.

Solebay, HMS

A transport ship in Jack Aubrey's squadron (TMC 6).
HMS Solebay, 32-gun, was launched in 1783 as HMS Iris. Withdrawn from active service in 1803, in 1809 she was re-named HMS Solebay (on the loss of her predecessor off Senegal) and then used as a general purposes transport and troop ship before being broken up in 1833. Her second name commemorates the Battle of Southwold (sic) Bay of 1672.

Solmes

An Admiralty official who questions Jack Aubrey over the sinking of the *Waakzaamheid*, revealing that Lieutenant Grant has now alleged that she was an unarmed transport rather than a man-of-war (SM 6).

Solomon, King

The biblical King referred to for his powers of judgement (TMC 5; DI 5), for his ownership, according to Jack Aubrey, of many porcupines (TGS 1) and for his polygamy (COM 5)
King Solomon (1033?–975? BC), the son of *David and Bathsheba, succeeded his father as King of Israel in about 1015 BC and soon established a reputation of the greatest of all its rulers. In the Old Testament Book of Kings, Solomon is said to have had a combined total of one thousand wives and concubines (perhaps he kept porcupines too), principally to cement alliances far and wide. His great wisdom was most famously demonstrated when he resolved the conflicting claims to a new-born baby of two women by observing which of them became most distressed at the prospect of the infant being cut in two.

Solon

The ancient Greek lawmaker, referred to by Jack Aubrey as one of his few pieces of classical learning (WDS 9).
Solon (638?–558? BC), one of the 'Seven Sages' of ancient Greece, was a famous Athenian politician who had spent his early years as a traveller and poet before becoming known in his home city as an expert conciliator and proponent of constitutional reforms. Indeed, he was later even offered the Kingship of Athens, an over-exalted position that he declined to accept.

Somers

1: the Honourable Mr Somers, a rich, well-connected officer appointed to Jack Aubrey's HMS *Worcester* as Third Lieutenant. A heavy drinker, he has a deserved reputation for very poor seamanship (IM 2–5). Soon reprimanded for his poor skills by Jack (IM 3), Somers goes on to have the ship miss stays in view of the whole fleet (IM 5). Again reprimanded, this time angrily and in public, he speaks back and makes as if to strike his Captain before being restrained. Jack relieves him of his duty and then allows him to exchange for Mr Rowan of HMS *Colossus*, but not before the Lieutenant has been derisively tagged by Worcester's crew as the 'Honourable Sod' (IM 5).

2: the Second Lieutenant of HMS *Bellona* (COM 5; YA 6,9) who later joins Jack Aubrey's *Surprise* as a volunteer (YA 10), remaining in her when she once again becomes a King's ship in Jack's Mediterranean squadron (HD 2,4,5,6).

Somers, John, William and Mr

William Somers is a seaman in *Surprise* whose shipmate brother John had been drowned at sea, an occurrence that he has later to report to their grand-father (COM 1).

Somerville

1: a Lieutenant in HMS *Oedipus* (SM 11).
2: a curate, the schoolmaster of the young John Daniel (HD 6).

Somerville, John

The Barcelona merchant and Catalan nationalist who had first introduced Stephen Maturin to intelligence work (TGS 4).

Sommers

A Midshipman in HMS *Leopard* (DI 3).

Sophia or Sophie

see **Aubrey, Sophia or Sophie**

Sophia, Princess

A Princess whose birthday is marked by HMS *Diane* at Pulo Prabang (TGS 7).

> *Princess Sophia (1777–1848) was the fifth daughter and twelfth child of King *George III and Queen Charlotte.*

Sophia, HMS

The name by which Maturin initially refers to HMS *Sophie* (M&C 2).

Sophie, HMS

HMS *Sophie*, a 14-gun, 2-masted brig-sloop, is Jack Aubrey's first ship as Commander (M&C 1+). Previously the Spanish *Vencejo* (M&C 2), she had been captured by the Royal Navy in 1795 (PC 1). Under Jack's command she takes the much larger Spanish xebec privateer *Cacafuego* (M&C 10), a famous victory for which she is given a very rare, full cheer by HMS *Amelia* (M&C 11), but is later forced to surrender to a French 74-gun, *Desaix* (M&C 11; *also* PC 1+; HMS 1+; TMC 2+; DI 3; IM 5,6,7; TH 4; FSW 5,6; LM 7; TGS 4,8; NC 1; WDS 4; COM 3,4,8,10; YA 9; HD 10).

> *The 'real' HMS* Sophie, *18-gun sloop, was the ex-French privateer* Consul, *captured by HMS *Endymion in 1798 and broken up in 1809. However, O'Brian models Jack *Aubrey's HMS* Sophie *on Thomas *Cochrane's HMS *Speedy.*

Sophonisba

A character in a novel by 'Blue Breeches' (LM 1).

> Sophonisba *(d.203 BC), the daughter of a defeated Carthaginian general, Hasrubal, killed herself rather than be taken captive to Rome. In the 17th and 18th centuries she became the heroine of a number of popular plays and novels.*

Sorley

A seaman in HMS *Diane*, an expert rock-climber (TGS 10).

Soules, Captain

A Captain of HMS *Minerva* under whom the young Jack Aubrey had served (WDS 1).

South

A well-known author of sermons (DI 5; IM 5; FSW 7; COM 8).

> *Robert South (1633–1716) was one of the most famous preachers of his time, renowned for both engaging humour and biting wit in his pulpit; for a time he served as a private chaplain to King *Charles II. Six volumes of his very popular sermons were published from 1679 to 1715, with other, posthumous collections following in 1717 and 1744.*

Southam

An army friend of Edward, Clarissa Oakes' childhood 'guardian' and molester. Southam had not only sexually abused the young girl but, after Edward's death, then consigned her to Mother Abbott's whore-house (C/T 6).

Southampton

A man in India who had offered Diana Villiers 'protection' (PC 2).

> *The name is possibly inspired by either Charles Fitzroy (1737–1797), 1st Baron Southampton or his son George Ferdinand Fitzroy (1761–1810), the 2nd Baron. Both were career soldiers although neither had a connection with India.*

Southampton, HMS

A ship of which Philip Broke had been Third Lieutenant at the Battle of Cape St Vincent (FW 7).

> HMS Southampton, *32-gun, was launched in 1757, supposedly the first true 'frigate' to be built in England. She fought in *Howe's great victory in 1794 at the Battle of the Glorious First of June and, now under Captain James Macnamara (d.1826 in the rank of Rear Admiral), at Jervis and *Nelson's triumph at *St Vincent in 1797. In 1812, under James Lucas Yeo (d.1818 as Sir James), she was wrecked on an uncharted rock off the Bahamas.*

Southcott, Joanna

A religious figure referred to by Martin (LM 5).

> *Joanna Southcott (1750–1814) was a religious fanatic who attracted a very large following, after about 1801, by her prophesies and supernatural claims. She died soon after having falsely claimed that she was about to give birth to a new 'Prince of Peace.'*

Sowerby, Jacob

A naturalist encountered by Maturin in Batavia, who goes on to name a fetid plant after the Doctor (NC 3,4).

> *Although Jacob Sowerby is portrayed as a wretch, the Sowerby family of the time were famous and highly-regarded English naturalists and artists, the most noted of whom was James Sowerby (1757–1822). However, the family had no particular connection with Batavia and no Jacob is recorded in its ranks.*

Spalding

Admiral Harte's secretary (PC 8).

Sparman

An author read by Maturin (TMC 3).

*Andreas Sparrman (sic; 1747–1820), a Swedish botanist who had studied under *Linnaeus, travelled as a collector to southern and central Africa and then accompanied Captain *Cook on his 1772 voyage to the South Seas. On his return to Stockholm, Sparrman published a meticulously accurate accounts of his earlier travels and then went on to hold a number of important scientific posts in his native land.*

Spartan

An American-French privateer that Jack Aubrey, in HMS *Surprise*, and Tom Pullings, in the prize *Danaë*, attempt to engage (RM 2,3). Having escaped, some time later she herself engages the Spanish *Azul* and is then taken by *Surprise*, now a private letter-of-marque (LM 1–4; TGS 2; NC 5).

Speedy, HMS

Lord Cochrane's 14-gun ship in which he had taken *Gamo* (FSW author's note).

HMS Speedy, *14-gun brig-sloop, was launched in 1782. Taken by the French in mid–1794, she was then re-taken by the Royal Navy in early 1795. In 1799 she was given to the newly promoted Commander Jahleel *Brenton and then, on his elevation to Post rank early in the following year, to Thomas *Cochrane. After taking the xebec-frigate El *Gamo on May 6th 1801, she was in turn taken just a few weeks later by the 74-gun Desaix, on June 24th. In 1802, re-named St Pierre, she was given by *Buonaparte to Pope *Pius VII as a gift; her fate thereafter is unknown.*

Speldin, Fintrum

A seaman in HMS *Worcester* (IM 7).

Spencer

1: a previous First Lord of the Admiralty (HMS 1).

*George John, 2nd Earl Spencer (1758–1834; Earl from 1783), came from a famous Whig family of socialites, politicians and military officers. His period as *First Lord (December 1794–February 1801) was thought to be a very successful one during which he gave full support to both Lord *St Vincent and his brilliant protégé *Nelson, as well as dealing effectively with the great mutinies of 1797 at Spithead and the Nore. After a period out of office, the Earl then served as Home Secretary from 1806 to 1807. Spencer's sister, Georgina, Duchess of *Devonshire, was the leading society hostess of her day; his direct descendent, Charles, the present 9th Earl (b.1964; Earl 1992), is the brother of the late Diana, Princess of Wales (1961–1997).*

2: Sir Spencer, *see* **Smith, Sir Spencer**

Spencer, HMS

A 74-gun ship of Saumarez' squadron (M&C 12).

HMS Spencer, *74-gun, was launched in 1800 and in 1805 was unlucky enough to be one of the ships—led by *Louis' HMS *Canopus—sent by *Nelson to re-supply at Gibraltar, thus narrowly missing the great victory of Trafalgar. Spencer, named for Earl *Spencer, the First Lord of the Admiralty at the time of her launch, was broken up in 1822.*

Spenser

The poet referred to by Maturin and Martin (RM 3).

Edmund Spenser (1552?–1599), an English administrator and poet, was the author of the Faerie Queen *(1591–1596), amongst many other works. In 1598 he had been High Sheriff of Cork in Ireland but was forced off his land in the Earl of Tyrone's rebellion, losing all his property, his health and perhaps one of his children too. Reduced to poverty, Spenser soon died in London.*

Spitfire

A cannon in *Surprise* (C/T 8).

Spitfire, HMS

A ship dispatched to Zambra by Admiral Ives (FSW 1).

Sponge, Old and Young

Names used by Jack Aubrey for the seamen Apollo and Turbid (M&C 6).

Spooner

A Midshipman in HMS *Surprise* (HD 4).

'Spotted Dick'
see **Richardson, Dick**

Spottiswood, Captain

The Captain of the Indiaman *Lord Nelson*, captured by the French privateer *Bellone* (PC 5).

*Robert Spottiswood (dates unknown) was Master of the *Lord Nelson *when she was taken by* Bellone *on August 14th 1803.*

Spry, HMS

A ship in Admiral Thornton's Mediterranean fleet (IM 5).

Square, John

A name used by Mr Whewell for a Krooman tribesman in Sierra Leone. He acts as a guide for Stephen Maturin (COM 8) and temporarily joins HMS *Bellona* as a seaman and inshore pilot (COM 8,9).

St

see under **Saint**

Stallard, Charles

An able seaman in HMS *Sophie* (M&C 3).

Standish

1: Mrs Standish, a member of Louisa Wogan's circle in London (DI 6).

2: the new Purser of *Surprise*, recommended by his friend Mr Martin to Jack Aubrey, who welcomes both his background as the son of a dead Royal Navy Lieutenant and his ability as a violinist (LM 8+). Yet eventually even his considerable talents on the fiddle do not overcome

Jack and Stephen Maturin's growing dislike of his sense of superiority and his clear incompetence at his job (TGS 1–4). However, he suffers so badly from sea-sickness that he resigns when the ship reaches Lisbon (TGS 3) and soon accepts a position in Spain as secretary to the British army officer, Lumley (TGS 4). Some time later Jack later refers to him as a convert to Catholicism (C/T 1).

Stanhope

1 a Master of Foxhounds in Hampshire (DI 4).
2: the newly appointed British envoy to Kampong — often referred to simply as 'His Excellency' — whom Jack Aubrey is charged with conveying to his post in his HMS *Surprise* (HMS 4+). In already fragile health, he is further reduced by acute sea-sickness (HMS 5+) and, despite some temporary improvement in his condition, is taken suddenly and gravely ill at sea. Landed in the cove of Pulo Batak on Sumatra, he dies and is buried there (HMS 8; *also* FSW 7; TGS 4; COM 3).
3: according to Philip Aubrey, the family name of the second wife of General Aubrey (YA 8).

Stanhope, Lady Hester

A lady discussed by Maturin and Dr Simaika (TH 7).

*Lady Hester Lucy Stanhope (1776–1839) was a niece of William *Pitt, the Prime Minister of Great Britain, and acted as his personal assistant (and brilliant social hostess) from the late 1790s until his death in 1806. In 1810 she left England, a country in which she had come to feel stifled, and then travelled widely in the Middle East before eventually settling in the Syrian Lebanon in 1814. Here she kept a 'court' of some very considerable splendour and established a reputation as a deeply eccentric magician and mystic. Her family connections and her own grand manner gained her some minor political influence in the region, which she deployed against the Ottoman Turkish rulers in Constantinople but equally often against any plans emanating from the British Foreign Office. However, SPILLMANN reports that, during *Buonaparte's 'hundred day' return in 1815, Lady Hester did arrange the assassination of a French secret agent operating in the area, one Colonel Vincent Boutin (1772–1815), thus cutting short his schemes to ally the Sultan of *Turkey with the newly restored Emperor. After many years in her Levant palace, Lady Hester's extravagant generosity had reduced her to penury and she died in some obscurity, abandoned by her many former friends and visitors.*

Stapleton

The Third Lieutenant of HMS *Guerrier*, met by Jack Aubrey in Molly Harte's salon (M&C 1).

State, the Secretary of

1: a British government minister (SM 4; HD 3).
In British usage 'Secretary of State' indicates the political head of a government department, almost always a member of the Prime Minister's Cabinet. It does not usually in-dicate a particular department unless expanded to, e.g., 'Secretary of State for Home Affairs,' a post more usually referred to simply as that of 'Home Secretary.' However, in HD Maturin appears to use it in sense #2, below.
2: a U.S. politician whom Johnson advises on political and intelligence matters (FW 6,7).
*In U.S. usage the 'Secretary of State' is the political head of the Foreign Service. From 1811 to 1816 the post was held by the former Governor of Virginia, James Monroe (1758–1831), who also held the post of Secretary of War from 1814 to 1815. In 1817 Monroe went on to succeed *Madison as President, serving until 1825.*

Stately, HMS

A 64-gun ship of Jack Aubrey's squadron, Captain William Duff (COM 3+).
HMS Stately, 64-gun, was launched in 1784. Reduced to a troopship in 1799 (although she did see a little purely naval service after that date), she was broken up in 1814.

Staunch, HMS

A brig that joins Jack Aubrey's squadron from Bombay. She is commanded by Lord Narborough, who, as Lord Garron, was a sometime shipmate of Jack and Stephen Maturin (TMC 7,8).
*HMS Staunch, 12-gun brig, was launched in 1804. In the early part of Commodore Josias Rowley's Mauritius campaign she was under Lieutenant Benjamin Street, later Commander of HMS *Emma. In 1811, now under Lieutenant Hector Craig, she was lost with all hands off Madagascar.*

Steel

The publisher of the *Navy List* (M&C 8; PC 9).
David R. Steel, or Steele, (fl.1780–1815) published his Navy List twice a year, giving details of all serving officers and their seniority as well as other naval events of note. He also published reference works on shipping in both the USA and Britain and other texts on aspects of seamanship.

Steller

A naturalist who had discovered a sea-cow now named after him (NC author's note, 2,8).
Georg Wilhelm Steller (1709–1746), a German naturalist and biologist, spent his active career in Russian exploration and science, especially in Siberia, the Bering Straits and Alaska. He discovered his massive (and soon to be extinct) sea-cow, hydrodamalis gigas, on Bering Island.

Stephen

see **Maturin, Stephen**

Stephen the Protomartyr, Saint

A saint referred to in passing (HMS 11; YA 1).
Stephen was supposedly the first ever (i.e., proto in Greek) martyr of the Christian faith, being stoned to death for his beliefs sometime between 35–37 AD.

Sterne

The novelist referred to by Martin (NC 9).
Laurence Sterne (1713–1768) was an Anglo-Irish vicar, novelist, historian, and traveller. His works, the most notable of which is the nine-volume Tristram Shandy, *show*

a man of great perception, wit, and originality. They also display a great affection for military men and their life-style, a characteristic perhaps gained in his early years following his soldier father from post to post.

Stevens

A warrant officer in HMS *Shannon* (FW 9).
William Stevens (d.1813), an elderly man who had once served under *Rodney, was the boatswain of HMS *Shannon. In *Broke's famous victory, he was hit by grape- and musket-fire whilst lashing his ship to USS *Chesapeake and later died in Halifax of his wounds.

Steward, Mr

A reference in a verse quoted by Farquar (TMC 5)
Here the reference is simply to the post of 'steward,' the chief administrator of a great estate.

Stewart, Bob

A seaman in *Surprise* badly wounded in the first action on Moahu Island (C/T 9).

Stindall

A seaman in HMS *Polychrest* on Lieutenant Parker's punishment list (PC 7).

Stirling, Charles

The Captain who presides over Jack Aubrey's court-martial for the loss of HMS *Sophie* (M&C 12).
Charles Stirling (1760–1833) was made Post in 1783. He commanded HMS *Pompee in the first of *Saumarez' two 1801 fleet actions but his ship was so badly damaged as to be unable to fight in the second successful action six days later. A little later, he presided over Thomas *Cochrane's court-martial for the loss of his HMS *Speedy. Stirling was promoted Rear Admiral in 1805 and Vice Admiral in 1810. Appointed to the command of the Jamaica station in 1811, in 1814 he was court-martialled on charges of corruption, convicted on several of them and sentenced to be placed permanently on the half-pay list, with no possibility of further promotion.

Stokes, James

A Master's Mate in HMS *Leopard* who dies of gaol-fever (DI 5).

Stone, Mr

Admiral Pellew's secretary, a minor intelligence functionary (RM 1). He acts as Deputy Judge Advocate at the trial of the HMS *Hermione* mutineers (RM 2).

Stopford

A yacht-owning Captain known to Billy Sutton and Jack Aubrey (FSW 1).
The reference is perhaps to Edward Stopford (d.1837), a Post Captain of 1811. He was the son of that Vice Admiral Sir Robert Stopford (1768–1847; full Admiral 1825) who had succeeded the deceased *Drury as Commander-in-Chief at Batavia in 1811.

Storr

A silversmith who engraves Jack Aubrey's presentation set of silver plate (LM 4).

Stourton

The new First Lieutenant appointed to HMS *Surprise* following Mr Hervey's promotion to Commander. He had formerly served in HMS *Narcissus*, a 'spit-and-polish' frigate (HMS 8).

Strabo

An ancient authority referred to by Maturin (M&C 11).
Strabo of Amaseia (63?BC–21?AD) was a Greek historian, geographer and Stoic philosopher who travelled extensively around the Mediterranean lands. His work is chiefly concerned with human and political (rather than physical) geography, with its main aim being to explain the Greeks and Romans to each other.

Strachan

The officer who had captured *Scipion* (YA 9).
Sir Richard John Strachan (1760–1828) was made Post in 1783 and soon established a reputation as one of the Royal Navy's most effective commanders. From 1793 to 1801 he led a small squadron that harried French coastal supply ships to great effect and from 1803 was given charge by *Nelson of the blockade of Cadiz. In late 1805, just a few days after the Battle of Trafalgar, Strachan (in HMS *Caesar) and his squadron encountered four French ships (*Scipion amongst them) that had avoided capture in that great action, taking them all in a brisk fight. For this victory Strachan, already a baronet by inheritance, was awarded a knighthood and a large pension; by co-incidence, he was also promoted Rear Admiral by seniority just a few days after the battle. In this rank Strachan led the North Sea fleet in the 1809 assault on the Dutch-French island of Walcheren, the army component of the force being led by the Earl of *Chatham. Although the General was quite rightly given most of the blame for the ensuing fiasco (the island taken but the victory not exploited, the loss of over 4000 men by malaria and the subsequent embarrassing withdrawal), Strachan was undoubted tainted by association and his sea-career soon ended (see also *Canning and *Castlereagh). He advanced by seniority to Vice Admiral in 1810 and full Admiral in 1821.

Strachey, William

A seaman and mutineer in HMS *Hermione* who is captured by Jack Aubrey from USS *Norfolk*, court-martialled in HMS *Irresistible* and then sentenced to hang (RM 2).

Stranraer, Vice Admiral Lord and Lady

The commander of the squadrons blockading Brest and thus Jack Aubrey's immediate superior (YA 2,4+). Before being ennobled, Stranraer was plain Captain Hanbury Koop, a former shipmate of the Duke of Clarence (YA 2,4), and, despite having seen relatively little action in his career, he has a reputation as a good seaman (YA 2). Stranraer suffers from a chronic heart complaint that was, sometime in the past, briefly treated by Stephen Maturin (YA 4), who now attends him again (YA 7+). The Admiral, an influential man chiefly on account of Lady Stranraer's wealth (YA 7), is the uncle of Jack's Dorset neighbour, Captain Griffiths. The pair are very much in favour of land enclosures (YA 2,3,4) and plot to prevent Jack's strong opposition to their schemes getting its day in Parliament (YA 3). When Jack's argument nevertheless prevails (YA 3), Stranraer becomes his open political and career enemy (YA 6+). A little later however, Lord Stranraer is later reported to have died of his illness (HD 1).

Streatham

An East Indiaman, Master Mr Dale, first captured by the French *Caroline* (TMC 3,4) and later re-taken by Jack Aubrey at Réunion (TMC 4).

> *Streatham, 850-tons and carrying 30 guns, completed four round trips for the East India Company between 1804 and 1818. Under John *Dale she was taken by the French in May of 1809 and then re-taken by the Royal Navy at Réunion in September of that year.*

Strobenius

A scientist referred to by McAdam (TMC 3).

Strode, Annie

A dinner guest at Mapes Court, either the wife or sister of the local parson (PC 3).

Strumpff

The author of *The Nearest Way to Heaven*, a work translated by Mr Scriven (PC 6).

Strype

The Commander of HMS *Vulture* (LM 6).

Stubbs

A seaman in HMS *Nimble* (TGS 4).

'Stupor Mundi'

A Latin reference by Stephen Maturin to the newly born son of Jack Aubrey (TMC 10).

> *In English, 'the wonder of the world,' a phase used in Roman Catholicism for *Jesus Christ.*

Styles, Jacob

A seaman in HMS *Leopard* whose tobacco and watch are stolen (DI 4).

Suakarta, Sultan of

A guest at a dinner given by Governor Raffles (TGS 6).

Sublime Porte *or* Porte

A term for the government of the Sultan of Turkey (IM 9,11; TH 1–7; HD 6).

> *The term is a French translation of the Turkish Babiali, the 'High Gate' leading to the main administrative com-*

*pound in Constantinople where the Sultan of *Turkey's Grand Viziers held sway.*

Success, HMS

A ship commanded by Sir Harry Neale in which Jack Aubrey had once served (M&C 7).

> *HMS Success, 32-gun, was launched in 1781, reduced to a convict ship in 1814 and broken up in 1820. She was the first ever Post ship of the notorious Hugh *Pigot, of HMS *Hermione mutiny fame, but was never held by *Neale.*

Sudden Death

A cannon in *Surprise* (LM 2; NC 7; C/T 1).

Sue

An imaginary person referred to by the mad Mr Lowndes (PC 8).

Suffren

A great seaman of a former time (HMS 7).

> *Pierre-André de Suffren Saint-Tropez (1729–1788) was a wealthy and aristocratic French seaman who, in a very active career, established a reputation for himself as one of the most aggressive and effective fighting captains and admirals of his age. In French naval lore, Suffren is the only native amongst the three 'immortal names' of the age of fighting sail, the others being *Nelson and de *Ruyter.*

Suleiman

1: a nephew of Sciahan Bey of Kutali (IM 11).
2: the loblolly-boy in HMS *Nutmeg of Consolation* (NC 5).

Suliman, Emperor of Morocco

A reliable ally of Britain (IM 4; FSW 1), although there is later concern that he may align himself with the newly restored Buonaparte (HD 1). His title is occasional used as a joking reference to exotic splendour (PC 6; SM 10).

> *Moulay Suleiman (d.1822) became Emperor of Morocco in 1792, establishing a reputation as a wise and benign ruler who not only abolished slavery but maintained effective alliances that ensured prosperity for his country.*

Sullivan

An Irish seaman in HMS *Sophie* (M&C 3).

Sullivan, Mary

An Irish nurse at Choate's hospital in Boston (FW 5).

Sultan, the

see **Pulo Prabang, Sultan of** *or* **Turkey, Sultan of**

Sultan, HMS

A swift-sailer in Admiral Thornton's Mediterranean fleet (IM 8).

> *HMS Sultan, 74-gun, was launched in 1807. After a long but uneventful career, she was reduced to a gunnery target ship in 1860 and finally broken up in 1864.*

Summerhays

A wealthy botanist who passes through Malta (TH 8).

Summerhays, Ned

An officer referred to by Jack Aubrey as a valued, former ship-mate whom he had wanted as a Lieutenant for HMS *Leopard* (DI 4).

Summers, Will

A seaman in HMS *Repulse*, a noted boxer (YA 3).

Superb, HMS

A British warship, Captain Keats (M&C 11+; PC 5). Later, now under Captain Charlton, she is said to be a most unhappy ship (IM 4).

> HMS Superb, *74-gun, was launched in 1798 and, under Captain Richard* *Keats, *played a brilliant role in Saumarez' victory off Gibraltar in late 1801. In 1808 she was also Keats' flagship when, as a Rear Admiral, he evacuated the Spanish troops from the Franco-Danish island of Fünen (see* *Casademon*). Superb* was broken up in 1826.

Superbe

A ship that had been sunk by HMS *Royal George* in a very brisk action (YA 5).

> Superbe, *a 70-gun launched in 1738, was part of the French fleet pursued into Quiberon Bay by Sir Edward* *Hawke *in November 1759. In a confused action fought in very rough weather (on account of which several ships on both sides foundered), she was sunk by just two broadsides from the British flag-ship, the 100-gun HMS* *Royal George.

Supply, HMS

A brig that had been with HMS *Sirius* when she was wrecked on Norfolk Island (C/T 1).

> The storeship HMS Supply *was purchased in 1786 for the voyage of the 'First Fleet' to Australia; when no longer needed, she was sold locally in 1792. For much of the outbound journey she was commanded by Henry Lidgbird* *Ball *and, being a swift-sailer, for a time even acted as the pennant-ship of Commodore Arthur Philip.*

Suraj-ud-Dowlah

A potentate whose gold palanquin is contemplated as a gift for the victorious Jack Aubrey (HMS 10).

> Siraj-ud-Dowlah *(1729–1757; a.k.a. Mirza Muhammad),* *Nawab of Bengal, *was the Indian Prince who in 1756 confined a number of British captives in the 'Black Hole of Calcutta,' leading to a number of agonising deaths (variously claimed to be between 43 and 123). In the following year, the Nawab was defeated by* *Clive *at the Battle of Plassy and was soon afterwards captured and executed by a rival Prince.*

Surel, John

A seaman in HMS *Sophie* (M&C 6).

Surprise, HMS

Surprise, whether as a King's Ship (HMS *to* RM; HD 1–9), a private letter-of-marque (RM *to* TGS)

or His Majesty's Hired Vessel (TGS *to* YA; HD 9,10), is Jack Aubrey's favourite command, first appearing in the eponymous *HMS Surprise* and then taking part, or being mentioned, in every book thereafter. Consequently most of the key incidents in her career are given under the main entry for Jack himself, with this entry being largely confined to a general summary and to certain details not to be found in that location.

1: *The career of* Surprise *under Jack Aubrey.*

Surprise is Jack's first permanent command as a Post Captain, obtained for him by the good offices of Sir Joseph Blaine. Long ago, Jack had served in her as a Midshipman, during which time he had carved his initials on the cap of the mast-head (HMS 4; *a period referred to many times thereafter*). Her first service under Jack, in the Indian Ocean (HMS 4+), is later several times referred to in those books in which she does not actually make an appearance (TMC 1,3,7; DI 1,3; FW 1; SM 1,7). *Surprise* next appears as an unhappy ship in the Mediterranean fleet under the command of Francis Latham (IM 5–8). During the abortive attempt to bring the French to battle, Latham and his First Lieutenant are both killed by a shot from *Robuste* (IM 8,9) and she is now given to Jack for a mission to the Ionian region (IM 9). Under her service nickname of *Joyful Surprise* (TH 5) she continues as Jack's ship in the Mediterranean (TH 1+), Atlantic and Pacific (FSW 1+; RM 1) but is soon due to be 'retired' on account of her age (TH 8; FSW 1; RM 1–3). Jack would like to buy her for himself but lacks the means to do so (RM 4–6) and is in any case soon ruined by his conviction for fraud and dismissal from the Royal Navy (RM 7). The newly rich Stephen Maturin *is* able to afford her and, with the expert help of Tom Pullings, acquires her (*though concealing his own role in the transaction*: LM 1) as a letter-of-marque. Charged with an (often to be postponed) intelligence mission to Peru, she is given to Jack as a private command (RM 7–10; LM 1+; TGS 1–3). When Jack is restored to the Royal Navy, *Surprise* is then temporarily given to Tom Pullings, and thus holds the curious status of a private ship commanded by a King's officer (TGS 3,4; NC 3,6,7). On Jack's re-assumption of command for the delayed Peruvian mission, she is then officially hired-in by the Navy (NC 8) and, at some unspecified point, somewhat unwillingly sold to Jack by Stephen (NC 9; C/T 1). Sometimes now commanded by Jack and sometimes by Tom Pullings, *Surprise* now conducts a variety of missions in the Pacific (C/T 1+; WDS 1+) before finally arriving back in England (COM 1,3,4,7; YA 5,8). Following France's capitulation, *Surprise* is next to be Jack's command on a mission to Chile, hired to the Admiralty Hydrographic Survey for the purpose (YA 10; *but the deal is done by Stephen, who appears to own her once again*). However, whilst at Madeira, the friends learn that Buonaparte has escaped from exile on Elba and, in consequence, Jack has been ordered to shift to HMS *Pomone* as a Commodore (YA 10). *Surprise* accompanies the new squadron to the Mediterranean, restored to the Royal Navy as a King's frigate (HD 1) and soon becomes Jack's pennant-ship for his various missions (HD 2–9). However, once Jack's squadron is dispersed, Admiral Lord Barmouth orders *Surprise* to be returned to her status of a private warship (HD 9). It is in this capacity (although she may perhaps have been even further reduced to 'hired survey vessel' again) that she enjoys the final triumph of taking the Moslem treasure-galley before resuming her South American voyage (HD 10).

2: ***The history of*** Surprise *before Jack Aubrey assumed command.* According to Jack, *Surprise* is older even than HMS *Irresistible* (RM 1), having been launched at Le Havre (YA 9) in the 1780s as the French *Unité* (HMS 5; RM 3) and captured by the Royal Navy in 1796 (WDS 3; *N.B., thus making it impossible for Jack to have served on her as a Midshipman:* HMS 4). She is famous for having retaken the mutinous HMS Hermione (e.g., HMS 5; FSW 10; C/T 2), an action for which she was given the nick-name of *Nemesis* (HMS 6,7) and then officially renamed successively HMS *Retaliation* and *Retribution* (LM 5,8).

Jack *Aubrey's HMS Surprise *is an amalgam of — and perhaps even something of a most understandable confusion between — at least two real ships, both at various times named* Unité: **a)** *the 24-gun corvette *Unité, launched at Le Havre in 1794, captured by HMS* Constant *in 1796, and taken into the Royal Navy as* Surprise *(and largely the model for Jack's favourite ship); and* **b)** *a rather older 36-gun frigate, launched at Rochefort as* Gracieuse *in 1787 (the same year as *Irresistible), renamed* Unité *in 1793 and then* Variente *in 1796, the year in which she was taken by HMS* Revolutionaire *and bought into the Royal Navy as HMS* Unity/Unite *(both spellings are seen). By a curious coincidence, both of these ships were then sold by the Admiralty during 1802, in February and May respectively, further adding to the ease of confusing the pair in the various service listings. In 1799, under Sir Edward *Hamilton,* Surprise *famously retook the mutinous HMS *Hermione and consequently acquired the nickname of* Nemesis, *a term meaning something very like 'retribution' in Greek legend. However, it was Hermione herself, not* Surprise, *that was successively re-named HMS *Retaliation and *Retribution.*

Susan, Miss
see **Christy**

Susanna
see **'Marriage of Figaro'**

Sussex, Duke of
A patron of both Blaine and Maturin (COM 2,4).

Prince Augustus Frederick (1773–1843), Duke of Sussex, was the sixth son of King *George III. The Duke became a political liberal, strongly opposing the slave trade and supporting religious emancipation. Also a noted patron of learning, he served as President of the Royal Society from 1830 to 1839.

Sutton
The Captain of HMS *Amphion* and a member of the squadron that takes Bustamente's Spanish treasure ships (PC 14; HMS 1).

Samuel Sutton (d.1832) was made Post in 1797 and spent the next several years as *Flag Captain to various Admirals until being returned to independent frigate commands in 1801. In 1803, after a short spell in command of HMS *Victory whilst she was being refitted for Lord *Nelson, he was appointed to the 32-gun HMS *Amphion and, in October 1804, took part in the capture of *Bustamente's squadron. Sutton was promoted Rear Admiral in 1821.

Sutton, Billy
The Captain of HMS *Namur*, an old friend of Jack Aubrey from their days together in HMS *Resolution*. Now MP for Rye, he returns to England to attend Parliament (FSW 1).

Sutton, Richard
A Lieutenant in HMS *Sophie* killed in action before Jack Aubrey's appointment to command (M&C 2).

Swainton
A London seller of weather-proof cloaks (LM 4).

Swallow, HMS
1: the sloop Carteret had commanded under Captain Wallis (NC 8).

HMS Swallow, *discovery vessel, was commanded by *Carteret during *Wallis's 1766–1768 circumnavigation. She became separated from Wallis's 24-gun frigate HMS *Dolphin and went on to make an important voyage of discovery on her own, returning to England in 1769 and being broken up later that same year.*

2: an aviso on the Brest blockade squadron in which Philip Aubrey serves as Midshipman (YA 8).

HMS Swallow, *18-gun brig-sloop, was launched in 1805 and broken up in 1815.*

Swammerdam
An author whose works are owned by Blaine (SM 4).

Jan Swammerdam (1637–1680) was a distinguished Dutch physician, anatomist and entomologist who produced a series of general works on the insect world as well as an important monograph on bees.

Swan of Avon

A cannon in HMS *Diane* (TGS 5).

The title is commonly applied to William *Shakespeare.

'Swedish Knight'
see **Smith, Sir Sidney** or **Sydney**

Sweeting

A Midshipman who had first spotted 'Sweeting's Island' (NC 8).

Sweeting, Emily and Sarah/Sal

Two little Melanesian girls, aged perhaps 5 or 6, found on the otherwise deserted and smallpox-ravaged Sweeting's Island and taken aboard HMS *Surprise* by Stephen Maturin. After a short trial of Behemoth and Thursday, they are finally named Emily and Sarah (NC 8). Stephen later attempts to place the unwilling girls in a Sydney orphanage but they immediately escape, re-join HMS *Surprise* (NC 9) and, apart from a short spell ashore in Peru (WDS 7,8), remain on board, attached to the sick-berth as efficient and well-liked helpers (C/T 1+; WDS 1+). Once they arrive in England, they are left in the care of Mrs Broad of the Grapes Inn (COM 1,2,5; YA 1,8,10), Stephen now regarding them as his god-daughters (YA 8).

Swieten, van

The author of a medical text consulted by Maturin (C/T 4), although later claimed by him to be unavailable (WDS 4).

Gerhard van Swieten (1700–1772) was an eminent Dutch physician, chemist and teacher, at one time the pupil and assistant of *Booerhaave. Although it is for his Commentaries on Booerhaave's ideas and methods that he is best remembered, he also published a text on the diseases of armies and made a number of innovations in the treatment of venereal disease.

Swiftsure, HMS

A ship that Lieutenant Nicholls says has recently called at Gibraltar (HMS 5) and that is later in sight of HMS *Ajax* when she takes *Méduse* (SM 11). Some years later still, Sir Joseph Blaine says she has recently captured a French vessel containing valuable scientific specimens (RM 7).

HMS Swiftsure, *74-gun, was launched in 1804. Under her Captain William Gordon Rutherford (1764–1818), she fought at Trafalgar in 1805, with her predecessor (see following entry) being present on the French side. *Blaine's later reference may be to her taking of the privateer* Charlemagne *in 1813.* Swiftsure *became a receiving ship in 1819 and was sold in 1845. Her name is said to be an Elizabethan English contraction of 'swift (pur)suer.'*

Swiftsure

A French 74-gun in Toulon Harbour, captured from the Royal Navy in 1801 (PC 4; HMS 2).

Le Swiftsure, *74-gun, was launched as HMS* Swiftsure *in 1787. In 1797 she fought under Benjamin *Hallowell in *Nelson's victory at The Battle of the Nile but in mid–1801, still under the same commander, was captured by a French squadron. She was retaken by the Royal Navy in 1805 at Trafalgar but, as she had already been replaced (see previous entry), was then re-named HMS *Irresistible, prison ship, until being finally broken up in 1816.*

Swiney

A Lieutenant in HMS *Raisonable* (TMC 3).

Sybille, HMS
see **Sibylle, HMS**

Sydney, Sir
see **Smith, Sir Sydney**

Sylph

A ship that had once fought *Flèche*. Mr Elliott of HMS *Diane* had been an officer on one or the other, wounded in the action (TGS 4).

Ships named *Sylph and *Flèche served at various times in both the British and French navies. I have been unable to find a record of an action between the two and so am uncertain in which Mr *Elliott had served.

Sylph, HMS

A ship in which Jack Aubrey and Billy Holroyd had served when boys (NC 8).

Two HMS Sylphs *are just possible, though neither seem likely: the first a 14-gun sloop purchased (as* Lovely Lass*) in 1776, re-named HMS* Lightning, *fireship, in 1779 and sold in 1783; the second an 18-gun sloop, purchased (as the cutter* Active*) in 1780 and captured by the French in 1782, serving in their navy until 1786. The* Sylphs—*a fanciful term coined by *Paracelsus—were beautiful, slender girls inhabiting forest glades.*

Sylphide, HMS

William Babbington's first ship as a Commander (SM 11).

Symonds

A seaman in HMS *Irresistible* who had once served with Jack Aubrey (RM 1).

after 118 AD

T

T_, Colonel

An officer referred to by Stephen Maturin as a closet Catholic (M&C 6).

Taafe, Ned

An Irish gentleman with whom Diana Villiers had hunted (COM 10).

Tabitha

1: Tabitha or Tabby, Admiral Sir John Thornton's pug-dog who, having often bitten Admiral Harte, now bites Jack Aubrey (IM 3,4).

2: a Java civet cat belonging to Governor Raffles (NC 4).

Tacitus

An historian referred to by Goodridge (PC 10).

Caius Cornelius Tacitus (55? AD–after 118 AD) was perhaps the greatest of the Latin historians. However, of his personal life we know almost nothing other than that he served as a fairly high-ranking government official under the Emperors Vespasian, *Titus and Domitian. Amongst his surviving works are most of his famous Annals, *a history of Rome from 14 to 64 (originally in 16 volumes) that shows a rare combination of profound insight into motivation and character and great narrative drive.*

Taft, Mrs

A Baltimore friend of Louisa Wogan and Diana Villiers (DI 5).

Taillandier

The head of the French intelligence network in Lisbon (TGS 3).

Taio

One of the younger members of the crew of the *pahi* that picks up Aubrey and Maturin when adrift in the South Seas. She and her companion, Manu, then save the pair from the fate intended for them — emasculation and death — before abandoning them on a small, deserted island (FSW 7).

Tallal ibn Yahya

The ruler of the small island of Mubara in the Red Sea whose family have traditionally extorted payments from passing shipping (TH 2,4). His son, possibly also named Tallal, has become a French ally, a matter of some concern to the British (TH 2).

Talleyrand or Talleyrand-Périgord

A French politician known personally to Stephen Maturin (SM 5) who, although nominally out of office, remains very influential and has a private intelligence organisation (SM 10). When held captive in Paris, Stephen Maturin learns that he, Aubrey and Jagiello are in the immediate custody of Talleyrand's faction — represented in the person of Duhamel — and are being kept safe as part of a plan to make contact with the exile Bourbon Court in England (SM 11). Talleyrand arranges the release of all three men and delivers a promise eventually to restore the 'Blue Peter' diamond to Diana Villiers (SM 11; RM 5,10; YA 10).

Charles-Maurice de Talleyrand-Périgord (1754–1838), Bishop of Autun (from 1788 to 1791) and Prince of Benevento, was an aristocratic French prelate and statesman renowned, amongst many other things, for his exquisitely refined powers of insult. Talleyrand, having supposedly only ever entered the Church because a severe limp prevented the pursuit of a military career, became known principally as a statesman and diplomat, usually following a distinctly independent line of policy that his enemies often characterised as devoid of any moral principle other than self-interest. Active in the Revolution, yet an enemy of its excesses, he later formed an alliance with *Buonaparte when the latter seized power in 1799, soon becoming Foreign Minister and Grand Chamberlain. In 1806 Talleyrand was created Prince of Benevento but in 1807 resigned his posts, supposedly feeling that Napoleon had over-reached himself and would eventually pay the price. Although he then held no further formal office under the Empire, his influence continued to be considerable, with no section of French or Allied opinion able to ignore either his machinations or his formidable skills as a negotiator. Instrumental in the restoration of *Louis XVIII in 1814–1815, Talleyrand resumed an active political life until 1834, usually in some degree of opposition to the extremely reactionary domestic policies of the *Bourbon monarchs.

Tallis

A composer whose vocal works are heard by Aubrey and Maturin in London (YA 10).

Thomas Tallis (1505?–1585), an English music publisher and church organist, was a composer of ingeniously complex vocal music, the best known example of which is perhaps his 40-part motet, Spem in alium.

Tamar, HMS

A ship referred to in passing (IM 2).

Of several possible ships, the reference is probably to the 38-gun frigate HMS Tamar, *launched in 1796 and broken up in 1810 (her somewhat smaller replacement not being launched until 1814, after* IM *is set). She was named for a river in southwest England, the boundary between Devon and Cornwall.*

Tamerlane

A reference by Maturin to tyranny (IM 2).

Timur/Tamerlane/Tamburlane (1336–1405; 'lane' is a corruption of Turkish lenc, *meaning 'the lame') was a Mongol tribal leader and warrior (from modern Uzbekistan) who first conquered much of Central Asia and then gradually extended his rule to the borders of China in one direction and the shores of the Mediterranean in the other.*

Like his supposed ancestor Ghengis Khan, Timur's essentially nomadic frame of mind perhaps induced in him a preference to seize, lay waste and move on: certainly, his reputation for ruthless cruelty was widespread and deeply feared. In some contrast, his 'official' capital of Samarkand (he himself scarcely spent any time there) rose in his lifetime to become a splendidly affluent and beautiful city, which his descendants soon turned into a world-famous centre of art and learning.

Tandy, Napper

A Protestant United Irishman. In the vain hope of diffusing a growing tension between the Irish Lieutenant, James Dillon, and his English Captain, Jack Aubrey, Stephen Maturin tells Jack that many United Irishmen were well-educated Protestants and not merely 'Catholic rebels,' as Jack might have supposed (M&C 3).

*James Napper Tandy (1740–1803) was a Dublin merchant who, from about 1782, became both a political activist in favour of reform in Ireland and an irregular soldier in pursuit of that same aim. At the end of 1791, he formed the United Irish Society with his fellow-Protestants *Tone and Russell and, after spending a period from 1795 in exile in the USA, travelled in 1798 to Paris in search of support for a military invasion of Ireland. Appointed a French General of Brigade in that same year, he then accompanied the abortive attempt on Donegal, a sally that almost immediately withdrew in disarray on hearing of the collapse of General Humbert's earlier incursion further to the south. Tandy retreated with the small French fleet to Hamburg, from where, having been detained on arrival, he was extradited to Ireland in 1799 to face trial. Condemned to death in the following year, Tandy nevertheless had his sentence commuted in 1801, when his French allies were able to link his case to the negotiation of the Peace of Amiens. Further pressure, combined with Tandy's age and ill-health, led to his release in 1802, after which he lived in Paris until his death.*

Tantalus

A character referred to by Maturin when he is yet again denied an opportunity to go exploring (TMC 4).

*King Tantalus of Sipylus was a son of *Zeus and one of the first of the mortals. Allowed as such occasionally to dine with the gods, he then abused this privilege either by letting slip a divine secret he had overheard or by testing the gods' discernment of palate by serving a stew of his own murdered son's flesh. In either telling of the legend, Tantalus is thereupon condemned to perpetual thirst, standing in a pond that recedes whenever he tries to drink and 'tantalised' with luscious fruit, dangling just out of reach.*

Tapetterie, de la

A French spy (HMS 1), later exposed by Mr Waring (HMS 4).

Tapia

A Polynesian seaman in the whaler *Truelove* (C/T 9).

Taplow

A seaman in HMS *Surprise* (TH 6).

Tartan, Mrs

The convenient name given to the lovely young woman accompanying the Master of the tartan (i.e., two-masted, lateen-sailed) merchantman *Pola*, intercepted and taken by HMS *Sophie* (M&C 10).

Tartarus, HMS

1: a bomb-ketch docked in Port Mahon (M&C 1), thought by Jack Aubrey to be more suited to the attack on *Fanciulla* than his own HMS *Polychrest* (PC 10).

HMS Tartarus, *8-gun bomb ketch, was purchased (as* Charles Jackson*) in 1797 and then wrecked on the sands off Margate in 1804. In Greek legend, Tartarus was a name both for a son of Gaia (earth) and Aither (air), and for the very deepest region of the underworld, below even Hades.*

2: an 18-gun sloop commanded by William Babbington (RM 6; LM 4).

HMS Tartarus, *16-gun fireship, was launched in 1806. Converted in 1808 to a sloop armed with 30 carronades and two regular light canon, she was sold in 1816.*

Tartini

A musician referred to by Jack Aubrey (NC 9; C/T 3; WDS 4).

Giuseppe Tartini (1692–1770), an Italian composer, virtuoso violinist and teacher, is credited both with designing a new type of bow and developing new harmonic techniques on his instrument.

Tattersall's

The location of stud sales (COM 2).

*Richard Tattersall (1724–1795), a former stud-groom to the last Duke of *Kingston, founded his famous horse auction ring at Hyde Park Corner in 1766. He rapidly developed a reputation for great integrity and became an intimate of the very highest ranks of English sporting society. The firm was continued by his son, Edmund (1758–1810), and many subsequent generations of the family until being sold in the 20th century.*

Taylor

1: an Admiralty official (HMS 4).
2: a Bishop of the diocese near Jack Aubrey's childhood home (LM 7).

Taylor, Isaac

A merchant whose mark is found on a floating barrel cast overboard by a Yankee whaler (WDS 5).

'Teapot'

see Lowndes, Mr

Teevan, Kevin

The surgeon of HMS *Leviathan* (HD 2).

Temminck

A naturalist for whom a pangolin (*scaly ant-eater*) is named (COM 8).

> *Conrad Temminck (1770?–1858) was a leading Dutch naturalist (as was his father before him) who published many important works on ornithology between 1807 and 1839 and, between 1825 and 1841, a catalogue of the preserved mammals to be found in the museums of Europe. He also published a number of monographs on the wildlife of the Dutch colonies in the East Indies.*

Temple, Captain

The Marine Captain in HMS *Bellona* (YA 5).

Tenedos, HMS

A ship at Halifax, Captain Hyde Parker (SM 1).

> *HMS Tenedos, 38-gun, was launched in 1812, only a few months before the outbreak of the war with the USA, and then commissioned by Hyde *Parker, who was to remain her Captain throughout that conflict. In 1815 (just before the end of hostilities) Tenedos was part of the small British squadron that harried Stephen Decatur's USS *President to defeat, being the ship to which he then actually surrendered. Tenedos, reduced to a convict hulk in 1843 and broken up in 1875, was named for an island in the far eastern Mediterranean.*

Tennant, Harry

The Captain of HMS *Despatch*, said by General Aubrey to be 'Harbrook's son,' his father presumably being a peer (RM 4).

Tepec

An Inca colleague of Eduardo (WDS 9).

Tereo

The Chief of Annamooka (C/T 6) and King of the Friendly Islands (C/T 7).

Terpsichore, HMS

A ship referred to by Aubrey as one of several very desirable frigates into which he would like to be made Post (M&C 11). Once the command of Captain Griffiths, she had mutinied under him (YA 2).

> *HMS Terpsichore, 32-gun, was launched in 1785, converted to a receiving ship in 1818 and broken up in 1830. In Greek myth Terpsichore was the muse of dance and song.*

Terrible, HMS

A 74-gun initially promised to Jack Aubrey for his squadron (COM 2) but soon diverted to other duties (COM 3).

> *HMS Terrible was launched in 1785 and, after a long but rather uneventful career, was reduced to a receiving ship in 1823 and a coal hulk in 1829, before being broken up in 1836.*

Terrier, HMS

A sloop referred to by Admiral Russell (LM 1).

Tessin, Countess

Jagiello's grandmother (LM 9).

> *The Tessins were a leading Swedish family of architects, diplomats and statesmen who had made their most notable contributions to public life during the 17th and early 18th centuries.*

Thacker's

A naval coffee house in London (PC 3).

Thales of Miletus

An ancient author (SM 8).

> *Thales of Miletus (640?–550? BC) was one of the 'Seven Sages' of ancient Greece, renowned as the most scientific of their number for his interests in astronomy, engineering, geometry and navigation (although this last may be a much later attribution).*

Thames, HMS

1: a ship with the fleet at Gibraltar (M&C 12).

> *HMS Thames, 32-gun, was launched in 1758. Taken by a French squadron in late 1793, she served as Tamise until her re-capture in mid–1796. In July 1801 she fought under her Captain Aiskew Paffard Hollis (d.1844 in the rank of Vice Admiral) in *Saumarez' second, successful action off Gibraltar. The very elderly Thames was broken up in 1803.*

2: a 32-gun frigate in Aubrey's squadron (COM 3+), commanded by the harsh disciplinarian, Captain Thomas (COM 4+).

> *The 32-gun, fir-built replacement for the old Thames, above, was launched in 1805. At about the time of COM (1813) she was commanded by Charles Napier (1786–1860), later to become famous as 'Black Charlie' or 'Mad Charlie,' a vain and deeply eccentric commander of fleets for both the British and Portuguese governments from the mid–1830s to mid–1850s. Napier died, in the rank of full Admiral, with no less than five knighthoods to his name (British, Portuguese, Austrian, Prussian and Russian), as well as having been created Viscount Cape St Vincent in the Lisbon hierarchy for a successful fleet action fought in 1833. His Thames was broken up in 1816.*

Themistocles

A classical figure discussed by Maturin and Graham (IM 10).

> *Themistocles (524?–459 BC) was an Athenian politician, orator and military commander, famous for his resistance to *Xerxes' Persian invaders in 480. After suffering a defeat on land at Thessaly and a stalemate at sea off Artemisium, he inflicted a decisive defeat on the Persian fleet at Salamis (having interpreted an oracle's call for a new 'defence of wooden walls' as referring to stoutly built, new ships). After this great victory, Themistocles, who already had a reputation for both cunning and corruption, fell out of favour and, by about 470, had been banished. Later, he was reported to be engaging in intrigues with the King of Persia and was condemned to death by Athens. He himself never returned to the city but one legend has him eventually committing suicide so that his family could return to their home town.*

Theobald

The one-legged Master of the East Indiaman *Seringapatam*, a former naval colleague of Jack Aubrey in HMS *Orion* (HMS 8).

Théodule, St

A saint whose church lies near the Temple prison in Paris (SM 10,11).

> The Catholic Church has at least ten saints named Theodulus, all relatively obscure early martyrs or moral exemplars.

Theopompus

A classical figure discussed by Maturin and Graham (IM 10).

> Theopompus (378?–320? BC), a highly regarded Greek historian, is best known for his (now largely lost) Hellenica, a continuation of *Thucydides' history of Greece, and for his Philippica, a 58-volume account of the times and achievements of King Philip I of Macedon (the father of *Alexander), a work that exists today only in numerous fragments.

Theresa of Avila, Saint

A saint known personally to a distant ancestor of Maturin (LM 2).

> Saint Teresa of Avila (1515–1582), a Spanish Carmelite nun and author canonized in 1621, was renowned for her mystic visions of God's love.

Theseus, HMS

A ship in which Jack Aubrey had once been Third Lieutenant (M&C 3; DI 7; IM 2) and which had served in Sir Sidney Smith's squadron at the Battle of Acre (TH 5). She is also mentioned several times in passing (DI 6; IM 5; LM 9).

> HMS Theseus, 74-gun, was launched in 1786. Under her Captain Ralph Willett Miller (d.1799) she was *Nelson's flagship off Cadiz in 1797 (when the great man lost his arm in an assault on Tenerife) and in 1798 took part in his victory at the Nile. In the following year she was present at *Smith's successful defence of Acre against General *Buonaparte but Miller himself was killed in an accidental explosion on the ship just a few days before the siege was lifted. After a subsequent career largely spent on blockade duty, Theseus was broken up in 1814. The ship was named for the native hero of ancient Athens, with a role in almost every early legend of the city.

Thetis

1: a ship referred to by the First Lord of the Admiralty (HMS 1).

> El Thetis, a Spanish 40-gun frigate laden with great quantities of treasure, was captured off the coast of Spain by a Royal Navy squadron in 1799 (see *Collins # 1). The following day the same squadron took her similarly rich companion, *Santa Brigida. (N.B., the reference in HMS 1 to there being some doubt over the legitimacy of these actions remains obscure to me, as both ships were routinely condemned, making the capturing crews temporarily affluent and their officers wealthy for life). In Greek myth, Thetis was a sea-nymph, the wife of Peleus and the mother of *Achilles.

2: a French ship once fought by HMS *Amethyst* with *Surprise's* Lieutenant Davidge aboard (C/T 2).

> Thétis, 40-gun, was launched in 1788. In November 1808, under her Captain Jacques Pinsum, she was forced to strike by Michael *Seymour's 38-gun HMS *Amethyst after a particularly bloody night-action during which three-quarters of the Frenchmen were killed or wounded. The captured ship was taken into the Royal Navy as HMS Brune, reduced to a troopship in 1810 and sold in 1838.

Thetis, HMS

A ship referred to by Jack Aubrey as one of several very desirable frigates into which he would like to be made Post (M&C 11). She is later mentioned several times in passing (PC 10,11; IM 6; COM 8).

> HMS Thetis, 38-gun, was launched in 1782 and, after a long if rather uneventful career, was sold in 1814.

Thévenot

The head of a French intelligence agency, possibly Lesueur's superior (TH 3).

Thomas

1: a seaman in HMS *Sophie* (M&C 9).

2: Miss Thomas, the unmarried sister of Mrs Williams (M&C 11).

3: the Williams family coachman and/or groom (PC 2).

4: the surgeon of HMS *Nymphe* (TH 9).

5: the Captain of HMS *Thames* (COM 4+), formerly of HMS *Eusebio* (COM 4), known in the service as the 'Purple Emperor' (or simply, 'Emperor') for his furious devotion to naval spit, polish and precedence (COM 4+). Jack Aubrey, his Commodore off Sierra Leone, regards him as incompetent (COM 5) and his crew are said eventually to be on the verge of mutiny (COM 9). From a family of slave owners and traders, he is by no means opposed to the practice the squadron are supposedly there to suppress (COM 7).

6: A seaman in HMS *Surprise* whose leg is amputated by Maturin and Jacob (HD 3).

Thomas, Moses

A seaman from the destroyed whaler *Intrepid Fox* (FSW 7).

Thompson

1: Maturin's assistant surgeon in HMS *Polychrest* (PC 10).

2: the gunroom steward in HMS *Surprise* (IM 9), possible the same man who later moves to in Jack Aubrey's temporary command, *Niobe* (TH 6).

3: an hotel-keeper at Gibraltar (HD 1,2).

Thompson, Thomas

A seaman in HMS *Sophie*, wounded in action (M&C 7).

Thomson
A Midshipman in HMS *Bellona*, the son of a Lieutenant in one of Jack Aubrey's former commands (YA 6).

Thorneycroft
A Lieutenant whom Jack Aubrey had wanted for HMS *Worcester* in place of the incompetent Mr Somers (IM 2).

Thornton
Admiral Saumarez' political advisor from the Foreign Office (SM 7,9).

Thornton, John
A Captain whom Jack Aubrey thinks may have taken himself out of the promotion stakes by becoming a Commissioner of a dockyard (YA 1).

Thornton, Admiral Sir John and Lady
The somewhat religious Commander-in-Chief of the Mediterranean fleet (IM 1–9) and his wife (IM 3,4). Old, worn out and now very ill, Thornton is determined to crown his career with a great fleet action (IM 4) but fails to bring the French to battle (IM 8). Initially furious with Jack Aubrey and William Babbington over what he sees as their failure at Medina, he soon comes to see that it was in fact his own second-in-command, Admiral Harte, who must bear most of the blame (IM 7). His frustrations and disappointments bring him to death's door (IM 9) and indeed he is soon reported to have passed away (TH 1; FSW 1).

Thorold, Jack
A seaman in HMS *Lion*, a noted boxer (YA 3).

Thrale, Mrs
A society figure who had married a Roman Catholic foreigner (M&C 4; COM 3).
> Mrs Hester Lynch Thrale (1741–1821) was a diarist and well known literary hostess, the close friend of Dr *Johnson. In 1784, three years after the death of her first husband, the wealthy brewing heir Thrale (see HD 9), she married Gabriel Piozzi, an Italian Catholic music teacher, causing great consternation to her many friends (she broke with Johnson over his reaction) and family, among the latter being her daughter Queeney Thrale, later Lady *Keith. Mrs Thrale's best-known works are Anecdotes of the late Samuel Johnson (1786) and Thraliana, a literary miscellany covering the period 1776–1809.

Three Brothers
1: a whaler met in the South Atlantic by HMS *Leopard* (DI 7).
2: a merchant ship, some of whose captured crew are forced to serve in Murad Reis' galley (HD 10).

Three Graces
A Liverpool merchantman in which Geary serves as surgeon (WDS 6).

Thucydides
The great classical historian (TH 6).
> Thucydides (460?–400? BC) was an Athenian historian who wrote an 8-volume account of the Peloponnesian War waged by Athens against Sparta from 431 to 404 BC, a war in which the author himself had fought as a relatively junior general. Thucydides' great work, renowned for its meticulous use of contemporary sources, was left incomplete as to events after 411, with several other sections showing signs of being finally compiled by an editor rather than the author himself.

Thunderer, HMS
A 74-gun in which Jack Aubrey had once served as a Lieutenant (M&C 1,3), Alexander Lushington as a Marine officer (SM 11) and William Grimshaw as a seaman (NC 4,5). She later carries Admiral Harte's flag in the Mediterranean, now with a reputation as an unhappy ship under her Captain Fellowes (IM 4; TH 1). Still under the same commander, she is afterwards met by *Surprise* and HMS *Berenice* at sea (COM 1).
> HMS Thunderer, 74-gun, was launched in 1783 and during her career fought in three famous fleet actions: Lord *Howe's victory at the Battle of the Glorious First of June in 1794 (under Captain Albemarle *Bertie); *Calder's indecisive pre–Trafalgar action in 1805 (under William Lechmere, d.1815 in the rank of Vice Admiral); and, just a few weeks later, at in *Nelson's great victory itself (under her First Lieutenant John Stockham (d.1814 in the rank of Captain), Lechmere having been sent home to give evidence at Calder's court-martial). Thunderer was broken up in 1814.

Thurlow, John
see **Ducks, Jemmy**

Thurlow
An East Indiaman in which John Robarts had served (FSW 3).
> Lord Thurlow, 805-tons, completed six voyages between England and India between 1789 and 1800. She was named for Lord Edward Thurlow (1732–1806), a British statesman and lawyer who served several times between 1778 and 1792 as Lord Chancellor.

Thurlows, the
A family who had given a dinner attended by Diana Villiers (IM 1).

Thursday
The name first contemplated for Sarah Sweeting (NC 8).

Thwaites
1: Mrs Thwaites, a lady who has died in childbirth near the Aubreys' home. She is perhaps the

local rector's wife, whose confinement is mentioned shortly beforehand (TMC 1).

2: a ship's boy in one of Captain Hanmer's commands who had lost his legs to a Red Sea shark (TH 2).

Thwaites, Joe
A seaman and boxer once beaten by Barret Bonden for the championship of the Mediterranean Fleet (YA 3).

Tiaro
The warrior Pakeea is said to be an under-chief of Tiaro (C/T 5).
*In the context, Tiaro looks like a slip for King *Tereo.*

Tia Udin
A character in a hunting tale told by Wan Da to Stephen Maturin (TGS 6).

Tib
A name initially contemplated for Mr Hollar's cat, Scourge (FSW 3).

Tibbets
The gunroom cook in HMS *Surprise* (FSW 3).

Tiberius
An Emperor whose reign Goodridge had studied in Tacitus (PC 10).
*Tiberius Claudius Nero (42 BC–37 AD) reigned as Emperor of Rome from 14 AD until his death. The step-son of the Emperor Augustus, Tiberius followed a distinguished career as a soldier before being made heir to the throne in 4 AD. In 26 he retired to the island of Capri (where he reputedly lived a life of the utmost debauchery), retaining the title of Emperor but never returning to Rome, where power was left in the hands of his infamous favourites, Sejanus and, later, Macro. On his death Tiberius was succeeded by *Caligula, his great-nephew.*

Tiddler, Tom
'Tom Tiddler's ground,' sailors' slang for a plentiful supply of stores (HMS 7; TMC 4; TGS 1).
'Tom Tiddler/Tickler/Tittler' is a children's game, a variant of 'king of the castle/hill' played to the refrain of, 'we're on Tom Tiddler's ground, picking up gold and silver!' OED records the earliest literary usage of the term as 1823 (of course, the phrase would have been in perfectly common parlance well before that date), with its transferred meaning of 'any place where goods are easily available' being common, especially in Charles Dickens, after 1848.

Tierney, Michael
An Irish seaman in HMS *Bellona* who had died off the African coast (COM 10).

Tiger, HMS
The former ship of Mr Allen, now Master of HMS *Surprise* (FSW 2).
*The reference may be either to the 50-gun HMS *Gram-*

pus, which was initially intended to be named Tiger, *or to HMS *Tigre, below.*

Tigre, HMS
A ship in Sir Sidney Smith's squadron at the Battle of Acre (TH 5).
HMS Tigre, *74-gun, was launched by the French in 1793 and captured by the Royal Navy in 1795. In 1799 she was Commodore Sir Sidney Smith's pennant-ship in the eastern Mediterranean, and in 1805, now under Captain Benjamin *Hallowell, she was one of those ships unlucky enough to miss the great victory at Trafalgar, being part of *Louis' small squadron sent for supplies to Gibraltar shortly before the battle.* Tigre *was broken up in 1817.*

Tillotson, Archbishop
The author of sermons typically preached by Mr Martin (IM 5; TH 5).
*John Tillotson (1630–1694), originally a *Calvinist who had married a niece of Oliver *Cromwell, later converted to the Church of England and rose to become Archbishop of Canterbury in 1691. Tillotson's sermons, immensely popular both in his own time and for many years afterwards, were regarded as models of lucidity and common-sense, standing in some contrast to the metaphysical rhetoric of many of his contemporaries.*

Timely, Mr
The bosun of HMS *Superb* (M&C 11).

Timmins, Wm
A Gosport clockmaker (IM 7).

Tindall, Mr
Sophia Williams' piano-teacher (PC 2).

Tippoo Sahib
The Indian Prince in a battle with whom both Diana Villiers' first husband and father had been killed (PC 1).
*Fateh Ali Tippu (1750?–1799), a.k.a. 'Tippu Sahib,' was the son of Hyder Ali, ruler of Mysore. Trained as a military officer by his father's French allies, between 1767 and 1782 he several times won victories over both the rival Maratha peoples and British armies. Having succeeded his father in 1782, he adopted the title of Sultan and in 1784 made peace with Britain. However, by 1789 he was back at war with his former foes and in 1792, on the verge of total defeat, was forced to cede half of his territory to Britain and her allies. Tippu Sahib had retained many contacts with the French and these soon proved his downfall for, once his negotiations with revolutionary Paris became known to Governor-General *Lord Mornington (the brother of the future Duke of *Wellington, who also made a great name for himself in this campaign), an all-out assault was launched, Tippu being soon killed at the head of his own troops.*

Tiresias
A character in Homer referred to by Maturin (FSW 9).
*Tiresias was the legendary, foremost seer of ancient Greece, closely associated with the city of Thebes. Blinded after catching a forbidden glimpse of the goddess *Athena*

bathing naked, the gift of prophecy had then being given to him in compensation. In *Homer, the ghost of Tiresias is consulted by the Greek hero *Odysseus.

Titian

An artist whose work has just been bought for the Keith's house in Bath (HMS 4).

Tiziano Vecellio (1488?–1576), the great Italian painter of portraits and mythological or religious scenes, is one of those relatively few artists not only to have achieved a towering reputation in his own lifetime but also never to have had that reputation in any way diminish in the centuries following his death. Spending almost his entire creative career in Venice (having been born just to the north of the city), Titian maintained to the very end of his life a prodigious output, always of supreme quality.

Tito

The title character of Mozart's *La Clemenza di Tito* (TGS 4).

*Mozart's opera is very loosely based on the Roman Emperor Titus' affair with the Berenice, the daughter of the King of Judea; it was first given in 1791, with the first London performance taking place in 1806. Titus (39–81 AD) was the son and successor, in 79, of Vespasian. A famously talented artist and singer (as well as an able general), Titus' short but popular reign was marked by private benevolence and great public works. There is another passing reference to Titus in the series: in SM 9 a guest at a dinner mutters 'non olet' ('it doesn't stink') in reponse to Admiral *Saumarez's remark on 'filthy lucre.' Titus is said once to have accused his father of being excessively grasping in having imposed a tax on the use of public urinals. The gruff old Vespasian then thrust a gold coin under the son's nose and asked him if he felt sick; when the young man, a famous spendthrift, replied that he did not, the father growled, 'so it comes from piss, boy, but doesn't stink?.'

Titus

The yeoman of the signals in HMS *Nutmeg of Consolation* (NC 6).

Titus Oates

The name used by *Surprise* when she disguises herself as an old whaler (C/T 9).

see **Oates, Titus** *for the name derivation.*

Toby

see **Raphael, Archangel**

Tolland

A court short-hand reporter (RM 8).

Tolly, Barclay de

see **Barclay de Tolly**

Tolson, Mr

A member of the London Entomological Society (HMS 1).

Tom

1: a carpenter's mate in HMS *Sophie* (M&C 2).
2: the hall-porter at the Admiralty (PC 6) who

moves Jack Aubrey's epaulette from his left to his right shoulder, thus marking his promotion from Commander to junior Post-Captain (PC 12).

Jack Aubrey's observation, that Tom's claim to have performed this service for Lord *Nelson himself cannot be true, is based on Nelson's having been made Post in 1779 by Admiral Sir Peter Parker whilst on the Jamaica station.

3: a seaman in a lugger that carries Maturin from Spain to England (PC 14).
4: a coachman (HMS 4).
5: Babbington's steward in HMS *Oedipus* (SM 11).
6: the hall-porter at Black's Club (RM 4,5), later said to be Head Porter (TGS 4).
7: Admiral Lord Keith's coxswain (YA 10).
8: a seaman in HMS *Surprise* (HD 4).
9: *see* **Christy, Tom**
10: *see* **Dalgleish, Tom**
11: *see* **Pullings, Tom**

Tomboy

A horse belonging to Diana Villiers (C/T 3).

Tom Cribb

A cannon in *Surprise* (LM 2) and HMS *Diane* (TGS 5).

see **Cribb, Tom** *for the name derivation.*

'Tom Fool'

A reference by Jack Aubrey to idiocy (HMS 2).

OED records the first literary usage of 'tom' for a 'clown' as being in 1820, though of course the term is likely to have been in common spoken use well before that date.

Tomkinson

The First Lieutenant of HMS *Otter*, promoted her Commander when Jack Aubrey makes Lord Clonfert Post into HMS *Néréide* (TMC 4). Later, whilst *Otter* is under repair, he is offered, but declines, the temporary command of the armed Indiaman, *Windham* (TMC 8).

James Tomkinson (dates unknown), a Lieutenant of 1805, was promoted Commander of HMS *Otter in March 1810 (as a reward for brave service as First Lieutenant of HMS Comet in 1808). Although JAMES notes his declining the command of Windham, this does not appear to have adversely affected his career (as Jack *Aubrey perhaps feels it should), for he was soon made acting Captain of the 32-gun HMS Ceylon (see *Bombay, HMS) and, in 1819, made Post.

Tompion

The maker of a clock in Black's Club (LM 4).

Thomas Tompion (1639–1713), known as the 'father of English watchmaking,' was equally distinguished for his very much rarer clocks. He was an innovator and craftsman of great international reputation.

Tompkins, Albert and Mr

Albert Tompkins, a Midshipmen in HMS *Cambridge*, had stolen a watch from the Master of a prize and has now been sentenced by Admiral Ives to both demotion and humiliating punishment, this despite the fact that his father is an Admiralty lawyer in Malta (FSW 1).

The incident exactly mirrors the punishment meted out to an errant Midshipman by Lord *St Vincent in 1798.

'Tom Postman'

The name used by the Williams family for the local mail deliverer (PC 3).

'Tom Tiddler'
see **Tiddler, Tom**

Tone, Wolfe

A Protestant United Irishman. In the vain hope of diffusing a growing tension between the Irish Lieutenant, James Dillon, and his English Captain, Jack Aubrey, Stephen Maturin tells Jack that many United Irishmen were well-educated Protestants and not merely 'Catholic rebels,' as Jack might have supposed (M&C 3,6).

*Theobald Wolfe Tone (1763–1798), an Irish Protestant lawyer, political activist and rebel, was born in Dublin and educated at the city's Trinity College and, later, in London. A descendent of one of *Cromwell's settler-soldiers, as a young man he had an ardent, yet thwarted, desire to join his brother, William, in the British East India Company's army and there to make his fortune as a '*nabob.' Indeed, he and William (who eventually died on active service in India in 1802) had once proposed to the British Government a somewhat ramshackle scheme for the military colonization of the South Seas, only to have it brusquely rejected. In 1790 Tone began to agitate in Ireland for both political reform and Catholic emancipation, soon developing the doctrine — most unusual and rather unpopular at the time but later central to Irish nationalist thought — that his home country should be completely independent of England, the land from whose rule he had come to believe that all her woes sprang. Under the heady inspiration of the events in France from 1789 onwards, Tone formed the United Irish Society with Thomas Russell and Napper *Tandy in about 1791. In 1795 he was forced into exile in the USA but by 1796 was in France to solicit military and financial aid for an Irish rebellion. In the following year he then played an active role (as a newly-appointed general in the French Army) in *Hoche's abortive French invasion of Bantry Bay but, in the equally unsuccessful 1798 invasion, was then captured by Sir John Borlase *Warren's (see **Warne, Admiral**) squadron aboard a French warship, the 74-gun Hoche. Tried and condemned to death, Tone attempted suicide in prison and, after a week's agony, died of his throat-wound. He remains the most famous of the Irish revolutionaries of the end of the 19th century, partly on account of his passionate and articulate proposals for complete Irish independence from English rule and partly because of the attractive and witty character revealed in his diaries.*

Tonnant, HMS

The ship in which Midshipman Ricketts had nominally served (M&C 2), whose later appearance in company with HMS *Colossus* forces the French-cap-

tured *Lord Nelson* Indiaman to strike to the little HMS *Seagull* (PC 5). We later learn that the young Jack Aubrey had, long ago, seen from her decks three HMS *Bounty* mutineers being hanged on HMS *Brunswick* (DI 1).

HMS Tonnant, 80-guns, was launched as the French Tonnant in 1789, and captured by *Nelson's fleet at the Battle of the Nile in 1798 (her Captain Aristide Dupetit-Thouars (1760–1798) fighting her, at the last, propped up in a tub of bran, having had both arms and an leg shot away) At the time of the Lord Nelson action, in late August 1803, she was commanded by Sir Edward *Pellew, who held her until late 1805, when she was given to Charles Tyler (1760–1835; a full Admiral of 1825). Under the latter, Tonnant fought in the thick of the action at Trafalgar, the Captain being severely wounded quite early in the fight. Up until the end of her career in 1821, she was then commanded by a number of well-known men, including Edward *Codrington and Edward Pelham *Brenton.

Tooke, Horne

A literary figure and friend of Louisa Wogan (DI 4,6).

John Horne Tooke (1736–1812) was a radical politician, an enthusiastic supporter (until a later falling out) of John *Wilkes. For a time after 1801, Tooke represented the famously 'rotten' borough of Old Sarum in Wiltshire, a constituency almost entirely without genuine voters. Tooke's literary reputation is based partly on his fame as a conversationalist and partly on his Diversions of Purley (1786–1805), a work of speculative philology that enjoyed great popularity in its day but which lacked any of the systematic approaches to the formation of language that characterised the burgeoning discipline in continental Europe.

Topaz, HMS

A ship in which Mr Whewell had served under Captain Dick Harrison (COM 7).

The 38-gun Topaze (sic) was launched by the French in 1790 and handed over to the Royal Navy in 1793 by the Royalists in Toulon. She was sold out of the service in 1814.

Torgud

A 30-gun Turkish frigate in the Ionian Sea, the main force of Captain-Bey Mustapha's very small squadron (IM 9–11). Under his command, she and her smaller consort, *Kitabi*, are engaged and defeated by Jack Aubrey's HMS *Surprise*, with *Torgud* being sunk and *Kitabi* captured (IM 11; TH 1,5; HD 1).

see also **Seahorse, HMS**

Torquemada

The Grand Inquisitor, one of whose distant family, Sor Luisa, was a childhood guardian of Stephen Maturin (NC 1).

Tomas de Torquemada (1420–1498), a Dominican monk, was made Inquisitor-General of Spain in 1483, becoming infamous for the both quantity and quality of his cruel persecution of religious opponents.

Tortoise

A transport ship escorted to Trieste by Aubrey's HMS *Surprise* (TH 9).

Tournajibashi

Ismail Bey's Keeper of the Cranes (IM 10).

Towser

A cannon in HMS Surprise (RM 3; C/T 8).

Towser has long been a popular English name for an especially large dog and has also come to mean any big, strong, hard-working fellow.

Trabucayres, the

A family of bandits (PC 4).

Trade's Increase

1: a merchantman with which HMS *Polychrest* collides (PC 9).

2: a merchant ship, some of whose captured crew are forced to serve in Murad Reis' galley (HD 10).

Travers, Jill

A sail-maker's wife who had served in Jack Aubrey's HMS *Bellona* (HD 2).

See also **Defiance, HMS**

Treacher

Sir Joseph Blaine's manservant (YA 1).

Trecothic, Henry

A quartermaster who had once sailed under Jack Aubrey, now manning a signal station on Réunion (TMC 9).

Trémarec

The French discoverer of Desolation Island (DI 9).

Yves-Joseph de Kerguélen-Trémarec (1734–1797) was a French naval officer and navigator who between 1771 and 1774 led two expeditions to the South Seas, discovering the remote and barren Antarctic islands know known as the Iles de Kerguélen, the largest of which is often called Desolation Island. On his return to France, he was prosecuted both for fraud and for having taken a young lady friend on the voyage. Dismissed the Royal service and briefly imprisoned, he later took up a career as a privateer before returning to naval service — as a Rear Admiral — from 1793 to 1796.

Tremendous, HMS

A 74-gun commanded by Jack Aubrey's friend, Edward Smith (TGS 1).

HMS Tremendous, 74-gun, was launched in 1784 and ten years later fought in Lord *Howe's great victory at the Battle of the Glorious First of June. In 1810 she was remodelled with *Seppings' system of diagonal bracing (hitherto only used on a very limited scale), a rebuild so successful that it was widely copied throughout the Navy for both repairs and new construction. In 1845 Tremendous was reduced to a 50-gun and renamed HMS Gram-

pus, before becoming a powder hulk in 1856 and finally being sold as late as 1897.

Trevor, Miss Anne

A lady who dines at Diana Villiers' London home (IM 1).

Although 'Anne Trevor' is scarcely an unusual name, it may perhaps have been inspired by its being the maiden name of the Countess of Mornington, the mother of both the Duke of *Wellington and his elder brother, the Earl of Mornington and Marquis Wellesley (see ***Lord Mornington***).*

Trilling

A seaman in *Surprise* (C/T 2).

Trimble

A neighbour of Aubrey and Maturin in Sussex (PC 1).

Triton

The classical figure, famous for swimming ability (TH 5; FSW).

In Greek myth, Triton was a son of *Neptune, half-fish and half-man.

Triton

An 30-gun English letter-of-marque, Captain Goffin, sailing in company with *Surprise* and then met at sea by Jack Aubrey and his HMS *Nutmeg of Consolation* (NC 6,7).

Triton, HMS

A ship referred to by Aubrey as one of several very desirable frigates into which he would like to be made Post (M&C 11).

This ship is something of a curious desire for Jack *Aubrey for HMS Triton, 32-gun, was launched in 1796 but, being experimentally fir-built, was soon found unseaworthy and, in 1800, sent for harbour service. She was sold in 1814.

Trollope

1: a Lieutenant in Jack Aubrey's HMS *Boadicea* (TMC 2+) who had been a Midshipman in HMS *Amelia* when Jack had HMS *Sophie* (TMC 2). He is later struck down by sunstroke (TMC 10).

2: a Marine in HMS *Surprise* (FSW 9).

Tromp, HMS

A Dutch-built 54-gun ship, Captain Billy Holroyd, met by HMS *Surprise* at sea (NC 8).

HMS Tromp, 60-gun, was captured from the Dutch in 1796. However, she had already been sent for harbour service in 1799 (well before NC is set), being finally sold in 1815. She was named for Admiral Marten Harpertzoon Tromp (1597–1653), the Dutch seaman renowned for both skill and courage.

Trotter

1: according to Mr Brown of the Port Mahon dockyard, an officer made Post chiefly for his frugality with ship's stores and equipment (M&C 2).

The name is possibly inspired by John Trotter (1757–1833) who, as a private businessman, won a monopoly for the maintenance of British Army supply stores lasting from 1787 to 1807. In that latter year the lucrative trade was 'nationalised' and Trotter was then appointed official Storekeeper-General of the Army. His nephew, Henry Dundas Trotter (1802–1859), entered the Royal Navy, eventually rising to flag rank.

2: a medical friend of Stephen Maturin (HMS 4,5).

*The reference is probably to Dr Thomas Trotter (1760–1832), who first entered the Navy in 1779 as a surgeon's mate. After a spell in the merchant service (on board a slaver, a period that turned him into an ardent abolitionist), in 1788 he took his M.D. degree at Edinburgh and soon rejoined the Royal Navy, being one of only four men in the service at that time with a physician's degree. In 1793 Trotter became a staff member at the Haslar Naval Hospital and was soon appointed by Lord *Howe as Physician of his Channel Fleet (and was thus present at the Battle of the Glorious First of June, later giving a detailed report of the casualties), a post he held under various Admirals until his retirement in 1802. He is best recalled for his* Medicina Nautica, *a medical— though not surgical— text and report, first published in three volumes between 1797 and 1803. Throughout his career Trotter was a tireless activist for improvements both in the health of seamen and in the status of naval surgeons.*

3: a seaman in HMS *Surprise* familiar with Yankee ports (WDS 5).

Troubridge, Admiral

A British commander notable for having risen from humble birth (DI 4).

*Sir Thomas Troubridge (sometimes 'Trowbridge'; 1758–1807), the son of a London baker, entered the Royal Navy in 1773 and soon made the acquaintance of the young Horatio *Nelson, one of whose 'Band of Brothers' he was later to become. Made Post in 1783, he later commanded HMS *Culloden at the Battle of Cape *St Vincent in 1797 and took her to Nelson's great victory at the Battle of the Nile in the following year. Here, unfortunately, his ship grounded on shoals before she could ever get into action and consequently missed the entire fight. A member of the Admiralty Board from 1801 to 1804, in that latter year Troubridge was promoted Rear Admiral and, in 1805, given a command in the East Indies. In 1807, whilst sailing from the Cape to Madras in the decrepit 74-gun HMS* Blenheim, *Troubridge, his *Flag Captain Austin Bissell (see *Racoon, HMS), and all hands were lost in a great storm. A son, Sir Edward Thomas Troubridge (d.1852), married a daughter of Sir Alexander *Cochrane and, in 1847, himself rose to Rear Admiral's rank.*

True Blue

A cannon in HMS *Surprise* (RM 3).

Truelove

A British whaler, Master William Hardy, held captive at Moahu by Kalahua and his French allies (C/T 5,8). Soon retaken by Jack Aubrey's *Surprise*,

she is sent to Batavia under acting Lieutenant Billy Oakes (C/T 9; WDS 1).

The fifteenth novel of the O'Brian's series was first published as Clarissa Oakes *in the United Kingdom and then, purely for marketing reasons, as* The Truelove *in the USA.*

Tullidge

The First Lieutenant of HMS *Africaine*, wounded in action against *Vénus* and *Victor*. With Forder and Parker, Tullidge had earlier asked Surgeon Cotton whether Captain Corbett might be relieved on the grounds of insanity (TMC 9). After Corbett's death in battle, he assumes command of the ship but is soon forced to strike to the French (TMC 9).

*Joseph Crew Tullidge (d.1845) entered the Royal Navy in 1793 as an ordinary seaman in HMS *Victory. He later rose on merit alone to Midshipman and, in 1800, was commissioned Lieutenant. Shortly after his 1810 defence of HMS *Africaine, during which he was four times wounded, Tullidge became First Lieutenant of Commodore Josias Rowley's HMS* America; *he was then promoted Commander in the following year. During the 'Hundred Days' of *Buonaparte's return in 1815, Tullidge and his sloop HMS* Clinker *ran the Duc de Douro, 200 Royalist officers and a large quantity of arms across to the French coast in support of King Louis XVIII. For these and other services, he then spent the rest of his life advancing a claim to further promotion and eventually, in 1842, was placed on the list of superannuated Post Captains.*

Tully

see **Cicero**

Tupac Amaru

An Inca who had recently led an unsuccessful uprising in Peru (WDS 9).

José Gabriel Condorcanqui (1740?–1781) was a wealthy and well-educated descendent of the last Inca ruler of Peru, Tupac Amaru, who had been executed in 1571. When Condorcanqui then led his own rebellion against direct Spanish rule, he was given the former Emperor's name by his followers. The revolt was unsuccessful and in 1781 the new Tupac Amaru was captured, hideously tortured and then executed along with his entire immediate family.

Tupec

A colleague of Maturin's Andean guide, Eduardo (WDS 9).

Turbid

A Greek sponge fisherman (a.k.a. 'Sponge'), now a seaman in HMS *Sophie* (M&C 3,6).

Turd, M.

An abusive nickname for Jean Dutourd (WDS 4).

Turkey, Sultan of

The ruler of the Turkish Ottoman Empire, whose mother is said to be French (IM 9–11; TH 2,5,7; COM 3). Jack Aubrey receives from him a valuable and striking diamond *chelengk* for his defeat of the rebel Mustapha Bey (TH 1). Later, the Sultan seems ready to ally himself with the newly restored Buonaparte (HD 1,6).

At the time Jack Aubrey is engaged in Turkish affairs (nominally 1813–1815) the Sultan of Turkey was Mahmud IV (1785–1839), ruler of the Ottoman Empire from 1808 until his death. With a reputation as a moderately liberal reformer at home, Mahmud's foreign policy was largely concerned with attempting to manage the decline of the span of his Empire, as the Balkans and Greece gradually won their independence and the Levant and Egypt moved towards virtual autonomy (see also *Codrington). However, some of the incidents and references in the text are rather more to the activities of Mahmud's immediate predecessors, his reactionary elder brother Mustafa IV (1779–1808), Sultan from 1807 until being deposed and strangled by Mahmud in mid-1808, and their cousin, Selim III (1761–1808), ruler from 1789 until 1807, when he was overthrown, and later murdered, by Mustafa. It was Selim who was said to have had a French mother, supposedly a high-born Provençal beauty, captured by Algerian pirates and sold into slavery. After a short spell as a British ally (it was he who in 1799 had awarded Sir Sidney *Smith a chelengk for the defence of Acre), in about 1803 Selim, always a Francophile in terms of culture and intellect, fell under *Buonaparte's personal spell, thereafter shifting several times between Imperial associate and uneasy neutral.

Turnbull

1: a Lieutenant in HMS *Leopard* (DI 3–9), of whose skills Jack Aubrey has a very low opinion (DI 4,8). When *Leopard* is holed by an iceberg,

Turnbull is one of those who leaves in the boats led by First Lieutenant Grant (DI 9) but, curiously, Jack later tells Admiral Drury that, of the ward-room officers, only Grant, Fisher and Benton had abandoned ship, neglecting to mention either Turnbull or Larkin, the Master (FW 1).

2: the Marine Lieutenant in HMS *Pomone* (HD 5).

Turnbull, Dick

A seaman in HMS *Surprise* who had cut free a shipmate's entangled pig-tail (HMS 6).

Turnbull, Harry

A former First Lieutenant of HMS *Agamemnon*, later killed at the Battle of the Nile (TMC 2).

Turnbull, Harry and Lucy

Two cousins of Jack Aubrey, married to each other. Harry, an MP, chairs the committee that rejects Captain Griffith's land enclosure proposals; Lucy was formerly Miss Brett (YA 3).

Tyndall

A senior Master's Mate in HMS *Bellona* (COM 9).

Tyrant, the

Napoleon Buonaparte, as referred to in Jack Aubrey's recruiting poster for HMS *Polychrest* (PC 7).

U

Ullastret, d'

see **Casademon, Ramon d'Ullastret**

Ulrike

Diana Villiers' maidservant in Sweden (LM 9).

Ulusan

The English-speaking subordinate of Capitan-Bey Mustapha (IM 10), who surrenders the defeated *Torgud* to Jack Aubrey's HMS *Surprise* (IM 11).

Ulysses

The cunning, warrior-hero of Homer's *Odyssey* (FW 1; SM 6; FSW 4,10), guessed at by Jack Aubrey as notorious for having mistreated Dido (TH 9).

Ulysses (in Latin Ulixes, in Greek, Odysseus), King of Ithaca, is one of the main heroes of *Homer's Iliad, in which he is shown as the most resourceful and diplomatic of the Greek leaders. Later the central character in the great poet's Odyssey, he is now portrayed, during his long journey home after the Trojan war, as a sly trickster; although ultimately, on his return to his Queen Penelope,

Ulysses still turns out to be the ideal king, wise and strong. Jack *Aubrey has somewhere in his mind the tale of the abandonment of Queen *Dido by *Aeneas, son of *Anchises.

Undaunted, HMS

The frigate, Captain Tom Ussher, that takes Buonaparte into exile on Elba (YA 10).

HMS Undaunted, 38-gun, was launched in 1807, then spending most of her war-service in the Mediterranean fleet. Given to Thomas *Ussher in 1813, she embarked the newly-abdicated Emperor Napoleon *Buonaparte at Fréjus on April 28th 1814 and then delivered him to his new, miniature island-kingdom of Elba on May 4th. Reduced to a gunnery target ship in 1856, Undaunted was finally broken up in 1860.

Undertaker, Khowasjee

A wealthy Parsee merchant and mathematical philosopher met by Maturin in Bombay (HMS 7).

Unité
see **Surprise**, HMS

United Kingdom
A merchantman taken by *Vénus* and *Manche* (TMC 5).

> United Kingdom, *an 820-ton British East India Company ship launched in 1801, was captured by the French in November 1809 and retaken at Mauritius by Admiral *Bertie's squadron in December 1810.*

United States, USS
A new American frigate, heavier than anything possessed by the Royal Navy (FW 2), that takes HMS *Macedonian* (FW 3; FSW 3).

> USS United States, *44-gun, one of the 'six original frigates' of the US Navy, was launched in 1797. Under Stephen Decatur, she took HMS *Macedonian off the Canary Islands in late October 1812, completely out-gunning her opponent in a brisk action. After the end of the war against England in early 1815, she then several times served as the flagship of the U.S. Mediterranean squadron. In 1861 the by-now scarcely seaworthy United States was captured at Norfolk Navy Yard by Confederate forces and used as a receiving ship; re-taken by the Union in the following year, she was scrapped in 1864.*

Upex
A senior Master's Mate in HMS *Bellona* (COM 9).

Upjohn
A seaman in HMS *Surprise* who had previously been confined as a lunatic on Gibraltar (FSW 6).

Ussher, Bishop
A source used by Goodridge for the dates of comets (PC 10).

> James Usher or Ussher (1580–1656), *an Irish scholar and churchman, became Professor of Divinity at Trinity College, Dublin, in 1607 and Archbishop of Armagh (and thus Protestant Primate of All Ireland) in 1624. Amongst his many works are the* Annals of the Old and New Testament *and a* Sacred Chronology. *After 1640 he lived exclusively in England, having been burned out of his home by Catholic rebels.*

Ussher, Tom
The Irish Captain of HMS *Undaunted*, an ex-shipmate of Jack Aubrey (YA 10).

> Sir Thomas Ussher (1779–1848), *a son of the great Irish astronomer Henry Ussher (d.1790), was commissioned Lieutenant in 1797 and soon made a fine reputation for himself by leading dashing small-boat attacks on coastal cannon-batteries, a practice he continued throughout his sea-career. Promoted Commander in 1806 and Post Captain in 1808, Ussher took command of HMS *Undaunted in 1813 and in late April of the following year conveyed the Emperor Napoleon *Buonaparte to his first exile on Elba. Knighted in 1831, he published in 1841 an account of his brief dealings with the fallen Emperor. Although he saw no sea-service after 1814, Ussher was promoted Rear Admiral by seniority in 1846.*

Usurper, the
Napoleon Buonaparte, as referred to in Jack Aubrey's recruiting poster for HMS *Polychrest* (PC 7).

Utile, HMS
A sloop that founders off Malta (M&C 11).

> In November 1801 HMS Utile, *16-gun brig-sloop, was sent under Commander Edward Jeykll Canes from Malta to Minorca with a very large sum of money for the payment of garrison wages. Shortly after leaving Malta she disappeared, presumed to have foundered with the loss of all hands. N.B., British sources usually identify this* Utile *as being a French privateer of the same name taken in 1799 by Sir Richard *Keats' HMS *Boadicea, but VICHOT states that two* Utiles *were taken by the English in 1799, with the ship that foundered in 1801 being taken not by* Boadicea *but by another, unknown ship on an unspecified date.*

Uzès, Madame d'
A lady who attends Maturin's lecture in Paris (SM 5).

V

Vaggers, Mr and **Mrs**
An elderly, highly experienced, Sethian ex-smuggler who serves under Jack Aubrey in *Surprise* (LM 5; NC 7) and HMS *Bellona* (COM 5). Mrs Vaggers remains in their home town of Shelmerston (COM 5).

Valençay
> Not in fact the name of a person, but rather a generic term for Talleyrand-Périgord's organisation, derived from his main place of residence (SM 11).

Valentinius
The founder of a Gnostic sect that Martin believes to be the remote origin of the Sethians (LM 5).

> Valentinius (d.160?) *was an Egyptian Christian mystic and famous Gnostic, for which doctrinal 'error' he was excommunicated in 140. The Gnostics, a loose school of heretical Christians who first became widely known in the 2nd century, claimed that *Jesus Christ had left a secret store of written knowledge (in Greek,* gnosis) *concerning the perpetual struggle between the forces of light and dark.*

Vancouver

An officer referred to somewhat unfavourably by Stephen Maturin as Captain Cook's successor (LM 8).

George Vancouver (1/58–1798) was an English navigator and explorer who had started his naval career as one of *Cook's Midshipmen, serving on the latter's first and second voyages to the South Seas. Commissioned Lieutenant in 1780 and made Commander in 1790, Vancouver's high reputation for seamanship and surveying was offset by his cold, often brutal ship-board discipline. Made Post in 1794, his A Voyage of Discovery to the North Pacific Ocean, 1790–1795 *was published shortly after his death. Vancouver Island is named for his confirmation there was in fact a clear passage between it and the Canadian mainland.*

Van Da

see **Wan Da**

Vandamme

A passing reference to a French General (SM 5).

Dominique-Joseph-René Vandamme (1770–1830), Comte d'Unsebourg, was one of *Buonaparte's most active and loyal soldiers, fighting in at least 18 major battles since first promoted General in 1793, including service under the returned Emperor during the 'Hundred Days' of early 1815. During his career he also acquired a well-deserved reputation as a foul-mouthed brigand, being suspended three times for theft and financial irregularities; when briefly taken prisoner by the Russians in 1813, he supposedly responded to the *Czar's charge of looting with a riposte of, 'Well at least no-one has accused me of killing my father!'

Vanguard, HMS

Nelson's flagship at the Battle of the Nile (TH 4).

HMS Vanguard, *74-gun, was launched in 1787. From 1794 to 1795 she was commanded by Charles *Sawyer, the notorious groper of young seamen. In April 1798 Rear Admiral *Nelson raised his flag in her, now with Edward *Berry as his *Flag Captain, but a few weeks later she was severely damaged in a gale off Toulon and had to limp to shelter in Sardinia. In a spendid feat of resourcefulness, Berry had her fighting-fit again by the beginning of June and was thus able to carry Nelson to his great victory at the Battle of the Nile on August 1st. When Berry was sent off with the victory dispatch, Commander Thomas Hardy (later of HMS *Victory at Trafalgar; see* ***Mutine, HMS** *for a note on his career) was made Post into her. Vanguard was reduced to a prison ship in 1812 and a powder hulk two years later, being broken up in 1821.*

Van John

A card game (DI 1).

Van John is an anglicised corruption of vingt-un, *a.k.a. 'blackjack.' Although the game was popular in England from at least the mid-18th century, OED gives the date of the first literary use of the term 'Van John' as 1853.*

Vargas

An agent who had been tortured and killed by Dubreuil (FW 7).

Vasa

The 'legitimate' Swedish Royal Family, referred to by Blaine (LM 4).

The family name comes from Gustavus Vasa, King Gustav I of Sweden from 1527. When the direct heir of King Charles XIII died in 1809, the Swedish Diet elected the French General *Bernadotte heir to the throne, favouring him over more distant Vasa family members.

Vauban

The military architect whose forts lie all over France (PC 10).

Sébastian le Prestre de Vauban (1633–1707) was King *Louis XIV's great military engineer. From a background lacking both education and cultural sophistication, Vauban made his early reputation as an aggressive siege engineer before turning his immensely practical talents to the design and construction of forts, fortified towns and castles all over France and its newly conquered territories. *Voltaire and others regarded Vauban as a new type of 'Enlightenment' public servant, distant by choice from the sycophancy of the Court yet wholly dedicated to the cause of his country: indeed the word 'citoyen'— in its sense of 'model citizen' rather than 'loyal subject'— was first coined to refer to him.

Vaux, John

An officer who had distinguished himself at the capture and fortification of the Diamond Rock some years previously, and is now made Post into HMS *Pomone* (HD 3–5).

Vauxhall

see **Raneleagh**

Veale

A seaman in *Surprise*, injured during a volcanic explosion in the South Seas (WDS 1).

Veale, Colonel

An acquaintance of Professor Graham in Malta (TH 3).

Vega, Garcilasso de la

An author in whom Maturin had read of the powers of coca leaves (FSW 5).

Garcilasso de la Vega, 'El Inca,' (1530?–1616?), born in Cuzco to one of *Pizarro's captains and an Inca princess, collected materials for a history of Peru and, in about 1560, obtained a salary from King Philip II of Spain to produce his Authentic History of the Origins of the Incas, *still an important source-work. He later wrote an account of the Spanish conquest of Florida.*

Vega

A London whaler from which Captain Palmer of USS *Norfolk* falsely claims to have news of the end of war between Britain and the USA (FSW 9,10).

Venable

The commander of a transport ship expected at

Kutali but intercepted by Capitan-Bey Mustapha (IM 11).

Vencejo

The previous name of HMS *Sophie* (M&C 2).

The Spanish 16-gun brig El *Vincejo was taken by the 20-gun HMS Cormorant *in 1799, war against Spain having been declared in 1796. Re-named HMS* Vincejo, *she and her Commander *Wright were re-captured by the French in Quiberon Bay in 1804. Possibly then re-named* Martinet *(VICHOT is unclear), she was sold in 1805. Also see* **Sophie, HMS**

Venerable, HMS

A 74-gun ship of Saumarez' squadron (M&C 12) in which Phelps of HMS *Worcester* had once served (IM 2).

HMS Venerable, *74-gun, was launched in 1784. She was *Duncan's flag-ship in his victory at the Battle of Camperdown in 1797 and fought under Samuel *Hood in Saumarez' 1801 actions off Gibraltar. In the second, successful action Venerable was badly battered and eventually grounded on shoals south of Cadiz, being then hauled off by HMSS *Caesar and *Spencer. In 1804 she was wrecked in heavy seas just off Torbay, drifting onto rocks when she tried to recover a Royal Marine who had fallen overboard. It is possible that Phelps served not in this ship but in her similar replacement, in service from 1808 to 1838.*

Vengeance

A ship that had badly damaged USS *Constellation*, being later herself taken by HMS *Seine* (FW 2).

Vengeance, 50-gun, was launched by the French in 1794 and, under her Captain F.M. Pitot, met Thomas Truxtrun's USS *Constellation off Guadaloupe in early 1800 (during the 'Quasi-War' of 1788–1801). After initially declining battle (for Vengeance was much encumbered by troops and passengers and also carrying a large quantity of gold back to France), Pitot was overhauled by the faster American and brought to action. The two ships battered each other for several hours until, just as she was about to try boarding, Constellation's mainmast collapsed and Vengeance was able to make off. American accounts of the battle report that Pitot had twice struck his flag during the long fight and was clearly beaten; French accounts regard the action as indecisive throughout, ending only when Constellation was too damaged to manoeuvre effectively (indeed, in his report, Pitot speculated that she may even have sunk). In August of that same year Vengeance was taken by David Milne's HMS *Seine in another long, evening action, this time fought off the coast of Puerto Rico. As the prison ship HMS Vengeance, she was badly damaged when stranded on shoals in 1801 and finally broken up in 1802.

Ventura, Bep

The owner of a Port Mahon warehouse (M&C 9).

Ventura

A slow mail-ship owned by Martinez, taken by the French *Murion* (M&C 11).

Venus

The subject of a side-show at an entertainment park (FW 7) and often a reference to sexual temptation (FW 8; SM 6; FSW 4; C/T 1; COM 1).

Venus was the Roman goddess of seduction and persuasion, primarily sexual but not always so.

Vénus

A new French 40-gun frigate (TMC 1+) that soon becomes Commodore Hamelin's pennant-ship in the Indian Ocean (TMC 5,8). In company with *Manche*, she takes the merchantmen *Windham*, *United Kingdom* and *Charlton* (TMC 5) and then arrives at a crucial point in the action at the Battle of Port South East, helping to secure the French victory (TMC 7). With *Victor*, she later takes HMS *Bombay* (TMC 9) but is soon beaten by Jack Aubrey's HMS *Boadicea* (TMC 9).

Vénus, 38-gun, was launched in 1806 and, as the pennant-ship of *Hamelin, was taken by Josias Rowley's HMS *Boadicea in September 1810. Taken into the Royal Navy as HMS *Néréide, she was finally broken up in 1816.

Venus, HMS

A hulk at Gibraltar (FSW 2).

This may be a reference to HMS Venus, *36-gun, an ex-Danish frigate of the same name taken by *Nelson at Copenhagen in 1801. Sent for harbour service in 1809, she was sold in 1828.*

Vernon, Edmund

A character in Paulton's novel (NC 9).

Vertueuse, HMS

The sloop into which Middleton is promoted Commander (M&C 2).

The name Vertueuse may be an amalgam of two captures from the French: Victorieuse, *a 12-gun brig-sloop launched in 1794, captured by the Royal Navy in 1795 and broken up in 1805; and* Vertu, *40-gun, launched in 1794, captured in 1803 and taken in as HMS* Vertu *(sometimes found as* Virtue*), and then broken up in 1810. In 1803 the Royal Navy also captured the French 2-gun schooner* La Vertu *but her fate is unknown.*

Vice, Mr

1: the proposer of the loyal toast in the wardroom of HMS *La Flèche* (FW 2).

2: a reference to Mr Adams, HMS *Surprise*'s purser and Vice-President of her temporary mess in the *Dromedary* transport (TH 4).

The junior Lieutenant on a ship traditionally served as Vice-President of the mess, being responsible for the chore of its everyday management. Mr Adams presumably takes the job whilst in Dromedary *as he would no doubt have organised the officers' private stores for the trip.*

Viceroy, the

The unnamed head of the Spanish regime in Peru (WDS 7+).

At the notional time of Maturin's expedition (1813–1814),

the Viceroy of Peru was José Fernando Abascal y Souza (1743–1821), who held the position from 1804 to 1816.

Victor

A French privateer from St-Malo once beaten off by the *Dromedary* armed transport (TH 4).

Victor, HMS or *Victor*

A 16-gun sloop under Admiral Bertie's command, not immediately available to Jack Aubrey's squadron (TMC 3+). Soon taken by *Bellone*, she is then given back her original French name of *Victor* (TMC 5). She later strikes to Clonfert's HMS *Néréide* at the Ile de la Passe but, unsecured in the mêlée, soon manages to escape (TMC 7). In company with *Vénus*, she then takes HMS *Bombay*, the latter's Captain Graham having the mortification of mistaking the sloop for a large frigate and striking to her (TMC 9,10). Some years afterwards she is once again in the Royal Navy, now commanded by a Captain Painter (RM 2).

HMS Victor *was the ex-French* Iéna, *launched in 1805 as* Revenant. *She was first captured by the Royal Navy in 1808, re-captured by* Bellone *in 1809 and then taken for the final time by Admiral Bertie's squadron at the fall of Mauritius in 1810, upon which she was almost immediately sold.*

Victory, HMS

The beautiful first-rate (TMC 1,3; TH 8; WDS 2), at various times the flag-ship of Admirals St Vincent (TH 10), Nelson (NC 7; WDS 2) and Saumarez (SM author's note).

HMS Victory, *100-gun, was launched in 1765, after six years on the stocks, but not then commissioned until 1778, when she became the flag-ship of Admiral Augustus *Keppel. In 1797 she was Sir John Jervis' flagship at the Battle of Cape *St Vincent and, after a short period as a hospital ship, was quite substantially rebuilt in 1801–1803 for service under *Nelson in his Mediterranean command. Under Captain Thomas Hardy (see ***Mutine, HMS** for a note on his career), she was then the great Vice Admiral's flag-ship for his final battle at Trafalgar on October 21st 1805, afterwards carrying his body home to England. Her next and final active service, after a further re-fit, was as *Saumarez' flag-ship in the Baltic from 1808 to 1812. In 1824* Victory *was sent for harbour service and then, in 1835, paid off to be used as the stationary base of the Commander-in-Chief, Portsmouth (the senior fleet post in the Royal Navy). In 1922, after years of deterioration and neglect (including a near-sinking in 1903 as a result of an accidental collision with a drifting ship), she was put into dry dock and then underwent a program of extensive restoration. She now remains in commission, still as the dock-side flag-ship of the Commander-in-Chief but also as a splendid 'museum ship,' open for public visits every day of the year. On the anniversary of Trafalgar itself,* Victory *is always dressed at the mast-head with a wreath of laurel, honouring her role in the 'Immortal Memory' of Viscount Nelson.*

Vidal, Henry and Ben

A master-mariner serving as a volunteer aboard *Sur-*

prise, later promoted to acting Second Lieutenant (WDS 2+). When his religious sympathies have later persuaded him to help Jean Dutourd to escape (WDS 7), Jack Aubrey allows him and two like-minded cousins — one of whom is probably young Ben Vidal (WDS 7) — to quit the ship (WDS 10).

Vilheim, Abraham

A seaman in HMS *Sophie* (M&C 3).

Ville de Paris, HMS

A line-of-battle ship in sight of HMS *Polychrest* when Jack Aubrey prevents a mutiny (PC 11).

HMS Ville de Paris, *104-gun, was launched in 1795, sent for harbour service in 1825 and broken up in 1845. She had retained the French name of her predecessor ('The City of Paris'), a captured first-rate that had foundered in 1782.*

Villeneuve

The French Admiral (HMS 1) who had met with Admiral Sir Robert Calder's smaller fleet and suffered a minor reverse (FW 3; COM 10).

*Pierre-Charles-Jean-Baptiste-Sylvestre de Villeneuve (1763–1806) was a career naval officer who had entered the Royal service in 1778. In 1793, in the midst of the Revolutionary turmoil, he was appointed to a senior Post Captaincy but almost immediately dismissed as having an aristocratic background. Re-appointed to command in 1795, he was promoted Rear Admiral in the following year. In 1798 he was one of *Brueys' subordinates at the Nile in his* Guillaume Tell, *one of only four French ships to escape being taken or destroyed by *Nelson. Having fled to Malta, he was taken prisoner when that island fell to the British in 1800 but soon exchanged. Promoted Vice Admiral in 1804, he was then given command of the Toulon squadron and charged by *Buonaparte with diverting the English fleets by slipping out of the Mediterranean across to the West Indies. Pursued, as intended, by *Nelson across the Atlantic, he then doubled back to Europe, had an inconclusive brush with *Calder's squadron and took shelter in Cadiz. The Emperor, now feeling that Villeneuve should have remained at sea to do battle with the main English force, accused the Admiral of cowardice, provoking him to set out again, now with his Spanish allies, to meet Nelson. This he did in late October, engaging the English fleet off Cape Trafalgar where he was soundly beaten and again taken prisoner. Freed in early 1806, Villeneuve returned to France and, facing the Emperor's furious opprobrium, there killed himself with six stab wounds to the heart.*

Villiers, Charles

The deceased, first husband of Diana Villiers (PC 1; HMS 1), a soldier related to Lady Jersey (PC 6).

*One branch of the Villiers family were Earls of *Jersey, with the contemporary peer being George Bussy Villiers (1735–1805), 3rd Earl from 1769. Another branch held the Earldom of Clarendon.*

Villiers, Colonel

A relative and former colleague of the deceased

father of Diana Villiers, with whom she now stays in Ireland (COM 10; YA 3).

Villiers, Diana (*often simply* **Diana**, **Di**, **Villiers** *or* **DV**)

Diana Villiers is the beautiful, dashing young widow of a young army officer, Charles, killed in India before he could come into a great inheritance (PC 1; *perhaps through his cousins, the Jerseys:* PC 6). Her father, a General, had been killed in the same engagement, both men dying in considerable debt (PC 1). Now about 27 years old, she lives in genteel, near-poverty in England, a not entirely welcome guest in the house of her aunt, Mrs Williams (PC 1+; *also, for her age, see* DI 1). Diana and her cousin, Sophie Williams, make the acquaintance of their nautical neighbours, Commander Jack Aubrey and Dr Stephen Maturin, with both women becoming strongly attached in friendship to each of the two men (PC 2+). Yet, in the marriage-stakes, only Jack Aubrey can be considered any sort of catch and Diana's dalliance with him brings her into furious conflict with Jack-besotted Sophie (PC 8), nearly breaks the heart of Diana-besotted Stephen (PC 6+) and brings the two men themselves close to a duel (PC 10). However, a prize far richer than Jack's modest prospects soon appears in the person of the wealthy, charming — and married — merchant, Richard Canning. Diana becomes intimate with him (PC 12) and the pair flee to India as lovers, leaving the family scandalised and Stephen Maturin crushed (PC 14; HMS 1,6,7). *(N.B., with the exception of* TMC, *Diana is from here on almost continually a subject of Stephen's thoughts and diary entries, even if seldom present herself.)*

A little later, in Bombay, Diana and Stephen renew their friendship, with Stephen offering marriage as an escape from the now overbearing and unfaithful Canning (HMS 7+). Although tempted by her genuine attachment to Stephen, Diana prevaricates, not least because she has recently formed an alternative liaison with yet another wealthy and powerful merchant, the American Harry Johnstone (HMS 10). Matters come to a head when Stephen and Canning duel, with the doctor dropping the merchant dead but being himself badly wounded in the encounter. Diana nurses her wounded friend, and even accepts from him a ring, but eventually throws in her lot with Johnstone, breaking with Stephen by letter and sailing off to America (HMS 10,11). Over the next several years Diana is reported to have met Stephen in London and again to have rejected him, even though she has discovered Johnson (*the spelling of whose name now changes*) to be yet another married man (TMC 7; DI 1). Whilst in England, she had also met and become friendly with the American spy Louisa Wogan, eventually drawing down suspicion and even brief arrest on

herself, before being cleared of any wrongdoing and returning to America to await Johnson's divorce (DI 2,3; FW 1,2).

When, some years later, Stephen and Jack Aubrey arrive in Boston as prisoners-of-war, Diana soon reveals that she is both home-sick for England and tired of Johnson's many other lovers (FW 6). In order to solve the problem of her having become an American citizen — to ease Johnson's complex, interminable divorce proceedings — and being thus subject to detention in Canada or England, Diana is again offered a marriage of convenience by Stephen, an offer that she now accepts (FW 6,7). When Stephen is revealed as an intelligence agent, Diana conceals him in her bed from pursuing French assassins (FW 8) and then escapes with him and Jack in a small boat out to the cruising HMS *Shannon*, desperately seasick all the while (FW 8,9). Once free, she renews her acceptance of Stephen's offer, now with some degree of emotional enthusiasm (FW 8,9). Yet, to ensure some degree of financial independence, she has taken the precaution of retaining the glorious diamond necklace, set with the 'Begum' stone, earlier given her by her American lover (FW 6,8).

Safely in Canada (SM 1), Diana confirms to Stephen his earlier suspicion (FW 8) that she is pregnant by Johnson, now stating that she cannot and will not marry whilst carrying another man's child; her hint at abortion is emphatically rejected by the Doctor (SM 2). Again prostrated with seasickness, she travels to England in the mail packet *Diligence*, narrowly avoiding capture by the vengeful Johnson's privateers (SM 3). Briefly detained as an enemy alien, Diana now accepts Stephen's suggestion that she accompany him to Paris — for three years her childhood home (SM 5) — and pass her confinement there as a guest of his old friend, La Mothe (SM 4,5). When Stephen later returns to Paris, but now as an endangered prisoner, she uses her beloved diamond (now 'Blue Peter') to bribe an influential politician into guaranteeing his safety and eventual release (SM 11). Whilst they are returning to England in HMS *Oedipus,* Stephen, having already learned that Diana has miscarried her child due to her recent arduous sea-journeys and acute sea-sickness, renews his marriage offer (SM 10,11). She finally accepts and the pair are wed in a ship-board ceremony, conducted by Commander William Babbington with Jack Aubrey and their dashing new Lithuanian friend, Captain Jagiello, in attendance (SM 11).

Following the marriage, Diana and Stephen agreed to maintain separate dwellings in London, for Diana is now rich and lives very stylishly whilst Stephen remains by temperament a scholarly batchelor (IM 1,2,11; TH 2+; *her wealth has presumably come from the sale of the remnants of Johnson's valuable jewels*). The Catholic Stephen also wishes to go through a further ceremony of marriage in his Church — for in its eyes, he remains a bachelor — but Diana steadfastly refuses (IM 1). Stephen now begins to receive anonymous letters stating that Diana and Jagiello have become lovers, a suggestion he dismisses out of hand (IM 5; TH 8). At this point too, Diana begins to show certain signs of being pregnant (IM 1) but later writes to the absent Stephen saying that this has turned out not to be so (IM 5). At home in London, she herself soon hears rumours that Stephen is having a public affair in Malta with the pretty Sicilian, Laura Fielding. Unfortunately her innocent husband's letter of denial and explanation never reaches England (FSW 1–9) and, insulted by the supposed dalliance, Diana accompanies Jagiello to Sweden (RM 1,5,10; LM 1+), entertaining herself there not by engaging in an affair with her dashing Lithuanian friend but by taking spectacular balloon rides (LM 4; *she also appears now to be somewhat impoverished*). Eventually she is tracked down by Stephen (LM 1+) but only after he is injured in a fall does his recuperation period draw the couple back together as man and wife, a process perhaps somewhat aided by the restitution of her beloved 'Blue Peter' diamond (LM 9).

Now properly Church-married to Stephen, Diana is soon heavily pregnant and in search of a country estate: she settles on Barham Down, an extravagant choice thought most unsuitable by her husband (TGS 1–4). During his next, long absence at sea, Diana gives birth to a daughter (TGS 9; NC 10) but soon tells Stephen, in somewhat distracted letters, that the child is a little strange (C/T 3+). Separately, Sophie Aubrey tells her husband, Jack, that her cousin is behaving both oddly and badly following the birth (C/T 3). Diana and little Brigid remain very much in Stephen's thoughts during his long voyage to South America and back to England, but often with a strong sense of apprehension and even foreboding (WDS 1,5,8,9). On his eventual return (COM 1), Stephen finds that Diana has fled Barham House, unable to cope with Brigid's withdrawn strangeness and convinced — wrongly — that her husband has had a ship-board affair with Clarissa Oakes, to whose care she has effectively abandoned the child (WDS 10; COM 2+). After an awkward separation, Diana and Stephen (who, in the meanwhile, has sent Brigid and the family fortune to Spain) are, almost by chance, re-united in Ireland and once again achieve a happy reconciliation (COM 10).

The couple now collect their much-improved daughter from her temporary exile but are prevented from doing the same with their money, returning to England to live in temporarily reduced circumstances at the Aubreys' Woolcombe House (YA 1+), with Diana soon having to pawn the 'Blue Peter' to raise cash for her preferred life-style of fast friends and fast horses (YA 3, 6). A little later, she and Clarissa Oakes — now her firm friend — persuade Sophie Aubrey to take a liberal view of Jack's past adultery with Amanda Smith (YA 8) and, when the long war with France seems finally over, the two families travel together in *Surprise* for a holiday on the island of Madeira. But here they learn of Buonaparte's escape from Elba, and the future looks once again most uncertain (YA 10).

Diana soon returns to England with the families but is almost immediately killed — along with her cousin Cholmondeley, Mrs Williams and others — in a coaching accident (HD 1,3). She is buried wearing her beloved 'Blue Peter' diamond (HD 7).

Vincent

1: the commander of HMS *Weymouth*, once court-martialed (M&C 12).

Nicholas Vincent (d. 1809) was made Post in 1748 and in 1757 appointed to HMS *Weymouth, 60-gun. In 1758 he fought under Admiral Sir George Pocock (1706–1792) in an indecisive squadron action against the French off Cuddalore. Pocock afterwards had Vincent (and two other Captains) charged with 'lack of promptness' in coming up to the fight: he was soon convicted and dismissed his ship. However, this decision was extremely controversial at the time, in that Pocock — in common with numbers of other unimaginative flag officers — had adhered so strictly to the 'Admiralty Fighting Instructions' that many sea-officers felt the rear-most ships of his squadron could never have got up in time, willing or not. Not without influential friends, Vincent got his case re-examined in 1766 and was soon re-appointed to a command, later seeing some brisk service: in 1779 his 74-gun HMS Yarmouth famously destroyed the American frigate Randolph. Promoted Rear Admiral in that same year, he then held no further sea commands, rising purely by seniority to Admiral of the Red in 1805. The other two captains also convicted after Cuddalore (and whose cases never seem to have been reviewed) were William Brereton of HMS Cumberland (reduced in seniority by one year) and George Legge of HMS Newcastle (dismissed the service). Brereton continued with a successful naval career, commanding the 90-gun HMS Duke at the Battle of Ushant in 1778 and being promoted Rear Admiral on the retired list in 1787; Legge, however, vanished from notice.

2: an officer in the French privateer *Bellone* (PC 5).

3: a seaman in HMS *Surprise*, a lay preacher at home in England (FSW 6).

4: see **St Vincent, Admiral Lord**

'Vinegar Joe'

According to Jack Aubrey, the service nickname of his friend Heneage Dundas (IM 10).

Vining, Dr

A member of Mr Savile's hunt, the doctor to the Williams family (PC 1,2,3).

Viotti

A man referred to by Jack Aubrey as a famous violinist (IM 2).

Giovanni Battista Viotti (1755–1824), an Italian composer and violinist, was the most influential virtuoso between *Tartini and *Paganini. For a time Viotti lived in Paris as accompanyist to Marie Antoinette, the consort of King *Louis XVI, but fled to London in 1792 when revolutionary turmoil threatened his life. Curiously, in 1798 he was then expelled from England as a *Jacobite sympathiser (with no real evidence to justify such an accusation) but managed to return in about 1801. Now almost entirely retired from performance, he took up full-time promotion of a wine business he had started some years before but this then failed spectacularly in 1818, leaving him in deep debt for the rest of his life. From his *Bourbon patrons, Viotti now secured appointment as Director of the Paris Opera, a post he held with indifferent success until 1821. In 1823, somewhat broken in both spirit and health, he returned to London, living with loyal friends until his death the following year.

Viper

A cannon in HMS *Surprise* (RM 3).

Viper, HMS

A large cutter commanded by Lieutenant Dixon (LM 2).

HMS Viper, 8-gun, was purchased as the Niger in 1809 and sold in 1814.

Viper, USS

A 12-gun ship referred to by Jack Aubrey (FW 2).

USS Viper, 12-gun, was commissioned in 1809 (having perhaps been bought into, rather than built for, the service) as Ferret, being re-named in 1810 on her conversion from schooner to brig. This re-rig was not successful and Viper was regarded thereafter as both slow and somewhat unseaworthy. In January 1813, under a Lieutenant Henby, she was taken by the 32-gun HMS Narcissus; her fate thereafter is unknown.

Virgil

The great Latin poet (M&C 9; FSW 4; TGS 5), referred to by Mr Mowett as 'Maro' (IM 3).

Publius Virgilius Maro (70–19 BC), usually known simply as Virgil, was the most celebrated poet of Imperial Rome. His Eclogues present an idealised picture of pastoral bliss; his Georgics maintain a passion for rural life, yet are also a little more down-to-earth; and his great 12 book epic Aeneid tells of the founding of Rome (by *Aeneas amongst others) and extols the new, imperial age of Augustus. It is this last great work that is on one occasion quoted in its entirety by the delirious Stephen Maturin (HMS 11).

Vizier

1: the Chief Minister of the Sultan of Pulo Prabang (TGS 6–8).
2: *see* **Hashin**

Voisin's

A fashionable restaurant in Paris (SM 10).

Volage, HMS

A ship of which Charles Fielding had once been Second Lieutenant (TH 9).

The reference could be to either of two ships: the ex-French 22-gun privateer Volage ('Flighty'), captured by the Royal Navy in 1798 and broken up in 1804; or her similar replacement, launched in 1807 and sold in 1818.

Volgardson

A Swedish seaman in HMS *Sophie* (M&C 5).

Voltaire

The great French writer (M&C 3; DI 5; FW 2) whose name is once used by Maturin's contact, Leclerc, as a greeting-code (IM 7).

Voltaire was the pen-name of François-Marie Arouet (1694–1778), the great French, poet, philosopher, historian, polemicist and playwright. In all his works Voltaire was a passionate advocate of a tolerant, secular society, to be composed of rational, practical men and women; yet he could be sweepingly caustic towards all enemies of this beloved 'Enlightenment.' At his death, the strength of both his pen and personality left him simultaneously one of the best loved and most hated men in Europe.

Vowles

1: a junior Lord of the Admiralty, a cousin of Admiral Drury (FW 1).
2: a bosun's mate in *Surprise* (C/T 8).

Vrijheid

A Dutch ship at the Battle of Camperdown that had badly mauled Midshipman Jack Aubrey's HMS *Ardent* (DI 6).

The 74-gun Vrijheid ('Liberty') was the flag-ship of Admiral Jan de Winter (1750–1812) at *Duncan's great victory off Camperdown in October 1797. In offering a very gallant resistance to the English onslaught, Vrijheid was herself so badly damaged that she was broken up by her English captors shortly after the battle. N.B., Jack *Aubrey nowhere else refers to his being at Camperdown and by that date had in fact already been a Lieutenant for five years.

Vulture, HMS

A slop-ship into which Jack Aubrey had once feared 'promotion' (M&C 1), later found sailing in company with Babbington's HMS *Tartarus* (LM 6).

A slop-ship was an armed supply ship, taking the nickname from 'slops' (originally sailors' working clothes, but later also any day-to-day goods, such as tobacco, available to seamen). Two HMS Vultures fit the dates here, although neither was a permanent slop-ship: the first, a 14-gun sloop, was launched in 1776 and sold in 1802; the second, a 16-gun sloop, was purchased as Warrior in 1803 and sold in 1814.

W, Mrs
see **Williams, Mrs**

Waakzaamheid
A Dutch 74-gun cruising in the South Atlantic (DI 5–8) that, before intercepting and pursuing Jack Aubrey's HMS *Leopard* (DI 6,7), has already encountered and damaged the frigate HMS *Nymphe* (DI 5). In monstrous seas, *Waakzaamheid*'s foremast is toppled by a single English cannon-shot, fired by Mr Moore, and she immediately founders with the loss of her entire crew (DI 7; FW 1; SM 4–6; LM 7,8). Much later, *Leopard*'s Lieutenant Grant, now unemployed, alleges that she was not a warship at all but rather an unarmed transport (SM 6).

> *Although this* Waakzaamheid *is invented by O'Brian, the name was well known to the Royal Navy. In 1792 the Governor of New South Wales hired the Dutch merchant snow* Waaksamheyd *(sic) to take the crew of the wrecked HMS* *Sirius back to England. By a curious co-incidence, in 1798 the new* *Sirius took a Dutch navy 24-gun corvette called* Waakzaamheid *(sic) off the Texel. She was then taken into the Royal Navy under that name, serving until being sold in 1802.*

Waddon
A Hampshire neighbour of Jack Aubrey, met by him in London (RM 4).

Wade, Miss
A dinner guest at Molly Harte's house (M&C 8).

Wade, Patrick
A seaman referred to in HMS *Sophie*'s log (M&C 2).

Wager, HMS
A ship in Anson's squadron (NC 1), in which Admiral Byron, then a Midshipman, had served with Tom Pullings' grandfather (DI 3).

> *HMS* Wager, *24-gun, was purchased for* *Anson's voyage in 1739 and then wrecked off the coast of Chile in 1741. Her loss and* *Byron's own account of his consequent adventures by sea and land form the basis of O'Brian's early novel,* The Unknown Shore.

Wagstaff, Captain
A guest at one of Laura Fielding's musical evenings (TH 3).

Wainwright
The Master of the whaler *Daisy*, an ex-Royal Navy officer, who meets Jack Aubrey and updates him on the situation at Moahu Island (C/T 5+; WDS 1).

Waites
1: a resident of Polton Episcopi (LM 1).
2: a Shelmerstonian seaman in HMS *Surprise* (NC 7).

Wakeley
The keeper of a tavern (or perhaps some other establishment) near the Marquess of Granby Inn (LM 1).

Wales, Prince of
see **Regent, the**

Waley, Colonel
A gaming partner of Harry Turnbull (YA 3).

Walker
1: a seaman in HMS *Surprise* (HD 4).
2: the surgeon of HMS *Polyphemus* (HD 9).

Walker, Ned
A member of the carpenter's crew of HMS *Diane* (NC 2), promoted carpenter of HMS *Nutmeg of Consolation* (NC 5+).

Walker, Thomas
Admiral Lord Keith's secretary, who signs Jack Aubrey's first commission as Commander (M&C 1).

Walkinshaw
The schoolmaster in HMS *Bellona* (YA 5,6).

Wall
1: the Governor of Minorca (M&C 8).
> *The name distantly echoes that of the notorious Governor Joseph Wall (1737–1802), an Irish colonial administrator and British Governor of Goree (Senegal). In 1782 Wall, an ardent flogger, arrested one of his own soldiers on a false charge and had him whipped to death. Although charged with cruelty and murder, Wall was not brought to justice until 1801, when he was sentenced to hang. Unsuccessful attempts were made by influential friends to secure his reprieve but the government probably could not risk light treatment of an officer convicted of cruelty, so soon after executing many common seamen for mutiny at Spithead and elsewhere.*
2: a Shelmerstonian seaman in HMS *Surprise* (NC 7).
3: a British diplomat or intelligence official referred to by Sir Joseph Blaine (YA 1).

Wallace
An ill seaman in HMS *Lively* (PC 12,13).

Waller, Mr and **Mrs**
1: Mr and Mrs Waller, the former employers of Maturin's new servant, Ahmed (TGS 4).

2: an English agent in Spain exposed by Diego Diaz (YA 7).

Wallis

1: a naval explorer (FSW 7; C/T 8) under whom Jack Aubrey's cousin, Admiral Carteret, had served when young (NC 8).

Samuel Wallis (1728–1795), an expert navigator, was made Post in 1757 and commanded HMS *Dolphin and a small squadron, including *Carteret's sloop HMS *Swallow, on its circumnavigation in 1766–1768; in 1767 he discovered both Easter Island and Tahiti. Wallis served as a Commissioner of the Navy from 1780 to 84 and from 1787 to 1795.

2: Admiral Drury's political advisor on Java, whom Stephen Maturin, an old intelligence associate, had once circumcised so that he could pass for a Jew (FW 1). Wallis has also produced a report on the situation in Catalonia, Stephen's own usual chief concern (FW 2).

Wallis, Admiral of the Fleet Sir Provo

The Nova Scotian Second Lieutenant of HMS *Shannon* (FW 9; SM 1,2), who will go onto to be a centenarian (FW author's note).

Sir Provo William Parry Wallis (1791–1892), the son of the chief clerk to the Naval Commissioner at Halifax and, supposedly, the grandson of a loyalist master shipwright of New York, was commissioned Lieutenant in 1808 and appointed to *Broke's HMS *Shannon in January 1812. As a reward for his part in the great victory over USS *Chesapeake in the following year, Wallis was almost immediately promoted Commander, being made Post in 1819. He then held sea-commands almost continuously until 1846, seeing a great deal of active service. A Rear Admiral of 1851, in 1857 he was briefly Commander in Chief, South America, until his promotion later that year to Vice Admiral, after which he never again served at sea (although he remained on the active list until his death). Having been being knighted in 1860, Wallis became a full Admiral in 1863 and rose to Admiral of the Fleet in 1877. The same Reverend J.G. *Brighton who had produced the Memoir of *Broke published a life of Wallis in 1892, the year of the Admiral's death.

Walsh

A seaman in HMS *Surprise* (FSW 4).

Walsh, Patrick

A name given to Padeen Colman in order to facilitate his escape from New South Wales (NC 10).

Walters, Samuel

A Royal Navy Lieutenant who wrote a book of memoirs containing some informative, if artistically indifferent, naval verse. The volume was not published until 1949, under the editorship of Professor Northcote Parkinson (IM author's note).

Samuel Walters (1778–1834) first went to sea in 1795 as a carpenter's mate on the East Indiaman Ocean, then under the command of John Bowen, a younger brother of James *Bowen and, like Walters, a native of Ilfracombe in Devon. Walters joined the elder Bowen's HMS *Argo in 1798, initially as an able seaman but very soon as a Midshipman, serving in her until 1802. After further service with some of Bowen's own patrons, Walters was commissioned Lieutenant in 1805, being posted to Josias Rowley's HMS *Raisonable and almost immediately serving in her during *Calder's indecisive, pre–Trafalgar action. Walters then continued in the ship for several years, serving in the Mauritius campaign of 1809–1810 before returning to England with her in the middle of the latter year to be paid off. Walters' final Royal Navy service was in Philip *Wilkinson's HMS *Courageux, from 1810 until early 1813 : it was her partial wrecking in 1812 that was the inspiration for Walters' stirring verse, later given by O'Brian to his Lieutenant *Rowan (IM 9). After 1813 Walters was unable to secure a ship and, again with Bowen's assistance, now took a post as an agent of the Transport Board, thus removing himself from the possibility of further promotion. Even this position did not long outlive the final conclusion of the wars in 1815, and Walters seems thereafter to have re-entered the purely merchant service for the rest of his sea-career. In 1833 he emigrated to Canada, where he already had relatives, but died at Montreal during a cholera epidemic in the following year. Like his well-known marine-artist nephew, also Samuel Walters (1811–1882; sometimes seen as 'Waters,' the usual pronunciation of the family name), 'our' Samuel was both water-colourist and poet: though, in truth, he cannot be said to have enjoyed outstanding talent at either, as *Parkinson's edition of his journals rather tends to show. There is one curious puzzle over Walters' career: SYRETT & DiNARDO give the date of his death as June 1st 1812 (sic), citing a notice, obviously mistaken, in the London Gazette.

(N.B., I am most grateful to Bob Huddleston, another regular contributor to the O'Brian internet discussion groups briefly mentioned in my Introduction, for supplying me with extensive raw material for this note, at the shortest of notice.)

Wand, Mr

An officer in the *Lord Nelson* Indiaman (PC 5).

Wan Da

A dignitary at the court of the Sultan of Pulo Prabang (TGS 6,8; NC 1+).

Wang

The aunt of Golden Flower of the Day (NC 2).

Wantage

A Master's Mate in *Surprise* who is thought to have been murdered at Madeira by his lover's husband (HD 3).

'Wapping Slasher'

A famous pugilist (FSW 9).

Ward

1: Jack Aubrey's clerk in HMS *Surprise* (IM 9,10; TH 4; FSW 3,6,9).

2: Dr Ward, a 'quack' manufacturer of pills and drops (M&C 1; HMS 4), for whom Olivia

Raffles says a form of the dropsy is named (NC 4).

*Joshua Ward (1685–1761) was a promoter and seller of remedies for illnesses of all kind. His famous, very commercially successful pills were a mixture of antimony and balsam, with wine added to produce the alternative drops; his similar 'fever powder' became regulation Royal Navy issue in 1753. 'Spot' Ward—so named from a birthmark on his face—became a popular society figure, enjoying the patronage of King George II whom he had cured of a painfully dislocated thumb that qualified doctors had diagnosed as gout. He may have obtained his formulas from learned Jesuits in Paris and they were seen as therapeutically successful enough to earn Ward the appellation of 'Doctor,' even though he lacked any medical qualification. During his long career, Ward amassed a considerable fortune, becoming a notable philanthropist. 'Dropsy' (which Mrs Raffles perhaps confuses with 'drops') was the contemporary name for congestive heart failure due to oedema, a complaint for which Dr William *Withering developed an effective treatment based on the digitalis content of foxglove leaves.*

3: the Captain of HMS *Dover*, a man disliked by Jack Aubrey, his Commodore. He and his ship leave the squadron in order to escort East Indiamen home to England (HD 2).

Wardle

An HMS *Surprise* quartermaster (TH 7).

Waring

The man whom Sir Joseph Blaine says is to be his successor as *de facto* Head of Naval Intelligence, with Admiral Sievewright becoming his nominal superior (HMS 4,6,7).

see also **Warren # 1**

Warley

The captain of the maintop in HMS *Surprise*, lost at sea off Cape Horn (FSW 5).

Warley

An East Indiaman in Commodore Muffit's merchant fleet (HMS 9).

Warley, 1200 tons, completed 9 round trips for the British East India Company between 1788 and 1814.

Warne, Admiral

A man referred to by Stephen Maturin as being corrupted by the long exercise of high authority (M&C 6).

*This may be a slip for Sir John Borlase Warren (1753–1822), an officer made Post in 1781, promoted Rear Admiral in 1799 and Admiral in 1810. Warren was unusual in being one of the very few Captains of the time with a university degree, an MA from Cambridge obtained after first serving as a Royal Navy Midshipman for about 4 years. In 1798 he had been in command of the squadron that had prevented any significant landings being made in Ireland from the small French invasion fleet, and had then captured Wolfe *Tone from the Hoche after a fierce battle. In 1800 Warren (somewhat contrary to *Maturin's*

*perception, a very popular and effective commander) joined the Mediterranean command, becoming Lord *Keith's deputy in the Western region around Minorca from 1801 to 1802. In 1806 he was in command of the squadron that captured the homeward-bound Admiral *Linois in his *Marengo and, in 1813, was appointed Commander-in-Chief, North American, serving in that post until his retirement from sea-service in 1815. Warren died suddenly in 1822 whilst on a visit to his old Mediterranean comrade Sir Richard *Keats, the Governor of Greenwich Naval Hospital. See also: **Warren, Lady Anne**.*

Warner

1: an officer, probably the First Lieutenant, in HMS *Eurydice* (DI 3).

2: the First Lieutenant of HMS *La Flèche*, a harddriving, severe disciplinarian. He falls out with Stephen Maturin, who later comes to suspect that his character is twisted by a natural paederasty, rigorously and necessarily suppressed aboard ship (FW 2). In 1779 he had been a Midshipman on the American Station under 'Foulweather Jack' Byron and, in Jack Aubrey's eyes, is a capital seaman (FW 2).

3: a secretary to Governor Raffles (NC 3).

Warren

1: the *de facto* Head of Naval Intelligence, who suffers a disabling stoke (DI 2; SM 4). He seems later to be fully recovered and assisting the once-again active Sir Joseph Blaine (TGS 3; YA 7; *unless these references are perhaps to Colonel* **Warren**, *below*). See also *Waring.

2: Colonel Warren, the Head of British Army Intelligence, said by Sir Joseph Blaine to be an eunuch (RM 9,10; COM 2).

3: a seaman in *Surprise* under particular obligation to Stephen Maturin for a past cure (LM 5).

4: the Master of HMSS *Diane* and *Nutmeg of Consolation*, in which latter ship he is killed in the action against *Cornélie* (TGS 4+; NC 2–6).

5: Mrs Warren, the cook at the Maturins' Barham House (COM 2).

Warren, Lady Anne

An admiral's wife met by Jack Aubrey at Molly Harte's salon (M&C 1).

*Although this is probably a reference to the wife of Admiral Sir John Borlase Warren (see *Warne, Admiral), this lady was in fact named Caroline (m. 1780, d. 1839). Sir John's mother was indeed called Anne, but she was neither the wife of an Admiral nor, in this titular sense alone, a Lady.*

Warren, Joe

A friend of Bonden who serves in USS *Constitution* (FW 3), probably the 'Boston Joe' who later shackles his old shipmate (FW 4).

Warren Hastings

A merchant ship (HMS 7) of the East India Company fleet due in Calcutta with Mrs Canning aboard (HMS 10).

No less than three East India Company ships were named for Warren Hastings (1732–1818), a linguist, administrator and soldier who rose from clerk in the company's Calcutta office to become, in 1773, the first British Governor-General of India. The ship in question was the second to bear his name, a 1064-tonner that made just 2 round trips from India to England between 1802 and 1804. Warren Hastings' career and administrations were deeply controversial (not least because his reforms began to limit the opportunities for vast corruption that had characterised India since *Clive's departure) and, on his retirement to England in 1785, he was impeached before the House of Commons for both financial irregularities and military atrocities. The ensuing trial, which lasted for a total of seven years from 1788 to 1795, was really intended and conducted as an enquiry into the whole conduct of British policy in the new dominion, with Hastings facing accusations (principally from the Whigs, led for this occasion by the Irish philosopher, Edmund Burke) of responsibility for many excesses of zeal in carrying out semi-official policy. Having in fact been personally involved in few serious scandals, Hastings was eventually acquitted (and went onto live out his years in prosperous retirement) but the trial marked the beginning of the end of the rather 'free-booting' style in which Britain had acquired India and the start of a period of rule inseparable from some higher notions of consequent responsibility.

Warwick, HMS

A ship that appears during Jack Aubrey's action with Maistral's squadron (COM 10).

No HMS Warwick was in service at the time of COM, the most recent ship of that name having been a 50-gun launched in 1767 and sold in 1802.

Washington

The American general under whom Michael Herapath, a distant relative, had served in the US Army against the French in 1798 (DI 5,6). He is later guessed at by Tom Pullings as being the serving President of the USA (WDS 10).

George Washington (1732–1799), a surveyor, explorer, career soldier and colonial politician, became in 1775 the Commander in Chief of the American armies during the Revolutionary War, fighting a strategically brilliant campaign (not, of course, without its setbacks) that for almost the entire conflict denied Britain the opportunities for both set-piece battles and the decisive victories that home opinion demanded and expected. Always maintaining a army intact in the field (often ramshackle, usually under-supplied, repeatedly in the most unforgiving territory), he eventually laid siege to Lord *Cornwallis' now somewhat demoralised forces at Yorktown in 1781 and, with French aid, soon achieved a victory that persuaded political opinion in London that the war was unwinnable. Military operations were largely discontinued in 1782 and in late 1783 a final peace was signed. From 1789 to 1797 Washington then served as the First President of the newly-formed United States of America. When hostilities with
France broke out in 1798, the retired Washington was again appointed Commander in Chief of a newly raised army, a post he accepted only with some considerable reluctance. He died, following a short illness, before that conflict was brought to a conclusion (in early 1801). Tom *Pullings' stab at the serving President is made during the term of James *Madison, in office from 1809 to 1817.*

Wasp

An armed schooner, Master Mr Fortesque, of the East India Company, attached to Jack Aubrey's squadron (TMC 4,5).

The 18-gun Wasp, under her Mr Watkins, was attached by the East India Company to Commodore Josias Rowley's squadron for the assaults on Réunion and Mauritius of 1809–1810.

Wasp, USS

A sloop that has taken HMS *Frolic* (FW 3).

USS Wasp, 18-gun ship-rigged sloop, was launched in 1806. In October 1812, under her Captain Jacob Jones (1770–1850), she used her superior gunnery technique in taking HMS *Frolic during a very bloody action in which every British officer was wounded or killed. However, just a few hours later, Captain John Poo *Beresford's 74-gun HMS Poitiers arrived on the scene and immediately took both battered ships. Wasp was taken into the Royal Navy as HMS *Peacock (as a replacement for the ship sunk a few months later by USS *Hornet) but foundered off the coast of South Carolina in 1814 with the loss of all hands.

Waterhouse

A gentleman, said by Maturin to have been Admiral Sir John Thornton's political and intelligence advisor, who had been captured and shot by the French (TH 8; IM 4).

Waters, Mr

The surgeon of HMS *Irresistible* who consults Maturin over his stomach tumour. Following an operation, he becomes gravely ill with sepsis (RM 1,2).

Watkins

A seaman and drummer in *Surprise* (C/T 9).

Watson

1: a Midshipman in HMS *Arethusa* (IM 1).
2: Jack Aubrey's carpenter in both HMSS *Worcester* (IM 6) and *Surprise* (IM 11).

Watt

1: HMS *Sophie's* bosun (M&C 1+), severely injured in the *Cacafuego* action (M&C 11).
2: the First Lieutenant of HMS *Shannon* who is first injured in the action against USS *Chesapeake* and then later killed by his own ship's fire as he fumbles in attempting to run the Union Jack up the beaten American's flagstaff (FW 8,9; SM 1).

George Topham Lawrye Watt was commissioned in 1806 and in early 1812, when a vacancy arose, *Broke promoted him from Second to First Lieutenant of his HMS

*Shannon. He was killed in action, just as described in the text, on June 1st 1813.

3: a name invented by Mr Welby for his anecdote about an Marine recruit (TGS 9).

4: a member of the Royal Society known to both Stephen Maturin and James Wright (HD 3).

*The reference is presumably to James Watt (1736–1819), the great Scottish engineer and scientist. Watt made his early reputation in Glasgow as an expert maker of mathematical instruments but also spent much of his spare time in general scientific study and in acquiring all the chief European languages. In 1764 Watt was given a small steam engine to repair by the University of Glasgow; from his work and experiments he soon produced a vastly improved machine, using the principle of separate condensation in order to channel hitherto wasted energy into, e.g., the movement of a piston and, eventually, the turning of a wheel and shaft. After 1768 Watt devoted himself wholly to civil engineering and surveying, commencing large-scale manufacture (with Matthew Boulton (1728–1809), his financial partner) of his patented steam-engine in 1775, an invention (much refined in the ensuing years) that not only made his fortune but also heralded the industrial age. Watt was elected a fellow of the Royal Society in 1785 and, after his retirement from business affairs in 1800, an associate of the Institut Français in 1814. His son and business successor, also James (1769–1848), was an enthusiastic Francophile in his youth, living in Paris during the Revolutionary years as an active member of the *Jacobin club; in 1792 he was forced to flee after a violent argument with Robespierre, who had accused him of being William *Pitt's spy.*

Waverly, HMS

A ship that arrives in Sydney from Madras (NC 10).

Weasel, HMS

1: a large cutter (HMS 2).

2: a ship met at sea by *Surprise* (COM 1).

*HMS Weazel (sic), 18-gun brig-sloop, was launched in 1805 and sold out of the service in late 1815. In 1813 she had made a great reputation for herself as an independent member of *Hoste's squadron, capturing a number of gunboats in a succession of dashing inshore operations. At this time she was under Commander James Black (d.1835), soon made Post for his work. Black had been a Midshipman at *Howe's victory at the Glorious First of June in 1794 and had later served as Second Lieutenant of the 74-gun HMS *Mars at the Battle of Trafalgar in 1805, being wounded in the action.*

Weatherall

A Midshipman in HMS *Boadicea* (TMC 3).

Weaver, Harry

A seaman in *Surprise* killed in action on Moahu Island (C/T 9).

Webber

1: HMS *Boadicea*'s gunner (TMC 3+).

2: The Second Lieutenant of HMS *Néréide* (TMC 7).

3: an HMS *Surprise* youngster, the son of an old colleague of Jack Aubrey (RM 3).

4: a seaman in *Surprise* (C/T 1).

5: Miss Webber, a young lady friend of Master's Mate Paddy Callaghan (YA 4).

Webster

1: a Midshipman in HMS *Surprise*, wounded in action (LM 3).

2: an officer referred to by Lieutenant Arrowsmith (HD 1).

Wedell, Arthur

A youngster found in Jean Dutourd's *Franklin*, who had been taken by him from a captured merchantman. He now joins Jack Aubrey's *Surprise* (WDS 3+).

Weightman

The ship's butcher in *Surprise* (C/T 6), later flogged for insolence (C/T 8).

Welby

The Marine Captain of HMS *Diane* and, later, HMS *Nutmeg of Consolation* (TGS 4+; NC 1–5).

Weld, Charles

The man who had shown Stephen Maturin the Pope's document concerning the Regent's marriage to the Catholic Mrs Fitzherbert (RM 9).

The reference is possibly a member of a leading Roman Catholic family of England, the Dorsetshire Welds, one of whose members, Thomas Weld (1773–1837), became a Cardinal of his Church in 1830. The name may also echo a later Charles Weld (1813–1869), the Irish born historian of the Royal Society, the institution of which so many of O'Brian's characters are members.

Welland

A visitor expected by Jack Aubrey at Woolcombe House (YA 2).

Weller

A Midshipman in HMS *Bellona* (YA 6).

Wellington

The Anglo-Irish (FW 2) commander of the British forces in Spain (SM 4,6,7), where he has recently inflicted a defeat on the French at Vitoria (SM 4). Later, despite a slow advance, his armies have penetrated well into France (YA 1, 7–9). After Buonaparte's return from exile in 1815, Wellington is again marching to meet his armies, this time in the Low Countries (HD 1). News of the ensuing great victory at Waterloo rapidly finds its way to the British fleet at Gibraltar (HD 10). Earlier in his career, Wellington had been famous for the unusually speedy embarkation of troops (TMC 6).

Sir Arthur Wellesley (1769–1852), Duke of Wellington, was the fourth son of the Anglo-Irish peer and musician, Garrett Wesley, 1st Earl of Mornington, and the younger brother of General Sir Richard Wellesley, later 1st Marquess Wellesley and 2nd Earl of Mornington (see *Lord Mornington; the spelling of the family surname was changed in about 1797). Wellesley followed his brother into the army in 1787 and, as was the way of the times, bought his way to a Lieutenant-Colonelcy in 1793, never having seen any action. However, in that same year he commanded his regiment during a disastrous retreat through the Netherlands, being shocked at the military ineptitude of the British officer class but establishing for himself a reputation as both brave and able. Wellesley went to India in 1797 to serve as a full Colonel in his brother's campaigns against *Tippoo Sahib and others, and then remained in the sub-continent until 1805 (having been promoted Major-General in 1802), there learning and mastering the trades of high command: visible leadership and a shrewd feel for ground, intelligence and logistics, personal courage and resilience. From 1805 to 1808 Wellesley served in two relatively minor European campaigns as well as engaging in political activities as Chief Secretary for his native Ireland and as an MP. In mid–1808 he was promoted Lieutenant-General and sent for the first time to the Iberian Peninsular, the theatre where he was soon to make his reputation as a steady and relentless master of the battlefield. Yet his start was uneasy for, although he immediately won a series of battles against the French in support of Britain's Portuguese allies, he was soon superseded and recalled to London to face an enquiry over what was seen as a premature ending of the campaign. Fully exonerated, Wellesley was sent back to the Peninsula, now as Commander-in-Chief. Again immediately successful, he was created Viscount Wellington in late 1809 and began, by a series of great victories and occasional judicious retreats, to build a formidable army that not only drained the stretched resources of *Buonaparte's empire but eventually was able to push the French from Spain, a successful drive eastwards and northwards culminating in the victory over Joseph *Buonaparte at Vitoria in June 1813. Wellington, already in 1812 created Earl and then Marquess, was now given a Dukedom and promoted Field Marshall. The ensuing fight to cross the Pyrenees was both slow and tough — the French were now led by the able and wily Marshal Soult— but in November 1813 Wellington entered France and gradually fought his way to Toulouse before learning of Buonaparte's abdication. Chief of the occupying army and British military representative at the Congress of Vienna, on Buonaparte's return from Elba during the 'Hundred Days' of early 1815 Wellington was appointed Commander of the allied forces in the Netherlands and Belgium. On June 16th he fought a stalemate against Marshal *Ney at Quatre Bras and then retired to what he considered more favourable ground at Waterloo. Here, two days later, Wellington faced for the first and only time armies led by the Emperor himself and, in a 'damn near-run thing' (to use his own words), inflicted a decisive defeat on the French, aided at the last by Marshal *Blücher's Prussians. Following the restoration of the *Bourbons, Wellington remained as military commander in France until 1818. Upon his return to England, he then commenced a purely political career (although he remained a serving military officer, being Commander in Chief from 1827 to 1852). A staunch and even reactionary Tory, Wellington served as a most unpopular Prime Minister from 1828 to 1830 and as Home and Foreign Secretary in 1834 and 1835. He continued to be influential

(and was occasionally in office) thereafter, being an especially close advisor to Queen Victoria and Prince Albert. Perhaps somewhat curiously, in his last political years Wellington was a firm opponent of all army reform, leaving Britain's forces wholly unprepared for the Crimean War that broke out shortly after his death. The 'Iron Duke' died at Walmer Castle, Kent, (his official residence as *Lord Warden of the Cinque Ports) and was given one of the most magnificent state funerals ever seen in England.

Wells

1: a guest at the Keith's Ball (PC 6).
2: the Port Admiral at Portsmouth (TMC 1).
   The reference, made in mid–1809, could perhaps be to either Vice Admiral Thomas Wells (d.1811) or to Rear Admiral Sir John Wells (d.1841 in the rank of full Admiral).
3: a naval parson who travels out to Gibraltar in Jack Aubrey's HMS *Worcester* in order to join his own ship, HMS *Brunswick* (IM 3).
4: a Midshipman in HMS *Surprise* (HD 2).

'Wellwisher'

The anonymous author of the regular letters to Stephen Maturin regarding the supposed affair between his wife Diana Villiers and the Lithuanian hussar Jagiello (FSW 4).

Wesley, Serena

A young lady in Sydney with whom Jack Aubrey had wished to dally (C/T 1).

West

1: HMS *Lively*'s bosun (HMS 3).
2: a former Royal Navy officer, dismissed the service for duelling, who joins Jack Aubrey's letter-of-marque *Surprise* as a Mate/Lieutenant (LM 1+; TGS 1–4; NC 7+; C/T 1+; WDS 1–3). For much of the cruise in the Pacific he is on appalling terms with his fellow Mate, Mr Davidge, over their mutual attraction to Clarissa Oakes (C/T 3+) but his good conduct as a seaman leads Jack to suggest he might eventually be re-instated in the Navy (WDS 1). However, he is almost immediately gravely wounded by flying debris thrown up by a great volcanic eruption (WDS 1), soon dies of his head injuries (WDS 2) and is buried at sea (WDS 3). Stephen Maturin remarks that West had fought at the Battle of Camperdown (C/T 4) but he himself gives only an entertaining account of service at the Battle of the Glorious First of June, as a Midshipman in Lord Howe's HMS *Queen Charlotte* (C/T 4).
3: a Parson and keen fisherman with a living near Jack Aubrey's childhood home (LM 7).
4: an army major in Batavia (NC 3).

West, John

The sometime Captain of HMS *Euryalus* (COM 7).
   Sir John West (1774–1862), a man from a large and dis-

tinguished military and naval family related to the *Hoods and the *Pitts, was made Post in 1796. From then until the end of his sea-service in 1814, he commanded HMSS Tourterelle, *Excellent and *Sultan, but not *Euryalus. Promoted Rear Admiral in 1819, Vice Admiral in 1830 and Admiral in 1841, in 1860 he rose to Admiral of the Fleet.

West, Lady
A friend of Diana Villiers (COM 2).

Westby, Mrs
An ironmonger in Portsmouth (RM 6).

Wetherby or Witherby
A youngster in HMS *Bellona* and *Ringle* (COM 3,7,9,10; YA 4,6,9) who follows Jack Aubrey into HMS *Pomone* (HD 1).

Wetherby
A Midshipman in HMS *Leopard* (DI 3; FW 1).

Wexford
An East Indiaman in Muffit's China Fleet, protected by HMS *Surprise* from Admiral Linois' French squadron. (HMS 9).
Wexford, 1200 tons, made 7 round trips from India to England between 1802 and 1815. The action is based on the defence of a Honourable East India Company merchant fleet against *Linois' attack in February 1804. However, no Royal Navy ship was present during the fight, the squadron being organised by the senior Master, Nathaniel Dance of *Earl Camden. On this occasion William Stanley Clarke was Wexford's Master.

Weymouth, Lord
An English politician whose department has its own intelligence organisation (IM 4).
At the time of IM Thomas Thynne (1765–1837) had been 4th Viscount Weymouth and 2nd Marquis of Bath since succeeding to his father's titles in 1796. Unlike several of his predecessors, this Lord Weymouth never held government office and appears simply to have led the life of a country gentleman.

Weymouth, HMS
1: the ship whose Captain Vincent had once been court-martialed (M&C 12).
HMS Weymouth, 60-gun, was launched in 1752 and broken up in 1772. *Vincent was somewhat infamously court-martialed for his supposed failure to get her up in time to engage in the Battle of Cuddalore, 1758.
2: a ship wrecked in the approaches to Lisbon (TGS 3).
HMS Weymouth, 56-gun, was the ex-Indiaman Lord Mansfield, purchased by the Royal Navy whilst on the stocks and launched in 1795. She was reduced to a 26-gun storeship in 1798 and in early 1800, under Commander Ambrose Crofton (d.1835 in that rank), was wrecked on Lisbon Bar.

Whately
A quartermaster in HMS *Surprise* (FSW 6).

Wheel 'em Along
A ship in which Phelps of HMS *Worcester* had recently served (IM 2).
'Wheel 'em Along' was naval slang for HMS Milan, a 38-gun French frigate captured by HMS *Leander as Ville de Milan (hence the pronunciation-based nickname) in February 1805. Launched as Hermione in 1803, she had been re-named a little later in the same year. Milan served in the Royal Navy until being broken up in 1815.

Whewell
A senior Master's Mate in HMS *Aurora*, an expert on the naval aspects of the slave trade from his former merchant career, who had also previously served in HMSS *Euterpe*, *Euryalus* and *Topaz* (COM 7,8,9). Promoted by Jack Aubrey into HMS *Bellona* as an acting Lieutenant (COM 7), he is given command of the brig HMS *Cestos* (COM 9). Although Whewell later continues as a Lieutenant in *Bellona*, with the implication that his acting rank has now been confirmed (YA 5,9), he also appears in *Ringle*, *Bellona*'s tender, when she is under the command of Paddy Callaghan, a Master's Mate properly Mr Whewell's junior (YA 4). When the war against Buonaparte ends, Whewell joins Jack's *Surprise* as a volunteer for the Chilean mission (YA 10), then serving as her Third Lieutenant when she is recalled to the King's service for Jack's Mediterranean mission (HD 2+).

Whiskers
A racehorse owned by Jack Aubrey (DI 1).

Whitaker
A seaman in HMS *Surprise*, an ex-smuggler (LM 1).

Whitby, Harry
A former Captain of HMS *Leander*, who had once been treated by Stephen Maturin. Later accused of firing illegally into a U.S. merchant ship and killing one of her crew, he had been acquitted of any offence at his politically motivated court-martial but left without a command until he could clear his name through his own efforts (FW 4).
Henry Whitby (d.1812) was in command of HMS *Leander off New York in April 1805. Whilst he was dining on the nearby HMS Cambrian, his First Lieutenant, John Smith Cowan (d.1821 in the rank of Commander), fired at an American coaster, Richard, killing one John Pierce with a splinter ripped from the taffrail. That Leander had probably not intended to hit the boat at all did little to assuage opinion in the U.S., furious at her vessels again being interfered with by a foreign power and doubly furious that the incident may well have taken place just inside U.S. territorial waters. Whitby was acquitted at a subsequent court-martial on the somewhat dubious grounds that, being out of his ship, it was not he who had given the actual order to fire the round. By 1810 he was in command of the 32-gun HMS *Cerberus in *Hoste's small Mediterranean squadron and in 1811 took part in

that officer's dashing victory at Lissa. (N.B., the fact and date of Whitby's promotion to Post Captain has been omitted from the SYRETT & DiNARDO list.)

White

1: Envoy Stanhope's Chaplain (HMS 5+). After Stanhope's death, White, being too poor to take passage home in one of the East Indiamen, temporarily remains aboard HMS *Surprise*, assisting Stephen Maturin during the actions against Linois (HMS 9).
2: a member of the barge-crew of Captain Baker's HMS *Iris*, chosen for his colourful surname (FSW 2).
3: the gunner of HMS *Diane* and later HMS *Nutmeg of Consolation* (TGS 6–9; NC 1–4).
N.B., at the beginning of NC 2 *Jennings says that White has just been killed in the Dyak/Malay attack. This must be a slip of the tongue, for it is Mr *Hadley, the ship's carpenter, who has died, as correctly reported by Jennings a few moments earlier.
4: a naturalist referred to by Mr Martin (WDS 4).
Gilbert White (1720–1793) was an English naturalist and writer famed for his graceful literary style. In 1789 he published his Natural History and Antiquities of Selborne *(the small Hampshire village in which he was born and where he later served as curate: see COM 5), with his reputation being confirmed after his death by* A Naturalist's Calendar *(selections from his journals, published in 1795). White's work (still in print today) was a favourite of the young Charles Darwin and is said by Patrick O'Brian himself to have greatly influenced his own writing style.*
5: the name of two Irish families known to Jack Aubrey (COM 10).

White, Abram
A seaman in HMS *Surprise* who falls into an alcoholic coma (HD 9).

White Knight, the
An Irish chivalric title referred to by Maturin (PC 8).

White's
1: a London club (PC 10; YA 7).
White's club, popular amongst the Whig political élite, had a reputation for high living and high stakes at the gaming table. It was founded as a public Chocolate House in 1693 by Francis White (orig. Francesco Bianco, d. 1711), with its private Club dating from a few years later. White's moved to its present premises in St James' Street in 1755.
2: a hotel in Halifax, Nova Scotia (SM 1).

Whiting
A Lieutenant in HMS *Worcester* (IM 2,3,6).

Whittington
Either the gunner or a Lieutenant in HMS *Raisonable* (TMC 4).

'Whoreson Prick'
A name by which HMS *Sophie*'s crew refer to Captain Harte (M&C 11).

Widdrington, Tom
A Royal Navy officer who congratulates Jack Aubrey on his victory over *Cacafuego* (M&C 11).

Widgery
A dockyard official at Plymouth (IM 2).

Wilberforce
An anti-slavery activist in Britain (COM 8).
William Wiberforce (1759–1833), the son of a wealthy merchant, entered Parliament in 1780, becoming there a supporter, though never a partisan, of his close friend, William *Pitt. In 1785, after a Continental tour, Wilberforce experienced a deep religious conversion and by 1787 had begun to dedicate himself to the abolition of the slave trade, an activity with which Britain was then intimately connected. Between 1790 and 1806 he introduced to Parliament several bills against the trade, but each was defeated, albeit sometimes only narrowly. On a change of administration from Tory to Whig, the mood of the house altered and in 1807 an Act was passed, now with overwhelming support, declaring the trade illegal: yet the practice of slavery went on, especially in Britain's Caribbean colonies. From 1813 until his retirement on health grounds in 1825, Wilberforce continued to agitate for the emancipation of existing slaves, dying in 1833 just as the final Abolition Act was passing through Parliament.

Wilbraham
Mrs Williams' business adviser (HMS 1) who later dies, leading to his client's fleecing by his replacement (TMC 1; COM 2).

Wilcocks
A seaman in HMS *Polychrest*, previously an attorney's clerk turned pick-pocket and now believed by Jack Aubrey to be about to mutiny (PC 11).

Wilcox
1: an hay-supplier in Hampshire (DI 4).
2: a seaman in *Surprise*, injured during the volcanic explosion (WDS 1). He is perhaps the same man who is later on the ship in the Mediterranean (HD 8).

Wilfred the Shaggy
A Catalan patriot of old, an ancestor of Maturin's godfather Casademon (SM 6) and a supposed distant ancestor of Hurtado (WDS 8).
The reference is to Wilfred the Hairy (873?–898?), Count of Barcelona and a founder of the dynasty that later became Kings of Aragon. Wilfred is regarded as a great national hero of Catalonia, which he partly unified through both family alliances and force of arms.

Wilful Murder
A cannon in *Surprise* (RM 3; LM 2; NC 7; C/T 3).

Wilkes

'Wilkes and Liberty,' a code phrase used by Stephen Maturin when he embarks on a boat from Spain to England (PC 14) and later yelled by the Aubrey children as they play at 'elections' (SM 4).

John Wilkes (1727–1797) was a renowned, even infamous, English populist politician and journalist. In 1763 Wilkes, an MP since 1757, was convicted of libelling King *George III in his journal The North Briton *(a paper established to hound the Scotsman, Lord *Bute). Expelled from Parliament, Wilkes was forced to flee the country but what was seen as Royal, and Government, persecution soon made him a huge favourite with the common people. Returning to England in 1768, Wilkes was re-elected MP but then immediately arrested, fined and again expelled from the House, with the pattern being repeated in 1769. Although the crowds of his supporters took up his case with the cry 'Wilkes and Liberty,' he remained rejected by the King and his political intimates. In 1774 Wilkes, now a somewhat less fiery character, given to denying that he himself was ever a 'Wilkesite,' was elected Lord Mayor of London and MP for the County of Middlesex: this time the Establishment relented, with Wilkes now enjoying a long career as an active and always independent-minded politician.*

Wilkins

1: a seaman in HMS *Polychrest* (PC 11).
2: a former colleague of Jack Aubrey and Mr Theobald in HMS *Orion* (HMS 8).
3: the senior gunner's mate in HMS *Surprise* (FSW 6), made acting gunner following Mr Horner's suicide (FSW 7).
4: a seaman in HMS *Surprise* who breaks his arm (NC 7).
5: cruel neighbours in New South Wales of Paulton's cousin, Matthews (NC 9).
6: Wilkins Brothers, a horse-yard in Sydney (NC 9).
7: a young seaman taken from the privateer *Franklin* into *Surprise*, later promoted acting Lieutenant on account of having reputedly once been a Master's Mate in HMS *Agamemnon* (WDS 4+; COM 1).
8: a senior Master's Mate in HMS *Bellona* (COM 7; *possibly the same character as* 7 *above*).

Wilkinson

1: a seaman in HMS *Surprise* (NC 8).
2: the sometime Captain of HMS *Courageux*, whose running onto a reef is the subject of a poem by Lieutenant Rowan (IM 9).

Philip Wilkinson (d.1846) was made Post in 1794. In 1811 and 1812 he twice ran his HMS *Courageux onto rocks, being reprimanded by court martial on the first occasion and losing his ship (too damaged to serve again) on the second. The poem given to Mr *Rowan is by Courageux's *Third Lieutenant of the time, Samuel *Walters. Wilkinson rose by seniority to Rear Admiral in 1813, Vice Admiral in 1821 and full Admiral in 1837.*

Wilkinson, Robt.

A seaman referred to in HMS *Sophie*'s log as having been lashed (M&C 2).

Wilks

An elderly seaman in HMS *Surprise* (HMS 8).

Wilks, Reuben

The 'lady of the gunroom' in HMS *Irresistible* (RM 1).

'Lady of the gunroom' was the traditional ship-board name for the mate in charge of the gunner's stores.

Will

The grandson of Harding, the head gamekeeper at Woolcombe House (YA 10).

Willet

1: a Midshipman in HMS *Worcester* (IM 7).
2: a rick-yard owner near Woolcombe (YA 3).

Willet, Harry

Diana Villiers' groom, the only survivor of the coaching accident that claimed his mistress' life (HD 1).

Willett

A gunner's mate in HMS *Diane* (NC 2).

Willett, Joe

A seaman in HMS *Surprise* (HD 4).

William

1: the name used by Jack Aubrey for his steward in HMS *Sophie* (M&C 11).
This is not a name elsewhere associated with Preserved *Killick, Jack's usual steward.
2: a servant at Mrs Moon's apartment building (DI 2).
3: the Master of the fishing vessel *Leviathan* (SM 3).
4: a seaman in HMS *Surprise*, a cousin of Grainger (WDS 3,5).
This is possibly a reference to William *Sadler.
5: a man at the Hand and Racquet pub in Woolcombe (YA 2).
6: Hetty's son, badly beaten by the game-keeper Black Evans (YA 3).
7: Lord William, an English official in Sicily in the recent past (HD 3).
This may be a slip by Maturin for Sir William *Hamilton, or even perhaps for Sir William Drummond (1770?–1828) who was Minister to Naples from 1801 to 1803 and in 1806, as well as Ambassador to Constantinople from 1803 to 1806. Both men dealt with the Carbonari, a secret society which led the opposition to French influence and, later, rule in the Kingdom of the *Two Sicilies.
8: Prince William, see **Clarence, Duke of**
9: Sir William, see **Hamilton, Sir William and Emma**, *or* **Pellew, Admiral Sir William**.
10: William or Uncle William, see **Babbington, William**
11: *see* **Reade, William**

William

An American merchantman taken by HMS *Java* (FW 3).

William, HMS

see **Royal William**, HMS.

William and Mary

A captured ship whose cargo had been bought by Guzman (LM 3).

> *The ship is named for King *William III and Queen Mary II, joint monarchs of England.*

William Enderby

A London whaling ship, recaptured from the Americans by Jack Aubrey (RM 1).

William III, King

A former King of England (YA 2) since whose time the Williams family had been settled at Mapes Court. He is known as 'Dutch William' (PC 10; TMC 1) or simply, by the Ulsterman McAdam, as 'King Billy' (TMC 7).

> *King William III (1650–1702) was born as the Protestant Prince William Henry of Orange (in Holland), a grandson of King Charles I of England. In 1677 he married Mary, the daughter of that James, Duke of York, who in 1685 then succeeded his own elder brother, *Charles II, as King *James II. James, a Catholic, became deeply unpopular in England and soon William and Mary, in what has become known as the 'Glorious Revolution of 1688,' were invited by the King's Whig opponents to invade England. In 1689, after very rapidly routing James's forces with scarcely any bloodshed, William and Mary were proclaimed joint monarchs of England, Scotland and Wales (the only time a joint monarchy has existed in the Kingdoms). In the following year, William defeated James' largely Catholic armies in Ireland at the Battle of the Boyne (thus giving rise to the modern tradition of Protestant 'Orangemen' in the North) and the former Stuart ruler retired to France. In 1694 Queen Mary II died of smallpox and in 1702 William died following a fall from a horse. He was then succeeded by Mary's younger sister, *Anne.*

Williams

1: the Port Mahon correspondent of Jack Aubrey's Gibraltar prize-agent (M&C 1,9).

2: a seaman in HMS *Worcester* who had been bitten by a camel at Barka (IM 7).

3: a seaman in *Surprise* (C/T 7), later injured (COM 1).

4: Miss Williams, *see* **Aubrey, Sophie**

Williams, Cecilia or Cissy

The middle and liveliest of the three Williams sisters (PC 1+; HMS 1,4), who tells Stephen Maturin that Diana Villiers has become Richard Canning's lover (PC 14). She accompanies her elder sister Sophie on a visit to Jack Aubrey's HMS *Surprise*, there being paid attentions by the Royal Marine officer, Mr Dredge (PC 14). A little later, now pregnant, she has recently married a penniless militia officer, the cousin of her sister Frances' new husband, Sir Oliver Floode (HMS 7; *also see the note under Frances *Williams, below*). The ensuing child, 'little Cecilia,' is afterwards left with Sophie Aubrey, her aunt, whilst her mother is away following her husband's regiment (TMC 1).

Williams, Frances or Frankie

The youngest of the three Williams sisters (PC 1+; HMS 1,4). She marries Sir Oliver Floode, an Ulster landowner and the MP for Antrim (HMS 7) and is later expecting a child (SM 4). A few years later she is referred to as both a new mother of a baby and a new widow, but now of a Mr Clotworthy (RM 6). In reduced circumstances, she runs a school in Ulster that the Aubrey girls attend (YA 1).

> *A speculation: perhaps it was really Cecilia *Williams who had married Mr Clotworthy and had then been left penniless, with a young child, on his death.*

Williams, Geo.

A seaman referred to in Captain Allen's HMS *Sophie* log (M&C 2,4).

Williams, Mrs

The ignorant, interfering and grasping mother of Sophia, Cecilia and Frances Williams and the aunt of Diana Villiers. She is most eager to marry off her moderately wealthy brood but only on the most iron-clad financial terms (PC 1+). Always lukewarm over the attachment of her eldest daughter to Jack Aubrey (e.g., PC 14), she continues in her opposition to the match (HMS 1,4,6,7), especially after meeting Jack's father, with his new wife and son (HMS 7). However, in due course, Mrs Williams is undone both by the course of true love and by her own financial folly (TMC 1+): by early 1809 she has gained Jack as a son-in-law but has lost the entire family fortune, having now to let out her home of Mapes Court to a 'commercial gentleman' and move in with Jack, Sophie and her three grandchildren (TMC 1; COM 2). Although the spoils of Jack's Mauritius campaign have later paid off the Mapes mortgage, Mrs Williams prefers to leave it rented out and continue to live, presumably free, at Ashgrove Cottage, to the despair of her family and its circle (DI 1). Sometime afterwards she spends a period in Ulster, awaiting the birth of Frances' child (SM 2,4). Her relative poverty in the middle years of the series gradually seems to break her spirit (IM 5; FSW 9; RM 3; LM 4; *especially* TGS 1,4; C/T 3), but the slow rise in the Aubrey family fortunes, together with a wicked ploy by Diana Villiers, put her back in the thick of things. Having moved to Bath with her friend Mrs Morris and the manservant Briggs, Mrs Williams takes over Diana's small, illegal gambling business, again to the despair and irritation of all around (COM 1–6). But we soon learn that Mrs Morris and Briggs have run off together, leaving Mrs Williams ill and distraught, bundled back to Woolcombe House by Sophie (YA 6). Here, in her sick-room, she eventually discovers old love letters once sent to Jack by an *amour* and, having immediately shown them to Sophie, provokes a furious row and temporary separation between the couple, before being herself packed off back to Bath by Diana Villiers (YA 8). A little while later Mrs Williams is killed, along with several others, in the coaching accident that takes Diana Villiers' life (HD 1,2).

Williams, Sophia, Sophie, or simply Miss
see **Aubrey, Sophie.**

N.B., as the eldest daughter of the family Sophia Williams is addressed formally as 'Miss Williams,' with her younger sisters being addressed 'Miss Cecilia' and 'Miss Frances.' In addition, 'Sophie,' a contraction of her proper given name of 'Sophia,' is at first used only by her closest confidants.

Williamson
1: a Midshipman in Jack Aubrey's HMSS *Worcester* and *Surprise* (IM 5+), the son of Jack's old friend Dick Williamson (IM 10). Due to play Ophelia in the *Worcester* production of *Hamlet* (IM 5), he falls ill with the mumps (IM 8). On Jack's Ionian mission Williamson goes wolf-hunting with the Turkish allies (IM 8) and, in the later action against the rebel frigates *Torgud* and *Kutali*, loses an arm (IM 11). Although he then continues in service with Jack, no further reference is made to any incapacity (TH 2+; FSW 2–7; RM 1+).
2: Williamson, Esq., Sir: the mistaken way in which Andréossy referred to a Whitehall mandarin (LM 7).
One cannot be both an 'Esq.' and a 'Sir.' Examples of possible correct modes of written address would be either plain 'Mr John Williamson,' or 'John Williamson, Esq.' ('Esquire' being an explicit indication that the addressee has the 'social rank' of 'gentleman'). If the addressee is a knight, then 'Sir John Williamson' is correct and may be shortened, in direct address, to 'Sir John.'

Williamson, Dick
An old shipmate of Jack Aubrey, whose son now serves as a Midshipman in Jack's HMSS *Worcester* and *Surprise* (IM 10).

Willis
1: Willis,' a gambling den frequented by Aubrey and Goole (RM 1), later said to be where Jack Aubrey had accused Andrew Wray of cheating at cards (IM 1).
*N.B., elsewhere the location is said to have been *Craddock's.*

2: a Commander known to Tom and Mrs Pullings (TGS 1).
3: a now-deceased expert on mental disorders who had once treated King George III (TGS 9).
*Francis Willis (1718–1807), a clergyman and theologian, became Vice Principal of Brasenose College, Oxford, in the late 1750s before receiving the M.D. degree in 1759 and turning full-time to his true passion, the sympathetic treatment of mental illness. After founding a centre in Lincolnshire that won great acclaim for its successes, Willis was in 1788 called in to treat King *George III, then suffering from his first debilitating bout of mania. Against the views of his more conventional colleagues (who regarded him as little more than a mountebank), Willis was convinced that the King could recover and that he should therefore be treated far less rigorously and contemptuously than was the grim norm of the time. When, in the following year, the King did in fact almost completely regain his faculties—at least for a time—Willis' reputation soared, enabling him to build a large and lucrative private practice. Two of his sons also became physicians specialising in insanity (see # 5 below) and another became a Rear Admiral in the Royal Navy (see # 6 below).*
4: the family name of friends of Diana Villiers (COM 2).
5: a Portsmouth specialist in the mental development of children (COM 3).
*The reference may be to one of two well-known doctors with large practices in treating mental disorders, the brothers John (1751–1835) and Richard Darling (1760–1821) Willis, sons of Francis Willis (see # 3 above). Both men followed their father in treating King *George III for his bouts of mania, although neither was able to repeat the earlier success of 1788. One of their other brothers, Richard, became an Admiral in the Royal Navy (see # 6 below).*
6: a Post Captain promoted Rear Admiral and immediately placed on the retired, or 'yellow,' list (YA 1).
Richard Willis (1755–1829), a son of the mad-doctor Francis Willis (see #3 above), was made Post in 1790 and, after a career of no noteworthy service, 'yellowed' to Rear Admiral in 1808 (some seven years before YA is set).
7: an officer in HMS *Pomone* (HD 1).
8: the Master of a school once attended by William Reade and a Royal Marine officer (HD 8).

Willis, Peter
A seaman in *Surprise* (C/T 2; WDS 2; COM 1).

Willougby
A Marine Lieutenant in HMS *Stately* who quarrels with the Second Lieutenant of HMS *Thames* (COM 8). They then duel, each inflicting a mortal wound on the other (COM 9).

Willoughby
A Captain mentioned by Molly Harte (M&C 1).

Willsea, Saml.
A seaman referred to in HMS *Sophie*'s log (M&C 2).

Willughby

A naturalist referred to by Maturin (M&C 2).

*Francis Willughby (1635–1672) was a celebrated British ornithologist, naturalist, mathematician and traveller, many of whose works, edited posthumously by his colleague John *Ray, were greatly admired by *Cuvier.*

Wilson

1: an American seaman in HMS *Sophie* who unsuccessfully petitions not to be flogged by King, the black bosun (M&C 11).

2: a seaman in HMS *Polychrest* (PC 9).

3: one of Colonel Keating's officers (TMC 4).

4: a landowner against whom some of HMS *Leopard*'s convicts had poached (DI 4).

5: an officer who, having escaped from imprisonment in France with Charles Fielding and Mr Corby, had then died of exposure in northern Italy (TH 9).

6: an official referred to by Sir Joseph Blaine (RM 5).

7: Jack Aubrey's cook in HMSS *Diane* (TGS 5) and *Nutmeg of Consolation* (NC 4+).

8: a seaman in *Surprise* (C/T 8; HD 2).

9: Diana Villiers' stud manager, supposed by Mrs Williams to be her lover (COM 2,3).

10: a member of Black's Club (YA 1).

11: Captain and Mrs Wilson, who had died, with all their children, of fever in the West Indies after the Captain had been nursed back to health from the loss of a foot by Poll Skeeping (HD 2).

Wilson, Frederick

The First Lieutenant of HMS *Surprise* when she cut out the mutinous *Hermione* (C/T 2).

*William Wilson (dates unknown), an officer commissioned in 1779, was acting First Lieutenant of *Hamilton's HMS *Surprise when she re-took *Hermione in 1799. Wilson, given the task of running his boat up to Hermione's anchor cables and cutting the ship free, instead engaged and pursued a Spanish gunboat before arriving late at the now-secured frigate. Although Captain Hamilton made no direct criticism of his conduct, he simply failed to mention the Lieutenant in the official report, an omission tantamount to a condemnation.*

Wilson, Isaac

A seaman in HMS *Sophie*, the subject of a note to Jack Aubrey from Captain Allen (M&C 1). He is later accused of sexual congress with the ship's goat and clapped into irons whilst Jack ponders the problem of his, and the goat's, fate (M&C 3; COM 9).

Wilton

A seaman in *Surprise* (C/T 9).

Windham

A merchantman taken by the French frigates *Vénus* and *Manche* and shortly afterwards retaken by HMS *Magicienne* (TMC 5). However, she soon falls yet again into French hands (TMC 7) before being finally retaken by Tom Pullings in his schooner (TMC 8). Jack Aubrey offers her to Tomkinson, the Commander of the temporarily disabled HMS *Otter*, but he declines the appointment (TMC 8).

*Windham, 823-tons, made 6 round trips for the East India Company between 1800 and 1815. During the Mauritius campaign she was first taken by the French in late November 1809 and retaken by the Royal Navy just a few weeks later, as described in the text. When, under John Stewart, she was again taken by the French in July 1810, she put up a stout resistance, only surrendering when she was badly battered and had sustained 24 injuries and deaths. She was again taken into British hands three weeks later by the boats of HMS *Sirius, led by Lieutenant John Wyatt Watling (dates unknown; a superannuated Post Captain of 1830). When *Tomkinson later declined command of the ship, it was a Lieutenant from HMS *Emma, Henry Lynne (a Commander of April 1811, d.1835), who filled the breach. Windham was named for William Windham (1750–1810), a British statesman who was Secretary of War from 1794 to 1801 and Secretary of the Colonies in 1806–1807.*

Winslow

A U.S. official who interrogates Jack Aubrey in Boston (FW 4).

Winthrop

An officer of the USS *Norfolk* (RM 2).

Wiseacre, Jean

A French seaman aboard *Santa Lucia* who mistakes HMS Sophie for the Danish brig *Clomer* (M&C 7).

Wiseman

A medical authority whose text is consulted by Stephen Maturin (C/T 4).

Richard Wiseman (1625–1686), known as the 'father of English surgery' published two books intended as manuals for naval and military surgeons. His Several Chirurgical Treatises *(1676) was the more general of the two, with the earlier* Treatise of Wounds *(1672) being promoted as especially useful for ships' doctors 'who seldom burden their cabin with many books.'*

Witherby

see **Wetherby**

Withering, Dr

An expert on the use of the drug *digitalis* for heart ailments (YA 8).

William Withering (1741–1799) was an English physician, botanist and scientist with a special interest in the medicinal uses of plants, a long-standing field of study that he helped now to systematise. Withering is best remembered for his researches into the use of the digitalis *component of foxglove leaves as a treatment for congestive heart failure or 'dropsy' (see also TH 8).*

Withers

The Dorsetshire attorney of the Aubrey family (LM 8; C/T 1), later reported dead (C/T 3).

Witsover, Abraham
A seaman in HMS *Surprise* (IM 9).

Witsover, John
A seaman who acts as a servant at Jack Aubrey's Melbury Lodge (PC 2).

Witsover, William
A seaman in HMS *Sophie* (M&C 3+).

Wittgenstein
A Heligoland seaman in Sir James Saumarez' Baltic flag-ship, loaned to Jack Aubrey's HMS *Ariel* for his local knowledge. Many years before, the young Midshipman Aubrey had in fact pressed him into the Royal Navy from a collier and, on one later occasion, only Wittgenstein's solid navigational abilities had saved Jack, now a very youthful prize-master, from disaster (SM 8). A very steady and able man, he is given command of *Minnie* in order to take Stephen Maturin into Grimsholm (SM 8) and later, when all are captives of the French, he is given charge of Jack's purse for the needs of *Ariel's* crew (SM 10).

Wodehouse
1: the Honourable Mrs Wodehouse, the fashionable wife of a naval officer, living in Halifax (SM 1)
*The reference is to the wife (details unknown) of the Honourable Philip Wodehouse (1773–1838), a son of Lord Wodehouse of Kimberley (a family title later upgraded to an Earldom). He was made Post in 1796 and from 1811 to 1819 served as *Commissioner at Halifax, resigning this North American position in late 1819 on his promotion to Rear Admiral. Wodehouse rose to Vice Admiral in 1830.*
2: the Captain of HMS *Orion* (IM 8).

Wogan
The estranged husband of the spy Louisa Wogan, a member of the American diplomat Mr Jay's mission to London (DI 4,6).

Wogan, Caroline
The baby born to Louisa Wogan and Michael Herapath aboard the whaler *La Fayette*. Although Louisa had told Maturin she was keen to have children (DI 8), she later appears not to be wholly attached to the reality of the experience. Furthermore, her new lover, Harry Johnson, is thought by Caroline's doting grandfather, George Herapath, to be profoundly uninterested in the support of any child not his own (FW 5–8).

Wogan, Louisa
An American spy, estranged from her diplomat husband, who has been living in London, sometimes with Michael Herapath — to whom she seems genuinely attached — and sometimes with a succession of well-connected lovers (DI 2+). According to Sir Joseph Blaine, she is originally from Philadelphia (DI 2,4) and a Roman Catholic (DI 6), occasionally showing herself to be an accomplished author under the name 'John Doe' (DI 2). Louisa's acquaintance with Diana Villiers draws down suspicion both on her new friend and even on Stephen Maturin (DI 2), especially when she herself is soon arrested. However, she then manages to plead to a lesser charge than spying in exchange for giving some details of her activities to the authorities (DI 2). With the intercession of a former lover, the 'D of C' (*the Duke of *Clarence is possible, as are the Dukes of *Cumberland, Connaught etc.*), she is sentenced to transportation to Australia — rather than immediate imprisonment or worse — and consigned to Jack Aubrey's HMS *Leopard* for the journey (DI 2+). Stephen Maturin has been deputed by Blaine to travel with her, in his 'disguise' as the ship's surgeon, in order to find out the full extent of her former activities (DI 2). He soon gains both her confidence and that of Herapath, who has stowed away in *Leopard* to be near her (DI 3+). Louisa uses the unwitting Herapath — by whom she is now pregnant (DI 8) — to send coded letters to the USA but these are intercepted by Stephen (DI 5) who, in turn, uses her loving dupe to plant false intelligence information in her own mind (DI 7). Stephen then arranges for the pair to 'escape' from Desolation Island in *La Fayette*, a passing American whaler (DI 10).

A little later, Jack and Stephen, now prisoners-of-war, encounter Louisa (here said to be a native of Baltimore: FW 4,5) in Boston (FW 1–8). Having given birth at sea to a daughter, Caroline, she seems most uneasy with the actual experience of parenthood (FW 5–8), despite her earlier desire for a child (DI 8). Louisa has also become attached to Diana Villiers' lover, Harry Johnson, perhaps in part because they are both closely associated with U.S. intelligence activities (FW 5,6). Together they try to recruit Stephen to their cause, all the while thinking it is Jack who is the wily British intelligence agent simply masquerading as a bluff sea-captain (FW 5+). However, with horror Louisa finally realises, presumably having been told by Johnson, that it is Stephen who has duped her all along (FW 7; *also* SM 4; NC 6; C/T 1).

Wood, James and Christine
The Governor of Sierra Leone, once a shipmate of Jack Aubrey and formerly Captain of HMS *Hebe* (COM 7,8,9; HD 3,6); he is soon reported by Dr Glover to have recently died (HD 1). His wife is the sister of the naturalist Edward Heatherleigh, and herself an anatomist of considerable ability (COM 9), as well as being related to the engineer James Wright (HD 1,3). Dr Glover also remarks that the marriage cannot have been a happy one, the Governor having been impotent (HD 1); Christine

Wood later features in a vivid dream of the newly widowed Stephen Maturin (HD 4).

At the time that COM is set, the Governorship of Sierra Leone had been out of Royal Navy hands since the resignation in 1811 of Captain Edward Henry Columbine, who had held the post since just after the slave trade was abolished in 1807 (Columbine's wife had died of fever shortly before his resignation and he himself died just a few weeks later, also of fever). After his tenure, the post passed into army hands until at least the late 1820s.

Wood, Joseph

An HMS Sophie seaman referred to in her log as having been lashed (M&C 2+).

Woodbine

The Master of Jack Aubrey's HMSS *Bellona* (COM 7,8,9; YA 5,6) and *Surprise* (HD 2–9). He is a Sethian from Shelmerston (HD 2).

Woods

An elderly seaman in HMS *Surprise* who contracts a fatal pneumonia (HMS 6).

Wool, Perpetual Curate of
see Lydgate

Woolcombe, Captain

1: the Captain of HMS *Laurel*, 22-gun, a ship that had been captured by *Cannonière* before Jack Aubrey's arrival in the Indian Ocean. He is court-martialed and honourably acquitted for her loss by a panel led by Jack (TMC 6).

*John Charles Woolcombe (dates unknown) was promoted Commander in 1804 and made Post later that year; his HMS *Laurel, 22-gun, was captured by the 48-gun *Cannonière in September 1808. Woolcombe went on to command the 38-gun HMS Revolutionnaire in operations off the coast of Spain during 1813.*

2: the name under which General Aubrey had been in hiding before his death (LM 8).

The alias is taken from Woolcombe House, the Aubrey family home near Dorchester, in the county of Dorset; the name is sometimes also seen as Woolhampton (PC 1; YA 2).

Woolton, Harry

The Captain of HMS *Mars* (YA 4).

Wooton

An English politician or civil servant who has fallen into the power of the spy Diego Diaz (YA 7).

Worcester, HMS

A decrepit 74-gun ship due for blockade duty in the Mediterranean of which Jack Aubrey accepts temporary command when his worsening finances necessitate a long spell at sea (IM 1–10). Built in Sankey's corrupt yard, she is one of the notorious 'Forty Thieves' (IM 1). Jack obtains for her a private supply of gunpowder from the stores of a recently deceased fireworks manufacturer: though effective when fired, it is spectacularly and alarmingly colourful (IM 2). In order to relieve the tedium of blockade, the *Worcesters*, a musical crew, embark upon preparation for a performance of Handel's *Messiah* (IM 5) but the event is interrupted by news that the French fleet has set sail from Toulon (IM 8). After participating in the abortive attempt to bring Admiral Emeriau to battle (IM 8), the storm-battered *Worcester* is sent to Malta to refit and Jack is then given his old HMS *Surprise* for a mission to the Ionian sea (IM 9). *Worcester* undergoes major and costly repairs (TH 1–3) before being condemned as a sheer-hulk by Admiral Ives (TH 4, 5,8; also RM 1; COM 7; HD 4).

HMS Worcester, 64-gun, was launched in 1769 and fought in no less than six fleet actions (five of them in the Indian Ocean in 1782–1783) before being reduced to a hulk in 1788 (well before IM, although she may have occasionally then been used as transport) and finally broken up in 1816.

Worlidge

1: a former shipmate of Jack Aubrey, now in service at Ashgrove Cottage (SM 4).
2: the Captain of HMS *Leopard* (LM 8).

Worsley

A member of Black's Club (TGS 4).

Wrangham or Wrangle, Captain

The Captain of HMS *Pomone*, ashore in Madeira with an injured leg (YA 10). He is superseded by Jack Aubrey (YA 10; HD 1).

Wray, Andrew (*on one occasion* Edmund)

Andrew Wray, an *eminence grise* for much of the series, is first met as a rising young Treasury official who has served in both the Admiralty and Patronage offices (DI 1,2). A frequenter of Craddock's gaming house in Portsmouth, he plays cards for high stakes with Jack Aubrey and others (DI 1,2) and is soon suspected by Stephen Maturin of cheating (DI 1). Directly accused of so doing so by Jack, who then expects to duel as a consequence, Wray fails to issue a challenge, with Stephen suspecting that he will have his revenge in some quieter way (DI 2; *oddly, Stephen later recalls that he knew nothing of the card incident between Wray and Jack until after the event, learning of it only at second hand:* TH 1). Wray soon rises to the important position of acting Second Secretary at the Admiralty (SM 1,4; IM 1) and starts to get his own back on Jack by arranging for his promised HMS *Acasta* to be given to another Captain (SM 4; *curiously, at one point Sir Joseph *Blaine asks Stephen if he recalls 'Edmund Wray,' a slip uncorrected by the Doctor: SM 4*). He also becomes Commander William Babbington's rival for the hand of Fanny Harte, the daughter of an Admiral (IM 5,11).

Wray soon assumes new responsibilities for intelligence matters and arrives in Malta (TH 1+), newly married to the unwilling and unhappy Fanny (TH 1,8). We now learn that Wray is a traitor, motivated in part by radical enthusiasms but not adverse to financial rewards: his main contact is the French spy Lesueur, from whom he learns of Stephen's past political activities (TH 2+). Sending Hairabedian as a spy on Jack's Mubara expedition, he ensures its betrayal is complete (TH 4). He also almost certainly betrays the later Zambra mission, bringing about, amongst other things, the death of his wealthy father-in-law, Admiral Harte (TH 8,10). At this stage Stephen does not entirely trust Wray, being as he is both a newcomer to intelligence work of doubtful judgement and honesty (TH 1,8) and either homo- or bi-sexual (TH 8; RM 6), but he does not suspect him as traitor (TH 10). Indeed, Stephen even asks him to carry to England an important letter to Diana Villiers assuring her that the rumours of an affair with Laura Fielding are false, a letter then left cruelly undelivered (FSW 1,2,4).

Back in London, Wray remains undiscovered as spy and now works in association with his more powerful and clever colleague, Ledward: Blaine and Stephen increasingly come to regard Wray himself as weak and unsound (RM 2,5). Indeed, when Stephen later pays him a visit, he is in a state of considerable nervous tension, trying unsuccessfully and all-too-openly to trick the Doctor into a trap in France (RM 5). He is soon revealed as being in deep financial trouble — his semi-estranged wife, Fanny, has sole control of her dead father's fortune and is still in love with William Babbington (RM 6; LM 2+) — with Stephen learning that large sums of secret government funds that he had entrusted to Wray's care (RM 5) have gone missing (RM 8). Finally, the French defector Duhamel reveals Wray and Ledward as both the long sought after traitors (RM 10) and also as the plotters of the recent disgrace and dismissal of Jack Aubrey from the Royal Navy (RM 7+; LM 2+).

A little later, somehow forewarned of their impending doom, Wray and Ledward have escaped to France and are both now to be part of the French mission to Pulo Prabang, rivals to Mr Fox, the British envoy (TGS 1–9). Wray himself, in a somewhat pitiful state of fear, is now thought to be relatively unimportant (TGS 3,4 6). Exposed by Stephen and Fox as the lover not only of Ledward but also, simultaneously, of the Sultan's cup-bearer and intimate, Abdul, Wray is left unprotected and killed, along with both of his *amours* (TGS 7,8). The two traitors, probably shot by Fox, perhaps with Stephen's assistance (TGS 9), are then dissected by Stephen and his fellow anatomist, van Buren, as a means of quiet disposal of the bodies

(TGS 8; WDS 7). Later still, Stephen discovers from Clarissa Oakes that Wray and Ledward had frequented Mother Abbott's whore-house with their secret patron 'Pilliwinks' (C/T 6,7,9), afterwards exposed as the Duke of Habachtsthal (COM 2,4,5).

Wray, Mrs Fanny
see **Harte, Fanny**.

Wray, Judge
A cousin of Andrew Wray, a card player at Craddock's (DI 1,2).

Wright
1: a seaman in HMS *Polychrest* (PC 9).
2: a Royal Navy Commander who had been captured by the French in 1805, held in the Temple prison in Paris and then almost certainly murdered there, much to the outrage of the British government (SM 10).
John Wesley Wright (1769–1805), an Irish officer, entered the Royal Navy in 1781 and from 1788 to 1793 spent a period of unemployment travelling in Russia and becoming an accomplished linguist. In 1794 he was invited by Sir Sidney *Smith to join his HMS Diamond as both Midshipman and confidential secretary. In April 1796 Wright then accompanied his Captain in a small boat attack on the Vengeur privateer lying in the mouth of the Loire. Unfortunately the captured Vengeur then drifted upstream with the tide into the path of other enemy ships and her English prize crew were soon captured. Smith and Wesley were sent to the Temple in Paris as state prisoners (rather than naval prisoners-of-war) but, after just a few weeks, managed a bold escape, soon returning to service in England. Wright was soon commissioned Lieutenant, in 1800, and then promoted Commander in 1802. In late May 1804, supposedly whilst attempting to land French partisans in Quiberon Bay, his 16-gun HMS Vincejo (see *Vencejo) was becalmed, surrounded by gun-boats and, after a fierce resistance, taken. Wright, denying that he was engaged in anything other than a routine naval operation, was once again consigned to the Temple, where (according to CLOWES) he soon received from London the consoling news that he was to be made Post. However, on October 28th 1805, just a week after *Nelson's great victory at Trafalgar, Wright was found dead in his cell, his throat cut and his hand clutching a razor. The French authorities reported this as suicide (saying that he had been driven to deep despair by the news of the surrender to *Buonaparte of the Austrian General Mack!) but the British government immediately alleged foul play, refusing until 1807 even to accept that Wright was necessarily dead. After the *Bourbon restoration of 1814–1815, Admiral Smith tried to gather hard evidence that his protégé had been murdered, prompting the exiled Emperor to issue a denial of what he thought to be a preposterous slur on his own character. Despite Smith's efforts, the circumstances of Wright's death remain obscure.

Wright, James
A famous engineer and Fellow of the Royal Society, currently visiting Port Mahon (HD 1). He is related to the newly widowed Mrs Christine Wood (HD

3). Wright offers to repair Stephen Maturin's broken narwhal horn (HD 3), a task expertly accomplished (HD 8).

Wriothesley, Sir John
A Justice of the Peace in Hampshire (COM 3).

Wrong
One of Canning's domestic tigers, the other being Right (HMS 10).

Wu Han
A banker in Pulo Prabang, an associate of Lin Liang (TGS 6–8)

X

Xaloc
A Barcelona smuggling vessel, owned by Mateu and protected by the privateer *Gloire*, eventually captured by Jack Aubrey's HMS *Sophie* (M&C 7).

Xenophon
An author referred to by Maturin as a famous horseman (HD 7).

Xenophon (430?–355? BC) was an Athenian soldier and historian, a pupil and friend of the great philosopher Socrates. His best-remembered work is the Anabasis, *an account of his service as a mercenary under the Persian prince Cyrus in his revolt against King Artaxerxes. After Cyrus' defeat, Xenophon led the Greek contingent of the rebel army to Anatolia, where they eventually took service with the Spartans, on one occasion against his own home state. Formally exiled from Athens as a result, between about 394 and his death he lived in retirement under Spartan patronage, as keen a huntsman as he was a writer both on the military events of his own lifetime and on the more general political and cultural milieu of Greece and Persia. Xenophon and Athens were reconciled to each other shortly before his death, at least in part because his son had been killed in the city's service in 362. In addition to the* Anabasis, *amongst Xenophon's many other works (all of which appear to be extant) are* Hellenica, Cavalry Commander, On Horsemanship *and* On Hunting.

Xerxes
A King who fought at Salamis (SM 8).

Xerxes I of Persia (ruled 486–465 BC) succeeded his father King Darius, continuing his plans for war against the Greeks (although, curiously, no Persian document mentions his expeditions, with our principal knowledge coming from the Greek historian, *Herodotus). In 480 BC Xerxes' armies crossed the Hellespont, swiftly dispatched Greek resistance and marched on to Athens. He then found that city to have been evacuated by its retreating citizens, trusting in *Themistocles plans to defeat the invaders at sea. After an indecisive engagement with the Greeks off Artemesium (an affair followed by a great storm), Xerxes quickly re-grouped his enormous fleet of some 1200 vessels but was soon heavily defeated off Salamis, a calamity that he is said to have witnessed from the shore. He then returned to Babylon (leaving his armies to continue the war for another year before retreating homewards), ruling for another 15 years before being assassinated in a palace coup.

Y

Yamina
The beautiful and intelligent horse given to Jack Aubrey for the overland portion of his Mubara expedition (TH 5).

Yann
A French royalist pilot attached to the English squadron blockading Brest (YA 5,6).

Yardley, John
The yeoman of the sheets in HMS *Surprise* (WDS 4).

'Yardo'
The 'parish bull' mentioned by Mr Williams regarding Jack Aubrey's amorous propensities (M&C 11).

Yarrow
Admiral Ives' secretary (TH 4,8; FSW 1,2), once a speech-writer for the politician Mr Addington (FSW 1)

Yates, Thos.
A seaman in HMS *Sophie* (M&C 5).

Yeats

A gardener pressed into Jack Aubrey's HMS *Worcester* who, as a boy, had served briefly in HMS *Hermione*. Taking pity on Yeats' plight, Stephen Maturin rejects him as unfit for service (IM 2).

Yeo

A Lieutenant in HMS *Néréide*, wounded in action (TMC 10).

York, Cardinal

A man believed by Princess Augusta to be the last barrier to the security of the Hanoverian dynasty (LM 7).

> *Henry Benedict Maria Clement Stuart (1725–1807) was the last surviving grandson of the deposed *James II of England (who had been Duke of York before succeeding to the throne). The son of James Edward Stuart, the 'Old Pretender,' and the brother of Charles Edward Stuart, the '*Young Pretender,' he spent his life in Rome, becoming a Cardinal of the Roman Catholic Church in 1747.*

York, HMS

The ship into which George Lucock had been pressed, that had then foundered in the North Sea with the loss of all hands (PC 7).

> *HMS York, 64-gun, was launched in 1796 (having been purchased on the stocks as the East Indiaman Royal Admiral). Last seen on December 26th 1803, she is presumed to have foundered in a North Sea gale some time during January 1804.*

Yorke, Charles

1: a man who writes a letter to Jack Aubrey (DI 1).

> *Charles Philip Yorke (1764–1834), an English lawyer and statesman, was the half-brother of Philip Yorke (1757–1834), 3rd Earl of Hardwicke. Charles Yorke served as an MP from 1790 to 1818, becoming in 1801 Secretary of War in *Sidmouth's administration and then serving as Home Secretary from 1803 to 1804, with a subsequent spell as *First Lord of the Admiralty under *Perceval from 1810 to 1811. In all three posts Yorke was as ineffective as he was unpopular. His younger brother, Admiral Sir Joseph Sydney Yorke (1768–1831), also served as an Admiralty Lord from 1810–1818, with his son, Charles Philip (1799–1873), eventually becoming both the 4th Earl of Hardwicke and a full Admiral in the Royal Navy.*

2: the somewhat idle and unambitious Captain of HMS *La Flèche*, a keen reader and musician (FW 1,2). He had once served with Jack Aubrey in HMS *Resolution* and had later been Third Lieutenant of HMS *Sybille* when she took *La Forte*. Having been Second Lieutenant of HMS *Orion* at the Battle of Trafalgar, Yorke gives a short account of the action to Jack and Stephen Maturin (FW 2). When his ship later catches accidental fire in the South Atlantic, he is the last man to leave her in the boats (FW 2) but it is later implied that he did not survive the ensuing journey (FW 6).

> *As Yorke (a fictional character) says, no two accounts of the Battle of Trafalgar are exactly alike; yet his own is a little*

odd in two respects. At the point when Captain *Codrington called his officers on deck, it was HMS *Ajax that lay immediately ahead of his HMS *Orion— which was lying 9th out of the 11 ships in *Nelson's windward division— with HMS *Minotaur ahead of her, although these positions gradually changed when the fleets opened fire just after noon. Orion's logbook notes that, just before battle commenced, she could see all 33 ships of the line in the enemy fleet, together with one frigate. However, the leading enemy ship was not the French *Bucentaure (as implied by Yorke) but the Spanish 80-gun Neptuno, with the rearmost ship being the 74-gun *San Juan Nepomuceno. Bucentaure in fact lay 11th in her line, almost dead ahead of Nelson's column (which was approaching the enemy fleet at right angles), and would consequently have been one of the most difficult enemy ships to see clearly from Orion.

Young

1: a seaman in HMS *Polychrest* (PC 9).

2: the author of *Night Thoughts* (COM 2).

> *Edward Young (1638–1765) was an English poet and clergyman whose most famous work is The Complaint, or Night Thoughts on Life, Death and Immortality, a popular and successful blank-verse, thought to commemorate his recently deceased wife, step-daughter and her husband. Amongst many famous lines, one in particular would undoubtedly be a favourite of Jack *Aubrey, 'Procrastination is the thief of time.'*

Young, Arthur

A friend of Jack Aubrey and an expert on the economics of land enclosure (YA 2), a practice he is later said by Lord Stranraer to favour (YA 4).

> *Arthur Young (1741–1820) was a leading English writer on the techniques and economics of agriculture, basing his work not only on his own experiences from 1765 onwards as an experimental (though largely unsuccessful) farmer in Essex, but also on extensive travels throughout the British Isles and France, on whose own land-use practices he had a great impact. He published widely on all aspects of the land and in 1784 issued the first of 47 volumes of his Annals of Agriculture, a popular and influential work (to which King *George III— 'Farmer George'— contributed under the name 'Ralph Robinson'). In 1793 Young became Secretary to the Board of Agriculture, a position from which he was able to promote his various schemes for improving productivity in raising crops and livestock, including widespread enclosure of hitherto open land. Young's Travels in France, 1787–1789 (1792) is especially valuable for the picture it draws of economic and social conditions in that country just as the Revolution is breaking out.*

Young, George

A seaman in *Surprise* badly wounded in the action on Moahu Island (C/T 9).

Young Pretender

The character adopted by William Babbington for a costume ball (LM 2), later said to be a Roman Catholic (COM 5).

> *Prince Charles Edward Stuart (1720–1788), a.k.a. 'Bonny Prince Charlie, the Young Pretender,' was a grandson of the deposed, Roman Catholic King *James II of England and the son of James Edward Stuart, the 'Old Pretender.'*

*Charles pursued his family claim to the English throne in the invasion and rising of 1745 (as his father before him had done in 1715) but, after its failure, lived out his life in dissolute exile in France and Italy. His younger brother, the last of the direct male Stuart line, was Cardinal *York.*

Yusuf

One of Mr Fox's Malay servants (TGS 5,6,8), by implication later killed with his master in the typhoon that strikes their small boat (TGS 10).

Z

Zealous, HMS

A ship dispatched to Zambra by Admiral Ives following Jack Aubrey's inconclusive battle (FSW 1). She is later on the Brest blockade (YA 4).

HMS Zealous, *74-gun, was launched in 1785 and in 1798 fought under her Captain Samuel *Hood in *Nelson's great victory at the Nile. Towards the end of that battle she engaged single-handed the four French ships that managed to escape capture or destruction, until being recalled to anchor by the Rear Admiral. Long part of the Mediterranean fleet, in 1805 she was one of those ships unlucky enough to be sent with *Louis' squadron to Gibraltar for supplies, thus missing Nelson's final victory at Trafalgar.* Zealous *was broken up in 1816.*

Zebedee

A reference, perhaps biblical, by Mr Burton (DI 7).

*In the New Testament, Zebedee, a Galilean fisherman, was the father of the Apostles *John the Divine and *James.*

Zeek

The harpooner of the American whaler taken by *Surprise* and *Franklin*. He promptly murders the ship's Master for having abandoned him and his boat-mates in an attempt to escape capture (WDS 5).

Zelenka, Dismas

A composer admired by Jack Aubrey (HD 3).

Jan Dismas Zelenka (1679–1745) was a Bohemian composer and double-bass virtuoso. After study in Prague and Vienna, he settled in Dresden, becoming church music composer to the Court in 1735.

Zeno

The Stoic philosopher (M&C 12), whose school is much admired by Maturin (RM8; WDS 10).

Zeno (335–263 BC) of Citium, in Cyprus, founded a philosophical school in Athens at the Stoa Poecile ('Painted Porch'), a location that gives rise to the term 'Stoic'. His philosophy, and that of his many pupils and associates, had branches of physics, metaphysics, logic and, most famously, ethics. In Zeno's uncompromising ethical system, all emotion is bad, only virtue is good, and virtue

alone is sufficient for 'happiness,' the latter concept somewhat idiosyncratically and variously defined. In the popular sense, 'stoicism' is characterised by the calm acceptance of the vagaries of fate whilst in the pursuit of some more certain purpose.

Zephyrus

A god invoked by Jack Aubrey in the hope of fair winds (WDS 1).

*In classical myth, the Zephyr, a son of Astreus and *Aurora, represented the west wind.*

Zeus

A god, one of whose temples lies at the Greek port of Kutali (IM 10).

*Zeus was the pre-eminent diety in the Greek pantheon, the great father, king and lord. The root of the name is something akin to 'bright sky' and for Greeks and Romans (to whom he was known as *Jupiter), Zeus controlled the weather, both in the everyday sense and in his ability to strike the recalcitrant with lightning or thunder, signs of his power and wrath. In early Greek legend, Zeus had to struggle for his power both against his own father, Cronus, and various giants and monsters and, having triumphed, thereby assumed the right to exert dominance over both the heavenly spheres and already-existing mankind. From his union with his sister, *Hera (the Roman *Juno), Zeus fathered *Mars, *Minerva, *Venus, *Apollo and many other gods, all of whom compete for his favour, often involving mortals in their elaborate plots.*

Zwingerius

A doctor referred to by Maturin (IM 2).

The Swiss Zwinger (often Latinised to Zwingerius) family were highly distinguished in the medical arts (as well as in many other aspects of scholarship) from the late 16th to at least the late 18th century. The reference here is perhaps to Theodore Zwinger (1658–1724), a physician, anatomist and botanist who held a series of professorships at Basle University from 1687 until his death, publishing extensively in his chosen fields.

Bibliography

In a reference work of the type here attempted it is neither possible (nor would it be especially useful) to list every work consulted, especially when many of these have only given me an idea of where next to look. However, everything in this biographical dictionary has been confirmed from one or more of the works listed below. In addition, a handful of works consulted on a single fact alone are detailed only in the main entries to which they refer.

Bank, David and Anthony Esposito. *British Biographical Archive* (London: K.G. Saur, 1984).

A four-volume index to an accompanying 1200 microfiche cumulation of 324 English-language biographical reference works published between 1601 and 1929 (including the multi-volume compendia of naval biographies by *O'Byrne — both the first and unpublished second editions — and Charnock). A second series of 268 sources — and about 1700 microfiches — is available, with its emphasis on the later 19th and the 20th centuries, although this currently lacks an index. Taken together, the two series contain 1.25 million pages of text (1998 will see enlarged versions of both series with a new, single index). In addition to this and DWYER, below, Saur have also published versions for Italy, the Iberian and Latin-American worlds, the Scandinavian countries, Germany and Australasia.

Batteau, J., M. Barroux and M. Prevost (originating editors). *Dictionnaire de Biographie Française* (17 vols., in progress; Paris: Letouzey, 1933–).

This major work is currently complete only through the early stages of the letter 'L.'

Bauer, K. Jack and Stephen S. Roberts. *Register of Ships of the U.S. Navy, 1775–1990, Major Combatants* (Westport: Greenwood, 1991).

Book of Saints (6th edition, compiled by the monks of St. Augustine's Abbey, Ramsgate; London: Black, 1989).

Brenton, Edward Pelham. *Life and Correspondence of John, Earl St. Vincent* (London: Colburn, 1836).

Brewer, E. Cobham. *The Dictionary of Phrase and Fable* (on-line version of 1894 edition; www.bibliomania.com/Reference/PhraseAndFable/).

Brighton, the Rev. Dr. *Memoir of Admiral Sir P.B.V. Broke, Bart., KCB, etc.* (London: Sampson, Low, 1866).

Chalmers, Alexander. *The General Biographical Dictionary* (32 vols; London: J. Nichols, 1812–1817).

Chandler, David G. *Dictionary of the Napoleonic Wars* (New York: Simon & Schuster, 1993; first pub. 1979).

Charnock, John. *Biographia Navalis* (London, c.1790).

Charnock, a rare volume, is also available in BANK & ESPOSITO's *British Biographical Archive* series noted above; its merits are briefly discussed under the main entry for the similar work by William *O'Byrne.

Clowes, William Laird (general editor). *The Royal Navy: A History from the Earliest Times to the Present* (7 vols.; London: Chatham, 1997; first published 1897–1903).

Colledge, J.J. *Ships of the Royal Navy, Second Edition* (2 vols; Annapolis: Naval Institute Press, 1987, 1989; Supplement published by World Ship Society at Kendal, 1986).

Cunningham, A.E. (ed.). *Patrick O'Brian: Critical Essays and a Bibliography* (New York: Norton, 1994).

This volume has contributions by O'Brian himself (a rare autobiographical essay as well as some other pieces), John Bayley, Stuart Bennett, A.E. Cunningham, Charlton Heston, Brian Lavery, Richard *Ollard, N.A.M. Rodger, William Waldegrave, and L.J. West.

Dann, John C. *The Nagle Journal* (New York: Weidenfield & Nicholson, 1988).

Drabble, Margaret (ed.). *The Oxford Companion to English Literature, Fifth Edition* (Oxford: OUP, 1985).

Dundonald, Earl of. *The Autobiography of a Seaman* (2 vols; London: Bentley, 1859–60).
Dundonald is of course Thomas *Cochrane.

Dwyer, Helen and Barry. *Index Biographique Français* (London: K.G., 1993).
A four-volume index to an accompanying 1200 microfiche cumulation of 180 French-language biographical reference works published from the 17th — early 20th century, similar in scope to that of BANK & ESPOSITO above.

Encyclopaedia Britannica
I have consulted the current *Britannica Online* (www.eb.com); the *11th, Cambridge University, Edition* (1910–11); and the *5th Edition* (1815–17, itself largely a supplemented reprint of the *4th Edition* of 1801–10).

Farnol, Jeffery. *Famous Prize Fights, or Epics of 'The Fancy'* (Boston: Little, Brown, 1928).

Fitzgerald, Arthur. *Royal Thoroughbreds: a History of the Royal Studs* (London, 1990).
Thanks are due to Liz Ross and Michael O'Neill for supplying me with extracts from this work on early bloodstock in England.

Ford, J. (ed.). *Selections from Pierce Egan's 'Boxiana'* (London: Folio Society, 1812–29).
A work on early pugilists and prize-fights.

France, Peter. *The New Oxford Companion to Literature in French* (Oxford: Clarendon, 1995).

George, J.N. *English Guns and Rifles* (Harris: Stackpole, 1947).

Gillispie, Charles Coulston (originating editor). *Dictionary of Scientific Biography* (New York: Charles Scribner's Sons, 14 vols + supplements, 1970–90).

Glendenning, Ian. *British Pistols and Guns 1640–1840* (London: Cassel, 1951).

Golding, Louis. *The Bare-Knuckle Breed* (London: Hutchinson, 1952).
A work on early pugilists and prize-fights.

Gosset, W.P. *The Lost Ships of the Royal Navy, 1793–1900* (London: Mansell, 1986).

Graham, Gerald S. and R.A. Humphreys (eds). *The Navy and South America, 1807–1823: Correspondence of the Commanders-in-Chief on the South American Station* (London: Naval Records Society, 1962).

Hibbert, Christopher. *Nelson: A Personal History* (London: Viking, 1994).

Hill, J.R. (ed.). *The Oxford Illustrated History of the Royal Navy* (Oxford: OUP, 1995).

Hoefer, Jean C.E. *Nouvelle Biographie Generale* (46 vols; Paris: Didot, 1852–1868).

Holweck, F.G. *A Biographical Dictionary of the Saints* (London: Herder, 1924).

Hornblower, Simon and Antony Spawforth (eds). *The Oxford Classical Dictionary* (3rd edition; Oxford: OUP, 1996).

HotBot (www.HotBot.com).
One of many available search engines for the World Wide Web. Information drawn from web sites has not been used for this work unless it is either directly taken from published and cited works of scholarship or can be confirmed as to its basic facts from such works. However, a 'web search' has often provided a useful pointer as to where best to look in the printed works for an otherwise deeply puzzling or obscure reference.

Hubback, J.H. and E.C. *Jane Austen's Sailor Brothers* (London: Lane, 1906).
A brief note on the Austen brothers, Admirals both, may be found under the main entry for HMS *Canopus.

Hughes, Robert. *The Fatal Shore* (New York: Knopf, 1987).
A work on the early history of the white settlement of Australia.

Hyamson, Albert M. *A Dictionary of Universal Biography of All Ages and All Peoples* (2nd edition; New York: Dutton, 1966).

James, William. *The Naval History of Great Britain* (3rd edition, 6 vols; London: Bentley, 1837).
*James' index (in all editions) is unhandy, in that it appears only in the final volume of the series and includes only the names of persons, not ships or places. A useful companion volume is therefore: C.G. Toogood and T.A. Brassey's *An Index to James' Naval History, 1886 edition* (London: Navy Records Society, 1895).

Johnson, Allen (general editor). *Dictionary of American Biography* (11 vols + supplements; New York: Charles Scribner's Sons, 1944–64).

Johnson, Rossiter (editor-in-chief). *The Biographical Dictionary of America* (10 vols; Boston: American Biographical Society, 1906).

Kavanagh, Peter. *Irish Mythology: a Dictionary* (Kildare: Newbridge, 1988).

Kelley, J.N.D. *The Oxford Dictionary of Popes* (Oxford: OUP, 1986).

Kemp, Peter. *The Oxford Companion to Ships and the Sea* (revised edition; Oxford: OUP, 1988).

Kennedy, Michael (ed.). *The Oxford Dictionary of Music* (2nd edition; Oxford: OUP, 1994).

King, Dean, John B. Hattendorf and J. Worth Estes. *A Sea of Words: a Lexicon and Companion for Patrick O'Brian's Seafaring Tales* (New York: Henry Holt, 1995).

King, Dean and Hattendorf, John B. *Harbors and High Seas: An Atlas and Geographical Guide to the Aubrey-Maturin Novels of Patrick O'Brian* (New York: Henry Holt, 1996).

King, Dean and John B. Hattendorf (eds). *Every Man Will Do His Duty: An Anthology of Firsthand Accounts from the Age of Nelson, 1793–1815* (New York: Henry Holt, 1997).

Langley, Harold D. *A History of Medicine in the Early U.S. Navy* (Baltimore: Johns Hopkins University, 1995).

Lavery, Brian. *Nelson's Navy: The Ships, Men and Organisation 1793–1815* (London: Conway, 1989).

Lloyd, Christopher (ed.). *The Health of Seamen: Selections from the Works of Dr. James Lind, Sir Gilbert Blane and Dr. Thomas Trotter* (London: Naval Records Society, 1965).

Lloyd, Christopher and Jack L.S. Coulter. *Medicine and the Navy 1200–1900: Volume III, 1714–1815* (Edinburgh: Livingstone, 1961).

Mackenzie, Robert Holden. *The Trafalgar Roll, Containing the Names and Services of all Officers of the Royal Navy who participated in the Glorious Victory of the 21st October 1805, together with a History of the Ships engaged in the Battle* (London: George Allen, 1913).

McLean, Ken. *Genetic Heritage* (Kentucky, 1996).
Thanks to Liz Ross and Michael O'Neill for supplying me with extracts from this work on early equine bloodstock in England.

Mahan, Alfred T. *Types of Naval Officers* (London: Sampson, Low, Marston, 1902).
This classic volume contains analyses of the careers of *Hawke, *Rodney, *Howe, *St. Vincent, *Saumarez and *Pellew.

Manning, T.D. and C.F. Walker. *British Warship Names* (London: Putnam, 1959).
Although this work is far less comprehensive than that of COLLEDGE, its special merit (even more useful than the very brief name derivations it contains) lies in its listing the battle honours of every ship covered.

Mariner's Mirror, The
The *Journal of the Society for Nautical Research*, running in quarterly parts (for most of its history) from 1911 to the present day, and now published by the National Maritime Museum, Greenwich, U.K.

Marshall, John. *Royal Navy Biography* (12 vols; London: Longman, 1823–1835).

*The merits of this work are discussed under Lieutenant *Marshall's main entry in the text.*

Mendiburu, Manuel de. *Diccionario Histórico-Biográphico del Perú* (11 vols + supplements; Lima: Enrique Palacios, 1931).

Michaud, J. F. *Biographie Universelle Ancienne et Moderne* (2nd edition, 45 vols; Paris: Desplaces, 1854 onwards).

Naval Chronicle, The (London: Joyce Gold, 1799–1818).
A work consisting of 40, six-monthly volumes, each containing accounts of the war, catalogues of ships in service, promotion lists, official letters and announcements, biographies, obituaries, and essays and review pieces on important nautical topics. In addition, the volumes have miscellany sections of anecdotes, poetry, correspondence etc. The *Chronicle* is a treasure-trove of information and clearly provides direct inspiration for minor incidents and scenes in O'Brian's work. However, the sheer amount of information, and the variable quality of its indexing, can make the books laborious to use for extensive 'fact checking'; much of its major material is incorporated in the general histories of JAMES and CLOWES.

Norie, J.W. *The Naval Gazetteer, Biographer and Chronologist; containing a history of the late wars from their commencement in 1793 to their conclusion in 1801 and from their re-commencement in 1803 to their final conclusion in 1815, and continued, as to the biographical part, to the present time* (2nd edition; London: J.W. Norie & Co., 1827).
This exceptionally useful, rare work is in four sections: (I) an alphabetical guide to names of Royal Navy officers, battles, campaigns and stations; (II) an annotated, chronological list of all the ships lost, taken or destroyed by each belligerent power from 1793 to 1815, together with a list of British commanding officers who were killed in action during the same period; (III) a similar account of all privateers taken or lost; and (IV) the texts of various treaties agreed during the war period.

O'Brian, Patrick. *Joseph Banks: a Life* (London: Collins Harvill, 1987).

O'Brian, Patrick. *Men of War: Life in Nelson's Navy* (New York: Norton, 1995; first published in 1974).
O'Brian's book is something of a slight work, intended primarily for the younger reader, and cannot really compete with LAVERY's later volume. It is, however, exquisitely illustrated, with the Norton edition having lavished a great deal of care on the quality of reproduction of paintings.

O'Byrne, William Richard. *A Naval Biographical Dictionary: comprising the life and services of every living officer in Her Majesty's navy, from the rank of admiral of the fleet to that of lieutenant, inclusive. Compiled from authentic and family documents* (London: Murray, 1849).
O'Byrne, a rare volume, is also available in BANK & ESPOSITO's *British Biographical Archive* series noted above; included here are entries from the otherwise un-

published 2nd edition of 1861. The merits of this work are briefly discussed under *O'Byrne's main entry in the text.

Oxford English Dictionary, 2nd edition (20 vols + supplements; Oxford: Clarendon Press, 1989).

Padfield, Peter. *Broke and the Shannon* (London: Hodder & Stoughton, 1968).

Palmer, Michael A. *Stoddert's War: Naval Operations during the Quasi-War with France, 1798–1801* (Columbia: University of South Carolina, 1987).

Pocock, Tom. *Horatio Nelson* (London: Bodley Head, 1987).

Pope, Dudley. *The Black Ship* (London: Weidenfield and Nicholson, 1963).
    An account of the mutiny of HMS *Hermione* under Hugh *Pigot and her recapture by Sir Edward *Hamilton's HMS *Surprise*. Pope himself was of course a leading author of naval fiction.

Porter, Roy (ed.). *The Cambridge Illustrated History of Medicine* (Cambridge: CUP, 1996).

Porter, Roy. *London: a Social History* (Cambridge, Mass.: Harvard UP, 1994).

Porter, Roy. *Health for sale: Quackery in England 1660–1850* (Manchester: Manchester University Press).

Radice, Betty. *Who's Who in the Ancient World* (London: Penguin, 1973).

Ralfe, James. *The Naval Biography of Great Britain* (4 vols; London: Whitmore, Fenn, 1828).
    The merits of this work are briefly discussed under the main entries for *O'Byrne and *Charnock.

Ross, Sir John. *Memoirs and Correspondence of Admiral Lord de Saumarez* (2 vols; London: Bentley, 1838).

Sadie, Stanley. *The New Grove Dictionary of Music and Musicians* (20 vols; London: MacMillan, 1980).

Schama, Simon. *Citizens: a Chronicle of the French Revolution* (London: Viking, 1989).

Shaw A.G.L. and C.M.H. Clark. *Australian Dictionary of Biography, 1788–1850* (Melbourne: Melbourne University Press, 1996).

Spillman, Général Georges. *Napoléon et l'Islam* (Paris: Perrin, 1969).
    A book that, as well as containing a scholarly monograph on its title subject, has a series of shorter sections on French intelligence activities in the Moslem world of the time.

Stark, Suzanne J. *Female Tars: Women Aboard Ship in the Age of Sail* (Annapolis: Naval Institute Press, 1996).

Stephen, Sir Leslie and Sir Sidney Lee. *Dictionary of National Biography* (22 vols + supplements; Oxford: Oxford University Press, 1967 reprint of 1885–1901 edition).
    Almost all the naval entries in the main series are by Sir John Knox Laughton (1830–1915); Mr. O'Brian himself contributed to the *'Missing Persons'* supplement. The 2-volume *Concise DNB* (1953 edition) is useful not only as an index to the main work but also for its giving separate entries for many minor characters whose details are subsumed under a single main entry in DNB itself. Where dates of promotion in DNB are at variance with SYRETT & DiNARDO's volume, I have usually followed the latter, as it is the meticulous listing of these details that forms its *raison d'être*. However, it should be noted that many differences between the two can probably be accounted for by Laughton's focus on the date on which a man assumed duty in a rank, with Syrett & DiNardo giving the date, earlier or later, on which any such appointment was officially confirmed.

Sutton, Jean. *Lords of the East: the East India Company and its Ships* (London: Conway, 1981).

Syrett, David and R.L. DiNardo (eds). *The Commissioned Sea Officers of the Royal Navy, 1660–1815* (London: Naval Records Society, 1994).
    See note to STEPHEN's DNB, above.

Taillemite, Etienne. *Dictionnaire des Marins Français* (Editions Maritimes & d'Outre-Mer, 1982).

Thomas, J. *Universal Pronouncing Dictionary of Biography and Mythology* (5th edition; Philadelphia: J.B. Lippincott and Co., 1930).

Thompson, J.M. *Napoleon Bonaparte* (Oxford: Basil Blackwell, 1952).
    One of the classic English-language studies of the great man, as elegantly written as it is meticulous in its research and balanced in its judgements.

Tomalin, Claire. *Jane Austen: a Life* (New York: Knopf, 1997).
    A brief note on Jane Austen's sailor brothers, Admirals both, may be found under the main entry for HMS *Canopus.

Thorne, R.G. *The History of Parliament: the House of Commons, 1790–1820* (London: Secker & Warburg, 1986).

Uden, Grant and Richard Cooper. *A Dictionary of British Ships and Seamen* (New York: St. Martin's Press, 1981).

Vichot, Jacques. *Répertoire des Navires de Guerre Français* (Paris: L'Association des Amis des Musées de La Marine, 1967).
    This work, in many ways the French equivalent of COLLEDGE, includes privateers as well as national ships.

Whipple, A.B.C. *To the Shores of Tripoli: the Birth of the US Navy and Marines* (New York: William Morrow, 1991).
    An excellent modern work that provides much background material on the politics and personalities of the Mahgreb and its various corsair fleets.